The Epistle
to the
Romans

LEON MORRIS

WILLIAM B. EERDMANS PUBLISHING COMPANY
GRAND RAPIDS, MICHIGAN

INTER-VARSITY PRESS
LEICESTER, ENGLAND

Copyright © 1988 by Wm. B. Eerdmans Publishing Co.
255 Jefferson Ave. S.E., Grand Rapids, Mich. 49503
All rights reserved
Printed in the United States of America

Reprinted 1995

Library of Congress Cataloging-in-Publication Data

Morris, Leon, 1914-
The Epistle to the Romans / by Leon Morris
p.   cm.
Includes indexes.
ISBN 0-8028-3636-4 : $27.95
1. Bible.   N.T.   Romans — Commentaries.   I. Title.
BS2665.3.M58 1987
227'.107—dc19   87-28076

First British Edition 1988 by Inter-Varsity Press,
38 De Montfort Street, Leicester, England, LE17GP

British Library Cataloguing-in-Publication Data

Morris, Leon 1914-
The Epistle to the Romans
1. Bible N.T. Romans — Commentaries
I. Title
227'.107

ISBN 0-85111-747-3

Contents

98845

Preface

Throughout the years I have frequently been occupied with Romans. I have worked with it extensively while writing books on theology (especially on the cross). I have lectured on it many times, and am indebted to students in Britain, Canada, the United States, and Australia for their interaction. But prior to this I have never written at length on Romans. Now in my retirement I have finally had the opportunity to devote time to a commentary on this great epistle. I offer it as my tribute to an apostle to whom I owe so much.

I have included the text of the New International Version as an aid to the reader. Occasionally I have made my own translation (without specifically drawing attention to it) in order to bring out some feature of the original. But the commentary is based on the Greek text, not the translation. It has been my aim to make clear to the general reader what I see in the Greek text, and it is my hope that this will be of some help to others who are grappling with the thought of this great epistle.

LEON MORRIS

Chief Abbreviations

ABR   *Australian Biblical Review*
Achtemeier   Paul J. Achtemeier: *Romans* (Atlanta, 1985)
Alford   Henry Alford: *The Greek Testament*[7] (London, 1874)
Althaus   Paul Althaus: *Der Brief an die Römer* (Göttingen, 1970)
ANF   Ante-Nicene Fathers (American repr. of the Edinburgh edn.; Grand Rapids, n.d.)
ARV   *The American Revised Version*
AS   G. Abbott-Smith: *A Manual Greek Lexicon of the New Testament* (Edinburgh, 1954)
ASV   *The American Standard Version*
BAGD   Walter Bauer: *A Greek-English Lexicon of the New Testament and Other Early Christian Literature*, rev. and aug. by F. Wilbur Gingrich and Frederick W. Danker from the 5th edn. (Chicago, 1979)
Barclay   William Barclay: *The Letter to the Romans* (Edinburgh, 1957)
Barrett   C. K. Barrett: *A Commentary on the Epistle to the Romans* (London, 1957)
Barth   Karl Barth: *The Epistle to the Romans* (Oxford, 1933)
BDF   F. Blass and A. Debrunner: *A Greek Grammar of the New Testament*, trans. and rev. R. W. Funk (Chicago, 1961)
Bengel   John Albert Bengel: *Gnomon of the New Testament*, II (Edinburgh, 1873)
Black   Matthew Black: *Romans* (London, 1973)
Bowen   Roger Bowen: *A Guide to Romans* (London, 1975)
Boylan   Patrick Boylan: *St. Paul's Epistle to the Romans* (Dublin, 1947)
Brown   John Brown: *Analytical Exposition of the Epistle of Paul the Apostle to the Romans* (Grand Rapids, 1981 repr. of 1857 edn.)
Bruce   F. F. Bruce: *The Letter of Paul to the Romans*[2] (Leicester, 1985)
Brunner   Emil Brunner: *The Letter to the Romans* (London, 1959)
Calvin   John Calvin: *The Epistles of Paul the Apostle to the Romans and to the Thessalonians* (Edinburgh, 1961)
CBQ   *The Catholic Biblical Quarterly*
CBSC   The Cambridge Bible for Schools and Colleges
CGT   Cambridge Greek Testament
Chamberlain   William Douglas Chamberlain: *An Exegetical Grammar of the Greek New Testament* (New York, 1941)
Christian Words   Nigel Turner: *Christian Words* (Edinburgh, 1980)

Cragg	*The Interpreter's Bible*, IX, "The Epistle to the Romans," exposition by Gerald R. Cragg
Cranfield	C. E. B. Cranfield: *A Critical and Exegetical Commentary on the Epistle to the Romans* (Edinburgh, I [1975]; II [1979])
Denney	James Denney: "St. Paul's Epistle to the Romans" in *The Expositor's Greek Testament*, II (Grand Rapids, 1979 repr.)
DM	H. E. Dana and Julius R. Mantey: *A Manual Grammar of the Greek New Testament* (New York, 1927)
Dodd	C. H. Dodd: *The Epistle of Paul to the Romans* (London, 1944)
Donfried	Karl P. Donfried: *The Romans Debate* (Minneapolis, 1977)
Earle	Ralph Earle: *Word Meanings in the New Testament*, III, *Romans* (Grand Rapids, 1974)
EGT	W. Robertson Nicoll, ed.: *The Expositor's Greek Testament*, 5 vols. (Grand Rapids, 1979 repr.)
ET	*The Expository Times*
Foreman	K. J. Foreman: *Romans, I & II Corinthians* (London, 1962)
Gamble	Harry Gamble, Jr.: *The Textual History of the Letter to the Romans* (Grand Rapids, 1977)
Gifford	E. H. Gifford: *The Epistle of St. Paul to the Romans* (London, 1886)
GNB	*Good News Bible (Today's English Version)*
Godet	F. Godet: *Commentary on St. Paul's Epistle to the Romans*, 2 vols. (Edinburgh, 1895)
Goodspeed	Edgar J. Goodspeed: *The New Testament: An American Translation* (Chicago, 1923)
Gore	Charles Gore: *St. Paul's Epistle to the Romans*, 2 vols. (London, I [1902]; II [1907])
Grammatical Insights	Nigel Turner: *Grammatical Insights into the New Testament* (Edinburgh, 1965)
Griffith	Gwilym O. Griffith: *St. Paul's Gospel to the Romans* (Oxford, 1949)
GT	*A Greek-English Lexicon of the New Testament*, being Grimm's Wilke's *Clavis Novi Testamenti*, trans. and rev. J. H. Thayer (Edinburgh, 1888)
Haldane	Robert Haldane: *The Epistle to the Romans* (London, 1966 repr.)
Harrison	Everett F. Harrison: "Romans" in *The Expositor's Bible Commentary*, 10 (Grand Rapids, 1976)
Harrisville	Roy A. Harrisville: *Romans* (Minneapolis, 1980)
Hendriksen	William Hendriksen: *New Testament Commentary: Exposition of Paul's Epistle to the Romans* (Grand Rapids, I [1980]; II [1981])
Hodge	Charles Hodge: *A Commentary on Romans* (London, 1972 repr. of 1864 edn.)
Hunter	A. M. Hunter: *The Epistle to the Romans* (London, 1975)
IBNTG	C. F. D. Moule: *An Idiom Book of New Testament Greek* (Cambridge, 1953)
IDB	*The Interpreter's Dictionary of the Bible*, 4 vols. (Nashville, 1962); Supplementary Volume (1976)

ABBREVIATIONS

JB	*The Jerusalem Bible*
JBL	*The Journal of Biblical Literature*
JTS	*The Journal of Theological Studies*
Käsemann	Ernst Käsemann: *Commentary on Romans* (Grand Rapids, 1980)
Kertelge	Karl Kertelge and Gerhard Schneider: *The Epistles to the Romans and Galatians for Spiritual Reading* (London, 1977)
Knox	*The Interpreter's Bible,* IX, introduction and exegesis by John Knox (Nashville, 1978)
Knox, R	R. Knox: *The Holy Bible, A Translation from the Latin Vulgate* (London, 1955)
LAE	A. Deissmann: *Light from the Ancient East* (London, 1927)
Lagrange	M.-J. Lagrange: *Saint Paul Épitre aux Romains* (Paris, 1922)
LB	*The Living Bible*
Leenhardt	Franz J. Leenhardt: *The Epistle to the Romans* (London, 1961)
Lenski	R. C. H. Lenski: *The Interpretation of St. Paul's Epistle to the Romans* (Minneapolis, n.d.)
Lightfoot	J. B. Lightfoot: *Notes on Epistles of St Paul* (London, 1904)
Lloyd-Jones	D. M. Lloyd-Jones: *Romans: An Exposition of Chapters 3:20– 8:39,* 6 vols. (London, 1970-75)
Loane	Marcus Loane: *God's Mere Mercy* (Blackwood, South Australia, 1986)
LSJ	*A Greek-English Lexicon,* comp. H. G. Liddell and R. Scott, rev. H. S. Jones and R. McKenzie, 2 vols. (Oxford, 1940)
Luther	Martin Luther: *Lectures on Romans* (Library of Christian Classics; London, 1961)
LXX	The Septuagint
M, I	J. H. Moulton: *A Grammar of New Testament Greek,* I, *Prolegomena* (Edinburgh, 1906)
M, II	*Ibid.,* II, *Accidence and Word-Formation,* ed. W. F. Howard (Edinburgh, 1919)
M, III	*Ibid.,* III, *Syntax,* by Nigel Turner (Edinburgh, 1963)
M, IV	*Ibid.,* IV, *Style,* by Nigel Turner (Edinburgh, 1976)
Manson	T. W. Manson: "Romans" in *Peake's Commentary on the Bible,* ed. Matthew Black and H. H. Rowley (London, 1980)
Metzger	Bruce M. Metzger: *A Textual Commentary on the Greek New Testament* (London and New York, 1971)
Michel	Otto Michel: *Der Brief an die Römer* (Göttingen, 1966)
Minear	Paul S. Minear: *The Obedience of Faith* (London, 1971)
MM	J. H. Moulton and G. Milligan: *The Vocabulary of the Greek Testament* (London, 1914-29)
Moffatt	James Moffatt: *The New Testament: A New Translation*
Morison	James Morison: *A Critical Exposition of the Third Chapter of Paul's Epistle to the Romans* (London, 1866)
Moule	Handley C. G. Moule: *The Epistle of St. Paul to the Romans* (London, 1896)
MS(S)	Manuscript(s)

MT	Ernest de Witt Burton: *Syntax of the Moods and Tenses in New Testament Greek* (Edinburgh, 1955)
Murray	John Murray: *The Epistle to the Romans,* 2 vols. (Grand Rapids, 1960 and 1965)
NASB	*The New American Standard Bible*
NBCR	*The New Bible Commentary Revised,* ed. D. Guthrie *et al.* (London, 1970)
NEB	*The New English Bible*
NIDNTT	*The New International Dictionary of New Testament Theology,* ed. Colin Brown, 3 vols. (Exeter, 1975-78)
NIV	*New International Version*
NPNF	Nicene and Post-Nicene Fathers
NTS	*New Testament Studies*
Nygren	Anders Nygren: *Commentary on Romans* (London, 1952)
Olshausen	Hermann Olshausen: *Studies in the Epistle to the Romans* (Minneapolis, 1983 repr. of 1849 edn.)
O'Neill	J. C. O'Neill: *Paul's Letter to the Romans* (Harmondsworth, 1975)
Parry	R. St John Parry: *The Epistle of Paul the Apostle to the Romans* (Cambridge, 1912)
Phillips	J. B. Phillips: *Letters to Young Churches* (Melbourne, 1952)
Rhymer	Joseph Rhymer: *Good News in Romans* (London, 1974)
Ridderbos	Herman Ridderbos: *Paul* (Grand Rapids, 1975)
Robertson	A. T. Robertson: *A Grammar of the Greek New Testament in the Light of Historical Research* (London, n.d.)
Robinson	John A. T. Robinson: *Wrestling with Romans* (London, 1979)
RSV	*The Revised Standard Version*
RThR	*The Reformed Theological Review*
RV	*The Revised Version*
SBk	H. L. Strack und P. Billerbeck: *Kommentar zum Neuen Testament aus Talmud und Midrasch,* 4 vols. (München, 1922-28)
Schonfield	Hugh J. Schonfield: *The Authentic New Testament* (London, 1956)
Scott	E. F. Scott: *Paul's Epistle to the Romans* (London, 1947)
SH	William Sanday and Arthur C. Headlam: *A Critical and Exegetical Commentary on the Epistle to the Romans* (Edinburgh, 1907)
Shedd	William G. T. Shedd: *Commentary on Romans* (Grand Rapids, 1980 repr. of 1879 edn.)
Simeon	Charles Simeon: *Horae Homileticae, XV, Romans* (London, 1847)
Smart	James D. Smart: *Doorway to a New Age* (New York, 1972)
Stott	John R. W. Stott: *Men Made New* (Downers Grove, 1966)
Synonyms	Richard Chevenix Trench: *Synonyms of the New Testament* (London, 1880)
Tasker	R. V. G. Tasker, ed.: *The Greek New Testament* (Oxford and Cambridge, 1964)

TDNT	*Theological Dictionary of the New Testament*, a translation by Geoffrey W. Bromiley of *Theologisches Wörterbuch zum Neuen Testament* (Grand Rapids, 1964-76)
TH	Barclay M. Newman and Eugene A. Nida: *A Translator's Handbook on Paul's Letter to the Romans* (New York, 1973)
Thomas	W. H. Griffith Thomas: *Romans*, 3 vols. (London, 1911-12)
Vaughan	C. J. Vaughan: *St. Paul's Epistle to the Romans* (London, 1880)
Vermes	G. Vermes: *The Dead Sea Scrolls in English* (Harmondsworth, 1972)
Way	Arthur S. Way: *The Letters of St. Paul* (London, 1921)
Wesley	John Wesley: *Explanatory Notes upon the New Testament* (London, 1977)
Weymouth	R. F. Weymouth: *The New Testament in Modern Speech* (London, 1907)
WH	B. F. Westcott and F. J. Hort: *The New Testament in the Original Greek* (London, 1907)
Wilckens	Ulrich Wilckens: *Der Brief an die Römer*, 3 vols. (Zürich, 1978-82)
Wilson	Geoffrey B. Wilson: *Romans* (Edinburgh, 1976)
WTJ	*The Westminster Theological Journal*
Wuest	Kenneth S. Wuest: *Romans in the Greek New Testament* (London, n.d.)

Quotations from the Talmud are from the Soncino edition, and the Mishnah is cited from Danby's translation.

The Epistle
to the
Romans

Introduction

It is commonly agreed that the Epistle to the Romans is one of the greatest Christian writings. Its power has been demonstrated again and again at critical points in the history of the Christian church. Augustine of Hippo, for example, was converted through reading a passage from this letter, and thus began a period of the greatest importance for the church. It is not too much to say that at a later time Martin Luther's spiritual experience was shaped by his coming to grips with what Paul says in this epistle. The Reformation may be regarded as the unleashing of new spiritual life as a result of a renewed understanding of the teaching of Romans. Again, John Wesley's conversion was triggered by hearing Luther's Preface to Romans read, a Preface, of course, inspired by the epistle. Nearer to our own day it was Karl Barth's coming to grips with the message of the book that ended an era of sterile liberalism and ushered in a more fruitful period of biblical theology. But Romans is not for great minds only. The humble believer also finds inspiration and direction in these pages. Romans is not an easy book. But it has always yielded rich dividends to anyone who has taken the time to study it seriously, and it does so still.[1]

It is one of a large number of letters, some 14,000 in all, that have come down to us from antiquity. Many are in copies only, but quite often we have the originals. Some letters are very private, being intimate communications within the family or among friends; others are plainly meant for a wider public. In the papyri private letters range in length from 18 words to 209.[2] More literary letters[3] tend to be longer, the subject matter obviously having an influence on length. Cicero's 796 letters average 295 words with a range from 22 to 2,530 words, while Seneca's 124 letters range from 149 to 4,134 words

---

1. The continuing relevance of Romans is illustrated by the articles in the January 1980 issue of *Interpretation*. This whole number is given over to Romans. The articles cover a wide range and leave no doubt about the fact that this epistle still plays a vital role in the life of the church.

2. The statistics in this section are taken from Alfred Wikenhauser, *New Testament Introduction* (New York, 1958), pp. 346-47.

3. For a discussion of types of letters in antiquity see especially William G. Doty, "The Classification of Epistolary Literature", CBQ, XXXI (1969), pp. 183-99; Martin Luther Stirewalt, Jr., "The Form and Function of the Greek Letter-Essay", Donfried, pp. 175-206. Doty discerns eight classes with up to seven subclasses grouped under his headings, and he does not claim to be exhaustive. He points out that the Hellenistic school handbooks included 21 and later 41 specific types (pp. 196-97).

with an average length of 995 words. The New Testament letters tend to be longer, though 2 and 3 John are quite short. The 13 Pauline letters average around 1,300 words. Clearly Paul took letter writing very seriously and made it much more of a vehicle for significant teaching than did most people of the ancient world. Romans is his longest letter, with about 7,100 words. Its length as well as the profundity of its subject matter marks it out as a most unusual letter.

AUTHORSHIP

The letter claims to have been written by the apostle Paul (1:1), and no serious objection appears ever to have been urged against this claim. The few who have objected have not been able to convince many that their arguments have weight. The style and contents are what we expect of Paul, and the tradition of the church has always accepted this letter as a genuine work of the great apostle.

DESTINATION

As it stands, the letter is addressed to the church[4] at Rome (1:7, 15). This is supported by the geographical note in which Paul writes of going to Spain

---

4. E. A. Judge and G. S. R. Thomas argue that there was no church in Rome when Paul wrote, nor indeed right up to the time when he came to Rome as a prisoner. That was when he formed the individual Christians in that city into a church ("The Origin of the Church at Rome: A New Solution?" RThR, XXV [1966], pp. 81-94). They point to the lack of reference to an ἐκκλησία at Rome, or to officials like bishops, priests, and deacons, or to ordinances like baptism (though cf. Rom. 6:3-4) and the Lord's Supper. But Paul rarely refers to these anywhere. He has general references to churches, but the only specific groups to which he applies the term are house churches (including Rom. 16:5) and those at Corinth, Cenchraea, Philippi, Laodicea, and Thessalonica. This despite the fact that his use of the plural (e.g., Gal. 1:2; 1 Thess. 2:14) shows that he saw the term as widely applicable. Apart from Rom. 6:4 the only occurrences of βάπτισμα in the Pauline corpus are in Eph. 4:5 and Col. 2:12, while the corresponding verb is used a number of times in 1 Corinthians, in Gal. 3:27, and nowhere else in the Pauline corpus except Romans. The discussion of the reference in Suetonius (see below, p. 4) I do not find convincing, while the failure of the Jews Paul met when he eventually came to Rome to mention a local church (Acts 28:22) does not mean that there was not one there. It may have been politic on their part to be silent on the matter, as William Neil thinks (The Acts of the Apostles [London, 1973], pp. 257-58). And Godet held that Roman Christianity was of Gentile origin; there had been no Christian preaching in the synagogues and thus no way the Jewish leaders would mention it (Godet, pp. 60-70). The article is a warning not to be overconfident and it reminds us that the small amount of evidence can be understood in more ways than one. But the best explanation of the evidence still seems to be that there was a church in Rome (Rom. 1:8). SH, of course, long ago suggested that Peter and Paul may have "founded" the church in Rome in the sense that they organized scattered groups into one whole (SH, p. xxxv).

and proceeds, "I hope to visit you while passing through" (15:24). Some scholars have been so impressed by the fact that the words "in Rome" (1:7, 15) are absent from a few manuscripts that they have concluded that the Roman church was not the epistle's original destination. They hold that it was meant as a circular letter, perhaps sent to Rome as one of its addressees. However, the evidence is not strong and there is no reasonable doubt about the text.[5]

But the question is not as simple as this, for there are many who deny that we should take the letter as it stands. Quite a few hold that chapter 16 was not originally part of this letter but was meant for the church at Ephesus (see below, pp. 24ff.). Usually this is understood to mean that all or part of a letter to Ephesus has somehow been attached to a letter to Rome. A different line is taken by T. W. Manson. From the fact that P[46] (our oldest copy of Romans) has the doxology at the end of chapter 15 he argues that Paul wrote a 15-chapter edition. Manson thinks that the apostle sent a copy to Ephesus with the addition of chapter 16 and sent another copy, without the addition, to Rome.[6] On this view we have the letter to Ephesus. I shall discuss this view more fully later. Here it is enough to say that the personal references in chapters 1 and 15 make it difficult to accept any circular-letter hypothesis. It would not have been insuperably difficult to remove them or, if this copy was meant for Ephesus, to replace them with matter more appropriate to that city. And we should not overlook the fact that even on Manson's view the bulk of the letter was intended for the Roman church just as much as for that in Ephesus.

We have no precise information about how and when and by whom the church was established at Rome. Acts 2:10 informs us that visitors from Rome were among those in Jerusalem who heard the Christians preach on the day of Pentecost. There is nothing improbable in the suggestion that some of them responded to Peter's sermon and became Christians, though we must immediately add that we have no knowledge of this. There is a tradition that Peter and Paul founded the church. But this epistle shows that the church was flourishing in Rome long before Paul visited that city. If Peter was the founder in the same sense as Paul, this can mean only that he was interested in the church, that he may have visited it at some time, and that it accepted his

---

5. The words in question are lacking in 1:7 in the MSS designated G 1739[ms] 1908[ms] it[g] Or[lat]. In 1:15 they are not found in G it[g] Or[lat]. The case against the words can, however, be made a little stronger. The reading in G it[g] in v. 7 may be translated "to all who are in the love of God". Now the reading of some MSS, "to all who are in Rome in the love of God", seems to be an adaptation of this reading to the more usual text (so, e.g., Bruce, pp. 25-26). If so, the scribes must have had both readings before them. We should also notice that the commentaries of Ambrosiaster and apparently also of Pelagius lacked the reference to Rome (see Gamble, p. 32). This is an interesting list, but even the combined testimony of these witnesses is scarcely enough to prove the point. They show that at some time the reference to Rome was missing. But the evidence of the overwhelming bulk of the MSS must be accepted as giving us the true reading.

6. See his article "The Letter to the Romans—and Others", BJRL, 31 (1948), pp. 224-40, reprinted in Manson's book *Studies in the Gospels and Epistles* (Manchester, 1962), pp. 225-41. Quotations are from this reprint. Cf. also Manson, p. 941.

teaching. It cannot mean that he was responsible for its first converts. This is in any case unlikely, for Peter's primary responsibility was to the Jews, just as Paul's was to the Gentiles (Gal. 2:7-8). It is most improbable that Peter settled in Rome as bishop of the church as some traditions hold, for he seems to have exercised a wandering ministry (1 Cor. 9:5). There is no record of his ever settling down anywhere. As for Paul, it is impossible to hold that he had much to do with the church in Rome in its early years. When he wrote this epistle he had never been to Rome (1:10-13), and he makes it clear that there was already a significant group of believers there (1:6, 7, 8; 15:14).

There is then no reliable tradition about the founding of this church, and we are left to speculation. The probability is that traders and other travellers first brought Christianity to Rome. As they witnessed to their faith they brought others to believe, and in this way a church was born. It seems likely that the first converts were won from among the Jews, and they may even have been organized as a synagogue (or synagogues).[7] This is speculation, but it is supported by a note in the Roman historian Suetonius. This man tells us that the Emperor Claudius expelled the Jews[8] from Rome because they "constantly made disturbances at the instigation of Chrestus *(impulsore Chresto)."*[9] Most scholars take "Chrestus" as equivalent to "Christus" (the two words had similar pronunciations), that is, Christ. If this understanding of it is correct, it would seem that the fairly large group of Jews in Rome[10] had

---

7. Any ten adult male Jews could form a synagogue (Mishnah, Meg. 4:3; Sanh. 1:6; Ab. 3:6). There were many synagogues in Rome (W. Wiefel gives the names of 13 of them [Donfried, p. 106]). In Rome the term "synagogue" seems to have signified the community, the place of worship being called a *proseucha* (see R. Penna, NTS, 28 [1982], p. 327). It would be strange if Jewish Christians did not form synagogues of their own. The term is, of course, used of a Christian assembly (Jas. 2:2).

8. For the relations between the Romans and the Jews see the note by Vincent M. Scramuzza, "The Policy of the Early Roman Emperors towards Judaism" (F. J. Foakes-Jackson and Kirsopp Lake, *The Beginnings of Christianity*, V [Grand Rapids, 1966], pp. 277-97).

9. *Life of Claudius* xxv.4 (Loeb translation). Dio Cassius denies that Claudius expelled the Jews, saying that there were too many of them (lx.6.6). But he mentions the danger of rioting and speaks of the repressive measures adopted by Claudius. Clearly there was trouble, and this is the main point. Our interest is in "Chrestus" rather than in the precise action Claudius took. W. Wiefel understands Dio Cassius to mean that the Jews lost their right to assemble. He thinks that this refers not to the initial trouble but to the situation when the Jews were permitted to return. As a first step they were allowed to come back to Rome, but "synagogue assemblies were prohibited for some time since they were seen as seedbeds of dispute" (Donfried, p. 111). Judge and Thomas argue that "Chrestus" cannot refer to Jesus Christ (RThR, XXV, pp. 84ff.). Rather, it signifies "some religious star whose appearance at Rome caused an upheaval among the Jews, but whose fame was sufficiently ephemeral for his precise identity to have been lost" (*ibid.*, p. 87). This is certainly possible. But riots instigated by Jews on account of Christian claims (like that at Ephesus, Acts 19:23ff.) seem more probable.

10. J. Juster estimated that there were 50-60,000 Jews in Rome in the time of Tiberius (*Les Juifs dans l'Empire Romain*, I [Paris, 1914], p. 209). Penna thinks this number too high, as also the 30-40,000 of S. Collon, but regards *Encyclopedia Judaica*'s estimate of 10,000 as too low. Reasoning from the 8,000 Jews mentioned by Josephus (*Ant.* xvii.299-303) and the 4,000 men of military age deported in A.D. 19 (*Ant.* xviii.81-84), he estimates the number as 20,000 in Nero's day (NTS, 28, p. 328 and p. 341 nn.51-53).

mixed feelings about Christianity. Some followed Christ. But others objected so violently that there were riots. Orosius's dating of this in A.D. 49 is generally accepted, so the passage points to an early establishment of the church in the capital city. An early establishment is indicated also by the fact that Paul says that he had for a long time wanted to visit them (1:13).

But if the first converts were Jews, this was a condition that did not last. By the time Romans was written a large Gentile element was clearly in the number (1:5-6, 13; 11:13-32; cf. 9:3ff.; 10:1-2; 15:15-16). The church can scarcely have been completely Gentile, as the many references to views held by Jews (Christian and otherwise) throughout the epistle show. Paul speaks of Abraham as "our" forefather (4:1) and writes to people who know law (7:1) and have "died" to the law (7:4; these passages may include others than Jews but they certainly include Jews). The charge of nullifying the law (3:31) looks like a Jewish charge, as do objections to Paul's view of freedom from the law (6:1–7:6). Justification by faith, not law, is said to be an argument against a Jewish position. It would not have been impossible for Paul to have written these words to Gentile Christians (cf. 1 Cor. 10:1), but at least they are congruous with Jewish recipients.[11] But when Paul writes "Accept one another" and goes on to speak of Christ as having "become a servant of the Jews on behalf of God's truth, to confirm the promises made to the patriarchs so that the Gentiles may glorify God for his mercy" (15:7-9), it is plain that he is writing to members of both groups. We should also bear in mind what W. G. Kümmel calls "the equal responsibility of Jews and Greeks before God",[12] which finds expression in a number of places (e.g., 1:16; 2:9ff., 25ff.; 3:29; 10:12). Such expressions are pointless unless representatives of both groups are to read the letter. It is not clear which group predominated,[13] though the general tone of the letter and the fact that Paul clearly believed that the Roman church had come within his sphere of responsibility as apostle to the Gentiles may be held to point to some preponderance of Gentiles.

DATE AND PLACE OF WRITING

The epistle seems to have been written in Corinth. Paul commends Phoebe, a lady from Cenchraea, the port of that city (16:1). His host is Gaius (16:23), and

---

11. It is sometimes urged that the Roman church was predominantly Jewish-Christian, as by Theodor Zahn (*Introduction to the New Testament*, I [Edinburgh, 1909], pp. 421ff.). So, more recently, William Manson (*The Epistle to the Hebrews* [London, 1951], pp. 172-84). But not many have been persuaded. Paul was the apostle to the Gentiles (11:13). Why would he have written such a considerable letter to a predominantly Jewish church?

12. *Introduction to the New Testament* (London, 1966), p. 219.

13. Cf. A. F. J. Klijn, "It is impossible to determine which group formed the majority" (*An Introduction to the New Testament* [Leiden, 1967], p. 76); Martin Dibelius, "it appears to me to be useless to look for an answer in Romans to the much-discussed question whether the Roman Christians were Jewish or Gentile" (*A Fresh Approach to the New Testament and Early Christian Literature* [London, 1936], p. 162; he goes on to suggest that "the character of the church in the Capital was continually changing").

Gaius is the name of a man Paul baptized at Corinth (1 Cor. 1:14). Erastus, Timothy, and Sopater were with Paul when Romans was written (16:21, 23) and also when he was in Greece (Acts 19:22; 20:2-4). Both times Paul intended to go to Jerusalem and then to Rome (Acts 19:21; Rom. 15:24-26, 28). The object of his immediate journey was to take money to the poor saints at Jerusalem (Acts 24:17; Rom. 15:26-28). All this makes it conclusive that Paul was writing from Corinth just before he travelled to Jerusalem.[14]

But dating this with any precision is something of a problem. The fixed point for Pauline chronology is the proconsulship of Gallio in Corinth, for there is an inscription that tells us that this man was in office in A.D. 52.[15] Proconsuls held office for a year, though on occasion their terms might be extended to two years. Depending on whether the inscription refers to a time near the beginning or end of Gallio's term of office, Paul would have been in Corinth at some time during the period A.D. 50-54. We do not know at exactly what point Paul was brought before him (Acts 18:12). But it is not unreasonable to suppose that it was early in his term of office (the Jews might hope to get their wish granted by a new official) and not so very long before the end of Paul's own ministry in the city. If Paul was before Gallio in the summer of A.D. 51[16] and left in the autumn for Antioch (Acts 18:18-22), his return to Galatia (Acts 18:23) would be in the following spring, that of A.D. 52. His visits to the churches and journey to Ephesus would bring him to that city at the autumn period. He stayed there for three months (Acts 19:8) and then apparently for two years more (Acts 19:10; cf. 20:31). This brings us to A.D. 55. It was apparently the Pentecost of that year that he wished to spend in Jerusalem (Acts 20:16). This means that the three months he spent in Greece just prior to the journey (Acts 20:3), during which he wrote Romans (he was about to go to Jerusalem, Rom. 15:25), would be the early months of A.D. 55.[17] This would be supported if Acts 24:27, "when two years had passed", means when Felix had been in office for two years (not when Paul had been a prisoner for two years), and if Festus succeeded Felix in A.D. 55.[18] There are, of course, many

14. Though perhaps we should notice the view of Robert M. Grant, who, on the basis of the names mentioned in ch. 16, judges it "likely that Romans was written not from Greece but from Macedonia, perhaps specifically from Philippi—or perhaps across the Aegean Sea, from Troas" (A Historical Introduction to the New Testament [London, 1963], p. 188). But the evidence is inadequate.

15. See Beginnings, V, pp. 460-61; C. K. Barrett, The New Testament Background: Selected Documents (London, 1956), pp. 48-49. Jerome Murphy-O'Connor, St. Paul's Corinth (Wilmington, DE, 1983), pp. 141-52, 173-76.

16. Cf. Kümmel, "Paul's encounter with Gallio perhaps took place in May or June of 51" (Introduction, p. 180).

17. Cf. Günther Bornkamm, "in the winter of A.D. 55/56" (ABR, XI [1963], p. 2). Bruce thinks that Acts 20:2 covers more than a year, "say from the summer of A.D. 55 to the late part of A.D. 56" (Commentary on the Book of the Acts [London, 1954], p. 405). This would place Romans in early 57, a date which J. A. T. Robinson accepts "confidently" (Redating the New Testament [London, 1976], p. 55). Cranfield regards the winter-spring of A.D. 55-56 or a year later as the most likely time (pp. 14, 16).

18. See Ernst Haenchen, The Acts of the Apostles (Oxford, 1971), pp. 661-63; Beginnings, V, pp. 464-67, 471 n.1.

uncertainties, and no dating can ever be more than approximate. Some date Romans as early as A.D. 53.[19] But A.D. 55 seems to satisfy the data as well as any year.

OCCASION

From its situation in the capital city the Roman church would have had good means of communication with the churches in other cities. Christians would be coming and going. This church might well have a widespread influence, and from the respectful way Paul addresses it the inference is that it had not only had such an influence but had used it well. It had set a good example to believers everywhere.

Two questions arise then. Why did Paul write to such a church? And if he did write, why write such a letter as this? It is curious that, despite the importance everyone concedes to this epistle, there is no agreement about the answers we should give.[20]

One searches the epistle carefully for information that might help with the answers. What emerges is that Paul had never been to Rome, though for a long time he had wanted to visit the Christians there (1:8-13; 15:23). He says that he had been hindered from coming to Rome (1:13; 15:22), which seems to mean that he had tried to come but had been stopped. When he wrote, however, he had the prospect of a trip to Spain (15:22-29), which would give him the opportunity to visit the Roman Christians along the way. Some of the things he says are not easy to harmonize with one another. Thus, on the one hand he wanted to impart some spiritual gift to the Roman Christians, to have "some fruit" among them, and to preach the gospel among them (1:11, 13, 15). On the other hand he says that it was not his custom to preach the gospel where Christ was already named lest he build on someone else's foundation (15:20). Why did the man who did not build on other people's foundations want to preach in the flourishing church in Rome? It is not at all obvious.

Romans does not deal with local issues in the manner of, say, 1 Corinthians. It is a majestic epistle, dealing with grand themes. It has proved relevant to the needs of Christians in a great variety of situations. But sometimes Paul addresses himself to specific difficulties in Rome. Most students feel, for example, that the discussion of the weak and the strong (14:1–15:13) shows that Paul had information about one of the problems at Rome.[21]

---

19. John Knox, IB, 9, p. 358. J. R. Richards argues for A.D. 54 (NTS, XIII [1966-67], p. 27).

20. Despite the fact that J. A. T. Robinson says cheerfully that the occasion, as well as the author and date of the epistle, "are fortunately all beyond serious dispute" (Robinson, p. 1).

21. In addition to this point Kümmel notes the references to "dissensions and difficulties, in opposition to the doctrine which you have been taught" (16:17-18); "Jewish errors and criticism of the gospel" (2:17; 3:1-31; 4:1; 7:13; 9:31-32; 11:11); "libertine-antinomian

From all this a broad classification emerges. Some scholars are impressed by the paucity of references to Rome and see the letter as originating in questions outside that city. Others hold that it was written to meet some specific need in the Roman church.[22] There is great variety in both camps and no approach to agreement. We notice a number of suggestions.

1. *A Compendium of Christian Teaching.* This is the traditional view.[23] Something like it has been expressed in recent times by Anders Nygren.[24] This approach is based on the steady treatment of great themes throughout the epistle. But it does not allow for the specific references to Rome. Nor does it appear why Paul should write such a compendium to Rome (Colossians, another letter to a church Paul had never visited, is quite different). Nor does it account for some important omissions. Much needs to be added in some areas for a compendium, such as christology (cf. Ephesians, Philippians, Colossians), the resurrection (1 Corinthians), the church (Ephesians), and eschatology (1 and 2 Thessalonians). Nothing is said about holy communion. If Romans is a compendium of theology, there are some curious gaps.

2. *Paul's Mature Thinking on Essential Christianity.* Günther Bornkamm calls it Paul's "last will and testament".[25] Bornkamm finds many topics in Romans already dealt with in earlier epistles, but there in polemical contexts. In Romans they are given "a strongly universal meaning".[26] Bornkamm thinks that Paul has gone back to his conversion experience and that Romans reflects his history and struggles. He sums it up in this way: "This great document, which summarizes and develops the most important themes and thoughts of the Pauline message and theology and which elevates his theology above the moment of definite situations and conflicts into the sphere of the eternally and universally valid, this letter to the Romans is the last will and testament of the Apostle Paul."[27] One cannot but agree with much of this. But

---

deductions from the message of the freedom of the Christians from the Law" (3:8, 31; 6:1,15; 7:7ff.); and "Gentile-Christian arrogance" (11:13ff.). He does not see this as the account of a situation frequently encountered and thus a statement drawn up in the first place for general use, then adapted for Rome (*Introduction*, p. 221).

22. Brevard S. Childs examines "The Problem of the Addressee" in this letter (*The New Testament as Canon: An Introduction* [London, 1984], pp. 260-63). He can say, "regardless of the concrete character of Paul's original addressee, in their present literary form, the chapters serve to denote a genuine ambiguity. The occasional addressee recedes within the larger context and a universal referent emerges which far transcends local Roman party rivalries in order to speak a word for all" (p. 262).

23. Cf. W. G. T. Shedd, "The object of the writer was to give to the Roman congregation, and ultimately to Christendom, a complete statement of religious truth" (Shedd, p. viii).

24. He sees the epistle as addressed to "the great problem of all Christendom. What is the new that entered with Christ? What is it that the congregation has by faith in Him? And what is the relation between the new way of salvation, the way of faith, and the way in which the people of God had hitherto walked, the way of works?" (Nygren, p. 8).

25. "The Letter to the Romans as Paul's Last Will and Testament", ABR, XI (1963), pp. 2-14.

26. *Ibid.*, p. 12.

27. *Ibid.*, p. 14. Barclay reminds us that Sanday called Romans "testamentary" and

it scarcely gives a reason why Paul should have written the letter. Granted that Romans contains the apostle's mature reflection on what Christianity is all about, we must still ask, Why did Paul set this mature reflection down in writing? And if he did, Why send it to Rome?

3. *A Discussion of the Church.* Franz J. Leenhardt finds the occasion in Paul's preparation for his missionary work in Spain. He had concluded his work in the East, where he had fully proclaimed the gospel from Jerusalem to Illyrica (15:19). Thus far the church had what we might call geographical unity. There was no problem in all the converts Paul had made looking to Jerusalem as the mother church. But "for regions as distant as Spain, what specific role could this church still claim?"[28] Where he might have written a "Doctrine of the Church" Paul preferred to tackle the problem another way. "The object of his letter is to show that all believers benefit from the promises made to Abraham and that, by faith and baptism, they are thus incorporated into the people of God, thanks to the secret operation of the Holy Ghost."[29] But it is not easy to see this in the letter. Baptism comes before us only in 6:3-4, while the term "church" is confined to chapter 16. It is not Protestant prejudice but careful attention to the language of the letter that compels us to see the aim elsewhere. And in any case, Why Rome? Leenhardt does not produce a sufficient reason for addressing a treatment of the nature of the church to the Roman Christians.

4. *A Circular Letter.* Some who emphasize the wide applicability of the letter see it as originally a circular. There is convincing evidence that at one time there was a 14-chapter edition and some indication also of a 15-chapter edition (see below, pp. 21ff.). It is also true that in some MSS the words "in Rome" are lacking in 1:7, 15 (see above, p. 3). The suggestion is made that Paul wrote an original letter of 14 (or 15) chapters to be sent to a number of churches. Rome was, of course, one of them, and it is in the form addressed to the church in that city that the letter has come down to us. T. W. Manson sees an original 15-chapter edition of which one copy went to Rome and another, with chapter 16 added, to Ephesus.[30] The letter was written at the end of a very controversial period, as we see from the earlier letters. Manson reminds us that throughout Romans Paul frequently answers objections, and he holds that "we have here a record made by Paul and his clerical helpers of a real discussion."[31] It represents Paul's summing up of positions he and his friends had reached. "Looked at in this way Romans ceases to be just a letter of self-

---

he comments, "It is as if Paul was writing his theological last will and testament" (Barclay, p. xxi). Gore quotes approvingly Hort's view that the writing has the character of "last words" (Gore, p. 5).

28. Leenhardt, p. 15.

29. *Ibid.*, p. 16. Later he asks, "Ought we to be surprised that the theme of the church, in spite of the absence of the word, should be as it were the horizon towards which all the main lines of the thought expounded in the letter tend?" (*ibid.*, p. 20). In all honesty I can answer only, "Yes, we ought."

30. See above, p. 3 n.6.

31. *Studies*, p. 240.

introduction from Paul to the Roman church, and becomes a manifesto setting forth his deepest convictions on central issues, a manifesto calling for the widest publicity, which the Apostle did his best—not without success—to give it."[32]

There is something undeniably attractive about such views. But the question persists, Why Rome? That Paul was setting down his deep convictions after a period of conflict is no reason for sending the result to a church to which he was a stranger. Further, there must be a reason for a circular, just as for a letter to a definite destination. What is the reason for this one? No really convincing suggestion has been made. Nor is there any real evidence that it was ever sent anywhere but to Rome. Most scholars find a decisive argument against all circular-letter theories in the very personal tone of some parts of the letter, for example, 1:8-15.[33] It is very difficult indeed to think that 1:10-11 was originally written to no one in particular. Moreover, it would be strange to have a record of controversies without one reference to a specific opponent.[34]

5. The Jerusalem Church. Paul was about to start for Jerusalem when this letter was written. He was taking a large sum of money for the church there but was obviously doubtful about the reception he would get. Some hold that it is this that gives us the key to Romans. Jacob Jervell entitles his study of our letter, "The Letter to Jerusalem".[35] He points to our inability to be certain about the composition of the church in Rome (was it Jewish? or Gentile? or both?) and its circumstances. We cannot accordingly show that Paul was writing with the circumstances of the Roman church primarily in mind. Moreover, "the letter itself states clearly that its raison d'etre does not stem from the situation in the Roman congregation, but is to be found in Paul himself at the time of writing."[36] His major concern at that time was the reception of his gift of money by the saints in Jerusalem.[37] Thus "The essential and primary

---

32. *Ibid.*, p. 241.

33. Interestingly, John Knox finds this section a principal argument for a circular letter (NTS, II [1955-56], pp. 191-93). He points to the fact that Paul does not indicate his destination anywhere in ch. 1; he says only that he "longs to see" the Romans (and similar expressions). He may accordingly be "leaving as it stood a letter which was originally composed for a type of Gentile church with which Paul is seeking to establish contact" (*ibid.*, p. 192). But Knox pays no attention to the warmth of the personal tone of this section. Could Paul say of every Gentile church with which he sought to establish contact, "your faith is being reported all over the world" (1:8)? Or "I long to see you" (1:11)? Or that he had often tried to come to them (1:13)? This is particular, not general language.

34. Cf. Bornkamm, "it seems to me very inadequate to understand Romans as a mere report and record of former controversies. In that case one would have to expect some concrete references to Paul's opponents in the East; and those are completely lacking in our letter" (ABR, XI, p. 9).

35. Donfried, pp. 61-74.

36. *Ibid.*, p. 62. James Moffatt from a different point of view sees Paul's own circumstances as primary, not anything in Rome: the aim is "to state, for the primary benefit of the Roman Christians, the χάρισμα πνευματικόν which Paul was conscious of possessing in his knowledge of the gospel" (*An Introduction to the Literature of the New Testament* [Edinburgh, 1927], p. 145).

37. A. J. M. Wedderburn stresses the importance of the collection. It was not only a matter of money, but had symbolic significance. It was too late for the Romans to contrib-

content of Romans (1:18–11:36) is a reflection upon its major content, the 'collection speech,' or more precisely, the defence which Paul plans to give before the church in Jerusalem."[38] Why then write to Rome? Because Paul wants the Romans to pray for him and to stand behind him so that he can claim their support. "Paul wants to represent the entire Gentile world in Jerusalem, including the West."[39]

It is, of course, highly probable that when Paul wrote to the Romans he had in mind that he would face a difficult task in Jerusalem. We need not doubt that some of the things he writes in Romans he would say in Jerusalem. But there still remains the stubborn question, "If his letter really was 'The Letter to Jerusalem' why send it to Rome?" That makes no sense. The reason Jervell gives is insufficient. In any case, nothing in Romans indicates that Paul wanted assurance that he would represent Rome in the coming debate. If he wanted Roman support, why does he not ask for it? And how would Roman support (if he could get it) be brought to bear, or even be known, in Jerusalem? This view points to some interesting facts, but it does not carry conviction. It does not account for the epistle as a whole.

6. *Personal Claims.* Another view which roots the origin of the letter in Paul's own circumstances is that of Käsemann. "The most important theological epistle in Christian history is undoubtedly also the record of an existence struggling for recognition and of an apostolicity called into question. Apart from this insight Romans cannot be interpreted correctly"[40] Käsemann holds that Paul continually asserts an apostolic authority which many in the church refused to concede to him. We may freely accept this without drawing the conclusion that Paul was continually worried and embarrassed by the rejection of his claims (his list of troubles in 2 Cor. 11:23-29 would not lead to such a conclusion). Romans does not read like the desperate product of a man on the defensive and worried that people will not recognize him. Its calm, magisterial tone has often been noted, and passages like 1:11-12 do not prove Käsemann's point.

7. *Apostolic Foundation.* Günter Klein is impressed by the statement that Paul does not build on another's foundation (15:20). But he does plan to preach the gospel in Rome (1:15). Klein sees the reconciliation of these passages in the fact that the Roman church had not been founded by an apostle. The situation was unique. Paul "was dealing with addressees whose faith was beyond question but who still were lacking the authentic apostolic stamp."[41] Paul's aim in this writing and in the preaching he planned in Rome was to give this "authentic apostolic stamp" to the church in Rome.[42]

---

ute, but they could at least support it and thus "endorse the Gentile mission and its gospel, whose fruits were being offered in the collection and in the persons of its bearers" (ET, XC [1978-79], p. 141).

38. Jervell, in Donfried, p. 64.
39. *Ibid.*, p. 74.
40. Käsemann, p. 20.
41. Donfried, p. 46.
42. "Paul's Purpose in Writing the Epistle to the Romans", *ibid.*, pp. 32-49.

11

But this is more than the letter says and it smacks of an ecclesiasticism that is foreign to all we know of Paul. It is more than difficult to see how, on New Testament premises, preaching the gospel to Christians whose faith was well known (1:8) and who were full of goodness and knowledge and able to admonish one another (15:14) could be justified. Klein simply says, "Paul can consider an apostolic effort in Rome because he does not regard the local Christian community there as having an apostolic foundation";[43] the Romans lacked "the fundamental kerygma."[44] He recognizes that his view points to "a shockingly authoritarian understanding of the apostolic office"[45] but gives no reason for seeing Paul in this shockingly authoritarian role. There must have been many churches in the first century which had been founded by itinerant Christians of the rank and file.[46] Must some apostle have visited each of them before it could be accepted as a Christian church?

A related but more acceptable view is that of A. Fridrichsen: "I believe that the main motive of Romans is to assert, in a discreet way, the apostolic authority and teaching of Paul in the church of Rome."[47] But even this way of putting it goes beyond the evidence. If the view of E. A. Judge and G. S. R. Thomas were accepted, namely that there was no church in Rome at the time Paul wrote,[48] it might be possible to work out the view that Paul wrote to gather the scattered Christians in Rome into a church. But in the form Klein gives it the theory can scarcely be accepted.

8. *The "Weak" and the "Strong"*. Quite a number of scholars have in recent times seen the key to understanding this letter in the references to the "weak" and the "strong" in 14:1–15:13.[49] They usually see the weak as Jewish Christians who had long been accustomed to the Jewish food regulations and to the observance of special days such as the Sabbath and the feast days laid down in the Old Testament. The strong, then, are the Gentile Christians who have no such inhibitions but enter more wholeheartedly into Christian

---

43. *Ibid.*, p. 44.
44. *Ibid.*, p. 48.
45. *Ibid.*, p. 49.
46. The church at Antioch is a fairly clear example. Luke appears to connect its founding with the preaching of Christians scattered by the persecution that arose in connection with the death of Stephen (Acts 11:19ff.). But he expressly says that the apostles were not scattered with the rest (Acts 8:1).
47. Cited in John Knox, NTS, II, p. 191.
48. See above, p. 2 n.4.
49. See Karris's list in CBQ, XXXV (1933), p. 155 n.6. Paul S. Minear gives an extended treatment of this theme in his book *The Obedience of Faith* (London, 1971). He distinguishes "at least five distinct factions, or, if faction be too strong a word, five different positions" (*ibid.*, p. 8), namely "The 'weak in faith' who condemned the 'strong in faith'", "The strong in faith who scorned and despised the weak in faith", "The doubters", "The weak in faith who did not condemn the strong", "The strong in faith who did not despise the weak" (*ibid.*, pp. 8-14). There is nothing improbable about such groups' coming into existence, but the evidence for them is not convincing. Minear's distinctions have not won wide acceptance, nor has his view that a number of passages in Romans are addressed primarily to one or another of these groups. Minear's treatment is stimulating, but comes short of being an acceptable solution.

freedom. Sometimes this is given precision by referring to the edict of Claudius which caused all Jews to be expelled from Rome (Acts 18:2).[50] The reasoning is that the Roman church consisted originally almost entirely of Jews who presumably worshipped in synagogues (see above, p. 4). When the Jews were driven out, the Gentile Christians remained. Their numbers grew. Then when the edict of banishment was rescinded, Jewish Christians returned and found Gentiles in control of the church. The two groups found it difficult to adjust to one another.[51] Wolfgang Wiefel thinks that at first the authorities did not permit the returning Jews to organize synagogues and that this stimulated the development of Christian house churches with a multiplicity of small congregations and obvious possibilities of friction.[52] This was assisted by the fact that the synagogues were originally independent and that in Rome there was no coordinating figure like the ethnarch in Alexandria.[53] Paul wrote to the Roman church to admonish the two factions to live at peace.[54]

50. This view is argued by, e.g., Willi Marxsen, *Introduction to the New Testament* (Philadelphia, 1980), pp. 95-104. Marxsen is supported by Karl Paul Donfried, "A Short Note on Romans 16" (JBL, LXXXIX [1970], pp. 441-49). Donfried is basically concerned to argue that ch. 16 is an integral part of Romans, and he maintains that this accords with the position of Marxsen.

51. Raymond E. Brown has difficulty with the idea of "Jewish Christian" and "Gentile Christian" as early as this (though he allows that the distinction may be acceptable in the second century). Hebrew Christians were of more than one type and differed from one another more than they differed from the Gentiles whom they converted. He finds four groups: (1) Jewish Christians and their Gentile converts who held to the full observance of the law of Moses; (2) Jewish Christians and their Gentile converts who did not insist on circumcision for Gentiles but required the keeping of some Jewish purity laws; (3) Jewish Christians and their Gentile converts who did not insist on circumcision or food laws for Gentiles; and (4) Jewish Christians and their Gentile converts who did not insist on circumcision or food laws for Gentiles and saw no abiding significance in the cult of the temple (CBQ, 45 [1983], pp. 74-79). Whatever be thought of his four groups, a good deal can be said for the view that Gentile converts would tend to agree with the Jews who had converted them and that a hard division that lumps all Jewish Christians together as distinct from all Gentile Christians is most unlikely. Brown sees Roman Christianity as essentially his group 2 (Raymond E. Brown and John P. Meier, *Antioch and Rome* [New York, 1983], p. 184).

52. Donfried, pp. 100-119.

53. According to Josephus, in Alexandria "a great part of the city has been allocated to this nation. And an ethnarch of their own has been installed, who governs the people and adjudicates suits and supervises contracts and ordinances, just as if he were the head of a sovereign state" (*Ant.* xiv 117; Loeb translation).

54. W. S. Campbell does not particularly stress chs. 14 and 15, but he holds that "A division had apparently arisen because the liberal-minded Gentile Christian majority (the strong in faith) were unwilling to have fellowship with the conservative Jewish Christian minority (the weak in faith)." Since the fault lay with the Gentile Christians, "Paul undertakes an exposition of the righteous purpose of God both for Jew and Gentile as fulfilled in Jesus Christ and revealed in the Gospel" (ET, LXXXV [1973-74], p. 268). Stephen Neill argues for three groups with different attitudes to Jewish observances, but uncertain how "to co-exist without friction". "Paul is the recognized authority on all such questions; the perplexed Christians have sent a message to him asking for guidance, and the Epistle to the Romans is the result" (*Jesus through Many Eyes* [Philadelphia, 1976], p. 63).

Against all such views is the fact that nowhere in Romans does Paul appear as the mediator between warring factions. He indicates that he wanted to come to Rome to preach the gospel (1:15) and to impart some spiritual gift (1:11). There is not a word, however, about bringing fighting factions together. It is, moreover, incredible that if such a problem existed, and indeed was the reason for writing the letter, he would wait until chapter 14 to deal with it. When he did face factions, as in the church at Corinth, he put off everything, even the letter the church had written to him with specific questions for which they wanted answers, until he had repudiated division in the strongest of terms. "Is Christ divided?" he asked. "Was Paul crucified for you?" (1 Cor. 1:13). There is no equivalent in Romans. There Paul's tone is consistently mild. It is also curious on this view that he addresses the Roman church as Gentiles (1:5-6, 13; 15:15-16). This is no way to maintain the balance between feuding factions.

It must also be borne in mind that it is far from certain that 14:1–15:13 refers to Jews and Gentiles.[55] The positions assigned to the weak are not known to have been held by Jews and some seem very difficult to assign to them, namely the use of vegetables and the abstention from wine. These practices could just as easily be seen as characteristic of Gentiles. Further, when Paul does refer to Jews, a good deal of what he says applies to non-Christian Jews, not Jewish Christians (especially in chs. 9–11). It is also true that views of this kind are usually far too confident in their descriptions of the church in Rome. The origins and early history of that church are lost in obscurity. It has never been proved that 14:1–15:13 refers to parties rather than to individuals, and if it does, to the precise membership of those parties. Robert J. Karris argues strongly against views which make this section the key to the epistle.[56] He holds that no such specific reference can be demonstrated. "Rom 14:1–15:31 has no specific referent within the Roman community. It is part of a letter which sums up Paul's missionary theology and paraenesis."[57] Karris is not so much outlining how he thinks the letter came to be written as denying that the section 14:1–15:31 describes a concrete situation with sufficient clarity for us to see in it the occasion for the letter. I do not see how his argument can be resisted.[58]

---

55. Cf. Karris, CBQ, XXXV, p. 172 n.73 where a number of writers are cited as raising objections to the hypothesis that the weak and the strong are Jews and Gentiles. Even if this be accepted, there are still problems: "Are the Jewish Christians legalists, liberals, apocalyptically-oriented or what? Are the Gentile Christians legalists, antinomians, Gnostic-influenced or what? What is the specific nature of the conflict between Jewish and Gentile Christians which Paul is supposed to have heard about and is trying to settle by writing Rom?" (CBQ, XXXVI [1974], p. 356; the words occur in a short article entitled "The Occasion of Romans: A Response to Professor Donfried", ibid., pp. 356-58).

56. "Rom 14:1–15:13 and the Occasion of Romans" (CBQ, XXXV [1973], pp. 155-78).

57. Ibid., p. 177.

58. Raymond E. Brown at one point says, "I would insist parenthetically that it is quite implausible that all Christian Jews were expelled from Rome by Claudius—only those zealous enough to be involved in disturbances (wherefore evangelists like Prisca and Aquila)" (Antioch and Rome, p. 109).

9. *Liberalizing a Reactionary Church.* Matthew Black thinks that the Roman church was a large one ("next to Jerusalem, it was probably the largest in the Empire"), and that it was, from Paul's point of view, "reactionary", "imperfect", "immature", "still probably little more than a sect within Judaism".[59] Paul wrote, accordingly, to win it over to his way of thinking. If the Roman church were as Black depicts it, we need not doubt that Paul would make strenuous efforts to see that it came to embrace the doctrine of God's free grace. But do we know all this about the Roman church? On the same evidence Judge and Thomas argue that there was not even a church in Rome, let alone a strong one.[60] We must accept the fact that we do not know how the Roman church compared with other churches in respect of size or ecclesiastical outlook. The hypothesis is an attractive one, but there does not seem sufficient evidence to sustain it.

10. *Rhetorical Genre.* In an article entitled "Paul's Rhetoric of Argumentation in Romans: An Alternative to the Donfried-Karris Debate over Romans",[61] Wilhelm Wuellner finds the Donfried-Karris discussion of the epistle "unfruitful" and suggests a new approach: "I propose to replace the traditional priority on propositional theology and the more recent priority on letters as literature with the new priority on letters as argumentation."[62] He speaks of three basic rhetorical genres: the forensic/legal, the deliberative/symbouleutic, and the demonstrative/epideictic. Romans belongs to the last mentioned, "the epideictic genre, which is concerned with judgments about some present situation. The traditional categories for judgment are called 'praise or blame'; we might call them today 'ok or not ok' judgments."[63] The argumentation "sets out to increase the intensity of adherence to certain values, which might not be contested when considered on their own but may nevertheless not prevail against other values that might come into conflict with them."[64]

This is an interesting approach and one which draws attention to features of Romans which have received scant attention. But it is possible to feel uneasy at the rigidity of literary style it ascribes to such an unlikely conformist as Paul.[65] And in any case this approach scarcely answers the main question. Granted that this was the way Paul wrote, why did he write at all? Why did he decide that an epideictic communication to the Roman church was what was needed? Did this arise from Paul's situation or that in Rome?

A more acceptable form of this view has been put forward by Robert

59. Black, pp. 22, 23.
60. See above, p. 2 n.4.
61. CBQ, XXXVIII (1976), pp. 330-51.
62. *Ibid.,* p. 330.
63. *Ibid.,* pp. 342-43.
64. *Ibid.,* p. 343.
65. Cf. Brevard S. Childs, "One is amazed by the formalistic quality of the argument which has virtually removed the interpretation from its historical and theological content" (*The New Testament as Canon*, p. 249).

Jewett.[66] He notes that there is a great variety in epideictic literature and demonstrates the point by reproducing Theodore C. Burgess's list of 27 subtypes. He holds that Romans is properly to be understood as an ambassadorial letter, though with features of other subtypes, "the passionate letter, the hortatory letter, and the philosophical diatribe."[67] The need to include these other subtypes perhaps shows that Jewett is oversimplifying; Romans is too complex to be regarded as simply an example of the ambassadorial letter. But Jewett has done us a service in drawing attention to the many diplomatic touches in this epistle, and specifically to Paul's acceptance of a variety of teachings as long as the essentials of the gospel are preserved. "It is the synthesis that constitutes Paul's distinctive perspective, the serious effort to unite the Gentile and the Jewish Christian confessions, hymns, and interpretive traditions."[68]

11. *A Dialogue with Judaism.* J. Christiaan Beker holds that Paul is concerned in this letter to respond to questions Jews might ask, such as "What is Israel's role in salvation-history?" and "What is the function of the Torah and circumcision?" He says that "Romans is a dialogue with Judaism" and again, "Romans must be characterized primarily as a dialogue with Jews."[69] It is a novel idea that this great Christian writing, possibly the greatest of them all, is really not directed at Christians but at Jews. The novelty need not disturb us, but the argumentation is not convincing. The letter is addressed to Roman Christians, and Beker has not given a convincing reason why it should not be understood as directed towards the addressees. While no one knows what the precise composition of the Roman church was at the time, it is usually held that there was a strong Gentile component. Moreover, Beker confines "The Jewish Character of the Argument" to 1:16–4:25, which leaves out most of the letter. And it includes 1:19-32, which most see as addressed to Gentiles (and which does seem pointless if directed at Jews; Beker's idea that it is Paul's intention here "to set a trap for the Jewish auditor"[70] is not convincing). The viewpoint is interesting, but the evidence does not support it.

12. *Preparation for a Visit.* Paul had never been to Rome, but for a long time he had wanted to visit the Christians there (1:8-13; 15:23). He had been hindered from coming to them (1:13; 15:22), which appears to mean that he had tried to come but had been stopped. But when he wrote, he had the prospect of a trip to Spain. He saw this as a good opportunity to visit Rome. When he headed West, it was unthinkable that he would pass by this great church which he had so greatly longed to see. The epistle must be seen, then, as a means of preparing the way for a visit. Paul wanted to exercise a ministry in Rome (1:11-15). This was to be more than a halt by the way as he enlisted support for his mission to Spain. He wanted to get to know the Roman church

---

66. "Romans as an Ambassadorial Letter", *Interpretation*, XXXVI (1982), pp. 5-20.
67. *Ibid.*, p. 9.
68. *Ibid.*, p. 19.
69. *Paul the Apostle* (Edinburgh, 1980), pp. 77, 86.
70. *Ibid.*, p. 79.

and to preach in the world's greatest city. He wanted the support of the Roman Christians in his further missionary work as he had had that of the church of Antioch in the preceding period.

Since Paul was not the most popular of men in the early church, it is likely that he had been criticized in Rome as elsewhere (cf. 3:8). He clearly regarded it as important that the Roman church support him on his Spanish mission (15:24). If they were to support him, it was not unreasonable that they should know what he preached. Accordingly he sets forth a clear but profound statement of the essential message of Christianity as he proclaimed it.[71] This will show the Romans where he stands. The result is one of the most important Christian documents ever written.[72]

With the experts so divided, it is plain that the evidence does not all point in one direction. In my opinion the last-mentioned view is on the whole the most satisfactory (which is not to say that it clears up all the difficulties; it does not). It takes cognizance of the fact that Paul had been a missionary for 20 years or so. With the completion of his mission to the East (15:19) an important chapter of his life had closed. It is not unreasonable to suppose that, with this work done and with a mission field in Spain before his mind's eye, Paul hoped to transfer his base from Antioch to Rome. But before anything else happened he had a little time when he could be quiet (the three months of Acts 20:3). He used the time to write to the Roman Christians to let them know of his plan to visit them and to set down in order something of what the gospel meant.[73] If Rome was to be his base, the Romans would need to be assured of his message and theological position. Thus such a weighty epistle is very much in place.

We may discern at least three things Paul specifically says he wanted to accomplish by his letter. First, he wanted to prepare the way for a visit to Rome (1:13; 15:22-24). Second, he wanted to secure the support of the Roman Christians for his Spanish mission (15:24). Third, he sought the prayers of the

71. Cf. Kümmel, "we need not doubt that Paul himself with this extensive, argumentative, and transcending representation gives an account of his gospel which he previously preached and which he is now bringing to the far West" (*Introduction*, p. 222); "Romans is the theological self-confession of Paul, which arose out of a concrete necessity of his missionary work" (*ibid.*, p. 221). Cf. James P. Martin, "Missionary vision for the whole world dominates Paul's description of his situation and hope at the time he wrote Romans" (*Interpretation*, XXV [1971], p. 303).

72. It is objected that Romans is too great for such a purpose. A much more modest missive would have sufficed to introduce Paul. So it would. But perhaps the objection minimizes Paul's missionary passion. His deep concern to preach in Rome and Spain meant that he spared no pains in preparing the way and perhaps said more than was strictly necessary. And if he had doubts about his capacity to survive Jerusalem (cf. Acts 20:25; 21:13), he may have wanted to make sure that his essential message was on record and would be read in Rome.

73. W. S. Campbell objects that Paul would not submit his gospel for approval and cites Gal. 1:8ff. (ET, LXXV, p. 264). But he overlooks the fact that, while Paul would not vary his gospel to secure human acceptance, he could and did submit it for approval (Gal. 2:2).

Romans, specifically prayers that he might be delivered from unbelievers, that the Jerusalem church would welcome the gift he was bringing,[74] and that he might come to Rome "in joy" (15:30-32).

CONTENTS

Romans is not greatly taken up with local issues (as is, e.g., 1 Corinthians). It is true that Paul is apparently not unmindful of certain happenings at Rome. Thus he has a good deal to say about positions taken up by Jews. It would be pointless to mention such views unless the Roman Christians knew that Jews did teach such things (2:17; 3; 4:1; 7:13; 9:31-32; 11:11, etc.). There are references to antinomian objections to Christian discipline (3:8, 31; 6:1, 15; 7:7ff.) and to Gentile arrogance over against the Jews (11:18ff.), and a warning against people "who cause divisions and put obstacles in your way that are contrary to the teaching you have learned" (16:17). Paul knows of the faith of the Roman Christians (1:8) and of their obedience (16:19). He speaks of the "strong" and the "weak" in such a way as to lead to the conclusion that both groups were represented at Rome (14:1–15:13). But, though such aspects of the epistle show that Paul had some knowledge of conditions at Rome, the letter is much more concerned with teachings which are timeless and which do not arise from contemporary Roman circumstances. It may be significant that Paul nowhere indicates that he had had communications from the church at Rome as he had had, for example, from the Corinthians (they had written to him, 1 Cor. 7:1; Chloe's people had given Paul news, 1 Cor. 1:11; and Stephanas and others had come from Corinth, 1 Cor. 16:17; there is no equivalent in Romans).

The letter is not to be understood apart from Paul's own experience. He had been brought up an orthodox Jew, a loyal Pharisee, fanatical to the point of persecuting the Christians. But on the Damascus road he had come face to face with the risen Christ. This encounter revolutionized his entire way of thinking and living. He saw now that God had been active in Christ and that it was through the cross that he had brought salvation to mankind. Grace, not

---

74. It is curious that the Jerusalem poor might raise difficulties about receiving a gift from the Gentile churches. But some conservatives there had opposed Paul at the Council of Jerusalem (Acts 15:1-2), and they may have grown stronger through the years. Conversions in Jerusalem would have been from among Jews. At the same time the Gentile churches had grown stronger and stronger. Under the leadership of men like Paul they would not have been willing to conform to Jewish attitudes to the law. Conservative Jews may well have been unwilling to countenance a Gentile-dominated church, or even a church that admitted Gentiles on equal terms. There were thousands of Jewish believers "all . . . zealous for the law" (Acts 21:20; cf. the request put to Paul, v. 24). They might well see acceptance of the money as countenancing an idea of unity which they did not accept. Cf. Günther Bornkamm, "Paul had to be prepared for reluctance on the part of the church in Jerusalem. They might be unwilling to go along with his demonstration of the solidarity of Jews and Gentiles. They might refuse to accept the collection" (*The New Testament: A Guide to Its Writings* [London, 1974], p. 109).

law, was decisive. Romans puts great stress on the divine initiative and on the centrality of grace. Paul is not taking his own experience as normative. An important section of the epistle is taken up with God's dealings with Abraham, and another with his activities with his own people Israel. But while God might deal with people in different ways, he has always acted by the way of grace.

By the time he wrote this letter Paul had been a Christian preacher for something like 20 years. He had three months without pressing commitments (Acts 20:3). He may well have felt that this was a good time, as the projected visit to Rome was a good occasion, to set out in order a summary of the gospel and its consequences as he understood them. In view of the uncertainties surrounding his reception at Jerusalem he may have thought that if he could secure the approval of the Roman Christians this would have good results at Jerusalem too (though there appears to be no way by which any Roman approval could have been known in Jerusalem in time to be of help to him).

After these preliminaries Paul states briefly the thesis of his letter, stressing the power of God manifest in the gospel and the importance of faith (1:16-17). Then he proceeds to a massive argument in which he shows that all people, Gentiles and Jews alike, are sinners and in danger of the judgment of God (1:18–3:20). This leads to the tremendous thought that by sending Christ to die on the cross God has opened the way for people to have right standing, "righteousness" before him. This means that their sin is put away, and that they are not required to earn their salvation by their own merit. Not that this is a new discovery. Paul goes back to Abraham to show that this had always been God's way.[75] Then he goes right back to Adam to show that the entail of sin which has shackled the human race from the very first has been broken in Christ. Though he puts such emphasis on justification by faith, Paul is not insensitive to the need for upright living; his doctrine that forgiveness is God's free gift in no way opens the door to a sluggard Christianity bereft of moral effort. He then goes on to the importance of a clean break with sin and to the gift of the Holy Spirit which enables the believer to walk in the ways of God (chs. 6–8).

Following this he gives himself over to a subject which clearly concerned him deeply, namely the problem posed by the fact that, though the Jews were God's own people, they had rejected God's Messiah when he came. For three chapters Paul wrestles with the question of whether God has rejected his people and concludes that God has acted and always will act in mercy (chs. 9–11). In the final major section of the letter (chs. 12–15) he writes of the way in which the life of faith is to be lived in the actual world in which we find ourselves, and he rounds it all off with a section of greetings and the like (ch. 16).

75. By contrast, "In Jewish tradition, Abraham, by his constancy in trial, had become the model of justification by works" (Wilfrid J. Harrington, *Record of the Fulfillment: The New Testament* [London, 1968], p. 265). Paul's example cut at the heart of the Jewish opposition to his central doctrine.

INTRODUCTION

This is a massive treatment of great themes, themes which are right at the heart of the Christian faith. Romans does not offer much that is new. In his earlier writings Paul has given expression to many of the themes he develops in this epistle.[76] But there is a sustained depth in Romans which is unmatched, and a concentration on the great, central doctrines of the Christian faith.[77] When these great thoughts are lost sight of, what remains is not authentic Christianity. But when they are affirmed, essential Christianity is proclaimed. Perhaps this is why Romans has a way of coming to the fore at any time of revival of vital Christianity.

One point that is often overlooked and should be stressed is that Romans is fundamentally a book about God.[78] It is obvious to all that Romans is concerned with the gospel, with salvation, and so on. But many students seem not to have noticed Paul's preoccupation with God. The thought of God dominates this epistle. The word "God" occurs 153 times in Romans, an average of once every 46 words. This is more often than in any other New Testament writing (except the short 1 Peter and 1 John). Acts has the word 166 times, but since it is so much longer this works out to once in 110 words. The only other books with more than 100 occurrences are Luke with 122 and 1 Corinthians with 105. And not only does "God" occur in Romans more frequently than in any other writing, it occurs more often than any other theme in that book. Apart from a few prepositions, pronouns, and the like,[79] no word is used in Romans with anything like the frequency of "God". Next is "law" (72 times), then "Christ" (65), "sin" (48), "Lord" (43), and "faith" (40). Statistics must always be used with caution, but these figures draw attention to the important fact that in Romans the one great theme is God. Paul writes on a number of topics, but everything is related to God. He sees law, for example, not in the abstract but in relation to the way of God. He sees Christ as bringing about "the righteousness of God". He sees sin as sin against God. And so on. Romans may truly be described in a way that no other book can be, as a book about God. It is perhaps this that gives it its importance and its appeal.[80]

76. Bornkamm lists 16 points in which Romans is related to the earlier Pauline writings (ABR, XI [1963], pp. 9-11).

77. Cf. A. M. Hunter, "in Romans we have the answer to the question, 'What is Christianity?' by the strongest thinker in the early Church" (Introducing the New Testament [London, 1945], p. 75).

78. Ralph P. Martin, discussing the plan of Romans, makes the point that "Much of Paul's thought is shaped along trinitarian lines. The Father purposes both to condemn and to save; the Son's obedience and righteousness lay the foundation of justification; and the Spirit's new life imparts a dynamic for victory over sin and death and a new social life-style in the church and society" (New Testament Foundations, II [Exeter, 1978], p. 194).

79. The only words which occur more frequently in Romans than θεός are the definite article (1,105 times), καί 274 times, ἐν 172 times, and αὐτός 156 times. Even common words like δέ and the verb εἶναι ("to be") occur less frequently (147 and 113 times respectively).

80. See further my essay "The Theme of Romans" in Apostolic History and the Gospel, ed. W. Ward Gasque and Ralph P. Martin (Exeter, 1970), pp. 249-63.

THE SHORTER EDITION(S)

There are problems at the end of Romans. From the fact that the doxology (16:25-27) is found at the end of chapter 15 in the very important P46 (the oldest extant MS of the Pauline epistles) some, notably T. W. Manson, have reasoned that there was at one time a 15-chapter edition.[81] This cannot be dismissed as impossible. It is easy to conjecture that Paul wrote a 15-chapter edition or that chapter 16 with all its local interest was omitted when the letter circulated outside Rome. But it remains conjecture, and the lack of supporting evidence tells against it. The occurrence of the doxology at the end of chapter 15 may be significant. On the other hand it may mean no more than that one scribe did not think chapter 16 suitable for reading to a congregation. And we must bear in mind that neither with nor without the doxology does the close of chapter 15 conform to Paul's normal way of closing letters.

There is more to be said for a 14-chapter edition.

1. *The doxology* is found at the end of chapter 14 in many MSS.[82]

2. *Marcion* appears to have had a 14-chapter edition. Tertullian says this,[83] and Origen lends support.[84]

3. *The Breves.* One MS of the Vulgate, the Codex Amiatinus, has the usual 16 chapters, but it also has some numbered summaries of sections of the epistle, which are called *breves.* No. 50 reads, "Concerning the danger of

---

81. For Manson, see above, p. 3, and the references given there. Throughout this section I am, of course, referring to our way of dividing the epistle. In the original there would have been no chapter divisions. In time students of the epistle produced a number of ways of dividing it. The modern chapter divisions in the New Testament appear to have been drawn up by Stephen Langton during the thirteenth century (see *The Cambridge History of the Bible*, II, ed. G. W. H. Lampe [Cambridge, 1969], pp. 147-48).

82. UBS cites the following as having the doxology here only: L Ψ 0209[vid] 181 326 330 451 614 1175 1241 1877 1881 1984 1985 2492 2495 *Byz Lect* it[dem] syr[h] mss[acc. to Origen lat] Chrysostom (Theodore) Cyril Theodoret John-Damascus. It is read both here and at 16:25 by A P 5 33 88 104 460[lat] arm; it is read only at 15:33 by P46; it is omitted entirely by F[gr] G (this MS leaves a space) 629 it[dc(?)[g]] Marcion[acc. to Origen lat] mss[acc. to Jerome [vid]]; it is read only at 16:25 by a large number of MSS led by P61 ℵ B C D D[abs [1]] 81 436 it[mss] vg syr[p] cop[sa.bo] eth Clement Origen[lat] mss[acc. to Origen lat] Ambrosiaster.

83. Tertullian refers to Rom. 14:10 as *in clausula epistolae*, "in the conclusion of the letter" (*Adv. Marc.* v.14). This need not mean that these were the very last words, but it is difficult to think that more than two chapters followed. Barrett, however, refuses to press this point on the ground that in later Latin *clausula* could be used for any division of a document (Barrett, p. 11; here, however, it is *clausula epistolae*, which does not look like a division). Tertullian repeats that Marcion has made serious omissions from Romans (*Adv. Marc.* v.13, 14).

84. Rufinus's Latin version of Origen's commentary on Romans tells us that "from that place where it is written 'all that is not of faith is sin'" (i.e., Rom. 14:23) Marcion "cut it away up to the end (*usque ad finem cuncta dissecuit*)" (cited from Gamble, p. 22). There is a tiny doubt here, for *dissecuit* strictly means "cut in pieces". But most take it here in the sense *desecuit*, "cut off". This appears to be what Origen is saying. We have evidence of a text lacking chs. 15 and 16, but not of one with a mutilated version of these two chapters. T. Zahn, however, took the word strictly and found it unthinkable that Marcion should have discarded all of chs. 15 and 16 (*Introduction*, pp. 396ff.).

grieving a brother by one's food, and that the kingdom of God is not food and drink, but righteousness and peace and joy in the Holy Spirit." This clearly refers to 14:13-23. No. 51, however, reads, "Concerning the mystery of the Lord kept in silence before the passion, his truth having been revealed after the passion."[85] This surely refers to the doxology (16:25-27). Thus these summaries are no doubt based on a shorter edition and not on the 16-chapter edition to which they are now attached.[86] They are found in a number of other MSS, so the system was widely used. Harry Gamble also points to Codex Fuldensis, in which Romans 1–14 is divided into 23 sections followed by the Amiatine divisions 24-51.[87] There are problems here, but since the Fuldensian divisions end at chapter 14 this is further evidence for a 14-chapter edition. We should add a reference to an ancient concordance to the Pauline epistles found in some Vulgate MSS where heading no. 42 refers to Romans 14:17ff., and no. 43 to the doxology.[88]

4. *Tertullian, Irenaeus, and Cyprian* make no quotations from chapters 15 and 16.[89] They have left rather full writings, and some of the matter in these chapters would have been useful to them. They stand in contrast to Clement of Alexandria, who has quite a number of citations from these two chapters. But early Western writers generally make no appeal to Romans 15–16. As Gamble puts it, "the cumulative *argumentum e silentio* is quite strong: there is a consensus of Western writers through the third century, no part of the text is quoted even where its appropriateness is obvious, and the extent of the text is such that silence on it can have but one explanation: chs. 15 and 16 of the Roman letter were not generally known in the West for a long time."[90]

5. *The Marcionite Prologue to Romans* says that the letter was written "from Athens".[91] This presupposes the 14-chapter edition, since the last two chapters so clearly point to Corinth as the place of origin (15:25-27; 16:1, 23).

All this convinces most students that a 14-chapter edition did at one time exist. But it is not clear how this was related to the longer edition. One suggestion is that the shorter form came first and that it was written as a

---

85. I have cited these *breves* from Gamble, p. 16.

86. F. F. Bruce adduces an argument from silence. "The *Book of Testimonies* ascribed to Cyprian (died AD 258) includes a collection of biblical texts which enjoin withdrawal from heretics; this collection does not include Romans 16:17, which might have been thought an apt text for his purpose. This argument from silence, which would have little weight if it stood alone, must be taken along with other pieces of evidence" (Bruce, p. 27). Gamble also draws attention to this (p. 20).

87. Gamble, p. 17.

88. *Ibid.*, pp. 18-19.

89. This is significant but its importance should not be exaggerated. None of the three quotes from 1 Cor. 16 either, but this is not usually seen as an argument that that chapter is unauthentic.

90. Gamble, p. 21. The only exception he can find is the Muratorian fragment, and even here there is dispute.

91. Cited from Alexander Souter, *The Text and Canon of the New Testament* (London, 1935), p. 206. There is, of course, doubt as to whether the prologues really are Marcionite, but it is usual to cite them under this name.

circular.[92] Those who hold this remind us of the absence of "in Rome" from some MSS. They suggest that when Paul wanted to write to the Romans, he adapted an original circular with the insertion of the appropriate words in 1:7, 15 and the addition of the last two chapters.

There are, however, strong objections. Thus it is not easy to think that the warm words of 1:8-15 were not originally meant for any specific people (see also 1:6). Again, there is not a great deal of evidence that the words "in Rome" were missing at the same time as chapters 15 and 16.[93] A very important consideration is that the argument does not break off at the end of chapter 14 but continues right on to 15:13. It is difficult to think of a reason why Paul should have ended the letter at 14:23. The authenticity of chapter 15 seems obvious to most students. But if Paul did not write it when he wrote chapters 1–14, when did he write it? There is no obvious answer. Some scholars add that they find affinities between 1:8-13 and 15:14-32. These are not so much repetitions and the like as the kind of thinking natural in two parts of the same letter. For such reasons we should reject the idea that the 14-chapter edition was original, though it was certainly used very widely.[94]

It seems, then, that we should take the longer edition as what Paul wrote. But this raises the interesting question of how the shorter edition came to exist. It is most unlikely that Paul himself should have cut off the end of his argument,[95] and in any case 14:23 is a curious place to end an epistle. A number of suggestions have been made.

1. Scribes found little of value for general reading in the last two chapters, and thus omitted them. Gamble thinks that the shortening was due to a desire to make the letter more general.[96] With the local features cut out, this great writing was seen to belong to the church at large. This is quite possible. But why stop at 14:23, in the middle of Paul's argument?[97] It would be a strange proceeding.

2. Some see the shortening as due to the demands of liturgy. When the letter was read during worship, the last two chapters were omitted as unsuitable for worship. This may be so, though it can never be more than a guess.

---

92. E.g., Morton Scott Enslin, *Christian Beginnings* (New York and London, 1938), pp. 266ff.

93. Gamble, however, links the two. He is impressed by "the testimony of the Pauline bilinguals, which, properly evaluated, attest the phenomena together" (Gamble, p. 33).

94. Gamble sums up: "The evidence is geographically widespread, representing Europe (the Amiatine *capitula*, the *Concordia epistularum*, Irenaeus, the bilingual and other Old Latin witnesses), Africa (Tertullian and Cyprian), and the East (the Byzantine text and Origen), and this form of the letter can be traced back with confidence at least as far as the second century in the testimonies of Tertullian and Origen" (Gamble, p. 33).

95. "It is to us inconceivable that St. Paul should have himself mutilated his own argument by cutting off the conclusion of it" (SH, p. xcv).

96. Gamble, pp. 115-24.

97. Dodd has a suggestion: "there is perhaps no answer but the illimitable stupidity of editors" (Dodd, p. xvi).

And again, why stop at 14:23? The early part of chapter 15 at any rate is quite suitable in the liturgy.[98]

3. Many consider Marcion to be the most likely candidate. He would not have liked the way the Old Testament is used in chapter 15 (the quotations in vv. 9-12, and especially the way it is described in v. 4). Nor would he have cared to refer to Christ as "a servant to the circumcised" (v. 8).[99] The principal objection to Marcion is that the shorter edition was used so widely. Could a heretic have had such a wide influence?

4. The shortening may have been accidental. The end of a papyrus scroll could easily be damaged and break off. Against this is the widespread use of the shorter version. Could one damaged copy have had such wide influence? Or several copies break off at exactly the same place?

None of the suggestions is entirely convincing. There are strong objections to them all. Perhaps the view with most in its favor is that Marcion was the culprit, but we can scarcely put it more strongly than that.

THE DESTINATION OF CHAPTER 16

Quite a different question is the original destination of chapter 16. Many scholars wonder whether this was meant for the Roman church, and some take it as axiomatic that it was not. Usually such hold that its original destination was Ephesus but that it has somehow become attached to Romans. The following points are relevant.

1. *The salutations* are surprisingly numerous when we recall that Paul had never been to Rome. He greets 26 individuals (24 by name) and five households or house churches. He speaks of three "fellow-workers", two "fellow-prisoners", three people whom he calls "beloved", and a lady he greets as his mother. "Had Paul's friends, it is asked, migrated in a body to Rome?"[100] It is felt that he is more likely to have this number of friends at Ephesus (where he had ministered extensively) than at Rome (where he had never been).

But there is more to it than this. We must ask, for example, what would have been the reaction on others at Ephesus if 26 of their number were greeted in a letter read out in the assembly.[101] Paul must have known more than 26 of

---

98. The Anglican *Book of Common Prayer* provides that Rom. 15:4-13 be read on the second Sunday in Advent (as in a number of other churches). *An Australian Prayer Book* (Anglican) has Rom. 16:25-27 as a reading for the fourth Sunday in Advent.

99. "Such a concentration of material offensive to Marcion can scarcely be paralleled in the Pauline writings" (Bruce, p. 29).

100. Dodd, p. xvii.

101. Cranfield makes the point against Ephesus that Paul had ministered extensively in that city and that it is inconceivable that he would have had no more to say to his friends than we read in Rom. 16. They would look for "some pastoral message specially appropriate to them" and "its absence is made all the more inexplicable by the fact that Paul had time to include so many greetings to individuals" (Cranfield, p. 11).

them quite well. It would have been invidious to make a selection. Moreover, Paul does not normally send greetings to members of churches he knew. Such a practice would create obvious difficulties. No such greetings are found in 1 and 2 Thessalonians, 1 and 2 Corinthians, Galatians, or Philippians. Indeed, the only Pauline letter with anything of the sort is Colossians, another letter to a church Paul had not visited. Even there he greets only one person by name (Nympha, Col. 4:15), the other greetings being from people Paul names.

2. *Connections with Rome.* Some point out that most of the names in Paul's list are found in the inscriptions in Rome. But it is fairly countered that there are so many names in this vast list that inclusion proves nothing. Most names occur in it somewhere. The most we can say is that there is nothing improbable about the names Paul lists.[102] Some of them may, however, be significant. For example, a Rufus (v. 13) is mentioned in Mark 15:21, apparently for no other reason than that he was known to Mark's readers (he does nothing in Mark). Since our second Gospel is usually connected with Rome, we may well have a link here. Again, Paul mentions the household of Narcissus (v. 11). This is the name of a powerful freedman who was executed by Nero. According to custom his slaves would have passed to the Emperor, retaining the name of their former owner.[103] There may be a similar link with Aristobulus (v. 10), for a grandson of Herod the Great bearing this name died in Rome. He was a friend of the Emperor Claudius, and his slaves may well have passed into imperial possession.

3. *Aquila and Prisca* (v. 3) seem to have been wealthy (they had a house large enough for a church to meet in it) and to have travelled widely.[104] They went to Ephesus with Paul (Acts 18:18), and they were there later on (1 Cor. 16:19, 2 Tim. 4:19).[105] Indeed, the last time they are mentioned they are at Ephesus, and that in both Acts and the Pauline writings (Acts 18:26; 2 Tim. 4:19). The church in their house there (1 Cor. 16:19) seems to indicate settled residence. It is this link with Ephesus which as much as anything inclines some to hold that the chapter was originally destined for that city.[106]

102. The Latin names are not a problem. Donfried draws attention to Harry Leon's study of 551 names of Jews in Rome which shows that there were more Latin names among them than Semitic and Greek names combined. "Leon's conclusion establishes the probability that the names in Romans 16 could easily belong to Roman Jews" (Donfried, p. 56). Roman Christianity, however, was predominantly Greek speaking until well into the second century, so that it is idle to look for too many Latin names in this church.

103. Bruce regards this as "Perhaps the strongest case" of identification with names known at Rome, for we know of a " 'family of Narcissus' in Rome at this very time" (Bruce, p. 256).

104. In support of the view that considerable travel took place in the Roman Empire of the time and that it was feasible among Paul's correspondents, Barrett cites Lietzmann for information about a migration from Asia Minor to Tusculum of a household of 500 persons, "a 'house-church' of initiates of Dionysius" (Barrett, p. 282).

105. 1 Corinthians is usually held to have been written from Ephesus (cf. Kümmel, p. 205); Timothy's knowledge of what was going on in Asia (2 Tim. 1:15; cf. 1 Tim. 1:3) seems to locate him in Ephesus.

106. Some argue that the names point to Ephesus. But the only names which can be

But this couple can be held to support Rome. They left the capital city when Claudius expelled the Jews (Acts 18:2), and there seems no reason why they should not have returned after that Emperor's death.[107] In fact, the expulsion of the Jews may be the explanation of Paul's knowledge of some, at least, of those mentioned in this chapter. They would have scattered widely, and he would have had the opportunity of meeting some of them. There is nothing improbable about his sending greetings to any he knew who had now returned to Rome. Many Jews lived in Rome early in Nero's reign, and some were well accepted at court.

4. *Ampliatus* (v. 8) is a name found on a very ancient tomb in the cemetery of Domitilla which may possibly go back as far as the end of the first century. Some hold this to be the very Ampliatus Paul mentions. This seems to be going too far (the name was not uncommon). But at least the name is connected with Christian circles in Rome at an early date.

Perhaps we should also notice the tradition of the Roman church which links Nereus and Achilleus with Domitilla, who was punished as a Christian under her cousin, the Emperor Domitian. The tradition goes back to the fourth century and may be older. It is not likely to depend on Romans since the two names are always linked in the tradition, as they are not in Romans.[108] But it is not conclusive.

All this means that there is nothing unlikely in Paul's knowing such a group of people in Rome as those mentioned in Romans 16. Some of the names do seem to have connections with that city. Certainly they do not prove Ephesus.[109]

5. *Epaenetus* is called "the first-fruits of Asia for Christ" (v. 5). Such a

---

linked with that city are Aquila and Prisca, and perhaps Epaenetus. But the first two are connected also with Rome, as are Rufus, Narcissus, Ampliatus, and possibly Nereus and Aristobulus (Dodd, p. xxiii). The argument has little weight.

107. It is even possible that they went back to Rome as advance agents of Paul. Thus Zahn thought it not impossible that "when Paul turned his attention toward Rome and prepared to give up his work in Ephesus, this couple left Ephesus, very soon after the sending of 1 Corinthians, at about the same time that Paul did, and returned to Rome, where they had resided earlier, in order to prepare quarters for the apostle there as they had done previously in Ephesus" (*Introduction*, p. 390). He thinks that Epaenetus may have accompanied them. Parry comments, "It is reasonable to conclude that when, at Ephesus, the plan of a visit to Rome was definitely formed (Acts xix.21), it was also decided that these two faithful companions and fellow workers should return to that city, to which at any rate Prisca probably belonged, prepare the way for S. Paul's own visit, and send him information as to the state of the church there" (CGT, p. xiii). As a possible link of Prisca with Rome Dodd points out that both Acilius (or Aquillius) and Prisca are names connected with the consul Acilius Glabrio, who "was a Christian in the time of Domitian." It is possible that Aquila and Prisca were freed slaves of the Acilii (Dodd, pp. xxi-xxii). It is not a strong link, but it is possible.

108. Cf. Dodd, p. xxiii.

109. Raymond E. Brown discusses the evidence and, after considering the names, writes, "Thus, overall the 16-chapter form of Romans has every reason to be considered as original" (*Antioch and Rome*, p. 108).

man, it is said, is more likely to be in Ephesus than in Rome. But this can be put too strongly. People travelled widely at this time, and it is not unlikely for someone to move from the province of Asia to the capital, Rome. In fact, something like this may be necessary if there is to be point in mentioning that he was Asia's firstfruits. In Ephesus this would be well known and scarcely worth mentioning. Not so at Rome.

6. *The commendation of Phoebe* (v. 1) would be more natural to a church Paul knew than to one where he had never been. To which it may fairly be retorted that Paul's commendation would carry weight anywhere. He was not exactly unknown in the early church.[110]

7. *The greeting in 16:16*, "All the churches of Christ greet you", looks like a warm expression of fellowship from the representatives of the churches gathered with Paul at the time he wrote his letter (Acts 20:3-4). It would be natural for the assembled provincials to send greetings to the church in the capital. But what would the words mean if written to Ephesus? Especially so as Ephesus was represented among Paul's companions (Trophimus, Acts 20:4, was an Ephesian, Acts 21:29; possibly Tychicus also).

8. *The antinomianism of 16:17ff.* seems more pronounced than anything in other parts of Romans. It is urged that it is more likely to be found in Asia than in Rome, and further that there are resemblances in Paul's words to the Ephesian elders (Acts 20:28ff.). It is also said that there are points of contact with the false teaching mentioned in 1 and 2 Timothy and that this should be located at Ephesus. It is not unlike that encountered in Colossians, a church in the same region. Again, Romans has a good deal to say about the relationship between Jews and Gentiles (who apparently had some difficulty in adjusting to one another), but there is nothing Jewish here. The tone is also said to be different from that earlier in the epistle (which is eirenic) and more akin to that in letters to churches of Paul's own foundation, like Galatians and Corinthians.

But all this is highly subjective. As a matter of fact we have no way at all of knowing how well the words applied in either place. Paul is speaking of a danger, a threat, not something that was in actual existence. Such a warning would be as conceivable addressed to Rome as to Ephesus. It is also true that from time to time in this epistle Paul clearly has in mind unethical tendencies (cf. 6:1-4, 15ff.; 8:5-13; 12:2). It would, moreover, be not in the least surprising if when he was warning against possible false teaching in one place (Rome) he were to couch his warning in terms derived from false teaching with which he was familiar in another place (Ephesus). The difference in tone should not be exaggerated. Warm appreciation is expressed in verse 19. And Gamble draws attention to Carl Bjerkelund's examination of the way the exhortation in

110. Cf. Donald Guthrie, "if Paul has no authority to commend anyone to a church where he is unknown he would equally have no authority to write to them as he has done in chapters i-xv" ("The Pauline Epistles," *New Testament Introduction* [London, 1961], p. 30). The very existence of the epistle is the refutation of the objection.

verses 17-20 is introduced. He shows that it "is not an expression of authoritative demand or admonition, but a fixed epistolary element which functions as a polite, 'urbane' expression of request. It carries no polemical import, and appears to be used by Paul when his authority is not in question."[111]

9. *15:33 Looks like the End of a Letter.*[112] Perhaps. But none of Paul's other letters ends like this. And for that matter 15:13 looks as much like the end of a letter as does 15:33. Other possible "ends" could doubtless be picked out.

10. *The Character of Chapter 16.* The objection of Hans Lietzmann is often quoted: "A letter consisting almost entirely of greetings may be intelligible in the age of the picture-postcard; for any earlier period it is a monstrosity."[113] Writing a letter in antiquity was not as easy as at present; thus when anyone did write he had something more serious to say than simply to pass on greetings. If it be retorted that an earlier part of the letter probably existed but that this is all that survives, it must be countered that this is to bolster up one hypothesis with another. There is no evidence of such a letter. It would be curious for the letter to be lost and the greetings to survive.[114]

Lietzmann's objection is not quite as strong as it seems, for there are examples of short letters with extensive greetings.[115] We must, however, notice the kind of letter. If chapter 16 is an entire letter, then it is a letter of commendation of Phoebe. But greetings are almost invariably absent from letters of introduction.[116] "Of the eighty-three letters collected by Kim only three contain greetings (. . . all third and fourth century), and these have only one greetings-phrase each. Also, Cicero's letters of recommendation characteristically lack greetings."[117]

---

111. Gamble, p. 52. The introductory words are παρακαλῶ δὲ ὑμᾶς, ἀδελφοί.

112. This is supported by the fact that the oldest MS of Romans, P[46], has the doxology after 15:33. This is taken (e.g., by T. W. Manson) to indicate that at one time the text on which this MS is based ended with ch. 15. But it is not to be overlooked that this MS does not in fact end at ch. 15 and that there may have been some other reason than the original end of the epistle for the appearance of the doxology at this place.

113. Cited from Dodd, p. xix. Gamble does not regard this as a strong objection; he points out that the comment is found only in the first edition (Gamble, p. 47 n.51). He further points out that those who see ch. 16 as a whole letter are able to rationalize the greetings in some way.

114. Cf. Guthrie, "some reasonable explanation must be given for the strange preservation of the greetings and the loss of the Epistle. Common sense would suggest the reverse" (*Introduction,* pp. 31-32).

115. Gamble notes some; P.Oxy. 1296, e.g., has 12 lines of greetings in a letter of 20 lines (Gamble, p. 91 n.156). It is not the number of greetings in itself that is the problem but the number of greetings in a letter of this character. It should also be borne in mind that Paul has nothing like it elsewhere. There must be some reason for such a lengthy list of greetings in a Pauline letter.

116. This point is overlooked by many who note the existence of letters of recommendation in antiquity, e.g., A. Deissmann, LAE, pp. 170-71; J. I. H. McDonald, NTS, XVI (1969-70), pp. 369-72.

117. Gamble, p. 87 n.137.

But if letters of commendation do not normally contain greetings, letters written for other purposes often contain commendations.[118] Paul himself does this sort of thing elsewhere (e.g., 1 Cor. 16:10-11, 15-18). Gamble concludes: "Thus in the secular letter tradition and in Paul's own letters we have precise analogies for the commendation in Rom 16:1-2 in form, content, and position within the letter's conclusion. We are thereby warned against detaching ch. 16 from the larger Roman letter on the grounds that it has the character of a note of recommendation. That vss. 1-2 have the character imposes no necessity and creates no likelihood that the chapter was originally independent."[119] The character of chapter 16, then, is such as to make it likely that from the beginning it belonged at the end of this letter.

11. Rhetorical Structure. We noted earlier that Wilhelm Wuellner argues that the rhetorical character of Romans is very significant. When he comes to deal with the constituent parts of the writing, he takes 15:14–16:23 as the peroration. He can say, "It is my thesis that the *pathos* section of the peroration in Romans extends from 15:30 to 16:23."[120] That such a position can be taken up shows from another angle that chapter 16 is not self-evidently detachable from chapter 15.

12. Epistolary Structure. Gamble has an important section in which he examines the endings of the Pauline letters. A good deal of attention has been given to the openings, but not so much to the endings. Gamble shows that the Pauline letters regularly end with the following sequence:

1. Hortatory remarks
2. Wish of peace
3. Greetings
4. Grace-benediction[121]

If the letter ended at 14:23 or at 15:33, the Pauline pattern has been disrupted. The ending sequence which is invariable elsewhere in Paul has then been abandoned on this occasion. Why? The other side of this argument is that Romans 16 contains the normal Pauline pattern for a letter ending (though with some minor problems like the possible double grace-benedic-

---

118. Gamble cites a number of examples, e.g., Plato, *Ep.* 13, which he describes as "a lengthy letter" and which ends: "Iatrocles, who along with Myronides was set free by me, is now about to embark with those sent by me. Therefore give him some paid employment since he is well-disposed toward you; and use him for whatever you wish" (*ibid.*, p. 86).

119. *Ibid.*, p. 87.

120. Donfried, p. 164. Wuellner has earlier said, "The peroration has been specified in Hellenistic rhetoric 'as the proper place for *pathos*,' i.e., the rousing of emotions for the purpose of stimulating the audience to action" (*ibid.*, p. 163).

121. Gamble, p. 83. Not all these elements are invariably present, but some of them always are and the sequence does not vary. Gordon J. Bahr has also given attention to the endings of Paul's letters ("The Subscriptions in the Pauline Letters", JBL, LXXXVII [1968], pp. 27-41). Of Romans he says, "As far as the form of ch. 16 is concerned, there is no reason to deny its authenticity" (*ibid.*, p. 39).

tion, vv. 20b, 24). But the chapter does not comply with what we normally find in a complete letter.[122] Its form indicates that, if it is not the end of Romans, it is the end of some other letter. Which?[123] We can sum up the position in this way. We have:

1. Romans 1–16, a Pauline letter with a Pauline ending
2. Romans 16, a normal Pauline ending
3. A manuscript tradition in which Romans 16 is invariably attached to Romans 1–15.

It is not easy to escape the conclusion that Romans 16 is the intended and original conclusion to the letter.[124]

13. The laudatory character of the greetings may be significant. Whenever Paul describes someone in this chapter to whom he sends a greeting, it is always complimentary (e.g., 16:4, 6, 7). This would result in the individual's being accorded respect in the community. But it also classed the person with Paul. The link might be expected to cause such people to be his advocates. "That epistolary greetings should be turned to this effect would hardly be comprehensible if they were addressed to a community whose recognition of himself Paul could have presumed. Only if addressed to the Roman church, where such recognition could not be assumed—a fact acknowledged in Paul's cautious and apologetic approach to it (15:14-21)—does the peculiar character of the greetings of Rom 16 make any sense."[125]

From all this it seems that we should regard chapter 16 as an integral part of Romans. It is true that some have put forward arguments of greater or

---

122. "Ch.16 has all the earmarks of an epistolary conclusion, as can be seen by comparing it with other conclusions. The same comparison, however, reveals the distinctiveness of Rom 16, a distinctiveness which can be accounted for only on the basis of the situation presupposed in the Roman letter" (Gamble, p. 91).

123. Gamble sums up in these words: "Thus, even though many have found considerations of content to be prohibitive of a Roman destination for ch. 16, in terms of letter-form and style everything speaks in favor of the integrity of the letter. That Paul had some acquaintances in Rome—and only a limited number of firsthand acquaintances need be supposed—is a smaller and more reasonable assumption than that ch. 16 was no original part of the Roman letter. If judgments based on content are inevitably somewhat subjective and inconclusive, the evidence of epistolary style is a much more demonstrable and reliable index for deciding literary-critical issues. In the case of Romans it provides as much certainty as can be had that Rom 1-16 preserves the original extent of Paul's letter to the Romans" (Gamble, pp. 94-95).

124. In an article entitled "Greetings as a New Testament Form" (JBL, LXXXVII [1968], pp. 418-26), Terence Y. Mullins looks at the usage in greetings both outside and inside the New Testament. He sees Romans as different from the other letters. As befits the longest letter, both the opening and the closing are longer than any others in the New Testament. On the basis of the greetings he thinks that the relationship between Paul and the Roman congregation "seems to be other than scholars have assumed, and no simple readjustment of our old notions is likely to bring it into focus. We can not, for example, simply lop off the last chapter or two and say that they are not part of the letter. The opening and closing are too obviously supplementary for such a solution to hold" (*ibid.*, p. 426). He thinks that problems remain, but for our present purpose the point is that the greetings agree with other evidence that ch. 16 is part of the original letter.

125. Gamble, p. 92.

less force to indicate that it should be seen as a separate letter or part of another letter. But the evidence for such views is not convincing. The presumption must always be that a writing that comes down to us as part of an ancient document is to be seen as part of that document until the contrary is proved.[126] In this case sufficient evidence is not forthcoming, while on the contrary there are some strong indications that chapter 16 belongs with chapters 1–15.

126. Donfried emphasizes this strongly in his "Methodological Principles II" (Donfried, pp. 122-23).

Analysis

I. **Introduction, 1:1-15**
  A. Salutation, 1:1-7
  B. Prayer, 1:8-15
II. **Thesis, 1:16-17**
III. **The Way of Deliverance, 1:18–5:21**
  A. Universal Sinfulness, 1:18–3:20
    1. *The Condemnation of the Gentile World, 1:18-32*
    2. *The Condemnation of the Jew, 2:1-16*
      a. The danger of judging others, 2:1-3
      b. The need for repentance, 2:4
      c. Judgment, 2:5-16
    3. *The Jew, 2:17–3:8*
      a. The Jew's confidence, 2:17-20
      b. The Jew's failure, 2:21-24
      c. The inward and the outward, 2:25-29
      d. The faithfulness of God, 3:1-4
      e. Objections, 3:5-8
    4. *Universal Sinfulness—Proof from Scripture, 3:9-20*
  B. Justification, 3:21–5:21
    1. *How Justification Is Effected, 3:21-31*
      a. The death of Christ, 3:21-26
      b. Faith, 3:27-31
    2. *Justification Proved from Abraham, 4:1-25*
      a. God's way is grace, 4:1-8
      b. Faith and circumcision, 4:9-12
      c. Faith and law, 4:13-17
      d. Faith and Abraham, 4:18-25
    3. *The Effects of Justification, 5:1-11*
    4. *Solidarity in Adam and in Christ, 5:12-21*
IV. **The Way of Godliness, 6:1–8:39**
  A. Shall We Continue to Sin That Grace May Abound? 6:1-14
  B. Shall We Sin Because We Are under Grace, Not Law? 6:15–7:6
    1. *We Are Not Slaves, 6:15-23*
    2. *An Illustration from Marriage, 7:1-6*
  C. Is the Law Sin? 7:7-12
  D. Did the Good Law Cause Death? 7:13-25
  E. The Holy Spirit in the Believer, 8:1-39

Romans 1

I. INTRODUCTION, 1:1-15

Letters in antiquity, as in every age, had a conventional form. Whereas we begin with our address and the date, after which we greet our correspondent as "Dear ————" (though he may be our worst enemy or a total stranger), the ancients had the sensible custom of starting with the name of the writer. They followed this with the name of the recipient and a greeting, giving the formula "A to B, Greeting." There was usually a little prayer. In letters of a formal character written to strangers that was all. But titles were added to the names in official letters and expressions of warmth and esteem in more personal letters. The prayer might be no more than conventional good wishes ("May the gods preserve you"). Or it might be a genuine thanksgiving for blessings received. Here is the opening of a letter which survives: "Serenus to his beloved sister Isidora, many greetings. Before all else I pray for your health. . . ."[1] Notice the use of the third person, which was normal.

Paul follows the usual pattern in all his letters, though with some significant modifications.[2] He takes his letter openings more seriously than do his more conventional contemporaries, and he makes them the vehicles of important Christian teaching. This ordinarily means a somewhat longer introduction than was normal. Nowhere is Paul's ability to use the framework more apparent than in Romans. This opening is longer and much more formal than in Paul's other letters—perhaps because he was not personally known to the Roman church, perhaps also because he did not want anyone to doubt his position as an apostle. It will be convenient to divide his opening into two parts, dealing first with his greeting and then with his prayer.

A. SALUTATION, 1:1-7

1Paul, a servant of Christ Jesus, called to be an apostle and set apart for the gospel of God— 2the gospel he promised beforehand through his prophets in the

1. *The Oxyrhyncus Papyri*, Part III, ed. Bernard P. Grenfell and Arthur P. Hunt (London, 1903), p. 264.
2. Thus a letter would begin with the names of the sender (in the nominative) and the recipient (dative) and a greeting, all in one short sentence. Paul expands this and adds a sentence invoking God's blessing or giving thanks or both. Strictly, Greek letters have their introduction in the third person, but Paul can use the first person (e.g., Gal. 1:1-2). In his differences from the Greek model Paul often conforms to Middle Eastern and specifically Jewish customs. For a study of Paul's opening thanksgivings see Peter Thomas O'Brien, *Introductory Thanksgivings in the Letters of Paul* (Leiden, 1977).

Holy Scriptures [3]*regarding his Son, who as to his human nature was a descendant of David,* [4]*and who through the Spirit*[a] *of holiness was declared with power to be the Son of God by his resurrection from the dead: Jesus Christ our Lord.* [5]*Through him and for his name's sake, we received grace and apostleship to call people from among all the Gentiles to the obedience that comes from faith.* [6]*And you also are among those who are called to belong to Jesus Christ.*

[7]*To all in Rome who are loved by God and called to be saints:*

Grace and peace to you from God our Father and from the Lord Jesus Christ.

[a]4 Or *who as to his spirit of holiness*

In this opening Paul speaks of his relationship to Christ and to the gospel, of the purpose God worked out in Christ's saving work, and of the nature of Christian service. These first seven verses are one complicated sentence in Greek (Paul often uses such long, complicated sentences).

1. Normally Paul associates others with himself in his opening greeting.[3] The absence of this feature marks Romans as highly personal. The name *Paul* is first used in Acts 13:9. The apostle's original name, "Saul", is from a Hebrew word with a meaning like "asked"[4] (cf. Samuel, 1 Sam. 1:20). It was not uncommon for a first-century Jew to bear two names, a Greek or Roman name as well as his original Hebrew name. Since Paul was a Roman citizen he would have had three names, but it is understandable that he would not have emphasized his superior status when writing to fellow Christians who were mostly from the lower orders. "Paul" derives from the Latin *paulus*, meaning "little". This may mean that the apostle was short of stature (is this meant in 2 Cor. 10:1, 10?),[5] or it may be due to nothing more profound than that the name had a sound resembling Saul.[6] For some reason he seems to have been known generally by his Latin rather than his Hebrew name.

He calls himself *a servant of Christ Jesus, servant* being a strong term meaning "slave"[7] (used in similar fashion in Gal. 1:10; Phil. 1:1; Tit. 1:1; Jas. 1:1; 2 Pet. 1:1; Jude 1). As the Christians used it, the term conveys the idea of

---

3. Others are linked with Paul in every letter except Ephesians and the Pastorals.

4. שָׁאוּל.

5. According to tradition Paul was "small of stature" (*Acts of Paul and Thecla* 3). There is, of course, no way of knowing how reliable this tradition is.

6. A. Deissmann argues from Σαῦλος ὁ καὶ Παῦλος (Acts 13:9) that Paul had the two names before the incident in which we first learn of them and thus that he did not adopt the second name in connection with Sergius Paulus (*Bible Studies* [Edinburgh, 1901], pp. 313-17). We should not see "Paul" as a new name adopted to help in his missionary work (though it was suitable, being a Roman name for the Roman world), nor as symbolizing his new nature or the like.

7. δοῦλος. This is a very striking thought in a Greek writing. Among the Easterners it was not uncommon for people to speak of themselves as the "slaves" of their god or king, but this was not the case among the Greeks. Proud in their freedom, they eschewed the language of slavery. On this word, cf. BAGD, " 'servant' for 'slave' is largely confined to Biblical transl. and early American times . . . in normal usage at the present time the two words are carefully distinguished."

complete and utter devotion,[8] not the abjectness which was the normal condition of the slave.[9] Paul is affirming that he belongs to Christ without reservation.[10] The term is applied to Abraham (Gen. 26:24), to Moses (Josh. 1:2), and to the prophets from the time of Amos (Amos 3:7; Isa. 20:3). Paul may thus be quietly affirming that he stands in the true succession of the prophets.[11] If this is in mind, it may be significant that he speaks of himself as the slave, not of God (as the prophets did), but of Christ. He puts Christ in the highest possible place.[12]

The probability is that he here calls his Savior *Christ Jesus*[13] (though some hold that the order of the words should be reversed). "Christ" of course means "Messiah", and many think that Paul normally uses the term as a title.[14] But Vincent Taylor argues convincingly that we should usually understand the word as a proper name in Paul.[15] This is supported both by the way Paul uses it and the frequency with which he employs it. In all Paul uses the term 379 times out of its 529 New Testament occurrences (65 in Romans). The highest total in any non-Pauline writing is 25 in Acts. It is thus to Paul that we owe our habit of calling our Lord simply "Christ". The Gospels show that during his lifetime the title was used of him but rarely and that Jesus himself preferred "the Son of man". In the other non-Pauline writings "Christ" is used on occasion, but some other name is more usual. But Paul habitually

---

8. K. H. Rengstorf speaks of the word as pointing to "unconditional commitment"; he comments, "the goal of redemption . . . is obedience rather than autonomy" (TDNT, II, p. 275).

9. Cf. T. W. Manson, " 'Slave' gives the wrong emphasis: in religious usage in both OT and NT the stress is not on one person's rights of property but on the total loyalty and unstinted service given of right to God by his prophets or to Christ by his apostles." Many share this point of view, but it is not easy to maintain. The word does mean "slave" (see n. 7). And it is applied not only to great people like apostles, but to ordinary Christians as well (cf. 6:22; 1 Cor. 7:22; Col. 4:12; 2 Tim. 2:24).

10. H. Moule comments, "To be a bondservant is terrible in the abstract. To be 'Jesus Christ's bondservant' is Paradise, in the concrete" (p. 11).

11. Käsemann denies that the title expresses humility or a placing of oneself on a level with other Christians. "Rather, he is using the honorific title of the OT men of God. . . . This title expresses (as in Revelation) election as well as the submission of an instrument to the will of God." But this overlooks its use for lowly Christians (see above, nn. 7, 9).

12. Deissmann calls attention to the use of the term in the Emperor cult. He cites an inscription from Phrygia in the imperial period which reads, "Agathopus, slave of the lord Emperor" (LAE, p. 376).

13. Cranfield accepts this order with P[10] B *pc c e* vg[codd] Ir Ambst Aug. He sees it as "quite probable that he adopted this order here with the intention of giving special emphasis right at the beginning of the epistle to the fact that the One, whose slave he was, was the fulfilment of God's promises and of Israel's age-old hope."

14. Cranfield does this, and he cites Cullmann and Bornkamm in support (p. 51 n.3).

15. *The Names of Jesus* (London, 1953), pp. 18-23. He points out, *inter alia*, that in the Gentile world the title was meaningless: "If Jesus was to be invoked, venerated, and worshiped, He must be called 'Lord' and 'Son of God'. The name 'Christ' could survive only by becoming a personal designation, charged with deep religious meaning by reason of its association with these titles" (*ibid.*, p. 23).

used the term, and from him it has passed into the common Christian vocabulary. This does not mean that he has forgotten that it is a title with the meaning "Messiah"; sometimes he uses it in the strict sense. But usually we cannot press it. *Jesus*, the human name, of course, means "Savior". Paul uses it 37 times (38 if 16:24 be accepted) in Romans and 213 (214) times in all (John with 237 references is the only writer with more). While he does not employ it as frequently as Christ, clearly Paul loves the human name. When he combines the two he prefers the order "Christ Jesus" to "Jesus Christ" by a margin of 73 to 18 (omitting 24 cases where the MSS are divided). But if he includes "Lord" the order is reversed, with "Jesus" coming first 49 times and "Christ" eight times.

He proceeds to say that he is *called to be an apostle*. Since the Greek has no "to be", we could take the words to mean "a called apostle" (as Boylan does). Nothing has to be supplied to get this meaning. But few accept it because it would imply that some other apostles were not called, and on Pauline premises this would be an absurdity. NIV is surely correct in supplying "to be". The idea of a divine call is important for Paul, as we see from the fact that he uses the adjective *called*[16] in seven of its ten New Testament occurrences. It stresses the priority of the divine ("neither self-appointed nor chosen by men", Hodge). We should notice that for Paul the idea of call includes the notion of response. The "called" are those who have not only heard but have obeyed the divine call. Paul thinks of an "effectual call".[17] In stressing the thought of call Paul is not making an innovation. Many Old Testament worthies were called by God, such as Abraham (Gen. 12:1), Moses (Exod. 3:4ff.), Jeremiah (Jer. 1:4ff.), Amos (Amos 7:15), and especially Isaiah (Isa. 6). Paul sees his task in life (like theirs) not as self-chosen, nor as mapped out for him by men (cf. Gal. 1:1), but as God's own call.

His call is to be an *apostle* (cf. 1 Cor. 1:1).[18] Paul makes a good deal of use

---

16. κλητός. If the word is read in Matt. 20:16, it occurs 11 times. The present passage is noteworthy for the idea of a personal call (as in 1 Cor. 1:1). In its other occurrences the word is plural and refers to groups. The idea that God calls individuals is found in the New Testament (e.g., 1 Cor. 7:17, 20ff.; Heb. 11:8). But it is interesting that so often the common Christian calling is in mind.

17. Paul's terminology differs from that in the Synoptic Gospels. There we read that "many are called, but few chosen". Paul's idea is not essentially different, but he does not use the term "called" in the same way. For him the call and the response go together.

18. MM find it "not easy to point to an adequate parallel for the NT usage of this important word" (ἀπόστολος). Etymologically it should signify "messenger", a meaning attested in two passages in Herodotus, one in LXX, and one in Symmachus. But its common use is for naval matters (see LSJ). All this makes it surprising that it is so common in the New Testament (79 times). F. Agnew cites some eighth-century secular papyri which have the word in the sense "messenger" and argues that the meaning we see in Herodotus persisted though it is not attested in the literature (CBQ, XXXVIII [1976], pp. 49-53). Perhaps the New Testament writers used an uncommon word because ἄγγελος was preempted for the sense "angel", and thus another term was needed. A surprising number of commentators see the background as the Jewish שָׁלִיחַ; they often appeal to Rengstorf, TDNT, I, pp. 413ff. But this official is not attested for the New Testament period, not earlier in fact than the third and fourth centuries. G. W. H. Lampe can say,

of this term. Perhaps surprisingly he rarely uses it of the Twelve. Mostly he uses it of himself or of apostles generally.[19]

The word means "someone who is sent, a messenger". Paul had been "sent" as well as "called". In the New Testament apostles were men of high dignity, owing their appointment directly to God (Gal. 1:1) and being mentioned first in the list of those appointed in the church (1 Cor. 12:28). They were concerned with establishing and caring for churches. The Twelve whom Jesus called were held in high honor, but Paul does not see his apostleship as in any way inferior to that of any (2 Cor. 11:5; 12:11). He had seen the Lord (1 Cor. 9:1) and had been commissioned by him (Gal. 1:1). He had manifested the signs "that mark an apostle" (2 Cor. 12:12). He had a special responsibility as "the apostle to the Gentiles" (11:13).[20]

Paul says that he is *set apart for the gospel of God*. He uses this verb of his being set apart "from birth" (Gal. 1:15; there also it is linked with the idea of call; cf. Jer. 1:5; Acts 9:15). It is used of the setting apart of Barnabas and Saul for missionary work (Acts 13:2). Interestingly, it is connected with the root from which the Pharisees delighted to derive their name. They held that "Pharisee" means "separated one",[21] and Paul would have regarded himself in this light when he was "a Hebrew of the Hebrews; in regard to the law, a

---

"The institution which we know in the fourth century almost certainly came into existence later than the time of the New Testament, and the 'shaliachate' in this sense is not likely to have contributed anything to the development of the Christian apostolate" (*Some Aspects of the New Testament Ministry* [London, 1949], pp. 15-16). In a Foreword to E. R. Fairweather and R. F. Hettlinger, *Episcopacy and Reunion* (London, 1953), A. M. Ramsey commends Dr. Fairweather because he "discards the *shaliach* argument used by the authors of *The Apostolic Ministry*."

19. The term ἀπόστολος is found 34 times in Paul out of the New Testament total of 79; the highest elsewhere is Acts with 28. The Gospels use the word rarely: Matthew, Mark, and John once each, Luke six times. In Romans it is found only here and in 11:13; 16:7. Paul uses the term in the following ways:

Of himself Rom. 1:1; 11:13; 1 Cor. 1:1; 9:1, 2; 2 Cor. 1:1; Gal. 1:1; Eph. 1:1; Col. 1:1; 1 Thess. 2:7; 1 Tim. 1:1; 2:7; 2 Tim. 1:1, 11; Tit. 1:1.	15
General Rom. 16:7; 1 Cor. 4:9; 9:5; 12:28, 29; 15:9 (*bis*); 2 Cor. 11:5, 13; 12:11, 12; Eph. 2:20; 3:5; 4:11.	14
The Twelve 1 Cor. 15:7; Gal. 1:17, 19.	3
Apostles of the churches 2 Cor. 8:23.	1
Epaphroditus Phil. 2.25.	1
	Total 34

20. For apostles see further my *Ministers of God* (London, 1964), ch. III and the literature there cited.

21. The verb is ἀφορίζω. But it is not clear from whom or what they were separated. They may have been separated from uncleanness in their devotion to the law, or the Hasidim may have used the term of their separation from the Maccabees. Some have seen a separation from priestly interpreters of the law. Others hold that the name really means "Persian" and was a nickname given on account of what their critics saw as Persian innovations. Cf. Matthew Black, IDB, III, p. 776, and for the literature, Joachim Jeremias, *Jerusalem in the Time of Jesus* (London, 1969), p. 246. Whatever the truth of the origin of the name, there is no doubt that in the first century the Pharisees firmly believed that they were in a special sense God's "separated ones".

Pharisee" (Phil. 3:5). Now, however, he is separated to a greater purpose. We often understand separation negatively, as separation "from" something. But here it is positive. Paul is separated "to" the gospel (cf. Acts 13:2). *Gospel* is a definitely Pauline word (60 times in Paul out of its 76 New Testament occurrences; nine times in Romans and Philippians is the most in any one book).[22] It is found in every Pauline writing except Titus. The word basically means "good news".[23] In a Christian context there is no good news to compare with the news of what God has done in Christ for man's salvation.[24] It is this for which Paul is set apart. Some understand this to mean "set apart to preach the gospel". It certainly includes this, but it is surely more. It means to be a gospel man, to live the gospel. Preaching is important, but then so is living. Paul's call was to a way of life as well as to a task of preaching.

The gospel is *the gospel of God* (as in Mark 1:14; Rom. 15:16; 2 Cor. 11:7; 1 Thess. 2:2, 8, 9; 1 Pet. 4:17). Elsewhere Paul sees it as "the gospel of his Son" (v. 9), "the gospel of Christ" (15:19; it centers on his saving work), and "my gospel" (2:16; 16:25; the preacher must make the gospel his own). When the gospel is spoken of as God's, it is referred to its ultimate source. It is rooted in God's eternal purpose. It is promised in Scripture (v. 2). It takes its origin in God's concern for his people and his will to save them.[25]

God is the most important word in this epistle.[26] Romans is a book about God. No topic is treated with anything like the frequency of God. Everything Paul touches in this letter he relates to God. In our concern to understand what the apostle is saying about righteousness, justification, and the like we ought not to overlook his tremendous concentration on God. There is nothing like it elsewhere.[27]

22. Normally the word εὐαγγέλιον has the article. It is without it in the New Testament only here, in 2 Cor. 11:4; Gal. 1:6 (both of which refer to "another" gospel), and in Rev. 14:6. Käsemann points out that the article is sometimes omitted in technical expressions (cf. BAGD in n. 31 below). But it is not easy to see why it should be omitted on this occasion.

23. There are some unsolved problems about the word. The combination of εὐ and ἄγγελος points to "good news", though the word seems often to have been used simply of "news", or "message" (it was also used of the reward given the bearer of good news). But there is no doubt that in the New Testament good news is in mind (though cf. Rev. 14:6). The absolute use, so frequent in Paul, is new. Paul finds the content of the word so central that he can assume that his readers know what it is.

24. In the Roman Empire εὐαγγέλιον was linked with the Emperor cult. It was "good news" when an heir was born or came to the throne. Deissmann quotes from an inscription dated 9 B.C. concerning the birthday of the Emperor Augustus: "But the birthday of the god was for the world the beginning of tidings of joy on his account" (LAE, p. 366). Cf. also G. Friedrich, TDNT, II, pp. 724-25.

25. The genitive θεοῦ might conceivably mean that the gospel is good news about God. But while there is truth in this, the expression more naturally refers to origin (BDF 163). The gospel is from God. Cranfield sees Barrett's the Good News "God is now setting forth" as "an unwarranted limitation of the sense".

26. See Introduction, p. 20.

27. E.g., in Matthew, Mark, and John "Jesus" is referred to more often than is "God". In Luke "God" is used more often than "Jesus" (122 times and 89 times respectively), but here the words for "man" occur as often as "God" (ἄνθρωπος 95, ἀνήρ 27), and this total is exceeded by those for verbs like εἰπεῖν (294) and εἶναι (361). There are no comparable phenomena in Romans.

2. **Paul's emphasis on the divine continues.** That the gospel is part of God's unchanging purpose is evident from the fact that it was *promised beforehand*[28] in the prophetic writings. It is God's gift, part of his purpose for his people. In that he has now fulfilled what he promised it is plain that God can be trusted and the gospel accepted. Notice that the prophets are called *his* prophets. Paul is not speaking of men of vision in general, men who by their innate abilities could discern the signs of the times. He is speaking of men who belong to God, the vehicles of his message. When a promise is given through (not "by") such men, then clearly it is the promise of God. We are probably right in interpreting the term *prophets* as not only the prophets in the strict, technical sense, but all the Old Testament writers (cf. Heb. 1:1).[29] So Paul proceeds to locate the promise in *the Holy Scriptures*, or, more exactly, in "holy writings".[30] The expression normally has the article (as NIV), but twice, in 16:26 and here, the Greek has the plural without the article, the noun being there qualified by the adjective "prophetic" and here by "holy". This use is distinctly exceptional. It would be possible to recall the original meaning of the word and translate here by "holy writings". But the reference to the prophets makes it clear that Paul has in mind the Old Testament. We should thus translate by "holy scriptures". But by omitting the article Paul is emphasizing the character of these writings as "holy" (for this term see on v. 7)[31] rather than following his usual practice of making them definite with the use of the article. It may well be that his gospel of grace had been misunderstood and that he had been accused of putting out teachings which destroyed the Old Testament. It was important to Paul, as to all the early Christians, that the gospel was the fulfilment of the Old Testament. It is the realization in action of what God had promised through his own prophets. It is the fulfilment of promises which had been recorded in writings which must be received with reverence, for they are holy.

3. **That the gospel concerns the Son**[32] points to the central role of the Son

---

28. The verb προεπαγγέλλομαι is not common in the New Testament; it is found elsewhere only in 2 Cor. 9:5.

29. So Lagrange, etc.

30. γραφή is found 14 times in the Pauline writings. It most commonly occurs in the singular with the article, "the scripture" (Rom. 4:3; 9:17; 10:11; 11:2; Gal. 3:8, 22; 4:30; 1 Tim. 5:18), while once we find "all scripture" (or "every scripture", 2 Tim. 3:16). Sometimes we have the plural with the article (Rom. 15:4; 1 Cor. 15:3, 4). It is unusual to have scripture characterized as "holy" (though cf. 7:12; 2 Tim. 3:15), and G. Schrenk can say: "We may thus conclude that the phrase αἱ ἱεραὶ γραφαί perpetuates in the Church a Jewish and Hellenistic rather than a specifically early Christian usage" (TDNT, I, p. 751).

31. "The absence of the article with γραφαῖς ἁγίαις emphasises the peculiar holiness of the Old Testament Scriptures" (Boylan; Schrenk, however, sees the absence of the article as "of no significance" [TDNT, I, p. 751 n. 7]). BAGD comment on ἱερὰ γράμματα, (2 Tim. 3:15), "because of the technical character of the expression no article is needed" (*sub* γράμμα 2.c).

32. Paul uses υἱός 12 times in Romans, of which seven refer to Christ. They are all qualified ("his", "God's", etc.), and the absolute use, "the Son", which is so common in John, is not found at all. Another difference from John is that Paul does not hesitate to use the term to denote the sonship to God that people may have. John prefers to speak of τέκνα θεοῦ, and he brings out some of the uniqueness of Christ by reserving the term υἱός for him

in salvation. The title is one of high dignity, as is fitting for one who accomplished so great a work. As Paul uses the term, it involves community of nature with the Father.[33] That the Messiah would be a *descendant of David* is taught in the Old Testament (Isa. 11:1, 10; Jer. 23:5-6; Ezek. 34:23-24, etc.) and elsewhere.[34] The idea is found in a number of places in the New Testament. Paul's expression here means "became[35] of the seed of David according to the flesh", "the seed of David" being referred to on a number of occasions besides the present passage (John 7:42; 2 Tim. 2:8). Jesus is also called the "Son of David" a total of 12 times,[36] and there are other references of a somewhat similar character.[37] Jesus does not call himself "Son of David" and indeed on occasion seems to distance himself from the title (Mark 12:35-37).[38] But we should not exaggerate the significance of this, for when the title was directly applied to him he did not reject it (Mark 10:47-52). The facts seem to indicate that it was widely expected that the Messiah would be of David's line and that Jesus knew that he was of Davidic descent. But presumably because of popular messianic expectations he put no emphasis on the fact.[39] The Davidic

---

alone. Perhaps Paul's use of the term points to the divine condescension in admitting the saved into membership in his family.

33. Cf. Käsemann, "Provisionally one might state that no NT author understood the unique divine sonship of Jesus otherwise than in a metaphysical sense"; he finds Son of God "as rare in Judaism as it is common in Hellenism". Robinson notices that Paul is the only one said in Acts to preach Jesus as the Son of God (Acts 9:20; 13:33; cf. Gal. 1:16). He asks, "Is this presentation peculiarly remembered as having been associated with Paul?" See also Jeremias, *Prayers of Jesus*, pp. 11-19; *Abba*, pp. 15-33.

34. It is attested in the Qumran literature, as in the commentary on Isa. 11:1-3: "(Interpreted this concerns the Branch) of David who shall arise at the end" (G. Vermes, *The Dead Sea Scrolls in English* [Penguin, 1972], p. 227; cf. pp. 224, 246). So also in the Psalms of Solomon, "Behold, O Lord, and raise up to them their king, the Son of David . . . and let Him reign over Israel thy servant" (17:23; J. Rendel Harris, *The Odes and Psalms of Solomon* [Cambridge, 1911], p. 155).

35. γενομένου. The verb γίνομαι is an exceedingly common verb (Paul uses it 35 times in Romans and 141 times in all). It has no necessary connection with descent, apparently being concerned rather with "transition from one state or mode of subsistence to another" (T. S. Evans, *Speaker's Commentary* on 1 Cor. 1:30). But this transition may be from the womb to the world and the verb may thus be used of being born, though it is not the usual way of denoting birth. It is used in this way of Abraham (John 8:58), as well as of Christ (Gal. 4:4). This may well be the way we should understand it here (as ARV, Moffatt, Way, etc.), though some suggest it means from a previous mode of existence (in heaven) to "coming to be" in human form. But this may be too subtle.

36. Matt. 1:1; 9:27; 12:23; 15:22; 20:30, 31; 21:9, 15 (a total of eight); Mark 10:47, 48 (two); Luke 18:38, 39 (two). This is probably implied in another three cases, Matt. 1:20; Mark 12:35; Luke 20:41. I have not included the occurrences in parallel passages.

37. Jesus' descent from David is mentioned now and then without being emphasized (Acts 2:29ff.; 13:22-23, 34; Rev. 5:5; 22:16).

38. Black comments, "Jesus himself appears to have found difficulty with this popular belief, and to have taken exception to it; he never used the term 'son of David' of himself". But Bruce can say that Jesus' "question about the scribal exegesis of Psalm 110.1 (Mk. 12.35-37) should not be construed as a repudiation of Davidic descent."

39. James D. G. Dunn has a good deal to say about this text in an important article, "Jesus—Flesh and Spirit: An Exposition of Romans 1:3-4" (JTS, N.S. XXIV [1973], pp. 40-68). He argues that we should not take κατὰ σάρκα here or elsewhere in a neutral

descent is thus of importance for an understanding of Jesus' messiahship. It is, however, an aspect of the Messiah which evidently did not mean much to Paul, for he does not specifically mention it elsewhere (though 15:12 comes close).

Many hold that in vv. 3b-4 Paul is not composing freely but making use of a primitive Christian creed. This is supported by the structure of the section (parallelism and the like), the reference to David, some un-Pauline vocabulary,[40] and some theological implications of what is written which scholars find difficult to ascribe to Paul.[41] It is quite possible that Paul is referring to a traditional summary of the faith familiar to the Romans. It would make good sense for him to assure them of his orthodoxy by citing words they accepted and with which they were familiar.[42] But the credal hypothesis is not as certain as many assume. There is no way we can be sure of it, and in any case there are difficulties. Thus we have no real evidence for fixed credal forms until a considerably later time. Such "credal" fragments as scholars discern in the New Testament differ from one another whereas it is of the essence of creeds that they do not (there is no point in having a creed if people are free to modify it as they will). Further, the question arises as to whether the "creed" Paul uses is Roman or, say, Corinthian. If it was Roman, how did Paul come to know it? If it was Corinthian, how would the Romans recognize it? Such questions may have answers, but we should not assume that they do not

---

sense, for Paul uses it pejoratively. He says, *"it must be judged highly probable that for Paul κατὰ σάρκα in Rom. i.3 carries its normal note of depreciation"* (p. 49). He holds that "Paul does not affirm the Davidic sonship of Jesus without qualification. He does not deny it either, but he makes it clear that to describe Jesus as 'born of the seed of David' is a dangerously defective and misleading half-truth" (p. 51). He sees the κατὰ σάρκα, κατὰ πνεῦμα antithesis as important here and remarks that these two expressions "denote not successive and mutually exclusive spheres of power, but modes of existence and relationships which overlap and coincide in the earthly Jesus" (p. 54). I am not sure that Dr. Dunn has allowed sufficiently for the possibility of neutrality in some of the examples of κατὰ σάρκα, but his article is thought-provoking. The idea that the earthly Jesus knew what it was during his time in the flesh to live κατὰ πνεῦμα, thus setting us an example, is very valuable.

40. Notably the verb ὁρίζω, which Paul uses nowhere else (Luke and Hebrews have it once each, Acts five times), and the expression πνεῦμα ἁγιωσύνης (not found elsewhere in the New Testament). Other features, such as "Son" and κατὰ σάρκα, are quite Pauline, however. See a concise summary of the evidence for the use of "an earlier statement" in Dunn, JTS, XXIV, p. 40.

41. Thus it is suggested that the formula expresses a pre-Pauline, adoptionist christology. Paul, it is said, does not refer to Christ's Davidic descent elsewhere (2 Tim. 2:8 is regarded as credal), nor does he connect Christ's status as Son of God with his exaltation. But (a) the words do not necessarily point to adoptionism, and (b) Paul certainly did not understand them in that way. In any case we should be very cautious about labelling anything in the New Testament "pre-Pauline". The date of Paul's conversion is estimated by competent authorities as c. A.D. 32, so there cannot have been much Christianity before him.

42. Käsemann has a good discussion of the issues; see also R. Bultmann, *Theology of the New Testament*, I (London, 1952), p. 49. See also Paul Beasley-Murray, "Romans 1:3f: An Early Confession of Faith in the Lordship of Jesus", *Tyndale Bulletin*, 31 (1980), pp. 147-54 and the article by Dunn noted earlier.

arise. And the possibility must be kept in mind that Paul was not so much quoting a creed as making free use of traditional expressions.[43] In any case, if Paul is quoting we have no reason for thinking anything other than that what he has quoted he has made his own.[44]

Paul proceeds to qualify his reference to Christ's descent with *as to his human nature*, or more literally, "according to the flesh". He uses the term "flesh" in a bewildering variety of ways and characteristically of the moral frailty which is so much a part of human life (see the note on 7:5). Here, however, the meaning will be as far as human nature, or perhaps physical descent, is concerned. On the level of flesh, of human life, Jesus really was a descendant of David (cf. 9:5). Theodoret, a fifth-century writer, pointed out that this way of expressing it carries the implication that there is more to be said. "The addition 'according to the flesh' is not predicated of those who are merely what they are seen to be", and he cites the absence of the expression from Matthew's genealogy to prove his point.[45] The words imply that Jesus was more than human. Otherwise it would be sufficient to say that he was of the seed of David.

4. The verb rendered *declared* has been variously understood. Cognate with the word for a "boundary", it means something like "bounded", "marked out", "designated"[46] (as RSV, NASB, NEB, GNB, Goodspeed, etc.). If we accept this, we will see the meaning as that the resurrection showed Jesus to be the Son of God. Others prefer the meaning "appointed" (as in Luke 22:22; Acts 10:42, etc.). If this be accepted, it will be in the sense that he who was Son of God in weakness and lowliness during his earthly life "Through the resurrection . . . became the Son of God in power" (Nygren).[47] Paul would not have accepted a view that Jesus was not divine until "appointed" Son of God (cf. Phil. 2:5-11).[48] Leslie C. Allen stresses the link with Psalm

43. Cf. V. S. Poythress, "Is Romans 1³⁻⁴ a *Pauline* Confession After All?" (ET, LXXXVII [1975-76], pp. 180-83).

44. Dunn rejects the idea that we can go back to an earlier form of the formula to determine Paul's meaning: "the primary object must be to discover what *Paul* understood by the saying. Only then can we begin to ask whether and how he has adapted and moulded the earlier formula" (JTS, XXIV, p. 43).

45. Cited from an unpublished thesis by Elmer Leroy Birney, *An Annotated Translation of Theodoret's Commentary on Romans 1–5* (in the library of Trinity Evangelical Divinity School, Deerfield, Illinois), May 1968.

46. ὅρος = "boundary"; ὁρίζω = "to separate, mark off by boundaries" (AS). BAGD give the meaning here as "declared to be the powerful Son of God". Some of the Fathers, whose language was Greek, take the word in this sense. Thus Chrysostom, "What then is the being 'declared'? being shown, being manifested, being judged, being confessed, by the feeling and suffrage of all" (p. 340).

47. In Acts 2:36 Jesus is "made" both Lord and Christ at the resurrection, although he has already been approved by signs, etc. (2:22).

48. Some take the words in the sense "appointed" and hold that they express an adoptionist christology, the view that Jesus was at first no more than a man, but that at the resurrection God "adopted" him into the heavenly family or "installed" or "appointed" him as a member. Thus Käsemann holds that the formula is pre-Pauline and that unlike Paul "the formula does not presuppose the preexistence and divine sonship of the earthly Jesus. . . . Jesus receives the dignity of divine sonship only with his exaltation and en-

2:7 and sees the meaning as *"decreed* to be the Son of God".[49] K. L. Schmidt argues that there is no great urgency to decide between "declaration or decree" and "appointment and institution" because "a divine declaration is the same as a divine appointment: God's *verbum* is *efficax*."[50] It would seem that *declared* is the better way to understand the expression, but that "appointed" is possible in a sense which safeguards the truth that Jesus was Son of God before as well as after the resurrection.[51]

There is an ambiguity in that the words *with power* might be taken either with *declared* ("powerfully declared", as NIV, GNB, SH, etc.) or with *Son of God* ("declared to be the powerful Son of God", as JB, Käsemann, etc.). Grammatically either view is possible. Perhaps it is a little more likely that Paul has the latter meaning in mind. There is a sense in which Jesus was the Son of God in weakness before the resurrection but the Son of God in power thereafter. Elsewhere Paul can say that Christ "was crucified in weakness, yet he lives by God's power" (2 Cor. 13:4), and it seems that he has in mind something of the same sort here. Jesus used the title *Son of God* very little (though cf. Matt. 27:43; John 10:36). He preferred "Son of man". But Jesus' own name for himself for some reason was not acceptable in the early church (it is found outside the Gospels only in Acts 7:56). Instead such a title as Son of God was favored, perhaps because it expressed so plainly what the early Christians thought about Jesus. The word here rendered *power* is used in the Synoptic Gospels for Jesus' miracles, the "mighty works".[52] Paul is fond of

thronement" (p. 12); "The reference here is to the enthronement of Christ as Son of God, and the Spirit of holiness was the power which accomplished this" (p. 11). If the words are understood in this way, they express without much precision the thought that it was the resurrection that showed Christ to be God's Son. Dodd speaks of it as "pre-theological". It is difficult to find evidence that any New Testament thinker really held an adoptionist position, and certainly in quoting these words Paul did not understand them in such a sense.

49. NTS, XVII (1970-71), pp. 104-8.

50. TDNT, V, p. 453. He goes on, "But behind the dispute there is an important point, for in the christological passages adduced, Ac. 10:42 and 17:31 as well as R. 1:4, the appointment of Jesus (Christ) as what He is to be must be equated with what He already is from the very beginning of the world, from all eternity in God's decree." Godet, however, rejects "declared" as insufficient: "For the resurrection of Jesus not only manifested or demonstrated what He was; it wrought a real transformation in His mode of being." He argues for "establishing". Moule uses the illustration of a coronation: one who is king by right of birth is yet "made" king by being crowned (p. 17). Geerhardus Vos has an important note on this passage (*The Pauline Eschatology* [Grand Rapids, 1953], p. 155 n.10). He says, "The resurrection (both of Jesus and of believers) is therefore according to Paul the entering upon a new phase of sonship characterized by the possession and exercise of unique supernatural power."

51. Murray rejects the meaning "declared" for the verb in favor of "appointed". But he avoids an adoptionist view by taking "with power" closely with "Son of God": "The apostle is dealing with some particular event in the history of the Son of God incarnate by which he was *instated* in a position of sovereignty and invested with power." He sees Acts 2:36 as analogous.

52. δύναμις. We might have expected that it would be primarily a Gospel word. But the greatest number of occurrences in any of the Gospels is 15 in Luke, whereas Paul uses it 48 times (eight in Romans).

contrasting mere words with power. The gospel does not simply offer people some bright ideas and then leave them to put them into practice as best they can. Christians live out their faith in a strength not their own, the power of God's Holy Spirit. Here the note of power receives stress. The resurrection introduces us to that which overcomes death, a power alongside of which the mightiest of human forces is seen for the puny thing it is.

Through the Spirit of holiness[53] introduces a further ambiguity. This might mean "according to his (the Son's) holy spirit" and refer either to the human spirit of Jesus[54] or to his divine nature.[55] Or it might mean "according to the Holy Spirit".[56] There are difficulties with all these views. The view that it refers to Jesus' human spirit is supported by the fact that there has just been a reference to "the flesh" which, it would seem, should be balanced by one to the spirit. Lagrange argues that just as "flesh" points to Christ's humanity, so does "spirit" to his divinity. But against such views Jesus' human spirit is never elsewhere referred to in terms anything like "a spirit of holiness" or "a holy spirit". This sounds so much like a reference to the Holy Spirit as to be confusing. It is objected to the view that the Holy Spirit is meant that he is not normally associated with the resurrection. This is usually reinforced by the requirement for an antithesis to "the flesh" in verse 3. Hodge, indeed, is so impressed by this that he thinks a reference to the Holy Spirit "destroys the antithesis". Paul, however, is not such a systematic writer that this is decisive. He quite often fails to supply antitheses we might think required, and we cannot insist on one here. And, while it is true that the Holy Spirit is not normally linked with the resurrection, it seems too much to say that he never can be.[57] Paul seems, then, to be speaking of the power of the Holy Spirit of God as shown in the resurrection and the designation of Christ as the powerful Son of God. A less probable alternative is that the sending of the Holy Spirit by the exalted Jesus (cf. Acts 2:33) is evidence that the Son has truly been exalted in power.[58]

53. ἁγιωσύνη is found elsewhere in the New Testament only in 2 Cor. 7:1; 1 Thess. 3:13.

54. Cf. Earle, "it seems best to take it as referring to Jesus' human spirit, which was completely holy"; so SH.

55. So Haldane, Hodge, etc. Cf. GNB, "as to his divine holiness". Murray notices and rejects the view that the expression refers to "the divine nature" of Christ. He sees it rather as characterizing "the phase which came to be through the resurrection"; "the lordship in which he was instated by the resurrection is one all-pervasively conditioned by pneumatic powers."

56. "*The Spirit of holiness* is the regular Hebrew way of saying 'the Holy Spirit'; Paul here reproduces the Hebrew idiom in Greek" (Bruce); "We should not try to be too subtle about the phrase 'Spirit of holiness' . . . Πνεῦμα ἁγιωσύνης is the exact replica of 'Holy Spirit'" (Leenhardt).

57. Black holds that "According to common Jewish belief, the resurrection of the dead was to be the work of the Holy Spirit." He cites I. Hermann in support. He sees the meaning here as "Christ was divinely decreed Son of God 'in power', i.e. miraculously, by a mighty act of God, through the work of the Holy Spirit effecting his Resurrection".

58. ἁγιωσύνη might refer to spirit as holy (Cranfield cites Ps. 51:11 [13]; Isa. 63:10-11; Test. Levi 18:7; Qumran scrolls, etc.), or if the latter view be held (as Cranfield suggests), to the work of sanctification the Spirit accomplishes in believers.

The words rendered *by his resurrection from the dead* could also be understood in the sense "from the time of the resurrection from the dead".[59] There is certainly some reference to time, but this is not primary. Rather, the emphasis is on the fact that the resurrection is that whereby Christ is seen to be the Son of God in power. There is no *his* in the Greek and the *resurrection from the dead* would normally be taken to refer to the general resurrection at the last day (the identical or almost identical expression is taken in this way in Matt. 22:31; Luke 20:35; Acts 17:32; 23:6; 24:21; 1 Cor. 15:12, 13, 21, 42; Heb. 6:2).[60] But the words apparently can mean the resurrection of one man (Acts 26:23).[61] This is the meaning required here. It is Jesus' own resurrection of which Paul is writing. But we should not overlook the fact that he chooses to do this in a way more commonly used to denote the general resurrection.[62] As Nygren puts it: "the resurrection of Christ and the resurrection of the dead are not two totally different things. . . . *For Paul the resurrection of Christ is the beginning of the resurrection of the dead.*" Elsewhere Paul speaks of Christ as "the firstfruits of those who have fallen asleep" (1 Cor. 15:20), and it may be that it is this that is behind the present expression (cf. 8:11). Christ's resurrection is no isolated event, but has important consequences for mankind at large. The emphasis is not, however, on this, but rather on the fact that the resurrection shows Jesus to be the powerful Son of God. In the light of the resurrection he is not to be classed with the generality of mankind.

Paul goes on to give him the full title *Jesus Christ our Lord*. For *Jesus Christ* see on verse 1. Paul uses the title *Lord* 275 times (out of 718 in the New Testament). This term could be no more than a polite form of address like our "Sir". But it could also be used of the deity one worships.[63] The really significant background, though, is its use in the Greek translation of the Old Testament to render the divine name, Yahweh. Where the Hebrew has this name of God the LXX frequently translates with "Lord". Christians who used this as their Bible would be familiar with the term as equivalent to deity. They were thus taking a significant step when they used it of Jesus. In referring to Jesus Paul is fond of compound expressions. He uses the combination *Jesus Christ* 15-19 times in this letter (the exact number depending on the resolution of textual problems) and the reverse, "Christ Jesus", 13-16 times. *Lord* is

59. The expression is ἐξ ἀναστάσεως νεκρῶν and the point at issue the meaning to be attached to ἐκ. It certainly can have a time reference, as we see from John 9:1, 32; Acts 24:10, etc. But since this is not its normal meaning, NIV is to be preferred. Only if the preceding words refer to the exaltation is the time reference to be accepted.

60. S. H. Hooke objects to translations which concentrate on Jesus' own resurrection and argues that Paul is saying "that it is the ἀνάστασις νεκρῶν, the resurrection of the dead, now made possible by the resurrection of Christ, that marks him out as Son of God" (NTS, IX [1962-63], pp. 371-72).

61. Sometimes 1 Pet. 1:3 is also cited, but the expression there is slightly different: δι' ἀναστάσεως Ἰησοῦ Χριστοῦ ἐκ νεκρῶν.

62. Cf. Bengel, "it is intimated, that the resurrection of all is intimately connected with the resurrection of Christ". Cf. Acts 4:2; 23:6; 26:23.

63. Cf. an invitation to dinner in the Oxyrhyncus Papyri, "Antonius son of Ptolemaeus invites you to dine with him at the table of the lord Sarapis . . ." (*The Oxyrhyncus Papyri*, Part III, ed. Bernard P. Grenfell and Arthur S. Hunt [London, 1903], p. 260).

combined with one or both of these names 17 times, to which "our" is added 12 times and "your" once.[64] In all he uses the full expression *Jesus Christ our Lord* about 68 times, whereas the rest of the New Testament has it but 19 times (CGT). From all this it is clear that Paul is fond of compound names. Perhaps they helped him bring out something of the majesty of the Savior.

5. *Through him* appears to mean that the gifts in question come from God the Father and that he gives them "through" the Son. This gives good sense and may well be right. But the Greek preposition rendered *through*[65] may on occasion denote the ultimate source (as it does in 11:36; 1 Cor. 1:9; Gal. 1:1). Paul may thus mean "from God". But even if the preposition has this meaning, Paul seems to have in mind that Christ is the giver. These uncertainties do not affect the main sense, namely that the apostle is speaking not of human achievement but of a divine gift. He often emphasizes that he owes all to Christ (e.g., 1 Cor. 9:1; 15:8; Gal. 1:1, 12, 16).

We should probably take his *we* as an epistolary plural with the meaning "I" (in English we have the royal plural and the editorial plural; in Greek the writer of a letter sometimes says "we" where we would use the singular). The point is that *apostleship* is not a gift common to Christians at large, so that Paul can scarcely mean "you Romans and I".[66] Some scholars think that the meaning is "we apostles". This is not impossible, but it does raise the question of why Paul should drag in a reference to other apostles which he does not follow up. This would be all the more curious in the salutation of a letter from Paul alone, not from Paul and other apostles.

Grace is a typically Pauline word. It is found in the apostle's writings no less than 100 times out of its 155 New Testament occurrences, so that Paul uses it approximately twice out of every three times it is found in these books. He uses it 24 times in Romans, the highest number in any one book (next is 2 Corinthians with 18, then Acts with 17). The word is cognate with that for "joy", and the basic meaning is "that which causes joy". We still retain some of this meaning when we speak of, say, a ballet dancer moving gracefully, that is, in a pleasing, "joy-giving" manner, or when we refer to "the social graces". In a Christian context nothing brings joy like that great, inexplicable[67] saving act of God in Christ in which he freely brings about our salvation without any contribution from our side. The term thus comes to us rich with ideas of joy and bounty. Grace may be specifically opposed to what is due (4:4), or again, to works (11:6). The thought is of something completely un-

---

64. "When, as here, a personal pronoun in the genitive is combined with it, the sense of personal commitment and allegiance is brought out" (Cranfield).

65. διά.

66. It is possible, however, to reason from the fact that "grace" applies to all Christians: "ἀποστολήν evidently applies to Paul himself, but the addressees and all Christians (4 τοῦ κυρίου ἡμῶν) are included in χάρις, so that he could not have written ἔλαβον χάριν" (BDF 280).

67. Cf. Barth, "Grace is the incomprehensible fact that God is well pleased with a man, and that a man can rejoice in God. Only when grace is recognized to be incomprehensible is it grace."

earned and unmerited. The word may be used of salvation in general ("by grace you have been saved", Eph. 2:8),[68] but here it is a gift for service.[69] It is the free, divine gift which enables Paul to carry out the task allotted to him (cf. 1 Cor. 15:10; Gal. 1:15; 1 Tim. 1:12-14). Here *grace* is linked with *apostleship*.[70] The meaning may well be that Paul received *grace* for his work as an apostle ("grace of apostleship"), though it is also possible that he refers to *grace* as that which enables him to live the specifically Christian life in common with other believers, and *apostleship* as the peculiar gift God had given him for his ministry. Either way *grace* is not regarded, here or elsewhere, as a gift given for the recipient's personal and private enjoyment. It is given in accordance with God's will and to further God's purposes.

Paul goes on to the purpose of the gift. The word rendered *obedience*[71] is not found in pre-Christian writings (apart from one occurrence in LXX and one in Aquila). Christians did not, of course, bring the concept of obedience into the world. This virtue was known and appreciated long before, even if it found expression in other words. But certainly Christians gave it a new emphasis. Obedience follows from the truth Paul expressed in his opening line when he described himself as a "slave" of Christ. Believers belong to Christ without reserve. Therefore they owe him the most complete obedience. It is not without interest that this epistle, which puts such stress on the free salvation won for us by Christ's atoning act, should also stress the importance of obedient response.

This is further brought out with a characteristic reference to *faith*.[72] In the New Testament this noun normally denotes the attitude of trust, though sometimes it refers to what is believed, that is, the faith (e.g., Jude 3). In the present passage the expression is literally "to obedience of faith",[73] an expression which recurs in 16:26 and which may be taken in any one of a number of ways.

(a) The genitive may be objective and faith mean "the faith", the body of teachings held by Christians. Thus Moffatt translates, "to promote obedience to the faith" (cf. 6:17; Acts 6:7). The absence of the article tells against this;

---

68. Cf. Cranfield, grace "characteristically denotes . . . God's undeserved love revealed in Christ and so may be said to sum up the whole gospel in a single word" (on v. 7).

69. Moule brings out these two aspects: "grace is God for us, grace is God in us" (p. 22).

70. ἀποστολή is a rather rare word, found only four times in the New Testament, three being in Paul.

71. ὑπακοή. AS notes that "The word is not found except in LXX, NT and eccl.". In the New Testament it occurs 15 times, 11 of which are in Paul, seven in Romans. Thus unusual attention is given to it in this letter.

72. πίστις is another Pauline word, for the apostle uses it 142 times out of the New Testament total of 243. Romans with 40 occurrences has it more than any other book (next is Hebrews with 32). Paul has a similar preponderance with πιστός, which might be translated "faithful" or "believing" (33 times out of 67; it is not used at all in Romans). Curiously this is not the case with the verb "to believe", which Paul uses but 54 times out of 241.

73. εἰς ὑπακοὴν πίστεως. Cf. 10:3; 16:26; Gal. 3:2; 2 Thess. 1:8; 1 Pet. 1:22.

therefore some adopt the variant, "obedience to the authority of faith", or even "obedience to God's faithfulness". The last two are possible, but they do not spring to the mind.

(b) The genitive may be subjective and denote origin, "obedience which springs from faith" (BAGD), or "obedience which faith demands".[74]

(c) The genitive might be epexegetic, meaning "obedience which consists in faith"[75] (so Murray, Cranfield, etc.).[76]

The absence of the article makes (a) less plausible. There is more to be said for (b), and in any case it expresses an important truth. Many favor (c), but there is a problem in that, while faith and obedience go together, they are not identical. Why use two words for one meaning? It seems rather that the gospel is seen as demanding the response of faith. Accordingly, the way to obey is to believe. But obedience is more than faith, and faith is more than obedience.

Whichever way we take the expression, obedience is not an option (cf. 1 John 3:23-24). It is binding on all Christians. "Faith's obedience" is a reminder that, as Paul understood it, faith is not an easy out for those who find a strict morality irksome. When anyone is saved through faith, it is with a view to obedience. The life is given in service to the Lord in whom one has come to believe. In some modern discussions Paul is seen as a charismatic, impatient of rules and institutions. Whatever be the truth about that, he clearly valued obedience. He was not free to innovate where God had made his will known.

For his name's sake means something like "for his sake".[77] In New Testament times "the name" had a much fuller significance than with us. We see it as a label, a way of differentiating one from another. But in antiquity generally it was held that in some undefined way the name summed up the whole person. That is the significance of changing a person's name. God changed people's names at times when he bestowed a new character on them (e.g., Gen. 17:5, 15; 32:28). When one person changed another person's name it

---

74. Cf. Black, "The words define the purpose and sphere of Paul's special apostleship: it was to bring the Gentile world to an obedience which springs from faith, in contradistinction to an obedience based on the external observance of the Law." JB has a note, "Subjective genitive: the obedience implicit in the virtue of faith".

75. Cf. G. Kittel, "the message of πίστις which consists or works itself out in ὑπακοή" (TDNT, I, p. 224). But these are not quite the same; "consists" is (c), but "works itself out" is (b).

76. Cf. Käsemann, "the obedience of faith means acceptance of the message of salvation . . . the characteristic linking of faith and obedience in Paul has a meaning which is not primarily ethical but, as is especially clear in 2 Cor 10:4-6, eschatological: When the revelation of Christ is accepted, the rebellious world submits again to its Lord". Cf. 15:18; 16:19; 2 Cor. 10:5, 6; 9:13; 1 Thess. 1:8-10.

77. The preposition ὑπέρ is characteristically Pauline, being found in the Pauline corpus 99 times out of its 149 New Testament occurrences (17 in Romans; the most in one book is 33 in 2 Corinthians, while the most in any non-Pauline writing is 13 in John). Paul often uses it to express the truth that Christ's death was substitutionary (see my *The Apostolic Preaching of the Cross*[3] [London and Grand Rapids, 1965], pp. 62-64). In the present passage, however, the more general sense, "on behalf of", is required.

emphasized his lordship (2 Kings 24:17, etc.). Here *name* stands for the whole person.[78] Paul's obedience was to all that Christ stands for.[79]

In Paul's case this was to be worked out *among all the Gentiles*. "All" is a word of which Paul is fond, and he uses it in over one third of its New Testament occurrences.[80] It may perhaps indicate the largeness of his vision. He was not apt to concentrate on some insignificant segment of any matter with which he was dealing.[81] The word *Gentiles* is one he shares with Acts.[82] Paul saw his vocation as specifically to the Gentiles (11:13; Gal. 2:9). This was a tremendous step of faith for a Jew, a Pharisee, and a Hebrew of the Hebrews (Phil. 3:4ff.). And when he turned to the Gentiles, he saw not a part only but all the Gentiles as coming within the scope of his commission. There was nothing small-minded about Paul.[83]

6. Paul's correspondents, whom he has not yet seen, come under the heading "Gentiles". This may mean that the church at Rome was predominantly Gentile (so SH, Barrett, Bruce, etc.). Or it may point to its geographical location at the heart of the Roman Empire, and thus of the Gentile world (Cranfield). The former seems more likely, but either way this justifies the apostle of the Gentiles in writing to the Roman believers. Actually the Greek is not unambiguous, and it may be that we should take *you also* not with the preceding ("the Gentiles among whom you also are") but with the following, as NIV, which groups the Romans with others who *are called*. But it seems better to take them with the preceding, as RSV, GNB, etc. In that case Paul is saying that the Romans are among the Gentiles and then goes on to refer to them as *called*. He used this word in verse 1 (where see note) of his own special call as an apostle. Now he balances this with the reminder that, while great apostles are certainly called by God, this is also true of every humble believer. When we think of our position as Christians we are inclined to think first of

---

78. Cf. Kertelge, "'his name' here means his 'person'". On the similar expression in 3 John 7 Westcott comments, "it is evident that 'the Name' is 'Jesus Christ'" (*The Epistles of St John* [London], 1892], p. 238). A little later he says, "This 'Name' is in essence the sum of the Christian Creed (comp. 1 Cor. xii.3; Rom. x.9)."

79. Michel takes the name to be that of God.

80. Paul uses πᾶς 460 times out of the New Testament total of 1,226. It is found 152 times in Luke, 170 times in Acts, and 128 times in Matthew, these being the only books which have more than 100.

81. Minear holds that the word "all" in this letter "carries a strong polemical thrust. He was fighting with his partisan readers and trying to persuade them to draw a much wider circle in their conception of the boundaries of the community of faith. As Paul saw it, that community embraced the two most hostile factions" (Minear, p. 45 n.4). But this depends on accepting Minear's view of the faction-ridden state of the Roman church (which is improbable), and it overlooks the fact that πᾶς is frequent throughout the Pauline writings, not only in Romans.

82. ἔθνος is found 162 times in the New Testament, of which 54 occurrences are in Paul (29 in Romans) and 43 in Acts. The highest number elsewhere is 23 in Revelation. This points to the truth that in Acts we see the Gentile mission at work and in Romans the theology that underlay that mission.

83. Notice how the thought of this verse recurs in 15:15-16.

what we do, and so we speak of our faith or our commitment or the like. But Paul stresses God's initiative. Christians are people whom God has called. He goes on to speak of being called *to belong to Jesus Christ*. There is a responsibility attaching to call. Those called belong to Christ. Their lives are his.[84]

7. We come to the address: *To all in Rome who are loved by God and called to be saints*. We have already noticed Paul's fondness for the word *all* (see on v. 5). He leaves out nobody as he greets the church.[85] He proceeds to speak of the Roman Christians as "God's beloved".[86] It is only because of God's self-giving love that the gospel, and hence the church, exists at all (cf. 5:5, 8; 8:35ff.). That Christians are loved by God is not a truism but a truth to be received with awe and wonder.

For *called* see on verse 1. The call of the rank and file of the Roman church balances that of the great apostle. Great leaders are called, but then so are all God's lowly people. *Saints* is a term frequently used in the New Testament to denote Christians in general. Some deduce from passages like 15:25 and Ephesians 2:19 that the word was used by Jews or Jewish Christians as a self-designation to link them with the saints of the Most High (Dan. 7:22; cf. 27). If so, Paul is putting the Gentile believers in the same class. The term reminds us of the essential character of being Christian. The word[87] basically signifies "set apart", "separated". We normally use this concept in a negative way and after "separated" we naturally supply "from". But the separation of which Paul writes is not so much a separation "from" anything as a separa-

---

84. Some understand the expression κλητοὶ Ἰησοῦ Χριστοῦ to mean "called by Jesus Christ"; they point out that the verbal adjective may take the genitive of agent (as in 3 Kings 1:49 [LXX], where this very word, κλητός, is used). Cranfield sees the refusal to accept this as "doctrinaire". Alford also accepts it, but most reject it (as SH, Lagrange, Barrett, NEB, etc.). The point is that normally Paul sees the Father rather than the Son as calling people (4:17; 8:30; 11:29; 1 Cor. 1:9; 2 Tim. 1:9). BDF 183 expressly differentiate this passage from those where the verbal adjective takes the genitive of agent because "the one calling is God". "Called to belong to Jesus Christ" is the meaning. Deissmann notes the use of the simple genitive Καίσαρος, "belonging to the Emperor" (LAE, p. 377), which may be part of the background against which the expression is to be understood (cf. 1 Cor. 1:12; 2 Cor. 10:7; Gal. 3:29; 5:24, etc.).

85. The words ἐν Ῥώμῃ are omitted in G 1739mg 1908mg its Or. Most of these authorities are late, and the words should certainly be read. See above, p. 3, for the support this reading lends to the theory of a circular letter. The reading ἐν ἀγάπῃ θεοῦ for ἀγαπητοῖς θεοῦ (G itcodd Ambstr Pel) is probably an attempt to smooth the text after ἐν Ῥώμῃ was omitted. The words are preceded by the participle οὖσιν, for which there seems no particular reason. But Paul uses this participle more than anyone else in the New Testament (61 times out of 152, 18 in Romans). He does not use the verb εἶναι as a whole in this way (560 times out of 2,450). We should take the presence of the participle accordingly as a mark of Paul's style rather than as having some profound meaning.

86. The construction is like that with κλητοί in v. 6. "God's beloved" seems to be the meaning. But NIV's *loved by God* is possible if we see this as an example of the verbal adjective taking the genitive to denote the agent as in, say, Luke 7:28 (cf. M, III, p. 234). ἀγαπητός is another word of which Paul is fond (27 times out of 61 in the New Testament).

87. ἅγιος is of course used of things as well as people. Thus it is used of scripture (v. 2), of the law and the commandment (7:12), of the firstfruits and the root (11:16), of the kiss with which Christians should greet one another (16:16). Its most notable uses are for the holy people (the saints) and for the Holy Spirit.

tion "to" God. It is positive, not negative. The saints are peculiarly God's. They are set apart for him, "called to be his dedicated people" (NEB).[88] The word contains a challenge to faithful Christian service, for *saints* should live in accordance with the character implied in being thus set apart. At the same time their being *saints* at all is by virtue of their divine calling, not their own moral achievement.

We should not overlook the plural. We sometimes speak of an individual man or woman as "a saint" or refer to "St. Peter", "St. Mary", or the like. This is not a New Testament usage. The word is never used there of any individual believer. It is always plural when used of believers, and the plural points to believers as a group, a community set apart for God. Again, the term does not convey the idea of outstanding ethical achievement which we usually understand by "saintliness". While the importance of right living is insisted on and may even be implied with this very term, the main thrust is not there. It is rather in the notion of belonging to God.

The rest of the verse contains Paul's standard greeting, a form which other Christians apparently took over from him. While in a general way it corresponds to openings to letters at large, the precise form Paul gives it is not found before his time. The Greeks normally began with "Greeting",[89] a word which in sound, though not in meaning, is close to "grace". "Peace" reflects the usual Hebrew salutation. Thus Paul's opening combines features from both groups.[90] For *grace* see on verse 5. The combination *grace* and *peace* is found already in Numbers 6:25-26.[91] *Peace* is only slightly less Pauline than is *grace*. Paul has almost half the New Testament occurrences of the word.[92] The Greeks generally understood peace as a negative thing, the absence of war. But in the New Testament the word has much of the positive connotation of

88. "When Paul writes to 'all God's beloved in Rome who are called to be saints', he is writing, not to people likely to figure in stained-glass windows, but to a somewhat motley collection of shop-keepers, minor civil servants, converted prostitutes, prize-fighters and slaves. These are the people called to be God's 'holy ones'" (S. Clive Thexton, ET, LXXXVIII [1976-77], p. 26).

89. χαίρειν is used in this way in Acts 15:23; 23:26; Jas. 1:1.

90. Käsemann, however, regards this view as "outmoded": "Paul is, rather, modifying an oriental-Jewish formula which remains intact in 2 *Apoc. Bar.* 78:2 and Gal 6:16: 'Mercy and peace be with you.'" But Käsemann's two examples both have "mercy" and not "grace"; they lack the critical word. We need not doubt that Paul's starting point was "an oriental-Jewish formula". But he modified it in a way which inevitably reminded readers of the Greek salutation.

91. Though we should notice that in LXX we have ἐλεῆσαι, "have mercy", rather than "grace".

92. Paul has 43 examples of εἰρήνη out of 91 in the New Testament. Gamble points out that the word tends to occur mostly in "the epistolary framework, that is, in the opening salutations and the concluding peace-wishes". He does not see it as frequent in "the primary vocabulary of Pauline preaching" (Gamble, p. 68). But we should not overlook Paul's frequent designation of God as "the God of peace" (15:33; 16:20; 1 Cor. 14:33; 2 Cor. 13:11; Phil. 4:9; 1 Thess. 5:23; cf. 2 Thess. 3:16). Peace was an important concept for him. He finds the making of peace a most important aspect of the work of Christ, who made peace through the blood of the cross (Col. 1:20). Indeed, he himself is "our peace" (Eph. 2:14; the whole section Eph. 2:11-18 is important for this concept).

the Hebrew *shalom*, which it constantly translates in LXX. For the Hebrews and the people of the New Testament *peace* was not so much the absence of war or strife as the presence of positive blessing.[93] In this greeting it always follows *grace*. It may not be pressing this unduly to see that it is only God's *grace* that brings real *peace*.

Among Christians the characteristic name for God is *Father*.[94] This term is, of course, far from being confined to Christians. Pagans also used it, but for them it was not typical and for Christians it was (and is). The word expresses something of the love and tender concern that God so constantly shows his people. In the first century it also conveyed the thought of absolute rule, for the father in those days was supreme in his family (among the Romans the head of the house even had the right to put members of his household to death, even if this was done very rarely; cf. Gen. 38:24). But the main thing is the love and care which God never fails to show. As he does habitually, Paul links *the Lord Jesus Christ* with the *Father* in this salutation.[95] We should not overlook the very natural way in which the two are linked. "St. Paul, if not formally enunciating a doctrine of the Divinity of Christ, held a view which cannot really be distinguished from it" (SH). The same writers see this as pointing to the Trinity: "There is nothing more wonderful in the history of Christian thought than the silent and imperceptible way in which this doctrine, to us so difficult, took its place without struggle and without controversy among accepted Christian truths."[96] In view of later church history this may be a trifle optimistic, but the New Testament usage is noteworthy. It is impossible to think of any other than Christ as being linked to the Father in this way. The formula tells us something important about the person of Christ.

B. Prayer, 1:8-15

> *8First, I thank my God through Jesus Christ for all of you, because your faith is being reported all over the world. 9God, whom I serve with my whole heart in preaching the gospel of his Son, is my witness how constantly I remember you*

93. Cf. Hunter, peace "was the normal Jewish greeting, but on Paul's lips it must mean that inner serenity which belongs to those who, through Christ, have made their peace with God."

94. Turner points out that normally when there is apposition a proper noun is anarthrous, while the apposition has the article (M, III, p. 206). He cites this passage as an example of the omission of the article "because a formula" (p. 174).

95. It is also Paul's normal practice not to have the article with either term. Colossians is an exception, for there most MSS omit any reference to Christ. 1 and 2 Timothy differ only in that the words "our Lord" are put after "Christ Jesus", while Titus reads instead, "Christ Jesus our Savior". In 1 Thessalonians the greeting ends at εἰρήνη. Paul's practice is thus not uniform, though reasonably consistent. Since the expression here is the standard form, perhaps it should not be pressed. There may be a glance at the quality of the two as Father and Lord rather than a stress on their individuality, but we can scarcely say more.

96. Cf. Black, "here is the germ of Trinitarian doctrine."

10in my prayers at all times; and I pray that now at last by God's will the way may be opened for me to come to you.

11I long to see you so that I may impart to you some spiritual gift to make you strong— 12that is, that you and I may be mutually encouraged by each other's faith. 13I do not want you to be unaware, brothers, that I planned many times to come to you (but have been prevented from doing so until now) in order that I might have a harvest among you, just as I have had among the other Gentiles.

14I am obligated both to Greeks and non-Greeks, both to the wise and the foolish. 15That is why I am so eager to preach the gospel also to you who are at Rome.

Some pious expression was often found at the beginning of a first-century letter. It might be a little prayer that things would go well with the recipient(s) of the letter,[97] or perhaps a thanksgiving for blessings received. Paul makes something very real of this feature of early correspondence,[98] and we find a thanksgiving at this point in all his letters except Galatians (which has instead, "I am astonished that you are so quickly deserting . . ."). It is not surprising to find him praying for his converts, but it is interesting that he here prays for the Roman Christians, whom he did not know. Clearly his prayers were wide-ranging. This prayer expresses some of the intensity of the feeling with which the apostle had longed to visit Rome to work among the Christians there and to preach the gospel to the heathen. We gather incidentally from his words something of the reputation the Roman Christians had at that time.

8. Paul proceeds to thank God for what he had done among the Romans. The apostle begins with *First*, but he never does get around to a corresponding "second".[99] This phenomenon may be due to a combination of the tumultuous way Paul's thoughts tumbled out and the method of writing, by dictation to a secretary,[100] a procedure which does not make for the smooth-

97. George Milligan gives the text of an early third-century letter which begins: "Serapias to her children Ptolemaeus and Apolinaria and Ptolemaeus, heartiest greeting. Above all I pray that you may be in health, which is for me the most necessary of all things. I make my obeisance to the lord Serapis, praying that I may receive word that you are in health, even as I pray for your general welfare" (*Here and There among the Papyri* [London, 1922], p. 35).

98. P. T. O'Brien has a detailed examination of this thanksgiving in his *Introductory Thanksgivings in the Letters of Paul* (Leiden, 1977), pp. 197-230.

99. BDF see the omission as "excusable or even good classical usage", perhaps "from the very outset" (447 [4]). Cf. 1 Cor. 11:18 and for a similar construction with τὰ μέν 2 Cor. 12:12. Some hold that we should see the meaning here as "first of all" or "before all" (as Boylan), but others think the corresponding second idea is found in v. 10 (as Godet). Lagrange rejects this solution.

100. It is uncertain how a secretary was used in antiquity. Many scholars hold that a trusted secretary took a rough copy on a wax tablet, wrote out the letter on papyrus with some freedom in the way the thought was expressed, then brought it to the author for correction, final approval, and the addition of a personal greeting. See, e.g., E. Earle Ellis, NTS, 26 (1979-80), pp. 498-99. Gamble cites a number of authorities on modes of dictation, all of whom "wish to allow for a considerable compositional role on the part of the

ing out of all grammatical irregularities. He begins with thanksgiving.[101] He has used the epistolary plural in verse 5, but here, writing more personally, he uses the singular. He addresses God as *my God*, an expression he uses but rarely (2 Cor. 12:21; Phil. 1:3; 4:19; Phlm. 4; some MSS of 1 Cor. 1:4). It reminds us that personal relationship is important in religion, a truth brought out by the frequent use of this kind of language in the Psalms.[102] He offers his thanksgiving *through Jesus Christ*, another unusual expression;[103] neither Paul nor anyone else can presume to approach God of himself (cf. Heb. 13:15). The matter of his thanksgiving is that the faith of the Roman Christians *is being reported*[104] *all over the world* (cf. 1 Thess. 1:8 and, from another standpoint, Col. 1:5-6). He uses two different words for *all* (in *all of you* and *all over the world*),[105] but there seems no difference in meaning; we should see the change as stylistic. Both are a trifle hyperbolic. Paul did not know all the Romans or indeed many of them. And it is possible that some parts of the world did not speak about their *faith*. But the statement is meaningful. It brings out the facts that Paul is happy with what he knows about the whole church and that it had a good reputation throughout the world of the day. *Faith* is what really matters, and clearly Paul could take it for granted that the Romans were in agreement on the point.[106] Without it neither a person nor a church has claim to the name "Christian". Sometimes the apostle's words are taken to mean that the Romans were outstanding, as when Barrett sees the meaning as, " 'the faith *as you hold it*', that is, the understanding, constancy, and charity with which you hold it." Barth's position is more in accordance with the text: "Paul does

---

amanuensis." While agreeing that there is room for "a fresh investigation" of the possible uses of amanuenses, he says, "the vigor, individuality, and consistency of style in the undisputed letters, which often bears the marks of oral speech, favor the view that these were dictated in the verbatim mode" (Gamble, p. 76 n.94). It is not easy to dispute this verdict.

101. εὐχαριστέω is yet another characteristically Pauline word, being found in the Pauline writings no less than 24 times out of its 38 occurrences in the New Testament (five in Romans).

102. Cf. Chrysostom, "with how much feeling he gives thanks: for he saith not 'to God,' but 'to my God' "; he adds "which also the Prophets do, so making that which is common to all their own."

103. O'Brien points out that this is the only occurrence of this formula in Paul's thanksgivings. He sees it as meaning that "Christ is, in some sense, the Mediator of the thanksgiving" (*Introductory Thanksgivings*, p. 204). Cf. Bruce, "As it is through Christ that God's grace is conveyed to human beings (verse 5), so it is through Christ that their gratitude is conveyed to God."

104. καταγγέλλεται. The word is used of proclaiming Christ (Phil. 1:18; Acts 17:3), the resurrection (Acts 4:2), the word of God (Acts 13:5), the gospel (1 Cor. 9:14), the Lord's death (1 Cor. 11:26), the mystery of God (1 Cor. 2:1), forgiveness of sins (Acts 13:38), and the way of salvation (Acts 16:17). It is thus the right verb to use of a serious and important proclamation. Shedd sees in the use of the verb "a proof that the Roman church had been in existence for some time."

105. περὶ πάντων ὑμῶν but ἐν ὅλῳ τῷ κόσμῳ. For πᾶς see on v. 5. ὅλος is not such a favorite word of Paul's (14 times out of 108 in the New Testament; four times in Romans).

106. Cf. O'Neill, "the opening thanksgiving for their faith is a sign that he can assume agreement about the fundamentals: the saints in Rome, as everywhere, live by faith."

not thank God for the piety of the Roman Christians. . . . He simply gives thanks for the fact that there are Christians in Rome" (so Nygren, Lagrange, Leenhardt, SH, etc.). It must have meant much to the scattered little Christian communities[107] that the church was established in the world's capital city. So they spoke of it with satisfaction, and Paul gives thanks for it. *World* is largely a Pauline and Johannine term in the New Testament.[108] In Romans the word normally means the world at large, as here, or else the inhabitants of the world; it is not used of the world in opposition to God as often in John and sometimes elsewhere in Paul (e.g., 1 Cor. 1:21).

9-10. Paul links this statement to the preceding in logical sequence with "For" (which NIV omits). It is a favorite word of Paul's[109] and one very much at home in the argumentative style of this epistle. Here it introduces a statement explaining what the writer has just said. He is very much in earnest, as his calling of God to witness shows. This is a kind of oath, a very solemn affirmation of the truth of a statement which could be known only to God.[110] The form is purely Pauline in the New Testament (with minor variants in 2 Cor. 1:23; 11:31; Gal. 1:20; Phil. 1:8; 1 Thess. 2:5, 10; but cf. Rev. 1:5; 3:14). On this occasion it is clearly very relevant, for (a) Paul had never yet been to Rome though for many years he had been "the Apostle of the Gentiles", and (b) even as he wrote he was about to go off in the opposite direction, to Jerusalem. As he preaches the gospel Paul has given his life to the service[111] of God, this God whom he calls to witness, and this in no shallow, surface manner but *with my whole heart*, or more exactly, "in my spirit".[112] This may

107. Paul is, of course, referring to what was known among believers. As for non-Christians we have the verdict of the Jewish leaders in Rome at a slightly later date, "people everywhere are talking against this sect" (Acts 28:22).

108. κόσμος occurs 185 times in the New Testament, of which 78 are in John, 24 in the Johannine epistles, and 47 in Paul (nine in Romans). Outside these two writers the most in any one book is eight in Matthew.

109. Paul uses γάρ 454 times out of a New Testament total of 1,036. It occurs 143 times in Romans, while the most in any non-Pauline writing is 124 in the much longer Gospel of Matthew. γάρ never stands first in its clause, its usual position being second. But it may come third (v. 19) or even fourth (2 Cor. 1:19). LSJ note examples of its occurring fifth, sixth, or even seventh. Modern translations for some reason often omit the term. Thus in Romans NIV omits it 58 times (more than 40% of the whole), and RSV 43 times. This tendency often obscures the connections in Paul's thought and prevents the reader from appreciating a Pauline distinctive. It is true that sometimes γάρ may legitimately be omitted in translation (BAGD, "oft. in questions, where the English idiom leaves the word untransl."). But these translations go too far and obscure the connections in Paul's argument.

110. "Paul appeals to God, as to a witness in court, since God is the one who can testify or *prove* that Paul always thinks of the Romans when he prays" (TH).

111. Paul's word for *serve*, λατρεύω, may mean "serve for hire" in secular writings (cf. λάτρον, "hire"; λάτρις, "hired servant"), but in the Bible it is nearly always used of the service of God or a god or gods (Deut. 28:48 is an exception). In LXX it is narrower than λειτουργέω in this respect, for the latter may be used when men receive the service (1 Kings 1:4; 19:21, etc.). But it is broader in that it is more often used of the service rendered by laypeople as well as priests (λειτουργέω usually, though not invariably, refers to the service of priests and Levites).

112. ἐν τῷ πνεύματί μου.

57

carry with it the thought that the service of God must be carried out in the spirit rather than the letter, as some think. It certainly stresses the thought that there is nothing superficial about the apostle's service. He serves God with his innermost being, with all his might. Hodge sees this as "opposed at once to an insincere, and to a mere external service", while Cranfield finds a reference to "his praying as being the inward side of his apostolic service contrasted with the outward side consisting of his preaching, etc."[113]

One may characterize the gospel in various ways (see on 1:1). Here Paul speaks of it as *the gospel of his Son* (cf. 15:19). It centers on Christ's atoning act. Without that there would be no gospel. In a very special sense it is Christ's own gospel. Paul speaks of his service of God as "in the gospel" (not *in preaching the gospel*; he says nothing about preaching, but simply that he serves in his spirit in the gospel). The gospel is central to the living out of the Christian life as Paul sees it; really to understand the gospel and accept it means a change in one's whole life. It is central to Paul's preaching, certainly (cf. 1 Cor. 1:17). But that is not his point here.

That for which Paul calls God to witness is the way he prays for the Roman Christians: *how constantly*[114] *I remember you in my prayers*. He never stops. *Remember* is more exactly "make[115] mention", and Paul uses his word for "mention"[116] seven times but it is found nowhere else in the New Testament. Since Paul has no special corner on any of the other words for remembrance, this is striking, though it is not easy to see whether this has significance. It is used of remembrance in prayer on every occasion but one (1 Thess. 3:6).

At all times[117] emphasizes that Paul's remembrance of the Romans is unvarying, not sporadic. His word for *prayers* is not found in the classical writers before the New Testament (though it does occur in LXX and the papyri); but the Christians found it congenial and used it often.[118]

At this point we notice an ambiguity arising from the way we punctu-

---

113. Michel sees prayer and preaching as particular forms of priestly service for Paul. Other suggestions are that his whole person is involved, that the reference is to the Holy Spirit, that his spirit (as opposed to the rest of him) accomplishes the service, and that Christians' service is spiritual whereas in other religions it is carnal. Hodge's view seems the best.

114. ἀδιαλείπτως does not mean "without intermission". MM cite its use of a cough. Paul uses it elsewhere of constant prayer (1 Thess. 1:2; 2:13; 5:17).

115. "Make" is ποιοῦμαι. The middle of this verb is used "mostly as a periphrasis of the simple verbal idea" (BAGD; cf. Eph. 1:16; 1 Thess. 1:2; Phlm. 4).

116. μνεία.

117. πάντοτε is another Pauline word. It is used by Paul 27 times out of 41 in the New Testament.

118. The noun is προσευχή. It occurs 36 times in the New Testament, of which Paul can claim the respectable total of 14 (he uses the corresponding verb only 19 times out of 86). He does not use the verb rendered *pray* in v. 10 (δέομαι) very often, but it yields another noun for prayer (δέησις) which he uses 12 times out of its 18 New Testament occurrences. Clearly Paul is more than a little interested in prayer. Perhaps we should notice that he says ἐπὶ τῶν προσευχῶν μου, which SH point out means "at my prayers"; it is not "in my prayers", but "when I pray", "at the time of" or "on the occasion of" (cf. Eph. 1:16; 1 Thess. 1:2; Phlm. 4).

ate. The most ancient manuscripts had no punctuation (or very little), and the punctuation we find in modern editions and translations is supplied by editors and translators. Paul says something very like: "how constantly mention of you I make always at my prayers asking. . . ." We could put a comma after "make" to give the sense: "how constantly I make mention of you, always at my prayers asking. . . ." Or we could put our comma after "prayers" thus: "how constantly I always make mention of you at my prayers, asking. . . ." Many modern translations favor the latter (as RSV, NIV, Moffatt), though it is also possible to opt for the former (with ASV, NEB). The difficulty with the former way is that there is nothing in the first clause to indicate that prayer is in mind, and it is further urged that it is doubtful whether Paul in his prayers invariably prayed to go to Rome. The problem with the latter is that "how unceasingly" and "always" appear very awkwardly in the same clause. But, however we resolve the problem, Paul is saying two things: in the first instance he prays for the Roman Christians constantly and in the second he asks God to let him visit them.

I pray renders a word which strictly points to petition from a sense of need,[119] though we should probably not stress this. Paul proceeds to pile up a group of Greek particles which are the despair of the Greek student and which NIV reduces to *now at last*.[120] Paul does not particularize the method or the time, but he does want to come to Rome. Notice, however, that he slips in the caveat, *by God's will*. His primary concern is to follow God's leading, not to fulfil plans of his own making. He wants to come to Rome, but only in the way and at the time God chooses. The verse contains an interesting combination of Paul's longing to visit Rome[121] and of respect for the will of God. And it is the will of God on which the emphasis is placed.[122]

---

119. δέομαι.

120. εἴ πως ἤδη ποτέ. εἰ = if; enclitic πως = somehow, perhaps; ἤδη = already; enclitic ποτε = at some time (Cranfield thinks this term "expresses the feeling that there has been enough time of waiting"). This is a formidable list, and it conveys an eager desire to come to Rome at any time God wills. Murray cites Meyer for the rendering, "if perhaps at length on some occasion." Harrisville sees "a cluster of conjunctions and adverbs here which yield the picture of a man champing at the bit". This accords with Käsemann's view that there is a suggestion of impatience. O'Brien similarly finds uncertainty and perhaps impatience (*Introductory Thanksgivings*, p. 217). Robertson includes the expression among those that show "the witchery of the old Greek particles" and thinks that ἤδη ποτέ has "more the notion of culmination ('now at last') than of time" (Robertson, pp. 1145, 1147). SH hold that "ἤδη = 'now, after all this waiting': ποτέ makes the moment more indefinite"; they render, "some near day at last." Clearly the complex expression brings out Paul's eagerness to get to Rome.

121. Paul is greatly concerned with God's will, and he uses θέλημα 24 times, somewhat curiously only four times in Romans, a book which is full of God. εὐοδόω means literally "make a good way", "be led along a good road", but in the New Testament the literal sense does not occur. It means rather "to prosper, be prospered, be successful" (AS). NIV brings out something of the original flavor with *the way may be opened*.

122. O'Brien comments, "Because of the uncertainty of journeys in ancient times, frequent and intensive prayers were offered to the gods for safe travel. Yet these requests were accompanied with very little assurance on the part of the person praying, so in order to account for any unforeseen circumstances, the rider ἐὰν θεοὶ θέλωσι was added." The difference in the case of Paul was that for him "God's will was not capricious, for it was

11. But the longing is there—a deep and strong desire (cf. Acts 19:21). Paul proceeds to speak of it, and he makes it clear that it is no selfish desire. He longs[123] to see his Roman friends, not primarily to get something out of them, but in order to impart something to them, *some spiritual gift to make you strong*. In this place *spiritual* can do no more than add emphasis, for the idea is already there in the noun. *Gift* renders *charisma*, the word normally used of the special gifts imparted by the Holy Spirit (such as those discussed in 1 Cor. 12; cf. also Rom. 12:6ff.), gifts of healings, miracles, speaking with tongues, prophecy, teaching, and so on. But the word may also be used in a wider and more general sense of the gift God makes to every believer (5:15; 1 Pet. 4:10). Paul speaks of each as having a gift which determines whether he should live the married or the single life (1 Cor. 7:7). There is no reason to think that Paul has the special gifts in mind here, and the indefinite form of the expression[124] favors the more general concept. Nor is there any indication that he could have imparted such a gift if he wished to; they seem to have been gifts given by the Holy Spirit when and how he chose. The term is used here in the more general sense of anything that builds up the spiritual life. Paul wanted the Roman Christians to be strengthened in the faith as a result of the gift God would give them through his ministry. He speaks of strengthening them (and gives that as the purpose[125] of his proposed visit—he was not aimless in anything he did). Life was not easy for first-century Christians. At Rome, as elsewhere, it was important that they be strong.

12. Paul explains his meaning a little more, for what he has just said, though sincere, might seem boastful or patronizing.[126] Some suggest that Paul checks himself from reasons of policy, but this is not a cunning ploy, calculated to secure a desired effect. It is the simple truth. When he went to Rome the traffic would not be all one way.[127] Paul would doubtless bring

---

through the will of God that he had been called to be an apostle. . . . Paul might therefore commend specific details of that apostolic calling (such as a journey to Rome) to God's will with true confidence" (*Introductory Thanksgivings*, p. 220).

123. This verse is full of characteristic Pauline language. Paul uses ἐπιποθέω seven out of its nine times in the New Testament, πνευματικός 24 out of 26, and χάρισμα 16 out of 17. This last mentioned is, of course, connected with χάρις, "a concrete instance of God's χάρις, a gift of God" (CGT). The combination χάρισμα πνευματικόν is found here only. Perhaps we should add ἵνα to the list of Pauline words. It is, of course, a common word and might be found anywhere. But Paul uses it more than anyone, 249 times out of 673; John is next with 147, a long way behind Paul's total.

124. ἵνα τι μεταδῶ χάρισμα. On the position of τί BDF comments, "Unemphatic (enclitic) pronouns and the like are placed as near the beginning of the sentence as possible . . . (they are not, however, placed first)" (473 [1]).

125. For εἰς with the accusative of the infinitive see the note on v. 20.

126. Paul uses the various forms of οὗτος quite often (268 times). He is far and away the greatest user of τοῦτο, which he has 114 times out of a New Testament total of 315, more than a third of the whole. We should thus add this to the characteristic Pauline language of this part of the epistle. The expression τοῦτο δέ ἐστιν is found here only in the New Testament. Leenhardt says that it "has not the meaning of τοῦτ' ἔστιν (that is to say) (cf. 7:18). It introduces not an explanation but a complement" (Cranfield accepts this, though Robertson, p. 705, finds no difference).

127. Cf. Calvin, "Note how modestly he expresses what he feels by not refusing to

something to the Roman Christians, but they would also help him. They would be *mutually encouraged*[128] *by each other's faith.*[129] The mutuality is strengthened by the addition "both yours and mine"[130] (which NIV omits, thus losing a Pauline emphasis). This is not required by the sense, for the faith in question had to be that of Paul and the Romans. But the addition makes it quite clear that the faith of both was to be a factor in the situation. Paul was sure that the Romans would help him just as he would help them. Actually the translation *that you and I may be mutually encouraged* slightly oversimplifies the Greek. Paul says, "that is, to be encouraged among you". He does not specify who is to be encouraged, though clearly he means himself (there is nobody else who is to be "among you"). But at this point he is thus putting more emphasis on his receiving from the Romans than on their receiving from him. He would certainly give them all he could. But he wants to leave no doubt but that he expected to be encouraged by their faith.[131]

13. *I do not*[132] *want*[133] *you to be unaware*[134] is an expression Paul uses four times (11:25; 1 Cor. 10:1; 12:1), while on two more occasions he differs only in

---

seek strengthening from inexperienced beginners. He means what he says, too, for there is none so void of gifts in the Church of Christ who cannot in some measure contribute to our spiritual progress." So also Cragg, "It may have been a wise approach, but it was an attitude dictated more by the nature of the gifts of which he writes than by the strategy which governed his mission. Benefit is never one-sided. . . . It is impossible to bless without being blessed."

128. συμπαρακαλέω may have the meaning "comfort" (as KJV) or "encourage"; it "is used of the inner strengthening of mind and spirit imparted by God" (Black). Hodge thinks that the word "expresses all that excitement and strengthening of faith and pious feeling, as well as consolation, which is wont to flow from the communion of saints."

129. Paul "piles up phrases to emphasise the reciprocity of benefit (συν., ἐν, ἀλλ., ὑ.κ.ἐ.)" (CGT).

130. "Emphatic ἐμοῦ does not appear in NT except in combination with another gen." (BDF 284 [2]). The meaning will be, "each through the faith of the other."

131. Käsemann, who sees "uncertainty and embarrassment" here, discerns a "sudden change from the stylized certainty of the prescript and the dignity of the thanksgiving"; "The planned visit is . . . definitely divested of any official character, in obvious contradiction of the real plans of the apostle and of the claims raised in v. 5" (p. 19). He rejects explanations like Paul's modesty, humility, tact and sensitivity, or caution induced by opposition. Instead he finds this to be Paul's reaction to widespread rejection of his apostolic claim. But this reads a good deal into the passage and is a far from obvious explanation of the words. Certainly some of the explanations Käsemann rejects are more convincing than the one he accepts. What *evidence* is there that Paul's claims were rejected at Rome?

132. Paul makes a good deal of use of the negative. He uses οὐ, οὐκ 121 times in Romans and 483 times in all (1,619 in the New Testament); next is John with 286. He is also far and away the largest user of μή, 77 times in Romans and 354 times in all (1,055 in the New Testament); next is Luke with 142. Paul has some resounding negatives, the reverse side of his positive message.

133. For οὐ θέλω some MSS, such as D* G d e g Ambrosiaster, Pelagius, read οὐκ οἴομαι. Tasker, explaining the rejection of the latter, says that the majority of his committee "thought that it was out of place for Paul to say that he believed the Roman church to be well informed about his movements; the required sense being that he wishes now to give such information to a church to which he was a stranger" (Tasker, p. 434).

134. Paul uses ἀγνοέω 15 times out of 21 in the New Testament, six being in Romans. Paul may also complain, "You do not know" (2:4; 6:3, etc.), while his "we know"

using the plural "we" (2 Cor. 1:8; 1 Thess. 4:13). He uses this expression as a rule when he is introducing his readers to something they might not be expected to know but which he regards as important. In this way he emphasizes it to some extent. Paul often uses *brothers*[135] as a form of address (in this epistle on no less than ten occasions), but it is rare outside his writings. Luke uses "men and brothers" and James "my brothers". Normally the term carries overtones of affection, but since Paul had never been to Rome we must take this as an indication of the warmth of feeling he had for all who were kin to him in Christ.

This leads to the statement that he had often[136] intended[137] to come to Rome (cf. Acts 19:21), but had always been *prevented*.[138] He does not say what had prevented him; his emphatic term, however, implies that he had tried hard to make the trip but that circumstances beyond his control had prevented it. His aim in seeking to come to Rome was *in order that I might have a harvest among you. Have a harvest* is perhaps more accurately rendered, "get some fruit"[139] (cf. John 15:16), a term which is not further defined. There may be something of a double meaning: the harvest would be his gain and theirs. Usually in the New Testament "fruit" refers to qualities of character or the like, as when Paul speaks of the fruit of the Spirit as "love, joy, peace . . ." (Gal. 5:22). It may be that this is in mind here, but on the whole it seems a little more likely that he is thinking of converts. He had been the means of bringing people to believe in Christ elsewhere in the Gentile world (for "Gentile" see on v. 5). Now he looks for the same thing to happen in Rome. *The other Gentiles* shows that Paul had had a very extensive ministry, but we need not take it to mean that he had worked among all the other Gentiles without exception. The expression also shows that the Roman church had many Gentiles in it, perhaps that it was predominantly Gentile.

14. There is no connecting particle, a fact which Godet takes to indicate

---

assumes knowledge shared with his readers (2:2; 3:19, etc.). Now and then he has "I know" (14:14; 15:29).

135. ἀδελφός is another Pauline word, for Paul uses it in 133 of its 343 New Testament occurrences. Käsemann sees it as "a primitive Christian term for a member of the community which has both Jewish and pagan analogies (Lietzmann)" (p. 20).

136. πολλάκις shows that the Roman church had been in existence for quite some time.

137. Cranfield thinks προεθέμην is "stronger than βούλεσθαι or θέλειν"; the implication "is that on a number of occasions Paul's wish to see them has actually been transformed into a more or less definite plan to visit them."

138. κωλύω is a strong term (GT, "cut off"). MM cite its use in senses like "stop" and "forbidden by law". In 1 Thess. 2:18 Paul speaks of having been hindered by Satan, but that is not said here. Indeed, he seems to mean that it was God who had stopped him because it was not yet time (cf. v. 10). In Acts 16:6 the apostle's movements were prevented by the Holy Spirit. A number of students hold that 15:22ff. may point us to the answer (e.g., Hunter, Hendriksen).

139. τινὰ καρπὸν σχῶ. CGT comments, "σχῶ, 'get,' as always." The metaphor of harvest is often used of the eschatological judgment (e.g, Isa. 27:12; Joel 3:13; Matt. 3:12; 13:30, 39; Mark 4:29), but also of the evangelistic activities of Christ's servants (Matt. 9:37-38; John 4:35-38).

feeling. Paul goes straight on to *I am bound both to Greeks and non-Greeks. I am bound* is more literally "I am a debtor."[140] Paul uses the concept of debt on a number of occasions (as in 8:12; 15:27; Gal. 5:3). Here he probably means that his commission as the apostle of the Gentiles put him under obligation to preach the gospel to the Gentiles, at Rome as elsewhere. For any of us to receive the gospel is to incur a debt, and Paul shared in this. "Obligation to him who died produces obligation to those for whom he died."[141] Earle speaks of "a vast amount of unnumbered blessings he had received from God" and adds, "All this put him under obligation." But we should not overlook the fact that Paul speaks of being a debtor not to God, but to the Gentiles. This gives point to Barclay's comment: "He was debtor because of all the kindness that he had received, and he was a debtor because of his obligation to preach to them." Cranfield rejects this and understands the words in the sense "having an obligation to them in the sense that God has laid upon him a duty toward them."[142] We need not tie Paul down too tightly and insist that his words be given the narrowest possible interpretation, but is this just to the fact that he speaks of himself as debtor *to the Gentiles*? It is better to see the thought as complex, certainly including all the implications of Paul's commission to be the apostle to the Gentiles, but with a glance also at what he owes the Gentiles in so many ways. They had contributed to his understanding of life. There may also be the thought that he had "got fruit" among many nations and was thus indebted to them.[143] It is not completely clear whether Paul's groups of people are meant to sum up all mankind or only the Gentiles. In favor of the Gentiles is his reference to them at the end of verse 13, but his language is quite general and there seems no real reason for excluding Jews. Perhaps the best understanding of the words is to see the gospel as imposing a debt on all who receive it, a debt which calls for repayment by passing the gospel on to someone else.

Paul lists some of those to whom he is indebted and begins with *Greeks*.[144] This term can have other meanings than "those of the Greek na-

---

140. ὀφειλέτης εἰμί.

141. Minear, p. 104. He later says, "To the extent that Paul was indebted to God for this call, to that very extent he was indebted to those Gentiles for whose sake God had called him." On the same page he cites A. Schlatter's suggestion "that the principle which Jesus had made binding on his disciples had become binding on Paul—that his purpose in giving a gift to one disciple was that he might give it to another. This is why Paul was indebted to all."

142. He adds, "His debt to them is constituted by the fact that God had appointed him ἐθνῶν ἀπόστολος."

143. Parry rejects Ramsay's view of a general benefit which Paul repays by preaching the gospel or a reference to 1 Cor. 9:16: "It is best taken in close connexion with καρπὸν σχῶ; cf. Phil. iv.17. He has already 'got fruit' from these classes: he pays the debt by sowing the seed more widely among such" (CGT). But the relevance of Phil. 4:17 is not obvious; it refers to credit the Philippians might claim for their service, not to any obligation resting on them.

144. Paul uses Ἕλλην in exactly half its New Testament occurrences (13 out of 26). An interesting feature of his use is that he never employs it with the article: it is always "Greeks", never "the Greeks". This puts an emphasis on the quality ("people like Greeks"). His use is "because the emphasis is always on the distinctive quality ('people like

tion". In the expression "Jew and Greek" it clearly means "Gentile" (cf.
v. 16). Now and then it appears to mean Greek-speaking Jews or Jewish
proselytes (John 12:20; Acts 17:4). At this period the Greek language and
culture were widespread and people in many places had adopted both. The
term could thus mean "people of culture", which is possibly the way we
should take it here. This is supported by the fact that it forms a pair with
"barbarians", and it would form a natural antithesis to see it as meaning
"cultured".[145] It is possible, however, that "Greeks and barbarians" should
be understood as NIV, *Greeks and non-Greeks,* and thus the totality of mankind. "Barbarian"[146] originally meant someone who did not speak the local
language. But it came to mean "one who lacks culture", just as is the case with
our word "barbarian". Greeks and barbarians form a natural pair of opposites
and sum up the world.[147] People are either cultured or uncultured.[148]

Paul has another pair of opposites, *the wise and the foolish.*[149] Paul may
decry worldly wisdom (as he does, e.g., in 1 Cor. 2), but he is deeply interested in true wisdom. He often reverts to the subject as he distinguishes
between the wisdom of this world which he sees as foolishness (1 Cor. 1:20)
and the true wisdom that comes from God. Here he is thinking of those the
world counts as wise, but he is not contrasting their kind of wisdom with that
which comes from God. He is accepting it for what it is and agreeing that it has
its values. It is only when people use it to reject the divine wisdom that it is to
be condemned. GT cites Aristotle's definition of wisdom as "mental excellence in its highest and fullest sense." It is something like this that Paul has in
mind here, along with the point that Trench makes, that there is an important
ethical element in wisdom.[150] By contrast, *the foolish* are those without under-

---

the Greeks' . . .) and not on the existing group as a collective whole, while in classical Greek
the arthrous form is the rule" (BDF 262 [2]).

145. TH renders, "to the civilized and to the savage, to the educated and to the
ignorant", and comments, "In the first two expressions, *civilized . . . savage* (literally
'Greeks . . . barbarians'), the distinction is not racial or national, but cultural. . . . The next
two terms, *educated . . . ignorant,* do not refer to innate intellectual capacities, but rather to
degrees of learning." But this is surely going beyond the evidence.

146. βάρβαρος seems to have been an onomatopoeic term, meaning someone
whose language is unintelligible; it sounds like "bar bar." Cf. 1 Cor. 14:11. But the barbarians on Malta (Acts 28:2, 4) seem to have spoken Greek, so the linguistic significance was
perhaps not strictly applied.

147. H. Windisch thinks that Paul "perhaps groups the Spaniards to whom he
plans to journey from Rome" along with others under this heading (TDNT, I, p. 552).
Leenhardt sees it as "certainly an allusion to Spain and the missionary plans of the
apostle."

148. Does Paul class the Romans as "Greeks" or "barbarians"? It is perhaps relevant that the church of Rome was Greek-speaking, as the very existence of this letter
shows. It was not until the third century that it seems to have become genuinely Latin. But
Haldane's comment is relevant: "He does not inquire or decide whether they ought to be
reckoned among the Barbarians or the Greeks, the wise or unwise; he was ready to preach
the Gospel to them all."

149. σοφός is another of Paul's characteristic words, being found in his writings in
16 of its 20 New Testament occurrences. He has ἀνόητος five times out of six.

150. "If σοφία includes the striving after the best ends as well as the using of the

standing. They are not schooled in the niceties of philosophical debate, but that does not mean that Paul owes them nothing. He is in debt to all people, and he wants to do something to discharge the debt. This second division of mankind is not identical with the first. There could be foolish Greeks and there could be wise barbarians!

15. *That is why* expresses consequence: "since I am bound to all men" (Hodge). *I am so eager* is perhaps a little stronger than Paul's words, which mean rather, "I am ready". There is a slight difficulty with the Greek, but it appears to mean something like "as concerns me there is a readiness. . . ."[151] Whatever had prevented Paul from going to Rome till now had not been his own fault. He himself was quite ready, but matters he could not control had till now prevented him from making the trip.[152] The reason he wanted to go to Rome was *to preach the gospel*[153] to the Romans. It is a revealing glimpse of his priorities. He has already said that he is separated to the gospel (v. 1), and it accords with this that when his thoughts turn to what he can do for those *at Rome*[154] it is preaching the gospel on which he seizes. That is the one thing that matters. The question arises, of course, "Why preach the gospel to Christians?" Our answer should probably be that in this sense he writes to his readers as Romans rather than as Christians (so Godet).[155] In Rome as elsewhere it is to nonbelievers that he would bring the gospel.

II. THESIS, 1:16-17

> 16*I am not ashamed of the gospel, because it is the power of God for the salvation of everyone who believes: first for the Jew, then for the Gentile.* 17*For in*

---

best means, is mental excellence in its highest and fullest sense (cf. Aristotle, *Ethic. Nic.* vi.7.3), there can be no wisdom disjoined from goodness, even as Plato had said long ago (*Menex.* 19)" (*Synonyms*, p. 283). He sees the use of ἀνόητος as significant, "for, while the ἀσύνετος need not be more than intellectually deficient, in the ἀνόητος there is always a moral fault lying behind the intellectual" (*ibid.*).

151. BDF notes κατά + accusative as "a circumlocution for the possessive or subjective gen. . . . it is virtually limited to pronouns in the NT"; "τὸ κατ᾽ ἐμὲ πρόθυμον = ἡ ἐμὴ προθυμία (τὸ πρόθυμον = ἡ προθυμία)" (224 [1]). Cranfield sees three possibilities: (i) τὸ κατ᾽ ἐμέ is subject and πρόθυμον is predicate; (ii) ἐγώ (understood) is subject and τὸ κατ᾽ ἐμέ is adverbial, "so far as it rests with me"; (iii) all four words are subject and (ἐστιν) . . . εὐαγγελίσασθαι is predicate, "my eager desire is. . . ." He accepts (iii).

152. Robert Jewett sees "I am eager, etc." as "a well-established bureaucratic formula for being prompt in following orders" (*Interpretation*, XXXVI [1982], p. 15).

153. Paul does not use the verb εὐαγγελίζω in the overwhelming majority of cases as he does the noun "gospel" (for which see on v. 1), but he still uses it appreciably often, namely 21 times out of 54 in the New Testament (next is Acts with 15).

154. The words ἐν Ῥώμῃ are omitted here by fewer MSS than in v. 7, namely G it^g Or^{lat}. It seems that the words should be accepted.

155. Turner disposes of the problem by understanding the verb as "tell"; he takes the text in the sense, "I am anxious to tell you in Rome also my own point of view" (*Grammatical Insights*, p. 92). But this is an unnatural meaning for the verb as Paul uses it, and it does not fit the context where εὐαγγέλιον in the sense "gospel" occurs five words later.

the gospel a righteousness from God is revealed, a righteousness that is by faith from first to last,ᵃ just as it is written: "The righteous will live by faith."ᵇ

ᵃ17 Or *is from faith to faith*   ᵇ17 Hab. 2:4

These two verses have an importance out of all proportion to their length. The weighty matter they contain tells us much of what this epistle is about. Barrett can say, "Most commentators recognize in them the 'text' of the epistle; it is not wrong to see in them a summary of Paul's theology as a whole." We have already noticed that the theme of Romans is God. This whole epistle is a book about God. But once that is recognized these verses may be held to give us the thesis of the epistle: they sum up for us what God has done to bring us salvation. Paul declares his adherence to the gospel (which he has already said is God's, v. 1) and points out that God's power is at work in it. It is a revelation of God's righteousness. Paul quotes from the prophet Habakkuk to show that it is no new-fangled fantasy, but God's way foretold from of old through God's prophets. All these are characteristic Pauline thoughts and will be developed as we go through the epistle.

16. The verse is introduced by "For", which NIV omits.[156] It is perhaps a little curious that Paul writes *I am not ashamed*[157] *of the gospel*. Why should he feel it necessary to utter this disclaimer? He gloried in the gospel (5:2, 11; 2 Cor. 10:17; Gal. 6:14; Phil. 3:7). But it may be that there were people in Rome who despised the simplicity of the message (there were certainly some elsewhere, Acts 17:32; 1 Cor. 1:18, 23). Such people would look down on the Christians and their unusual gospel.[158] Whatever be the case with others, Paul emphatically stands by the message. It had brought him neither ease nor comfort: "Paul had been imprisoned in Philippi, chased out of Thessalonica, smuggled out of Beroea, laughed at in Athens. He had preached in Corinth

---

156. This γάρ is important because it links what follows with what precedes and gives a reason. Cf. Chamberlain, in vv. 16 and 17 γάρ "occurs three times: the first instance introduces the reason for Paul's eagerness to preach the gospel in Rome; the second, his reason for not being ashamed of the gospel; the third, the reason for the dynamic of the gospel" (Chamberlain, p. 154). Harrisville holds that the construction "for . . . not" reflects a pattern in this epistle. Except in 6:14, he says, it introduces an argument; it is often preceded or followed by another clause with "for", "indeed", or "but"; often there is a "whoever" and usually the copula (one or more of these characteristics is sometimes absent) (Harrisville, p. 254 n. 1).

157. Jesus recognized the possibility that some would be ashamed of him: "If anyone is ashamed of me and my words in this adulterous and sinful generation, the Son of Man will be ashamed of him when he comes in his Father's glory with the holy angels" (Mark 8:38); cf. also, "do not be ashamed to testify about our Lord"; "I am not ashamed, because I know whom I have believed . . ." (2 Tim. 1:8, 12). The natural man is repelled by "the offence of the cross" (Gal. 5:11), and such scriptural warnings are much to the point.

158. "The gospel of a crucified carpenter in the streets of Imperial Rome—is not the idea so incongruous as to make one ashamed at the prospect? No, he is not ashamed, for the gospel is a divine POWER . . ." (Hunter). Chrysostom comments, "Paul was going to preach Jesus, who was thought to be the carpenter's son, who was brought up in Judea, and that in the house of a mean woman, who had no body guards, who was not encircled in wealth, but even died as a culprit with robbers, and endured many other inglorious things".

where his message was foolishness to the Greeks and a stumbling-block to the Jews, and out of that background Paul declared that he was proud of the gospel" (Barclay). He had certainly had his share of trouble as he proclaimed the message. But the gospel had proved adequate for the needs both of himself and his hearers, and Paul was far from being ashamed of it. Some have thought that he was troubled at coming to so splendid a place as Rome, the capital city of the world, with so simple a message. But, as Adolph Schlatter pointed out, "Reasons for deliberating whether he ought to be ashamed of the gospel were as real in the lowliest house of worship of the Jews as they were in the Roman Forum. Their root lay in the message he came with, in what he called its foolishness."[159] That might tempt Christians anywhere to be ashamed. But Paul was not of that number.

The *gospel* is *the power of God*[160] for salvation (for *gospel* see on v. 1 and for *power* on v. 4). Paul is fond of contrasting mere words with power (e.g., 1 Cor. 2:4; 4:19-20; 1 Thess. 1:5; power and the gospel come together again in 15:19; 1 Cor. 1:18, 24; 2:5; cf. 2 Cor. 13:4; Eph. 3:20; Col. 1:11; 2 Tim. 1:7). No such contrast is explicit here, but Paul makes it plain that he is greatly interested in the power he sees in the gospel. The gospel is not advice to people, suggesting that they lift themselves. It is power. It lifts them up. Paul does not say that the gospel brings power but that it *is* power, and God's power at that. When the gospel is preached, this is not simply so many words being uttered. The power of God is at work.[161] When the gospel enters anyone's life, it is as though the very fire of God had come upon him. There is warmth and light in his life.[162]

The power of God of which Paul writes is not aimless but directed to *salvation*. It issues in salvation. This is the general term of which justification, redemption, and the like are particular aspects. Leenhardt sees it as signifying "all the blessings which God alone can give in answer to the need and longing of man, who is oppressed and in anguish in face of a destiny which sharpens his need of supernatural beatitude in proportion as it does nothing to satisfy it."[163] Salvation is a very positive affair; it brings a rich variety of blessings

---

159. Cited in Nygren.

160. Luther comments, "'power of God' does not mean that power by which he is powerful in himself but that power by which he makes powerful and strong"; for examples he cites Luke 1:35; 24:49; Acts 1:8; 4:23.

161. The word for *power* is δύναμις (from which we derive words like "dynamic"). Knox comments that Paul "thinks of the message, the preaching, as he calls it in 1 Cor. 1:21ff., as being itself a part of the continuing dynamic event."

162. Theodoret remarked that "many things have their own operation hidden from the senses." He chooses pepper as an illustration, for "pepper outwardly seems to be cold, and to those who are unaware it gives no outward appearance of heat. But the person who crunches it between his teeth experiences the sensation of burning fire" (*Commentary*, pp. 29-30). The illustration might not strike us all as obvious, but it certainly makes the point.

163. Cf. Moule, "The word is here probably used in its largest meaning, including the whole process of mercy from the time of belief onwards; deliverance from doom, sin, and death" (CBSC; he goes on to notice future and present positive aspects and notes that the meaning is concerned with rescue rather than amelioration).

from God (5:10-11; 1 Cor. 1:18; Eph. 2:13, etc.). But it also has negative aspects. People may be saved from wrath (5:9), from hostility to God (5:10) or alienation from him (Eph. 2:12), from sin (Matt. 1:21), from being lost (Luke 19:10), from futility (1 Pet. 1:18), from "a yoke of slavery" (Gal. 5:1), from demon-possession (Luke 8:36), from sickness (Luke 8:48), from danger (Matt. 8:25-26), from a "corrupt generation" (Acts 2:40). Salvation has many facets. There is a sense in which it has already been achieved (Eph. 2:5), and another in which it is a present, on-going process (1 Cor. 1:18; 2 Cor. 2:15), but often the New Testament writers see it as future (13:11; 1 Cor. 5:5; 2 Tim. 4:18, etc.).

The scope of salvation is universal. It is open to *everyone who believes.* Paul brings this out further by saying that it is *first*[164] *for the Jew,*[165] *then*[166] *for the Gentile* (literally "the Greek"). The combination stands for the totality of mankind. The gospel is for all and knows no limitation by race. In the matter of salvation God puts no difference between one nation and another. Paul assigns a certain priority to the Jew but immediately balances it with his reference to the Greek. Historically the gospel came to the Jews first, but Paul seems to mean more than this. The priority was in God's plan. An electing purpose is expressed in it. But there is not one gospel for Jews and another for Gentiles. All who are saved are saved by the one gospel and are brothers and sisters in Christ. Just as it is true that it is *first for the Jew, then for the Gentile,* so it is true that "There is neither Jew nor Greek . . . for you are all one in Christ Jesus" (Gal. 3:28). But if *everyone* marks the universality, a restriction is indicated by *who believes.* The powerful salvation of which Paul writes is not the possession of any unbeliever. Each person must make it his own by his act of faith. This does not mean that faith is like another kind of law, but easier, as though God and man were cooperating to bring about salvation. "It is not man's faith that gives the gospel its power; quite the contrary, it is the power

164. πρῶτον assigns priority to the Jew, but this is balanced with τε καί, which coordinates the two. Curiously Lenski takes πρῶτον to apply to both, "in the first place for both Jew and Greek" (understanding "Greek" in terms of culture, he reasons that the gospel goes first to the combination of religious Jews and cultured Greeks; if even they needed it, so did "the lower classes"). This is unconvincing. The word πρῶτον is missing from some MSS, namely B G g sah Tertullian Ephraem. The best suggestion is that it was omitted by Marcion, who would have found it quite unacceptable (so, e.g., Metzger). It is interesting that Paul, the apostle of the Gentiles, writing to a group made up largely of Gentiles (v. 13), should not hesitate to speak of the priority of the Jew. Cf. Matt. 15:24; Luke 24:47; John 4:22; Acts 1:8; 13:46. John H. Stek examines the priority of the Jew, mostly in material from the Gospels, in "To the Jew First", *Calvin Theological Journal,* 7 (1972), pp. 15-52.

165. Ἰουδαῖος occurs 11 times in Romans, the most in any Pauline writing. The apostle is greatly concerned with the Jews in this letter. But the term is much more frequent in other writers (Acts has it 79 times and John 71).

166. καί. GT notes that καί "is *conjunctive,* τέ *adjunctive.* . . . καί introduces something new under the same aspect yet as an external addition, whereas τέ marks it as having an inner connection with what precedes" (*sub* τέ). Cranfield comments, "The word τε (though its presence is simply ignored by RV, RSV, NEB and JB) is suggestive of the fundamental equality of Jew and Gentile in the face of the gospel (the gospel is the power of God unto salvation for believing Jew and believing Gentile alike)". BDF (444 [2]) draw attention to καί . . . καί in 1 Cor. 10:32, "where the distinction between the members is retained, whereas with τε καί the distinction is rather set aside."

of the gospel that makes it possible for one to believe" (Nygren).[167] Paul is not saying that people achieve power by their own believing effort.[168] He is saying that the power of God is at work in the gospel.

17. Paul proceeds to an explanation, giving the grounds for what he has just said (*For* keeps the argument in logical sequence). The statements of v.16 are seen to be true because of what Paul now affirms. For the *righteousness of God* see Additional Note A. In this passage it is not completely certain whether we should understand the expression in the sense of a quality or attribute of God or of a right standing which God gives. It makes good sense to say, "In the gospel it is revealed that God is a righteous God." But it also makes good sense to say, "In the gospel it is revealed that people get a right standing, a status of being right, from God."[169] The following reference to faith seems to show that the righteousness that God gives is primarily in mind, as does the quotation from Habakkuk. Cranfield sees as decisive the further point that the argument of the epistle as a whole supports this view. Up to 4:25 Paul is concerned with the man who by faith is just (it is only after this that he emphasizes that the just "will live").[170] Here Paul is saying that in the gospel God has acted decisively for our salvation and in a way that is right. The "rightness" of the way of salvation will be further brought out in this epistle as Paul develops the concept of justification. We should further notice that the righteousness of God is here said to be "revealed" in the gospel. That is to say, it is something new, not simply a repetition of Old Testament truth (important as that is).[171]

This righteousness *is revealed*.[172] It is not something that people know

---

167. Cf. Cranfield, "it is of the very essence of faith as Paul understands it, that it is opposed to human deserving, all human establishing of claims on God. . . For Paul man's salvation is altogether—not almost altogether—God's work; and the faith spoken of here is the openness to the gospel which God Himself creates." He later says, "And yet this faith, as God's work in a man, is in a real sense more truly and fully the man's own personal decision than anything which he himself does of himself; for it is the expression of the freedom which God has restored to him—the freedom to obey God."

168. O'Neill seems to countenance such views by saying things like "the men who live by faith live righteously in God's sight"; "To the objection that Paul wants to speak only of God's action and not at all of man, I answer that this context is about faith, what man has to do if he would live before God."

169. Cf. Lenski, "Δικαιοσύνη θεοῦ *is the status of righteousness into which faith and the believer are placed by the judicial verdict of God*" (Lenski's italics).

170. Hodge sees righteousness as both ἐκ θεοῦ (Phil. 3:9) and παρὰ τῷ θεῷ (2:13; 3:20; Gal. 3:11). Here he sees both "a righteousness, which God gives, and which he approves". But this seems tautological. How could God give a righteousness of which he did not approve?

171. NEB renders, "God's way of righting wrong". Black sees it as "the triumph of God (over Satan, sin and death)". But this perhaps relies too much on connecting these words with certain Old Testament passages such as Judg. 5:11; Ps. 103:6, which link righteousness and deliverance. From another point of view Käsemann speaks of "the fact that the δικαιοσύνη θεοῦ appears in Rom. 1:17; 10:3ff. in personified form as Power" (*New Testament Questions of Today* [London, 1969], p. 169). But his "fact" goes beyond the evidence. Paul does not say that God's righteousness is power, but that the gospel is power.

172. The present tense ἀποκαλύπτεται points to an ongoing process. We proclaim the gospel, but the revelation is something God does. The verb is found in Paul in exactly half its New Testament occurrences (13 out of 26).

naturally or can find out for themselves. Unless God makes it known they will never discover it. NIV repeats the word *righteousness* though it occurs but once in the Greek: *a righteousness from God is revealed, a righteousness that is by faith.* This may well be the way the passage should be understood, for righteousness and faith are certainly linked elsewhere (e.g., 3:22). But we should notice that the word order is "righteousness of God in it is revealed from faith to faith." This makes it possible to take *is revealed* and *faith* together, with the meaning that only faith apprehends the revelation.[173] While this is true, it does not appear that this is what Paul is saying. It is much more likely that we should accept the sense of NIV and see a reference to that righteousness or right standing which is ours by faith.

NIV's *by faith from first to last* is the translation of a very difficult Greek expression.[174] It means literally "out of faith into faith" or "from faith to faith". Some have stressed this literal meaning and have argued that Paul means that the gospel spreads by a process in which the faith of one reaches out to bring another to faith. Some see the words as pointing to growth in faith (so SH), others that faith is both ground and goal. Manson favors "a revelation that springs from God's faithfulness and appeals to man's faith" (similarly Barth and others). An ancient interpretation is "from an Old Testament faith (cf. the quotation from Habakkuk) to a New Testament faith (the gospel)". There are other views. Such interpretations, however, do seem to be reading something into the expression. It seems much more likely that Paul is simply emphasizing the place of faith: "faith through and through" or, as Ronald Knox renders it, "faith first and last". The centrality of faith is important and must be clearly seen. Dodd finely remarks that for Paul "faith is that attitude in which, acknowledging our complete insufficiency for any of the high ends of life, we rely utterly on the sufficiency of God. It is to cease from all assertion of the self, even by way of effort after righteousness, and to make room for the divine initiative." See further on verse 5.

Following his custom Paul drives home what he is saying with a quotation from Scripture. His almost invariable habit is, as here, to introduce it with *just as it is written.*[175] It is not necessary for him to say where it is written. The central place assigned to Scripture in the early church made that unnecessary. On this occasion he quotes from Habakkuk 2:4 the words, *The righteous will live by faith* (quoted again in Gal. 3:11; Heb. 10:38).[176] This message has been

---

173. Murray, e.g., finds it "more natural . . . to couple 'from faith to faith' with the word 'revealed'." He is not arguing that revelation depends on faith, but that it is made known only through faith.

174. ἐκ πίστεως εἰς πίστιν. Similar constructions are ἐκ δυνάμεως εἰς δύναμιν (Ps. 83:8 [85:7]); ἐκ θανάτου εἰς θανάτον . . . ἐκ ζωῆς εἰς ζωήν (2 Cor. 2:16); cf. ἀπὸ δόξης εἰς δόξαν (2 Cor. 3:18).

175. καθὼς (or καθάπερ) γέγραπται occurs 14 times in Romans and simple γέγραπται twice. In 10:5 Paul has Μωϋσῆς γὰρ γράφει.

176. The passage was clearly regarded as important in some later circles in Judaism. Thus we are told that R. Simlai saw the 613 commandments in the law as reduced to 11 by David (Ps. 15), to six by Isaiah (Isa. 33:15-16), to three by Micah (Mic. 6:8), to two by Isaiah again (Isa. 56:1), and to one by Amos (Amos 5:4). But R. Naḥman demurred and saw the

understood traditionally as "The just shall live by faith" (KJV), but many now hold that it should be taken as "He that is just by faith shall live." Grammatically it is slightly easier to take the words as KJV.[177] But the point is not decisive, all the more so since Paul is quoting and may have felt obliged to reproduce the words of the prophet in the text known to him.[178] But a number of reasons may be urged for taking the words in the sense "he that is just by faith shall live." First, there is the context. Paul is talking about that righteousness which is "from faith to faith", and he is citing the prophet in support. He is not talking about the way God's people should live. Second, there is the point made by Nygren that in chapters 1–4 the faith words ("faith", "to believe") occur "at least 25 times" and the life words ("life", "to live", "to preserve alive") twice, whereas in chapters 5–8 the figures are exactly reversed.[179] The inference is that at this stage of the epistle Paul is concerned

---

reduction to one as effected by Habakkuk, citing our text (Makk. 24a). But these are third- and fourth-century rabbis, and we have no way of knowing how far back this kind of exegesis goes.

177. The Greek is Ὁ δὲ δίκαιος ἐκ πίστεως ζήσεται. Strictly, if the sense "he that is just by faith" were required, ἐκ πίστεως should be between the article and δίκαιος or else have an article of its own. But such an article is not invariable in the New Testament and the point cannot be insisted upon. Lightfoot summarizes the reasons in favor of taking the words in the sense of KJV as follows: "(1) the original seems certainly so to intend it; and in the LXX . . . it appears so to be taken. This is also the construction in the Targum Jonathan. (2) Ἐκ πίστεως here corresponds to ἐκ πίστεως in the former part of the verse, where it belongs, not to the predicate, but to the subject. It is here separated from ὁ δίκαιος, as it is there separated from δικαιοσύνη. (3) Ὁ δίκαιος ἐκ πίστεως is not a natural phrase, and, I think, has no parallel in St Paul. (4) The other construction takes the emphasis off 'faith,' which the context shows to be the really emphatic word, and lays it on the verb 'live.'" The reading has eminent support; see, e.g., ASV, Moffatt, Hendriksen, Leenhardt, Michel, Murray, SH. R. M. Moody has a strong defence of this understanding of the text (ET, 92 [1980-81], pp. 205-8).

178. It is not certain exactly what text Paul had. The Hebrew means "the righteous will live because of his faith (or faithfulness)" and appears to signify that the servant of God must await God's time for deliverance. Till then his trust in God must sustain him. In our text of LXX μου is attached to πίστεως, which might mean (with God as the speaker) "because of my faithfulness" or "because of his faith in me". Paul lacks the μου both here and in Gal. 3:11. It is not clear whether he had a different text or whether he understood the passage in a different way.

179. I am not sure whence Nygren derives his statistics (except that he tells us that he does not include the life words in "the thematic verse"). But the words occur as follows: Chs. 1–4: πίστις is found in 1:5, 8, 12, 17 (ter); 3:3, 22, 25, 26, 27, 28, 30 (bis), 31; 4:5, 9, 11, 12, 13, 14, 16 (bis), 19, 20, a total of 25. πιστεύω is found in 1:16; 3:2, 22; 4:3, 5, 11, 17, 18, 24, nine times in all. The total of the faith words is thus 34. ζωή occurs in 2:7, ζάω in 1:17, and ζωοποιέω in 4:17, a total of three.

Chs. 5–8: πίστις is found in 5:1, 2 and πιστεύω in 6:8, a total of three. ζωή occurs in 5:10, 17, 18, 21; 6:4, 22, 23; 7:10; 8:2, 6, 20, 38, a total of 12. ζάω is found in 6:2, 10 (bis), 11, 13; 7:1, 2, 3, 9; 8:12, 13 (bis), which totals 12, while ζωοποιέω is found in 8:11, which makes the total of the life words in these chapters 25.

The figures then appear to be
chs. 1–4 faith words, 34; life words, 3
chs. 5–8 faith words, 3; life words, 25

Some allowance must be made for textually doubtful passages (I have simply cited Moulton and Geden). But when this is done, it is plain that the figures favor Nygren's position somewhat more strongly than he says, even if there is not an exact reversal.

with the fact that it is by faith that God saves people rather than with how they live. Third, the whole teaching of Romans is such as to lead us to connect "righteous" with "faith". Paul keeps insisting that a person is righteous only by faith (3:20, 22, 24, 28; 4:2-3, 13, etc.; 5:1 is especially important, for in summing up the argument to that point Paul speaks explicitly of being justified by faith). There is no corresponding emphasis on the righteous as living by faith.

The traditional view is sometimes supported by an appeal to the meaning of the original. The Greek which Paul quotes reflects a Hebrew word rendered "faith" but which most agree denotes fidelity rather than trust, or, as Gifford puts it, "the faith which may be relied on, rather than the faith which relies." But this is not decisive. Long ago J. B. Lightfoot pointed out that the two meanings are not as far apart as they may at first seem, for "constancy under temptation or danger with an Israelite could only spring from reliance on Jehovah."[180] It should also be borne in mind that Habakkuk is contrasting the man who is "puffed up" with the man of faith. So, however we translate his words, he is speaking of an attitude of lowly dependence on God. Which is basically what Paul is saying. Bruce can say: "The terms of Habakkuk's oracle are sufficiently general to make room for Paul's application of them—an application which, far from doing violence to the prophet's intention, expresses the abiding validity of his message."

It is quite clear that Paul is stressing the primacy of faith.[181] He is telling us that God's righteousness is shown in the gospel, that gospel which tells us that people must come to God in faith. It is this that he cites Habakkuk to support. It seems, then, that we should take the words in the sense "he that is just by faith will live."[182] Paul is speaking of the way a person is made righteous, namely by faith, and assuring us that it is the one who is made righteous in this way who will live.[183]

III. THE WAY OF DELIVERANCE, 1:18–5:21

Some modern discussions reduce the Christian salvation to the level of a commonplace. God was always ready to welcome sinners, we are told, and the gospel is simply the proclamation of something already well known,

---

180. *Saint Paul's Epistle to the Galatians* (London, 1902), p. 155.

181. Contrast the interpretation of the Qumran sect. The commentary on Habakkuk explains the words "The righteous shall live by his faith" in this way: "this concerns all those who observe the Law in the House of Judah, whom God will deliver from the House of Judgment because of their suffering and because of their faith in the Teacher of Righteousness" (Vermes, p. 239). It is the Law that matters, specifically in the way the Teacher expounded it.

182. So RSV, GNB, Black, Bruce, Feuillet (NTS, 6 [1959-60], pp. 52ff.), Hunter, Lagrange, Nygren, Harrison, Robinson, Wuest, TH, etc. JB renders, "The upright man finds life through faith."

183. The verb $\zeta\acute{\alpha}\omega$ is used 23 times in Romans, the most in any one book (140 times in the New Testament; 17 in John). It can refer to physical life, but it is also used "of the supernatural life of the child of God" (BAGD; they class this passage under "have eternal life").

indeed something of a truism. God is a forgiving and compassionate God, and he is well aware of the good intentions people have even when their performance falls short. He makes allowances. All we have to do is come back to him. There is, of course, a measure of truth in this, but such ways of describing the Christian salvation overlook the fact that the gospel tells us of something that happened. The cross is at the heart of it. Christ died for us. His death is meaningful; it is God's great saving act. That sin was a very real problem is shown by the fact that God's Son came to die as the means whereby it would be put away. Paul will expound this gospel, but before he comes to the remedy he makes his diagnosis of the disease. He has a careful argument that we are all sinners and this despite our opportunities for better things. Salvation means being saved from real peril. It is only when we realize in the depths of our being that we are lost that we are ready to receive the salvation that God gives. Not until we come to see that our search for God is and must be completely unsuccessful will we discover that God is searching for us.

A. UNIVERSAL SINFULNESS, 1:18–3:20

Paul is about to expound a wonderful salvation. But first he establishes the need for it by showing that all people are sinful.[184] Many of his contemporaries did not agree, with the result that his message seemed foolishness to them. Many of our contemporaries do not agree with him either, with the result that his words are incomprehensible to them, too. It has always seemed to most people that they are, on the whole, pretty decent people. They may not be perfect but they have done no great wrong. Since they are conscious of no really disastrous sin, they feel that they must be right with God. But for Paul the significant thing is not that people have met their own standard but that they have not met God's. They have come short of his demand. They are in the greatest of danger because they are subject to his wrath.

1. The Condemnation of the Gentile World, 1:18-32

18*The wrath of God is being revealed from heaven against all the godlessness and wickedness of men who suppress the truth by their wickedness,* 19*since what may be known about God is plain to them, because God has made it plain to them.* 20*For since the creation of the world God's invisible qualities—his eternal power*

184. O'Neill maintains that Paul was not the author of 1:18–2:29. If the argument were that all Gentiles are sinners he thinks there would perhaps be a connection, "but the writer is not arguing that all Gentiles are sinners. The argument is that idolaters are prone to immorality, not that all Gentiles are immoral." But this ignores the fact that the section is introduced with the revelation of God's wrath "against all the godlessness and wickedness of men" (v. 18). Idolaters are certainly castigated, but the language includes other sinners as well (cf. vv. 28-32). O'Neill is isolated in his view. Barrett is much more representative when he says, "Paul's argument is developed in a clear and consistent way. The Gospel rests upon a manifestation of righteousness; to those who believe, it proves to be the power of God unto salvation (cf. 1 Cor. i.18); to those who do not believe, but are disobedient and rebellious, it means God's wrath (cf. 2 Cor. ii.16)."

and divine nature—have been clearly seen, being understood from what has been made, so that men are without excuse.

21For although they knew God, they neither glorified him as God nor gave thanks to him, but their thinking became futile and their foolish hearts were darkened. 22Although they claimed to be wise, they became fools 23and exchanged the glory of the immortal God for images made to look like mortal man and birds and animals and reptiles.

24Therefore God gave them over in the sinful desires of their hearts to sexual impurity for the degrading of their bodies with one another. 25They exchanged the truth of God for a lie, and worshiped and served created things rather than the Creator—who is forever praised. Amen.

26Because of this, God gave them over to shameful lusts. Even their women exchanged natural relations for unnatural ones. 27In the same way the men also abandoned natural relations with women and were inflamed with lust for one another. Men committed indecent acts with other men, and received in themselves the due penalty for their perversion.

28Furthermore, since they did not think it worthwhile to retain the knowledge of God, he gave them over to a depraved mind, to do what ought not to be done. 29They have become filled with every kind of wickedness, evil, greed and depravity. They are full of envy, murder, strife, deceit and malice. They are gossips, 30slanderers, God-haters, insolent, arrogant and boastful; they invent ways of doing evil; they disobey their parents; 31they are senseless, faithless, heartless, ruthless. 32Although they know God's righteous decree that those who do such things deserve death, they not only continue to do these very things but also approve of those who practice them.

It is usually held that throughout this section Paul has the Gentile world in mind. This seems to be indeed the case, but we should notice that he does not specifically name the Gentiles here (as he does the Jew in 2:17) and further that some of the things he says had certainly been applied to the Jews (cf. v. 23 with Ps. 106:20; Jer. 2:11). By keeping this section general Paul is really indicting all mankind. He places special stress on two evils: idolatry and immorality. The language he uses is especially applicable to the Gentiles, and we need not doubt that he has them primarily in mind. As a rule they saw no problem in sin. The religions of the day seem to have had easy-going standards, so that people were not troubled by the lives they lived. As long as they avoided the worst excesses they felt that their gods were not going to be unduly concerned. Sometimes, indeed, they thought of their gods as so remote as not to care much what their worshippers did. They were too great to be bothered with the frailties of mortal men. So mortal men were not bothered either. Paul shows that such views are shallow and superficial. Sin is real. It has dreadful consequences. Even though the Gentiles have not had God's law revealed to them as the Jews have, they know enough about what is right and what is wrong to be in serious trouble when they reject the right way.

18. Once again NIV omits an opening "For". This word is important because it links this statement to the preceding one and gives a reason for it.[185] The gospel is necessary *because* there is such a thing as the wrath of God, because only the gospel of salvation by grace through faith (vv. 16-17) brings deliverance from that wrath.[186] Agar Beet perceptively remarks, "the entire weight of *vv.* 16, 17, which contain a summary of the Epistle, rests upon the assumption that all men are, apart from the Gospel, under the anger of God."[187] This is the plight of mankind. Apart from this the gospel has no meaning. And since the wrath of God is being revealed against all sin, there can be no way of salvation other than the way that deals with that sin, that is, the gospel.

This is the one place in Romans where we find the expression *the wrath of God*, but "the wrath" means much the same.[188] Whichever way he chooses to express it, the idea of the divine wrath is important in this epistle.[189] Paul is clear that God is not passive in the face of sin. God is implacably and vigorously opposed to every evil.[190] Ultimately everyone must reckon with this reality. Paul's reference to revelation, his genitive *of God*, and his *from heaven* are ways of emphasizing that the wrath is a divine activity. God is doing something in opposition to sin, not leaving sinners to their own devices.

Some, however, point out that the expression *the wrath of God* does not occur very often in Paul (again in Eph. 5:6; Col. 3:6) and that God is never the subject of the verb "to be wrathful". They suggest accordingly that Paul thought of wrath in more or less impersonal terms. For example, Dodd tells us that he prefers to translate "the wrath of God" rather than "God's anger" (Moffatt) "because such an archaic phrase suits a thoroughly archaic idea." He sees "wrath" as denoting "some process or effect in the realm of objective facts" rather than "a certain feeling or attitude of God towards us," though he

---

185. Cf. Shedd, γάρ "introduces the reason why God has revealed the δικαιοσύνη spoken of: namely, because he had previously revealed his ὀργή. This shows that mercy is meaningless except in relation to justice, and that the attempt, in theology, to retain the doctrine of the divine love, without the doctrine of the divine wrath, is illogical." This may be getting a bit much out of the conjunction, but the point is worth pondering.

186. Curiously Moffatt translates γάρ with "But", and even more curiously Dodd bases his comment on the mistranslation: "The adversative conjunction 'but' in i.18 shows that the revelation of God's 'anger' is contrasted, and not identified, with the revelation of His righteousness." It is true that γάρ can very occasionally have some adversative force. Thus when in a response a "No" is omitted, γάρ may supply the reason for the omitted negative (see examples in LSJ). Clearly there is nothing of the sort here. This is rather a typical case of giving a reason for the foregoing. Barrett renders, "A clear signal of the revealing of God's righteousness is the fact that his wrath. . . ." This may be something of an overtranslation, but it indicates the force of the word.

187. *A Commentary on St. Paul's Epistle to the Romans*[8] (London, 1892), *in loc.* Cf. G. Bornkamm, in Rom. 1:18–3:20 "the keyword is the 'revelation of God's wrath' " (*Paul* [London, 1971], p. 122).

188. Cf. Barrett, "When Paul speaks of wrath, it is in general quite clear from the context that the wrath is God's; so, for example, iii.5; ix.22. Wrath is God's personal (though never malicious or, in a bad sense, emotional) reaction against sin."

189. Paul uses ὀργή in 21 of its 36 New Testament occurrences, of which 12 come in Romans; all 12 appear to refer to the divine wrath.

190. Cf. Manson, "The 'wrath' is the obverse of the 'righteousness of God': his creative goodness is matched by his inflexible opposition to evil."

admits that this is "a peculiar extension of meaning." He sums up the process as he sees it in the writings of the prophets: "sin is the cause, disaster the effect." Paul, he thinks, had much the same idea, and the apostle retains the concept of wrath "not to describe the attitude of God to man, but to describe an inevitable process of cause and effect in a moral universe."[191] Views like these are widely accepted (cf. Bowen, p. 221). They fit the mood of our time. People today tend to see the truth that "God is love" as the one significant thing. They quite overlook the unyielding moral demand that runs through Scripture.[192]

It is, of course, true that God is love. But it is not true that this rules out any realistic view of God's wrath. We must bear in mind that the opposite of love is not wrath, but hate. Wrath is perhaps not an ideal term, for with us it so easily comes to denote an emotion characterized by loss of self-control and a violent concern for selfish interests. But these are not necessary constituents of wrath, and both are absent from the "righteous indignation" which gives us the best human analogy.[193] In any case "wrath" is the word the Bible uses, and we need the strongest of reasons for abandoning it. It is a term that expresses the settled and active opposition of God's holy nature to everything that is evil.[194] Until some better suggestion is made we do well to stick to the biblical term to convey the biblical idea. What we should not do is to abandon the idea that the wrath is personal. This leads to the position that God does not care about sin, or at least does not care enough to act. It is impossible to reconcile such a morally neutral position with the scriptural teaching about God. The Bible in general and Paul in particular see God as personally active in opposing sin.[195]

We should not overlook the further fact that the revelation of the wrath of God is in this context linked with the gospel. We see some revelation of the divine wrath, it is true, in the suffering, frustration, and sheer disaster that are so often the consequence of sin. But Paul is saying rather that it is the cross

191. Käsemann categorically rejects such views: "Our starting point should be that the manifestation of this wrath is described in vv. 24ff. . . . The thrice-repeated παρέδωκεν αὐτούς shows incontestably . . . that in the apparently purely immanent causal connection God himself is at work. . ." (p. 37).

192. Cf. Hunter, "The truth is that we dislike the phrase because we have sentimentalized our conception of God in a quite un-biblical way. Wrath—the strong and continuous reaction of the holy God against evil in every shape and form—a wrath operative now and not only at the Last Judgment, is an essential part of any truly biblical idea of God."

193. Cf. Trench, God "would not love good, unless He hated evil, the two being so inseparable, that He must do both or neither" (Synonyms, p. 134).

194. Cf. BAGD, wrath is "the divine reaction toward evil; it is thought of not so much as an emotion as in terms of the outcome of an angry frame of mind (judgment)." The lexicon goes on to point out that this is "a legitimate feeling on the part of a judge". God is doing something in opposition to sin, not leaving sin to work out its consequences. Cf. Nygren, "wrath is also God's own work, which He himself discloses from heaven. It is God and not some alien powers, who has laid the old aeon under condemnation."

195. See further my Apostolic Preaching, chs. V and VI; R. V. G. Tasker, The Biblical Doctrine of the Wrath of God (London, 1951); NIDNTT, I, pp. 105-13; TDNT, V, pp. 382-447; H. Ridderbos, Paul, pp. 108-14.

that shows us the measure of God's wrath. It is in the events of the gospel that the revelation occurs. Forgiveness is no cheap gesture. It is as costly as the cross. It is meaningless without the wrath (whether we use that term or not—it is the reality that counts). Unless there is something to be saved from, there is no point in talking about salvation. There is considerable agreement that we should understand the wrath in eschatological terms (cf. 2:5-9). That is, of course, true, but we should not overlook the other truth that it is also a present reality, as this passage shows (cf. the present tense, *is being revealed*, and vv. 24, 26, 28).

The reference to revelation shows that *the wrath of God* is not a human discovery. It is something that God has made known. The present tense indicates that it is a continuing process. Paul has just referred to righteousness as being revealed (v. 17), and there appears to be a connection. It is part of the revelation in the gospel that God's attitude towards sin is one of righteous wrath.[196] In that situation his love brings us a righteousness we could never earn. Both the righteousness and the wrath are a matter of revelation.[197] The present tense in both cases indicates that Paul is talking about present realities, not remote possibilities. And this wrath is divine: the use of the phrase *from heaven* is a reverent way of referring to God (cf. Luke 15:7, 10).[198]

God's wrath is aroused by *all the godlessness and wickedness of men*. If the two nouns are used strictly, they combine the thoughts of sin against God and sin against men.[199] Both matter. But probably Paul is simply indicating the variety of evil and is not trying to divide it carefully. His *all* is important. There are no exceptions. Nothing is overlooked. We cannot say that God does not mind some evils. His wrath is revealed against every wrong.

Paul characterizes sinners as those *who suppress the truth by their wickedness*. There is a problem with the meaning of the verb translated *suppress*.[200] It

---

196. Boylan, however, denies that this revelation is made in the gospel: "The revelation of God's anger is made in the moral degradation of the Gentiles depicted in *vv.* 24ff."

197. Cf. Robinson, "the full laying bare of the fearful truth and final consequences of the alienation of human society from God is but the other side of the very same revelation which is God's way of righting wrong."

198. G. Dalman examines "Evasive or Precautionary Modes of Referring to God" and gives attention to the use of "heaven" (*The Words of Jesus* [Edinburgh, 1902], pp. 206-20). Specifically he sees "from heaven" in its usage in the Gospels as signifying "derivation from God" (*ibid.*, pp. 219-20). It will not differ here.

199. ἀσέβεια is strictly "impiety" or "lack of reverence for God", and ἀδικία "lawlessness" or "wickedness". Some commentators see them used strictly here to give such meanings as "impiety against God and injustice against man. Thus humanity is at once a religious and a moral failure" (Griffith-Thomas). But most see them here as pointing to much the same thing; e.g., Hendriksen, both mean "sin, rebellion against God".

200. κατέχω has a number of meanings. (1) The κατά may have perfective force, giving the meaning "possess" (as in 2 Cor. 6:10) or "hold fast" (in a good sense, Luke 8:15; in a bad sense, Rom. 7:6). (2) This may lead to the thought of occupying a place (Luke 14:9). (3) The κατά may signify "down", giving the meaning "hold down" or "hold back" (2 Thess. 2:6, 7), "restrain", "hinder" (Luke 4:42).

is a compound of the verb "to have" and could possibly be taken in the sense "possess" (as Hodge, e.g., notes). This would give the sense "who possess the truth but act unrighteously".[201] The problem with this is that Paul does not appear to have in mind people who hold true beliefs but live evil lives. Rather, he is describing sinners who, far from responding to God's truth, oppose it. *Suppress* (NIV, RSV, etc.) is perhaps too strong. It implies that sinners are successful. Better is "hinder" (Moffatt) or the like. These people do not like the truth and do what they can to oppose it. By repeating the word *wickedness* Paul brings out that their sinfulness leads to their deeds. It is not possible to have a general attitude of unrighteousness without this finding expression in deeds opposed to God's purposes. However we translate, we should take the verb as conative. Paul is speaking of what sinners attempt, not of what they succeed in doing (cf. Hendriksen, "attempting to suppress").

The truth[202] here is the general truth that is open to all people, not the truth God has revealed in Christ and the gospel. People are guilty because they sin against the truth they have, not the truth they do not have.[203] Paul evidently thinks of truth as dynamic, for it can be hindered, which means that it must be doing something. This sort of thing may be in mind also when he pictures truth as rejoicing with love (1 Cor. 13:6).

19. The interpretation of verses 19-20 has been the cause of endless controversy.[204] Some maintain that they point to a revelation which God has made to all people whereby, if they give due heed to it, they will come to a place of salvation. The words are taken as a charter for a doctrine of "natural revelation". Others take the opposite view, that Paul is denying any saving revelation of God in nature. They affirm that he sees God as known in Christ, and in Christ alone. What he speaks of here is not a saving knowledge of God at all.

It does seem clear that Paul is not here speaking of a saving knowledge of God. The context is concerned with the condemnation of the Gentile world, not its salvation. The apostle is arguing from the necessity of the saving work

201. Parry notes that κατέχω means (1) to possess, and (2) less frequently to restrain. He comments, "Here the sequence of thought is decisive in favour of the first meaning; it is essential to the argument that the primary condition which makes an act or state sinful, should be set down here; namely, that the sinner knows what he is doing" (CGT). But this is not convincing. Translations like "suppress" or "hinder" also presuppose that the suppressor or hinderer knows what he is suppressing or hindering.

202. ἀλήθεια occurs 109 times in the New Testament, of which Paul accounts for 47, John's Gospel 25, and John's epistles 20. Paul does not use the word very often in any one writing, but it occurs in all his epistles except 1 Thessalonians and Philemon. See further Additional Note B.

203. Cf. Lenski, "'Αλήθεια is 'truth' in the sense of 'reality,' that which is actually so"; Calvin, "*The truth* of God means the true knowledge of God".

204. Richard N. Longenecker examines the question of whether Paul is indebted to Hellenism for his approach. He points to coincidences of language and thought but decides that such parallels are secondary. Basically what Paul says comes from Hebraic sources (*Paul, Apostle of Liberty* [New York, 1964], pp. 54-58).

which God accomplished in Christ. He is laying it down that God has revealed enough of himself to the Gentiles for them to be blameworthy when they sin and reject his leading. He is not facing the question whether there was enough in the revelation for them to be saved. That is quite a different question, and we should not torture Paul's words into giving an answer to a question he is not facing. It would probably be a fair paraphrase of his argument to say that people have never lived up to the highest and best that they have known. But God intends that they should. They are guilty in his eyes when they do not. And nobody can say, "I did not know." Our condemnation in each case lies in the fact that we have sinned against the light we have, not against the light we have never received. Thus, though the Gentiles did not receive the full revelation in the law of the Old Testament, they did receive enough illumination to know what was right. And they followed the wrong.[205]

Paul's *since*[206] introduces the reason for the preceding. He proposes to substantiate what he has just said. It is a matter of dispute whether the following expression is correctly rendered *what may be known about God* or whether it means "what is known about God". Paul's Greek term[207] strictly means "that which may be known", "that which is knowable". But in the New Testament it is mostly used more loosely in the sense "that which is

---

205. Some see a contradiction with the report of Paul's speech at Athens (Acts 17:22-31). But this is surely overreaction. There he is appealing to pagans for a hearing; here he is writing to believers. A difference in emphasis is inevitable. The point in the Athenian address is that God has given sufficient revelation for people to "seek him and perhaps reach out for him and find him" (v. 27). This had led to their altar "to an unknown god", whom Paul proceeds to proclaim to them (v. 23). Here he is saying that God has revealed himself to all people clearly enough for them to be guilty when they make their idols. It is like the approach to the people of Lystra: God "has not left himself without testimony" (Acts 14:17).

206. διότι is equivalent to διὰ τοῦτο ὅτι, "on this account", "for". Other possibilities have been pointed out ("wherefore" or "that"), but in the New Testament it seems always to mean "because". It is found 24 times, of which ten are in Paul, five being in Romans. "Because" may refer back to the earlier part of v. 18 and give the reason for saying the wrath is revealed. Or it may refer to the immediately preceding words and give the reason for affirming that people hinder the truth in unrighteousness. Either is grammatically possible and both give good sense, but the second seems more probable.

207. The verbal adjective γνωστός. Cf. W. Gunion Rutherford, "The verbal adjective in -τός normally denotes that the action expressed by the verb is possible"; he contrasts it with that in -τέος, which marks obligation. He gives as examples a form ending in -τός, yielding the meaning "the river may be crossed"; the corresponding form in -τέος means "the river must be crossed" (*First Greek Grammar Syntax* [London, 1935], p. 153). Neither form is very common in the New Testament. When γνωστός is used in other New Testament passages it means "known". This is the one place where Paul uses it, and thus we do not know whether he employs it in the same way as do other writers or not. Bultmann thinks that "the meaning is perhaps 'clearly recognisable'" (TDNT, I, p. 719). BDF have a note on another aspect of the use here: "Peculiar to Paul (Heb) is the use of a neuter sing. adjective like an abstract mostly with a dependent gen." They cite Origen, "what is known (knowable) of (or about) God is manifest to them" (263 [2]). Turner notes that the construction is characteristic of Paul and Luke, infrequent in the Gospels, and not attested in the papyri (M, III, p. 13).

known". Against the former suggestion it is argued that in that form the statement is simply not true. Many things about God are "knowable", though not known to people generally since God has not revealed them. Against the latter it is urged that it is tautology ("what people know . . . they know"). A decision is not easy, but on the whole it seems best to take the word here strictly (as NIV, RSV, Käsemann, etc.). There are things about God which cannot be made known in the natural order, but what can be made known God has made known.[208]

Such truth *is plain to them, because God has made it plain to them.*[209] His action matches the result.[210] There is a slight problem with the first *to them*,[211] for the Greek might well be understood as "in them" or "among them". "In them" would signify that the revelation takes place basically in people's minds (so R. Knox, "is clear to their minds"). On this view God is at work in them whenever natural revelation takes place. It is God who brings conviction, not some objective feature of the created universe. But some argue strongly for "among them". The revelation in question takes place, they say, not by some inward knowledge but in the creation in the midst of which they find themselves (so, e.g., Cranfield). But we must bear in mind that Paul uses the preposition "in" very frequently (988 times; this is more than a third of the New Testament total of 2,713). He seems to use it almost from habit, and we cannot always insist on a precise meaning. Since the grammarians usually regard it here as equivalent to the dative case, we should accept *to them* as the meaning.[212]

Paul proceeds to emphasize that it is God who has given them this knowledge. In this book about God it is natural that it should be made plain that it is not people's innate ability or cunning that enables them to rise to the knowledge of God. God can be known only as he chooses to make himself known. The initiative is with him.

20. Paul presses the point. His *For* explains the "God has made it plain" of verse 19; he has made it plain in that his *invisible qualities . . . have been clearly seen.* Paul takes the revelation right back to the beginning of things with his *since the creation of the world.* Some, it is true, argue that this expression indicates not so much the origin in time as a seeing of the universe as "the source

---

208. Barth insists on the reality of the knowledge: "When we rebel, we are in rebellion not against what is foreign to us but against that which is most intimately ours. . . . Our memory of God accompanies us always as problem and as warning."

209. Note that the adjective φανερόν and the verb ἐφανέρωσεν are from the same root.

210. For γάρ see on v. 9. Its position after ὁ θεός puts a little more emphasis on θεός than if the more normal order had been followed.

211. ἐν αὐτοῖς.

212. Cf. BDF, "Occasionally ἐν appears also to stand for the customary dat. proper". They see this passage as "probably" an example (220 [1]). BAGD hold that ἐν with the dative stands for the ordinary dative and cite Aesop here, τ. φανερὸν ἐν πᾶσιν = "evident to all" (ἐν IV.4a).

of knowledge—the basis of a deduction".[213] This is supported by the fact that the word for *creation* elsewhere in the New Testament seems mostly to have the meaning "what has been created" rather than "the act of creation" (though the form really points to the latter).[214] This leads on to an understanding like that of Gifford: " 'The creation of the world,' viewed as a whole, is first presented as the *source* from which man derives a knowledge of the unseen God." The more natural meaning of the Greek, however, makes the reference temporal ("being understood from what has been made" is Paul's way of referring to creation as the source). These words mean that the universe has always borne upon it the imprint of God's handiwork. While many translators refer to *the world*, Paul's meaning is, of course, "the universe".[215] Order in the heavens as well as on earth bears witness to God. This whole mighty universe has always reflected its Creator.

God's invisible qualities is a slightly overconfident rendering of a rather indefinite expression.[216] KJV translates it more literally with "the invisible things of him". The meaning we give the expression will be determined by our understanding of the following *his eternal power and divine nature*.[217] Paul's word for *eternal* is unusual.[218] The more common word[219] (found, e.g., in the expression "eternal life") is derived from the word for "age". Here, where Paul is speaking of God's essential being, he may well have felt that a word with a fundamental connection with time was not quite what he wanted. He prefers a word with a meaning like "always-ness". His word for *divine nature* is another unusual one, found only here in the New Testament. In distinction from *power* (for which see the note on v. 14), which points to "a single attribute", it "is a summary term for those other attributes which constitute

213. Moule, IBNTG, p. 73. The problem is the meaning of ἀπό. It can be used in a causal or instrumental sense, but most take it here of time.

214. Nouns in -σις denote activity, while nouns in -μα (κτίσμα) properly point to the result of the action. But the distinction is often blurred, and usage, not formation, is decisive. κτίσις is used of (1) the act of creating (Mark 10:6), (2) the totality of what was created (Col. 1:15), or (3) an individual created thing (Rom. 8:39).

215. κόσμος originally meant "ornament" and was used of the universe as the greatest jewel. Since for people the most important part of the universe is this world, the same term came to denote "the world". But here the wider meaning is required.

216. τὰ γὰρ ἀόρατα αὐτοῦ. For verbal adjectives see on v. 19; ἀόρατος strictly means "that cannot be seen", "invisible", though it may be used loosely in the sense, "that is not seen". Most understand it here in some such sense as "his invisible attributes" (NEB, Phillips); RSV has "his invisible nature". Bultmann sees the meaning as "He the Invisible" (TDNT, I, p. 719), which Turner quotes approvingly (*Grammatical Insights*, p. 132).

217. ἥ τε ἀΐδιος αὐτοῦ δύναμις καὶ θειότης. For τέ see on v. 16. Hodge points out that ἥ τε is explanatory; it does not add a new idea.

218. ἀΐδιος. It is derived from ἀεί, "always", and occurs in the New Testament again only in Jude 6. In LXX it occurs only in Wis. 7:26 and as a variant in 4 Macc. 10:15. In Greek generally it is found from early times (LSJ). According to MM it is frequent in inscriptions but rare in the papyri.

219. αἰώνιος.

Divinity" (SH).[220] Paul is laying it down that what is revealed is God himself. In nature we see something of nature's God.

Have been clearly seen[221] translates a verb, found here only in the New Testament, which is used of vision with the physical eye. With such vision we see the things God has created. But "being understood" refers to inner perception. The verb means *"to perceive* with the mind, *understand"* (AS). Paul is saying that we see certain outward things and thereby perceive things invisible.[222] What we see is defined as *what has been made.*[223] The expression is quite general and does not limit the revelation to any part of creation. God has left his imprint on the entire created universe. But Paul's main point is that seeing, people do not see; perceiving, they do not perceive. They see creation (cf. Job 40:15-41; Pss. 8; 19; 104; Isa. 40:21-26, etc.).[224] But because they reject the knowledge of God they have thrown away the key to it all.

Most translations of the concluding part of the verse give the impression that Paul is referring to the result of the preceding. But the construction normally expresses purpose rather than result.[225] If we accept purpose here,

220. SH see θειότης as denoting "Divine nature and properties", whereas θεότης (Col. 2:9) is "Divine Personality". Earle supports the distinction, but the two words are translated by the same English term in KJV and RSV. They seem to differ only as much as "divinity" and "deity".

221. The Greek is νοούμενα καθορᾶται. καθοράω is found here only in the New Testament, νοέω 14 times (five times in Paul). It is not easy to bring out in English the play on words, ἀόρατα . . . καθορᾶται; it is something like "his unseeable things . . . are clearly seen".

222. Cf. Boylan, "By looking on the visible world they can see the invisible" (on v. 19). Cranfield, however, points out that the action of the participle is naturally understood as prior to or contemporaneous with that of the verb in the indicative; he rejects the idea that it is subsequent. Thus νοούμενα and καθορᾶται both point to physical sight, though noting that usage favors mental perception in νοούμενα. NEB prefers mental perception, rendering "visible . . . to the eye of reason"; cf. Murray, "it is the seeing of understanding, of intelligent conception".

223. τοῖς ποιήμασιν is dative of means or instrument. The visible is the means of our perception of the invisible.

224. Wisdom 13 is often adduced as a parallel, but there the thought is slightly different. The writer says, "For from the greatness and beauty of created things comes a corresponding perception of their Creator" (v. 5). But he is referring to man's search after God ("as they live among his works they keep searching", v. 7), Paul to God's revelation of himself. In Wisdom if man does not come to know God that is simply a mistake, in Paul it is the rejection of what God has made known.

225. εἰς τό + infinitive. Moulton finds this construction three times in Matthew, once each in Mark, Luke, and Acts, twice each in James and 1 Peter, eight times in Hebrews, and 43 times in Paul. It is thus very much a Pauline construction. And Paul almost always uses it to express purpose. This is not invariable (cf. 12:3), but we need a reason if we are to see consequence. Specifically in the present passage Moulton says we must see purpose, "for this belongs to the category of passages dealing with Divine action, in which contemplated and actual results, final and consecutive clauses, necessarily lose their differentia" (M, I, p. 219; earlier he has quoted Westcott, "ἵνα appears to mark in each case the direct and immediate end, while εἰς τό indicates the more remote result aimed at or reached" [*ibid.*, p. 218]). It would be expected that if ἵνα can lose its telic force even more so could εἰς τό, but on the whole this does not appear to be the case. SH see here "not direct and primary purpose but indirect, secondary or conditional purpose. God did

as we apparently should, then Paul is telling us that God has so made the universe that we are responsible people. This means all people, not only those who have the Bible to guide them. God intends that they will be guilty if they reject the light given them and fall into sin.[226] The sinner may plead that he is ignorant. He does not know God. But Paul's first point is that his ignorance is culpable. God has given a revelation in nature but people have closed their eyes to it. How then could they possibly see? But it is their own fault that they do not. They are *without excuse*.

21. Having made the point that there has been some revelation of God to all mankind, Paul goes on to show that this has not been followed by willing obedience.[227] People refused to accept the way of God and suffered the inevitable result. They acted foolishly, and idolatry with all its attendant evils was the consequence. Paul's *For*[228] carries on the argument in logical sequence. He affirms that people had real knowledge[229] of God. It is a truth on which he is insisting, for in this passage he has said it four times in one way or another. But, having this knowledge, they reacted in the wrong way. They did not "glorify[230] him as God". This means a little more than that they did not "honor" God (as RSV, etc.).[231] They knew enough about him to know that

---

not design that man should sin; but He did design that if they sinned they should be without excuse." Lenski argues strongly for result: if it were purpose, "the purpose would be monstrous"; if it be regarded as conditional, then "Paul left out an essential point—a thing he never does." But this is not the way it appears to quite a few commentators. Thus Nygren says, "according to Paul it is actually the will of God that he who turns away from God be without excuse". Cf. Turner, here "it is better to retain the usual near-final meaning of εἰς τό, whatever theologians may say: i.e. RV text is correct against RSV and NEB" (M, III, p. 143; in *Grammatical Insights*, pp. 12-13 he argues that the construction does not always express "the result of strict causality" in Romans). Cranfield, Burton, Lagrange, Hendriksen, etc., however, favor result.

226. Cf. Barclay, "In the world we can see God. It is Paul's argument—and it is completely valid—that if we look at the world *suffering follows sin*. Break the laws of agriculture—the harvest fails. Break the laws of architecture—your building collapses. Break the laws of health—your body suffers. Paul was saying 'Look at the world! See how it is constructed! From a world like that you know what God is like.' The sinner is left without excuse."

227. The tenses in this section are mostly aorist, but GNB consistently uses the present: "The force of the Greek aorist in this context is to indicate that these actions are typical of what men have done at all times throughout history; for the English reader the present tense is more natural in expressing such events" (TH). I doubt whether this is justified.

228. διότι = because. It explains the previous statement (and covers vv. 21-23).

229. The aorist participle γνόντες means "having come to know". This preceded their failure and made it more blameworthy. The knowledge of God in the sense of v. 20 is in mind, not a knowledge like that of John 17:3. Paul makes a good deal of the concept of knowledge. He uses γινώσκω a total of 50 times. John uses it 56 times, while another 26 occurrences are in the Johannine epistles. It is thus very much a Pauline and Johannine word (221 times in the New Testament).

230. δοξάζω is another word Paul shares with John: Paul has it 12 times, John 23 times; next is Luke with nine. Paul uses the corresponding noun, δόξα, 77 times, so it is clear that he is quite interested in glory.

231. ὡς θεόν receives emphasis both from its position and from coming so soon after τὸν θεόν.

"glory" was his due, but they withheld it from him. They may perhaps have said polite things about him, but they did not ascribe to him the glory that was his due. They did not act on the knowledge of God they had, but preferred their own way. Presently Paul will show that this led to idolatry. People preferred a "religion" of their own making rather than the divine revelation. "Thus 'religion' is born, springing from a rejected knowledge of the true God and finalizing man's seizure of God, the triumph of gods over God" (Leenhardt, on vv. 22-24). With this Paul links another negative—*nor gave thanks to him*. It is interesting to see thanksgiving included as a response that might have been expected to God's revelation of himself, though not as surprising as it might be in another author, for the apostle is fond of this concept.[232] He sees people, then, as always ready to take up an irreligious attitude toward the universe in which they live, despite the many marks it bears of the Creator's hand.[233]

But[234] *their thinking became futile*. When people rejected God, it affected their minds as well as other things. The word for *thinking* (more exactly "thoughts") is neutral in itself and may be used of all kinds of thoughts. But in the New Testament it is mostly used of evil,[235] which fits this context. This is the one occurrence in the New Testament of the verb "to become futile" (Phillips, "became fatuous").[236] But Paul uses other words of the word group fairly often. The basic idea is that of pointlessness. The practice of idolatry is inherently futile. What else can be said of offering worship to what one's own hands have made? Paul is about to refer to idolatry (v. 23). Idolaters are out of touch with divine reality and shut themselves up to futility.

Not only was their thinking futile; it was characterized by darkness.[237] The New Testament often sets light over against darkness and equates sin with the latter. Sin is never an enlightened procedure despite the attitude of

---

232. He uses εὐχαριστέω 24 times out of its 38 New Testament occurrences, and the corresponding noun 12 times out of 15.

233. Cf. Dodd, "their attitude to life and the world is an irreligious one, though the impulse to religion was present in the very *data* of life and the world."

234. The strong adversative ἀλλ' (in Paul 311 times out of 635 times in the New Testament; Romans has it 69 times).

235. διαλογισμός. Cf. G. Schrenk, "The sense of 'evil thoughts' is predominant in the NT. . . . In view of the more flexible LXX usage, it is striking that the NT uses διαλογισμός only in the negative sense for evil thoughts or anxious reflection" (TDNT, II, p. 97). W. F. Howard cites H. A. A. Kennedy for the view that ἐν here is causal; he cites this verse among passages meaning "because of, by reason of, for the sake of" (M, II, p. 463).

236. The verb is ματαιόω (used of turning to idolatry in LXX of Jer. 2:5). The μάταιος word group is especially characteristic of Paul. For its meaning cf. O. Bauernfeind, who notes that it is "what is against the norm, unexpected, offending what ought to be. κενός means worthless, because without content, μάταιος worthless because deceptive or ineffectual" (TDNT, IV, p. 519). μάταιος is used of idols in Acts 14:15 (cf. 2 Kings 17:15; Amos 2:4, LXX).

237. Cf. Shedd, "The relation between sin and mental blindness is that of action and re-action. Each is alternately cause and effect." Parry comments, "missing the true aim, they lost the true light." Salvation means rescue from darkness (cf. Col. 1:13).

"advanced" secularists. It always represents a darkening of some part of us. *Foolish*[238] signifies "unintelligent", and this brings out another facet of sin. It is never bright to walk in the ways of evil. What is characterized as *foolish* is translated *hearts* in NIV (so RV, ARV, etc.), but "minds" in RSV, Moffatt, Phillips, etc. It is the normal word for "heart".[239] But whereas with us the heart is used metaphorically of the emotions, this was not the case with the Greek term. In the ancient world the emotions tended to be located lower down, in the entrails (cf. the old-fashioned "bowels of compassion"). The heart stood rather for the entire inner life; in some contexts the emotions are more prominent (e.g., 2 Cor. 6:11-12), in some the intellectual (Rom. 10:8), and in some the volitional (1 Cor. 7:37). The heart is the center of the inner life; from it the person's direction is determined, his whole course shaped, his basic commitments formed. This passage perhaps places some emphasis on the mind, but the term is comprehensive. When anyone rejects God, not only is his thinking awry but his whole inner life has taken a jolt. His emotions and will are affected, too. The comprehensive word is significant. Dodd reminds us that instances of what Paul had in mind are not hard to find. Though the apostle was not speaking specifically about the higher forms of Greek philosophy, in practice this philosophy "easily came to terms with the grossest forms of superstition and immorality . . . just as it is a grave count against the lofty philosophy of Hinduism that it utters no effective protest against the most degrading practices of popular religion in India today."[240] All too often in the history of mankind a high level of philosophy has been found consistent with all the degradation of polytheism. The ability to think clearly does not necessarily deliver from superstition.

22. People do not always recognize the realities of their situation. *Although they claimed to be wise, they became fools* (cf. 1 Cor. 1:21; Eph. 4:17). NEB renders, "They boast of their wisdom, but they have made fools of themselves". "Boast" is perhaps too strong for the Greek, which rather means "affirm".[241] But it is not much too strong. Clearly these people prided them-

---

238. ἀσύνετος is from alpha-privative and σύνετος, and σύνετος from συνιέναι, *"bring* or *set together"* (LSJ).

239. καρδία. The singular is used here in a distributive sense. "Contrary to normal Greek and Latin practice, the NT sometimes follows the Aram. and Heb. preference for a distributive sing." (M, III, p. 23). Paul has the singular here, but he prefers the plural of καρδία in such constructions (20 times including a quotation from LXX; he has the singular eight times; also in some MSS of Col. 3:16). In Romans the only other passage Turner includes with the singular in this construction is that with σῶμα in 8:23.

240. Cf. Godet, "all the labour of the sages did not prevent the most civilized nations, Egyptians, Greeks, Romans from being at the same time the most idolatrous of antiquity."

241. φάσκω, which Paul uses only here (its only other New Testament occurrences are in Acts 24:9; 25:19). It is cognate with φήμι. The construction is an example of the omission of the subject with a dependent infinitive when it is identical with that of the main verb. We should also notice that the predicate σοφοί is nominative even though it goes with the infinitive, since it refers to the main subject (cf. Turner, M, III, p. 146; BDF 405).

ʀᴇlves on their wisdom, as the self-sufficient so often do. In the process they *became fools*.[242] This verb is used by Paul of God's making foolish the wisdom of this world (1 Cor. 1:20); in its only other New Testament occurrences it is used of the salt losing its savor (Matt. 5:13; Luke 14:34). There is the notion of insipidity about it. Those who in their "wisdom" reject God's revelation do not enter a wonderfully exciting new life, but a life which, in comparison with the service of God, is flat, tasteless, insipid. Their attempt to be wise makes fools out of them.

23. The summit of their folly was realized in their acceptance of idolatry. They *exchanged*[243] *the glory of the immortal God for images*. . . . Paul sees it as stupid to make a god of one's own.[244] It is to exchange something of real worth (the glory of God) for something of no value (an image). The word rendered *immortal*[245] is more literally "not corruptible". From the thought of not decaying it is an easy transition to immortal, so we need not cavil at the translation. But it is worth noting that Paul is speaking not so much of eternity of being as of the total absence from God of that liability to decay which is inseparable from our physical existence and which is incompatible with the glory of which he writes. "The glory of the incorruptible God" is a striking expression, bringing out something both of the greatness and the majesty of God.

They exchanged all this for *images made to look like mortal man*. . . , or, more literally, "for the likeness of an image of corruptible man". The "likeness" and the "image" are much the same,[246] but the tautologous expression

242. ἐμωράνθησαν. In the classics the word signifies "to be foolish" (LSJ); in the New Testament it means "to make foolish" (or "flat" or "tasteless").

243. ἀλλάσσω = "to other", either by exchanging (as here) or by transforming. The construction is normally ἀ. τί τινος or ἀ. τί ἀντί τινος. ἐν is unusual. It may be instrumental ("they 'othered' God by means of images") or an imitation of the Hebrew הֵימִיר בְּ (as in Ps. 106:20). A number of scholars agree that the construction is Hebraic but point to the same thing in Sophocles (e.g., BDF 179 [2]).

244. In the manner of Isa. 40:19-20; 44:9-20 the author of Wisdom ridicules the idolater. He speaks of the woodcutter as making something useful from the wood of a tree: "But a castoff piece from among them, useful for nothing, a stick crooked and full of knots" he shapes in his leisure time into the likeness of a man or animal, "giving it a coat of red paint and coloring its surface red and covering every blemish in it with paint". He makes a niche for it: "So he takes thought for it, that it may not fall, because he knows that it cannot help itself. . . . For health he appeals to a thing that is weak; for life he prays to a thing that is dead; for aid he entreats a thing that is utterly inexperienced; for a prosperous journey, a thing that cannot take a step; for money-making and work and success with his hands he asks strength of a thing whose hands have no strength" (Wis. 13:11-14). Such polemic effectively illustrates the point Paul is making—the folly of idol worship.

245. ἄφθαρτος. It occurs four times in Paul and three times in 1 Peter.

246. ὁμοιώματι εἰκόνος. The former word is Pauline in five of its six New Testament occurrences, four being in Romans; the latter is Pauline nine times, while Revelation has it 20 times and no other New Testament writing more than once. εἰκών can be used of the "likeness" of the Emperor on a coin, but it is also used often of an image, as here. G. Kittel sees ὁμοίωμα as the copy and εἰκών as what is copied, to give the meaning "the copy of the figure of men and animals" (TDNT, II, p. 395). Käsemann, however, sees the distinction as pedantic (p. 45). Boylan sees perhaps an identity, "a likeness which is an idol". Better is Barrett's view, "the mere shadowy image". He comments, "Perhaps he uses the two words

emphasizes the unreality of it all. It was for nothing more substantial than an imitation that they exchanged that wonderful reality, the glory of God. And the imitation was "corruptible"[247] at that, forming a further contrast with "the incorruptible God". When people could and should have worshipped a God not subject to decay of any sort, they chose to worship not even man, but the image of man who wastes away. But the sorry story does not end even there. To the images of man idolaters added those of *birds* (amply documented in Egyptian worship), of *animals* (cf. Ps. 106:20), and of *reptiles* (cf. the serpent of Gen. 3; for the general concept cf. Deut. 4:16-18; Jer. 2:11). Paul links these with "and"; idolaters make all these kinds of images. It adds up to a determined substitution of their own way for that of God.[248]

24. People cannot reject God and go scatheless. Paul proceeds to draw out the consequences of the pagan world's refusal to worship God as he is. He draws a horrifying picture of a variety of vices. Contemporary records show that he is not exaggerating. All he says can be documented from the world of his day, and indeed other sins could be added. It is sometimes objected that this is not a balanced picture; the pagan world could do better than this. Of course it could, and Paul shows us something of this in the next chapter. But here he is not trying to picture the total scene. He is pursuing his theological purpose of showing that all people are sinners. In pursuit of this aim he concentrates on that part of the picture which is relevant. This is not to deny that other features exist; it is simply to say that they do not belong here. The good that people do is never a problem. It is something to be thankful about, not something people must be saved from. But sin is another thing altogether. It is a problem wherever it is found. It is Paul's purpose to show that it exists, and that it exists universally. Wherever pagans are to be found, the kinds of sin of which he speaks will be found also. People are not saved from sin by idolatry.[249]

---

but means no more than either would have suggested separately; perhaps (as the translation suggests) the reduplication emphasizes the inferior, shadowy character of that which is substituted for God." Morna Hooker has an article, "Adam in Romans 1" (NTS, VI [1959-60], pp. 297-306), in which she draws attention to a number of links between Paul's language in this chapter and the Adam story. Specifically she says, "our examination has lent additional weight to C. K. Barrett's point that the words convey the impression of the shadowy nature of that which is substituted for God" (*ibid.*, p. 303). She has a further note (NTS, XIII [1966-67], pp. 181-83) in which she argues that Ps. 106 is behind the present passage and the following verses. Harold Roberts also argues that we must see the Genesis reference to "image" as the background to this passage (ET, LXI [1949-50], pp. 74-77).

247. φθαρτός, "perishable, corruptible" (AS). Cf. also D. J. W. Milne, "Genesis 3 in the Letter to the Romans", RThR, XXXIX (1980), pp. 10-18.

248. William Baird sums it up this way: "The act of God which ought to be most meaningful to the pagan, then, is creation, for this has to do with the very nature of man himself. Here perceptive man should see that he is creature, that his very existence is dependent upon the Creator. Yet man has sinned; he has rejected this revelation; he has turned from the Creator to the creature" (*Paul's Message and Mission* [New York, 1960], p. 35).

249. In Wis. 14:27 the worship of idols is "the beginning and cause and end of every

Another feature of his treatment of the subject is his insistence that this is not simply an inevitable process of cause and effect which takes place while God stands by, more or less a spectator. God is in all of life. He does not contract out. We have already noticed that God willed that if people sin certain consequences follow (see the note on v. 18). This is a moral universe; sin has inevitable results. But three times Paul says, "God gave them up" (vv. 24, 26, 28). God is active in the process whereby sin's consequences follow sin.

Therefore[250] introduces the reason for what follows and links it with what has preceded in logical order. It was on account of their rejection of the divine revelation and of their preferring idols to the true God that God gave them up to the results of their folly. The verb *gave them over*[251] shows that God is active and not passive in the process (cf. Ps. 81:12; Acts 7:42). This does not mean that he is vindictive. That would be untrue both to the facts of the case and to the apostle's thought. Throughout this epistle Paul insists that God's purpose is one of mercy (cf. 11:32). Elsewhere the situation is viewed from another angle: people gave themselves up to licentious behavior (Eph. 4:19); they are responsible human beings. But here the thought is that God is active in the process. He shuts people up to the consequences of their sin so that they will see their error and look to him for mercy and for a better way. Notice that Paul does not call on God to punish sinners. Rather, he has the profound thought that their immersion in their sin is itself their punishment (cf. "one is punished by the very things by which he sins", Wis. 11:16). The first point is that they are given up *in*[252] *the sinful desires of their hearts to sexual impurity.* Paul's word for *sinful desires*[253] is a strong one, denoting "the passionate desire for forbidden pleasure" (Barclay). The addition, *of their hearts* (see v. 21), shows that Paul is thinking of deep-seated desire, not a surface impulse. They were given up "to uncleanness",[254] a general term suitable to this introduction. At this point Paul is not being precise about the result of people's sins, but he leaves the reader in no doubt that it is impurity of some kind, with a strong hint at sexual impurity (NIV is too definite). The sinful desires

---

evil." Like Paul, the writer has a long list of specific sins associated with idolatry.

250. διό is another word of which Paul is fond; he uses it 27 times out of its 53 New Testament occurrences.

251. παραδίδωμι means "to give or hand over". It is used for a number of ways of viewing the giving of Jesus over to his death. See the note on 8:32.

252. Turner comments, "There may be a causal ἐν in Ro 1²⁴ (*because of the lusts of their hearts*)" (M, III, p. 262). Or the meaning may be, "immersed in their lusts"; cf. Lenski, "God finds them *in* these lusts and so hands them over *to* uncleanness."

253. ἐπιθυμία is Pauline in exactly half its New Testament occurrences (19 out of 38). It denotes strong desire, occasionally for good (e.g., 1 Thess. 2:17), but usually for evil, so that it frequently means "lust".

254. εἰς ἀκαθαρσίαν. Paul uses the noun in no less than nine of its ten New Testament occurrences. It is linked with πορνεία in 2 Cor. 12:21; Gal. 5:19; Eph. 5:3; Col. 3:5. Paul is probably not unmindful of the sexual immorality that was such a common accompaniment of idol worship. But the term is a wide one and will not be limited to this.

lead to *the degrading of their bodies*.[255] People cannot give themselves to impurity and go scatheless. Consequences follow. *Degrading*, or more precisely "dishonoring",[256] is another general term; it may indicate an insult, whether in word or thought or deed. But, though the term is general, in the context of the rejection of God's revelation which leads to idolatry and then to the dishonoring of their bodies,[257] there can be little doubt but that Paul is referring to the practice of ritual prostitution which was all but universal in the idolatrous systems of the first century (he was writing from Corinth where more than a thousand sacred prostitutes were said to have been attached to one large temple). "Man has mocked the honour of God by deifying the bodies of creatures erected into idols; God therefore abandons man to passions which dishonour his own body" (Leenhardt). This represents the attempt of man to control his destiny in independence of God. He rejects the revelation God has made and this leads to idolatry as he manufactures idols in the likeness of his body. This in turn leads to immoral types of worship.[258] In the nature cults, for example, people thought that they had the secret of fertility. By the use of appropriate rituals (which included the sex act) they held that they could secure growth and vitality. They had become masters of themselves and their environment, or so they thought. They did not realize that they had thrust themselves into the depths of degradation. In every age an equivalent mistake is possible.

Perhaps we should add that in the catalogue of vices which Paul here begins he is following a fairly common custom among the moralists of the time. Dodd points out that it was a usual practice to divide vices into the sensual and the antisocial (p. 27). While there is a slight uncertainty about the

255. τοῦ + infinitive probably expresses result here. The construction is found 23 times in Luke, 21 times in Acts, and 13 times in Paul. Elsewhere Matthew has it six times, Hebrews twice, and James, 1 Peter, and Revelation once each. It is thus Lukan and to a less extent Pauline. In Greek writers generally it denotes purpose, but Moulton finds no certain example of purpose in Paul (though purpose is possible in some passages; M, I, pp. 216ff.). "So as to" will usually express Paul's meaning. Some take it here as purpose (Lagrange, Godet), and others see it as epexegetic (Moulton, Shedd, Murray), but we should probably see it as result (as BDF 400 [2]; BAGD [sub ὁ II.4.b.γ]; Turner [M, III, p. 141]).

256. The form ἀτιμάζεσθαι could be either middle or passive. Cranfield points out that the use of this verb in the middle is not found in ancient Greek and prefers to see it as passive, a view which should probably be accepted. But Lenski asks, "Who does this dishonoring?" It cannot be God; it must be the people themselves. He reasons, then, that if we take the verb as passive, it must be in the sense of the middle. Murray sees it as passive, "that their bodies should be dishonored among themselves".

257. NIV's *with one another* is based on accepting ἐν ἑαυτοῖς (with Dᶜ E F G K L P etc.), a view supported by RSV, GNB, and others. Hodge sees the possibility of accepting this reading and taking it as equivalent to ἐν ἀλλήλοις (cf. v. 27), i.e., "they dishonored one another, as to their bodies". However, there seems good reason for accepting ἐν αὐτοῖς (with ℵ A B C D* etc.), which gives the sense "among them" (so SH, Cranfield, UBS, etc.).

258. Cf. Num. 25:1-2. We see the idea also in the Wisdom of Solomon: "the idea of making idols was the beginning of fornication" (Wis. 14:12).

precise meaning of some of the terms he uses, it seems that Paul is following some such division. He speaks of sensual sins in vv. 24-27 and of the antisocial in vv. 29-31.

25.[259] *They exchanged*[260] *the truth of God for a lie* (cf. v. 23). There are three ways to understand "the truth of God". (1) Taking the abstract for the concrete, we might understand it as "the true God" (as NEB) (Hendriksen sees the genitive as one of apposition and renders, "God, [who is] the truth", which is much the same). (2) It may mean the truth God has made known, or, as Cranfield puts it, "the reality consisting of God Himself and His self-revelation".[261] (3) Some (like RSV and Kertelge) see the expression as meaning "the truth about God". The second view has the most to be said for it. For Paul truth is an important concept (see Additional Note B), something not known to us naturally but only as God has revealed it. It is usually connected with God himself.

These people might have responded to God's leading and have entered the joy of the service of God and of all that is true. Instead they gave all this away, and for what? For what Paul calls "the lie".[262] Most versions read "a lie" (NIV, KJV, RSV, etc.), but Paul uses the definite article. He is not thinking of idolatry as no more than one falsehood among many. It is *the* lie. Elsewhere he speaks of "putting away the lie" and "speak[ing] truth" (Eph. 4:25); again he speaks of some who "will believe the lie" (2 Thess. 2:11). In each case, as here, he is contrasting the lie with the truth. He does not see heathen religion as a partial truth. It is the lie that leads people away from the truth of God. The true God stands in contrast with idols (1 Thess. 1:9). To exchange the worship of God for the lie is the final disaster.

What is meant in this exchange is explained. They *worshiped and served created things rather than the Creator*. The verb rendered *worshiped* is unusual (here only in the New Testament),[263] but its meaning is not in doubt. They

259. There is a dispute about connections here. Cranfield starts a new paragraph with v. 25 (though noting that SH, Lagrange, and Michel connect it with v. 24), since v. 24 already has been given a reason by its διό, which looks back to vv. 22-23. Further, διὰ τοῦτο (v. 26) connects with vv. 25 and 26. He renders οἵτινες "They actually" (with the other division it would mean "seeing that they"). The reasons he gives for separating v. 25 from v. 24, however, scarcely seem adequate. It is better to retain the more usual division. The relative of quality is frequent in Paul (44 times), almost always in the nominative. BAGD class it here under the heading "to emphasize a characteristic quality, by which a preceding statement is to be confirmed" and translate "since indeed they had exchanged".

260. "Exchanged" here renders μετήλλαξαν (in the New Testament only here and in v. 26), which scarcely differs from ἤλλαξαν in v. 23. The same construction with ἐν is found there as here.

261. Käsemann comments, "ἀλήθεια again means the self-disclosing reality of God, not an attribute of God nor his 'true nature.' Hence τὸ ψεῦδος is not the false conduct of man, nor abstractedly the false god, but the deception which objectively conceals the truth, especially in Gentile religion" (p. 48). Parry sees the expression as comprehensive, "the truth about God and themselves and their relation to Him".

262. For idolatry as ψεῦδος cf. Isa. 44:20; Jer. 13:25; as ψευδής cf. Jer. 10:14; 16:19.

263. ἐσεβάσθησαν. The usual word is σέβομαι, but no difference of meaning is apparent.

accorded religious veneration to the creature. *Served*[264] is a word which originally applied to the service of gods or people. In the New Testament, however, it is always used of the service of God, so that its meaning is much like that of the previous verb. Paul is simply emphasizing that these people worshipped in the fullest sense. And they gave their worship not to the Creator,[265] to whom it was due, but to the creature, in fact to that which they themselves had fashioned, idols.[266]

The mention of the Creator leads Paul into a little doxology (as is not uncommon with him): *who is forever praised. Amen* (cf. Ps. 89:52). This is in part Paul's protest against the failure of the heathen to give God his due. He salutes God as *forever praised.*[267] All the meaning we can put into "blessing" belongs to God, and that not for a moment but forever.[268] Paul often tacks *Amen* on to the end of a doxology, but it is not easy to see why. It is really the response of a congregation when a leader says something, usually a prayer, on its behalf. "Amen" is the congregation's way of giving assent. It makes the words uttered by the leader its own.[269] But in a doxology like this one there is nobody to respond. It is all Paul's. It certainly ends the doxology on a solemn and devout note, and this may be its purpose; it is "the response of worship" (Murray).

26. *Because of this*[270] carries the argument along logically, as often in

264. λατρεύω meant originally "serve for hire" (λάτρον) and then generally "to serve" either gods or people. It was used alike of the service of slaves and free people.

265. παρά in the sense "rather than", "instead of" (BAGD III.3; Cranfield doubts whether all the instances cited are acceptable, but agrees for this passage). Cf. Luke 18:14. Phillips has "instead of" the Creator.

266. Barth sees something like this still, for "In their general view of the world scientists and historians are in far closer agreement with philosophers and theologians than is normally recognized. It is not merely that the world exists side by side with God: it has taken His place, and has itself become God, and demands 'the same devotion which the old-fashioned believer offered to his God' (Dr. F. Strauss)."

267. εὐλογητός. The form of the verbal adjective might give the meaning "capable of being blessed", but the usage of the verb shows that it means simply "blessed". In the Old Testament it may be used of blessing people (e.g., Gen. 12:2; 1 Sam. 15:13), but in the New it always refers to God or Christ (μακάριος is the word for people, 4:7, 8; 14:22). As to its meaning, H. W. Beyer says, "We best bring out its religious significance along the lines of Luther that God is praised in Himself but that we pray here that He may be praised among us" (TDNT, II, p. 764).

268. εἰς τοὺς αἰῶνας, "into the ages". Paul uses the noun 38 times, so it is a congenial term. Sometimes he uses the singular "into the age" (1 Cor. 8:13; 2 Cor. 9:9), but he prefers the plural (9:5; 11:36; 2 Cor. 11:31), while he uses the more sonorous εἰς τοὺς αἰῶνας τῶν αἰώνων (16:27, vl.; Gal. 1:5; Phil. 4:20; 1 Tim. 1:17; 2 Tim. 4:18; all these are doxologies). Behind all these forms is the idea that the present age is to be followed by a final age or ages. Anything that lasts from now into that age (or ages) lasts "forever".

269. ἀμήν is the transliteration of a Hebrew expression of which A. Jepsen says, "The form of this word is qaṭil, which could suggest an adjectival meaning. However, the use of this word in certain passages suggests that it is to be interpreted as a particle, so that no certain conclusion can be drawn about the meaning of 'amen from its form" (TDOT, I, p. 320). It was used to give assent to what someone else had said, and specifically it was used liturgically as the assent of the congregation to a prayer uttered by the leader of worship.

270. διὰ τοῦτο.

Paul. The reason in question is not, of course, given in the doxology, but in the idolatry referred to immediately before it. The punishment for the conduct involved in idolatry was their being given over to *shameful lusts*.[271] *Shameful* is cognate with "degrading" in v. 24, and, while there is no kinship of language, *lusts* recalls the "sinful desires" of that verse. Paul is still moving in the same realm of ideas. He goes on to particularize with his reference to women exchanging *natural relations*[272] *for*[273] *unnatural ones*.[274] He uses the adjectives "female" and "male" rather than the nouns "women" and "men", possibly because he is concentrating on sexual differentiation. Hendriksen points out that "A person's sexual orientation, whether heterosexual or homosexual, is not the point at issue. What matters is what a person does with his sexuality!" He goes on to remind us that "According to the plain teaching of Scripture sexual intercourse was intended for a husband and his wife, for no one else!" Paul mentions the degradation of women before he deals with that of men. Hodge thinks the reason for this is that "they are always the last to be affected in the decay of morals, and their corruption is therefore proof that all virtue is lost." There may be something to this, but it seems more likely that Paul is giving emphasis to the male perversion by putting it last and dealing with it at greater length.

27. The sin was not confined to women. The males engaged in the equivalent evil.[275] Paul's word for *abandoned* is a rather strong one.[276] It is common in the New Testament, but Paul uses it five times only. He has quite a bit of unusual vocabulary here, and his words for *were inflamed* and *lust* are found here only in the New Testament.[277] The former word has the notion of burning and seems to be used in the literal sense much more often than in the metaphorical sense Paul is giving it here; it is a very vivid term (cf. 1 Cor. 7:9 for much the same idea, though with a different word). *Lust* (a word with the notion of reaching out to grasp something) signifies strong and eager desire. It can be used in a good sense but also, as here, in a bad sense. Paul is saying in strong terms that the men were burned up with a powerful but unnatural

---

271. πάθη ἀτιμίας, where the genitive is a genitive of quality. πάθος is found three times in the New Testament, all in Paul. BAGD define the word as "1. that which is endured or experienced, *suffering* . . . 2. *passion* . . . esp. of a sexual nature", here "disgraceful passions". GT sees it as the passive side of a vice, whereas ἐπιθυμία is the active: "ἐπ. is (evil) desire, π. ungovernable desire". See further my NICNT commentary on 1 and 2 Thessalonians, pp. 124-25.

272. For χρῆσις used of sexual relations see BAGD 3. It occurs only in vv. 26 and 27 in the New Testament.

273. For παρά in the sense "instead of" see n. 265 above.

274. Paul uses both φυσικός, "natural", and φύσις, "nature", more than anyone else in the New Testament (the former two out of three times; the latter 11 out of 12). φύσις is connected with φύω, "grow", and indicates "what things grow into", "essential nature".

275. τε . . . τε "places the elements so connected in a parallel relationship (often = 'as . . . so')" (BDF 444 [1]; here they prefer the variant δέ, perhaps wrongly).

276. ἀφίημι.

277. ἐκκαίω and ὄρεξις (cf. ὀρέγω, "to stretch out" [AS]).

passion.[278] He does not define the evil practice that resulted[279] but speaks only of *indecent*[280] *acts*. But there can be no doubt about the particular kind of shamelessness he has in mind. So he says that these sinners received *the due penalty*[281] of their misdeeds *in themselves*. Paul is not so much calling for a penalty as thinking of sexual perversion as itself a penalty (being a sinner is the punishment of sin!). This is sharply different from the general attitude among Greeks and Romans of the day, for they preferred this kind of love to heterosexual love. Paul's language is perhaps a little stronger than *due penalty*. He is speaking of a requital which is "necessary".[282] The thought is one of compulsion. Thayer points out that it can signify "a necessity of law and command", but he sees it here as pointing to "the recompense due by the law of God" (GT). Once more Paul is thinking of what God has decreed rather than simply of the natural result of people's actions. He refers to such actions as "error" (NIV, *perversion*); sinners have wandered from the right way.

28. *Since* (perhaps "as" is better)[283] points to exact correspondence: "The cases are parallel; *as* they deserted God, so God abandoned them" (Hodge). There is nothing arbitrary about God's actions. *Think . . . worthwhile* renders another word Paul uses often.[284] It means first "test", then "approve" as a result of the test, and so simply "approve", as here, without any strict notion of test. Paul puts the word *God* in an emphatic position. It was no less than God whom they did not approve to "have in knowledge". This latter is an unusual expression, found here only in the New Testament. It is stronger than "know",[285] and thus a number of versions have "acknowledge". But Paul's thought is not so much this as that they refused to have God in their knowledge. They thrust him out of their circle of acquaintance. Their ignorance of God was not due to a lack of opportunity to know him, but to their

278. Barclay makes the point that what Paul says is all documented in Roman writers: "There is nothing that Paul said about the heathen world that the heathen moralist (*sic*) had not themselves already said. And vice did not stop with the crude and natural vices. Society from top to bottom was riddled with unnatural vice." He adds, "Fourteen out of the first fifteen Roman Emperors were homosexuals."

279. The verb κατεργάζομαι is frequent in Romans (11 times; in Paul 20 out of 22 times in the New Testament). In form it is stronger than ἐργάζομαι (having κατά perfective prefixed), giving meanings like "carry out", "accomplish". But in practice the two verbs are often synonymous.

280. ἀσχημοσύνη is a strong word. Elsewhere in the New Testament it occurs only in Rev. 16:15; there it refers to the private parts.

281. ἀντιμισθία is found only in the New Testament and Christian authors. The preposition stresses the idea of requital.

282. ἔδει. Paul and Luke are the great users of this verb. It occurs 102 times in the New Testament—18 in Luke, 22 in Acts, and 25 in Paul. But it is not prominent in Romans (three times).

283. καθώς, a frequent word in Paul (84 times out of 178 in the New Testament). It means "just as" = "since" (BDF 453 [2]).

284. δοκιμάζω is found in Paul 17 times out of 22 in the New Testament.

285. The noun is ἐπίγνωσις (in Paul 15 times out of 20 in the New Testament). It may denote knowledge directed towards (ἐπί) a particular object but in usage does not differ significantly from γνῶσις. It is the combination ἔχειν ἐν ἐπιγνώσει that is striking and significant.

deliberate refusal. They preferred other things to the knowledge of God. And, because they rejected the knowledge of God, God *gave them over* (the third use of this terrible expression) to the consequences of what they had done in both thought and action, namely to a *depraved mind, to do what ought not to be done.* The word *depraved* meant originally "that has not stood the test" (it is related to that rendered *think . . . worthwhile*[286] in the earlier part of the verse). It was used of coins that were substandard. The choice of words is another of Paul's ways of bringing out the fitness of things. They did not "approve" to know God and they came to have an "unapproved" mind.[287] Paul is not talking about an arbitrary process but about people who received the due result of their evil deeds. *Mind* is the usual word for the thinking faculty, but it can mean "the intellectual part of conscience" (SH). It is sometimes combined with "conscience", as when we read of certain people that "both their minds and consciences are corrupted" (Tit. 1:15).[288] The result, then, of their refusal to accept the knowledge of God is seen in the way they came to think and the things that their consciences came to approve. Their minds became quite unable to make trustworthy moral judgments. Robinson remarks, "reason as much as anything requires to be justified by faith before it can function truly as reason." They had cut themselves off from all the joys of the knowledge of God. They were delivered over in consequence to the narrow, joyless existence of base minds and improper conduct.[289] It was the only course they left open to themselves. They continually did what is not becoming, not fitting, not acceptable.[290]

286. It is not easy to bring out in English the wordplay ἐδοκίμασαν . . . ἀδόκιμον. The effect is to indicate that there was nothing arbitrary about their punishment. Cf. Denney, "As they did not think fit, after trial made . . . to keep God in their knowledge, God gave them up to a mind which cannot stand trial". Paul took care that he himself should not be ἀδόκιμος (1 Cor. 9:27).

287. Cf. C. S. Lewis, "In creating beings with free will, omnipotence from the outset submits to the possibility of such defeat. What you call defeat, I call miracle: for to make things which are not Itself, and thus to become, in a sense, capable of being resisted by its own handiwork, is the most astonishing and unimaginable of all the feats we attribute to the Deity. I willingly believe that the damned are, in one sense, successful, rebels to the end; that the doors of hell are locked on the *inside*. I do not mean that the ghosts may not *wish* to come out of hell, in the vague fashion wherein an envious man 'wishes' to be happy: but they certainly do not will even the first preliminary stages of that self-abandonment through which alone the soul can reach any good. They enjoy forever the horrible freedom they have demanded, and are therefore self-enslaved" (*The Problem of Pain* [London, 1943], pp. 115-16). Both God's activity and man's are involved, and either can receive the stress in a given passage. Here God's act is emphasized.

288. Cf. Foreman, "The worst penalty for sin is to love sin".

289. The Stoic moralists used τὸ καθῆκον as a technical term for what is seemly. H. Schlier points out that Paul is not using the exact technical term, for "what is contrary to καθῆκον is always τὸ παρὰ τὸ καθῆκον" (TDNT, III, p. 440). He gives Paul's meaning as "that which is offensive to man even according to the popular moral sense of the Gentiles, i.e., what even natural human judgment regards as vicious and wrong." Paul's expression is not found elsewhere in the New Testament, but there are similar words in Acts 22:22.

290. For Paul's use of negatives see on v. 13. This is his first use of μή.

29. Paul launches into a detailed list[291] of the sins he has in mind.[292] He first speaks of the sinners as *filled with*[293] wickedness, showing that he does not think of them as half-hearted about their sin. They were wholly given over to it. Their exclusion of God left room for nothing else. We should probably not try to delimit too closely the words that follow, for Paul is more concerned to bring out the truth that those who reject God give themselves over to all manner of evils than he is to tell us precisely what those evils are. There must, however, be some significance in his choice of words, and it is worth looking into them accordingly. *Wickedness* is a comprehensive term,[294] so comprehensive indeed that in the opinion of some commentators it includes all that follows. The rest of the list, then, is no more than a filling out of what is meant by wickedness. This may be going too far, but at least we can say that the term covers a great variety of evils.

There is some dispute about the second and fourth members of the list, *evil* and *depravity*.[295] Some hold that the former points to an active form of wrongdoing while the latter means rather a vicious disposition. Others, however, almost reverse the distinction. It is safest, therefore, not to insist on too sharp a distinction between them.[296] What is plain is that both terms denote

291. He has lists of vices in 13:13; 1 Cor. 5:10-11; 6:9-10; 2 Cor. 12:20; Gal. 5:19-21; Eph. 4:19, 31; 5:3-5; Col. 3:5, 8; 1 Tim. 1:9-10; 6:4-5; 2 Tim. 3:2-5; Tit. 3:3.

292. The way to group the vices in the list is a matter of dispute. Some even hold that there is no order; Paul has simply put down unconnected vices as they occurred to him. Minor variations in word order in the MSS only compound the problem. Thus some MSS read πορνεία in v. 29 (cf. KJV), but this should be rejected; the attestation is insufficient and the vice has already been covered. Paul begins with πεπληρωμένοις, and attaches four vices to it (each is in the dative, giving the meaning "filled with"). Then comes μεστούς, followed by five more (each in the genitive, "full of"). Next is a group of 12 (in the accusative in apposition to αὐτούς). Some take the last four as a subgroup or a group of their own (each begins with alpha-privative). It is possible to see further groupings, e.g., by taking some consecutive terms together, such as "god-hated insolents" (v. 30). What is clear is that Paul has constructed his list with some care. He may have meant such refinements as the last-mentioned, but we cannot be sure. Of the 4-5-12 division we can be certain, but it is difficult to go beyond that. There are no references to sexual sin in the list, but these have been dealt with earlier.

293. πεπληρωμένοις may go with αὐτούς, "He gave them up, filled with all unrighteousness", or with ποιεῖν, "so that, filled with all unrighteousness, they should do. . . ." There is not a great deal of difference.

294. ἀδικία is here "put first in the list of offences as 'violation of the divine law and its norm'" (G. Schrenk, TDNT, I, p. 155).

295. πονηρία and κακία. It is perhaps worth noting that πονηρός, the adjective corresponding to the first term, is commonly used of Satan, who is "the evil one", and that it occurs in the Lord's Prayer, "deliver us from evil" (Matt. 6:13).

296. G. Harder notices a number of suggested distinctions between the two words and rejects them all. He points out that both terms occur in LXX as translations for the same Hebrew words. "The translators of the various books show preferences for the one term or the other but no fundamental distinction is made between πονηρία and κακία" (TDNT, VI, p. 564). BAGD class κακία here under the heading, "a special kind of moral inferiority . . . someth. like *malice, ill-will, malignity*".

thoroughgoing evil and that they include both the inner disposition and the active doing of harm to others. Incidentally the two are linked again in 1 Corinthians 5:8. The remaining term, *greed*,[297] means the inordinate desire to have more. It is selfishness unlimited. Although it is often translated "covetousness" (as RSV), we not infrequently use this word in a rather restricted sense, and we should be clear that Paul is talking about the desire to have more as a settled disposition. This covetous person pursues his own desires with a complete disregard of the effect on other people. He does not care about others but is a complete egotist. Paul is talking about one who is never satisfied. He is always anxious to have more of something, and no matter what he gets he remains unsatisfied. Which is, of course, an excellent illustration of Paul's point that the sinner is handed over to his sin. Evil is its own punishment. The word occurs in conjunction with *evil* again in Mark 7:22.

Full of[298] introduces another list of terms denoting individual sins. The adjective probably does not differ very greatly in meaning from the participle rendered *they have become filled* at the beginning of the verse. It simply marks a stage in the argument. *Envy*[299] reminds us that evildoers are not just one happy band of brothers. There is a divisiveness about evil which sets people apart from one another. Evil people are apt to be envious rather than appreciative. From such attitudes springs *murder* (cf. Mark 15:10), the ultimate outcome of *strife*.[300] *Deceit*[301] is basically *"bait* for fish . . . hence, *any cunning contrivance for deceiving* or *catching* . . . in the abstract, *craft, cunning"* (LSJ; they point out that it was used of such stratagems as the Trojan horse). There is nothing straightforward about sin, and sinners do not hesitate to deceive one another if their purposes can be advanced. NEB renders "treachery". *Malice*

---

297. πλεονεξία, from πλέον + ἔχω, means, in the first instance, "having more" (i.e., than one's fair share), "receiving more", then "the desire to have more". In the New Testament this word and its two cognates are basically Pauline (15 out of 19 occurrences). G. Delling holds that here it is "one of the basic facts in which the total abandonment of the human race by God works itself out. It occurs in a group of four nouns which comprehensively describe the power of sin in the ravaging of human relationships" (TDNT, VI, p. 272). Covetousness is idolatry (Col. 3:5), and the covetous person an idolater (Eph. 5:5; cf. 1 Cor. 5:10, 11; 6:9-10). All this is to be seen in the context of Jesus' words about the impossibility of serving God and mammon (Luke 16:13). MM cite examples of the word, including one in an "illiterate" papyrus, and speak of it as "a true vernacular word".

298. μεστός, "full", may refer to material objects (John 19:29; 21:11), but it is also used metaphorically (Matt. 23:28; Rom. 15:14, etc.).

299. φθόνου and φόνου are apparently placed beside one another because of the similarity in sound. But we should not overlook the fact that envy can lead to murder; there is a connection.

300. ἔρις signifies "strife, wrangling, contention" (AS). MM cite it in a papyrus of the second century B.C. They translate, "know that I have a heart unconquerable when hate takes hold upon me", an interesting example of that glorying in sin which Paul is deploring. In the New Testament the word is confined to Paul (nine times).

301. δόλος is used of craftiness or deceit in LXX as in the New Testament.

(Phillips, "spite") is "conscious and intentional wickedness."[302] *Gossips*,[303] more literally "whisperers", is a term which may be used in a good or a neutral sense (it was an epithet of the god Hermes). Here, however, it plainly refers to slander, whispering what one does not wish to be heard openly. Some think it refers to slander of those present as against slander of those not present (which is denoted by "slanderers" in v. 30), but most see the distinction rather as between secret slanderers and open slanderers (Phillips is picturesque with his "whisperers-behind-doors" and "stabbers-in-the-back").

30. For *slanderers*[304] see the note on the previous verse. The word is not attested before this passage, so Paul is not employing a well-known term. He may even have coined it himself. The meaning is clear enough. Evil people are prone to speak evil of others, and it is this to which Paul is objecting. *God-haters*[305] translates another compound word not found elsewhere in the New Testament. The meaning is not certain, for the form could mean "hated by God" (as NEB, "hateful to God"; Moffatt, "loathed by God") or "hating God" (RSV, "haters of God"; JB, "enemies of God"). The difficulty is that in all earlier references it means something like "hateful to God", "hated by a god", "god-forsaken" (BAGD), but in the immediate context all the words refer to human rather than divine activity. On the whole it seems that we should understand it in this second sense, for this is a list of vices. Hating God comes under this heading, but hated by God does not.[306]

The next three words are all concerned with some aspect of pride. *Insolent*[307] refers to a lofty sense of superiority out of which the insolent

---

302. W. Grundmann, TDNT, III, p. 485. The term is κακοήθεια. SH, Michel, and others, following Aristotle, see it as "the tendency to put the worst construction upon everything". Cranfield, however, rejects this as "clearly a special connotation" and favors "its ordinary general sense of 'malice', 'malignity', 'spite'".

303. ψιθυριστής. Theodoret, the fifth-century commentator, takes the term to mean "those who whisper in the ear and speak ill of some who are present", while he sees καταλάλους as "those who unscrupulously make false accusations against those who are absent".

304. καταλάλους. Both this word and the preceding ψιθυριστάς are found only here in the New Testament.

305. θεοστυγεῖς.

306. Cf. Calvin, "The word θεοστυγεῖς undoubtedly means *haters of God*, for there is no reason to take it in its passive sense *(hated by God)*, since Paul is here proving men's guilt by their obvious wickedness." Turner argues that "we should take the word passively in a subjective, not an objective sense: *out of favour with God*" (M, III, p. 234). But he appears to be arguing simply from the form of the word and taking no account of context. Some solve the problem by taking the term closely with the following words to give the sense, "god-hated insolents" (e.g., Lenski). Others appeal to its use in 1 Clement, but that passage is not very helpful, as Kirsopp Lake's translation shows. Clement speaks of casting away "evil-speaking, hatred of God (θεοστυγίαν), pride. . . . For those who do these things are hateful to God (στυγητοὶ τῷ θεῷ)" (1 Clem. xxxv.5-6).

307. Cranfield points to its use in classical Greek tragedy for the insolent pride that brings νέμεσις, "the retribution of the gods", upon the person who exercises it. According to G. Bertram, ὑβριστής "denotes a man who, sinfully overestimating his own powers and exaggerating his own claims, is insolent in word and deed in relation to gods and men" (TDNT, VIII, p. 296). Here he takes it closely with θεοστυγεῖς and says, "The expression

person treats all others as beneath him. It is the pride that is totally unaware of its limitations and "goes before a fall". *Arrogant*[308] does not differ greatly. Barclay quotes Theophrastus, who says that this vice means "a certain contempt for everyone except oneself." *Boastful* derives from a word meaning "wandering"[309] and apparently goes back to the extravagant claims made by wandering men: merchants with something to sell, quacks with claims to heal, and wanderers in general with tall tales to tell. Since there is no way of verifying or refuting what such people say, they are sometimes given to making claims that cannot be substantiated. The word includes the thought of evil intent; it is not used of harmless, amusing exaggeration.

They invent ways of doing evil suggests a certain ingenuity in devising wrong.[310] These people are not content to go on in the established paths of evil, but are eager to strike out on new and worse ways. To this Paul adds, *they disobey their parents*. In a world which took very seriously the obligation to honor one's forebears this was a grievous sin. It indicates a readiness to be false to those to whom one owes the most. It implies a lack of gratitude and a contempt for family authority.

31. Paul uses four adjectives, each of which commences with a prefix corresponding to the English "un-". It is difficult to capture the force of this construction in English, though NIV's succession of words ending in "-less" comes pretty close. *Senseless*[311] means without intelligence; it refers to those who act stupidly (cf. v. 21). Lagrange asks why it is a vice to be unintelligent. The answer must be that Paul includes a moral element as well as an intellectual one. He is saying that to cut oneself off from God is a stupid and wicked procedure. *Faithless*[312] is concerned at base with the breaking of agreements. When people enter into solemn undertakings, they should do what they say they will do. Satisfactory living comes to an end when people cannot be trusted to keep their pledged word. But such considerations do not trouble the wicked. Where they see personal advantage, keeping faith does not matter to them. *Heartless*[313] means "without natural affection". There is every

---

θεοστυγεῖς ὑβριστάς presupposes rebellion against God, for the reference is to the disruption of human fellowship as a result of ungodliness" (*ibid.*, p. 306). Paul had formerly been ὑβριστής (1 Tim. 1:13).

308. ὑπερήφανος may be used in a good sense, "pre-eminent, splendid" (AS). But in Scripture it is always used in the sense "arrogant".

309. ἀλαζών is connected with ἄλη, "*wandering* or *roaming* without home or hope of rest" (LSJ). The transition from wanderer to vagrant to charlatan to boaster is a series of easy steps.

310. ἐφευρετὰς κακῶν (Moffatt, "inventive in evil"). Cf. the address to Antiochus Epiphanes, "you who have contrived all sorts of evil (πάσης κακίας εὑρετής) against the Hebrews" (2 Macc. 7:31).

311. ἀσύνετος means "*senseless, foolish*, implying also a lack of high moral quality" (BAGD); cf. Manson, " 'Foolish' implies lack of conscience even more than of common sense".

312. ἀσύνθετος, here only in the New Testament, means not keeping συνθῆκαι, "covenant-breaking". The term is used of faithless Judah in Jer. 3:7 (LXX).

313. ἀστόργους. It means "people lacking στοργή", a term for love which does not

reason to expect that members of a family (or other natural group) will be united in bonds of love and affection, and it is an evil thing when they are not. *Ruthless*, a word found here only in the New Testament, means "without pity", "without mercy". It is significant that, in an epistle that will stress God's mercy throughout, the list of vices should be rounded off with "merciless". This is the very depth of evil. The person who shows no mercy can scarcely go lower.

32. We come back to the thought that these sinners do not act out of ignorance.[314] Granted that no evildoer ever understands all the implications of the wrong he is doing, it still remains that he knows enough to know that he is doing wrong. It is the point that Paul has been stressing throughout this chapter, namely that God has revealed enough of himself for people to know what is right and what is wrong. *Decree*[315] is a legal term. It is one of the righteousness words and has a meaning like "righteous (or just) ordinance". It sometimes means a verdict or declaration that a person is just, but here *decree* is clearly the meaning. Paul affirms that the decree is God's. God is sufficiently interested in what people do to lay down his decree for them.[316] Paul does not, of course, mean that the Gentiles had a codified system of divine laws as the Jews did. He is not concerned at this point with the way knowledge came to them, nor with the precision with which they had apprehended it. He is concerned only with the fact that they have enough knowledge to be sure that they should not act in the way in which they were in fact acting. They know that people who act as they do *deserve death*. Paul uses this word *death* 22 times in Romans, which is more than in any other book of the New Testament. Mostly he employs it in connection with sin, as he does here. Of his 22 uses of the word in this epistle, no less than 18 are related to sin (four concern the death of Christ, one of which connects also with sin, and one is linked with baptism).[317] Many of the "sin" passages are vivid, picturing death as a tyrant reigning over sinners. Here the thought is simply

---

occur in the New Testament (for its meaning see my *Testaments of Love* [Grand Rapids, 1981], pp. 114-17). But this passage, along with 2 Tim. 3:3, shows that the virtue it denotes was prized. It is the love that binds people in a natural grouping, notably the family. Many draw attention to the fact that in the pagan world it was an accepted practice to expose babies whom the parents did not wish to keep. Such killing forms an excellent illustration of the meaning of Paul's word. The Christians repudiated all such practices.

314. οἵτινες denotes the class. Cf. Parry, "οἵτινες κ.τ.λ. define once more the root of the evil—rejection of known truth—here as to the fixed judgment of God on such acts and persons" (CGT).

315. δικαίωμα, which Paul uses five times in Romans (ten times in the New Testament). AS says that it means "a concrete expression of righteousness, the expression and result of the act of δικαίωσις, 'a declaration that a thing is δίκαιον, or that a person is δίκαιος' ". From this he derives the meanings "ordinance" and "sentence" (of acquittal or condemnation).

316. Cf. G. Schrenk, "In Paul's eyes it is important to emphasise that there is for the Gentiles a recognisable divine order which is to be embraced, not as a sum of commands, but (in the sing.) as the one divine will" (TDNT, II, p. 221).

317. The word is linked with sin in 1:32; 5:12 (*bis*), 14, 17, 21; 6:9, 16, 21, 23; 7:5, 10, 13 (*bis*), 24; 8:2, 6, 38; with the death of Christ in 5:10; 6:3, 5, 9; and with baptism in 6:4.

that death is the desert of sin. Some think of physical death as the meaning; it was sin that brought death. Others think of spiritual death. More probably Paul is not defining death closely but simply viewing it as a horror. It tyrannizes the human race and keeps people from the life that is life indeed, whether we think of this world or the next.

Only[318] is another typical Pauline word. Here it is part of a statement that brings out the enormity of the offence. Not only do these sinners do[319] evil things, but they also take pleasure in other people who do[320] them. The Greek possibly means a little more than NIV's *approve*. It is rather "have pleasure in them that do them" (KJV) or "applaud such practices" (NEB). There are thoughts not only of full support but also of enjoyment. The word certainly includes the encouragement to do wrong. Through the centuries Paul's statement has caused difficulty.[321] Many have felt that it is far worse to do an evil thing than simply to express approval when others do it. But Paul is not talking about people who do not practice vice themselves but simply encourage others. He is talking about those who do evil things (*continue to do these very things*). Then, not content with vice in themselves, they actively encourage it in others. They heap up vice beyond their own power.[322]

Additional Note A: THE RIGHTEOUSNESS OF GOD

James P. Martin remarks that "The term *dikaiosune theou* (*tou theou* in 10:3) is crucial in Paul's theology, central in Rom., and the subject of intense discus-

318. μόνον is found in Paul in 36 of its 66 New Testament occurrences. It is not easy to see why a word like "only" should be used more by Paul than by others, but we should notice that he uses "not only" often when he is adding another point to the preceding.

319. Most of the verbs from v. 24 on are in the aorist, but Paul finishes the section with two present tenses, ποιοῦσιν and συνευδοκοῦσιν. There is some emphasis on the habitual attitude.

320. Paul uses two words which do not greatly differ in meaning and which NIV here translates as *do* (ποιέω) and *practice* (πράσσω). It is often said that the latter means "to do habitually" and the former simply "to do", but this is not easy to establish from the usage of the two terms. It may perhaps be more relevant that πράσσω is often used of actions that are blameworthy. C. Maurer points out that the verb is never used of God's actions: "This colourless word is used only with reference to man's action, and a predominantly negative judgment is implied." Here he comments, "the οἱ πράσσοντες of v. 32 refers to the mass of those who are rotting in the general swamp of pagan vices. On the other hand, the action of those who know God's righteous demands involves wilful transgression, and ποιεῖν is used for this" (TDNT, VI, pp. 635, 636).

321. O'Neill is an example of a recent scholar who sees a problem. He regards the statement as "a gloss that has crept into the text from the margin". There is, of course, no evidence for this, and it has every appearance of a desperate determination to get rid of it.

322. Cf. Murray, who says that when we do these things, "To put it bluntly, we are not only bent on damning ourselves but we congratulate others in the doing of those things that we know have their issue in damnation. We hate others as we hate ourselves. . . ."

sion."[323] It is found eight times in this epistle (1:17; 3:5, 21, 22, 25, 26; 10:3 [bis]), as against twice in the other Pauline letters (2 Cor. 5:21; Phil. 3:9) and three times in the rest of the New Testament writings (Matt. 6:33; Jas. 1:20; 2 Pet. 1:1). The noun *righteousness* is especially characteristic of Romans where it is used 33 times, the next highest total being seven each in 2 Corinthians and Matthew. It is a term which must be understood carefully. With us it is an ethical virtue, as it was for the Greeks generally. But among the Hebrews righteousness was first and foremost a legal standing.[324] The righteous were those who secured the verdict when they stood before God. This terminology applied even in an earthly court, and "the righteous" and "the wicked" in the Old Testament often mean much what we mean when we speak of "the innocent" and "the guilty" (cf. Deut. 25:1). In the final analysis what matters is the verdict of the heavenly court, and the man who is ultimately righteous is the one who is acquitted when tried at the bar of God's justice. Such a man will, of course, be upright, and the righteousness words sometimes express the character involved in such conduct. But more typically they point to status. For example, a woe is pronounced on them that "take away the righteousness of the righteous from him" (Isa. 5:23, ASV; NIV paraphrases). Righteousness in the sense of moral character or ethical achievement cannot be taken from anyone. What is meant is that wicked judges will take away the "right standing", the status of being right before the law, from people who are entitled to it.

All this must, of course, be modified if the term is to be applied to God, for he is judged by no one. But even when people speak of God's righteousness the legal flavor is not quite lost, for the term is often linked with judgment. Thus the Psalmist can say, "the heavens proclaim his righteousness, for God himself is judge" (Ps. 50:6), or again, the LORD "comes, he comes to judge the earth. He will judge the world in righteousness" (Ps. 96:13). God acts in accordance with right. It is not that some law is set over him to which he must conform. The Bible always regards God as supreme and sees nothing as superior to him. Rather to act rightly is part of his very nature. "Will not the Judge of all the earth do right?" (Gen. 18:25). For the people of the Old Testament the answer was never in doubt.

We should also notice that in the Old Testament righteousness in God is not uncommonly linked with salvation. Thus the LORD says, "my salvation

323. *Interpretation*, XXV (1971), pp. 308-9 n.15. This footnote gives an excellent summary of much in recent discussions.

324. Cf. Käsemann, "in biblical usage righteousness, which is essentially forensic, denotes a relation in which one is set, namely, the 'recognition' in which one, for example, is acknowledged to be innocent." He adds, "In Jewish apocalyptic this understanding is applied to the verdict of justification at the last judgment" (p. 24), and he finds the eschatological approach very important. I find it difficult to go along with Käsemann's emphasis on apocalyptic. Granted that Paul (in common with the men of Qumran) is interested in apocalyptic, it does not follow that this permeates his view of "the righteousness of God". Closer to the facts is Günther Bornkamm's view that, while Paul "sounds the note of apocalyptic", the truth that the gospel *is* God's power for salvation "does not fit into any apocalyptic pattern" (*Paul* [London, 1971], pp. 114, 115; see also T. W. Wright in *Themelios*, 7 [1981-82], p. 10).

will last forever, my righteousness will never fail" (Isa. 51:6). Again we read, "The LORD has made his salvation known and revealed his righteousness to the nations" (Ps. 98:2; this passage contains three important words found in Rom. 1:17, "salvation", "righteousness", and "revealed", as does Isa. 56:1). The thought in such passages is that God will not abandon his people. Since he is righteous, he will certainly deliver them.[325]

Paul's concentration on righteousness in Romans, and specifically on the righteousness of God, is part of the way he brings out the point that when God saves he does so in a way which accords with right. Much modern theology so stresses the note of victory in the atonement that it almost gives the impression that when God saves us, "might is right". He is strong enough to defeat all the forces of evil (however these be understood), and he does so. God does, of course, defeat evil. That is true. And it is an important truth. But it is not the whole truth. One of the truths Paul insists on is that God is righteous in the way he saves as well as in the fact that he saves.

I wonder whether perhaps Käsemann's well-known treatment goes astray at this point. Constantly linking power with righteousness, he can sum up his interesting discussion of "The Righteousness of God in Paul" in these terms: "His doctrine of the δικαιοσύνη θεοῦ demonstrates this: God's power reaches out for the world, and the world's salvation lies in its being recaptured for the sovereignty of God. For this very reason it is the gift of God and also the salvation of the individual human being when we become obedient to the divine righteousness."[326] Though he elsewhere says some important things about forensic aspects of justification and righteousness, when he comes to sum it all up he omits all reference to any such thing and concentrates on power and sovereignty. Granted that power is important and sovereignty is important, neither of these is basic to the biblical concept of *righteousness*. The connection with right is.

It is important to see that the righteousness of God is shown in the death of Christ (3:25, 26; cf. 3:22). Many discussions overlook this connection and thereby go grievously astray. As James Denney puts it, "In Paul the divine righteousness which constitutes gospel for sinners exposed to the divine wrath is revealed in Christ, and nowhere else."[327] We are not to understand

325. See further my *The Apostolic Preaching of the Cross* (London and Grand Rapids, 1965), ch. VIII. It is perhaps worth adding that the Qumran sect on occasion produced profound sayings expressive of the grace of God in salvation. Thus in the Hymns we read, "I know (that) righteousness is Thine, that in Thy mercies there is (hope for me), but without Thy grace (destruction) without end" (Vermes, p. 186); "By Thy goodness alone is man righteous" (Vermes, p. 192); "I lean on Thy grace and on the multitude of Thy mercies, for Thou wilt pardon iniquity, and through Thy righteousness (Thou wilt purify man) of his sin" (Vermes, p. 164). Unfortunately this standpoint is not uniformly maintained; cf. the note on 1:17. H. Conzelmann has an interesting comment after quoting passages from Qumran, "Here the pious admits his sinfulness in radical fashion and knows himself to be fully dependent on God's 'righteousness.' But Qumran knows no 'from faith alone'; here justification means radical submission to the law and not liberation from it" (*Interpretation*, XXII [1968], p. 182).

326. *New Testament Questions of Today* (London, 1969), pp. 181-82. The link between righteousness and power runs right through this discussion.

327. *The Christian Doctrine of Reconciliation* (London, 1918), p. 151.

the righteousness of God as an abstract quality or even as a general divine activity. It is preeminently to be seen in the atoning work of Christ; to overlook this is to miss a central thrust of Romans.

The expression "the righteousness of God" is ambiguous. It could mean "the righteousness which God himself exercises", "righteousness as an attribute of God or a quality in God". We have seen this meaning in Genesis 18:25, and it reappears in Romans 3:5, 25, etc. But the genitive "of God" might also denote origin,[328] in which case the whole expression means "a righteousness from God", "the right standing which God gives", a meaning which is required in Romans 3:21, 22; 10:3, etc. and is made abundantly plain by the use of the preposition in Philippians 3:9.[329] Some passages are not quite clear as to which meaning we should understand, but the important thing is the plain fact that Paul uses the expression in certain significant passages to bring out the truth that in the death of Christ God brings about a righteousness for those who believe.[330]

Additional Note B: TRUTH

Paul has three great thoughts about truth, one of which connects it with God, a second with the gospel, and a third with the Christian way of life.

1. Truth and God. Paul has the notable expression "the truth of God" (confined to Romans, 1:25; 3:7; 15:8). With this we should perhaps take his reference to the judgment of God as being "based on truth" (2:2). All these passages associate truth closely with God. It is not to be understood in purely human terms but only in connection with God. Sometimes it is linked with Christ, as when Paul says that he speaks the truth in Christ (9:1) or when he protests his reliability "as truth is in Jesus" (Eph. 4:21; NIV has "the truth that

---

328. BDF 163 see God as the originator. Cf. BAGD, *"the righteousness bestowed by God. . . .* In this area it closely approximates *salvation"*. Bruce cites H. K. Moulton's comment on the Pidgin translation of the New Testament for New Guinea, "We salute strokes of genius such as the translation of 'Justification': 'God 'e spik em olrite'" (p. 74 n.2).

329. ἐκ θεοῦ.

330. On 1:17 Luther remarks, "Here, too, *'the righteousness of God'* must not be understood as that righteousness by which he is righteous in himself, but as that righteousness by which we are made righteous (justified) by Him". Parry, however, comments, "'God's righteousness' i.e. righteousness as belonging to the character of God and consequently required by Him in the character of men" (CGT). SH argue strongly that we should understand both senses. Denney draws attention to an important consideration favoring the position of Luther: "The righteousness of God, conceived as a Divine attribute, may have appeared to Paul the great difficulty in the way of the justification of sinful men. God's righteousness in this sense is the sinner's condemnation. . . . What is wanted (always in consistency with God's righteousness as one of His inviolable attributes—the great point elaborated in iii.24-26) is a righteousness which, as man cannot produce it, must be from God. . . ." The divine attribute of righteousness means opposition to all unrighteousness and is bad news for sinful man. The passage requires the sense "that righteousness by which we are made righteous."

is in Jesus"). This is often misquoted in the form "the truth as it is in Jesus". But this distorts the sense. Paul is not saying that the truth is manifold and that we see part of it in Jesus. He is saying that we see truth, real truth, in Jesus (or in God), and that we see it nowhere else. Truth is inseparably connected with God.

2. *Truth and the Gospel.* When Paul speaks of "the truth of the gospel" (Gal. 2:5, 14), he probably means much the same as when he refers to "the word of truth" (Eph. 1:13; cf. "truthful speech", 2 Cor. 6:7, NIV). The same meaning is probably intended when we read of rightly dividing "the word of truth" (2 Tim. 2:15).[331] There can be no doubt when we read of "the word of truth, the gospel" (Col. 1:5; better, "the word of the truth of the gospel"). Clearly Paul sees a close connection between the gospel, God's way of saving people, and the truth, which, as we have just seen, must be understood in relation to God. The truth is seen in a special way in the gospel. This appears to be in mind also when Paul speaks of coming to the knowledge of truth (1 Tim. 2:4; 4:3; 2 Tim. 2:25; 3:7; Tit. 1:1), or of believing the truth (2 Thess. 2:12, 13). It is probably not out of sight also when he speaks of recognizing the grace of God in truth (Col. 1:6). He can set side by side "the word of God" and "setting forth the truth" (2 Cor. 4:2), apparently as equivalent statements.

Unfortunately, however, people do not always obey the gospel. This appears to be the case in some of Paul's references to truth. Thus he can ask, "Who cut in on you and kept you from obeying the truth?" (Gal. 5:7). Those who reject the gospel "refused to love the truth" (2 Thess. 2:10); they "reject the truth" (Rom. 2:8). As we might have expected, false teachers have lost their hold on truth ("have been robbed of the truth", 1 Tim. 6:5, NIV). They have turned away from the truth (2 Tim. 2:18; 4:4; Tit. 1:14). Paul declares that he is "for the truth" (2 Cor. 13:8). By contrast evil people "oppose the truth" (2 Tim. 3:8); it is difficult to imagine that the gospel is not primarily in mind in this passage, though the thought may include more. This is also the case with those wicked people who hinder the truth (Rom. 1:18).

3. *Truth and the Christian Life.* The third large group of passages connect truth with the way Christians live or should live. Paul speaks of the new man as "created to be like God in true righteousness and holiness" (or better, "in righteousness and holiness of the truth", Eph. 4:24); again he says that "the fruit of the light consists in all . . . truth" (Eph. 5:9). Paul is a teacher of the Gentiles "in faith and truth" (1 Tim. 2:7; NIV has "a teacher of the true faith"). Christians are to "keep the Festival" (a striking way of bringing out the joyful character of the Christian life) "with bread without yeast, the bread of sincerity and truth" (1 Cor. 5:8). So central to the Christian way is truth that the church may be characterized as "the pillar and foundation of the truth" (1 Tim. 3:15). And Paul can speak of the Old Testament law as "the embodiment of knowledge and truth" (Rom. 2:20). Christians should understand that the law gives guidance as they seek to live in the service of God.

---

331. So, e.g., the commentaries by D. Guthrie, M. Dibelius, J. N. D. Kelly, *in loc.* That it means the Old Testament is less likely.

There are, of course, passages in which Paul uses truth in much our sense, such as when he refers to telling the truth (2 Cor. 7:14; 12:6; Phil. 1:18). But it is clear that often he gave the term a richer and fuller meaning than we normally do. And it is equally clear that for Paul truth is given its definitive shape by what God has done in Christ.

Romans 2

2. The Condemnation of the Jew, 2:1-16

There is considerable discussion as to whether the opening part of this chapter refers to the Jew (who is not specifically addressed until v. 17) or the Gentile (who is certainly in mind in vv. 12-16; cf. vv. 9-10). One view is that Paul has in mind neither of them as such, but "men of moral insight and ideals" (Foreman).[1] Such people would applaud Paul's condemnation of blatant sinners of every race (ch. 1). But does that mean that they were guiltless? Not at all. Paul now moves on to show that those who sit in judgment on their fellows are as guilty as those they judge. There is a natural tendency to justify ourselves for the wrong we do by condemning people who do other evils that we think are worse. "The Pharisee is always present in each one of us" (Leenhardt). Even when we try to help people, we do not start with the premise that we as well as they are sinners needing God's forgiveness; we simply try to improve their moral conduct. Paul's point is that we are all involved in a solidarity of sin that embraces the whole human race. He is concerned with the gospel as God's way for the whole person and for the whole of mankind (not with self-justification or minor moral improvements).

But, while all this is true and some of it was probably in Paul's mind, it seems more likely that he is thinking here primarily of the Jew.[2] The way the term "Jew" is used in verse 17 does not look like the introduction of a new topic (and cf. "the Jew first", vv. 9, 10). Jews would have agreed heartily with all that Paul has had to say about the Gentile world. They were always ready to condemn the Gentiles, but they saw themselves as on a much higher plane. A Jew could write, "Now therefore weigh in a balance our iniquities and those of the inhabitants of the world; and so it will be found which way the turn of the scale will incline. When have the inhabitants of the earth not sinned in thy sight? Or what nation has kept thy commandments so well?" (2 Esdr.

---

1. Foreman sees the Jews as in mind in 2:17–3:20; Paul, he says, "does not fully explain his argument, nor logically prove it. He just tosses out the hand grenade and lets the splinters hit where they will." The Reformers, such as Calvin and Luther, view the words as applying generally (they do not refer specifically to the Jews); in modern times such views are shared by scholars like Barrett, Leenhardt, Lenski, and Harrisville. O'Neill calls in a glossator to account for some of the words, leaving the remainder to follow on logically from ch. 1.

2. That the passage refers to the Jews is held by Barclay, Cranfield, Dodd, Käsemann, Lagrange, and others.

3:34-35). The sufferings of the Jews were seen as different from those of the Gentiles: "For when they [i.e., the Israelites] were tried, though they were being disciplined in mercy, they learned how the ungodly were tormented when judged in wrath. For thou didst test them as a father does in warning, but thou didst examine the ungodly as a stern king does in condemnation" (Wis. 11:9-10). The whole of Wisdom 11–15 accords with this,[3] a parallel which Nygren regards as "quite decisive" (p. 114). The Jew seems to have combined two attitudes, one which stressed the community and the other the individual. He thought of his nation as the community of the saved. When he stood before God it was not simply as an individual, to be dealt with on the grounds of his personal record in keeping or not keeping the law. He belonged to God's own people and would be saved along with the rest of that people. His circumcision placed him firmly within the saved community. He might be punished for his sins, but he would not be eternally lost, for "All Israelites have a share in the world to come" (Sanh. 10:1).[4] But if the Jew put an emphasis in this way on the communal aspect, he did not mind stressing the individual in concrete situations. He regarded himself as on a different level from any Gentile with whom he happened to be confronted, and indulged in the luxury of despising him. A further point to be kept in mind is that what Paul says bears interesting resemblances to some aspects of the teaching of Jesus (e.g., Matt. 7:1-4; Luke 6:41-42), and this was certainly addressed to Jews.

Thus on the whole it seems best to think of the Jews as primarily in mind throughout this section. But the language is general enough to have an application to everyone, and sometimes Paul glances at the wider world (notably in vv. 9-10, 12-16).[5] His style throughout is lively, and many commentators see here the use of the diatribe form, a form which allows for spirited argument between the writer and his readers.[6]

a. The danger of judging others, 2:1-3

> [1]You, therefore, have no excuse, you who pass judgment on someone else, for at whatever point you judge the other, you are condemning yourself, because you who pass judgment do the same things. [2]Now we know that God's judgment against those who do such things is based on truth. [3]So when you, a mere man,

3. Many students of Rom. 2 are impressed with this. They find it incredible that a Jew should so consistently reproduce points of superiority claimed for his nation in Wisdom 11–15 and not have Jews in mind.

4. Cf. Justin, "they beguile themselves and you, supposing that the everlasting kingdom will be assuredly given to those of the dispersion who are of Abraham after the flesh, although they be sinners, and faithless, and disobedient towards God" (*Trypho* 140; ANF, I, p. 269).

5. Paul is "thinking—especially, yet not exclusively—of the Jews" (Brunner). A similar position is taken by Bruce, Murray, Parry, Knox, and others.

6. But see the note on 3:1-4.

pass judgment on them and yet do the same things, do you think you will escape God's judgment?

Paul begins by pointing out that those who engage in the luxury of condemning others are putting themselves in jeopardy, for in doing so they condemn themselves. It is always easier to see the mote in someone else's eye than the plank in our own.

1. *Therefore* links this with the preceding; what Paul says now arises out of what he said at the end of the previous chapter. There is a difficulty in that it is not obvious how the guilt of the Gentile world brings the Jew under condemnation.[7] We seem to require that those addressed here are included in the previous section. The explanation may be that, while it is true that in chapter 1 Gentiles are primarily in mind, the sins of all people are castigated, and here, while the Jews are at center stage, all who judge others are condemned.[8]

The word translated *have no excuse* is often used in a legal sense. It means "without reasoned defence". Paul has already used it of the Gentiles (1:20; see the note in Earle), and his use of it now with respect to the Jews shows that there is no difference. The Jew is in just as indefensible a position as are the Gentiles. When he condemns somebody else he condemns himself. Paul adopts a device he uses quite frequently, that of an address to an imaginary opponent.[9] BDF note this as a way of taking something universal and making it vivid by referring it to an individual.[10] "O man" (RSV; GNB paraphrases with "my friend", while NIV reduces it to *you*) is far from being a usual form of address; indeed, this "O" of address is found no more than 15 times in the entire New Testament (three times in Romans). It often lends something of an emotional tone to the address, but this is not obvious here.[11] "Whoever you are" (RSV) keeps the address general. But RSV's "when you judge another" (like NIV) is not as accurate as KJV's "whosoever thou art that judgest". Paul is not addressing a specific person and qualifying this by referring to those occasions on which he judges. He is addressing anyone who judges and addressing him because he judges. Preeminently he has the Jew in mind, though we should not overlook the fact that he expresses the idea very generally. Anyone who judges, whether Jew or Gentile, puts himself in danger,

---

7. But cf. Nygren: *"Precisely 'therefore,'* because that which has been said about the Gentiles is also true as to the Jews, 'therefore' the Jew is himself without excuse, when he judges."

8. Others suggest that διό has lost its force (Michel), or that it anticipates the following (Haldane; perhaps "proleptic", Knox; Murray sees this as possible, but Cranfield asks for evidence that διό is used in this manner). SH, Lenski, and others see it as referring, not to the immediately preceding, but to the whole of 1:18-32. Barrett views 1:32b as a parenthesis, so that the connection is with 1:32a. Käsemann and others think it may be part of "an early marginal gloss" (p. 54).

9. Cf. 2:17ff.; 8:2; 9:19-20; 11:17ff.; 13:3-4; 14:4, 10, 15, 20-22.

10. BDF 281. The first person singular may also be used in this way.

11. BAGD see it as "mostly expressing emotion (at the beginning of a clause)"; Turner sees "no great emotion" here (M, III, p. 33), and BDF 146[1b] is similar.

for[12] in passing judgment he condemns himself. Passing judgment[13] on another person[14] means condemning oneself.

This is because the person judging does *the same things*. This would be a startling charge to a Jew. He was sure that the Gentile did all manner of wicked things, as Paul has made plain in chapter 1. But he himself lived in a very different way, he thought. He was especially firm in having nothing to do with idolatry, which Paul has castigated so severely. But when he condemned the other person, the Jew was committing basically the same sin, even though the formal expression was different; "The sin of the Jews was the same, but their sins were not" (Denney).[15]

2. Paul not infrequently appeals to his correspondents' knowledge (*we know;* cf. 3:19; 6:6; 7:14; 8:22, 28). He varies his approach by using the participle "knowing" (5:3; 6:9; 13:11). Or he can say "you know" (2:18) or ask the question "Do you not know?" (6:3, 16; 7:1; 11:2; cf. 2:4). All this is an invitation to sweet reasonableness. Where the occasion demands it, Paul can be dogmatic and issue authoritative instructions. But he likes to enlist the intelligent cooperation of his readers and have them see the point for themselves (as when he tells the Corinthians, "I speak to sensible people; judge for yourselves what I say", 1 Cor. 10:15).

"The judgment of God"[16] is an expression which occurs again in verse 3 and nowhere else in the New Testament (though cf. 1 Pet. 4:17; Rev. 18:20). But, though the expression is rare, it is everywhere assumed that the judgment is God's and that it is "according to truth"; no sinner can face it with equanimity. Dodd sees this verse as the Jew's complacent utterance, with Paul's retort coming in the next verse. Others put the words in quotation marks,[17] but the meaning appears to be much the same. Such a position is possible, but it seems more likely that Paul is making these words his own and using them with deadly seriousness. The Jew is in real danger, for "God condemns that sort of behavior impartially" (JB; cf. v. 11). God's judgment is

12. ἐν ᾧ may mean ἐν τούτῳ ἐν ᾧ, "in that in which" (Denney); or ἐν τούτῳ ὅτι, "thereby". Or it may have a temporal meaning, "while" (as in Mark 2:19; John 5:7). BDF 219 [2] see ἐν as instrumental and the meaning as "while, because"; Turner also sees it as meaning "because" (M, III, p. 253).

13. Lenski insists that it is the passing of judgment that matters, whether the judgment is favorable or unfavorable. To pass judgment is to take up a position of superiority, whatever the verdict. It implies that the judge is in the clear. Cf. also Barrett, "Behind all the sins of 1:29ff. lies the sin of idolatry, which reveals man's ambition to put himself in the place of God and so to be his own Lord. But this is precisely what the judge does when he assumes the right to condemn his fellow-creatures."

14. Strictly ἕτερος means the other of two and is used to contrast one definite person with another; here the contrast is with αὐτός, and the meaning "one's neighbor" or "one's fellow" (BAGD).

15. Cranfield points out that there are more ways than one of breaking the seventh commandment (cf. Matt. 5:27-28). Of course, the same is true of the other commandments.

16. Strictly κρίμα denotes the sentence rather than the process of judging (κρίσις). But the two are not sharply distinguished.

17. E.g., Moffatt. Barrett also does this, and comments, "it is perhaps not wrong to say, the Jew in Paul himself".

"according to truth";[18] that is, it is just, and it is exercised toward all those who do the kind of thing Paul has been talking about. In judgment it is not nationality or privilege that matters, but deeds.

3. The verb translated *think* (which comes first in the Greek) is quite Pauline.[19] It is properly an arithmetical word and means "to count", "to reckon". But it is often used metaphorically where numbers are not in question with a meaning like "take into account", "reckon", "consider". It is a word that invites to reasoning, which may be why it turns up so often in Romans. It is suited to the argumentative style that Paul adopts throughout this letter.

NIV has altered the meaning a little with its *when you . . . pass judgment . . . and yet do. . . .* It is not so much *when* as "you who do such things". Throughout this section Paul is not speaking of someone who does a variety of things and addressing him *when* he does this or that. He is speaking to one whose characteristic is that he does certain things, specifically that he judges others. To this he links the further thought *and yet do the same things.*[20] The judge is as guilty as those he judges. When Paul goes on to say *you will escape,* his *you* is emphatic:[21] "Do you think that *you* of all people will escape. . . ?" Some Jews did expect precisely this: "even if we sin we are thine" (Wis. 15:2). Haldane points out that three things are implied in what Paul says: the Jew can avoid neither judgment nor being condemned nor the carrying out of the sentence. For "the judgment of God" see the note on v. 2.

b. The need for repentance, 2:4

> 4*Or do you show contempt for the riches of his kindness, tolerance and patience, not realizing that God's kindness leads you toward repentance?*

An important part of the teaching of this epistle is that God is a merciful God; his purposes are always purposes of mercy. He may at times be engaged in activities like judgment that seem to the casual observer to be directed against the sinner. But even God's judgments must be seen in a context of mercy; they are meant to lead people to repentance and forgiveness. God

18. κατὰ ἀλήθειαν. Knox comments, "The impressive 'according to truth' (KJV) is to be preferred to the more casual 'rightly' of the RSV. . . . Paul's point is that God's judgment is not according to race or nationality (cf. vss. 10-11), but is based on the moral facts."

19. λογίζομαι occurs 40 times in the New Testament, of which 34 are in Paul, 19 in Romans. It is thus a word that is very much a part of the argument of this epistle.

20. "The knowledge of the good is not the good itself" (Brunner). There is one article with the two participles—the same person both judges and does the things in question. NIV is not correct with *the same things*, which would be τὰ αὐτά; the Greek is simply αὐτά.

21. He uses the pronoun σύ only 24 times out of 173 in the New Testament. Its use here is thus not due to a stylistic preference of the apostle, and his sparing use of the term means that when he does employ it, it is with full meaning. He wants to emphasize it.

never punishes for the sake of punishment. And if this is the case with judgment, much more is it so with God's forbearance. So, before he brings out what is in store for the impenitent sinner, Paul has a short section in which he speaks of God's kindness as leading people to repentance.[22]

4. Paul's *Or* may pose a sharp alternative: either the Jew must consider himself immune from judgment *or* he must despise God's kindness. But more probably it is used to make much the same point as the preceding.[23] Anyone who thinks he will escape judgment despises God's kindness, treats it as of no account. *Riches* properly denotes material wealth, but it is often used metaphorically (cf. 9:23; Eph. 1:7, etc.). Here the meaning is that God's *kindness* and the other qualities mentioned are in no short supply. *Kindness* (cf. 11:22) renders a word that is difficult to translate exactly.[24] The basic thought is that of goodness (this same word is translated "good" in 3:12). But it is the goodness that is goodness of heart, not that which is austerely correct. The translation "kindness" brings out this benevolent aspect, but we should not be unmindful of the fact that goodness is also involved.[25] Paul is thinking of God's goodness, which is seen in the kindness he shows to his people.

Tolerance[26] translates a term found twice only in the New Testament, both in Romans. In Greek usage generally it denotes *"stopping, esp. of hostilities . . . armistice, truce"* (LSJ). God does not punish the sinner immediately after he sins. He holds back his final judgment and thus gives the sinner an interval in which he can repent and turn to God. But the important thing to notice about this word is that it points to a truce, not a peace. It is temporary. It implies a limit. If the sinner does nothing but sin, if he rejects the invitation to repent (cf. Eccl. 8:11), then in due course he must face God with all his sin

---

22. This is one of the sections that lead many to think that Paul was referring to Jews. Granted that God is rich in mercy to all people, could any Jew use language like this without recalling God's mercy and longsuffering towards his people throughout the Old Testament?

23. BAGD class this with passages "to introduce a question which is parallel to a preceding one or supplements it". Cf. Murray, "The purpose of this 'or' is not that of proposing alternatives; it is rhetorical like the questions themselves. And the effect is to press home upon the Jew in *crescendo* fashion the impiety of which he is guilty. In other words, these are not alternative ways of interpreting his attitude but different ways of stating what his attitude is."

24. χρηστότης is "not the attribute by which God is good (holiness), but by which he does good (benevolence)" (Shedd). K. Weiss says that in the Pauline corpus it "denotes God's gracious attitude and acts toward sinners", and that its meaning is the same as that of the corresponding adjective later in the verse (TDNT, IX, p. 490). In the New Testament it is used only by Paul (ten times, five in Romans).

25. Trench differentiates χρηστότης from ἀγαθωσύνη and sees Christ as showing the latter when he drove the traders out of the temple or denounced the scribes and Pharisees. We see his χρηστότης in his reception of the sinful woman (Luke 7:37-50) (*Synonyms*, pp. 234-35). Barclay makes the same distinction.

26. ἀνοχή (again in 3:26) "is the forbearance which suspends punishment" (Denney). It is not forgiveness but the suspension of penalty; the penalty may be imposed later. Cf. Trench, it "by no means implies that the wrath will not be executed at the last; nay, involves that it certainly will, unless he be found under new conditions of repentance and obedience" (*Synonyms*, p. 200).

about him. God's forbearance is wonderful, and eloquent of his deep concern for people. But it is not forgiveness.

Patience[27] renders a word which literally means something like "long-tempered" (as against "short-tempered"). It means patience with people, the ability to bear long in the face of disappointment and opposition. Paul sees God as enduring with patience the continuing failure of sinners, and more specifically sinners from his own people Israel, to turn away from their sin. The combination with the two preceding nouns gives a wonderful picture of God's refusal to punish and of his goodwill towards people, even sinful people.

Not realizing is more literally "not knowing", and the ignorance is culpable; the person ought to know[28] (for Paul's appeal to knowledge see the note on v. 2). The word translated *kindness* is not the same as the one earlier in this verse, though it is related.[29] There seems no significant difference, and the addition of the cognate word simply puts emphasis on the idea that both convey. That which is good and kind in God is directed towards bringing[30] people to *repentance*. This term means a change of mind, specifically a change of mind about sin.[31] It refers to that change which comes over a sinner when he sees his wrongdoing no longer as attractive but as damnable. He turns away from it. This means abandoning the security of the old way; God's demand for repentance is a demand that we trust him, even though it means forsaking our human securities. In the New Testament repentance is not simply negative. It means turning to a new life in Christ, a life of active service to God.[32] It should not be confused with remorse, which is a deep sorrow for

27. μακροθυμία, a comparatively late word and one that is rare outside the Bible (in the New Testament it occurs 14 times, ten in Paul). J. Horst says that it "takes on a distinctive depth in biblical usage" (TDNT, IV, p. 376). As in 9:22, it is here related to wrath. God's is angry with all evil indeed, but his anger must be understood in conjunction with his longsuffering which gives people ample opportunity to repent.

28. Cf. Lenski, "Is it too much to say that ἀγνοῶν means, 'will not see'?" The person in question does not want to be shaken out of his self-satisfied, sinful state.

29. The word is χρηστόν, the neuter of the adjective used as a noun. Perhaps we should notice that both this word and μακρόθυμος are used of God's attitude to the Jews in Wis. 15:1. "Peculiar to Paul (Heb) is the use of a neuter sing. adjective like an abstract, mostly with a dependent gen." (BDF 263 [2]). They further say, "χρηστότης is used in the same vs. in a different sense", but do not say what the sense is. Others hold that the sense is much the same (e.g., Turner, M, III, p. 14).

30. The present tense of the Greek is the basis of NIV *leads* (cf. KJV, "leadeth"). But increasingly people are understanding the verb in some such sense as RSV, "is meant to lead you". This takes the present as conative, which Moule sees used "of action attempted, but not accomplished"; he understands the meaning here as *"is trying or tending to lead"* (IBNTG, p. 8). For the thought of God leading people to repent cf. Wis. 11:23; 12:10, 19. Repentance is God's gift (Acts 5:31; 11:18; 2 Tim. 2:25).

31. In the New Testament μετάνοια is basically Lukan (Luke five times, Acts six times); Paul has it four times. The change it denotes does not come easily. As Käsemann says, "The danger of the pious person is that of isolating God's gifts from the claim which is given with them, and of forgetting to relate forbearance and patience to the Judge of the last day" (p. 55).

32. Hendriksen, who understands the word to mean "conversion" here, says,

sin (cf. 2 Cor. 7:10) but lacks the positive note in repentance. It is this thoroughgoing attitude to which God's goodness is leading people.[33]

c. Judgment, 2:5-16

> [5]But because of your stubbornness and your unrepentant heart, you are storing up wrath against yourself for the day of God's wrath, when his righteous judgment will be revealed. [6]God "will give to each person according to what he has done."[a] [7]To those who by persistence in doing good seek glory, honor and immortality, he will give eternal life. [8]But for those who are self-seeking and who reject the truth and follow evil, there will be wrath and anger. [9]There will be trouble and distress for every human being who does evil: first for the Jew, then for the Gentile; [10]but glory, honor and peace for everyone who does good: first for the Jew, then for the Gentile. [11]For God does not show favoritism.
>
> [12]All who sin apart from the law will also perish apart from the law, and all who sin under the law will be judged by the law. [13]For it is not those who hear the law who are righteous in God's sight, but it is those who obey the law who will be declared righteous. [14](Indeed, when Gentiles, who do not have the law, do by nature things required by the law, they are a law for themselves, even though they do not have the law, [15]since they show that the requirements of the law are written on their hearts, their consciences also bearing witness, and their thoughts now accusing, now even defending them.) [16]This will take place on the day when God will judge men's secrets through Jesus Christ, as my gospel declares.

a6 Psalm 62:12; Prov. 24:12

Paul points to what the impenitent are doing to themselves and goes on to the general principle involved. Judgment means that those who have acted in accordance with God's will will be rewarded, whereas those who have opposed God will be punished.

5. *But* is an adversative conjunction; what follows stands in contrast to the preceding. Instead of repentance there is hardness and impenitence. *Because of*[34] makes a causal connection. *Stubbornness*[35] translates a word found here only in the New Testament (though the cognate verb occurs in 9:18 and elsewhere). Its original meaning seems to have been what is hard to the touch, or rough. But it came to be used metaphorically of hardness of heart,

---

"Conversion indicates a complete turnabout". So it does, but μετάνοια is concerned with that aspect of the "turnabout" which means forsaking sin. By "repentance" Hendriksen appears to understand what is better termed "remorse".

33. Behm points out that for the Stoic "the wise man is above a μετάνοια. This . . . would represent him as the victim of error, which as the opposite of the virtue of wisdom is beneath the dignity of the sage" (TDNT, IV, p. 980). Repentance is a biblical distinctive, not a commonplace.

34. κατά may be used of the norm, "according to, in accordance with", but it may also mean simply "because of, as a result of, on the basis of" (BAGD, who see this meaning here).

35. The word is σκληρότης; it is applied to Israel in LXX of Deut. 9:27; cf. 31:27.

which of course is its meaning here.[36] *Unrepentant* is another word found only in this passage in the New Testament; indeed, as far as our present knowledge goes, this is its first occurrence in Greek literature. It often has the meaning "irrevocable" in its later usage, but here the meaning is clearly as NIV. For *heart* see the note on 1:21; it will mean here the whole inner life. In the case of those Paul has in mind the inner life is directed away from God. There is a hardness, a refusal to forsake sin and take God's way.

In this context *storing up* is a picturesque word. It is connected with the idea of "treasure" and means "to lay up as treasure" (cf. "riches", v. 4).[37] The person Paul has in mind is laying up for his treasure—the wrath of God! For *wrath* see the note on 1:18. It signifies God's settled opposition to all that is evil, and not some irrational passion. We should not miss Paul's point that sin will inevitably reap its due reward, and that God will be active in the process. *The day of wrath* (there is no *God's* in the Greek) is an unusual expression, found here only in the New Testament (Rev. 6:17 has "the great day of their wrath"). There is no real doubt that it refers to the Day of Judgment,[38] and that it views that day from the aspect of the punishment of evil. Many things might be said about that day, but one is certainly that then God's settled opposition to evil will reach its consummation.

That day will be not only one of wrath but of revelation (Paul says "day of wrath and revelation"). "Revelation" is another typically Pauline word;[39] it signifies the making known to people of something previously existent, but not known. God's righteousness in judgment was always a fact, but people have not always appreciated it, nor will they until the day of revelation. Then it will be clear beyond all doubting. *Righteous judgment* is one word in the Greek, the compound being found here only in the New Testament and not often in any earlier writing.[40] The meaning is probably much the same as

36. Earle reminds us that "arteriosclerosis" ("hardening of the arteries") derives from this word, and he speaks of "spiritual sclerosis", the "hardening of the spiritual arteries".

37. Stählin refers to the Jewish idea of a person's accumulation of capital in heaven by his deeds: "While the interest on this capital (קרן), acc. to the Jewish view, is already enjoyed on earth in the form of merit and reward, and only the capital will be paid back at the end, the capital of wrath grows until the Last Judgment and will then be paid with compound interest; hence this day is the ἡμέρα ὀργῆς, R. 2:5" (TDNT, V, p. 438). The word is used in LXX of Prov. 1:18 of people who store up evil for themselves.

38. Barth, however, takes the words closely with "store up". The meaning then will be that at this present time when the gospel is being preached, these people, by rejecting God's offer, keep storing up wrath. Cranfield sees this as a serious option and one which does no violence to the Greek, but he opts for the eschatological meaning.

39. Paul uses ἀποκάλυψις 13 times out of its 18 New Testament occurrences; no book has it more often than Romans, 1 Corinthians, and 1 Peter, each with three occurrences.

40. δικαιοκρισία is found in Hos. 6:5 in the Quinta of Origen's Hexapla (see Hatch and Redpath), and in Test. Levi 3:2; 15:2. MM say, "The emphasis which this compound lays on the character of the Judge rather than on the character of the judgment in Rom 2⁵ . . . receives support from two passages in the Oxyrhyncus papyri" (the passages are dated A.D. 303 and fifth century A.D.).

when Paul uses the two words instead of the compound (2 Thess. 1:5).[41]

6. With a quotation from Psalm 62:12 Paul sums up what judgment means. His verb *give* (RSV, "render"; JB, "repay") has about it the air of requital, the payment of what is due. *To each person* makes this personal; recompense is an individual matter, not a collective punishment. And this just requital, this paying back of what is due, will be done to each *according to what he has done* (cf. Job 34:11; Prov. 24:12; Jer. 17:10, and the New Testament passages cited on p. 147). It is the invariable teaching of the Bible and not the peculiar viewpoint of any one writer or group of writers that judgment will be on the basis of works, though salvation is all of grace. Works are important. They are the outward expression of what the person is deep down. In the believer they are the expression of faith, in the unbeliever the expression of unbelief and that whether by way of legalism or antinomianism. The Jew held that salvation was bound up with the law. Very well. Let him look at what this means. It means that a person's works, not his claims to belong to a favored group, are of the greatest significance, for God will render to each according to those works. The Jew cannot rest in any fancied security of privilege but must look to the day when his works will be subjected to the divine scrutiny. Paul is inviting him to consider how those works will stand up on the Day of Judgment.

7. Paul proceeds to particularize and to divide those being judged into two classes.[42] His word for *persistence* denotes an active, manly fortitude. It is used of the soldier who, in the thick of a hard battle, gives as much as he gets; he is not dismayed by the blows he receives, but fights on to the end. Linked as it is here with *doing good*, it is seen by BAGD as meaning "perseverance in doing what is right."[43] Barrett translates, "those who with patient endurance look beyond their own well-doing". He sees this word as "the vital word", and he also says: "Those who view their own activity with patient endurance attest thereby that they are seeking what is not to be found in any human being and doing. . . . The reward of eternal life, then, is promised to those who do not regard their good works as an end in themselves, but see them as marks not of human achievement but of hope in God. Their trust is not in their good works, but in God, the only source of glory, honour, and incorruption."

I am not sure that all this is to be found in the word, but it seems that this is Paul's basic thought (cf. Matt. 24:13; Heb. 3:14). He is certainly not speaking of law works as so many ways of acquiring merit. He is speaking of an attitude, the attitude of those who *seek* certain qualities, not of those who keep certain laws or try to merit a certain reward. Their trust is in God, not in their own achievement. He refers to those whose lives are oriented in a certain

41. SH see a difference. They think that the compound denotes "not so much the character of the judgement as the character of the Judge." This would agree with the context and may be right, but the word formation looks rather to the act of judgment. Cranfield disagrees with SH and sees no difference of meaning from 2 Thess. 1:5.

42. Cf. Bruce, "Paul is not teaching salvation by works here, but emphasizing God's impartiality as between Jew and Gentile."

43. The word is ὑπομονή; cf. BDF 163; M, III, p. 212.

way. Their minds are not set on material prosperity or the like, nor on happiness, nor even on being religious. They are set on glory and honor and immortality, qualities which come from a close walk with God. The bent of their lives is towards heavenly things.

Paul speaks of doing *good*, employing a word he uses often in Romans.[44] He goes on to link *glory*[45] with honor (as is done in v. 10; 1 Tim. 1:17; Heb. 2:7, 9; 1 Pet. 1:7; 2 Pet. 1:17, and several times in Revelation). *Glory* might refer to something that is ascribed to God, and perhaps *honor* also, but *immortality*[46] would be a curious word to use in this connection. People do not "seek" God's immortality, though they may seek immortality for themselves. We should take all three as the objects of our search. This linking of glory,[47] honor, and immortality points to a search that is not done from selfish motives (as the worldly-minded seek their favorite pleasures). It springs from a sense of values that arises from the conviction that nothing can compare with these qualities and that these are attained only as the gifts of God.

God gives *eternal* life, the adjective being characteristic of Paul and John.[48] Strictly it means "pertaining to an age", and it was applied to the age to come (rather than to the age before creation or the present age). Since that age was not thought of as coming to an end, the expression "into the age" was a way of saying "forever". Similarly the life that "pertains to an age", the age to come, is life that will not end; thus "eternal" is a reasonable translation. But we should not overlook the fact that life in the age to come is characterized by much more than longevity. It is life of a special quality, life lived in the very presence of God.[49] *Life* is another word often used by both Paul and John.[50]

44. ἀγαθός is found 104 times in the New Testament, 47 being in Paul. He has it 21 times in Romans, though no more than four times in any other epistle. Clearly in this letter he is taking a marked interest in what is and what is not good.

45. δόξα occurs 77 times in the Pauline writings (16 in Romans), out of a New Testament total of 165 (next is John with 18); clearly it is an important concept for Paul. In Greek generally it has a meaning like "opinion", but in the New Testament "the word is used for the most part in a sense for which there is no Greek analogy whatever . . . it denotes 'divine and heavenly radiance,' the 'loftiness and majesty' of God, and even the 'being of God' and His world" (G. Kittel, TDNT, II, p. 237). This seems to arise because in LXX it so often translates כבוד and picks up some of its meaning. When it is used of people in the New Testament, Kittel finds participation important: "Participation in δόξα, whether here in hope or one day in consummation, is participation in Christ" (*ibid.*, p. 250). Cf. G. Henton Davies, "the glory in Christians is Christ in them, and this in turn is the hope of glory (Col. 1:27)" (IDB, II, p. 402). Paul often uses "glory" to denote the final blessedness of the believer, but rarely uses terms like "heaven" (though cf. 2 Cor. 5:1).

46. ἀφθαρσία = "incorruption" (used in 1 Cor. 15.42 of the resurrection body). The word denotes "the state of not being subject to corruption" and thus immortality.

47. JB has "renown" in place of "glory". TH, however, says that this "would seem to suggest a wrong emphasis, since 'renown' is the praise which men give, whereas 'glory' is the gift of God."

48. αἰώνιος is found 70 times in the New Testament, of which 21 occurrences are in Paul and 17 in John. The word is the adjective of αἰών, "an age".

49. Cf. Nigel Turner, ζωή αἰώνιος "is the life to come, though we may have the promise and foretaste of it now. The expression stands primarily for a quality of life" (*Christian Words*, p. 456). See also the note in my *The Gospel according to John* (Grand Rapids, 1971), pp. 226-27.

50. Paul uses it 37 times and John 36 times; the New Testament total is 135.

117

They are both interested in the fact that the gospel brings people life. To believe on Jesus Christ is to enter an experience so transforming that one can be said to live only then. And since this new quality of life is *eternal*, it is permanent.

8. As Paul turns to those who do not seek the things of God, he uses the word *But* to introduce the contrast. The word translated *self-seeking* is not common; in the New Testament it occurs five times in Paul, twice in James, and nowhere else. Its meaning is disputed. Traditionally it has been held to mean "factious", but in recent times "selfishness" and the like have many supporters.[51] There does seem to be an attitude of self-centeredness about it, perhaps coupled with a contentious spirit. Paul uses the noun (not the adjective, as NIV) with a meaning like "those who are of" the quality, "those whose conduct is rooted" in it.[52] People thus motivated *reject*[53] *the truth*. How can they obey it? They have put themselves in the opposite camp; they have given their allegiance to evil, not to God. Out of their wrong motive they disobey the truth and give their obedience to unrighteousness. For *evil* see the note on 1:29 (where it is translated "wickedness").

At this point there is an interesting change of construction. Paul said that God "will give eternal life" (v. 7), but when he comes to *wrath and anger* he has no verb and most translators supply *there will be*.[54] It may be that Paul is reluctant to ascribe this punishing activity to God in quite as direct a manner as the giving of eternal life (cf. 9:22-23 where he has the active with God as subject when he speaks of "the objects of his mercy" but the passive when he

---

51. The word is ἐριθεία. This word looks as though it might be derived from ἔρις, "strife", which would lead to a meaning like "factious". But many contend that the word is derived from ἔριθος, "a hired laborer", from which we get the verb ἐριθεύομαι, "to work for hire". Politicians sometimes hired people to promote their cause; thus the verb came to be used for doing things for the sake of money (and thus for self-interest) or for the sake of the man who pays. This means the promotion of a cause without regard to principle, and leads to party spirit or factiousness. The correct derivation is not known for certain, but that from ἔριθος is favored in recent times. Barrett takes this as correct and argues that the word means "those who are out for quick and selfish profit on their own account" (cf. GNB, "selfish"). Büchsel understands it as " 'base self-seeking,' or simply as 'baseness', the nature of those who cannot lift their gaze to higher things" (TDNT, II, p. 661). Käsemann recognizes that "selfishness" or "selfish ambition" is widely held to be the meaning, but "baseness" (Büchsel) and "striving for recognition" (Schlier) "also call for consideration" (p. 59). We cannot be sure of the derivation, but the way the word is used in the New Testament favors something like "factiousness" (2 Cor. 12:20; Gal. 5:20; Phil. 1:17; 2:3; Jas. 3:14, 16).

52. ἐκ here denotes origin; these people have their root in factiousness. Contrast ἐκ πίστεως in 3:26, and cf. 4:12, 14; Gal. 3:7.

53. The verb is ἀπειθέω, "disobey". BAGD say, "in our lit. the disobedience is always toward God or his ordinances"; "since in the view of the early Christians, the supreme disobedience was a refusal to believe their gospel, ἀ. may be restricted in some passages to the mng. *disbelieve, be an unbeliever*. This sense, though greatly disputed (it is not found outside our lit.) seems most probable" in certain passages, "and only slightly less prob. in Ro 2:8. . . ." MM do not cite this meaning from the papyri.

54. Or ἀποδώσεται. We might also, with Godet, regard it as "better still, an exclamation: 'for them, wrath!' " Turner sees it as "Nom. for accus. (a slip)" (M, III, p. 317).

turns to "the objects of his wrath—prepared for destruction").[55] For *wrath* see
the note on 1:18. The word translated *anger*[56] is very close in meaning, and
indeed many assert that there is no difference between them.[57] Etymologically there is, for *anger* derives from a root conveying the idea of boiling
up. It is thus suited to the idea of a passionate outburst. It is the more vivid
term. *Wrath* has about it the idea of a swelling, such as the swelling of buds as
the sap rises and in due course causes them to burst. This word is more readily
applicable to an anger that proceeds from one's settled nature. It is more
suited to the thought of the wrath of God and in fact is almost always the word
used for this wrath.[58] In the present passage there is no great difference in
meaning; the two words reinforce one another and give emphasis to the
thought. When they come together they may be set side by side as passions
Christians should avoid (Col. 3:8); or they may occur in parallel clauses (Rev.
14:10); there may also be a genitive relation, "the fury of his wrath" (Rev.
16:19; 19:15). Thus the expression used here has no real parallel. The linking
of the two words gives emphasis to the reality of the wrath that will be poured
out on sinners.

9. Paul rushes on with no proper connective. He is not bothered by
grammatical niceties; great thoughts come pouring out with scant regard for
syntax. *Trouble*[59] is a strong word, with a meaning like pressure to the point of
breaking; it is thus used of dire calamity. *Distress*[60] is not nearly as common a
word. It conveys the idea of being cramped for lack of space, and thus of
extreme affliction.[61] The combination (found again in 8:35; 2 Cor. 6:4) adds up

---

55. Hodge comments, "God gives eternal life; indignation and wrath come as
earned by man, so to speak, *Deo nolente*. God wills all men to be saved. Comp. Rom.
vi.23."

56. Paul uses θυμός five times, once in each of five epistles. It occurs ten times in
Revelation, the only New Testament book to have it more than once. This is the only place
in the New Testament outside Revelation where it refers to the wrath of God.

57. So Büchsel, "There is no material difference between them" (TDNT, III, p. 168).
Stählin, however, sees at least a different nuance: "one might very well say that θυμός, to
which there clings the concept of passionate outburst, was well adapted for describing the
visions of the seer, but not for delineating Paul's concept of the wrath of God" (TDNT, V,
p. 422).

58. See further my *The Apostolic Preaching of the Cross*[3] (London and Grand Rapids,
1965), chs. V and VI.

59. θλίβω in the literal sense means "press", "squash" (as in the treading of
grapes), so that θλῖψις denotes not minor discomfort, but acute suffering. In the New
Testament it (and the corresponding verb) is almost invariably used in a figurative sense to
denote serious trouble. Tribulation is inevitable for the Christian (John 16:33); it is a filling
up of what is lacking in Christ's afflictions (Col. 1:24). Sometimes affliction is eschatological (Matt. 24:9, 21); occasionally, as here, it is the lot of the wicked at the Last
Judgment (cf. 2 Thess. 1:6).

60. στενοχωρία (twice each in Romans and 2 Corinthians but only there in the New
Testament) means literally "narrowness of space", and thus "difficulty", "hardship".

61. Those who see a difference in meaning cite 2 Cor. 4:8 to show that στενοχωρία
is the stronger word. Thus SH hold that it means "torturing confinement", though they
notice that "the etymological sense is probably lost in usage." Cranfield mentions as
having "considerable plausibility" the view held by Aquinas, Calvin, and Barth that

to rather severe trouble, and this Paul tells us is *for every human being*[62] *who does evil*. The universality of this punishment is further brought out with *first for the Jew, then for the Gentile*. The word *Jew* occurs first in 2 Kings 16:6. Strictly it means a member of the tribe of Judah, but it came to be used of all Israelites. They clearly accepted it gladly and took pride in it (v. 17). The meaning is connected with praise (cf. v. 29). In the New Testament the word has a curious distribution. It is used 79 times in Acts and 71 times in John, apart from which Romans with 11 instances uses it more than any other book. Paul has an interest in the Jews (all told he uses the word 26 times),[63] and it certainly comes out in this epistle. In view of the Jewish expectation that it was the Gentiles who would be judged by God, while they themselves would escape, it is noteworthy that Paul sees the Jew as the first recipient of judgment. This accords with the teaching of the Old Testament (e.g., Jer. 25:29; Amos 3:2).[64] But first-century Judaism did not find this strand of Old Testament teaching congenial and neglected it. The combination of *Jew* and "Greek"[65] here embraces the whole of mankind, for "Greek" is used in the sense *Gentile* (as NIV). It may perhaps put some stress on culture, for "Greek" could denote the cultured as against the uncultured (cf. 1:14). If Paul has this in mind he will be hinting that people, even at their cultural best, do not naturally belong to the people of God, and, further, that no matter how cultured they are, they stand under judgment.

10. Once again *but* introduces a contrast. Paul is turning from those who do evil to those who are right with God. For *glory* and *honor* see the notes on verse 7, and for *peace* see on 1:7. The combination points to a totality of bliss and blessing. Perhaps the first two refer mainly to what is outward and stress status, whereas *peace* is more the inward state, though the external relationship of peace with God will not be out of mind. As with the troubles of the previous verse, the blessings of this verse are not restricted, as is brought out in their application to both Jew and Greek.[66]

"when Paul uses the two words together he intends by θλῖψις outward affliction and by στενοχωρία inward distress or anguish." This may be so, but I see no reason for moving here from the outward to the inward. It seems more likely that the combination simply emphasizes the magnitude of the trouble. Denney discovers the same idea in both, "only intensified by the reduplication." G. Bertram finds it "well-nigh impossible to differentiate" between them here; "The use of the two synonyms together is for increased effect" (TDNT, VII, p. 607).

62. Literally "every soul of man", which some have taken to mean that it is in the soul that we are punished (cf. Lagrange). But this is reading something into the expression; NIV is right.

63. Cf. W. Gutbrod: "When he speaks of the Ἰουδαῖος, he does not have in view specific adherents of this nation and religion. He is thinking of a type abstracted from individual representatives" (TDNT, III, p. 380).

64. Commenting on "first", Lagrange notes that the bad deeds of the Jew are the more blameworthy because they are done despite the greater enlightenment he has received.

65. See the note on 1:16 for the two words and also for their being linked by τε . . . καί.

66. Leenhardt sees the principle of retribution here as not in contradiction of free

11. God's judgment is impartial. The word translated *favoritism*[67] has so far been found only in Christian writers and does not occur before the New Testament; it is apparently a Christian coinage. It is made up of two words meaning "to receive" and "face". It thus signifies giving someone a gracious reception, but in the New Testament it is always used in the bad sense of showing partiality or preferring someone without good reason. In the ancient world it was far from axiomatic that justice would be done in the law courts. In fact the opposite would be expected. Why would anyone think that a judge would treat a rich and important person in the same way as a poor and insignificant person? There are many exhortations to just judgment in the Old Testament; for example, "Do not pervert justice; do not show partiality to the poor or favoritism to the great, but judge your neighbor fairly" (Lev. 19:15). It is this kind of evenhanded justice that Paul ascribes to God. He will not weight things in favor of the rich or the poor. Nor will he favor any one nation, be that nation Jew or Greek. In the end we can rely on the fact that justice will be done. And for the sinful that is very frightening.

12. Paul now proceeds to show that it does not matter greatly whether people have received the law in a formal sense or not: all are under condemnation. The Gentile, it is true, cannot be accused of breaking the law, for he does not have the law. But when he does the right, as he sometimes does, this shows that he in fact knows what right is. He may not have the law, but his conduct shows that what the law requires is written in his heart. He is guilty when he does wrong. The Jew cannot claim that he will automatically be saved because God has given him the law: he has not kept it! Nor can the Gentile automatically be saved because he never had the law and so did not break it: he sinned against the light he had. People are judged according to the light they have, not according to the light they do not have.[68] So all are caught up in final condemnation.

Paul first sets forth in general terms the point of the paragraph: those who sin[69] suffer the consequences, whether they know the law or not. *Apart*

---

justification: "The two principles have not the same object. In his present discourse Paul is describing the condition of men before God quite apart from the divine grace of redemption."

67. προσωπολημψία. The Old Testament has a number of expressions that include "face", such as פנים נשׂא. This can be used in a good sense (Deut. 28:50; Job 42:8-9), but also in a bad sense ("do not show partiality to the poor", Lev. 19:15; cf. Deut. 10:17; Ps. 82:2; Prov. 18:5). LXX can render it by πρόσωπον λαμβάνειν, and it seems that the New Testament derives a group of words from this (cf. Acts 10:34; Eph. 6:9; Col. 3:25; Jas. 2:1, 9; 1 Pet. 1:17). The verb προσωπολημπτέω and the noun προσωπολήμπτης as well as our word "are not found in the LXX, and may be reckoned amongst the earliest definitely Christian words" (MM).

68. "The Gentile does not perish for the reason that he lacks the law which the Jew possesses, but because he sins" (Harrison). The Jews sometimes held that the Gentiles rejected the law, but they insisted on the reality of Gentile sins, e.g., "each of the inhabitants of the earth knew when he was transgressing. But My law they knew not by reason of their pride" (2 Bar. 48:40); "Thy law which they have transgressed shall requite them on Thy day" (2 Bar. 48:47).

69. This is Paul's first use of ἁμαρτάνω in this letter, a verb he uses seven times in

from the law renders an adverb that is found twice in this verse and nowhere else in the New Testament.[70] In the classics it appears to have the meaning "impiously", but here the meaning is clearly "without having the law". Paul is speaking of people outside Israel who do not know the law that God has revealed to his ancient people. These, he says, *will also perish apart from the law*. He does not explain what he means by *perish*, but this verb is used at times for the ultimate fate of the wicked (e.g., John 3:16; 1 Cor. 1:18). It signifies eternal loss without defining that loss. We should not, of course, take perishing as an exact description of the final fate of the impenitent and conclude that they simply cease to exist. Their fate is spoken of elsewhere in terms of "hell, where 'their worm does not die, and the fire is not quenched'" (Mark 9:47-48). It is described as the darkness outside (Matt. 8:12) and in other ways. The New Testament does not tell us how the same reality can be described by such different pieces of imagery, but it warns us that the fate of the finally impenitent is a horrible one.

When Paul speaks of those *who sin under the law*[71] (see Additional Note C), it is clear that the law in mind is the law of Moses. The Gentiles are not under this law, but the Jews are. The mere possession of the law does not mean eternal security (as some Jews thought). Law means judgment. Because they have the law and know what God demands in the law, *they will be judged by the law* (cf. Acts 7:53). Paul's Greek means "through (the) law".[72] He is not saying that the law itself judges, and his "through" points to the truth that God is the Judge. The law is the means God uses; it is his instrument to direct those to whom he has given it. It is not a charm guaranteeing salvation. On the contrary, it means condemnation for those who have it and do not obey it.

In this verse we see clearly that all will be judged according to their response to the revelation God has given them. The Gentiles have not been given the law. Therefore they will not be judged by the law. They will be judged by the light they have, and, because they have not acted in accordance with that light (as Paul has shown in ch. 1), this means that they will be condemned. The Jews have the law. They were tempted to say, "even if we sin we are thine, knowing thy power" (Wis. 15:2). Paul reasons differently.

Romans and 17 times in all out of its 42 New Testament occurrences (next is 1 John with ten instances). He uses the noun ἁμαρτία 64 times, 48 in Romans, out of 173 times in the New Testament (next is Hebrews with 25). Clearly he is deeply concerned with the fact and the problem of sin. It is not only a matter of statistics: in 1:18-32 he has developed an argument about sin, though without using the term, a phenomenon that recurs throughout his writings.

70. The word is ἀνόμως. The corresponding adjective ἄνομος is used in the sense "lawless", "wicked" (e.g., Luke 22:37; Acts 2:23), but also with the meaning "not having the law" (1 Cor. 9:21).

71. ἐν νόμῳ. Paul uses ἐν 988 times (172 in Romans), which is more than 36 percent of the New Testament total. Clearly he uses the word so often that it does not always have a precise meaning. Perhaps here the sense is "in the area of law".

72. διά is another of Paul's hard-worked prepositions. He has it 291 times out of 666 in the New Testament (about 43%), the next being Acts with 74. He uses it 91 times in Romans.

They have not kept the law God has given them; therefore that power of God which they valued so highly will be exercised for their condemnation. People will be condemned, not because they have the law or do not have the law, but because they have sinned.

13. *For* ties this in with the preceding and explains it. *Those who hear the law*[73] reminds us of the circumstances of the day. People did not normally read for themselves (the scribe was a member of a skilled profession). They heard it read. For *righteous* see the note on 1:17. It means the state of being "right" with God, of being acquitted when tried by him. The hearing of the law is not enough to bring this about; it is *those who obey the law* who are accepted (cf. Lev. 18:5). The expression is more exactly "the doers of the law" (AV, NASV). The word "doers" is not common; in fact Paul uses it only here (James has it on four of its six occurrences; cf. Jas. 1:22-25 for the importance of "doing"). When he says that doing the law matters much more than hearing it, Paul is stating a position often put forward by Pharisaic teachers. Josephus tells us that Eleazar of Galilee said to Izates (a convert to Judaism who became king of Adiabene in A.D. 31), "you ought not merely to read the law but also, and even more, to do what is commanded in it" (*Ant.* xx.24). Similarly the Mishnah cites a saying of Simeon, son of Rabban Gamaliel (under whom Paul studied, Acts 22:3): "not the expounding (of the Law) is the chief thing but the doing (of it); and he that multiplies words occasions sin" (Ab. 1:17).[74] But there seems to have been some dispute, at any rate in the early second century, and sometimes hearing was regarded as most important. Thus Eleazar of Modiim said, " 'If you will hear' (Exod. 15:26) is the most universal rule (the fundamental principle), in which the (whole) Law is contained."[75] Such a position must have had its attractions. But actions speak louder than words, and Paul is making it clear that the Jew cannot plead his privileged position. If he is relying on the law as his way of salvation, then his concern must be with keeping the law, not preening himself on the fact that he possesses it; even hearing it constantly will not do. Paul is not saying that people are saved by law-keeping. He is laying down the principle from the standpoint of law.

---

73. νόμου lacks the article. BDF note the anarthrous use with abstract nouns, other than when used in the generic sense. Paul tends to omit the article with ἁμαρτία and νόμος, and sometimes with θάνατος, but, they say optimistically, the reason is recognizable (258 [2]). Here the reason is perhaps that Paul is referring to law in general as well as the Mosaic law.

74. See SBk, III, pp. 84ff. for the views of the rabbis.

75. Cited from SBk, III, p. 87 (Dodd also has this quotation). The Mishnah has a reference to "honouring father and mother, deeds of loving-kindness, making peace between a man and his fellow", to which is added, "and the study of the Law is equal to them all" (Peah 1:1). The Talmud records a discussion in which R. Tarfon held to the primacy of practice and R. Akiba to that of study, with the decision of the elders: "Study is greater, for it leads to action" (Kid. 40b; the Soncino edition has a footnote, "This was a practical problem during the Hadrianic persecution, when both study and practical observance were forbidden, and the question was for which risks should sooner be taken").

Where the law is concerned, deeds, and deeds only, matter.[76] For *declared righteous* (= "justified") see Additional Note D.

14. NIV makes a parenthesis of vv. 14-15, and many others as well hold that these verses are an aside. But it seems better to take them as a continuation of the argument. The word "for" (which NIV renders *Indeed* and JB "For instance") ties the following words into the argument. Paul has just shown that for the Jew it is not a matter of hearing the law but of doing it. What then of the Gentiles who do not have the law?[77] Paul proceeds to show that they know enough about what is right for them to be judged by the same general principle, if not the same precise law.

When is more exactly "whenever".[78] Gentiles do not always do what is right, but sometimes they do. *Gentiles* really brings us to one of Paul's deep interests. As we saw in 1:5 (where see note), he uses the term in one third of all its New Testament occurrences, and he uses it especially often in Romans (29 times). The word is always plural in Paul (except in two quotations from LXX, both in 10:19), and most frequently it has the article,[79] but here it lacks it. As he is thus departing from his custom of seeing the Gentiles as a definite group, we must take this as significant. It is not the Gentiles as a whole that Paul has in mind here, but people who have the quality of being Gentiles. Hodge denies that the form without the article means here "some Gentiles". It includes them all, for "Men generally, not some men, but all men, show by their acts that they have a knowledge of right and wrong." We should probably deduce this also from the absence of the article with *law*. While the reference is to the law of Moses, it is its quality as law, and not this particular law as distinct from all other law, on which the emphasis falls. Doing *by nature*[80] *things required by the law*[81] refers to those occasions when a Gentile does

76. Cranfield, however, takes the words differently: Paul is "thinking of that beginning of grateful obedience to be found in those who believe in Christ, which though very weak and faltering and in no way deserving God's favour, is, as the expression of humble trust in God, well-pleasing in His sight." This way of understanding the passage is possible, but it does not spring to the eye. It seems that Paul is speaking of the way people are in fact condemned, not of the way they are in fact justified. He does not believe that people are ever justified by the way of law (3:20).

77. Turner points out that the construction ἔθνη τὰ μὴ νόμον ἔχοντα (with the article following the anarthrous noun) is rare in the New Testament and much more common in the papyri than in the classics. The construction with the repeated article (ὁ ἀνὴρ ὁ ἀγαθός) he finds common in the New Testament but rare in the papyri (M, III, pp. 8, 185).

78. ὅταν. It is used "of things which one assumes will readily occur, but the time of whose occurrence he does not definitely fix" (GT).

79. In Romans it lacks the article 16 times, seven of which are in quotations; thus Paul himself omits the article nine times (outside Romans he omits it six times out of 25 or 26).

80. For φύσις see on 1:26. There is a question whether it here goes with the preceding ("who by nature do not have law") or the following ("by nature do the things of the law"). It is usually assumed that the latter construction is correct, but the former is quite possible (cf. Bengel), and elsewhere in Paul φύσις may be held to support this (v. 27; Gal. 2:15; Eph. 2:3). In the end we must leave both possibilities open.

81. τὰ τοῦ νόμου, not νόμου. Paul is not saying that they do the law, but "the things

something that is also prescribed in the law. Thus he may honor his parents or refrain from stealing.[82] He does these things *by nature* (i.e., "by native instinct or propension, by spontaneous impulse as distinguished from what is induced by forces extraneous to ourselves", Murray), not because he is trying to obey the divinely given law. He cannot. He does not know it. Many commentators point out that this is not unlike "the unwritten law" mentioned by many pagan authors. They think of something within people that points them to the right way, though it is not embodied in written statutes, and often see that something as more important than any written code. Paul's point is that the Gentile knows enough to know that this is the kind of thing he ought to do. He is not consciously fulfilling the law, but nevertheless he is keeping some of the law's provisions (some only, for his thoughts still "accuse" him, v. 15). Paul does not say that he has a law of his own; in fact, twice he says that he does not have a law. He says that he *is* a law in himself, or perhaps for himself or to himself.[83] As Barrett puts it, "The fact is that the Gentile is not really outside the sphere of law, though he is of course outside the sphere of the law of Moses."[84] We see the sort of thing Paul has in mind in the words of Peter in the house of Cornelius, "God does not show favoritism but accepts men from every nation who fear him and do what is right" (Acts 10:34-35).[85] The Gentile does not have the law revealed in the Old Testament, but his conduct shows that he knows right from wrong. God is at work in him. He knows enough of "law" to be guilty when he sins, even though he may not know the God who prescribes right conduct, or even that there is a God who prescribes it.[86] Manson comments, "If they are loyal to the good they know, they will be acceptable to God; but it is a very big 'if'."

---

of the law", i.e., actions which in fact the law prescribes, but not done in obedience to the law, for they do not have it. It is not the law as a whole that they do, but actions which correspond to the parts of the law that prescribe those actions.

82. Calvin gives as examples religious rites, laws against adultery, theft, and murder, and the commendation of good faith in business affairs.

83. Black and others quote Aristotle: "the cultivated and free-minded man is, as it were, a law to himself"; Black adds, "i.e. he does not require rules to be imposed from outside, but has his own self-imposed discipline." W. Gutbrod says that the Gentiles in question "are herewith ἑαυτοῖς νόμος, i.e., 'the' Law, not 'a' law, to themselves. If νόμος without article implied here a generalisation of the concept of law, the train of thought would be broken" (TDNT, IV, p. 1070).

84. Cranfield accepts the view he finds in Ambrosiaster, Augustine, and Barth that the reference is to Gentile Christians and the works "are the expression of their hearts' faith." But it is not easy to see in the simple ἔθνη Gentile Christians; τὰ ἔθνη in 11:13; 15.9 is no real parallel since the context there indicates that believers are in mind. This is not the case here.

85. Cf. Käsemann, for Paul "everything depends on the fact that the Gentiles also experience the transcendent claim of the divine will and thus become, not *the* law or *a* law, but law to themselves. . . . They sense that a person is set in question and that a demand is laid on him from outside, and paradoxically they do so in their inner beings" (p. 64).

86. Barclay adds this comment: "And here is the answer to those who ask what is to happen to the people who lived in the world before Jesus came into the world and who had no opportunity to hear the Christian message. The Christian answer is that a man will be judged by his fidelity to the highest that it was possible for him to know."

15. *Since*[87] ties the words that follow to the preceding, and *show*[88] points to a continuing reality. The expression translated *the requirements of the law* is more exactly "the work of the law" (KJV), an unusual expression found here only in the New Testament (though the plural, "works of law", occurs in 3:20, 28; Gal. 2:16 *[ter]*; 3:2, 5, 10, and the reverse, "law of works", in 3:27). NIV gives the sense of it. The singular "work" may hint at the unity of the law—it is not a haphazard series of unrelated regulations; but perhaps this is reading too much into it. Though they are not trying to obey God's revealed law, Gentiles at times do the thing the law requires. And this, Paul says, is *written on their hearts* (cf. Jer. 31:33; 2 Cor. 3:3). There seems to be a mixture of two constructions here; Paul is saying two things at once: these people manifest the work of the law (they do what the law requires), and further they show that what the law requires is written on their hearts (they act out of a deep-seated conviction that such-and-such things are right). He is not saying that the law is written on their hearts,[89] as people often say, but that "the work of the law", what the law requires of people, is written there. Theodoret pointed to Joseph's brothers and to Abimelech (Gen. 20:4-5) as people who gave evidence of knowing right and wrong and who lived long before the giving of the law by Moses.

Their consciences also bearing witness (cf. 9:1). Conscience is not an Old Testament concept; it is one of the few Pauline concepts that are Greek rather than Jewish (though Leenhardt does not agree; he says, "the Pauline conscience is a ripe fruit of the Israelite ethic").[90] The word translated "consciences" can have any one of a number of meanings. It sometimes refers to consciousness, as in "consciousness of sin" (Heb. 10:2, see RSV). Or it can denote moral consciousness or conscience. Sometimes it means "conscientiousness", but this does not seem to occur in the New Testament (it is found in the late papyri; see BAGD). Here the meaning is "conscience", but this must be properly understood.[91] V. P. Furnish notes the opinion of M. Enslin that the term always looks back on completed acts, and that of W. D. Davies that it sometimes has a future reference. He himself thinks that Paul "never establishes conscience as a firm principle or guide for moral action. Its chief function is to *evaluate* actions (e.g. Rom. 2:15; I Cor. 8:7ff.; 10:25ff.) or persons

---

87. The word is οἵτινες (see on 1:25) = "who are of such a quality as to".
88. ἐνδείκνυνται is present, "show now".
89. γραπτόν agrees with ἔργον, not νόμου.
90. MM have a different objection: they do not find the word in Epictetus or M. Antoninus. They proceed, "The word would seem, therefore, to have been 'baptized' by Paul into a new and deeper connotation, and to have been used by him as equivalent to τὸ συνειδός. . . ."
91. Bruce points out that the word is not classical and that it appeared only shortly before Christianity. He goes on, "It meant 'consciousness of right or wrong doing', but Paul uses it (and perhaps he was the first to do so) in the sense of an independent witness within, which examines and passes judgment on one's conduct. In Christians this examination and judgment should be specially accurate because their conscience is enlightened by the Holy Spirit" (cf. 9:1).

(e.g. Rom. 9:1; II Cor. 4:2; 5:11), not to identify and define 'the good' or 'God's will' either abstractly or concretely. Conscience has a strictly limited and provisional place in the Christian's life."[92] This should be pondered in an age like ours when the conscience of the individual is often elevated to the supreme place and almost any course of action becomes permissible on the grounds that it does not offend one's conscience. No one, of course, argues that conscience may be ignored. If a prospective course of action troubles one's conscience, then it should not be pursued. But if we are looking for the proper line of conduct, we should notice that in the Bible it is the revelation God has made that is to be our guide, not any subjective process. A conscience may be oversensitive (1 Cor. 10:25) or not sensitive enough (1 Tim. 4:2); it pronounces on other people's activities (2 Cor. 4:2; 5:11) as well as one's own (2 Cor. 1:12). Certainly here Paul is using the term for passing judgment on actions already committed, not as expressing a preference for actions yet to be performed.[93]

Bearing witness translates a Greek word meaning "bearing witness with", but Paul does not add what it is with which conscience is in accord. It may well be the law of which he has just spoken (so Barrett), or the good life (Hodge), or the "heart" (Leenhardt).[94] In general it seems either that Paul is using the verb in the sense "witness" ("with" simply strengthening the idea),[95] or that he is linking conscience with the act that shows that the work of the law is written on people's hearts. Both form evidence that the Gentile has no excuse when he does wrong. And Paul proceeds to a third witness.

There is a problem, for some hold that we should understand the apostle to refer to "conflicting thoughts" (RSV), a process that takes place within the individual, others that we should see the meaning as, "their thoughts the mean while accusing or else excusing one another" (KJV),[96] a process involving other people. The context favors RSV, for Paul is not speaking of the way we regard or should regard our neighbor; he is speaking of the way a person's thoughts back up the witness of his better actions and his conscience in

92. *Theology and Ethics in Paul* (Nashville, 1968), p. 229.

93. Cf. the important work by C. A. Pierce, *Conscience in the New Testament* (London, 1955); C. Maurer in TDNT, VII, pp. 898-919; Margaret E. Thrall, NTS, 14 (1967-68), pp. 118-25.

94. Barrett says, "the conscience bearing witness with the divine law whose imprint it is"; Hodge, "the *honestas vitae*, the moral acts of the heathen"; Leenhardt, "the 'heart' suggests a decision; the conscience supports it by its own testimony"; cf. Moule, "Individual consciences affirm the common conviction of moral distinctions which they find around them" (CBSC).

95. For συν- in compounds with a perfective sense cf. M, I, pp. 113, 115-16. Cf. also BAGD, "the prefix συν- has in the highest degree the effect of strengthening" (*sub* συμμαρτυρέω).

96. Boylan argues that μεταξὺ ἀλλήλων means "in (their) intercourse with one another". He sees conscience as part of the evidence and holds that this is supported by the verdicts Gentiles pass on one another's conduct. He finds it difficult to see how "contending judgments" show the person to be a law to himself: "it would rather show that he is a creature of caprice". Murray inclines to this view (p. 76 n.30), and it is supported by Haldane, Denney, Parry, and others.

pointing to what is right. It does this whether these thoughts accuse or excuse him. Leenhardt comments, "This dialogue which man conducts with himself, this debate in which he is in turn the accuser and the defender of himself, shows that, for the appreciation of his conduct, he has at his disposition some objective term of reference, something in fact which God has ingrained in his heart and to which his conscience brings a subjective confirmation".[97] The verbs Paul uses, *accusing* and *defending*, are both legal terms, used for bringing charges in court and for offering a defence in court. Paul is fond of imagery from the law courts, though here this cannot be pressed. He is simply pointing out that those who have no law nevertheless have convictions about what they do. Their thoughts about their actions sometimes take the form of severe accusation and sometimes of acquittal.

The Gentile, though he lacks the divinely given law that was so important for the Jew, is not without guidance: "there are criteria for a person which he himself has not set" (Käsemann, p. 66). His upright actions show that deep down in his heart there is that which points to the right. His conscience bears witness to him of his past acts. And there are his conflicting thoughts. Often they accuse him, sometimes they excuse[98] him, but all the time they form a witness to right and wrong. This threefold witness shows quite clearly that the Gentile has all he needs to guide him along the right way and to leave him without excuse when he does the wrong. He cannot say: "I did not have the law, and therefore I did not know what was right."

16. *The day* is the Day of Judgment. Paul does not use this name, but he describes the day with reference to its function. Most interpreters connect this rather closely with verse 13 and take verses 14-15 as a parenthesis (as NIV does); KJV makes the parenthesis verses 13-15. O'Neill removes verses 14-15 as a marginal gloss. Moffatt puts verse 16 before verse 14, as does Barclay. As one can see, there is a good deal of confusion among expositors. At the same time there is a tendency to overlook the fact that we must not always expect perfect connections in a lengthy piece of dictated matter. Perhaps we would have expressed it otherwise, but the connection is there. Parry, for example, regards verses 14-15 as "strictly necessary to the argument", and Black can say, "there is no justification for detaching the clause from its present place" (he rejects Moffatt's suggestion). The connection between verses 15 and 16 is in fact quite a good one. Whatever their conscience may do in the meantime, it will certainly be a witness against sinners on Judgment Day. The strong eschatological note runs through the whole section.

The connection of judgment with the gospel should not be over-

---

97. Cranfield sees the witness of conscience and that of conflicting thoughts as both referring to Judgment Day. This makes the transition from v. 15 to v. 16 easy and removes a difficulty.

98. ἤ καί, "or even", may imply that excusing is less likely; cf. RSV, "or perhaps excuse them". It is worth noticing that Paul uses κατηγορέω here only, and ἀπολογέομαι, "make a legal defence", only once elsewhere; he delights in legal imagery, but it is not the excitement of the court that attracts him. It is the facts of God's law as the standard and of acquittal through grace.

looked.[99] We are apt to set the two in opposition to one another and to think that the one excludes the other. But the gospel does not preclude the thought of judgment. Indeed, it demands it. Unless judgment is a stern reality, there is nothing from which sinners need to be saved and accordingly no "good news", no gospel (for *gospel* see the note on 1:1). Paul speaks here of *my* gospel (as in 16:25). He has appropriated it and made it his own. He does not mean that he thought it up or that it belongs to him in any special way or that there is some peculiarity in the way he sets it forth.[100] He means that he knows it really and not theoretically. He espouses it wholeheartedly and not formally. To preach the gospel effectually it is necessary to make it one's own.

It is God who will judge. The verb may be a present (as RSV) or a future (as NIV),[101] but the meaning will be the same. Paul is not speaking of judgment as a present activity but of the judgment that will take place at the end of the age; if his verb is present, that is for greater vividness. *Men's secrets* reminds us of the searching nature of that judgment. Nothing can be kept hidden on that day. It is this that makes it so serious. We may present a respectable front to the world so that people do not know about the things of which we are ashamed. If those things could remain hidden we would fare so much better in any judgment. But they cannot remain hidden at the end. God will judge all things, hidden from men or not. This judgment will be done *through Jesus Christ* (cf. John 5:27; Acts 17:31). This is the distinctive Christian teaching about judgment. The Jews taught that in the end God alone would judge the world; he would commit judgment to no one, not even the Messiah. When the Christians taught that God would judge through Jesus the Messiah, they were introducing a new teaching (cf. John 5:22).[102] In one sense it mitigates the judgment. Our Judge will be the one who died for us, so we could not look for anyone more predisposed in our favor. All that can be done for sinners he will certainly do. But this adds a note of solemnity to the judgment. Since he has done so much for us, we cannot expect to get by with a shabby attainment, a half-hearted attitude to the duties we have shirked.

99. The precise connection has been understood in different ways. Paul may mean that the gospel includes the thought either (1) that God will judge, (2) that he will judge men's secrets, (3) that he will judge Gentiles as well as Jews, or (4) that he will judge through Jesus Christ. Certainty may be unattainable, but the word order favors the last. The main point, however, is the connection of judgment with the gospel.

100. Elsewhere he insists that there is but one gospel (1 Cor. 15:11; Gal. 1:6-9). This is overlooked by some who seek to interpret this verse by finding something peculiar to Paul. They put too much emphasis on μου, overlooking the fact that the enclitic is not emphatic. In a sermon on these words R. Bethune emphasizes Paul's point that there is but one gospel and that personal appropriation of the gospel message is in mind here (ET, LXVIII [1956-57], pp. 22-23).

101. κρινει is usually accented as a present (κρίνει), but there seems no reason why it should not be read as a future (κρινεῖ). In either case there is a future reference (cf. BDF 323 for the futuristic use of the present).

102. Cf. SBk: "According to the Rabbinic view it is exclusively God who will judge the world. . . . In Rabbinic literature there is no passage which unambiguously places the judgment of the world in the hand of the Messiah" (II, p. 465). Cf. also S. Mowinckel, *He that Cometh* (Oxford, 1959), pp. 313, 319, 336, etc.

3. The Jew, 2:17–3:8

As we have seen, Paul appears to have the Jew basically in mind from the beginning of this chapter. But some of what he has said refers to the Gentile and some is perfectly general, which leads some scholars to conclude that Paul is not thinking about the Jew in that section. But there can be no doubt about what he says from this point on. He names the Jew explicitly, and the way he writes about circumcision and the like makes it plain that he is talking about the Jew. He emphasizes that to be a member of a chosen race is to have a position of responsibility, not simply of privilege. One must not only know the right but do it.[103]

a. The Jew's confidence, 2:17-20

> [17]*Now you, if you call yourself a Jew; if you rely on the law and brag about your relationship to God;* [18]*if you know his will and approve of what is superior because you are instructed by the law;* [19]*if you are convinced that you are a guide for the blind, a light for those who are in the dark,* [20]*an instructor of the foolish, a teacher of infants, because you have in the law the embodiment of knowledge and truth—* . . .

The apostle begins this section with an enumeration of those things on which the Jew typically prided himself, and which he thought gave him superiority over the Gentile.[104]

17. Paul's *if*[105] throws no doubt on the proposition.[106] The construction implies the truth of what is supposed. Then he reverts to the construction he has already used in verse 1 (where see note) whereby an imaginary opponent is addressed for the sake of greater vividness. For *Jew* see the note on verse 9. *Call yourself* is probably the right way to translate the verb, though some see it as passive (cf. KJV, "art called a Jew"). But NIV is probably correct; it is the

---

103. Althaus thinks that this is the sort of thing Paul would have preached in the synagogue.

104. A number of scholars see this section as ironical (e.g., Boylan, Murray, Hendriksen), but this is perhaps unnecessary. Paul had a high view of the place of the Jew in God's plan, and there seems nothing here on which he would cast doubt. The view that he is using irony is rejected by scholars such as Nygren, O'Neill, and Käsemann.

105. The late MSS, it is true, often read ἴδε (cf. KJV, "Behold"), a reading treated respectfully in BDF 467: "in R 2:17ff. it is possible to transform what appear to be protases without a correct apodosis (21?) into independent clauses by adopting the reading ἴδε". But Metzger accepts εἰ δέ and comments on ἴδε, "This reading arose either as an itacism (ει and ε were pronounced alike) or as a deliberate amelioration of an otherwise extremely long and drawn out sentence (with the apodosis in ver. 21)." This is surely the way it should be understood.

106. εἰ + present indicative, "If (as is the case). . . ." Cf. TH, "these 'if' clauses are equivalent in force to an affirmative statement". GNB is so sure of the point that it dispenses with the "if": "You call yourself a Jew, you depend on the Law. . . ." The Greek has only one "if", though some translations agree with NIV in inserting the conjunction several times.

claim of the Jew, not the way others look at him, that is in mind (cf. Rev. 2:9; 3:9). The verb incidentally is found here only in the New Testament. The following verb, *rely on*, is also unusual, being found elsewhere in the New Testament only once (Luke 10:6). It conveys the notion of "rest upon", which aptly characterizes the attitude of the Jew to the law. It was the basis of all his hopes, for he did not see the law as his accuser (cf. John 5:45). For him it was the most signal mark of God's favor to the nation.

The verb *brag* is a favorite word of Paul's.[107] Sometimes it has a meaning like "rejoice", but typically it signifies "boast", as here. The Jew thought of one God and of that one God as having a special regard for this one nation, so he took pride in that God. "Boast" does not here have the meaning of a vainglorious but empty utterance; rather, it conveys the notion of a deeply felt pride, almost a legitimate pride. The form of expression is "boast in God", rather than *about your relationship to God*. Paul is not referring to relationship to God, but to God himself; cf. NEB, "are proud of your God".[108] The Jew thought he knew God and exulted in the thought (cf. Jer. 9:24; Mic. 3:11).[109] His boast was in the God whom he knew and whom he thought nobody else knew. But he did not take sufficiently into consideration the character of God: God is the Judge, the Judge of Jew as well as of Gentile (cf. Hos. 12:2; Amos 3:2, etc.).

18. The Greek says simply "know the will", but no doubt NIV is right with *know his will*. The will of God is so central for Paul that when he says simply "the" will, it can be only the divine will.[110] He is very interested in God's will and the way it works out in this world. Notice that he does not say

---

107. καυχάομαι. He uses it in no less than 35 of its 37 New Testament occurrences, and he has a similar near monopoly on other words from the same root; he has καύχημα ten times out of 11 and καύχησις also ten times out of 11. The word group may indicate a boasting that is laudable, such as boasting in God (5:11), in Christ (15:17; Phil. 3:3), or in the cross of Christ (Gal. 6:14). Christians can boast in tribulations (5:3) and generally in the things that show their weakness (2 Cor. 11:30; 12:5, 9). Paul sees his converts as a "crown of boasting" (1 Thess. 2:19). Christians can boast in one another (2 Cor. 1:14; 7:4, 14; 9:2, 3), and they can boast in the hope of future glory (5:2). But where boasting centers on one's own achievements, as it so often does, it is blameworthy. Cf. Bultmann, "For Paul καυχᾶσθαι discloses the basic attitude of the Jew to be one of self-confidence which seeks glory before God and which relies upon itself." He goes on to say that Paul sets in contrast πίστις "which is appropriate to man and which is made possible, and demanded, by Christ" (TDNT, III, pp. 648-49). M. Bouttier thinks the word means here not so much boasting, which "hardly brings out the existential content; it is a question of knowing what we make the basis of our life, what gives it its *raison d'être* and value" (*Christianity according to Paul* [London, 1966], p. 16). But this scarcely accords with the meaning of καυχάομαι. See further E. A. Judge, ABR, 16 (1968), pp. 37-50; Minear, p. 59.

108. Turner sees the meaning of ἐν here as "because of" (M, III, p. 253). TH seems to be in error when it rejects "boast about God", saying that the Jews were characterized rather by "boasting about their particular relationship with God" (cf. also NIV, RSV). While the Jews may well have had this characteristic, it is not what Paul is saying at this point.

109. This exultation is found also outside Scripture, e.g., Ps. Sol. 17:1: "O Lord, thou art our King, now and for ever: for in thee, O God, our soul shall glory."

110. Paul uses θέλημα 24 times, of which 20 or 21 refer to the will of God.

only that the Jew claims to know the will, but that he actually does know it. In that, of course, is his high privilege (and his severe condemnation when he fails to act on it).

The word translated *approve* (see on 1:28, where it is translated "think worthwhile") basically means "to test". But it is to test with a view to approving, and thus the word acquires the secondary meaning "to approve". There is a similar ambiguity about *what is superior*. This translates a participle from a verb[111] which means first "to differ", and then (since when things differ one is better than another, a usage we have in English when we speak of "someone who is different") "to excel". The total expression then might mean "You test out the things that differ",[112] in which case Paul would be saying that the Jew does not take things at face value but tests them to see what is right. This is possible, but it seems more likely that we should accept the meaning "approve what is excellent" (RSV; cf. Phil. 1:10).[113] It is more probable that the Jew would pride himself on giving approval to what is really excellent than simply on knowing right from wrong. And this is more likely to follow *know his will* than a reference to expertise in casuistry.

The verb *instructed*[114] strictly means "instructed orally", "instructed by word of mouth", though there is no emphasis here on the manner of the teaching. Yet we should remember that teaching at that time was normally done orally. The teacher spoke what had to be learned, and the class echoed it until it had learned it. More important than the method was the subject matter, and Paul goes on to tell us that this was *the law*. We make a distinction between worship and education, but it is worth bearing in mind that the synagogue was both a school and a place of worship. And the law was both the center of education and the heart of worship.

19. From the way the Jew sees himself over against God Paul turns to his attitude to people of other races than his own, an attitude of certainty regarding his inherent rightness: Paul says, *you are convinced*.[115] This is the apostle's

---

111. διαφέρω.

112. Shedd prefers this meaning "because the reference is to casuistry, or the settlement of nice questions in morals, upon which the Jew plumed himself." So also Robinson, Moule, Godet, etc. Cf. NEB, "you know right from wrong." Michel thinks Paul means making the distinction between Judaism and paganism, but this seems unlikely.

113. With ASV, RSV, Hodge, Gifford, etc. Denney holds that "There are no grounds on which we can decide positively for either"; Bruce also sets out the alternatives without expressing a preference.

114. κατηχέω. H. W. Beyer says that Paul always uses it in the sense "to give instruction concerning the content of faith", here of pre-Christian Judaism (TDNT, III, p. 638). In due course it became an important Christian word (cf. "catechism", "catechumen"). Lagrange points to the present tense as indicating that he is constantly instructed (contrast Apollos, Acts 18:25). Among the Jews great emphasis was given to oral repetition, which fits the meaning of the verb. Cf. Birger Gerhardsson, Jewish study of the oral Torah "is in principle oral repetition: the teacher's instruction, the pupil's learning—in fact all study and maintenance of knowledge within the discipline—rests on the principle of oral repetition" (*Memory and Manuscript* [Copenhagen, 1964], p. 28; cf. also pp. 115-16, chs. 10 and 11).

115. The 2nd perfect of πείθω is used with present meaning, "be convinced, be

one use of the term *guide*, and also of *blind*[116] (this latter term is fairly common in the New Testament; for the combination cf. Matt. 15:14; 23:16, 24). He maintains, then, that the Jew sees his position as one of superiority. All other people are blind, and he, the sighted one, is their guide. There is, of course, an important truth in this. The Servant was to be "a light for the Gentiles, to open eyes that are blind" (Isa. 42:6-7; cf. Isa. 9:2; 49:6; 60:3), and in part, at any rate, this sets before us the role that Israel should perform. To this nation was given the revelation that was to teach all mankind about God. That revelation was never meant to be the private treasure of one nation, which it could withhold from all others. Israel was to bring the light of God into the world's darkness; it was to share its revelation with the multitudes that did not have it.[117] But this could be done only in a spirit of humility, always bearing in mind that the Jew who had received the revelation would have been just as much in the dark as any Gentile, were it not for what God had done. There should accordingly be exultation in what God had done, not in the Jew's privileged position. The trouble with assuming that one is a guide to others is that it so easily leads to the assumption that one is naturally superior to them. But the Jew had no natural superiority, and Paul complains accordingly.

A light for those who are in the dark makes essentially the same point, but the imagery is more congenial to Paul than that in the previous expression (he uses *light* 13 times and *darkness* 11 times). He now sees the Jew as proud of the fact that he lives in the light while Gentiles inhabit darkness. The Jew does not take account of the fact that the light is not of his making. It is the gift of God, and should therefore be received with gratitude and humility.

20. The *instructor* disciplines and corrects as well as teaches, and the term not uncommonly has the idea of correction or discipline (as in Heb. 12:9, its only other New Testament occurrence). Here, however, Paul has instruction in mind. The *foolish* strictly are the unintelligent (NEB, "stupid"), those lacking the ability to think things out. But clearly Paul is not contrasting the Jew with the Gentile as the intelligent over against the unintelligent. The thought is rather that of perception in spiritual things (Phillips, "You can instruct those who have no spiritual wisdom").[118]

Paul uses the word *teacher* here only in Romans (and six times elsewhere). It is, of course, most common in the Gospels. *Infants* is more Pauline

---

sure, certain" (BAGD 2.*b*). It is joined to the preceding with τέ, which links clauses "thereby indicating a close relationship betw. them" (BAGD); "In the connection of clauses, τε indicates rather close connection and relationship" (BDF 443 [3]").

116. For the Jews' view of their role as leaders of the blind etc., see SBk, III, pp. 98-105.

117. In Wis. 18:4 the Jews saw themselves as those "through whom the imperishable light of the law was to be given to the world."

118. The word ἄφρων = alpha-privative + φρήν ("mind", "thought"); it means "mindless", "thoughtless". Here it signifies the Jew's "judgment on the pagan world around which is designed to express the accusation of ungodliness" (G. Bertram, TDNT, IX, p. 231). He considers ungodliness stupid. "ἄφρονες are, as in the O.T. . . . persons without moral intelligence" (Denney).

(ten times out of 14 in the New Testament). Strictly it denotes very little children, babies, or infants (cf. Matt. 21:16). But it is also used metaphorically of those who have little knowledge of the subject being discussed. Paul uses it of those who are "babies in Christ" (1 Cor. 3:1; cf. Eph. 4:14; Heb. 5:13). It may be used in a good sense (as of those unspoiled by sophistry, Matt. 11:25). But it is also used quite often of the immature, and that will be the sense of it here.[119] Since he had the treasure of the law, the Jew saw himself as the teacher of the immature Gentiles, people with no knowledge of the living God.

Paul goes on to what it means to have the law.[120] *Embodiment* is a good translation of an uncommon Greek word.[121] It refers to the outward, but to the outward as giving expression to the inward rather than the merely outward that contrasts with the inward. *Knowledge* is another of Paul's characteristic words (he has it 23 times out of its 29 New Testament occurrences). It can be used of specific knowledge such as that of the Christians. At a later time it became a technical word for the "knowledge" of the Gnostics (who, indeed, derived their name from this word, *gnōsis*). Here, however, it does not appear to be used in any technical sense; it is the general sense that is meant, though with some relationship to the law. For law see Additional Note C, and for truth Additional Note B. Paul is not speaking of one form of knowledge among many, one piece of truth among the rich deposits of truth in the world.[122] It was the pride of the Jew that in the law he had the very embodiment of fundamental knowledge and truth (Phillips, "the basis of true knowledge"). The Jew saw himself not as having produced yet another form of knowledge and truth which might compete with the various philosophies of the day. He saw himself as standing before the world holding in the book of the law that truth which is God's truth, the knowledge which God himself has made known. His place was thus supreme.[123] Paul is not disagreeing. He saw the advantage of the Jew as a very real one (3:2). It is a priceless privilege to be the recipient of God's revelation.

b. The Jew's failure, 2:21-24

> [21]*you, then, who teach others, do you not teach yourself? You who preach against stealing, do you steal?* [22]*You who say that people should not commit*

119. So NASV, NEB. Cf. Cragg, "it is not wise to forget that there are many who need the kind of moral and religious teaching that children receive."
120. Calvin takes the participle causatively, "because you have the form of knowledge" (so NIV).
121. μόρφωσις occurs in the New Testament elsewhere only in 2 Tim. 3:5. J. Behm sees it here as "a physical representation, indeed, the actual embodiment of absolute knowledge and truth, as the true depiction and representation of the idea of a divine norm." He adds that this "is stated with obvious irony by Paul" (TDNT, IV, p. 754), a judgment from which many dissent.
122. Paul often omits the article, but he is very definite here: he speaks of *the* embodiment of *the* knowledge and *the* truth in *the* law. The effect is to put emphasis on the supremacy of the revelation God has given in the law.
123. Cf. Manson, "With his pure religion and his lofty moral code he is uniquely fitted, he claims, to assume the spiritual leadership of mankind."

adultery, do you commit adultery? You who abhor idols, do you rob temples?
23You who brag about the law, do you dishonor God by breaking the law? 24As it
is written: "God's name is blasphemed among the Gentiles because of you."ᵃ

ᵃ24 Isaiah 52:5; Ezek. 36:22

There is a considerable measure of truth in the position taken up by
Paul's Jew.[124] In the law he did have a revelation from God, a special treasure,
rightly to be valued above all earthly possessions. But for this treasure to be of
any value it had to be used rightly. Paul now comes to the point that the Jew
has not done this.[125] In a series of biting questions the apostle makes it plain
that at point after point the Jew has failed to live up to the teaching of the law.
Instead of being humble at the condescension of God and seeking to show his
gratitude by living in accordance with the precepts contained in the revelation, the Jew gloried in his position of spiritual privilege and displayed a
totally unwarranted spiritual pride. He did not realize that in his conduct he
was denying the teaching of the law on which he prided himself and causing
the name of the great God he worshipped to be blasphemed by the
heathen.[126]

21. Paul breaks off his construction. His "if" of verse 17 is not followed
up in strict grammatical sequence.[127] Clearly Paul feels deeply about this
matter, and he is not concerned to express himself in the tidy way the grammarians would wish. He begins with a general question. The Jew has a place
as a teacher[128] of the nations, as Paul has just pointed out. Now he asks
whether the teacher teaches[129] himself (cf. Matt. 23:1-3). RSV makes the

124. O'Neill sees the whole section 2:17-29 as written by someone other than Paul
(as also 1:18-32; 2:1-16). He thinks that this was "a traditional tract which belongs essentially to the missionary literature of Hellenistic Judaism." But no sufficient reason is urged
for this position. The whole section is an integral part of Paul's argument that all people
are sinners, and without it he would scarcely have made his point.
125. Käsemann does not think that vv. 21ff. give us a true picture of contemporary
Jews. He says, "In general the life of the Pharisees was strict and not infrequently even
attracted Gentiles". But here "an apocalyptic approach is again presenting what may be
empirically an exception as representative of the community" (p. 69). Käsemann's over-
emphasis on apocalyptic has perhaps led him astray at this point. While some Jews
certainly lived exemplary lives, there is no evidence that the Jews as such were admired
and much that they were unpopular and widely criticized. Cf. n. 126 below.
126. Cf. the sorrowful words of R. Johanan b. Zakkai (died c. A.D. 80), in SBk, III,
p. 106. Dodd speaks of this discourse as "delivered probably not much more than ten
years after the date of this letter, in which he bewails the increase of murder, adultery,
sexual vice, commercial and judicial corruption, bitter sectarian strife, and other evils."
127. οὖν here is probably resumptive. The particle is often inferential, but this sense
is not strong here. Paul is quite fond of οὖν and uses it 112 times (47 in Romans), which is
more than anyone else in the New Testament other than John (194 times).
128. Thomas brings out the importance of the teacher with a quotation from
Nathaniel Hawthorne: "Let us reflect that the highest path is pointed out by the pure ideal
of those who look up to us, and who, if we tread less softly, may never look so high
again."
129. Leenhardt follows Michel in differentiating διδάσκων as instruction from
κηρύσσων, preaching, and λέγων as "authorized quotation and its explanation"; TH sees
teaching, preaching, and "exegesis or interpretation", but both are getting a lot out of
λέγων. Käsemann sees only "a rhetorical distinction" (p. 71), which seems right.

question a future (or an exercise of the will), but Paul uses the present tense. Phillips brings out the sense of it: "But, prepared as you are to instruct others, do you ever teach yourself anything?" The verb *preach*[130] is perhaps unexpected in this context. The term applied originally to the proclamation of a herald (cf. Rev. 5:2), and it came to be used of public proclamation in general. Since the herald did not originate the message, but simply proclaimed authoritatively what had been given him to say, the word was a very suitable one for the proclamation of the gospel and is normally used in this way in the New Testament. The object of the preaching that Paul singles out is that a person should not steal. The verb[131] properly denotes the activity of a sneak thief (rather than, say, a bandit), but here the thought is that of dishonesty generally. It is easy to preach honesty to other people, but not nearly so easy to be scrupulously honest in all one's own dealings. We are always tempted to grade honesties. And by a strange coincidence our own dishonesties have a way of coming out as the minor ones, while those of other people are serious.

22. Paul changes his verb to *say*, but the essential meaning is the same. *Adultery*[132] was widely practised in the ancient world and in many places was taken as quite normal (i.e., for a man; with a curious lack of logic it was reprobated in a woman). The Jews had a higher standard than the Gentile world in this respect, but were far from blameless (cf. Ps. 50:18).[133]

The Jews were known for their abhorrence[134] of idols. They prided themselves on their monotheism, and it was a major plank in their religious platform that they totally rejected all idols. But Paul can ask whether their practice was all that it should be. He does not speak of worshipping idols, for Jews would not do that. But they might profit from idols; they might *rob temples*.[135] This may be meant to be understood of pecuniary profit. It would

---

130. κηρύσσω is used of Jewish preaching (Acts 15:21), of the preaching of John the Baptist (Matt. 3:1), and, of course, of Christian preaching, that of Jesus himself (Matt. 4:17) and of his followers (Mark 6:12). Paul uses the verb 19 times out of its 61 New Testament occurrences (four in Romans). It is not easy to see why RSV inserts "while" into this question; the construction is the same: "You, who preach. . . ."

131. κλέπτειν is an infinitive because of the command implied in κηρύσσων. It is interesting that theft, adultery, and sacrilege are linked by Philo (who adds murder; *On the Confusion of Tongues*, 163). JB makes this a statement, not a question: "You preach against stealing, yet you steal", and so with the following.

132. Paul often denounces sexual sin and advocates purity, but he rarely uses the terminology of adultery. This is the one passage where he uses the verb μοιχεύω, and he has μοιχός once only; he never uses μοιχάω or μοιχεία.

133. Consider these statements from the Psalms of Solomon: "his eyes are upon every woman immodestly" (4:4); "all of them committed adultery with their neighbours' wives" (8:1); "they left no sins which they did not commit, and even worse than the Gentiles" (8:14).

134. The verb βδελύσσομαι (only here and in Rev. 21:8 in the New Testament) is connected with βδέω, "break wind", and words denoting a smell. It means to turn away from something on account of the stench, and thus to abhor, detest.

135. LSJ define ἱεροσυλέω as "rob a temple, commit sacrilege". Our problem is that these two meanings are not the same and it is not easy to see which of them Paul has in mind in this passage. BAGD, discussing the cognate ἱερόσυλος, note the general meaning "one who commits irreverent acts against a holy place"; MM see a similar meaning in the verb here.

not be easy for a Jew literally and physically to rob a temple, though some see this as the meaning. Thus Parry says, "The charge seems to be that, though they regard idols as 'abominable' things, they do not hesitate to make pecuniary advantages out of robbing temples". But the tractate *Abodah Zarah*, both in the Mishnah and the Talmud, has a good deal to say about Israelites and idols, and, for example, speaks of an Israelite as taking an idol and selling it to a Gentile (53b). The Israelite would profit and the Gentile would worship the idol. In such ways a Jew might profit from promoting idolatry even though he himself did not make or worship the idol.[136] The town clerk at Ephesus thought that "robbing temples" was an accusation that might well be brought against a Jew, and he says that Paul and his companions have not been guilty of it (Acts 19:37). Clearly some people held that a Jew might well make profits from dishonest practices connected with idolatry, and Paul may well have had this in mind.[137]

But some scholars think that we should see the meaning in a radical approach to the commandments like that found in the teaching of Jesus (e.g., Matt. 5:21-48). On this view Paul is not referring to a literal robbing of temples, but to the withholding of what is due to God (cf. Mal. 3:8), what Hodge calls "profanation, the irreverent disregard of God and holy things". To rob God of his due is to act sacrilegiously. When we take seriously what God demands of us, we see that we are sinners all. Paul is saying, then, that the Jews were in their own way sacrilegious.[138] Since both ways of understanding the verse have supporters, I see no way of deciding the point. We must keep both possibilities in mind.

23. Now Paul points to inconsistency at the heart of the Jewish way, the practice of the law.[139] Paul has spoken about the Jewish boast in God (v. 17); now he refers to boasting in[140] God's supreme revelation, *the law*. But, as he

136. Josephus says that Moses forbade Jews to rob temples or take treasure dedicated to any god (*Ant.* iv.207; cf. Deut. 7:25-26), from which many draw the conclusion that Josephus was opposing a contemporary practice. This historian also records the slander of Lysimachus that the original name of Jerusalem was Ἱερόσυλα (because of its inhabitants' temple robberies) and that this was later altered to Ἱεροσόλυμα (*Ap.* i.311; cf. 319).

137. G. Schrenk holds that we should take the word here in the strict sense of robbing temples (TDNT, III, p. 256). Cf. Moule, "'do you plunder temples', entering the polluted precincts readily enough for purposes at least equally polluting?" (p. 68).

138. Cf. Barth, "thy righteousness is robbery, for who does not steal? thy purity is adultery, for who is rid of sexuality? thy piety is arrogance, for where is the piety which does not approach God too nearly? Is there any advantage in distinguishing before the judgement seat of God a higher and a lower form of worldliness?"; "If God be not for thee, all is against thee." The Psalms of Solomon refer to people "plundering the House of God's Holiness" (8:12).

139. In the previous two verses Paul has used participles, but he now switches to the relative pronoun and the indicative. Some think this means a change from questions to statements (e.g., NEB, SH, Cranfield, etc.). It seems more likely that it is a stylistic variation, for apart from this the structure remains as in the preceding. C. F. D. Moule says it is "clearly an exact parallel to the preceding clauses" (IBNTG, p. 106); that it is a question is accepted by RSV, GNB, Hendriksen, etc.).

140. Turner sees ἐν here as causal, "because of" (M, III, p. 253).

has been insisting, it is one thing to have the law and quite another to keep it. As the law was God's supreme gift, to break the law is to *dishonor God*. The Jew held that he alone of all people had the right attitude to the one God, so this accusation hits at the heart of his religious understanding. Whatever else he did or did not do, he would have held that he gave God the place of highest honor. Paul maintains that his practice denies his profession.

24. Paul proves[141] his accusation with a quotation (which seems to be from Isa. 52:5, though it also resembles Ezek. 36:20, 23).[142] The accusation is made the more serious by this demonstration that it has scriptural support. For *name* see the note on 1:5; it stands for the whole person. The verb "blaspheme" may be used of defaming people (3:8), but more usually and more seriously it is used of a wrong attitude to God, as here. For *Gentiles* see the note on 1:5. Israel should have been the source of blessing to the Gentiles, bringing them to praise God. Instead, Israel caused them to blaspheme.[143]

How accurate was Paul in making such a charge? Barrett thinks that Jewish living as well as Jewish monotheism impressed the Gentiles. He sees the point of Paul's charge in the fact that "there is no man who is not guilty" of theft, adultery, and sacrilege when these are "strictly and radically understood" (cf. for theft Mal. 3:8-9, and for adultery Hos. 1–3; Jer. 3:8). The other point of view is put by Dodd, who says that the charges "are startling, but Paul would have stultified himself by making them if they had no ground. . . . There is in Paul's words an added tone of bitter indignation— the indignation of the high-minded Jew who moved about among the great cities of the pagan world and found the very name of Jew made a byword by the evil ways of its bearers". Gifford points out that Paul does not say that the Jews' sins were more flagrant then than at other times or than those of other nations, only that they *were* flagrant.[144]

The apostle ends with his usual formula when quoting Scripture, *As it is written*. NIV has moved it to precede the quotation, which is its normal position; indeed, this appears to be the only place where Paul has it after the quotation. The reason for this is not clear.[145]

---

141. He uses γάρ, "for, because", which NIV omits. For Paul's use of this conjunction see the note on 1:9.

142. The quotation differs from LXX of Isa. 52:5 only in minor points: δι' ὑμᾶς is differently placed, LXX has μου where Paul has τοῦ θεοῦ, and it includes διὰ παντός, which Paul lacks. None of these differences is major, but the thought of the passage is different. If the resemblance to the language of Isa. 52:5 is close, the resemblance to the thought of Ezek. 36:20-23 is closer.

143. The Qumran community was warned not to harm or rob Gentiles "lest they blaspheme" (Vermes, p. 114).

144. Denney comments, "As if the heathen were saying: 'Like God, like people; what a Divinity the patron of this odious race must be'."

145. Some hold that the position indicates that Paul is making a free quotation (e.g., SH, Lagrange, Lenski). Denney, however, rejects this and proceeds: "it is rather that there is a challenge in the words, as if he had said, Let him impugn this who dare contest the Word of God."

c. The inward and the outward, 2:25-29

> 25*Circumcision has value if you observe the law, but if you break the law, you have become as though you had not been circumcised.* 26*If those who are not circumcised keep the law's requirements, will they not be regarded as though they were circumcised?* 27*The one who is not circumcised physically and yet obeys the law will condemn you who, even though you have the^a written code and circumcision, are a lawbreaker.*
>
> 28*A man is not a Jew if he is only one outwardly, nor is circumcision merely outward and physical.* 29*No, a man is a Jew if he is one inwardly; and circumcision is circumcision of the heart, by the Spirit, not by the written code. Such a man's praise is not from men, but from God.*

^a27 Or *who, by means of a*

Circumcision, the sign of admission to the covenant (Gen. 17:9-14), was regarded by the Jews as having the utmost importance. It was unthinkable that a man, duly circumcised and admitted to the covenant, should fail of his salvation. Paul now takes this central ceremony and points out that it is completely ineffective if the spiritual state to which it points is not a reality. The inward is more important than the outward.

25. Circumcision[146] may mean the act of circumcising, the state of being circumcised, or those who have been circumcised. The word may also be used metaphorically to denote those in a right relationship to God (Phil. 3:3; cf. Gal. 6:15). Here the physical act is in mind. Paul sees circumcision as profitable, but only if the law is kept (cf. 1 Cor. 7:19; Gal. 5:3). It admitted to membership of the covenant people, but this is of no avail unless one lives as a member of that covenant people. Theodoret likens circumcision to a seal, and points out that the use of the seal depends on having something valuable to seal: "When we have gold, silver, precious stone, or expensive clothing, we usually attach seals, but when none of these is stored within, the attaching of seals is superfluous."[147] Paul's "if" construction is quite general; it implies nothing as to the fulfilment or nonfulfilment of the condition.[148] The rabbis attached great value to circumcision and made many statements like this one of R. Levi: "In the Hereafter Abraham will sit at the entrance to Gehenna, and permit no

---

146. περιτομή is a Pauline word, being used by the apostle 30 times out of its 35 New Testament occurrences. It means "a cutting around". Here it is followed by μέν, to which BAGD give the significance "for indeed". Paul also has γάρ, "for" (which NIV omits), which according to Hodge answers to what is implied rather than to what is explicitly said: "You are exposed to condemnation, *for* circumcision. . . ." Lagrange thinks it is probably because circumcision itself is enjoined in the law.

147. Theodoret, *Commentary*, p. 47.

148. ἐάν with the subjunctive. Paul is fond of ἐάν and uses it 95 times (20 in Romans). He is even more fond of εἰ, which he has 213 times (46 in Romans). It is a mark of his argumentative style that he so frequently uses conditionals, as he does here.

circumcised Israelite to descend therein" (Gen. Rab. 48:8).[149] Paul's view is in sharp contradiction: for the circumcised to break the law[150] is for them to become uncircumcised.[151] He does not attach saving value to the physical act. He looks for obedience to the revealed will of God, not simply the acceptance of a privileged position. It is perhaps worth bearing in mind that circumcision did not originate with Israel nor end there. The Egyptians, for example, practised it, and Ishmael was circumcised (Gen. 17:23). It was membership in the covenant of which circumcision was the sign that mattered. And covenant membership meant keeping the covenant. Without that, even the circumcised Israelite had no standing with God. Many commentators point out that Christian readers should remember that what is said here of circumcision applies with equal force to baptism.

26. Now we have the other side of the coin. If the circumcised can by their deeds become effectually uncircumcised, is not the reverse process just as possible?[152] *Those who are not circumcised* (actually Paul says "the uncircumcision") may *keep*[153] *the law's requirements.*[154] He is not, of course, advocating salvation by works and saying that those outside Israel may live such good lives that they merit salvation. The law is God's revealed will; it points to the way in which God would have people go, and this way is the way of trusting him, as the fuller revelation in the gospel makes so plain. The Gentile, despite his lack of the law, may respond to what God has made known to him, and this, for Paul, is the real circumcision. To respond with love and faith is to possess all that circumcision means (cf. Col. 2:11).[155] Murray follows Godet in seeing a reference to Gentile Christians. This may be the correct way to understand it, but it seems that Paul's words are wide enough to include people like Cornelius (Acts 10:34-35). See the notes on verses 7 and 14 above.

149. The rabbis did find a way of consigning the very wicked to perdition. The same passage says that Abraham "will remove the foreskin from babes who died before circumcision and set it upon (the sinners), and then let them descend into Gehenna". But this is distinctly exceptional. The normal, circumcised Israelite had nothing to fear.

150. παραβάτης has regard to the law; it refers not to evildoers in general, but to someone who "transgresses a specific divine commandment" (J. Schneider, TDNT, V, p. 741).

151. The word is ἀκροβυστία (= τὸ ἄκρον τῆς βύστης ἔχων, "having the foreskin"). GT points out that in the classics the word is ἀκροποσθία and think the New Testament word a variant from those who pronounced πόσθη (the male organ) as βύστη. LSJ, however, think it is probably "from ἄκρος and a Semitic root, cf. Bab. *buštu* 'pudenda', Heb. *bōsheth* 'shame'". MM note the word (with a fresh suffix) in Hippocrates, and say, "When a word containing a *vox obscoena* was taken from medical vocabulary into popular religious speech, it was natural to disguise it."

152. For the connective οὖν (which NIV omits) see the note on v. 21. RSV has "So". The following words are the logical consequence of what has just been said.

153. The verb is φυλάσσω, which means "guard, protect", but not infrequently is used of guarding a law from being broken, i.e., by observing its provisions.

154. For δικαίωμα see on 1:32; here it means "righteous ordinances".

155. Paul uses αὐτοῦ, though the grammatical antecedent is the feminine noun ἀκροβυστία; it is equivalent to ὁ ἀκροβυστίαν ἔχων (cf. BDF 282 [2]). Turner thinks it "has no expressed antecedent but again is vague in reference" (M, III, p. 40). Notice further that εἰς is here used of result.

27. NIV makes this a statement (as do RSV, NEB, JB, Gifford, SH, etc.), but others see the words as a question (KJV, ARV, Moffatt, Godet, etc.). The Greek is capable of either meaning; Paul's "and" (which NIV omits and RSV renders with "Then") may carry on the question, or it may introduce the conclusion. If it is a question it is rhetorical and the answer is not in doubt. The people he has described in verse 26 are a standing condemnation of those in verse 25. It is not *the one who is not circumcised physically*[156] as such, but the one who in addition *obeys the law* who brings about the condemnation. The verb rendered *obeys*[157] may be used here in something like its strict sense, "bring to its appointed end".[158] The uncircumcised man that Paul has in mind trusts God and obeys him, which is what the law is all about. Paul's *you* keeps up the personal address to the Jew. He will not let him evade the point. The Greek has the forceful expression, "you, the transgressor through letter and circumcision". Paul is saying that the Jew, for all his possession of the letter of the law and the physical act of circumcision,[159] cannot be described as anything other than "the transgressor". He is guilty before God. The "letter"[160] is "the literally correct form of the law" (BAGD); we might say it is the physical and external form of the law, just as circumcision is the physical and external form of covenant membership. Paul is emphasizing that the physical and external (on which it was so easy for the Jew to rely) is not enough. The man who lacks the written law and has never received physical circumcision but who acts in accordance with the spirit of the law will by that fact stand in judgment[161] on those privileged members of the circumcised group who for all their privileges transgress before God (cf. Matt. 12:41-42).

28. Parry's comment hits the mark: "The grammar is ambiguous, but the sense is clear." Since Paul is using an elliptical construction, we can fill in the gaps in more ways than one. We can take the words to mean "For not the Jew in what is outward is (the Jew)", or "For not he who is outwardly (a Jew)

156. ἐκ φύσεως means "from nature", not "physically" (though RSV supports NIV). The reference is to the man who is naturally uncircumcised, not the one who *becomes* uncircumcised (v. 25) by breaking God's law.

157. τελοῦσα; the participle has here something of the force of a conditional, "if it accomplishes".

158. τελέω means "to bring to its τέλος", its end or aim. The verb may thus be used in such a sense as *"bring to fulfilment* or *perfection," "bring* a child *to maturity"* (LSJ 5).

159. διά will be used here of "attendant circumstances" (so Black, Cranfield, etc.). G. Schrenk rejects this view in favor of "an instrumental significance. It is precisely through what is written and through circumcision that the Jew is a transgressor" (TDNT, I, p. 765). But there seems no reason for taking the word this way, and few have been persuaded.

160. γράμμα may denote a letter of the alphabet, a document, a letter in the sense "epistle", or a book. Or it may denote what is literal over against "spirit" and the like.

161. The translators of GNB saw the reference to judgment as so significant that they made it a separate clause and began the verse with it: "And so you Jews will be condemned by the Gentiles. . . ." This may be supported by the emphatic position of κρινεῖ, but perhaps Paul is saying that, far from being in a favored position, it is "judged that the Jew will be. . . ." JB has "a living condemnation", but the reference seems to be to final condemnation, not a present happening.

is a Jew"; there is a similar ambiguity about the reference to circumcision. But, though we cannot be sure where we should supply the missing words, the meaning is not in doubt. Paul is saying that it is not the outward but the inward that matters, and this whether we are talking about being *a Jew* or about *circumcision. Outwardly*[162] translates an expression that points to what is in the public domain, what is open and visible and thus known widely. *Outward* has a similar meaning, but *physical* is rather "in the flesh".[163] But the important thing is not there. It is in that which is inward and thus not open to public inspection.

29. *No* is really "But", the justification for NIV being that the strong adversative is used.[164] Paul is setting forth the opposite and doing so emphatically. The essence of being a Jew is that which is inward, and so with circumcision, which in this context means much the same as being a Jew (cf. Gal. 6:15-16; Phil. 3:3). *Of the heart* points to the inward and recalls some Old Testament passages (e.g., Deut. 10:16; 30:6; Jer. 4:4; 9:25-26; Ezek. 44:7; cf. also Acts 7:51). Then comes a contrast between "spirit" (which it is) and "letter" (which it is not). There is a difference of opinion whether we should understand a reference to the Holy Spirit (as NIV)[165] or in some such way as RSV, "spiritual and not literal".[166] That is to say, Paul's contrast may be between the Jew's strict adherence to the letter of the law and the action of the Holy Spirit which takes place within a person, or it may be between the outward and the inward. Possibly there is more to be said for a reference to the Spirit (cf. 2 Cor. 3:6). Either way gives a good sense. And either way Paul is making the point that there can be a scrupulous conformity to the outward requirements of the law which completely misses the point. He goes on to say that the person[167] who is in the right gets praise *not from men* (cf. Matt. 23:5; John 5:44), *but from God.* There appears to be a play on the meaning of the name "Jew", which derives from "Judah" = "praise" (cf. Gen. 29:35; 49:8).[168] The right kind of praise has its origin[169] not in men, but in God. It is the

---

162. ἐν τῷ φανερῷ. BAGD note τὸ φανερόν as "the open, public notice". In the received text ἐν τῷ φανερῷ is opposed to ἐν τῷ κρυπτῷ a number of times (Matt. 6:4, 6, 18), but this passage in Romans appears to be the only New Testament occurrence in the older MSS.

163. ἐν σαρκί.

164. ἀλλ᾽, "on the contrary". BAGD give as one meaning "The neg. answer is omitted as obvious: *(no,) instead of that"* (ἀλλά 1.a).

165. As do GNB, NEB, NASV, Murray, Robinson, etc. Cf. Odes Sol. 11:1-2: "My heart was circumcised . . . for the Most High circumcised me by his Holy Spirit".

166. So JB, Moffatt, Goodspeed, Barrett, Haldane, etc.

167. οὐ grammatically must refer back to Ἰουδαῖος, but it is probably meant to include "the circumcised man".

168. Barrett tries to bring this out with ". . . a Jew, whose due. . . ." SH think Gifford was the first to point this out, but it is older. It is found, e.g., in Haldane. Käsemann, by contrast, rejects it, saying that it would not have been intelligible to the Romans (but Gen. 29:35; 49:8 connect praise with Judah, though without using ἔπαινος, and LXX is freely quoted in this letter as apparently something the Romans would recognize).

169. ἐκ denotes the origin.

contrast between the inward and the outward again. It is not the outward, which alone people see, that counts, but the inward, that which only God sees, and which he esteems of greater significance than the outward.

Additional Note C: THE LAW IN ROMANS

Paul uses the term *law* in a bewildering variety of ways. Typically it is the law of Moses, the law of the Old Testament. Thus, even though neither Moses nor the Bible is mentioned, plainly this is meant when he speaks of the Jews as having "in the law the embodiment of knowledge and truth" (2:20). It is difficult to be certain of all the occasions when he means the law of Moses, for the context does not always put the matter beyond doubt, and we must bear in mind that in this epistle he never speaks of "the law of Moses" in set terms. Nor can we say that "the law" as opposed to "law" means the Mosaic law, since both usages can apply either to the Mosaic law or to law in general.

Law is especially important in Romans, where Paul uses it 72 times[170] (all told he has it 119 times out of 191 in the New Testament; Galatians is next with 32 occurrences, so that the frequency in Romans is noteworthy). It is not easy to see why Paul inserts or omits the article with this noun. In Romans it has the article 31 (or 32) times and lacks it 41 (42) times, but of the 31 (32) times with the article 15 come in chapter 7. Apart from this one chapter Paul prefers the term without the article. Sometimes he does this to keep the reference to law quite general, as when he says that no one will be justified "by works of law" (3:20; many translations insert the article, but the Greek does not have it). Here he is certainly saying that no one will be justified by works done in accordance with the law of Moses, but he is probably saying something more, namely that no one is justified by any works of law, the law of Moses or any other. But while one can conjecture a reason for the absence of the article on some occasions, this by no means applies universally. Thus in 2:23 Paul uses "law" twice, the first time without the article and the second time with it, but it is more than difficult to see different meanings.

All this means that it is not easy to classify Paul's use of the term with any exactness. But it seems to me that there are 51 places in Romans where the term is best understood of the Mosaic law (though sometimes with a glance at a wider meaning).[171] In addition, in some passages the apostle speaks of "the law of God" (7:22, 25; 8:7). Sometimes "law" seems perfectly general, as

---

170. This is the figure in Morgenthaler's *Statistik,* but Aland's *Vollständige Konkordanz* lists 74.

171. The law of Moses seems meant in 2:12 *(bis),* 13 *(bis),* 14 *(bis),* 15, 17, 18, 20, 23 *(bis),* 25 *(bis),* 26, 27 *(bis);* 3:19 *(bis),* 20 *(bis),* 21 *(bis),* 28, 31 *(bis);* 4:13, 14, 15, 16; 5:13, 20; 7:1 *(bis),* 4, 5, 6, 7 *(ter),* 9, 12, 14, 16; 8:3, 4; 9:31 *(bis);* 10:5; 13:8, 10. Cranfield holds that "It is safe to assume that in Paul's epistles νόμος refers to the OT law unless the context clearly shows this to be impossible" (p. 154 n.2). He is opposing the view that the arthrous form means the Old Testament law and the anarthrous form law in general.

when Paul says, "where there is no law there is no transgression" (4:15; cf. also 3:27; 5:13; 6:14, 15; 7:2, 8; 10:4).

But in addition to these more or less straightforward uses of the term Paul has a number of other expressions. Thus he can speak of "the law of faith" and of "the law of works" (3:27; NIV translates with "principle", and Hodge thinks the word here means "a rule of action"). He refers to "the law of sin" (7:23, 25; in 8:2 it is "the law of sin and death"), and again to "the law of the Spirit of life" (8:2). There is "a law to me who wish to do good" (7:21), there is "in my members another law" (7:23), and there is "the law of my mind" (7:23). A woman is bound by "the law of her husband" (7:2). And once Paul says that the Gentiles "are a law for themselves" (2:14).

It seems clear that for Paul *law* meant primarily the Mosaic law, but that this did not prevent him from using the term in a variety of ways. In their treatment of the word, after the general concept "of any law" BAGD have "2. *a rule* governing one's actions, *principle, norm*" (they cite as an example "the tune that the bird sings"!).[172] Some of Paul's usages certainly come under this heading, but basically he is concerned with what God has revealed.[173]

Law is very important, and Paul can organize all history around it. In Romans 5:12ff. he sees a time before the law, the time after the giving of the law, and the time after Christ came. In the first period sin was not reckoned (5:13; cf. 4:13). Then came the heyday of the law, the time from Moses to Christ, a time when people sinned "in the law" (2:12), but this was followed by the coming of Christ who is "the end of the law" (10:4). Paul has some perplexing things to say about the law, but he is clear that it is God's law (7:22, 25; 8:7). To have this law is one of the high privileges of Israel (9:4); the law is meant for life (7:10), it is holy (7:12), spiritual (7:14), and good (7:16); it is a source of instruction (2:18) and of truth (2:20). People will be judged by it (2:12), which leads to the thought that it is important to obey it (2:13, 25-27; 10:5).

But for all that the law does not bring salvation. Repeatedly Paul links sinning with the law, as when he speaks of people sinning "in law" (2:12) or transgressing law (2:23, 25, 27). Indeed, the law came in so that trangression might abound (5:20), and where there is no law there is no transgression (4:15; 5:13). What he calls "the passions of sins" are "through the law" (7:5), and the law "works wrath" (4:15), that is, it brings the wrath of God on the sinner. Sin is dead apart from the law (7:8); it lacks all power; Paul can speak of being alive apart from the law (7:9). It was not the function of the law to justify (3:20), but rather to give knowledge of sin (3:20; 7:7).

---

172. Hodge thinks that law, "as used by the apostle, means *the rule of duty,* the will of God revealed for our obedience; commonly, however, with special reference to the revelation made in the Scriptures" (p. 53).

173. There is a notable discussion of νόμος in Ernest de Witt Burton, *A Critical and Exegetical Commentary on the Epistle to the Galatians* (Edinburgh, 1959), pp. 443-60. Burton thinks that the great majority of New Testament references come under the heading "Divine law, the revealed will of God in general, or a body of statutes, ordinances, or instructions expressing that will" (p. 455). See also Douglas J. Moo, WThJ, 45 (1983), pp. 73-100.

For Paul the really wonderful thing is that Christ is the end of the law (10:4), the end of any seeing of the law as the way of salvation. So believers "died to the law through the body of Christ" (7:4); they are not under law but under grace (6:14-15). Another way of putting this is to say that the righteousness of God is "apart from the law" (3:21, 28). It is important for Paul that this has always been God's way: the promise that came to Abraham was "not through law" (4:13). In other words, God's way has always been the way of grace, and we misunderstand the law if we see it as the way of earning salvation. It is rather God's way of showing us our shortcomings so that we turn to Christ for our salvation. This does not mean an abolishing of the law; on the contrary, faith establishes the law (3:31). It is only when we experience the love of God in Christ, that love which we see so vividly on the cross, that we come to see the place of the law and find that love is the fulfilment of the law (13:8, 10).

Paul has a good deal to say about the law in his other writings, but it is clear that it is an especially important concept in Romans. In this calm and reflective letter we get important insights into the meaning of the law and into its relation to love.

Additional Note D: JUSTIFICATION

All told Paul uses the verb δικαιόω in 27 of its 39 New Testament occurrences, 15 of which are found in Romans (the next most frequent is Luke with five). Clearly Paul uses the term significantly more often than does anyone else, and equally significantly it is an important category in Romans. The word is a forensic or legal term with the meaning "acquit".[174] It is the normal word to use when the accused is declared "Not guilty". We see its significance in an Old Testament passage: "When men have a dispute, they are to take it to court and the judges will decide the case, acquitting (or, justifying) the innocent and condemning the guilty" (Deut. 25:1). Here the legal meaning is plain, and this remains with the word throughout the range of its biblical use. Some argue that it means "to make righteous", but this cannot be demonstrated.[175] The impossibility of making righteous is clear when the word is

---

174. Cf. Barrett, "the reader may be reminded that 'righteous' describes a relation not a quality, and that accordingly 'to make righteous' does not mean 'to make virtuous', but 'to grant a verdict of acquittal'" (p. 50). The verb is used 15 times in these early chapters of Romans and in the summing up in 8:30-33, but not at all in 12:1ff. where Paul deals with the formation of Christian character.

175. It is sometimes urged that the verbs ending in -οω are always factitive, with the meaning "to make—". This is so with a large number of these verbs, but not where some moral quality or the like is in mind. Thus ὁμοιόω means not "to make like" but "to declare to be like" or perhaps even "to show to be like". Similarly, ἀξιόω means not "to make worthy" but "to deem worthy", "to count as worthy". There should be no doubt that δικαιόω means "to declare righteous", not "to make righteous". Usage is decisive. It is the ordinary word for "to acquit", "to declare not guilty". When the accused is acquitted he is not "made righteous" but declared to be righteous.

used of God (3:4). It is plain also in the use of the future tense "will be justified" (2:13), for the reference is to Judgment Day and no one will be "made righteous" on that day. Moreover, that passage refers to "the doers of law" as "justified", but by definition "doers of law" are righteous: they cannot be "made" righteous.[176] The declaratory meaning is clear.[177] It is to be inferred also from the fact that it stands in opposition to condemnation. "To condemn" does not mean "to make wicked", but "to declare guilty"; similarly, "to justify" means "to declare just".

Paul is quite definite that "no one will be justified in (God's) sight by works of law" (3:20; cf. 4:2).[178] Justification, on the contrary, is God's good gift: people are "justified freely by his grace" (3:24). Several times Paul links justification with faith, making it quite clear that it is only by believing that anyone can appropriate this gift of God (3:26, 28, 30; 4:5; 5:1). The cross plays a necessary part in justification, for "we have now been justified by his blood" (5:9). Paul repeats the truth that justification is brought about by God (3:26; 8:30 [bis], 33), and this is, of course, implied when justification is used with reference to grace or to faith. The grace in question is always the grace of God, and the faith is faith in God; Paul stresses faith because that is the means whereby the sinner appropriates the gift of God.

In some modern discussions justification is understood in eschatological terms.[179] This is to be accepted inasmuch as there is certainly a future, eschatological aspect to justification (3:20; Gal. 3:11; cf. Rom. 1:17; 5:9-10). Nowhere do the early Christians see justification as something fully realized in the here and now. Its eschatological dimension is important, and it would be a poor, maimed thing if it were bounded by this life. But this must be held in conjunction with the other reality that believers are justified now. Their justification can be spoken of with a past tense (5:1, 9; 8:30; 1 Cor. 6:11). It is characteristic of the New Testament view that justification has been established by Christ's saving work.[180]

176. Any person who is justified in the New Testament sense is, of course, a changed person. As Calvin put it, "those who imagine that Christ bestows free justification upon us without imparting newness of life shamefully rend Christ asunder" (p. 121). Justification and sanctification belong together, and one cannot be justified without being in principle sanctified. That the believer lives on an ethically higher plane than before believing is not in doubt; that this is conveyed by δικαιόω is not supported by the evidence.

177. "Justification makes no actual change in us; it is a declaration by God concerning us" (Lloyd-Jones, *Romans 3:20–4:25*, p. 55).

178. Among the rabbis obedience to all the law was important, as Minear points out (p. 93). He cites the saying: "a proselyte who takes upon himself all the commandments of the Law with a single exception is not to be admitted."

179. See, e.g., R. Bultmann, *Theology of the New Testament*, I (London, 1952), pp. 273-74.

180. Bultmann brings this out: "by his thesis that *righteousness is a present reality* Paul, nevertheless, does not rob it of its *forensic-eschatological meaning*. The paradoxicality of his assertion is this: God already pronounces his eschatological verdict (over the man of faith) in the present; the eschatological event is already present reality, or, rather, is beginning in the present" (*ibid.*, p. 276). He sees the difference between the Jews and Paul in that "what for the Jews is a *matter of hope* is for Paul a *present reality*—or, better, is also a present reality" (*ibid.*, p. 279).

The justification of sinners is the great basic problem for all religion. God is good and man is not. How then can man, the sinner, stand before the high and holy God? Every religion must answer this question, and its value for us depends on the adequacy of the answer. What characterizes Christianity is that its answer centers on the cross. Justification does not take place because people in some way work out a means of dealing with sin. They do not and cannot. They can neither overcome it so that for the future they will live without it, nor blot it out from their past. But God can and does. Paul sees justification as brought about by Christ's death, for it is in this manner that our sin is done away. We are thus "acquitted", declared "not guilty". It is not that sin is treated as though it did not matter. No one who takes the cross seriously can think that. But the cross means that sin has been dealt with and put away.[181] Since this is so, it no longer remains to disqualify people and thus they can be said to be justified.

Justification by way of the cross means that God saves us in a way that accords with right. He does not save us at the price of saying "Morality does not matter. Though people have sinned they will be accepted just as they are." Sin is an evil, and God never condones it. It must be dealt with. When we speak of justification by way of the cross, we are saying that it has been dealt with. "Will not the Judge of all the earth do right?" asked Abraham (Gen. 18:25). In the cross we see that he has done so.[182]

Additional Note E: JUDGMENT

The judgment of God is a reality with which Paul spends some time. He gives attention first of all to the general principle, setting forth the position uniformly taken up in the New Testament that judgment is on the basis of works (Matt. 7:21; 16:27; 25:31-46; John 5:28-29; 2 Cor. 5:10; 11:15; Gal. 6:7-9; 2 Tim. 4:14; 1 Pet. 1:17; Rev. 2:23; 22:12, etc.). He goes on to show that this has consequences for everybody, Jew or Gentile. Romans 2 presents difficulties.

---

181. This point is sometimes overlooked. Thus Bowen sees justification as similar to the action of a judge who sentenced an old friend to a heavy fine, then paid the fine himself. But this is not justification; the man is guilty and he is sentenced accordingly. The justified sinner is one whose sin has been dealt with so that it no longer exists. He is "Not guilty". The illustration is defective in another way, for in our jurisdictions there are some crimes for which fines are prescribed and it does not matter who pays them. But where imprisonment or the death penalty is involved, it does matter who pays. Such a penalty must be paid by the offender, and "the wages of sin is death" (Rom. 6:23).

182. See further my *The Apostolic Preaching of the Cross* (London, 1965), chs. VIII and IX; V. Taylor, *Forgiveness and Reconciliation* (London, 1946), pp. 29-69; N. H. Snaith, *The Distinctive Ideas of the Old Testament* (London, 1950), pp. 51-78; E. C. Blackman, "Justification", IDB, II, pp. 1027-30; J. I. Packer, "Justification", IBD, II, pp. 841-44; G. Quell and G. Schrenk, TDNT, II, pp. 164-225; J. A. Ziesler, *The Meaning of Righteousness in Paul* (Cambridge, 1972); Hodge, pp. 81-86; Morison, pp. 161-99; Gavin Reid, ed., *The Great Acquittal* (London, 1980).

Paul has put considerable emphasis on the truth that salvation is God's free gift. But if people are saved by grace through faith, why should they be judged by their works? How does this judgment relate to salvation by grace? A number of suggestions have been offered.

1. *Direct Contradiction.* Some hold that Paul is setting forth two completely incompatible ideas. Of 2:6-16 Foreman says, "At two crucial points it does not fit Paul's teaching about faith and righteousness." But Paul is engaging in a sustained argument that all are sinners and need God's help (1:18–3:20). It is not easy to think that he would lose sight of a central tenet in the middle of his argument. In any case the view has not commended itself widely; it so obviously does not fit the passage.

2. *Purely Hypothetical.* Others think that Paul is not speaking of the way things are, but setting out in forthright terms the way things would be apart from grace. Leenhardt speaks of "the conduct of a humanity responding to God's general revelation" (p. 78), and adds, "the state of humanity here envisaged has never been realized in our human history." Knox sees Paul as "speaking largely hypothetically" (p. 409). But Paul says God "will render", not "would render". His words point to a fact, not a hypothesis.

3. *Law, Not Gospel.* "He is expounding the law, not the gospel" (Hodge, p. 50). This comes close to no. 2, for salvation is not by way of the law, which makes it hypothetical. But Paul is speaking of a real judgment, and one that applies to everybody.

4. *The Entrance and the Life.* Godet puts it this way: "justification by faith alone applies to the time of *entrance* into salvation through the free pardon of sin, but not to the time of judgment. . . . God demands from [the sinner], as the recipient of grace, the fruits of grace" (vol. I, p. 196; he further says, "faith is not the dismal prerogative of being able to sin with impunity"). A variant of this position sees the reference to "goodness of life, not however as meriting God's favour but as the expression of faith".[183] This accords better with the apostle's thought and may well be the way we should understand what he says here.

5. *Justification Is with Power.* When God justifies anyone, this is more than mere words; it is a work of power (1:16); the saved person is a new creation (2 Cor. 5:17). When he is judged he is judged for what he is, that is, by his works. Judgment shatters all illusions.[184]

183. Cranfield, p. 147. He later looks at ten interpretations of the passage and favors "not their faith itself but their conduct as the expression of their faith" (p. 151). Cf. Black, who says that people are saved by faith alone, but "in the life that follows 'works', as the spontaneous expression of the life of faith (the 'fruit of the spirit'), are no less an integral part of the life which will one day be judged by God—only they are no longer simply the result of an external conformity to a legal code" (p. 55).

184. Cf. Käsemann, "the difficulties in exposition are largely connected with a failure to pay due regard to the power-character even of the righteousness of God received as a gift, since this involves a radical separation of gift and Giver, and of Giver and Judge" (p. 58). He cites Gal. 5:5 to show that "faith itself waits for its definitive justification from the eschatological future." Cf. also Althaus, "Alongside 'by faith alone' there stands with equal emphasis 'by works alone'" (p. 24).

It seems that either 4 or 5 gives a satisfactory meaning to the passage. For Paul there can be not the slightest doubt that salvation is by grace; there is no other foundation than Christ (1 Cor. 3:11). But equally, what is built on that foundation is of importance, and people differ in what they build. Judgment Day will sift out the "gold, silver, costly stone", and separate it from the "wood, hay or straw" (1 Cor. 3:12; cf. vv. 13-15). It is important not to surrender the great truth that God saves by grace, but it is important also to bear in mind that final judgment is a reality. We are accountable.[185]

185. Klyne R. Snodgrass has emphasized the importance of taking Paul's teaching on judgment with full seriousness; it is an important topic (NTS, 32 [1986], pp. 72-93).

Romans 3

d. The faithfulness of God, 3:1-4

¹What advantage, then, is there in being a Jew, or what value is there in circumcision? ²Much in every way! First of all, they have been entrusted with the very words of God.

³What if some did not have faith? Will their lack of faith nullify God's faithfulness? ⁴Not at all! Let God be true, and every man a liar. As it is written:

> "So that you may be proved right in your words
> and prevail in your judging."ᵃ

ᵃ4 Psalm 51:4

In arguing that all people are sinful Paul has drawn attention to the place of the Jew. He is a member of the chosen people, but this does not avail if he sins. But this poses a problem. If a member of the chosen people can be rejected ("become as though . . . not . . . circumcised", 2:25), then what is the advantage of belonging to the chosen people? Paul will face this question more fully in chapters 9–11; here he uses a series of lively rhetorical questions in an animated treatment of objections that might be urged against his position.[1] It is not unlikely that these questions reflect objections Paul had actually

---

1. It is usually said that Paul uses the method of the diatribe, so common in the philosophers, wherein a series of imaginary objections is raised and answers given to forward the argument. But David R. Hall rejects this view ("Romans 3:1-8 Reconsidered", NTS, 29 [1983], pp. 183-97). He points out that in the diatribe the objection is put briefly and replied to in detail, whereas in Rom. 3:1-8 the objections are given in detail and the replies are brief. Again, Paul elsewhere does use the introductory formulas common in the diatribe such as ἀλλ' ἐρεῖ τις (1 Cor. 15:35) and ἐρεῖς οὖν (Rom. 9:19; 11:19), but here he has τί ἐροῦμεν, "a formula which introduces an internal debate rather than an external objection" (p. 183). While Paul is influenced by his debate with the Jews, he is basically concerned with objections within himself. S. K. Stowers has shown how the passage could be construed as a diatribe (CBQ, 46 [1984], pp. 707-22; see especially p. 715), though without considering Hall's objections. If we are to see the passage as a diatribe, Stowers's version is surely the way to take it. But Hall leaves a large question over this whole approach.

faced in his dialogue with the Jews, though, of course, we have no way of being sure. Be that as it may, Paul looks first at the objection that, if all people are sinful, the Jew has no advantage. He rejects this outright; the Jew has a very real advantage. A second objection is that, since God has promised to bless his people, he must do this irrespective of what the Jews do. Otherwise he would cease to be faithful.[2] Paul will have nothing to do with such a suggestion. God will always prove to be faithful.

1. Paul has listed some of the things on which the Jew[3] prided himself (2:17-20), and has shown that such things are of no importance if the Jew breaks the law of God. Being circumcised matters only if one keeps the law (2:25). So the apostle comes to the logical question, What is the advantage *in being a Jew* or *in circumcision?* There is no great difference in meaning between *advantage* and *value*[4] in this context. Paul is simply posing the question whether Jewishness or circumcision matters any longer in view of the arguments he has so far adduced. *Circumcision* has the article; this may signify "the circumcision already referred to" or, better, "the circumcision that admits to the people of God" (there were other circumcisions, such as that practised by the Egyptians).

2. Logically we expect the answer, "Nothing at all." But Paul surprises us with *Much*[5] *in every way!*[6] It is an important answer: if the Jew had no advantage, then either the Old Testament cannot be relied on or else God does not keep his promises. Paul has just rejected the notion that the Jew, because of his race and quite apart from the way he lives, can expect favored treatment from God. But Paul never goes to the other extreme of maintaining that to be a Jew does not matter. So, after rejecting decisively some of the Jew's most cherished illusions, he goes on to speak of the very real advantages God has given his ancient people. "The Jew has an advantage which can never be taken away, that is that it was to him that God first gave His word of promise. Thereby circumcision is seen in a new light. By the circumcision

2. Cf. Gore, "What he is arguing against is the claim of the Jews that God was bound to their race."

3. NIV has *a Jew*, but the Greek is τοῦ 'Ιουδαίου. This is a "collective (generic) singular", a "not unclassical usage" (BDF 139).

4. περισσός means that which surrounds a thing and thus is not part of it; it is over and above. From this it is but a step to *advantage* (cf. Eccl. 6:11, LXX). ὠφέλεια is sometimes used in the sense "assistance" or "help", and thus "profit" or "value" (ὠφελεῖ is used of circumcision in 2:25). Neither noun is common in the New Testament (twice each).

5. Paul is fond of πολύς (82 times, 20 in Romans). He does not hesitate to use the neuter adverbially (cf. 2 Cor. 8:22) or the plural (15:22; 16:6), but he prefers πολλῷ (5:9, 10, etc.). Godet takes πολύ here as an adjective agreeing with περισσόν.

6. τρόπος is connected with τρέπω, "to turn", and means "way", "manner". The expression here indicates a many-sided advantage. Cranfield points out that it does not mean "of every sort". The Jew had the many-sided advantage that Paul proceeds to name, but he does not face the question of whether the Gentile might have advantages of other kinds.

Israel became the people of promise" (Nygren).[7] *First of all*[8] leads us to expect a list, but Paul never gets past his *first;* he speaks of the great, supreme privilege of the Jew, that of being entrusted with God's revelation to mankind. The verb is the usual one for "believe", but it may be used in the sense "entrust". Thus Paul uses it of various things with which he is put in trust—a responsibility (1 Cor. 9:17), the gospel (1 Thess. 2:4), the gospel of the uncircumcision (Gal. 2:7), the message (Tit. 1:3; cf. also Luke 16:11; John 2:24). What the Jews were entrusted with was *the very words of God*, or, as RSV has it, "the oracles of God",[9] an expression Paul uses here only. Among the Greeks a god was thought to utter short sayings (e.g., the responses at Delphi). A short pregnant saying was thus characteristic of divine utterances, and in time the word for "a short saying" came to mean "a divine saying", "an oracle". Paul is referring to the fact that God has spoken and that the record[10] of what he has said was entrusted to Israel, and to Israel only. Some understand "the oracles" to refer to God's promises (Brown, Robinson), others to the messianic prophecies (cf. Boylan), others to the law (Chrysostom), or the

7. Barrett finds points of theological importance here: "If the Old Testament is to be believed God did choose the Jews out of all mankind and did bestow special privileges upon them. To reduce them therefore to the level of other nations is either to accuse the Old Testament of falsehood, or to accuse God of failing to carry out his plans." He sees the Jew's advantage as "a terrible one. He is first in election, first in judgement; instructed out of the law, judged by means of the law." These are valuable comments, but we should not overlook the fact that the one thing Paul mentions here is τὰ λόγια τοῦ θεοῦ. Knox finds Paul's answer "certainly not very convincing", but this is to underestimate the importance of Old Testament revelation. Smart has a better grasp of the argument when he says that the Jew "is to be the custodian of the treasure beyond all other treasures, the knowledge of God which alone makes a truly human life possible." Scott has the helpful comment, "by their possession of the Law the Jews have an advantage over the heathen, much as the educated man has a better chance in life than the one who has never been at school." Whatever use the Jew (or the educated man) makes of it, the advantage is real.

8. πρῶτον μέν looks for a following ἔπειτα δέ with a list like the one in 9:4-5. But, as in 1:8 (where see note) and 1 Cor. 11:18, *first* is not followed up. KJV takes the adverb to mean "chiefly" (so also Calvin), but NIV is surely correct.

9. τὰ λόγια τοῦ θεοῦ. λόγια is unlikely to be the neuter plural of λόγιος (which means "learned" in its only New Testament occurrence, Acts 18:24). Many see it as a diminutive of λόγος, though the normal diminutive is λογίδιον. SH think this last is a strengthened form, developed when λόγιον acquired the special sense (arising from its meaning "a brief utterance") of "an inspired utterance", "an oracle". A. Debrunner denies that the word is a diminutive, but gives the meaning "λόγος '(longer) narrative'— λόγιον '(shorter) individual utterance'" (TDNT, IV, p. 137 n.1). G. Kittel says that the sense "oracular saying" disappears in LXX where the term "has become a vehicle for the biblical conception of revelation by Word" (*ibid.*, p. 138). In LXX it apparently differs little from λόγος. Godet also denies that the word is a diminutive and takes it to mean "a *divine* saying". Whether the word is a diminutive or not is not clear, but the meaning is plain enough; it is a divine utterance. T. W. Manson has a summary of its use in the Old and New Testaments, the Apostolic Fathers, and the Apologists (*Studies in the Gospels and Epistles* [Manchester, 1962], pp. 87-104).

10. Murray emphasizes this: "For Paul the *written* Word is God's speech, and God's speech is conceived of as existing in the form of a 'trust' to Israel; divine oracles have fixed and abiding form"; "above all else . . . the Jew's privilege as an abiding possession . . . was his entrustment with the Word of God."

ten commandments (Barclay), or the covenant (Calvin). It is better not to restrict the expression but to see it as referring to the whole Old Testament revelation (Lagrange, Murray).[11]

3. Paul turns to the situation in which *some*[12] Jews failed to respond to God's goodness in giving them these oracles. What[13] are we to say of this situation? Paul speaks of some as not having *faith*,[14] or lacking a proper response to God's mercy. Scholars are divided on whether we should see the meaning here as "were unfaithful" (RSV, Moffatt, Hodge, Bruce, etc.; cf. Lightfoot, "were untrue to their trust"), or as "did not believe" (NIV, NASB, Morison, Cranfield, etc.). The context strongly favors the former meaning. Paul goes on to use a cognate word for God's *faithfulness* (KJV has "faith", but most agree that the meaning is really "faithfulness"), and the suggestion is that this term must be understood in the same way. But in the context the emphasis is on the unbelief of the Jews and their refusal to accept the promises of the Old Testament as fulfilled in Christ. Elsewhere Paul shows concern over Israel's unbelief (chs. 9–11), and this could be in mind here. It is pointed out that the verb occurs elsewhere in the New Testament seven times and means "disbelieve" on every occasion but one. However, we should bear in mind that these two meanings are not far apart, and it is possible that Paul was not trying to distinguish between them. Both are true. The noun rendered *lack of faith*[15] has meanings corresponding to those of the verb. On the ground that Paul goes on immediately to contrast this attitude with the faithfulness of God, many hold that "unfaithfulness" is the meaning here.[16] This is certainly possible, but it is equally possible that Paul has in mind Jewish unbelief, the failure to trust, despite the revelation God had given.

It is quite in the Pauline manner that the rhetorical question about the situation of the Jews should be followed by another, *Will their lack of faith*

11. Cf. Barth, the oracles "are the comprehensible signs of the incomprehensible truth that, though the world is incapable of redemption, yet there is redemption for the world."

12. Paul does not say that all Jews were without faith but that τίνες were (cf. 1 Cor. 10:7; Heb. 3:16). It is something like the Old Testament idea of the remnant; there were always some who were faithful, even though many were not. Nestle-Aland divide the text with a question after γάρ, but NIV, RSV, etc. take all the words up to τίνες in the first question. Not much depends on the way we resolve the point, for the meaning is much the same.

13. This is one of the situations where it is not easy to render γάρ in English. The word is "oft. in questions, where the English idiom leaves the word untransl. . . . Esp. τίς γάρ; τί γάρ . . . transitional, *what, then, is the situation?*" (BAGD 1f). But Haldane sees it as important here, and gives the meaning: " 'For what if some have not believed;' that is, 'the unbelief of some is no objection to my doctrine.' " εἰ introduces a condition accepted as factual, "if, as is the case. . . ."

14. The verb is ἀπιστέω, here only in Romans. Bultmann says that the sense "to be untrustworthy" is not attested in the classics where the verb means "to be distrustful", "unbelieving". In the New Testament the meaning is usually "not to believe" (TDNT, VI, pp. 178, 205; he thinks the meaning here, however, is "to be unfaithful").

15. ἀπιστία. It occurs five times in Paul (four in Romans), and 11 times in the New Testament. In these other passages it seems always to mean "unbelief".

16. J. Gwyn Griffiths argues for this meaning (ET, LIII [1941-42], p. 118).

nullify[17] God's faithfulness?[18] To ask the question, for Paul, is to answer it. The faithfulness of God is basic. Without that nothing makes sense. We must, of course, bear in mind that "faithfulness" means faithfulness in keeping his promises to judge the wicked, as well as those to bless those who love him. We should also remember that God in his faithfulness can use Israel's unbelief to promote his purposes (cf. 11:11, 15).

4. Paul gives the suggestion an emphatic negation, *Not at all!* (Moffatt, "Never!"; RSV, "By no means").[19] It is Paul's most emphatic repudiation of any idea to which it refers. He will have nothing to do with the suggestion that God might be unfaithful. *Let God be*[20] *true*, he says, where he means "Let God be seen to be what he is, true." It is interesting that this word *true* is applied to God (as in John 3:33; 8:26; to Christ, Matt. 22:16; Mark 12:14; John 7:18; to people, 2 Cor. 6:8). Truth is a quality of persons (and of actions, John 3:21) as well as of words. Here it stands for complete reliability. God is to be accounted thoroughly reliable, whatever the consequences when we come to people. Here *every man* is set over against God,[21] and characterized as *a liar* (cf. Ps. 116:11). This is the opposite of *true*. All perfection, all reliability is in God, and every one of us by contrast must be regarded as falling short. When in his lack of faith (v. 3) anyone stands over against God, he is shown in all his falseness. But this cannot interfere with God's faithfulness. If people's actions could prevent God from carrying out his promises, God would not be faithful. But he is faithful, even if this means that everyone on earth is a liar.

17. καταργέω is a difficult word to translate. It occurs 27 times in the New Testament (25 in Paul) and is translated in 17 different ways in KJV. RV got rid of eight of these, but introduced three new renderings of its own, and the process has been repeated with other translations. I now have a list of more than 80 ways in which reputable versions have rendered it in English. It may help to consider the way the word is formed. We start with ἔργον, "work". With the alpha-privative prefix and the verbal ending we get ἀργέω, "to be idle", "to do no work". The perfective prefix κατά brings us to "to do absolutely no work" or, causatively, "to make to do absolutely no work". Thus the verb has meanings like "nullify", "render null and void", "make inoperative". Here NIV's *nullify* brings out the meaning. Morison says, "The word rather means *to make inefficient*, than *to make without effect*. It negatives the idea of *agency* or *operation*, rather than the idea of *result* or *effect*." But this seems to narrow it unduly. G. Delling sees its religious meaning as "to make completely inoperative", "to put out of use" (TDNT, I, p. 453).

18. The question is introduced by μή, which shows that a negative answer is envisaged.

19. With but one exception (Luke 20:16) μὴ γένοιτο occurs exclusively in Paul in the New Testament (Romans, ten times; Galatians, three times; 1 Corinthians, once). Burton maintains that in 12 of its 14 occurrences in Paul "it expresses the apostle's abhorrence of an inference which he fears may be (falsely) drawn from his argument" (MT, 177). It is a strongly emphatic expression with the meaning "Let it not be!" It is rendered in English in a variety of ways: "Never!" "Not at all!" "Certainly not!" "Of course not!" etc.

20. γινέσθω. The verb expresses the idea of transition from one state of being to another, of "becoming". But God cannot pass from being untrue to being true. Paul is speaking of what comes to be seen, what is apparent. Cf. Lightfoot, "'be found,' i.e. become, relatively to our apprehension". The verb also comes to mean "to be", which is the justification for NIV. Some hold that the imperative is here equivalent to an indicative with a meaning like "God is true". Lightfoot seems to give the right sense.

21. The adversative δέ marks the contrast.

Characteristically Paul sheets this home with a quotation from Scripture (Ps. 51:4; it is exactly as LXX).[22] The Psalmist confesses his sin, acknowledges that it is sin only against God, and goes on to the conclusion that God is "proved right" and "justified". This fits neatly into Paul's argument. He has shown that both Gentiles and Jews are sinners, and it is pertinent that in the process of condemning sinners God is shown to be righteous. He is *proved right* (or "justified") in[23] what he says. The declaratory meaning of justification (see Additional Note D) is plain; it would be quite impossible to "make God righteous". God's *words* are the means whereby he is seen to be in the right.

Parallel to this is *prevail in your judging*. The forensic sense is clear, though the precise meaning is disputed. There is a complete triumph and *prevail* has a forensic sense, as the reference to judgment shows (NEB, "win the verdict").[24] The verb rendered *judging*[25] might be middle, "get judgment for yourself" (Lightfoot), or passive, "when thou art judged" (RSV, Denney). Whichever way we take it, Paul is saying that when God is put to the test he is vindicated. Paul entertained no doubt about the Davidic authorship of Psalm 51; he is saying that, though David's sin was certainly punished (2 Sam. 12:9-12), God did not withdraw his faithfulness from him (2 Sam. 7:1-17; 23:5). God never condones evil, but his punishment of sin is part of his faithfulness, not a negation of it. Käsemann understands all this in terms of apocalyptic: "At this point one sees plainly that Paul regards history as God's trial with the world which will come to an end only in the last judgment and will result solely in the victory or defeat of one or the other party" (p. 81). But

---

22. The quotation is introduced with ὅπως ἄν, which indicates purpose. In the classics it is often followed by the future indicative, but in the New Testament the subjunctive is more common; here we have both. The Hebrew text of Ps. 51:4 conveys the meaning "be clear (or justified) when you judge", but Paul, as he usually does, follows LXX (where it is 50:6). There is not the great deal of difference between the two which is sometimes alleged; either way God is seen to be just, whether as Judge (Hebrew text) or as litigant (LXX).

23. δικαιόω is followed by ἐν in Acts 13:39 (where τούτῳ refers to Christ or Christ's forgiveness), Rom. 5:9 (Christ's blood), 1 Cor. 4:4 (where τούτῳ refers to Paul's unawareness of anything against himself), 1 Cor. 6:11 (the name of Christ), Gal. 2:17 (Christ), 3:11 (not the law), 5:4 (law again), 1 Tim. 3:16 (spirit or Spirit). This is a mixed bag, but basically in this construction ἐν has a meaning like "by means of". This suits the present context well.

24. Vaughan finds here "the only clear example in Scripture of the classical use of νικᾶν as a forensic expression, *to gain a cause*" (so AS, BAGD 1b).

25. ἐν τῷ κρίνεσθαι. The construction ἐν τῷ + infinitive is sometimes said to be not classical, but Moulton notes it six times in Thucydides, 26 times in Plato, and 16 times in Xenophon (M, I, p. 215). BDF 404 say, "Attic does not use ἐν τῷ in this way". Robertson points out that Moulton minimized "the fact that in the O.T. ἐν τῷ occurs 455 times (45 in the Apocrypha) and that it exactly translates the Hebrew בְּ" (p. 1072). He goes on to notice that Moulton qualified his position in the second edition of his book, at the place where he said that the construction is "possible but unidiomatic Greek" (*ibid.*). See also M, II, p. 451. Hebrew employs בְּ with the infinitive (see Gesenius-Kautzsch 114, 2), which LXX renders ἐν τῷ + infinitive. This doubtless accounts for its frequency in the New Testament. It is mostly temporal, and means "while" (cf. BDF 404). Here, of course, it is LXX.

this is not exegesis; it is a reading of Käsemann's eschatological scheme into words which do not mean it. And I wonder whether we should not at this point insert, "Your God is too small." Paul's God is not one engaged (as Käsemann says he is) in a "struggle for vindication" (ibid.); he is supreme; he is true even if this means that every man on earth is a liar. We must not lose sight of the greatness of God as Paul sees him in the interests of an edifying eschatological struggle.[26]

e. Objections, 3:5-8

5But if our unrighteousness brings out God's righteousness more clearly, what shall we say? That God is unjust in bringing his wrath on us? (I am using a human argument.) 6Certainly not! If that were so, how could God judge the world? Someone might argue, "If my falsehood enhances God's truthfulness and so increases his glory, why am I still condemned as a sinner?" 8Why not say—as we are being slanderously reported as saying and as some claim that we say— "Let us do evil that good may result"? Their condemnation is deserved.

The objections continue. Paul now envisages an objector who reasons that if sin brings God's righteousness into focus and magnifies his glory, then it is surely not right for God to punish the sinner (where would God's righteousness be without the sin?). Then he considers another whose line is that people should sin more so that good (i.e., forgiveness to men and glory to God) may result. The apostle decisively rejects both.

5. Paul's first objector reasons that our unrighteousness brings out God's righteousness more clearly. His but if[27] is another argumentative supposition as he goes on to the curious reasoning that our sin is valuable, for it shows us the righteousness[28] of God in a way we would not have known had it not been for sin. The gospel that tells of salvation for sinners speaks also of God's righteousness (1:17; see Additional Note A). Had there been no sin there would have been no place for the gospel and we would never have known or at least never have known so well what God's righteousness means. Notice that Paul says our, not "your"; he has a habit of classing himself with those of whom he

---

26. Käsemann appears to concede this with "Paul already knows the outcome" (ibid.). A little later he says, "The justification of the ungodly means God's victory over the world that strives against him. It is to be seen from the perspective of the forensic situation which plays so great a role in our text. Always and everywhere it implies that mankind is presented as deceived by illusion regarding itself and God, that God's truth is manifested in his word, and that God's right prevails over rebels who have to give him the right" (p. 82). There are, of course, important truths here, but Käsemann appears to be confusing legal and military metaphors. Justification is a forensic term; it means getting the verdict when brought to trial. It does not mean getting a victory over rebels.

27. εἰ δέ.

28. RSV has "the justice of God"; Turner sees this as "more like a possessive gen.: the justice which God dispenses" (M, III, p. 211).

is speaking.[29] This might mean "we Jews", "we men", or even "we Christians" (so Lenski). The word translated *unrighteousness* can mean "injustice" (as in 9:14; Luke 18:6), but here it clearly has the wider sense of iniquity of any sort, as in 1:18, where it is translated "wickedness" (see the note). The meaning may be that our sin is the means whereby we come to see what God's righteousness is (as NIV), or the verb[30] may mean "commend" (as KJV) and signify that our sin not only shows God's righteousness for what it is, but commends it to people; if God has saved sinners like us, then he can save sinners like you. The question *what shall we say?*[31] is an expression Paul keeps on using in Romans, where it fits in well with the general argumentative style.

If the main result of sin is to advance God's purpose in some way, then it would seem that *God is unjust* when he punishes it.[32] Sin is simply giving God the opportunity of showing how righteous he is, the objector reasons, and so he ought not to punish the sinner. It is not right for him to use sin as a means of promoting his purposes and then to punish the sinner (who on this view is simply God's instrument). Paul does not go into the nature of the fallacy involved in claiming that God is unjust. Some commentators hold that it is not sin itself that shows God's righteousness, but the way God deals with it. Others think the attitude of the sinner is what is important; he does not intend a demonstration of God's righteousness, so he cannot claim any special consideration when this comes about. Paul goes on to speak of God as *bringing his wrath* (cf. 1:18; 2:8), where his verb is unusual in such a connection.[33] Indeed, it is so unusual that Dodd sees it as evidence that Paul is viewing "the wrath" as an objective thing, and he finds no place where the verb is used to mean "to vent one's passions on a person" (p. 22). But the Greeks did in fact use the verb of punishment,[34] so Dodd's argument cannot be sustained. The most we

29. Thus he can class himself with those who will be dead when Christ returns (1 Cor. 6:14) as well as with those who will be alive (1 Thess. 4:17). He does not know when the parousia will come, but he is one with believers whether he will be alive or dead then. He also classes himself with those who provoke the Lord with their eating and drinking in idols' temples (1 Cor. 10:22); it is Paul's way of saying "we sinners" rather than "you sinners" (though on occasion he can say this too).

30. συνίστημι means "stand together" and thus may mean "commend", "recommend", the bringing together of persons, as when Paul commends Phoebe (16:1). Deissmann notices the use of this verb in letters of commendation (LAE, p. 235 and n. 2). Or it may mean "show", "prove" (as in 5:8). The verb is Pauline in 14 of its 16 New Testament occurrences.

31. τί ἐροῦμεν is found seven times in Romans and nowhere else in the New Testament. It may be used to introduce a conclusion Paul rejects (6:1) or one that he accepts (9:30).

32. μή introduces a question looking for a negative reply. Paul asks the question, but does not think there is anything in the suggestion. Hall makes this part of his argument that Paul is not using the method of diatribe (NTS, 29, p. 190). An objector would not speak in this way.

33. The verb is ἐπιφέρω. It is not only unusual in such a connection; it is found again only in Jude 9 in the whole New Testament.

34. MM and LSJ both cite its use for inflicting πληγάς. It is perhaps worth noticing that the use in Jude is for bringing an accusation, which is a personal activity, not the impersonal activity Dodd envisages here.

can say is that Paul has chosen an unusual verb to make his point. For *wrath* see the note on 1:18. The expression is literally "the wrath", but NIV is surely right in seeing this as *his* wrath.

God's justice is so important for Paul that even to raise the hypothetical possibility of divine injustice requires an explanatory apology. "I am speaking according to man", he says ("in a human way, from a human standpoint", BAGD, who add that it "emphasizes the inferiority of man in comparison w. God"; the exact expression occurs again in the New Testament only in Gal. 3:15, but cf. 1 Cor. 9:8; 2 Cor. 11:17; Rom. 6:19).[35] That God might be unrighteous is so wide of anything that is possible that Paul asks pardon for even mentioning it.

6. It is unthinkable that God should be unjust (cf. Abraham's question, Gen. 18:25, and that of Elihu, Job 34:17), and thus we again have the emphatic repudiation, this time translated *Certainly not!* (the same Greek as that rendered "Not at all!" in v. 4, where see note). Paul shows how impossible it is to think of God as unjust by pointing to the consequences if the unthinkable were to happen. *If that were so*[36] the further question would arise, *how could God judge*[37] *the world?* For Paul this clinches the argument. For both him and his opponents it was axiomatic that there would be a judgment day when some would be acquitted and some condemned. Paul reasons that this points to the necessity of "the wrath". God could not engage in a real judgment of sinners without punishing some, so the wrath must be a reality. Some understand the question as "If God is not just, how can he judge the world?" (GNB), but this does not seem to be what the Greek means and it is not convincing. There is no theoretical reason why an unjust deity should not preside in an unjust judgment. Paul's point is rather that, assuming as all do that God will judge the world, some must be punished. Unless this happens, what occurs will not be judgment. It is the exercise of wrath, not the character of God, that is the point of it all.

The judgment of which the apostle writes is no parochial affair, but a judgment of *the world*. Back of this is the position taken up by the Jew that, while God would punish Gentile sinners, he would save him despite his sin; otherwise God would not be faithful. But the Jew's assumption could be made

---

35. D. Daube rejects the contention of SBk, III, p. 136 that this is not a technical expression (*The New Testament and Rabbinic Judaism* [London, 1956], pp. 394-400). He says, "The phrase is an apology for a bold statement which, without such an apology, might be considered near-blasphemous—be it because it is too anthropomorphic or be it because it sounds otherwise lacking in reverence for God or an established religious idea" (*ibid.*, p. 394).

36. There is just one word in the Greek, ἐπεί (= ἐπί + εἰ). The term can mean "because" or "since", and it is used elliptically here: "*for* (if it were different), *for otherwise*" (BAGD, who note that the usage is classical). The word is common in Hebrews (nine times), and Paul uses it ten times (three in Romans).

37. BDF 385 (1) cite this passage to illustrate the point that "The future indicative is often used in the NT where in Attic a potential optative could have been used". κρινεῖ could be accented as a present and some take it so, but the reference seems rather to final judgment.

by all mankind, for God is always working out his purposes, and he does this through the bad deeds people do as well as the good, and through the bad deeds of the Gentiles as well as those of the Jews. Every sinner can plead that his sin has been made to serve a good purpose, and on this premise there could be no judgment. But since all agreed that there would be a final judgment, the argument of the Jew could not be sustained. With his wide-ranging vision it is not surprising that *the world* is one of Paul's leading concepts (see the note on 1:8).

7. There is nothing in the Greek to justify NIV's *Someone might argue;* the justification for the words is that most agree that Paul is not stating his own position but citing an objection that might be urged against it.[38] It is essentially the same argument as that in v. 5, but stated this time in terms of *falsehood* and *truthfulness* (or "truth").[39] These two terms set in strong contrast the falseness and sin of people on the one hand, and the complete reliability and truth of God on the other. The argument is that my failure to be what I should be gives more scope for God's saving activity and thus for his reliability. This may be no more than a caricature of Paul's doctrine of salvation by God's free grace, urged by his enemies. Or it may have arisen from some who saw themselves as his disciples and friends but who unwittingly distorted his teaching. If all I am doing is giving greater scope for God's truth to be known, they may be reasoning, then it *increases his glory.* NIV has recast the Greek and added another verb; RSV is closer to the original with "But if through my falsehood God's truthfulness abounds to his glory. . . ." My falsity shows the truthfulness, the reliability, of God to be very great,[40] and this brings *glory*[41] to him. God's truthfulness, his complete and utter reliability, is one of the constituent elements of his greatness; it shows something of his glory.

Why then *am I*[42] *still condemned as a sinner?* In view of the good that

---

38. There is a textual problem at the opening of the verse. εἰ δέ is read by Nestle-Aland with the support of ℵ A 81 etc.; εἰ γάρ is supported by B D G and many others. The former reading makes this verse parallel to v. 5, a repetition of what has just been denied in μὴ γένοιτο; the latter makes v. 7 an explanation of the objection in v. 6. Metzger says that the majority of his committee accepted εἰ δέ, thinking that the argument "requires a parallel between verses 5 and 7"; they saw εἰ γάρ "as a rather inept scribal substitution, perhaps of Western origin." We should probably accept εἰ δέ (cf. RSV, "But if . . ."). εἰ γάρ is behind KJV, LB, etc.

39. ψεῦσμα means "lie", but BAGD note its use in the sense "lying, untruthfulness, undependability". Something of the sort is necessary here since there is no reason for thinking that Paul has in mind any one lie. Cf. Wesley, "*my lie,* that is, practice contrary to truth". It is not a common word, being found here only in the New Testament. For "truth" see Additional Note B and cf. v. 4. ἐν here will denote the means or instrument.

40. περισσεύω is a thoroughly Pauline word (26 times out of 39 in the New Testament; three times in Romans). It derives from περί, "around"; since what is around is beyond, this readily leads to the thought of abundance (cf. the note on περισσός, v. 1).

41. For δόξα see the note on 2:7. It is an important word for Paul and here points to the majesty, splendor, and sublimity of God. εἰς here will denote result; the abounding of God's truth results in his glory.

42. This is one of only two examples of κἀγώ in Romans. It puts emphasis on the subject, *I* of all people. Moule cites this as an example of Paul's "displacement of a καί which ought logically to cohere closely with the verb", and he gives the meaning as "not *why am I* also. . . ? but *why am I* actually judged. . . ?" (IBNTG, p. 167). Barrett is similar.

results from my action, the plausible argument is made, Why should I be condemned? We sinners display incredible ingenuity as we try to justify ourselves. The verb means "judged", but no doubt a negative judgment is meant. The word sinner[43] sometimes means one who is "especially wicked", but often also "one not free from sin", which appears to be its meaning here.

The false teaching opposed here is not dissimilar to that in chapter 6, though there is a difference. There it is a question of what free grace means and how it works out in practice. Here Paul is concerned with God's righteousness and a possible blasphemy against God on account of the way his grace operates. The two are related but not the same.

8. Wherever people have followed Paul in emphasizing that human merit has no part in bringing about our salvation and that we are saved by grace alone, some have drawn the conclusion that it does not matter whether we sin or not. It seems that the same conclusion was drawn by some of Paul's contemporaries and that they accused him of actively fostering sin in order to give the greatest possible scope for grace; they affirmed that he was saying, "Let us do evil[44] that good may result" (cf. Barrett, "Why not increase God's goodness by contributing as generously as possible to the stock of human sin?"), or, "The end justifies the means."[45] Paul repudiates this firmly;[46] it is a calumny; he is being slanderously[47] reported. Paul goes on to say, Their condemnation is deserved (perhaps better "just", as RSV; NIV does not bring out the link with justice that is important in Paul's argument).[48] There is an ambiguity here, for when Paul says "whose condemnation . . .", it is not completely clear to whom "whose" refers. Grammatically it could refer back to the slanderers, as JB, "Some slanderers . . . but they are justly condemned."[49] Or it might refer to those who advocate doing evil that good may result, "The

43. ἁμαρτωλός is found often in Luke (18 times), but Paul uses it only eight times, four being in Romans.

44. κακά is plural and may (along with ἀγαθά) indicate habitual practice, though the aorist cf the verb tells against this. κακός is especially characteristic of this letter, where it occurs 15 times, nearly one third of the New Testament total of 50 (Paul has it 11 times in his other letters).

45. The rabbis sometimes came close to this. In a comment on Ps. 51:4 the Talmud records a curious reason for David's sin: "David pleaded before the Holy One, blessed be He: 'Thou knowest full well that had I wished to suppress my lust, I could have done so, but, thought I, let them (the people) not say, "The servant triumphed against his Master"'" (Sanh. 107a). That is to say, David sinned in order that God might not be shown to be in the wrong.

46. It is not easy to see the force of the μή which introduces the statement. The parenthetical clause (καθώς) may somehow be mixed up with indirect discourse: "perhaps from μὴ λέγομεν (λέγωμεν) ὅτι 'do we say perhaps (should we perhaps say)' (with ὅτι recitativum), or from τί (7) οὐ ποιοῦμεν or μὴ ποιήσωμεν 'we surely do not want to do evil?' (G vg Or etc. thus with omission of ὅτι, smoothing the construction)" (BDF 427 [4]).

47. For βλασφημέω, "blaspheme", see the note on 2:24.

48. The word is ἔνδικος, only in Heb. 2:2 elsewhere in the New Testament. It signifies what accords with right and thus is "just" (RSV).

49. Godet holds that ὧν must have τινές as its antecedent. There may be a touch of irony in Paul's argument: the Jews who accused him of in effect doing away with God's law were in effect doing the same thing themselves, for they held that they would be saved despite their own law-breaking (cf. Hall, NTS, 29, pp. 194-95).

condemnation of those who would so argue is just" (Weymouth; cf. LB, Shedd, etc.). Or it might refer to the things they say, as Phillips, "such an argument is quite properly condemned" (so Moffatt). Again, Paul does not say whether the condemnation is men's or God's; perhaps both are involved.

Throughout this paragraph Paul has not mentioned the Jew. His language is general enough to embrace anyone (cf. the reference to "the world", v. 6). But to many commentators the form of expression and the type of objection urged point strongly to the Jew as being primarily in mind. If this be accepted, the reason will be as Käsemann has it: "Only from the perspective of the Jew as the representative of the religious person can universal godlessness be proclaimed" (p. 85).[50]

4. Universal Sinfulness—Proof from Scripture, 3:9-20

> [9]What shall we conclude then? Are we any better[a]? Not at all! We have already made the charge that Jews and Gentiles alike are all under sin. [10]As it is written:

> "There is no one righteous, not even one;
> [11]   there is no one who understands,
>   no one who seeks God.
> [12] All have turned away,
>   they have together become worthless;
>   there is no one who does good,
>   not even one."[b]
> [13] "Their throats are open graves;
>   their tongues practice deceit."[c]
>   "The poison of vipers is on their lips."[d]
> [14]   "Their mouths are full of cursing and bitterness."[e]
> [15] "Their feet are swift to shed blood;
> [16]   ruin and misery mark their ways,
> [17] and the way of peace they do not know."[f]
> [18]   "There is no fear of God before their eyes."[g]

> [19]Now we know that whatever the law says, it says to those who are under the law, so that every mouth may be silenced and the whole world held accountable to God. [20]Therefore no one will be declared righteous in his sight by observing the law; rather, through the law we become conscious of sin.

[a]9 Or worse   [b]12 Psalms 14:1-3; 53:1-3; Eccles. 7:20   [c]13 Psalm 5:9   [d]13 Psalm 140:3   [e]14 Psalm 10:7   [f]17 Isaiah 59:7, 8   [g]18 Psalm 36:1

Paul rounds off this important opening section of his letter with a series

50. Cf. Kertelge: "The infidelity of the Jews is being established in a legal action brought by God. . . . In the legal proceedings the Jew represents not just his own people but all mankind. In the face of God's righteousness all mankind's efforts simply demonstrate their own deep-rooted unrighteousness."

of quotations from Scripture that hammer home his point that all people are sinners. For him it is important that his readers be clear about this. Unless there is something to be saved from, there is no point in preaching salvation (or in embracing it). Paul's argument has been that all people, Jew and Gentile alike, are sinners, and he now shows that this is no private opinion but one well grounded in Holy Writ.

9. *What shall we conclude then?* is actually a much more concise "What then?" (as RSV),[51] though the sense is the same as that of the more verbose NIV. The following expression has puzzled expositors for centuries and its meaning remains uncertain. Our problem is that the verb used in the one-word second question[52] can be taken in more ways than one, and the context does not make it clear in which sense we should understand it here. The word means literally "to have before", which readily yields the meaning "to excel", and this is the normal sense of the active of the verb. But the verb here is not active; the form is either middle or passive. In the middle it concerns defending oneself and means "to have or place (something) before one", that is, for protection. Metaphorically this comes to signify "to put forward as a defence (or excuse)". The question "Have we (something) as a defence?" would make sense in this context, but there is a considerable objection. When used in this way, the verb requires an object. One must state what the "something" is; one cannot simply assume it. But there is no object here.[53] Despite this some do accept the verb as a middle. They point out that, however we take the verb, there is something anomalous about it, and they hold that the absolute use of the middle is not stretching probability too far. Godet, for example, takes it this way and gives the meaning, "Have we a shelter under which we can regard ourselves as delivered from wrath?"

But the verb might be passive, in which case the meaning will be as RV, "Are we in worse case than they?" (cf. NIV mg.). The passive was accepted by Lightfoot, SH, Manson, Goodspeed, LSJ, and others; recently Black has

---

51. τί οὖν; This makes a little pause in the argument for reflection. It should be read as a distinct question and not taken up into the following (see n. 53 below). προκατέχομεν περισσόν is read by D* G Ψ 104 etc., but most agree that this substitutes an easier question for προεχόμεθα; οὐ πάντως, which should be read (the reverse alteration is most improbable).

52. προεχόμεθα. The verb occurs only here in the New Testament.

53. An object could be found if we ran the two questions together: τί οὖν προεχόμεθα; But the question, "What then do we have as a defence?" cannot be answered with "Altogether not"; it needs "Nothing (οὐδέν)" or the like. Morison argues for the middle sense, and holds that an example of this use is found in Herodotus ii.42. He holds that, whether this be accepted or not, "there can be no reasonable room for doubting that the word is used absolutely by the Apostle Paul in the passage before us, and that it means, *Do we put forth pleas in self-defence?*" O'Neill takes the verb as middle and incorporates it with the previous question to give the meaning "What, then, do we put up as a defence?" He sees "Not completely" as a "nonsensical remark" and ascribes it to a glossator. Perhaps we should notice here the reading προεχώμεθα (A L), which "looks like an attempted improvement by someone who understood the verb in its proper middle sense and so felt a deliberative question was required" (Cranfield). It is evidence for an early understanding of the verb as a middle.

maintained that this is "Grammatically the least unsatisfactory solution". One problem with it is that the passive of this verb is so rare as to be almost nonexistent (Turner cites Field for one example in Plutarch, but he finds no others [*Grammatical Insights*, p. 106]). It is further urged that Paul is unlikely to have asked such a question. He has asked whether the Jew has any advantage and answered that he has much (vv. 1-2); why in the light of that would he now ask whether the Jew is at a disadvantage? It is, of course, not certain that "we" means "we Jews" (it might mean "we Christians" or simply "I, Paul"),[54] but most take it in this sense and indeed "Jews" is often inserted into the translation (e.g., RSV). But even accepting this, it cannot be said that the view that the verb is passive is completely convincing.

Thus neither the middle nor the passive is free from difficulties. Today most scholars think that the verb must be taken in the active sense despite its form and understand the sense as NIV, or as RSV, "Are we Jews any better off?" It is sometimes objected that there is no known example of the middle of this verb used in the active sense, and further that there seems no reason at all why Paul should not have used the active if that was his meaning. To this it is retorted that it is not uncommon for the New Testament authors to use the middle voice in the sense of the active and even that the "New Testament writers are not happy in their understanding of the middle voice".[55] This point of view is not, however, accepted by all,[56] and, while it is widely held, it is not beyond doubt. A further objection is that this understanding seems to be at variance with Paul's answer in verses 1-2. It is not easy to see why he should now answer "Not at all!" to the question "Have we Jews any advantage?" when he has just said that their advantage is "Much in every way!" It could be argued that the advantage there is of a different sort; here it is a question of sinners escaping the judgment of God and in that respect having no advantage. Not all find this convincing, but despite the difficulties most scholars today find this the best of an unfortunate group of choices (so, e.g., Barrett, Cranfield, Harrison, Maurer in TDNT, VI, pp. 692-93). It also appears in the majority of recent translations.

It is plain that whichever way we understand the verb we are involved

---

54. We see something of the difficulty when we notice that H. Moule has "we Christians" in his volume in *The Expositor's Bible* and "probably 'we Jews' " in CBSC. "We Christians" is understood by Hendriksen, Lenski (who makes the point that Christians as well as Jews had the Word), and others. There seems no reason to take the expression as "we Gentiles"; our choice is between "we Jews" and "we Christians".

55. Turner, *Grammatical Insights*, pp. 106-7.

56. Thus BDF say, "NT authors in general preserve well the distinction between middle and passive. The middle is occasionally used, however, where an active is expected" (BDF 316). This is quoted approvingly by Robertson (p. 805), and by Moulton who says, "the NT writers were perfectly capable of preserving the distinction" (M, I, p. 158). Turner holds that "the New Testament abounds in instances where a middle voice is used when there is an active form of the verb available" (*Grammatical Insights*, p. 106). But this is not quite the same as saying that they often use the middle in the sense of the active and that is the point at issue. Moule sees the distinction between active and middle as "blurred by the N.T. period" (IBNTG, p. 24).

in difficulties. There is no straightforward interpretation of this passage that solves all the problems. Perhaps as good an understanding as any is to take "we" as "we Christians"[57] and the verb as middle. Not enough attention appears to have been given to the fact that the immediate context strongly favors "we Christians". In verse 8 "we" who are "slanderously reported" are clearly Paul and his Christian associates, and the "we" in verse 9 who have "already made the charge" are just as clearly Christians. Why should the "we" that comes between them and is so close to them be understood of someone else? To understand it as "we Christians" is surely the most natural way of taking it. The meaning will then be "Are we (who are slanderously accused) making a defence (or . . . making excuses)?"[58] (as though claiming to be blameless; this leads on to "Not at all!"). This suits the context better than the other suggestions and does as little violence to the grammar as any.[59]

Most agree that the answer is *Not at all!* There is a problem here, too, for the Greek looks as though it should mean "not altogether". Indeed, after some hesitation Cranfield accepts this, and CGT suggests "not altogether that, either".[60] But NIV seems to give the sense required in this context. A

57. Barrett finds this suggestion "attractive", but thinks there would probably have been an emphatic ἡμεῖς or other "clear pointer" if so. But can we demand such consistency of a writer like Paul? In any case, there is something grammatically strange here.

58. Ronald Knox translates, "Well then, has either side the advantage?" This at least ingeniously preserves some of the possible shades of meaning. Barth takes the verb as middle and comments: "'Do we excuse ourselves' when we perceive that the faithfulness of God persists even in the apostasy of men? . . . Men are not deprived of one security, in order that they may immediately discover for themselves another." BAGD put this view in these terms: "if the 'we' in 9a must of necessity be the same as in 9b, i.e. Paul himself, he is still dealing w. the opponents whom he has in mind in vss. 7, 8, and he asks ironically: *am I protecting myself?, am I making excuses?* He is able to answer this question w. a flat 'no', since his explanation in vs. 9b is no less clear and decisive than his earlier statements" (*sub* προέχω 2). Lenski rejects this, but holds that the verb is middle: "Paul is asking: 'Have we Christians in our own persons an advantage in having the Word (the objective advantage the Jews, of course, also had)?" He sees the answer, "Not in every way." F. C. Synge also holds that Paul is the "we" and that the verb is middle voice. Paul is then asking, "'Am I setting (one group) ahead of the other, am I setting Jew before Gentile or Gentile before Jew?' And he answers his own question, 'No I am not, emphatically not, for I have already insisted (προητιασάμεθα) that both groups are equally under sin'" (ET, LXXXI [1969-70], p. 351).

59. In an important discussion of the passage N. A. Dahl argues for the middle with the meaning "What, then, do we hold before us as a defence?" (M. D. Hooker and S. G. Wilson, eds., *Paul and Paulinism* [London, 1982], pp. 184-204). He holds that to ask the question is to answer it (we humans "have nothing that we can plead as a defence or an excuse before God" [p. 195]), and he sees οὐ πάντως as an early gloss.

60. οὐ πάντως has a meaning like "not altogether" (cf. 1 Cor. 5:10). BAGD give the meaning as "not at all" and cite 1 Cor. 16:12; but in that passage the order is πάντως οὐ, which is not the same. BDF get rid of the difficulty by resolving the textual problem into τί οὖν προκατέχομεν; πάντως ἡτιασάμεθα Ἰουδαίους (433 [2]). This is a much easier text and for that reason probably wrong (it is not easy to see how such a straightforward text would be corrupted into the one we have). But MM cite an example of the expression from the papyri giving a complete negative, and this seems the way we should take it here. Turner holds that the words "must be reversed or taken separately: *no! absolutely* or *certainly not* (*not in all cases* is scarcely possible)" (M, III, p. 287). He thinks that the unusual expression may have occurred through the exigencies of dictation (M, IV, p. 86).

reason for the negative is given in the "for" (which NIV omits). Paul has *already made the charge*[61] that all are sinners, and this removes any advantage or defence. The language is legal, as in much of this part of Romans. For *Jews and Gentiles* see the note on 1:16 (the meaning of the plurals here is much the same as that of the singulars there). Together they make up all mankind, so that Paul is speaking of universal sinfulness. He speaks of charging them all with being *under sin* (see Additional Note E). He is regarding sin as a tyrant ruler, so that sinners are "under" it (JB, "under sin's dominion"); they cannot break free.[62]

10-12. Characteristically Paul reinforces what he has to say with an appeal to Scripture. He follows here a common rabbinical practice of stringing passages together like pearls.[63] He indicates their authority by introducing them with *As it is written*, and by linking passages of similar import he drives home his point that Scripture consistently stresses the fact that we are sinners all. He is saying something like "If you ask 'Who are the enemies of God?' look in the mirror!" Barth comments, "The whole course of history pronounces this indictment against itself"; he goes on to point to the fact that no serious thinker holds that people are good.

The first quotation (vv. 10-12) is from Psalm 14:1-3 (= 53:1-3), though it is not exactly as in our texts. This is especially true of the words in verse 10, and these may well be Paul's summary of what the passage is all about rather than part of his quotation. The differences, however, are minor. The point of the quotation is that there is not one *righteous* person, *not even one*, a sentiment with which this section begins and ends.[64] In between we read that *there is no one who understands*,[65] for surely no one would really choose sin if he fully understood what he was doing. The lack of understanding is coupled with a

---

61. KJV renders "proved", but it is the laying of a charge (αἰτία) beforehand that προαιτιάομαι signifies. The verb is found here only in the New Testament; it does not occur in LXX, nor is it cited from the classics. Did Paul coin it?

62. The expression is ὑφ' ἁμαρτίαν; cf. 7:14, "sold under sin". BAGD say that ὑπό + accusative may be used "of power, rule, sovereignty, command, etc. *under*" and cite Luke 7:8a etc. as well as this passage. The construction resembles that in which Paul speaks of being under law or under grace (6:14, 15, etc.). Paul has ὑπό in 74 of its 217 occurrences, 12 being in Romans.

63. Cf. A. Edersheim, "A favourite method was that which derived its name from the stringing together of pearls *(Charaz)*, when a preacher, having quoted a passage or section from the Pentateuch, strung on to it another and like-sounding, or really similar, from the Prophets and the Hagiographa" (*The Life and Times of Jesus the Messiah*, I [London, 1890], p. 449).

64. The rabbis could reach this truth. When R. Eliezer asked R. Akiba, "Akiba, have I neglected anything of the whole Torah?" Akiba replied, "Thou, O Master, hast taught us, *For there is not a just man upon earth, that doeth good and sinneth not*" (Sanh. 101a; the words in italics are a quotation from Eccl. 7:20). H. J. Schoeps takes this to mean that R. Eliezer was "a rabbinic exponent of the Pauline doctrine of the general sinfulness of mankind", but sees this as exceptional (*Paul* [London, 1961], p. 185).

65. The participle is usually accented συνίων (from συνίω), though some read it as συνιῶν (from συνιέω). But BAGD reject this, and Moulton sees it as "faulty accentuation" (M, I, p. 202).

failure to seek God.[66] Sinners do not look for God; their interest is elsewhere. They have *turned away*, a verb[67] that often conveys the idea of deliberate avoidance (e.g., 1 Pet. 3:11). Perhaps we cannot press this here, but the word is a strong one and certainly means more than that they accidentally missed their way. *Together*[68] they became *worthless*[69] or useless. This, of course, is to be understood in an ethical sense, a point further brought out with the following *no one who does good* (for this last term see the note on 2:4). The barrenness of this landscape is underlined with the melancholy *not even one*.[70] There is nothing to lighten the picture. The six negatives make a striking and impressive sequence.

13. From counting the number of the righteous Paul turns to the poisonous character of the wicked. He cites from Psalm 5:9 words that describe the *throats* of the wicked as *open graves* (the Psalm uses the singular in each case; curiously NIV retains this in the Old Testament but changes to the plural in this quotation).[71] *Open* translates a perfect participle which points to what stands open. If this means permanently open it is perhaps unlikely for a tomb, but very apt for a wicked mouth, a mouth permanently bringing out unclean things.[72] But an open tomb may be thought of as a tomb ready to receive the dead; taken this way the words point to the murderous impulses of the wicked (cf. Luther, "they devour the dead"; they "teach deceitfully" and they "destroy the people who listen to their teaching"). Either understanding is possible. It is not easy to see why the Psalmist referred to the "throat"[73]

---

66 This is Paul's one use of the verb ἐκζητέω. Some idea of diligence seems to be involved in the ἐκ. But these people are not in earnest. They do not want to find God.

67. ἐκκλίνω.

68. ἅμα denotes the coincidence of two actions in time or in place (this is the one instance in the New Testament of the latter use). Paul uses it six times in all, but only here in Romans.

69. The verb ἀχρειόω is derived from alpha-privative + χρή, "use", and thus means "make useless", or "unprofitable". A number of commentators draw attention to its use for milk that has gone sour. Barclay comments: "Human nature without Christ is a soured and useless thing." The word for *good* is χρηστότης, which is an admirable foil to ἠχρειώθησαν since it goes back ultimately to χράομαι (also derived from χρή), and signifies basically "what is useful". It is, of course, used here in an ethical sense, but it has added force in that it so firmly opposes what is said in the previous expression.

70. ἕως can be used "of degree and measure, denoting the upper limit" (BAGD). Thus in Matt. 18:21-22 ἕως ἑπτάκις means "as many as seven times". Here the upper limit is one, and even that is not attained! BAGD cite a papyrus οὐ . . . ἕως ἑνὸς νομίσματος, "not even a single coin".

71. See M, III, pp. 23-24 for this use of the singular. "Contrary to normal Greek and Latin practice, the NT sometimes follows the Aram. and Heb. preference for a distributive sing. Something belonging to each person in a group of people is placed in the sing." (cf. the singular of "heart" in 1:21 and "body" in 8:23).

72. Cf. Haldane, "What proceeds out of their mouth is infected and putrid; and as the exhalation from a sepulchre proves the corruption within, so it is with the corrupt conversation of sinners." LB reads, "Their talk is foul and filthy like the stench from an open grave". Cf. the reference to λόγος σαπρός (Eph. 4:29), where the adjective means "decayed, rotten" (BAGD).

73. λάρυγξ originally meant the larynx, but came to mean the throat, the gullet. It is used here only in the New Testament.

rather than to the mouth (which would more normally be used of speaking). Perhaps he wanted to indicate a deep-seated evil. With *their tongues* he moves to a more obvious organ of speech (and we should perhaps bear in mind that both life and death are linked with the tongue in Prov. 18:21). The change from the singular with "throat" to the plural with *tongues* is probably stylistic. *Practice deceit* renders yet another word in this string of quotations used here only in the New Testament.[74] It carries with it the thought of treachery (which NEB brings out: "they use their tongues for treachery").

Paul's third quotation is from Psalm 140:3. The word for *poison*[75] is used of the corrosion of metals in James 5:3, but poison is clearly the meaning here (as also in Jas. 3:8). The poison is that of vipers,[76] which we should probably understand of poisonous snakes in general and not of one particular species. NIV says that the poison is *on their lips*, but Paul locates it "under" them, on which SH comment that the quotation rightly describes the position of the serpent's poison bag. Used symbolically, the expression indicates that wicked people speak evil, even poisonous things. In their own way they are as venomous as snakes.

14. This little quotation comes from Psalm 10:7. The word "mouth" is used much more often in the New Testament than is "lip" (v. 13); both have to do with speaking.[77] *Cursing* is another word found only here in the New Testament, and *bitterness* appears only four times (twice in Paul). It is used of things with a bitter taste, and sometimes symbolically, as here. The verb translated *are full* points to a generous supply. Paul is complaining that those of whom he speaks do more than utter a bitter curse now and then; this kind of speech is habitual with them.

15-17. Next comes a somewhat shortened form of a denunciation of evil men from Isaiah 59:7-8. The passage refers to the *feet*, which are shown to act in harmony with the throat, tongue, lips, and mouth of the previous quotation (and with the eyes of the following one). Paul picks out their speed[78] to engage in homicide.[79] It is not that, when driven to it, they would take desperate measures; rather, they were eager for this form of wrongdoing. Naturally enough, *ruin and misery* result. Both words are uncommon (once and twice respectively in the whole New Testament). The first points to destructive activities, and the second to the wretchedness that follows. The

---

74. ἐδολιοῦσαν. Note the imperfect in -οσαν (cf. John 15:22, 24).

75. BAGD show that the word (ἰός) was in wide use and that it might denote literal poison, or metal corrosion; or it might be used metaphorically.

76. ἀσπίς is used here only in the New Testament. BAGD define it as "*asp, Egyptian cobra* gener. of venomous snakes".

77. στόμα occurs 78 times in the New Testament (13 in Paul, of which six are in Romans), but χεῖλος only seven times (two in Paul, one in Romans).

78. ὀξύς is found seven times in Revelation, but here only in the rest of the New Testament. In that book the meaning is "sharp", referring to a sword or sickle, but here it is "speedy".

79. ἐκχέω is the older form, but some parts of the verb are from the later Hellenistic form ἐκχύν(ν)ω. The aorist is ἐξέχεα (see M, III, p. 215), which yields the unusual infinitive we have here.

combination adds up to bad business. Their *ways* are their manner of life; they not only engage in wrong acts from time to time, but live in such a way that destruction and unhappiness are characteristic. But another way, *the way of peace*, is quite foreign to them. It is not only that they do not tread it—they do not even know it. Their interest is in bloodshed and destruction, not in peace. From which we see that sin not only separates people from God but from one another as well.

18. The final passage in the catena is from Psalm 36:1. We are told that the fear of the Lord is the beginning of wisdom (Prov. 1:7). Thus these people lack not only wisdom, but even wisdom's starting point. They have no reverence for the Supreme Being. *Fear* in this Psalm is not to be understood in the sense of "reverence" but of terror.[80] Evildoers would do well to have a healthy fear of him who will determine their eternal destiny, but they have none. It is a little curious that *fear* is connected with what is *before their eyes*; perhaps there is a contrast with "I have set the Lord always before me" (Ps. 16:8). "While a believer sets his course towards God Himself, this man does not take even 'the terror of the Lord' into account."[81] Along the line of his advance there is no fear of God.

19. His quotations ended, Paul considers a possible objection from a Jewish opponent. The things said are true enough, such a person might reason, but they refer to Gentiles, not Jews. Paul appeals to common knowledge *(we know);*[82] he retorts that what the law says it says to those who are subject to it. His *whatever*[83] is comprehensive; nothing in the law is excluded. For *the law* see Additional Note C. Here the term is used in its comprehensive sense to denote the whole Old Testament, for most of the quotations are from the Psalms and none is from the Pentateuch (cf. the use in 1 Cor. 14:21). All that the law says,[84] then, it says to *those who are under the law*, or more exactly those who are "in" the law (Moffatt, "inside the Law").[85] Presumably this

---

80. "The word *pachad* denotes terror inspired by God, not reverence for God. . . . Transgression persuades the wicked man that there is no need for him to dread God's judgments" (A. F. Kirkpatrick, *The Book of Psalms* [Cambridge, 1910], p. 184).

81. Derek Kidner, *Psalms 1–72* (London, 1973), p. 146. Kidner proceeds, "This is the culminating symptom of sin in Romans 3:18, a passage which teaches us to see this portrait as that of Man (but for the grace of God) rather than of an abnormally wicked type. All men as fallen have these characteristics, latent or developed." C. A. and E. G. Briggs comment, "He ignores God, can no longer see Him as present" (*A Critical and Exegetical Commentary on the Book of Psalms*, I [Edinburgh, 1907], p. 316).

82. This is Paul's second use of οἴδαμεν δέ (see the note on 2:2); he likes to appeal to what is common knowledge. He uses the verb οἶδα predominantly to appeal to well-known facts.

83. ὅσα. This word may be qualified by πάντα (Matt. 7:12 etc.), but even without it the absolute use may mean "all those who" or "everything that" (BAGD).

84. There seems no real difference between λέγει and λαλεῖ. Paul uses λέγω 100 times, 34 being in Romans, and λαλέω 60 times, three in Romans. The latter verb is thus rare in this epistle, but it is not easy to assign a reason other than that of style. Paul uses λαλέω 34 times in 1 Corinthians, 24 being in the discussion of tongues in ch. 14. If we deduct these, it is plain that Paul has a marked preference for λέγω in normal discussions.

85. οἱ ἐκ νόμου (4:14) is explicable, but τοῖς ἐν τῷ νόμῳ is more difficult. The same

means that the people in question center themselves on the law, have their whole being in the law. What the law says is certainly addressed to them, not to someone else who is outside the sphere of the law. Some hold that Paul means everyone in the world (e.g., Murray, Hendriksen), but it is unlikely that Paul's readers would have held that anyone other than the Jew was *under the law*. The law, being from God, has its relevance for all mankind, certainly. But Paul's point here is that the Jew cannot rest on a fancied security, holding that he is safe while the Gentile will come under the judgment of God. The law under which he lives, the law that is addressed to him and on which he prides himself that it is given to him and not to other people, convicts him as well as the Gentiles. *The whole world* (and not merely the Gentile world) is convicted. The construction introduced by *so that* indicates purpose.[86] It is God's plan to convict people of sin and so to silence *every mouth*. More literally the expression means "that every mouth may be stopped", which is forceful and intelligible though found but rarely (cf. Heb. 11:33, of stopping the mouths of lions, where the same verb is used though in a different sense). Indeed, there does not appear to be a comparable passage in the New Testament (2 Cor. 11:10, the only other passage with this verb, is perhaps the closest, but it probably means "this boasting will not [let itself] be stopped", BAGD). In Job 40:4, where Job spoke of putting his hand over his mouth, the imagery is slightly different but just as clearly affirms that before God the speaker has nothing to say. Paul is saying that the law speaks to those in its orbit, not those outside. Accordingly, those to whom the law is given have nothing to say. It stops their pleas. This is important, for the Jews could hold that at least some of their number were sinless, as when we read: "thou, O Lord, God of the righteous, hast not appointed repentance for the righteous, for Abraham and Isaac and Jacob, who did not sin against thee" (Prayer of Manasseh 8). Paul is opposing all such notions.

With this is coupled *and the whole world held accountable to God*. The Jew accepted that the Gentile was subject to God's judgment. Now that Paul has shown that the Jew who received the law is also guilty, the whole world is *accountable*.[87] This last term means not quite "guilty" (KJV) and not quite "answerable" (Moffatt); it refers to the person who has not been judged, but who knows what he has done wrong and that in due course he must answer for it.[88] The Jews, of course, recognized that they would give account of

---

preposition is used in 2:12, 23; Gal. 3:11, but the meaning is different in those passages. Käsemann says that ἐν νόμῳ "denotes the sphere of the law's validity as a factor in salvation history" (p. 87).

86. ἵνα commonly denotes purpose. Some students see result here, but there seems no reason for taking the term in anything other than its usual sense.

87. ὑπόδικος is found here only in the New Testament. Vaughan points out that in classical Greek it takes a dative of the person injured, "Thus τῷ θεῷ here expresses not the Judge before whom the case is tried, but the Person against whom the sin has been committed." It is a forensic term. Parry comments, "The dative seems always to be used of the person injured, not of the judge. The metaphor, then, suggests a trial as between God and His people." For Paul God is, of course, both the wronged Person and the Judge.

88. "ὑπόδικος here denotes more than a general unspecified liability to punishment

themselves to God. But they did not see themselves as guilty; for them it was a foregone conclusion that they would be saved. It is this to which Paul is objecting. *The whole world* (no exceptions!) will be silent as it comes under God's scrutiny, knowing at last that it has nothing to say in the judgment.

20. The consequence[89] is that no one will be accepted before God on account of his observance of the law, a truth Paul expresses in words reminiscent of Psalm 143:2. No law gives automatic acceptance by God.[89a] *Declared righteous* in this passage has obvious reference to the law, and once again we see that justification must be understood as forensic.[90] It clearly means "acquittal". *By observing the law* is more literally "from works of law", and the very general form of the expression may be significant (cf. BDF 258 [2]). It is true that observing the Jewish law will not bring salvation. Paul is certainly opposing the Jewish view that exalts deeds done in obedience to the directions of the Torah. But what he says is true of "law works" of any kind. No one[91] will be saved by the way of law.[92] *Rather*[93] would be better translated "for" (or "since", RSV); it introduces the reason for the preceding. As Paul's argument has shown, what law does is to bring recognition (see the note on "knowledge" in 1:28) of sin. A consideration of what the law requires and of what the student of the law actually performs leads us to see sin for what it is

---

but less than definitive condemnation. It describes the state of an accused person who cannot reply at the trial initiated against him because he has exhausted all possibilities of refuting the charge against him and averting the condemnation and its consequences which ineluctably follow" (C. Maurer, TDNT, VIII, p. 558). Morison argues for the meaning "liable to pay penalty to God".

89. For διότι see on 1:19. SH argue that it does not mean "therefore" but "because", giving the sense, "Mankind is liable for penalties as against God, because there is nothing else to afford them protection." BAGD see it here "in place of causal ὅτι" (which is not far from SH). BDF 456 (1) have it as "for" rather than "because" (the subordination is "very loose"). Paul is not drawing a conclusion from the preceding (which would require "therefore"), but giving a reason for it ("for"). Cf. Thomas, "Justification must be by something other than works, for law only reveals, it cannot redeem."

89a. J. D. G. Dunn says, "The 'works of the law' must be a shorthand way of referring to that in which the typical Jew placed his confidence, the law-observance which documented his membership of the covenant, his righteousness as a loyal member of the covenant" (NTS, 31 [1985], p. 528). Dunn stresses the importance of sociological factors and draws attention to the way Paul homes in on circumcision and food laws. It is, of course, true that such matters were important to Jews and marked them off from other people groups. But it may be doubted whether this aspect of Paul's thought explains the present passage. Paul is arguing that all are sinners, Gentiles and Jews alike, and while it is true that "works of law" will not save the Jews, it is also true that "works of law" (interpret the expression as widely as you will) will not save the Gentile.

90. The verb is δικαιωθήσεται; see Additional Note D.

91. οὐ . . . πᾶσα σάρξ is a Hebraism meaning "nobody" ("all flesh will not" = "nobody will"). Turner sees here an exception to the rule that "the negative precedes what is negatived" (M, III, p. 287). He also notes that οὐ . . . πᾶς is a "peculiarly Biblical Greek phenomenon" (*ibid.*, p. 196).

92. *In his sight* translates ἐνώπιον αὐτοῦ. The preposition has a curious distribution, being found not once in Matthew or Mark and once only in John, but occurring 22 times in Luke, 13 times in Acts, and 34 times in Revelation. Paul has it 17 times, three being in Romans.

93. γάρ.

and ourselves for what we are, sinners (cf. 5:20; 7:7-11; Gal. 2:16; 3:21). Phillips has a striking paraphrase: "it is the straight-edge of the Law that shows us how crooked we are."

B. JUSTIFICATION, 3:21–5:21

Having made it devastatingly clear that all mankind is caught up in sinfulness, Paul turns his attention to the way sinfulness is overcome. It is central to his understanding of the Christian way that no human merit can ever avail before God, but that the death of Christ on the cross changes all that. He sees the death of Christ as a great divine act that may be viewed from many angles. Indeed, one of our problems in working out what Paul thought the cross did is the fact that he speaks of it as doing so many different things and never bothers to work them into a unified system. There is no doubting that he saw Christ's salvation as fully meeting our need, however that need be understood, and equally there is no doubting that he saw the divine provision for meeting that need as complex. One of his ways of viewing it is as a process of justification. This is not confined to Paul, but in Paul's hands it takes on an importance that makes it central. It is a way of saying that man has no merit at all; his sin has disqualified him in the heavenly court. But because of what Christ has done, he can now face that court with assurance. The verdict that will be rendered on the believer is "Not guilty". In the section we now begin Paul works out in some detail what this means.

1. How Justification Is Effected, 3:21-31

In a very important passage Paul deals with the process of justification. He reiterates his point that all are sinners and goes on to show how the death of Christ copes with that sin, so that all who come in faith are righteous before God. He takes up in a different way the thought of 1:17, where he had emphasized the meaning of the gospel for sinners. Now that he has demonstrated that all people are sinners, he goes back to the content of the gospel.

a. The death of Christ, 3:21-26

> 21But now a righteousness from God, apart from law, has been made known, to which the Law and the Prophets testify. 22This righteousness from God comes through faith in Jesus Christ to all who believe. There is no difference, 23for all have sinned and fall short of the glory of God, 24and are justified freely by his grace through the redemption that came by Christ Jesus. 25God presented him as a sacrifice of atonement,a through faith in his blood. He did this to demonstrate his justice, because in his forbearance he had left the sins committed beforehand unpunished—26he did it to demonstrate his justice at the present time, so as to be just and the one who justifies the man who has faith in Jesus.

a25 Or as the one who would turn aside his wrath, taking away sin

In what is possibly the most important single paragraph ever written,[94] Paul brings out something of the grandeur of Christ's saving work. He speaks of the righteousness of God, the sin of man, and the salvation of Christ. He views this salvation in three ways: as justification (imagery from the law court), as redemption (imagery from the slave market), and as propitiation (imagery from the averting of wrath).

21. *But now*[95] may be understood logically (Shedd, Godet); it is then seen as moving to the next step in the argument, not the next point in time. Or it may be temporal (Boylan, TH),[96] moving to the next point in time. Or it may be both (Barrett): Paul is contrasting what people knew before the gospel came with what the gospel has revealed (cf. 16:25-26). The argument of the epistle up to this point has emphasized that the natural man, Jew or Greek, is a sinner who stands under the wrath of God. "But now" God has intervened. The human predicament has been radically transformed because of the saving act of God in Christ, which Paul proceeds to develop. He speaks of *a righteousness from God* (see Additional Note A), and the context makes it plain that here this means the right standing that comes from God[97] (though, of course, that God is himself righteous is not out of sight; the gospel involves

94. There is a question as to how much of the paragraph is due to Paul. R. Bultmann suggested that vv. 24-25 were non-Pauline traditional matter (*Theology of the New Testament*, I [London, 1952], p. 46). Käsemann enlarged on the point (he refers to *Exegetische Versuche und Besinnungen*, I [1960], pp. 96-100), and this view appears to have been widely accepted in Germany (see the list in N. H. Young, ABR, XXII [1974], p. 25 n. 7), and to some extent in the U.S.A. (e.g., Charles H. Talbert, JBL, LXXXV [1966], pp. 287-96; John Reumann, *Interpretation*, XX [1966], pp. 432 52). Cf also A. M. Hunter, *Paul and his Predecessors* (London, 1940), pp. 120-22; J. A. Ziesler, *The Meaning of Righteousness in Paul* (Cambridge, 1972), pp. 209-10, though these British writers do not give firm support to the view; interestingly, both relegate discussion of it to an appendix. More recently see Ben F. Meyer, NTS, 29 (1983), pp. 198-208. Young examines the hypothesis critically and concludes "that despite its wide acceptance, in Germany especially, the fragmentary hypothesis of Bultmann and Käsemann is invalid and that Rom. iii.24f. is a genuine insight into Paul's own peculiar thought" (ABR, XXII [1974], p. 32). O'Neill thinks a glossator has been very busy, and he attempts to resolve a number of the difficulties by accepting readings supported by one or two MSS and even on occasion by none (e.g., omission of "himself" in v. 26). But his suggestions do not commend themselves. There are difficulties in the text, but it is better to face them than to emend the text to one we like better. Even if Paul picked up these ideas from other people, he has made them his own.

95. The Greek is νυνὶ δέ. νυνί is a strengthened form of νῦν, but it is not easily distinguished in meaning from the simple form. In the New Testament it is found 15 times out of 18 in Paul, six being in Romans (no other writing has it more than twice). Paul always follows it with δέ. He is here contrasting (δέ is adversative) the situation under the law, which he has just said brings only a recognition of sin, with that under the gospel, where sin is really dealt with. Lloyd-Jones considers this contrast so important that he devotes several pages to it (3:20–4:25, pp. 23-29, 39-43).

96. TH comments, "For Paul all time is divided into two parts: the time before the revelation of the way in which God puts men in the right with himself, and the time after that."

97. Cf. Robinson, "'righteousness' does not primarily designate the ethical standard but the religious standing, the status of being right with God. It is not so much goodness as God-acceptedness."

both). This right standing is given quite *apart from law*.[98] In the first instance this means quite apart from the Jewish law, the law of Moses. It has been part of Paul's method to demonstrate in the section leading up to this point of the argument that that law cannot bring salvation. It can show up the problem; it can and does make clear that all are sinners. But it can do no more. The word *law* (not "the law") is general. What is true of the Jewish law is true also of all other law. The way to God is not the way of law (cf. the way "works of law" is treated in v. 20). No one can take refuge in law and the way he thinks he has kept it. This is not a human discovery; Paul is not congratulating himself on having uncovered an important spiritual law. It *has been made known* (for the verb cf. 1:19); that is to say, it is a matter of revelation. This means more than that it has now been discovered. It means that it is something in the secret counsels of God from of old (cf. Eph. 1:4-5). But whereas it has always been true, it has only now been "manifested". Paul is making the point that the gospel is no afterthought. God had always planned[99] to save people by the way of grace. It is the making of this known that is recent.

That it was always God's way is clear from the fact that testimony is borne to it by *the Law and the Prophets*, an expression that means the whole Old Testament (cf. Matt. 5:17; 22:40; Luke 24:27). The law was the heart of the Jewish religious system and the prophets were its outstanding religious teachers. And both, says Paul, point to the truth that right standing comes from God. Nygren points out that Paul's great example, Abraham, is from the law, and his great text, 1:17, is from the prophets. What Paul is saying is soundly based. It is not some minor truth tucked away in an obscure corner of Scripture, but a great truth blazoned forth in both law and prophets. And the present participle "being witnessed to" indicates that the testimony of the Old Testament continues.

22. Paul moves[100] to an explicit statement of Christ's involvement. This *righteousness* is one that *comes through faith in Jesus Christ*. There is, however, a question as to precisely how we should understand this. The Greek translated *in Jesus Christ* is a genitive ("of Jesus Christ"), a genitive which most students understand as objective (as NIV, RSV, etc.).[101] But it could be subjective, referring to the faith Jesus exercised,[102] and the word translated *faith* could be

---

98. Grammatically χωρὶς νόμου could be taken with the verb ("has been manifested apart from law"), but most agree that it is better taken with the noun.

99. Notice the perfect tense πεφανέρωται; the manifestation is of continuing force. Some see a reference to the incarnation (e.g., Lagrange), but it is rather to be understood of the atonement.

100. δέ here marks transition rather than contrast (BAGD, it is used "to insert an explanation *that is*"), though there may also be "an explanation or an intensification ('but', 'and . . . at that')" (BDF 447 [8]).

101. Harrison argues for the objective genitive. He thinks that what settles the point is "the precedent in Galatians 2:16, where we find the identical phrase 'through faith of Jesus Christ' followed by the explanatory statement, 'we believed in Christ Jesus.'" See also C. F. D. Moule, ET, LXVIII [1956-57], p. 157.

102. L. T. Johnson takes it in this way (CBQ, 44 [1982], pp. 77-90). George E.

taken in the sense "faithfulness". If this last suggestion were adopted, we could understand it either of "God's faithfulness in Jesus Christ" or of "the faithfulness of Jesus Christ".[103] There are thus several possibilities. If the word is used of God it must, of course, mean "faithfulness" (there is no question of God "believing in" anyone; cf. 1 Cor. 1:9; 10:13). If it is used of Christ it could still mean "faithfulness" (cf. Heb. 2:17; 3:2, etc.), or it might mean "faith" and be a reference to an important aspect of his genuine humanity (cf. Johnson, cited above). A reference to Christ is supported by the fact that the words *all who believe* may be held to be redundant if we translate *faith in Jesus Christ* in the immediately preceding section. Rather than a redundancy, it is urged, we should see a reference to Christ's faithfulness or to his faith.

Such an understanding of the words is not impossible, but perhaps in all our discussions we are making too sharp a distinction between the subjective and the objective genitives. It is not beyond the bounds of possibility that Paul saw that the expression might be taken in either of two ways and still used it (some speak of a "mystic" genitive; cf. Althaus). It is even possible that the distinction that seems so obvious to us with our quite different constructions did not loom so large to a Greek speaker. We should bear in mind that Paul is here not describing Christ, but outlining what Christ has done in bringing about salvation, so that we must understand, at least as part of the meaning, the objective genitive. *Faith in Jesus Christ* is certainly in mind. But there would be no place for the exercise of this faith were it not for "the faithfulness of Jesus Christ" and for "God's faithfulness shown in Jesus Christ".[104] The right standing God gives is connected with his faithfulness and that of Christ, and it certainly is linked with the faith of believers in Christ.

This is the first time in this epistle that faith is specifically linked to Christ. Paul is not referring to faith in general terms, or seeing it as a general

---

Howard cites favorably an argument that πίστις Χριστοῦ "refers to Christ's faith as opposed to man's faith in him. The faith of Christ, it was suggested, refers to the divine faithfulness to the promise given to Abraham that in him all the nations of the earth will be blessed" (JBL, LXXXVIII [1969], p. 335). It is not easy to see this meaning in the present passage.

103. Barth takes it in the former way, as does T. F. Torrance, ET, LXVIII (1956-57), p. 113, while the latter is espoused by Richard N. Longenecker, *Paul, Apostle of Liberty* (New York, 1964), pp. 149-50, and others. D. W. B. Robinson argues that Paul is saying, "Christ's faithfulness, in death itself, makes possible an atoning sacrifice which redeems lost men" (RThR, XXIV [1970], p. 80). Similar is G. Howard, ET, LXXXV (1973-74), pp. 212-15.

104. Cf. Turner, "God's act of redemption is seen to be motivated not only by the willingness and faithfulness of Christ by offering himself on behalf of all those who believe in him, but is seen also in the response of men who put their faith in Christ" (*Grammatical Insights*, p. 111). Of "the controversial phrase, 'the faith of Jesus Christ'" he says, it is "difficult to comprehend it within the limits of either the subjective or objective genitive exclusively"; he suggests that it may share in the qualities of both (*ibid.*, p. 122). Käsemann rejects the idea that the genitive is both objective and subjective, arguing that this view is correct only in "that for Paul the Giver always comes on the scene with the gift". He sees v. 26 as supporting an objective genitive (p. 94).

trust in God's overruling; he is linking faith to the one who came to earth to die for sinners, and, as he will make clear in the succeeding verses, thus brought about justification and redemption and propitiation. Paul puts his trust in the Savior whose activity on behalf of sinners is so clear, so costly, and so decisive. So important is *faith*, and so opposed to the way of law (which in one way or another is almost universal among mankind), that it is emphasized with the addition *to all who believe*.[105] The verb *believe* is used absolutely; it is not necessary to say in whom or what they believe. Paul is fond of this construction, pointing to the centrality of faith as it does (cf. the description of Christians as "believers"). *Through* is important.[106] It points to the fact that faith is not a merit, earning salvation. It is no more than the means *through* which the gift is given. Other expressions refer to our righteousness as being "on" (i.e., on the basis of) faith, or "from" faith. The variety of ways of connecting faith and righteousness should put us on our guard against placing too great an emphasis on any one of them. Together they bring out the important point that from the human side faith and faith alone is the requirement. Look at it how you will, only faith is required of us. Faith is the indispensable attitude.

Paul goes on to assure his readers that there is *no difference*.[107] This could refer back to the way of faith. All, without distinction, must come by that way. But it seems more likely that we should take the words closely with those that follow: Paul is speaking of all alike as sinners.

23. *All have sinned*[108] sums up the human tragedy. *For* gives the reason for the lack of difference. The common factor is sin. The aorist pictures this as past, but also as a completion. It certainly does not mean that sin belongs

---

105. εἰς is probably "with respect to" (BAGD 5), or perhaps destination, "extending unto all" (Hodge). πίστις εἰς means "faith in" Christ (Acts 20:21; Col. 2:5), but this is a different usage. Some MSS add καὶ ἐπὶ πάντας to εἰς πάντας (which is the text behind KJV, "unto all and upon all them that believe"). The attestation of the shorter text is superior and is generally accepted, though Nygren prefers the longer text (thinking it more likely that one of two similar expressions was dropped than that an apparently redundant expression was added. Morison holds that the shorter text may have arisen by homoioteleuton, the eye of the scribe moving from the first πάντας to the second). Wesley accepts the longer text, understanding the first "all" to refer to the Jews and the second to the Gentiles; but there is no reason for this. Better is Lightfoot: "reaching unto and extending over all."

106. Hodge sees significance in the use of the genitive after διά, whereas διὰ πίστιν would have meant "on account of faith". We have the same construction in Phil. 3:9, which also has ἐπὶ τῇ πίστει. Paul also uses ἐκ πίστεως (Rom. 9:30; 10:6) and the simple genitive (4:11, 13).

107. διαστολή is used of the truth that there is no distinction between Jew and Greek (10:12), and again of a distinction between musical sounds (1 Cor. 14:7). In the matter of being sinners there is no distinguishing between one person and another.

108. Shedd insists on "the aoristic meaning" of ἥμαρτον and sees an allusion to the sin of Adam as in 5:12, where the same words are used. Burton regards this as "a collective historical Aorist", one "evidently intended to sum up the aggregate of the evil deeds of men" (MT, 54). Bengel gives the word a full meaning: "Both the original act of sin in paradise is denoted, and the sinful disposition, as also the acts of transgression flowing from it."

wholly in the past, for Paul goes on to a present tense when he says *fall short*[109] *of the glory of God.*[110] Elsewhere in Romans the glory is often future (2:7, 10; 5:2; 8:18, 21). But there is also a present glory, for God "made his light shine in our hearts to give us the light of the knowledge of the glory of God in the face of Christ" (2 Cor. 4:6; cf. 2 Cor. 3:18; John 17:22). But this is something Christ produces in believers. Sinners fall short of it. Not only did all sin in the past, but they continually come short of God's glory. The linking of God's glory with man's sin is intriguing. It would seem that God intended people to share in his glory (as we see in the story of Eden).[111] But sin cut Adam off from all that, and sin cuts his descendants off still. This clear statement of universal sinfulness is basic to Paul's understanding of the human predicament and also of the salvation Christ brought. Were it not for our sin there would have been no need for Christ's redemptive activity; because of our sin there is no possibility of our achieving salvation by our own efforts. This is "the point of departure for the whole redemptive work of God. No one has anything to offer which could elicit the love of God" (Nygren).[112]

24. From tragedy to triumph. People who could not help themselves are *justified* (see Additional Note D),[113] or declared to be in the right. This does not mean that they are "made righteous" in the sense "made virtuous". It is a declaration that, on the basis of Christ's saving work, believers are right with

---

109. Gifford takes ὑστεροῦνται as a middle and gives it subjective force, "to *feel want*". He contrasts the complacent young ruler who asked, "What lack I yet?" (Matt. 19:20, ὑστερῶ) with the Prodigal who felt his destitution (Luke 15:14, ὑστερεῖσθαι). Denney, however, points out that this "is not borne out by the use of the N.T. as a whole." Here the point is that they come short, whether they feel it or not.

110. There are divergent translations. Thus GNB reads, "is far away from God's saving presence"; Phillips, "has fallen short of the beauty of God's plan"; JB, "forfeited God's glory", with an added note citing Exod. 24:16, "that is to say, God as present to human beings and communicating himself to them more and more, a process that can only reach its climax in the messianic era."

111. There are other ways of interpreting the expression: (1) "The radiance which according to the apocalyptic view awaits the justified in heaven" (Käsemann, p. 94; cf. Gifford). But the present tense tells against this, and Godet points out that it then really means to lack the qualifications for glory, which, of course, is not the same as to lack the thing itself. (2) "The divine standard for human life" (Thomas). (3) "Conformity to (God's) image" (Murray) or to "the divine likeness" (Dodd). (4) The approval of God (as John 12:43); so Hendriksen; cf. Black, "they have lost the divine favour". (5) "The presence of God and communion with Him" (Leenhardt). (6) "Sanctifying grace" (Boylan). Commentators tend to read their own meaning into the passage.

112. H. Moule puts it like this: "The harlot, the liar, the murderer, are short of it; but so are you. Perhaps they stand at the bottom of a mine, and you on the crest of an Alp; but you are as little able to touch the stars as they" (p. 97).

113. Grammatically δικαιούμενοι should go with πάντες. But while it is certainly the case that all sin, it is not the case that all are justified. The meaning appears to be that all who are justified are justified in this way. Or there may be a reference back to the πιστεύοντες of v. 22 (so SH, Murray, Denney). If we ask, "Who are the δικαιούμενοι?" we must answer, "The πιστεύοντες". The use of the participle rather than the indicative links this closely with the foregoing: "being justified" in the way that follows is evidence that all are sinners and come short of God's glory.

God.[114] That this is due to no merit of their own is brought out in more ways than one. First, it is done *freely*, which means "in the manner of a gift".[115] It is not earned; we receive it as we receive gifts. Second, it is *by his grace* (see on 1:5). This points to free, unmerited favor, to the generous goodness of God towards those he has made. Earlier Paul referred to grace as received "through" Christ (1:5), so that the essential source of grace is the Father. Here *his* must refer back to "God" in the previous verse, so that we have the same truth. The position of *his* in the Greek puts some emphasis on the word: it is the grace of none other than God that brings us salvation. We often refer to "the grace of our Lord Jesus Christ", which is, of course, both proper and scriptural. But we should not overlook the connection of grace to the Father as well. The linking of the two comes out quite naturally here in that the Father's grace operates "through" Christ's redeeming work.

In this verse we have two of Paul's great categories for the interpretation of the work of Christ. At the beginning of the verse he speaks of that work as justification, a metaphor from the law court.[116] He is saying that when believing sinners are tried at the bar of God's justice they will be acquitted because of Christ's saving work which they have appropriated by faith. We should not be afraid of the legal metaphor. It is not the entire way of understanding Christ's work, but it is a valid perspective and one that means a great deal to Paul, as we see from his frequent references to it. He is sure that one day we will all face God and that we will have no merits of our own to plead. But it is Christ's wonderful gift to us that he has met the law's full claims on our behalf and therefore we will be acquitted.[117]

---

114. Sometimes justification is said to be "a creative act" or the like, and the impression is left that it is the powerful act whereby God brings about a new creation (2 Cor. 5:17) or makes the new man (Eph. 2:15; 4:24). But if it is creative, it is, as Barrett says, "a creative act in the field of divine-human relations". The imagery is forensic. The new creation is not described in the New Testament in terms of justification.

115. δωρεάν is the accusative of δωρεά, "gift", used as an adverb (cf. NASB, "as a gift").

116. Curiously Thomas comments, "sin is . . . a debt. . . . The debt requires to be paid, and this may be called justification." But justification is a legal term; it is not the language of commerce. He does better when he says, "To justify means to declare, or pronounce righteous." Precisely. It has nothing to do with debt, though, of course, from another point of view sin may be regarded as a debt and accordingly we pray, "Forgive us our debts. . . ." Käsemann says that δικαιοῦσθαι here "can only mean 'to be made righteous'", and he cites Barrett and Cambier in support. But this is to import into the expression a meaning derived elsewhere; it overlooks the fact that the verb is a forensic term, a fact that Käsemann later recognizes when he says, it is "incontestably forensic 'declaring righteous'" (p. 96). It is true that the Christian salvation includes being "made righteous", but it is not this truth to which justification points us. We must not confuse justification with sanctification.

117. Some minimize the force of justification, perhaps in a laudable attempt to safeguard the truth that the Christian salvation means a mighty miracle: the power of God transforms the sinner into a person whose life is characterized by good works. They are repelled, too, by suggestions of a "legal fiction", and hold that when God says a person is "righteous" he is righteous. But no reasoning along these lines can alter the fact that justification is a legal term. Paul does not share our inhibitions, but full-bloodedly speaks

Paul goes on to speak of *redemption*, which he here says is "in Christ Jesus".[118] This picturesque statement had its origin in the release of prisoners of war on payment of a price (the "ransom"). It was extended to include the freeing of slaves, again by the payment of a price.[119] Among the Hebrews it could be used for release of a prisoner under sentence of death (Exod. 21:29-30), once more by the payment of a price. There are also metaphorical uses, but the idea of freedom after payment of a price is what gives them meaning.[120] As used of Christ there is, of course, no thought that the price was paid to Satan, as some have held. Never is there any mention of the recipient of the price.[121] Therefore we must regard redemption as a way of looking at the cross which brings out certain aspects of Christ's work but which cannot be pressed in every detail.[122] What it tells us is that a great price was paid (Moffatt, "ransom") to purchase sinners out of their slavery to sin (7:14), out of their sentence of death (6:23). Now they are to live in freedom (notice the connection between being set free with "the freedom of the glory of God's children" and redemption, 8:21-23).[123]

25. The verb translated *presented* (or "put forward", RSV)[124] may indeed have this meaning. But it is also used in the sense "to set before the mind, to purpose", and this is its meaning in both of its other New Testament occurrences (1:13; Eph. 1:9). This would give good sense here, and it is adopted in

---

of God as "acquitting the guilty" (cf. 4:5). He does not soft-pedal the truth that God's power transforms us (cf. 2 Cor. 5:17). But for that he uses other terminology. And so should we. There is no value in trying to turn the legal term into something nonlegal, even when we recognize the paradox involved.

118. BAGD include this occurrence of ἐν under the heading "causal or instrumental—1. introducing the means or instrument". Where a person is involved they think it means "with the help of", and translate here, "through Christ" (III.1b). For *Christ Jesus* see the note on 1:1.

119. It is often suggested that we should discount any reference to the freeing of slaves since Paul used Old Testament categories rather than those derived from the Hellenistic world. But the apostle would not have been unaware of the associations the term would have for freed slaves in the Christian communities.

120. Morison thinks the term points to "deliverance which is effected *in a legitimate way*, and *in consistency with the rights and claims of all parties concerned*" (p. 254).

121. Gore sees redemption and propitiation as "mutually corrective", each counteracting the possible misuse of the other. Propitiation (of the Father) prevents us from seeing the ransom as paid to the devil, while redemption, the idea that the Father gave the Son to buy us out of slavery to sin, makes it impossible to think that "the mind of the Father needed to be changed towards us" (pp. 152-53).

122. "The word implies the cost of redemption to him that brings it about; and does not involve (as used) a price paid to the alien master" (CGT).

123. The normal New Testament word for redemption is ἀπολύτρωσις, used here. What is not always noticed is that this is an unusual word, being found ten times in the New Testament and cited about ten times in all Greek literature outside the New Testament. Perhaps the early Christians refrained for the most part from using the normal terminology, thinking that there was something special about the redemption that Christ wrought. I have examined the ten non–New Testament passages in *The Apostolic Preaching of the Cross* (London and Grand Rapids, 1965), pp. 16-18.

124. προέθετο. GNB translates "offered", but the word is not usually a sacrificial term (though BAGD see this as a possible use of the active, at least).

some translations (as NEB, "God designed him"; Phillips, "God appointed Him"; Cranfield also prefers this meaning).[125] But the context seems to be concerned with the accomplishment of God's purpose rather than its origin; and it has a number of expressions that convey the idea of a public act ("made known", v. 21; "demonstrate", vv. 25, 26). We should probably accept the meaning of NIV and RSV.

There are problems with the next expression, which KJV rendered "a propitiation" and which nearly every modern translation waters down.[126] Part of the trouble is that "propitiation" is neither a well-known nor a well-used word today, and translators like to employ something simpler. But the major reason is that propitiation means the removal of wrath and, as we saw earlier (see the notes on 1:18), some commentators find the concept of the divine wrath distasteful and unworthy; so they write it out of Scripture.[127] If there is no wrath there is no propitiation.[128] There are two major reasons for rejecting this approach. One is the meaning of the word Paul uses. The detailed examinations mentioned in n. 126 show that the word means "the removal of wrath". The other is the context. Paul has mounted heavy artillery in the section 1:18–3:20 to show that all are sinners and subject to the wrath of God. But unless the present term means the removal of wrath he has left them

125. Hendriksen has a long note in which he argues for this meaning. So Lagrange.

126. The word is ἱλαστήριον, elsewhere in the New Testament only in Heb. 9:5. For this word see my article in NTS, II (1955-56), pp. 33-43; *The Apostolic Preaching*, chs. V and VI and the literature there cited. See also David Hill, *Greek Words and Hebrew Meanings* (Cambridge, 1967), ch. 2; C. F. D. Moule in *The Parish Communion To-day*, ed. David M. Paton (London, 1962), pp. 78-93. TH says that this word group "is sometimes used by pagan writers in the sense of propitiation" and that "it is never used this way in the Old Testament." The first statement is misleading: only two passages in all the range of Greek literature seem ever to be claimed as supporting a meaning other than propitiation (see *The Apostolic Preaching*, pp. 145-47). The second is simply wrong. Surely no serious student can doubt the meaning "propitiate" in, e.g., Zech. 7:2; 8:22; Mal. 1:9. I have tried to show that this meaning is characteristic in the Old Testament (*ibid.*, pp. 155-74).

127. T. C. G. Thornton cites evidence from Jewish sources that prayers and sacrifices can be seen as propitiatory; nevertheless he rejects the idea of propitiation here (and in 1 John 4:10), since if the words "in these passages had any propitiatory significance, they would imply that God was indirectly propitiating Himself, an idea for which I can find no parallel in Jewish or New Testament literature" (ET, LXXX [1968-69], p. 54). We should set aside the absence of any Jewish parallel, for Paul is talking about something unique: Judaism knows nothing of a Messiah on a cross. But many authors have difficulty with the idea of God propitiating himself (as I do myself). There is certainly a paradox here. But how else are we to account for two things: (a) God's wrath is directed towards sinners, and (b) the removal of that wrath is due to God himself? It may sound paradoxical to say that God provides the propitiation, but it accounts for the facts. It is significant that Thornton does not take the wrath of God into consideration in his discussion.

128. K. Grayston has an interesting discussion of propitiation in "ἱλάσκεσθαι and Related Words in LXX" (NTS, 27 [1980-81], pp. 640-56). He ends with the view that in the present passage Paul perhaps took ἱλαστήριον from "a traditional formulation and modified it by adding διὰ πίστεως: 'an act of propitiation when interpreted by faith'" (*ibid.*, p. 653). While I am glad that he recognizes the propitiatory force of the term in the present passage, it should perhaps be added that the comment on God's propitiating himself in n. 127 applies to some of Grayston's own argument (e.g., p. 655 n.23).

there, still under God's wrath. Nothing else he says means the averting of wrath. On both accounts we should see Paul as saying that from one point of view Christ's death means the removal of the divine wrath from believing sinners.[129]

A number of translations see a reference to sacrifice. This may be justified by the use of the term "blood" here, and further by the fact that a verb cognate with the noun we are discussing is commonly used in LXX to say that such-and-such a sacrifice was offered "to make atonement". It must, however, be borne in mind that the verb in such expressions means "to make atonement", not "to offer sacrifice", and further that the noun we have here is not the atonement word, but is only related to it. Usage is decisive, and the usage of this noun shows that it means "propitiation".[130] We must not lose sight of this. While I see no reason for denying that sacrifice may well have been in the back of Paul's mind, it was in the background, not the forefront. If we are to grasp what he is saying, we must not lose sight of this. Those who advocate a meaning like "propitiatory sacrifice" may well be right; they are certainly doing more justice to Paul's language than do translations like NIV or RSV. However we translate, it is most important that we bring out the thought that what God did in Christ averted the divine wrath from sinners.

Some hold that the word should be understood as "mercy seat" on the grounds that it has this meaning in LXX,[131] and that this was the view of many early Greek commentators.[132] But a close examination of the evidence shows that this is not solidly based. The same Greek word is used of the "mercy seat" indeed, but in LXX it is the context that makes this clear; there is no example of the word unqualified (as it is here) referring to the mercy seat.[133] Moreover, the same word is used in LXX of other things, such as the ledge of

---

129. Whether ἱλαστήριον is to be seen as an adjective or a noun is a matter of dispute. If an adjective, it might agree with ὅν (Denney) or with "sacrifice" understood (Cranfield). A few examples of the adjective are cited, but they are rare. It is much more likely that we should see the term here as a neuter noun with a meaning like "the removal of wrath". Some regard it as a masculine noun, "propitiator", but this has had little acceptance.

130. But such considerations do not stop O'Neill from saying: "In the supreme and key relationship with God we need to find a sacrifice. The news entrusted to the apostles is that God has put Jesus Christ before us as a sacrifice. We are able to offer him." Besides the firm identification of ἱλαστήριον with sacrifice we have here the thought that we do the offering. Could anything be further from the thrust of this passage?

131. This is sometimes exaggerated, as when J. A. Ziesler says: "In the Greek OT it is invariably used for the lid of the Ark of the Covenant" (ET, 93 [1981-82], p. 358). It is not so used, e.g., in any of the five occurrences in Ezekiel, nor in Amos 9:1. Ziesler recognizes that propitiation is not an impossible explanation, though he prefers something like expiation.

132. See Barth, Gifford, Bruce, T. W. Manson (JTS, XLVI [1945], pp. 1-10), etc. Calvin prefers "mercy-seat" but leaves the question open, for "God, apart from Christ, is always angry with us" and "we are reconciled to Him when we are accepted by His righteousness."

133. Cf. Denney, "A 'mercy-seat' is not such a self-evident, self-interpreting idea, that the Apostle could lay it at the heart of his gospel without a word of explanation."

the altar (Ezek. 43:14, etc.). It seems clear that the word is understood to signify "means of propitiation" or "propitiatory thing". This is a description that could on occasion apply to the mercy seat, but it could also refer to other things (and sometimes does). We need more than the simple, unqualified use of the word to see here a reference to that article of tabernacle furniture. We should also bear in mind that the mercy seat was hidden from the public gaze (nobody ever saw it but the high priest, and he only once a year), whereas here the context stresses what is in the open. Shedd remarks that a comparison to the mercy seat "upon the face of it seems incongruous." Few of those who hold to this view really face the fact that an unexplained likening of Christ to a blood-sprinkled lid would be very curious. "Means of propitiation" is surely the meaning.

Through faith repeats the construction of verse 22 (where see note).[134] Once more Paul reminds us of our inability to do anything to merit our salvation. We receive the propitiation through faith. Grammatically it is possible to take *in his blood* as qualifying *faith* (as KJV; so Hodge), but it is an unlikely understanding of the words. For Paul faith is in Jesus Christ, and it is not easy to see him speaking of faith in blood.[135] It is better to see it as referring to propitiation. The propitiation is effected (a) through faith, and (b) in[136] Christ's blood. *His* is emphatic from its position: it is the blood of none less than Christ that brings propitiation. In some quarters great emphasis is placed on the Old Testament texts that connect life and blood (e.g., Lev. 17:11) and the conclusion is drawn that we should see a reference to Christ's life rather than his death. But a close examination of the relevant passages shows that this view is untenable.[137] We should understand the expression to refer to the death of the Savior.

God did this, we are told, *to demonstrate his justice* (the Greek word is that translated "righteousness" in vv. 21 and 22).[138] The saving act did many things, one being that it showed[139] that God is just. The point is that God is a

---

134. There is not the same discussion here as in v. 22 as to whether the genitive is subjective or objective, most interpreters simply assuming the latter. It would be possible, though, to understand it as subjective and think of the Father's faithfulness, or that of Christ.

135. If we take the expression in this way, it is best to see the meaning, with Haldane, as "we believe that His death is a sacrifice which makes atonement for us".

136. ἐν will denote the means (cf. 5:9; Heb. 9:22; Rev. 7:14) or the price (BDF 219 [3]; M, III, p. 253). Moule classes it "Of accompaniment, attendant circumstances", perhaps meaning "to deal with sin . . . by his blood" (IBNTG, p. 78); he further thinks that ἐν indicates the sphere rather than the object of faith (*ibid.*, p. 81).

137. See my *The Apostolic Preaching*, ch. III and the literature there cited. Leenhardt is one commentator who sees blood as "the sign of a life which is at first offered to God and then given back by God, renewed, restored and forgiven." This sort of thing sounds impressive, but proof that it is Paul's meaning has not been produced.

138. εἰς might indicate purpose or result.

139. ἔνδειξις is used only by Paul in the New Testament (four times). A number of grammarians draw attention to the rule of Apollonius Dyscolus: where nouns are in regimen, both have the article or both lack it; but this may be modified, as here, so that the first is anarthrous and the second has the article (see M, III, p. 180).

forbearing[140] God. He does not hurry to punish every sinner, and *the sins*[141] *committed beforehand unpunished*[142] (cf. Acts 17:30) present a problem for the person who has a firm grasp on the truth that God is just. When God does not punish the sinner, that might well show him to be merciful or loving. But just? It would mean that God condones evil. Justice demands that the guilty be punished just as it demands that the innocent go free. So God might be accused of being unjust. Not any more, says Paul. The cross shows us God's inflexible righteousness in the very means whereby sin is forgiven. *Committed beforehand* translates an unusual verb,[143] and the perfect tense points not only to the sins in question as having taken place at an earlier time, but to those sins as somehow persisting. "Old sins cast long shadows", as the proverb puts it. Though done in earlier days the sins linger, for they have made those who committed them sinners. Luther holds that the reference is to "the sins that we have done in the past"; others hold that we should see it rather as a description of the sins of people in the days before Christ. The language could refer to either, and it scarcely seems profitable to try to differentiate. What Paul says is true of both.

26. "In the forbearance of God" in the Greek of this verse refers back to the previous expression. "Forbearance", of course, means God's withholding of punishment when he might have inflicted it. Paul sees this as a problem solved by the cross of Christ. Once again he says that God brought about salvation in Christ to[144] *demonstrate his justice.* Clearly the point means a good deal to him. *At the present time* stands over against "the sins committed beforehand". The sins were done at an earlier time, but the demonstration of God's righteousness is present. The saving act, Paul says, is in order to[145]

140. For ἀνοχή see the note on 2:4.
141. ἁμάρτημα occurs here only in Romans and only twice in Paul. It does not differ from ἁμαρτία except that it is confined to acts of sin and is not used of the principle.
142. πάρεσις differs from ἄφεσις as "passing over" differs from "forgiveness". It means that consideration of the sins in question is set aside for the time being; they may subsequently be either punished or forgiven. V. Taylor rejects the idea that the word here could mean forgiveness and points out that in that case διά + accusative would be prospective, "with a view to", a meaning rare in the classics and not found in LXX or MM. He considers it much more likely that it is used here in its "almost invariable *causal* sense, 'because of,' with reference to something which has already happened" (ET, L [1938-39], p. 298). Barrett sees a real difference between πάρεσις and ἄφεσις and points out that to take the meaning "pretermission" allows διά to have its more usual meaning and gives a better sense. Others (e.g., Hodge) see the two words as meaning much the same, but this is unconvincing. We perhaps get something of the force of the word when we notice that ben Sirach uses the corresponding verb in praying that his sins be not passed by (Sir. 23:2). He was certainly not praying that he would not be forgiven; rather, he looked for suitable chastisement (not condonation) so that he would be deterred from serious sin. Cf. also Wis. 11:23, "thou dost overlook men's sins, that they may repent."
143. προγεγονότων, found here only in the New Testament. Most see the reference to the sins of people in past days.
144. The preposition is πρός, which BAGD say is used here "of the goal aimed at or striven toward -a. with conscious purpose, *for, for the purpose of*". The article used here (but not in the previous expression) signifies "the demonstration just mentioned".
145. εἰς τό may indicate purpose or result (BDF 402 [2]), with purpose predominat-

bring about the demonstration. God's righteousness (or justice) is manifested in order that he may be[146] (and, of course, be seen to be) *just and the one who justifies*. We should take *and* in the sense "and also" rather than "and yet", "although" (as Shedd, Hodge, Cranfield). There is no antithesis between God's justice and his mercy. Paul is saying that it is not simply the fact that God forgives that shows him to be just. Indeed, that fact by itself raises a question about God's justice. As Barclay puts it, "The natural thing to say, the inevitable thing to say, would be 'God is just, and, therefore, condemns the sinner as a criminal.'" But if God had simply punished sinners, while that would have left no doubts about his justice, it would have raised questions about his mercy, and the God of the Bible is both just and merciful. What Paul is saying is that the cross shows us both.[147] It is the fact that he forgives by way of the cross that is conclusive. Grace and justice come together in this resounding paradox (cf. Ps. 85:10; Isa. 45:21; Zech. 9:9).[148] God saves in a manner that is right as well as powerful. The claims of justice as well as the claims of mercy are satisfied.

The person who is saved is *the man who has faith in Jesus*, more literally "who is of faith in Jesus".[149] This means not simply the person who believes, but the person whose characteristic is faith, whose whole position proceeds from faith. Paul has no patience with people who want to mix up faith and law or add faith to law. Those who are saved are those "of faith".

b. Faith, 3:27-31

> [27]*Where, then, is boasting? It is excluded. On what principle? On that of observing the law? No, but on that of faith.* [28]*For we maintain that a man is justified by faith apart from observing the law.* [29]*Is God the God of Jews only? Is*

---

ing in Paul. There is no doubt that purpose is in mind here. Turner classes this among passages where the construction is "final or very near it" (M, III, p. 143), though Lenski sees result.

146. εἰς τὸ εἶναι αὐτὸν δίχαιον points to more than manifestation. It is important that God not only be seen to be just, but that he *be* just. Cf. Tom Wright, in Romans "Paul presents justification as God's answer to his own, not merely to man's problem" (Gavin Reid, ed., *The Great Acquittal* [London, 1980], p. 23).

147. Simeon comments that in the light of the cross God's forgiveness is not only a matter of mercy: "It is not an act of mercy, but of justice, to liberate a man whose debt has been discharged by a surety."

148. Cf. Brown, "what to him who paid the ransom is justice, may be grace, pure grace, to him for whom it was paid" (pp. 38-39).

149. τὸν ἐκ πίστεως Ἰησοῦ. The expression ἐκ πίστεως is found a number of times (cf. 1:17). But this expression, preceded as it is by the article, is rare. Indeed, in this precise form it is found here only in the New Testament. τῷ ἐκ πίστεως Ἀβραάμ is found in 4:16, but this refers to the faith exercised by the patriarch, not to trust in him. οἱ ἐκ πίστεως occurs in Gal. 3:7, 9 (cf. Gal. 2:16; 3:22; Phil. 3:9). ἐκ πίστεως is rare outside Paul. Similar expressions are found for other qualities, e.g., οἱ ἐξ ἐριθείας (2:8). The meaning of the expression here does not seem to be in doubt, but it is certainly unusual. Turner discovers the sense "*belonging to* (-*ists*, of a sect or school)" and explains it here: "the noun after ἐκ expresses the character or standards of these men" (M, III, p. 260). L. T. Johnson sees a subjective genitive with the meaning "'the one who shares the faith of Jesus,' meaning 'one who has faith as Jesus had faith'" (CBQ, 44 [1982], p. 80). Linguistically this is possible, but an objective genitive (as NIV) is more in accordance with Paul's thought.

he not the God of Gentiles too? Yes, of Gentiles too, 30since there is only one God, who will justify the circumcised by faith and the uncircumcised through that same faith. 31Do we, then, nullify the law by this faith? Not at all! Rather, we uphold the law.

Paul has insisted that salvation comes only through Christ's death and that that death can be viewed from a variety of angles. He has said that we appropriate salvation only through faith, and he comes back to that thought now. He shows that there is no room for human boasting or the like and that a right understanding of faith is necessary if we are to uphold the law.

27. Paul resorts to one of his favorite devices, the rhetorical question,150 as he turns to the truth that Christ's saving death has removed from mankind any possibility of *boasting*.151 If the cross has done all that is needed (Michel), if God has revealed in the Old Testament that human effort is futile (Cranfield), there is no place for man's effort and accordingly for man's extolling of his own effort. In any religion of law the worshipper may legitimately feel satisfaction in his personal achievement, but this is a satisfaction that can lead to pride. For those saved by grace, however, that is impossible. Grace leaves no place for satisfaction in one's own achievement, for salvation is all of God. For the Jew it was a matter of pride that he had received the law (2:23; cf. 2:17), a pride that he could not but regard as legitimate because no other people had received this great gift. From this it was an easy step, and a very natural one, to pride in the extent to which one kept the law. Some such pride is the besetting sin of all religious people, no matter what their religion. But as the hymn writer puts it, "When I survey the wondrous cross . . . I pour contempt on all my pride." To understand what grace and faith mean is to reject the way of pride and boasting. And so Paul says that boasting *is excluded*.152 There is a decisiveness about his aorist tense: the possibility is excluded once and for all (cf. Jer. 9:23-24).153 This leads to a second question, *On what154 principle?* (literally "law";155 see Additional Note C). Paul seeks for the law, the reg-

150. He introduces it with ποῦ, a word he uses ten times, but only here in Romans. His οὖν is important: his question is devastating in light of what he has just said. It is because of Christ's act that there is no place for human initiative.

151. καύχησις is a favorite Pauline word: he uses it in ten of its 11 New Testament occurrences (the other is in James). For the corresponding verb see on 2:17. Bultmann points out that "καύχησις denotes boasting as an act; καύχημα is what is said in boasting . . . or the object of pride or boasting", though the distinction is not invariable (TDNT, III, p. 649 n.35). He says further, "Paul's rejection of boasting is not motivated, as is that of the Gks. . . . by the fact that boasting violates dignity and makes a man an ἀνελεύθερος, bringing him into dependence on others . . . but by the fact that it violates the divine glory and brings man into dependence on the σάρξ" (*ibid.*, p. 650 n. 40).

152. ἐξεκλείσθη. The verb is found again in the New Testament only in Gal. 4:17.

153. Calvin sweeps away distinctions between different kinds of merit such as "congruous merit" and "condign merit", for "Paul is not concerned with the diminution or moderation of merit, but does not leave a single particle remaining."

154. ποῖος is not common in Paul (twice only; here only in Romans). It really means "what kind of?" though it is often equivalent to τίς, "what?"

155. Hendriksen translates "basis".

ularity, that enables him to exclude boasting so decisively. His answer is another question, "Of works?" This is very compressed, but clearly he means the way of salvation by conforming to the works of the law, the typical Jewish understanding of God's dealings with his people.[156] At the same time his use is general, and Nygren is probably too restrictive with his statement: "'The principle of works' is only another name for 'the law'" (p. 162). The expression is wide enough to cover all doctrines of salvation by works, Jewish or any other. Works are important, but they do not merit salvation, and they thus form no basis for human pride. Paul rejects his suggested answer with an emphatic negative,[157] followed by a strong adversative.[158] Not that way lies the answer. Boasting is excluded because of what *faith* means.[159] Paul introduces "law" again: "through the law of faith" (cf. 8:2; Gal. 6:2). He so delights in the concept of law that he uses it in many places where we would not. When he excludes boasting he looks for a "law" to cover the situation and finds it in faith. This may be understood in some such sense as "principle" (NIV, RSV).[160] But it is also possible that "law" here directs us to the way of faith. Both the law and the prophets point us to that righteousness which is God's gift (v. 21). Paul may well be saying that the law points us to faith and thus cuts us off from all boasting.

28. Paul introduces a supporting argument.[161] *We maintain*[162] intro-

---

156. Barrett rejects the translation "principle" because it is too philosophical for Paul, and further he would not change his meaning between v. 27 and v. 28 where νόμος must mean "law". Since, however, Paul sets two "laws" over against each other, it cannot simply be the Jewish law: "The fact . . . is that here and elsewhere for Paul law (νόμος) means something like 'religious system', often, of course, though not always, the religious system of Judaism." Some who accept the interpretation that points to "religion" go beyond Barrett and press the view beyond what is legitimate. They sometimes take God's justification of the ungodly (4:5) to mean that it is those without religion, not those with it, whom God saves. But Paul's point is that religion is irrelevant; what matters is faith. Neither the religious nor the irreligious as such are saved, but either way they may be justified by faith.

157. οὐχί, which is found in Paul 17 times out of the New Testament total of 53 (three in Romans).

158. ἀλλά.

159. Barth speaks of the "law of the faithfulness of God", which is the same as the "law of faith", "the place where we are established by God." There seems, however, no reason for taking πίστις here in the sense of "faithfulness"; the meaning surely is "faith". But that Paul means "we are established by God" is not in dispute.

160. W. Gutbrod sees νόμος here as "meant in the broader sense of the divine ordinance which describes faith, not works, as the right conduct of man, to the exclusion of self-boasting before God" (TDNT, IV, p. 1071). I hesitate over the description of faith as "the right conduct of man"; it seems that Paul is saying rather that no conduct of man can bring him justification. Faith is not so much "the right conduct" as the abandonment of all reliance on conduct. It is trusting God, not one's conduct.

161. The connective in some good MSS is οὖν (B C Dᶜ etc.), but most recent critics accept γάρ (א A D* etc.), partly because the attestation is considered somewhat better and partly because "ver. 28 gives a reason for the argument in ver. 27, not a conclusion from it" (Metzger).

162. λογίζομαι is thoroughly Pauline (see the note on 2:3). Morison says that Paul "not only represents himself as *thinking*, he realizes that he was *thinking reasonably*"

duces a contention of Paul's own, but the use of the plural loosely associates Christians in general with him. He is not giving a purely individual opinion, but stating a truth that "we Christians" hold. *A man* is any member of the human race; the term is quite general. Justification is brought about in the same way for all, *by faith.*[163] We can do nothing to merit it, and the insistence on *faith*[164] emphasizes that we simply receive it as God's good gift. *Apart from*[165] *observing the law*, more literally "apart from works of law",[166] is virtually equivalent to "apart from law" (v. 21). There is perhaps a little more emphasis on the activity of the man, but the expression means that all such activity is of no avail. Justification takes place apart from law works of any kind.[167]

29. In an unexpected line of approach Paul tackles the subject from the standpoint of monotheism. Since there is only one God, it is unthinkable that the way of approach to him should be such that in principle only a small proportion of the people he has made can approach (as the Jews held with their view of the law). Monotheists must beware of the accusation "Your God is too small!" The Jews insisted that there was only one God; they rejected the gods of the heathen as no more than idols. Very well. Paul invites them to reflect on what that means. He introduces the verse with "Or" (which NIV omits) and on which SH comment, it "presents, but only to dismiss, an alternative hypothesis on the assumption of which the Jew might still have had something to boast of." *Of Jews* is in an emphatic position: "Or, *of Jews* is he the God only?" Can monotheists really hold that the one God is the God

---

(p. 374). H. W. Heidland holds that here the word stands for "the 'judgment of faith'" and that all questions "are framed in terms of such a conclusion: What are the consequences of the crucifixion for the righteousness of man (R. 3:28)?" (TDNT, IV, p. 288). The term points to a process of reasoning, but as Paul uses it it is not a secular process; it is the reasoning of a believing person, one saved through the cross.

163. Paul has spoken of faith in connection with salvation a number of times, but this is the first time he has used the simple dative. The same construction is used with respect to introduction (5:2), standing by faith (11:20; 2 Cor. 1:24), being founded in faith (Col. 1:23), established in faith (Col. 2:7), being sound in faith (Tit. 2:2). But this appears to be the only place in the New Testament where the dative πίστει is used in connection with justification (the dative πίστει occurs, but in expressions like those noted and in "strong in faith" and the like, as in 4:19, 20; 14:1; 2 Cor. 8:7; Phil. 1:27; again the dative is used with justification, but it is "by grace", v. 24; Tit. 3:7).

164. As is well known, Luther translated "by faith alone" and came in for criticism for adding to the text. But whether we add "alone" or not, that is surely the meaning of the text, for if we see anything at all in addition to faith as needed for justification it is not "by faith" that we are justified. Luther, of course, did not originate the addition, which goes back to Origen and was espoused by Roman Catholic writers before the Reformation (see the references in Morison, pp. 378-79; Hodge, etc.).

165. Barth sees this as "the 'No', which is, nevertheless, the 'Yes'." He goes on, "It is God who pronounces and speaks and renders, who selects and values according to His pleasure."

166. Hodge comments, "not by works which the law produces, but works which the law demands".

167. Joachim Jeremias speaks of "the first basic sentence of Paul: not the deeds of the law but the faith in Him who died for our sins is the way to justification. *Sola fide* we are justified" (ET, LXVI [1954-55], p. 369).

exclusively of any one people? *Is he not the God of Gentiles too?* is a question looking for an affirmative answer, and Paul obligingly supplies it himself, *Yes, of Gentiles too.* It follows from Jewish insistence on monotheism that the God the Jews worshipped could not possibly be no more than "the God of the Jews". Since there was no other God, he must be the God of the Gentiles also, a corollary that does not seem to have occurred to the Jews.[168] Monotheism means that God is not the exclusive property of any one nation (cf. Gen. 18:25; Ps. 96:1, 7-8; 97:5; 98:2-3; 100:1; Jer. 10:7, etc.). Neither *Jews* nor *Gentiles* has the article; it is the quality of belonging to one group or the other and not the definite groups (*the* Jews, *the* Gentiles) that Paul has in mind.[169] Monotheism is important to Paul, and so are its consequences. It means that the God the Jews had always worshipped is the God of the Gentiles throughout the world. And that is an important conclusion.

30. Paul carries on with the sentence he began at the end of the previous verse. *Since*[170] gives the logical ground for seeing Yahweh as the God of the Gentiles: "if indeed (as we all agree) God is one" (cf. Deut. 6:4). It is interesting that as he speaks of the one God Paul goes on to characterize him in terms of his activity of justification. He has shown that no man can secure his own justification, so that if anyone is justified, be he Jew or Gentile, it must be by God and there is but one God. This God then *will justify the circumcised by faith* (actually he says "circumcision", but the meaning is as NIV; for the word see on 2:25). Paul is not saying that all the circumcised are justified, but that all the circumcised who are justified are justified in this way. And the same God will justify *the uncircumcised* ("the uncircumcision") *through that same faith. Faith* the second time has the article ("through the faith"), which is the reason for NIV's *that same.* Paul is saying emphatically that there is no real difference. What God requires of the Jew is faith. What God requires of the Gentile is faith. Faith is the only way.[171]

---

168. Indeed, they were capable of drawing a very different conclusion: R. Simeon b. Yoḥai said: "The Holy One, blessed be He, said to Israel: 'I am God over *all* earth's creatures, yet I have associated My name only with *you;* for I am not called 'the god of the idolaters' but 'the God of Israel'" (Exodus Rabbah xxix.4).

169. Cf. BDF 254 (3).

170. εἴπερ is a strengthened form of εἰ and means "if indeed, if after all, since" (BAGD). There is a variant, ἐπείπερ, but its meaning is not significantly different. NEB has "if it be true", but the particle conveys the meaning of certainty rather than doubt (cf. TH).

171. Paul has ἐκ πίστεως of the Jew and διὰ τῆς πίστεως of the Gentile. Both prepositions have elicited a good deal of discussion. SH see a significant difference: the Jew is "justified ἐκ πίστεως διὰ περιτομῆς: the force at work is faith, the channel through which it works is circumcision. The Gentile is justifed ἐκ πίστεως καὶ διὰ τῆς πίστεως: no special channel, no special conditions are marked out, faith is the one thing needful, it is itself 'both law and impulse.'" Moule, however, thinks "credulity is strained" by the distinction (IBNTG, p. 195), and most agree that there is no essential difference. Paul uses both prepositions freely with πίστις (ἐκ, 1:17; 3:26; 4:16; 5:1; 9:30; 10:6; διά, Gal. 2:16; 3:14, 26; Eph. 2:8; Phil. 3:9; 2 Tim. 3:15). It is not easy to see a significant difference. Moreover, in Gal. 2:16 he says that "we Jews" know that "a man" is justified "by faith (διὰ πίστεως) in Christ Jesus" and that, knowing this, we "have put our faith in Christ Jesus that we may be justified by faith (ἐκ πίστεως) in Christ"; both prepositions are used of the Jews. Again,

31. What does all this do to the law? To the Jew it was a deeply held conviction that the law came from God and accordingly it showed the chosen people God's way of salvation. When Paul lays it down that all that is asked of people, Gentile as well as Jew, is faith,[172] this seems to the Jew to imply that the law has no place. It is done away. Paul's view is, however, far different. It is only as we see God's way of salvation in Christ that we see the true purpose of the law.[173] Paul has already laid it down that the law (as well as the prophets) witnesses to this salvation (v. 21). The law is the divine preparation for the way of salvation in Christ, but it is not itself the way of salvation. Jesus said that he came to fulfil the law (Matt. 5:17), and he did so in his life and in his death. Paul has been insisting, as the law does, that all people are sinners. He has pointed out that the righteousness from God, the divinely worked out way of salvation, is attested in the law (and the prophets, v. 21). Christ's atoning death means the working out of what the law really means. When we see this, we see the place of the law—"we establish the law." But not until then. It is also worth noticing that the law sets a standard of living which it is not able to produce in those who try to keep it. But, as Paul will show later, those who come by faith receive the gift of God's Holy Spirit, and in the power of the Spirit are able to produce it (cf. 8:3-4). In this second sense, too, the law is established.[174]

In this verse *law* lacks the article both times.[175] What Paul says has reference to the Jewish law, but also to law in general. The first occurrence of

in Gal. 3:8 he speaks of the Gentiles as justified ἐκ πίστεως, the very expression used of the Jews here. Turner, however, while recognizing the strength of the other view, suggests that we should take seriously the change of preposition and the fact that πίστεως has the article on the second occasion but not the first. He suggests the translation, "God will justify the Jews as a direct result of their faith and then will justify the Gentiles by means of *that same* faith" (i.e., by the faith of the Jews); "The Jews are justified by their faith, and the Gentiles by the faith of the Jews" (*Grammatical Insights*, pp. 108, 109). But if SH may be accused of being oversubtle in their distinction between prepositions, perhaps a similar charge may be directed against Turner in his distinction between the arthrous and the anarthrous nouns.

172. Lloyd-Jones points to the article ("the faith") and holds that Paul "means this message" (p. 139).

173. Cf. Charles H. Giblin, "Law itself is established (vs. 31) in the sense that a juridical arrangement and norm of action is definitely realized or fulfilled in God's disclosure of his own unique justice in the bond of faith in Jesus Christ" (CBQ, XXXVII [1975], p. 545).

174. The verb *uphold* translates ἱστάνομεν, from ἱστάνω, a variant of ἵστημι. Paul uses it six times in Romans and 16 times in all. It means "to make to stand". NEB translates, "we are placing law itself on a firmer footing". Cranfield's comment on this seems justified: this "is surely to put into Paul's mouth a self-important utterance which is quite out of character."

175. Turner argues that the absence of the article the second time indicates that the second occurrence does not have the same meaning as the first. He sees the first "law" as the Torah and the second as "a principle". The meaning then would be: "Are we then . . . setting the Torah at nought? Oh, no! At least we have established a *principle*" (*Grammatical Insights*, p. 109). But this seems oversubtle. We need more than the absence of the article to show that two occurrences of the same word so close together indicate such a radical difference in meaning.

law is in an emphatic position: *"law* do we nullify?" (for *nullify* see on 3:3), a position Paul negatives with the emphatic *Not at all!* (see on 3:4).

Additional Note F—SIN

"Nowhere do we see more clearly the difference between paganism and Christianity than in the conception of sin."[176] These words highlight an important point, for in the ancient world generally sin was not thought of as a very serious matter, certainly not nearly as serious as it was in the Christian understanding of things. We do not always realize how distinctive of Christianity was its attitude towards evil of every kind.

In the New Testament no one takes sin as seriously as does Paul, and nowhere does he treat it as fully as in Romans, especially chapters 5–7. The noun ἁμαρτία occurs 173 times in the New Testament, of which 64 are in Paul and no less than 48 in Romans. This is far and away the largest number in any one book, the next most frequent being Hebrews with 25. Paul similarly has a preponderance of the occurrences of the verb ἁμαρτάνω, with 17 (seven in Romans) out of 42 (1 John has it ten times); he has ἁμάρτημα twice (out of five). Paul sees all people as sinners; that is the thrust of his sustained argument from 1:18 to 3:20. He points out that the Gentiles (who do not have God's law as revealed to Moses) are sinners, but so are the Jews (who have that law and break it). Universal sinfulness is the subject of an explicit statement in 3:23 as well as being implicit in many places. Sin is our basic problem, for it pervades our members (6:19; 7:23); it affects our thinking (1:21; Eph. 4:17-18); it is a ruling power (5:21) tyrannizing people as its slaves (6:20; 7:14, 23, 25). People may will the good but find evil at hand (7:21); they may will, but not do the good (7:18). Sin is allied to death (5:21; 6:23; 8:10; 1 Cor. 15:56; Eph. 2:1), and indeed it kills people (7:11). It is linked, surprisingly, to law (7:8). It is also linked to flesh (7:25), which is important because "the mind of the flesh is enmity against God" (8:7). The connection between sin and flesh is emphasized in Paul's list of the "works of the flesh" (Gal. 5:19-21; notice that the list includes sins like anger and selfishness as well as more gross sins like fornication). Paul can use "sin" of a particular act (2 Cor. 11:7), but he is much more likely to use it of the general principle, the power that does us so much harm.

He sees the origin of sin in Adam, and in 5:12-19 he has a strong argument that Adam's sin infected the whole race and brought death in its train. The result is that man is a sinner "not only because of what he *does,* but also because of what he *is*".[177] He has inherited from Adam a sinful nature (5:12). Sin lives in people (7:17, 20), and people live in sin (7:25). They are "by nature" children of wrath (Eph. 2:3). Paul insists that God is active in punish-

176. F. X. Steinleitner, TDNT, I, p. 295 n.86.
177. Leon Morris, *The Cross in the New Testament* (Grand Rapids, 1965), p. 185.

ing sin, and he has a good deal to say about the wrath of God, which, of course, is directed at sinners. In Romans 1 he tells his readers three times that God gave sinners up to the punishment of their sin (1:24, 26, 28).

But Paul's really great thought about sin is that Christ has overcome it. Christ died for our sins (1 Cor. 15:3; Gal. 1:4); and, in a difficult expression, God made him sin for us (2 Cor. 5:21).[178] Because of Christ's death sin no longer reigns (Rom. 6:12, 14); believers are free (6:18, 22; 8:2). Christ's death once and for all avails for sin (6:10; cf. 1 Cor. 15:3; Gal. 1:4). This is the heart of the gospel that Paul gave himself over to proclaiming. It would seem that in his early life as "a Hebrew of the Hebrews" Paul did not see sin in quite the same way as he later came to view it. He could think of himself then as "blameless" (Phil. 3:6). But the cross changed all that. The cross shows the love of God for what it is, but also the evil of sin for what it is. Sin must be a very horrible thing indeed if it took the death of the Son of God to put it away. Grundmann sees Paul's view of sin as "orientated to the revelation of God in Christ. Hence it is not an empirical doctrine of sin based on pessimism." He goes on to sum up Paul's view in two propositions: "1. The Christ event comes upon man in a specific reality, i.e., his reality as a sinner. 2. It comes upon him in an event which rescues him from this reality and reconstitutes him" (TDNT, I, p. 308).

This means more than forgiveness. The "righteous ordinance of the law" is fulfilled in Christians (8:4); believers are new creatures (2 Cor. 5:17; cf. Col. 3:10-11). They have died to an entire way of life and risen to a new one (6:2-11). They are transformed and their mind is renewed (12:2; cf. Col. 1:13). As those who have been bought at a great price, they are to glorify God in their bodies (1 Cor. 6:19-20). So it is that while the preaching of the cross seems folly to perishing sinners, those being saved find it "the power of God" (1 Cor. 1:23-24).

A tension arises from all this, for the believer is both delivered from sin and at war with sin: "if Christ is in you, your body is dead because of sin, yet your spirit is alive because of righteousness" (8:10). Christians do not lead defeated lives, constantly at the mercy of every temptation. They are liberated, triumphant. But that does not mean a life of ease, free from all temptation. The decisive victory has been won, but the war still drags on. Temptations still come, and evil must be defeated every day. Yet Paul sees final victory as assured and knows that in due course the fulness of glory will be revealed (8:18, 30). But for now the Christian must be on guard, knowing what victory is like but still waging the war.[179]

---

178. "All the sin of man rests on Him, whether past or present" (W. Grundmann, TDNT, I, p. 312).

179. The literature on the subject is enormous, but the following may be consulted: articles in TDNT, I, pp. 267-335; IDB, IV, pp. 361-76; IBD, III, pp. 1456-59; Leon Morris, *The Cross in the New Testament* (Grand Rapids, 1965), ch. 5; C. Ryder Smith, *The Bible Doctrine of Sin* (London, 1953). The relevant sections of theologies of the Old Testament and of the New Testament are also useful; see, e.g., Donald Guthrie, *New Testament Theology* (London, 1981), pp. 187-218.

Romans 4

2. Justification Proved from Abraham, 4:1-25

It is central to Paul's position that the way of salvation he has just been outlining, the way of salvation by God's grace, is no innovation. He is not prepared to jettison the Old Testament or the Judaism in which he had been raised. He holds that the true understanding of the Old Testament is that which sees it as pointing forward to what God would do in Christ. The true Jew is not the one who conforms to the outward regulations of contemporary Judaism but the one who is a Jew inwardly (2:28-29). Such a Jew recognizes that Jesus is the Messiah and responds to what God is doing in Christ. Paul has made it clear that he sees God as saving by grace. Now he proceeds to show that this was true of Abraham, the great progenitor of the race. If God had acted in grace towards Abraham, if Abraham had been justified by faith, then Paul's point is established; whereas if Abraham had been accepted on the ground of his works, Paul's point that God had always acted in grace would not stand. Abraham is critically important.

a. God's way is grace, 4:1-8

1What then shall we say that Abraham, our forefather, discovered in this matter? 2If, in fact, Abraham was justified by works, he had something to boast about—but not before God. 3What does the Scripture say? "Abraham believed God, and it was credited to him as righteousness."a

4Now when a man works, his wages are not credited to him as a gift, but as an obligation. 5However, to the man who does not work but trusts God who justifies the wicked, his faith is credited as righteousness. 6David says the same thing when he speaks of the blessedness of the man to whom God credits righteousness apart from works:

7 "Blessed are they
      whose transgressions are forgiven,
      whose sins are covered.
8   Blessed is the man
      whose sin the Lord will never count against him."b

a3 Gen. 15:6; also in verse 22   b8 Psalm 32:1, 2

Paul begins by showing that according to Scripture Abraham's righteousness before God was due to his faith, not his works. The Jews as a whole would probably have regarded faith as a work,[1] but Paul has a different idea. He sees the grace of God as active, and Abraham's faith as simply Abraham trusting God. So Paul contrasts grace and works or obligation, and goes on to find his doctrine in David as well as in Abraham.

1. Typically Paul opens with a question,[2] and his *then* links what he is saying with the previous argument. If it is true that he is establishing the law with his doctrine of salvation in Christ, *then* something must be said about Abraham. There are textual problems in this verse: some MSS omit the verb translated *discovered* and the words are in varying order.[3] But it seems that the verb should be read. It is surprising to find the word *discovered* (or "found") used in this way, though we should bear in mind that it is sometimes used of intellectual discovery as well as physical (and that it is used specifically of Abraham in Gen. 18:3; cf. Michel). It seems to refer here to Abraham's finding the way to God (though some think it is the reward he found from God). *Forefather* is an unusual word in the New Testament, found only here in fact. It points to kinship with this great man of the remote past, the words "according to the flesh"[4] describing him as the physical progenitor of the Jewish race.

1. Darrel J. Doughty says, "the meaning of πίστις was well determined by its place of central significance within Jewish religion. Traditionally πίστις referred to the recognition of the one true God and to obedience to the will of God as expressed in his commandments" (NTS, XIX [1972-73], p. 165). The Jewish scholar H. J. Schoeps quotes approvingly A. Meyer's words, "faith becomes a zealous obedience in the matter of fulfilling the law, and its individual prescriptions" (*Paul* [London, 1961], p. 203). He finds Paul's position difficult: "this new tearing asunder of polarities, this absolute opposition between faith, on the one hand, and the law, on the other, quite contrary to the continuous meaning of the Biblical narrative, has always been unintelligible to the Jewish thinker" (*ibid.*, p. 202). See further, C. K. Barrett, *From First Adam to Last* (London, 1962), pp. 22-45.

2. For τί οὖν ἐροῦμεν see the note on 3:5.

3. εὑρηκέναι precedes Ἀβραάμ in ℵ A C D G etc. ("Abraham our forefather according to the flesh has found"; cf. KJV); it follows ἡμῶν in K P and many cursives ("Abraham our forefather has found according to the flesh"; cf. ASV); and it is omitted by B 1739 Or Eph. Curiously the omission is favored by many recent translations (as RSV, NEB, JB, Goodspeed, Moffatt), but not by most commentators. Metzger and his committee argue for the retention of the verb; they see no reason why copyists should add it in various places if it did not belong to the text and further that the omission could be accidental, arising from the similarity of the beginnings of the two successive verbs. Those who argue for the omission urge the tendency of scribes to supply what they see as lacking in an elliptical expression and the varying position of the verb in the MSS. R. R. Williams finds the position so difficult that he sees conjectural emendation as our only hope; he suggests εἰργάσθαι ("that Abraham has worked"; ET, LXIII [1951-52], pp. 91-92). But such suggestions have not convinced many. Our best course is to accept the word. Lenski gives another understanding of the text when he takes the subject of the infinitive εὑρηκέναι from the preceding verb and translates, "What, then, shall we say? That we have found Abraham (to be) our forefather (only) according to the flesh?" This is a possible, but unlikely, understanding of the Greek and difficult to fit in with v. 2. Some MSS read πατέρα instead of προπάτορα, but this looks like the substitution of a familiar word for a less common one, and in any case the meaning is the same.

4. κατὰ σάρκα (see the note on 1:3). A contrast may be intended with the different kind of fatherhood that will be mentioned in v. 11.

It is possible, however, to take this phrase with *discovered* to give the meaning "What shall we say that Abraham discovered according to the flesh?" that is, from a human point of view, by his human efforts. Godet argues that the context requires a reference to the way in which Abraham became righteous, not the nature of his paternity (which comes later), but Cranfield rejects this view since it does not suit the sequel. TH remarks that no modern translation accepts this understanding of the words.

2. Paul looks at the supposition that Abraham *was justified by works*. This is not a view he can accept, but it was widely held by Jewish teachers. They saw Abraham as an outstanding person who had kept the provisions of the law before the law was in fact laid down: "we find that Abraham our father had performed the whole Law before it was given" (Kidd. 4:14); "Abraham was perfect in all his deeds with the Lord" (Jub. 23:10).[5] If this view is right, then Paul is very, very wrong. But if Paul can show that Abraham was justified freely by God's grace, the apostle will have gone a long way towards establishing his position. He begins[6] by assuming for the moment that Abraham was justified in this way,[7] and then asking what follows. In that case Abraham would have *something to boast about*.[8] He would be able to take credit for having accomplished his justification before God by his own efforts. But Paul raises this possibility only to dismiss it. No man can boast before God. It is unthinkable that anyone, even Abraham, could have matter for boasting in God's presence, so Paul exclaims, *but[9] not before God*. His language is highly compressed, and these words are exclamatory, giving emphasis to an utter impossibility. Paul is not implying (as some hold) that Abraham had something to boast about before men; such a contrast with God does not seem to be in mind here. He is saying emphatically, as part of his argument, that Abraham had nothing to boast of before God. He will go on to point out that Scripture makes this clear and that the consequence is that no one is justified by his works (if Abraham was not, who could be?).

3. Characteristically Paul turns from human suppositions to the teach-

---

5. Cf. also Jub. 24:11, "And in thy seed shall all the nations of the earth be blessed, because thy father obeyed My voice, and kept My charge and My commandments, and My laws, and My ordinances, and My covenant" (words spoken by God to Isaac). Abraham "kept the law of the Most High, and was taken into covenant with him; he established the covenant in his flesh, and when he was tested he was found faithful" (Sir. 44:20; v. 19 says, "no one has been found like him in glory"). Abraham, Isaac, and Jacob were seen as men "who did not sin against" God (Prayer of Manasseh 8). There are many such passages; see SBk, III, pp. 186ff.

6. NIV translates γάρ as *in fact*, but it is better rendered "for" (as RSV).

7. The conditional clause is not easy (εἰ with the aorist in the protasis and a present in the apodosis). Robertson classes it as "Determined as fulfilled"; he points out that there was a good deal of liberty regarding the tense in the apodosis (p. 1009). For the sake of the argument, he thinks, Paul is allowing for the moment that Abraham was justified by works and proceeding to see what follows.

8. This translates one word, καύχημα. It is akin to καύχησις in 3:27, where see note.

9. Note the strong adversative ἀλλά.

ing of Scripture. He employs an argumentative conjunction which NIV omits but which is important.[10] Paul's argument proceeds along the lines "Does Abraham really have matter for boasting before God? Not at all, for Scripture says. . . ." For Paul's use of *Scripture* see the note on 1:2. He usually employs the singular, as here, for an individual passage (cf. 9:17; 10:11; 11:2).[11] He seems to use the word of the Old Testament almost as an independent entity expressing itself through the passage he is dealing with, as when he says that the Scripture speaks to Pharaoh (9:17). It may be too much to press the use of the present tense here, but it fits in with the vital role Paul assigns to Scripture. It still speaks. His quotation is from Genesis 15:6 (and agrees substantially with both the Hebrew and LXX).[12] The Jews interpreted the passage of a meritorious work. Thus we read: "The faith with which your father Abraham believed in Me merits that I should divide the sea . . ."; or again, "our father Abraham became the heir of this and of the coming world simply by the merit of the faith with which he believed in the LORD . . ."[13] (both passages go on to quote Gen. 15:6). Notice that both these passages (like many others) explicitly speak of Abraham's faith as a merit. But for Paul faith is not a good work; it is trust in God. The construction with the verb *believed* (the simple dative) strictly means "believe to be true", "accept what is said as correct". But really to believe what God says means to trust him, and Paul makes this clear as he develops his argument throughout this chapter. Abraham did not perform

10. The word is γάϱ, which Barrett sees as "a genuinely argumentative particle: Abraham has no ground of boasting before God, *for* Scripture says. . . ." The alternative, "Yes, Abraham would then have some ground for boasting, but on the human level only; not before God", takes away the "argumentative force" of the γάϱ and introduces a distinction between boasting before men and before God "which does not seem to be in Paul's mind." Lightfoot regards v. 2 as parenthetical and connects γάϱ with the question of v. 1, "What account then are we to give of Abraham our forefather? Why, what does the scripture say?" But it is better to take it with οὐ πϱὸς θεόν, "not towards God, *for*. . . ."

11. Käsemann, however, sees the singular as pointing to Scripture as a whole, not the individual passage (p. 106).

12. Except for the minor points that Paul has δέ where the LXX has ϰαί, his spelling is 'Αβϱαάμ where LXX has 'Αβϱάμ, LXX has the passive where the Hebrew has the active of the verb "reckoned", and LXX has the name 'Αβϱάμ where the Hebrew says "he".

13. Mekilta Exod. 14:15, 31 (cited from Cranfield; the first passage is attributed to R. Shemaiah, c. 50 B.C.). Sometimes works and faith are linked (2 Esdr. 13:23) and once there is the interesting reference to a man being saved "on account of his works, or on account of the faith by which he has believed" (2 Esdr. 9:7). Some writers esteem faith very highly; e.g., "Those who trust in him will understand truth, and the faithful will abide with him in love, because grace and mercy are upon his elect, and he watches over his holy ones" (Wis. 3:9). But such passages are not typical, and it is more common to have faith understood as a work, e.g., in the well-known Qumran comments on Hab. 2:4, "the righteous will live by his faith", which when interpreted "concerns all those who observe the Law in the House of Judah" (Vermes, p. 239; the passage goes on to refer to "their faith in the Teacher of Righteousness"). Schoeps cites as "typical of Jewish piety" a saying of R. Nehemiah (c. A.D. 150): "He who fulfils a commandment in faith merits highest praise before God" (*Paul*, p. 204). He holds that "With Paul the faith of the pious believer (in the Messianic status of Christ) replaces the Jew's fidelity to the law and becomes the sum of all truth and wisdom" (*ibid.*, pp. 204-5).

some great work of merit, but simply trusted God.[14] The verb *credited*[15] is used in the keeping of accounts. It was set down to Abraham's account[16] that he was righteous. *Righteousness*[17] here clearly points to status. Nothing is said about Abraham's deeds or the like. And a righteousness that is reckoned must be a right standing (an ethical virtue cannot be "reckoned"; it must be acquired by upright living). Harrison points out that to say that faith was credited to Abraham as righteousness "means that faith itself is not righteousness" (so Käsemann, "one may not infer from the 'reckon' that God treats faith as though it were righteousness", p. 111; Hunter is not correct in saying that the passage "equates faith with righteousness"). Paul is not saying that, because sinners could not produce the good works necessary to merit salvation (i.e., righteousness), God allowed them to substitute faith as an easier option. He is saying that God gives salvation freely and that faith is the means whereby we receive the gift (cf. 10:10, "with the heart one believes unto righteousness").

4. Paul proceeds[18] to contrast the way of works with the way of grace. When anyone works, his wage is his as a right; it belongs to him. It is not reckoned *as a gift*. Paul actually says his way is not "according to grace". While one cannot cavil at NIV's rendering, it is important to notice that the word for it is "grace", the same grace Paul has in mind throughout this section. To say that Abraham exercised faith would not necessarily get his point over, for the Jews often held that faith was a good work (as we have seen). They saw it as implying obedience to God's commands. But to say that he was saved not by works, but by grace, was another matter. There was no way of misinterpreting that. The reference to grace is important and should not be overlooked. But grace is not the way for the person who relies on works. For the one who works the wage is *an obligation;* it is what is due, what is owing to him (cf. F. Hauck, TDNT, V, p. 565). It might fairly be said that

14. Derek Kidner notes that in both Gen. 15 and Rom. 4 faith is presented "not as a crowning merit but as readiness to accept what God promises." He proceeds, "Note that Abram's trust was both personal (*in the Lord,* AV, RV) and propositional (the context is the specific *word of the Lord* in verses 4, 5)" (*Genesis* [London, 1967], p. 124). Godet speaks of faith as "a simple receptivity".

15. For λογίζομαι see the note on 2:3. It is used of Phinehas in Ps. 105 (106):31. The verb is a deponent, but is used here with passive force, a construction rare in the present tense (v. 4), though more frequent in the aorist (here; cf. M, III, p. 58). Paul uses it 11 times in this chapter; it is very much in his mind at this point. There is a useful discussion by H. W. Heidland (TDNT, IV, pp. 289-92).

16. Godet comments, "It is possible to put to one's account what he possesses or what he does not possess. In the first case it is a simple act of justice; in the second, it is a matter of grace. The latter is Abraham's case, since God reckons his *faith* to him for what it is not: for *righteousness.*"

17. Turner cites this passage as an example of the use of εἰς + accusative "in place of the predicate nominative owing to the Hellenistic tendency towards greater expressiveness" (M, III, p. 253).

18. δέ is a transitional particle here, with the meaning "now"; it does not have adversative force.

Genesis does not speak of God as owing anything to Abraham or of Abraham as meriting anything from God, so that it was not works that saved the patriarch. But Paul does not stop to point this out. He moves on to the next stage of his contrast between the two principles.

5. There is a slight shift of meaning in the word *work*. In v. 4 it was quite general, as Paul drew his principle from ordinary secular life where work and wages are linked. Here he is referring more specifically to matters religious; he is speaking of the person who does not perform law-works, works he sees as building up merit for him in the sight of God. The contrast[19] is not between the worker and the nonworker (Paul is not canonizing laziness), but between the one who trusts in his works and the one who trusts in God. The trusting person does not stand before God in the capacity of a paid laborer, receiving his due for work done, but as a believer. He has no good works to plead. None. A single article governs the two participles, making the point that it is one individual who does not work but believes (not one who does not work and another who believes).[20] His trust is in God,[21] *who justifies the wicked—* "acquits the guilty", as we might say (GNB has "declares the guilty to be innocent"). The word rendered *wicked*[22] is a strong term. Paul is speaking of the justified as completely without merit. God's saving activity does not operate solely on the most promising material. He justifies the impious, even those actively opposed to him. This is all the more striking in that the Old Testament says that God does not justify the wicked (Exod. 23:7; LXX has "Thou shalt not justify the ungodly", making it a command); it forbids people

19. δέ occurs twice in this verse. The first δέ sets this whole verse in opposition to the preceding, and the second sets "believing" over against "working".

20. πιστεύω is here followed by ἐπί, as in v. 24; 9:33; 10:11, etc. The construction rests faith upon God, so to speak. Hodge comments, "The faith which justifies is not mere assent, it is an act of trust." He thinks that the singular is used because "God does not justify communities." While we should not underestimate the importance of the beloved community, it is still true that faith is a personal activity. Moulton sees the use of prepositions after this verb as largely a Christian practice, arising because it was necessary for Christians to be able to distinguish between "believe" and "believe in". He says, "To repose one's trust *upon* God or Christ was well expressed by πιστεύειν ἐπί, the dative suggesting more of the state, and the accusative more of the initial act of faith; while εἰς recalls at once the bringing of the soul *into* that mystical union which Paul loved to express by ἐν Χριστῷ" (M, I, p. 68).

21. He has spoken of faith in Christ (3:22, 26); now he speaks of faith in God. Both, of course, are objects of faith for the Christian, and the fact that faith may be directed to Christ as to the Father with no appreciable difference in meaning tells us something about the way Paul regarded Christ.

22. ἀσεβής, defined as "destitute of reverential awe towards God, contemning God, impious" (GT). Strictly it does not denote wickedness in general, but a basically wrong attitude to God (though in LXX it is often used of wickedness in general). The Jews could regard Abraham as a proselyte, for he spoke of himself as "a stranger (גֵּר)" (Gen. 23:4), and he was not circumcised until he was 99 years old (Mekilta Exod. 22:20, cited in G. F. Moore, *Judaism*, I [Cambridge, 1958], p. 344). He might thus be regarded as "ungodly" (cf. Josh. 24:2-3). And David, who is about to be referred to, gave occasion to men to blaspheme (2 Sam. 12:14). The singular is used in the generic sense, but it applies to the two great ones Paul names.

from doing it (Prov. 17:15; 24:24; Isa. 5:23). Paul is not enunciating a religious commonplace, but giving expression to a resounding paradox.[23] He is pointing to a unique divine work. The believer's *faith is credited as righteousness*. This is not to regard it as a meritorious work; it is the very absence of all work, of all claim on God. Whereas systems of justification by works all look to the worshipper to produce the desired righteousness, Paul is speaking of a system that requires him to produce nothing. All he does is to reach out in faith for God's good gift.

6. Paul finds this[24] in David[25] as well as in Abraham.[26] David "pronounces a blessing" (RSV)[27] on the saved person, *the man to whom God credits righteousness apart from works*. The Psalm speaks of sins being forgiven, not being "counted against" the sinner, and Paul takes this as the crediting of righteousness. They are the two sides of the same coin. The example of David is significant for Paul, for in his case there is no question of salvation by works. The blessing is not concerned with someone who has good deeds to urge as meriting favor, but with one whose evil deeds are not imputed. Murray points out that the logic of Paul's argument here demands that " 'to impute righteousness' has the same force as 'to justify' ".

7. The quotation is from Psalm 32:1-2, in a form agreeing with both the Hebrew and LXX. It does not refer to faith or to righteousness, so there is a difference from the case of Abraham, but it does use the verb "credit" with respect to God and this is apparently the connection.[28] It is a blessed thing when God forgives and does not "credit" a person with sin. And, of course,

23. Denney comments, "The whole Pauline gospel could be summed up in this one word—God who justifies the ungodly. . . . The paradoxical phrase, Him that justifieth the ungodly, does not suggest that justification is a fiction, whether legal or of any other sort, but that it is a miracle."

24. He introduces the verse with καθάπερ = κατά + ἄπερ = "just as"; Paul uses this 16 times out of 17 New Testament occurrences, six times in Romans. Robertson sees it as "thoroughly Attic and a slight literary touch" (p. 967). καθάπερ καί is found again in 2 Cor. 1:14; 1 Thess. 3:6, 12; 4:5. The "also" is important here; it links David with Abraham.

25. Moule comments on the linking of David with Abraham: "David in the guilt of his murderous adultery, and Abraham in the grave walk of his worshipping obedience, stand upon the same level here. Actually or potentially, each is a great sinner. Each turns from himself, unworthy, to God in His promise" (p. 106).

26. Simeon holds that we may go back to Adam, and find "no hope but in 'the Seed of the woman, who would bruise the serpent's head.' There has been but one way of salvation for fallen man from the beginning of the world: nor shall there be any other as long as the world shall stand" (p. 98).

27. It is not easy to arrive at a satisfactory translation of this expression. Many translators agree with NIV, *speaks of the blessedness*, but μακαρισμός does not mean "blessedness", which is rather μακαριότης (SH, Cranfield). Black rejects RSV, "pronounces a blessing", and NEB, "speaks of the happiness", in favor of "being pronounced blessed by God". F. Hauck says that "the special feature" of the word group "in the NT is that it refers overwhelmingly to the distinctive religious joy which accrues to man from his share in the salvation of the kingdom of God" (TDNT, IV, p. 367).

28. A number of commentators draw attention to the rabbinic practice called g^{e}zerah shawa'. When the same word occurs in two passages, each may be used to explain the other. Since λογίζομαι occurs in both passages, each may be called on to explain the other.

the passage refers to free forgiveness. The Psalmist is not speaking of a reward for good works, but of God's grace towards sinners (cf. vv. 5, 7). He speaks of certain people as "blessed",[29] using "the highest term which a Greek could use to describe a state of felicity" (SH, who note that Aristotle uses it of the gods). This is the state of those whose *transgressions are forgiven*. The word for *transgressions*[30] strictly means "lawlessnesses". Here it is in a quotation and is parallel to *sins*, so the strict meaning can scarcely be insisted on; but the word certainly depicts evil as a lack of conformity to God's law. Paul does not often speak of forgiveness.[31] Perhaps he prefers positive imagery like justification or freedom from sin's control. But the idea is more widespread than the use of the word, and he certainly makes the thought that Christ has dealt with our sins central. Parallel to this is the statement that the blessed have their sins covered.[32] The imagery is different: the sins are not visible to God. But the basic thought is much the same: the transgressions, the sins have been put away.

8. The Psalm moves to the singular, but this is surely no more than a stylistic device. The application is still quite general, and *man*[33] means anyone at all. For *Lord* see on 1:4; here it refers to Yahweh, as commonly in LXX. The quotation uses an emphatic negative;[34] God will certainly not count the sins in question against the man of whom the words are written.[35] In the previous verse we have the positive: the sins are "forgiven" or "covered"; here we have the corresponding negative: they are not counted. The change to the singular, *sin*, is probably stylistic, though of course the word sometimes refers to the principle rather than to individual evil acts. But this distinction does not appear to be in mind here.

29. μακάριοι. G. Bertram says, "characteristic biblical beatitudes refer simply to the one who trusts in God, who hopes and waits for Him, who fears and loves Him" (TDNT, IV, p. 366). The word may refer to secular happiness, but the characteristic Old Testament use is for blessedness before God.
30. ἀνομία. Paul uses it six times in all, twice in Romans.
31. He uses the verb ἀφίημι five times out of 142 in the New Testament, and only here in the sense "to forgive". The noun ἄφεσις, "forgiveness", occurs twice in the Pauline writings.
32. For *sins* see Additional Note F. ἐπικαλύπτω is used here only in the New Testament. It will scarcely differ in meaning from the uncompounded verb.
33. This is Paul's first use of ἀνήρ in this epistle, where he uses it nine times (59 times in all, out of 216 times in the New Testament). He uses ἄνθρωπος much more often (27 times in Romans and 126 times in all).
34. οὐ μή. The double negative occurs frequently in the LXX, but in the New Testament it is rare apart from quotations from LXX and the words of Jesus. Moulton has a detailed examination of the construction (M, I, pp. 187-92). He shows that in the New Testament 90 percent of the occurrences are in quotations from LXX and sayings of Jesus. He suggests that in both there is "a feeling that inspired language was fitly rendered by words of a decisive tone not needed generally elsewhere" (p. 192). In Paul, apart from quotations from LXX, it occurs only four times.
35. The MSS are divided. Some read οὗ, "whose sin" (as JB); others, ᾧ, "to whom" (as KJV, Phillips). It is not easy to be sure, but perhaps Lightfoot is right in accepting ᾧ in the Psalm and οὗ in the way it is quoted here.

b. Faith and circumcision, 4:9-12

9Is this blessedness only for the circumcised, or also for the uncircumcised? We have been saying that Abraham's faith was credited to him as righteousness. 10Under what circumstances was it credited? Was it after he was circumcised, or before? It was not after, but before! 11And he received the sign of circumcision, a seal of the righteousness that he had by faith while he was still uncircumcised. So then, he is the father of all who believe but have not been circumcised, in order that righteousness might be credited to them. 12And he is also the father of the circumcised who not only are circumcised but who also walk in the footsteps of the faith that our father Abraham had before he was circumcised.

The Jews put a good deal of emphasis on circumcision, that divinely ordained ceremony which formally admitted one to membership in the people of God. It was this that marked him off from other people and that was the seal of his place before God. No matter who a man's parents were, if he was not circumcised he was not a Jew.[36] Those outside the people of God could be called simply "the uncircumcised" (1 Sam. 31:4; Isa. 52:1; Acts 11:3). The Jews could say explicitly, " 'uncircumcised' is but used as a name for the gentiles" (Ned. 3:11). But Paul insisted that it is faith (and by implication not any outward ceremony) that brings salvation and makes people members of the people of God. Now he points out that Abraham was accepted by God before he was circumcised and shows some of the implications of this.

9. Paul rushes on (his sentence has no verb, though it is easy to understand one). He has cited Scripture to show that the blessing David pronounces comes not on those whose good works merit it, but on those whom God has forgiven. In the light of this[37] he now asks whether the blessing in question comes on the circumcised or those not circumcised (he uses the terms "circumcision" and "uncircumcision", but clearly he is here referring to the people, not the act).[38] In view of his line of argument it is important to

36. "And every one that is born, the flesh of whose foreskin is not circumcised on the eighth day, belongs not to the children of the covenant which the Lord made with Abraham, but to the children of destruction; nor is there, moreover, any sign on him that he is the Lord's" (Jub. 15:26). Rabbi (i.e., Judah the Patriarch, 2nd cent. A.D.) said, "Great is circumcision, for despite all the religious duties which Abraham our father fulfilled, he was not called 'perfect' until he was circumcised" (Ned. 3:11; another is reported as saying that but for circumcision God would not have created the world). It was laid down that "Unless the seal of Abraham is inscribed on your flesh, you cannot taste" the Passover (Exod. R. xix.5). Again, "No Israelite man who is circumcised will go down to Gehinnom." What then of the few very wicked in Israel who deserve Gehinnom? They cannot go down to that place of doom circumcised, so God "sends an angel who stretches their foreskin and then they descend to Gehinnom" (Exod. R. xix.4). Jews held that the circumcised could not possibly end in the place of torment. For the place of circumcision see further SBk, IV, pt. 1, pp. 23-40.

37. Despite its omission in NIV, RSV, etc., οὖν is meaningful.

38. He has used the principle of *gᵉzerah shawa'* to enable Ps. 36 to shed light on Gen. 15. Now he reverses the process and shows that the blessing of which David speaks is to be explained in terms of faith like that of Abraham.

make the point that circumcision with its implied obligation to keep the whole law (cf. Gal. 5:3) is not God's chosen way to save people. Paul's emphasis on faith is not some new-fangled innovation. God has always saved people by the way of grace, as the case of Abraham shows. So now the apostle reverts to the words of Genesis 15:6 that he used in verse 3. The wording is not identical (he has the noun *faith* instead of the verb "believed"), but the meaning is the same.

10. Paul asks two questions that do not seem to have occurred to the Jews of his day. *Under what circumstances . . . ?*[39] directs attention to Abraham's condition[40] at the time of his acceptance with God, and *Was it after he was circumcised?* brings us explicitly to circumcision. He answers this question with a negative followed by a positive: "not in circumcision but in uncircumcision." These are the only possibilities, and Paul is in no doubt as to which is right. Abraham's circumcision was not commanded until long after he was accepted by God (Gen. 17:10-11), and was not performed until later still (Gen. 17:23-27). His acceptance on the grounds of his faith (Gen 15:6) was apparently before the birth (or even the conception) of Ishmael (Gen. 16), and Abraham was 86 years old when the child was born (Gen. 16:16). But he was not circumcised until he was 99 (Gen. 17:24).[41] It is thus plain that God's reckoning of Abraham as righteous took place years before there was any question of circumcision. It was not this rite that gave the patriarch standing before God.

11. But circumcision cannot be ignored. Every Jew knew that it had been commanded by God. If Abraham was accepted without it, then what did it mean? Why was it enjoined? In agreement with Genesis 17:11 Paul says that it *was a sign*. This is an important word, and Paul puts it in an emphatic position: "A sign he received. . . ."[42] It was not circumcision as such that was important, for in antiquity other nations than Israel were circumcised (IDB cites the Egyptians, most of the ancient Semites, and the people adjacent to Israel except the Philistines); it was the circumcision given by God as a sign that mattered. This *sign* is further explained as a *seal*.[43] In antiquity a seal was

39. GNB renders, "When did this take place?" which is a curious translation. πῶς means "how?" not "when?", there is no "this", and λογίζομαι does not mean "take place".

40. On each occasion ἐν will have a meaning like "in a state of". ὄντι most naturally refers to a continuing state.

41. According to the chronology accepted by the Jews, the interval was 29 years. They saw the patriarch's age as 70 at the time of the dividing of the sacrifice (Gen. 15:10; *Seder Olam R.* 1, cited in SBk, III, p. 203).

42. The genitive περιτομῆς means something like "a sign consisting in circumcision". Moule points out that this is more than an adjective: "it represents nothing less than a second noun in apposition to the first" (IBNTG, p. 38).

43. SH quote a prayer used at the circumcising of a child: "Blessed be He who . . . sealed His offspring with the sign of a holy covenant." There are rabbinic references to circumcision as a seal, and, while explicit attestation is late (Käsemann, p. 115), this was probably as early as New Testament times (circumcision is called a seal in Ep. Barn. 9:6, which is not far removed; cf. Michel, p. 119 n. 4; G. Fitzer, TDNT, VII, pp. 947-48). In the

often a mark of ownership, as when a man sealed property to show that it was his. But it was also a means of attestation, and it seems that this is the way we should take it here. God gave the sign of circumcision and by doing so set his seal[44] on the righteousness imputed to the patriarch. This righteousness was of faith (cf. Phil. 3:9).[45] It is important to see that the whole point of circumcision is its relation to righteousness and to faith, that faith which Abraham had while he was still uncircumcised. This is the point Paul is concerned to emphasize. Circumcision had nothing to do with Abraham's acceptance by God (cf. Gal. 5:6). It was while he was still uncircumcised that God accepted him.

There is a divine purpose[46] behind this. God did this in order that Abraham might be the father of all believers, circumcised or uncircumcised, and Paul singles out for mention those who *have not been circumcised*. Even that ordinance which was most typically Jewish was for the purpose of embracing the Gentiles! The true children of Abraham are not those who took his circumcision as a model, but those who received God's gift in faith as he did. Paul could be seen as a pattern of faith (1 Tim. 1:16), but Abraham was more; he was the spiritual father of all believers (cf. Gal. 3:7), the father of the household of faith. Fatherhood can, of course, be understood in more ways than one. We get light on the way Abraham was the father of uncircumcised believers by reflecting that Jabal was the father of tent-dwellers and breeders of livestock, while Jubal was the father of musicians (Gen. 4:20-21). In neither case was the paternity literal; it was concerned rather with the characteristics of the people in question. And it is characteristic of uncircumcised believers that they are like Abraham. Abraham was not the first to exercise faith (cf. Heb. 11:1-7), but he was the spiritual father of the community of faith.[47] It must have been startling to Jewish readers, who often referred with pride to "Father Abraham" (cf. Luke 3:8; 16:24, 30; John 8:39, 53, 56; Acts 7:2; Jas. 2:21), to hear Abraham described as *the father* of uncircumcised people.

A second construction of purpose (this time translated as *in order that*) brings out the truth that God intended to reckon righteousness to them. The emphasis on the divine purpose in this verse should not be overlooked. Paul sees it as God's purpose that justification should be by grace, by faith, and he

early church baptism was, of course, often referred to as a seal, and this may possibly reflect Jewish terminology (so Käsemann).

44. Cf. Leenhardt, "By the sign God speaks to the outside world; the sign is the distinctive mark. By the seal, God speaks rather to the believer himself; the seal is the mark which guarantees authenticity."

45. It is grammatically possible to see faith as τῆς ἐν τῇ ἀκροβυστίᾳ, but it is better to see a reference to righteousness, as NIV, RSV, etc. (cf. Cranfield, "it is Abraham's righteousness, not his faith, which is directly at issue").

46. The construction εἰς τό + infinitive, it is true, can on occasion express result, and this is the justification for NIV's *So then*. But it more often expresses purpose; thus RSV is surely right in translating "The purpose was. . . ." See the note on 1:20. Purpose is seen here by Turner (M, III, p. 143), Cranfield, and others; result by Lagrange.

47. Cf. T. Wright, "Abraham is no mere example of faith. He is the father of the worldwide covenant family which God has always promised and now has established in Christ" (G. Reid, ed., *The Great Acquittal* [London, 1980], p. 24).

holds that the way God justified Abraham brings this out for all who have eyes to see.[48]

12. Now comes the second aspect of Abraham's fatherhood. He was *also the father of the circumcised*.[49] The construction expressing purpose which was applied to the uncircumcised in the previous verse carries over to the circumcised here. The same divine purpose is in action. But it is not the circumcised[50] as such[51] who are in mind; it is circumcised believers (just as it was not the uncircumcised as such but uncircumcised believers who were said to be justified). They are those *who*[52] *also walk in the footsteps*[53] *of the faith that our father Abraham had*. Paul is unwearied in his emphasis on faith. Circumcision or uncircumcision matters little, but faith is all-important. "To walk in the steps of" is a natural metaphor for close imitation. And what is singled out for imitation is Abraham's faith (even though it means a rather curious metaphor—"walking in the steps of the faith . . ."). Even when dealing with the circumcised, Paul points to the faith that is to be imitated as that which Abraham had while uncircumcised.[54]

c. Faith and law, 4:13-17

> [13]It was not through law that Abraham and his offspring received the promise that he would be heir of the world, but through the righteousness that comes by

48. δι' ἀκροβυστίας will be the διά of attendant circumstances, "for all their uncircumcision."

49. Lightfoot comments, "The genitive περιτομῆς does not describe Abraham's progeny, as many commentators take it, but his own condition." He was "a father belonging to circumcision, himself circumcised."

50. Literally, "to those not of the circumcision only", which may be an imitation of a Hebrew construction, "father to", or a dative of advantage (Hodge).

51. On οὐκ . . . μόνον Bengel comments, "Abraham, therefore, is not the father of *circumcision* to such as are merely of the circumcision, and do not also follow the faith of Abraham." Burton says that in the New Testament οὐ μόνον occurs regularly rather than μὴ μόνον when the phrase applies either to an infinitive or "to some limitation of the infinitive" (MT, 481).

52. The construction is difficult, for the repetition of τοῖς before στοιχοῦσιν strictly means that those who walk are different from those who not only are circumcised; clearly this is not what Paul means. He is speaking of one group, not two. The MS tradition is unanimous, which is surprising. WH thought that the original may have been αὐτοῖς and the present reading a corruption, but this is difficult to accept. Others think that a very early scribe, perhaps even Tertius himself, made a mistake and all others copied it. C. F. D. Moule speaks of it as "an *intrusive* article" (IBNTG, p. 110). Cranfield draws attention to the fact that the second τοῖς is "ruled out grammatically . . . by the position of the earlier τοῖς in relation to οὐκ . . . μόνον" (Hodge is similar). It fits neither grammatically nor theologically and must be rejected.

53. The verb στοιχέω (in Paul four times out of five in the New Testament) means "orig. 'be drawn up in line', in our lit. only fig. *be in line with, stand beside* a pers. or thing, *hold to, agree with, follow*" (BAGD). SH speak of it as a military term meaning "march in file".

54. Cf. Bengel, "*Circumcision* was at least a sign, *uncircumcision* was not even a sign." At the time God accepted him Abraham had nothing.

faith. [14]For if those who live by law are heirs, faith has no value and the promise is worthless, [15]because law brings wrath. And where there is no law there is no transgression.

[16]Therefore, the promise comes by faith, so that it may be by grace and may be guaranteed to all Abraham's offspring—not only to those who are of the law but also to those who are of the faith of Abraham. He is the father of us all. [17]As it is written: "I have made you a father of many nations."[a] He is our father in the sight of God, in whom he believed—the God who gives life to the dead and calls things that are not as though they were.

[a]17 Gen. 17:5

With these verses Paul turns to the law, which mattered so much to the Jews. He might have urged a historical argument similar to the one he has used with regard to circumcision, for the law was 430 years after Abraham's acceptance with God (as he points out elsewhere, Gal. 3:17). Instead, he chooses to argue that law and grace (or promise) are incompatible. As the case of Abraham shows, God's way is that of grace. Therefore law cannot be the way.

13. Paul now emphasizes that Abraham acted on the principle of faith, not law. His use of "For" (omitted in NIV, RSV, etc.) links this to the preceding. Abraham was the father of all the faithful, *for* he acted in the way he did, in conformity with faith, not law. Paul is still rushing on, and this sentence has no main verb. *Not through law* is quite general. Just as Abraham's acceptance by faith was independent of circumcision, so it was independent of the Mosaic law. It was not through that law that he received the promise; indeed, it was not through any law. On the contrary,[55] it was through "the righteousness of faith". That is God's chosen way.

The *promise* is important for Paul (he uses the word in exactly half of its New Testament occurrences; 26 out of 52). It forms part of his understanding of the way of grace. We may rely on this way, for it is the result of God's promise. The promise is not only to Abraham, but also to *his offspring* (his "seed"). Paul quite often uses this expression for the descendants of Abraham and in one important passage for *the* Descendant, Christ (Gal. 3:16). Scholars like Käsemann, Michel, and Murray reject the messianic view here, but whichever way we take it, it has nothing to do with the law. The context of the promise is *he would be heir of the world*,[56] a form of expression that goes beyond the words of the Old Testament (Gen. 18:18; 22:17-18), though it may be held to agree in sense. *Heir* strictly means someone who secures posses-

---

55. The strong adversative ἀλλά sets this over against *through law*.

56. BDF 399 (1) see τὸ κληρονόμον αὐτὸν εἶναι as epexegetical to ἐπαγγελία, the article both times designating what is well known. They speak of the nominative and accusative of the substantivized infinitive (without preposition) as "found sporadically in Mt and Mk, somewhat more frequently in Paul, and almost never elsewhere." RSV translates, ". . . to Abraham and his descendants, that they should inherit the world" (Phillips and LB are similar). But this ignores the singular αὐτόν; the promise refers to Abraham.

sion after the death of the owner, but in the New Testament it is often used of secure possession without regard to the way the possession is obtained. *Heir of the world* is not a particularly easy expression. It could be understood as an enthusiastic description of great material prosperity, but we expect something in the way of spiritual blessing here. Perhaps material blessing is used as a symbol of spiritual blessing. It is possible to see the prosperity in terms of the family of faith that Abraham would beget, a worldwide family (Cranfield sees the best commentary on these words as 1 Cor. 3:21b-23).[57]

14. Paul advances his argument by pointing out that the promise means that no way of law can be the way to God. If the way of law is correct, there is no place for promise (Paul has a similar argument in 11:6, that grace and works are mutually exclusive; cf. Gal. 3:18). He speaks of "those of law", which means those characterized by law, *those who live by law.* Paul is not speaking of those who observe the law indeed, but whose center is elsewhere; he is speaking of legalists, people who regard law as central.[58] The Jews, of course, thought of Abraham as a man of law ("he kept the law of the Most High", Sir. 44:20); Paul's insistence on Abraham's faith is a direct denial of this view. If those who rely on law be the *heirs,* then faith has been "made empty";[59] there is nothing in it (cf. 1 Cor. 15:14). This of itself makes it impossible for Paul to hold it. For him it is plain that Scripture has said that faith is meaningful and anything that conflicts with Scripture is invalid. There is another consequence: *the promise is worthless.*[60] God's promise was not made on condition of law-keeping. If now it is the legalists who are in the right, God's promise to Abraham will not stand, and that is unthinkable. It would negate the very idea of promise, for that which comes as the due reward of work done is not a promise. A promise points to a gift given freely (of course, a promise may have conditions, but none was attached to the promise made to Abraham).

15. Now[61] we come to the true function of law. It *brings wrath.* Hodge sees this as working out in two ways: (a) our imperfect obedience brings the law's curse on us, and (b) law "excites and exasperates the evil passions of the heart". The law has its place in the way God brings people salvation, but that place is not the provision of a means whereby people may so prove themselves virtuous that they receive salvation as a merited reward. Rather, law shows up our inadequacies and makes us see our need of a Savior. Paul adds

57. Harrison takes strictly the application to Abraham (it is not his descendants who will inherit the world) and understands the world he will inherit to mean "the multitude of those who will follow Abraham in future generations in terms of his faith." Murray speaks of "the worldwide dominion promised to Christ and to the spiritual seed of Abraham in him." Denney rejects participation in the sovereignty of Messiah.

58. Cf. the note on the expression τὸν ἐκ πίστεως Ἰησοῦ in 3:26.

59. κενόω is confined to Paul in the New Testament (five times, here only in Romans). The perfect tense points to a permanent voiding of faith.

60. The verb is καταργέω; see the note on 3:3.

61. This is the third consecutive verse which is linked to its predecessor by γάρ; Paul is following a logical train of thought.

that *where*62 *there is no law there is no transgression* (cf. 5:13). This is beautifully simple and quite compelling. *Transgression*63 is the right word for overstepping a line, and thus for breaking a clearly defined commandment. If there is *no transgression*, there is no need of salvation. Law shows us where we stand, but it does not save us.

16. Again we have a verbless sentence; Paul's argument is rushing on.64 "On account of this", he says (NIV, *Therefore*), but it is not easy to see what his "this" is. Perhaps it takes in the sense of the preceding—because of the impossibility of salvation by law.65 "It is of faith", Paul says, but he does not stop to say what is "of faith". NIV supplies *the promise;* other suggestions include the inheritance, the divine plan, righteousness, and the way of salvation. Clearly Paul is referring to blessing in some form, but he does not stop to define it. He goes on to say that the purpose66 of the promise was grace (see the note on 1:5).67 A further construction indicating purpose68 brings out the point that the grace was in order that the promise *may be guaranteed*69 *to all Abraham's offspring*. This last word (= "seed") is perhaps unexpected, but the Jews put a good deal of emphasis on the fact that they were Abraham's seed, and Paul is insisting that the true seed of Abraham are those who come by faith, not the physical descendants of the patriarch. He proceeds to bring out the meaning of "all the seed" with a combination of the negative and the positive. First, it is not only70 *those who are of the law*. The reference to *the law* will point to Jews, but Paul is speaking of believing Jews, not of Jews who put their trust in the law. He has already negated that way, and he is not going back on what he said before. He is saying that some of those who treasured the law are people of faith and so true descendants of Abraham. The positive is "that which is of Abraham's faith". His *but also* is an unexpectedly strong antithesis;71 Paul is emphasizing that faith is the only way. Those who come

62. Turner notes this as one of very few instances where a dependent clause introduced by οὖ precedes the main clause; in Paul this occurs again in 5:20, cf. 9:26 (M, III, p. 344).
63. παράβασις. "In the NT the word denotes 'sin in its relation to law, i.e., to a requirement or obligation which is legally valid or has legal force'" (J. Schneider, TDNT, V, p. 739; the quotation is from Cremer-Kögel, *Biblisch-theologisches Wörterbuch,* 183).
64. The language is very compressed; Paul simply says "on account of this, of faith, that by grace". He highlights the important words and leaves out what can be understood.
65. Cf. Denney, "because of the nature of law, and its inability to work anything but wrath." Cranfield takes it with what follows: "For this reason . . . , namely, in order that".
66. ἵνα indicates purpose. Grace was always God's plan; it was no afterthought.
67. κατὰ χάριν, "according to grace", is found in v. 4, and with the article in 12:6; 1 Cor. 3:10; and 2 Thess. 1:12. It is thus a Pauline turn of expression, though not a common one. It signifies "by way of grace", "freely".
68. This time, as in v. 11, the expression is εἰς τὸ εἶναι.
69. A. Deissmann has shown that βέβαιος and its cognates are used of legally guaranteed security (*Bible Studies* [Edinburgh, 1901], pp. 104-9). Cf. also MM; H. Schlier, TDNT, I, pp. 600-603.
70. For οὖ . . . μόνον see the note on v. 12.
71. ἀλλὰ καί.

by the way of law are not saved. He is saying to the saved Jews, "Those Gentiles who come by the way of faith are saved just as much as you are." All who are saved are saved by grace, by God's promise, a promise that is accepted in faith. There is no other way. Thus Abraham is *the father of us all*. The way of faith which he exemplified is the only way we may come to God. *All* is a significant word. There is no distinction.

17. Characteristically Paul proves his point with an appeal to Scripture. He applies Genesis 17:5 to the many nations from whom Abraham's spiritual children would come. His quotation agrees exactly with LXX (whereas the Hebrew means "a multitude of nations"). There is a note of permanence about the perfect tense of the verb *I have made*; this is not a passing thought, but God's final word (cf. Calvin, it "denotes the certainty of the divine counsel"). So Paul speaks of Abraham as *our father in the sight of God, in whom he believed*.[72] He proceeds to characterize God in terms of his giving life to the dead.[73] Paul may have in mind the typical Jewish estimate of the spiritual state of the Gentiles; spiritually they may indeed be dead, but God is the God who gives life. There may also be a glance at Ezekiel 37, where God gives life to a great army of the dead. And a reference in the New Testament to God as giving life to the dead must always be understood against the background of the raising of Jesus. Paul goes on to speak of Abraham and Sarah in terms of death (v. 19), so they must be in mind, too. *The dead* is a general term and embraces both the physically dead and the spiritually dead. Consider death how you will, God is the life-giving God and he overcomes it. *Calls* is linked with *gives life* under the one article; God is the one who both gives life and calls. Both activities are characteristic of him. The verb *calls* can signify to name or to summon. But it can also signify to call into existence, and this is the meaning we find here.[74] When Paul uses the verb he usually has in mind the idea of effectual call. God's purpose in calling is completely accomplished. Those who are called respond. Paul's terminology differs from that of the Synoptic Gospels, where "many are called but few chosen", but his thought is not essentially different. His "called" are much like the Synoptists' "chosen". *Things that are not*[75] points to the nonexistence of the called before

---

72. The Greek is not straightforward, there being an attraction of the relative into the case of the antecedent, together with the omission or displacement of the antecedent: κατέναντι οὗ = κατέναντι θεοῦ ᾧ. Moule sees the omission of the antecedent as "common enough" and "where necessary, the relevant noun is then placed *after* the relative pronoun"; he cites Matt. 7:2; Rom. 2:16; 16:12 (IBNTG, p. 130). Some take the Greek as equivalent to κατέναντι θεοῦ κατέναντι οὗ ἐπίστευσεν. This is less probable (cf. Lightfoot), but the sense will be much the same.

73. Cf. the second of the Eighteen Benedictions: "Blessed art Thou, O Lord, who quickenest the dead." Cf. also 2 Cor. 1:9.

74. K. L. Schmidt regards καλέω as "a technical term for the process of salvation" (TDNT, III, p. 489). Philo speaks of creation and goes on, τὰ γὰρ μὴ ὄντα ἐκάλεσεν εἰς τὸ εἶναι (*De spec. leg.* iv.187).

75. RSV has "calls into existence the things that do not exist", and this is favored by Cranfield, Earle, and others. The difficulty with this interpretation is ὡς ὄντα, which is not a natural way of saying "into existence" (though ὡς can be used "of an actual quality"; BAGD III.1). Murray argues from "calleth the things that are not *as* being" to the meaning "the things determined by God to come to pass but which have not yet been fulfilled."

the call came. Paul is speaking of God as creating something out of nothing by his call. This applies to the physical creation, though that does not seem to be particularly in mind here. It certainly applies to God's calling of his people into existence, for Paul goes on to speak of both Abraham and Sarah in terms of being dead (v. 19). On the human level their potential for procreation was nil, but God called *many nations* into existence through them. Some see an application to Abraham's readiness to sacrifice Isaac and, as it were, receiving his son back from the dead (Gen. 22; Heb. 11:17-19), but Paul does not seem to be thinking of this, for he makes no reference to it. There will certainly be an application to the countless host of believers through the centuries. They did not exist at the time God called Abraham, but in due course God called them *as though they were*. God's own have no qualifications of their own to urge; they are *things that are not*. But *as though they were* indicates the very opposite. When they are called they are as those who lack nothing.

Käsemann sees here "the full radicalness of Paul's doctrine of justification", which is "an anticipation of the resurrection of the dead, which as no other event deserves to be called a creation out of nothing and presents the eschatological repetition of the first creation" (p. 123). When people really accept the reality of justification by faith, "there is unavoidably linked with it a reduction to nothing which deeply shakes the righteous by associating them with the ungodly. No one has anything of his own to offer so that a new creation is both necessary and possible." Whatever other allusion we may discern, surely this is primary. The justified bring nothing; they are as dead, as those who do not exist. But because of God's creative call they are brought to newness of life.

d. Faith and Abraham, 4:18-25

> [18]*Against all hope, Abraham in hope believed and so became the father of many nations, just as it had been said to him, "So shall your offspring be."[a]* [19]*Without weakening in his faith, he faced the fact that his body was as good as dead—since he was about a hundred years old—and that Sarah's womb was also dead.* [20]*Yet he did not waver through unbelief regarding the promise of God, but was strengthened in his faith and gave glory to God,* [21]*being fully persuaded that God had power to do what he had promised.* [22]*This is why "it was credited to him as righteousness."* [23]*The words "it was credited to him" were written not for him alone,* [24]*but also for us, to whom God will credit righteousness—for us who believe in him who raised Jesus our Lord from the dead.* [25]*He was delivered over to death for our sins and was raised to life for our justification.*

[a]18 Gen. 15:5

Paul links Abraham's faith with hope (an important concept for him) and brings out the truth that neither was a truism—Abraham and Sarah were as good as dead with respect to procreation when they received the promise of God. Abraham's faith was profound and its being reckoned to him for righteousness has meaning for all subsequent believers.

18. *Hope* is a decidedly Pauline word, and a word found more often in Romans than in any other New Testament book.[76] The concept is often linked with faith (cf. 5:2; 15:13; Gal. 5:5; Eph. 1:18-19; Col. 1:23; 1 Tim. 4:10; Heb. 11:1; 1 Pet. 1:21), and not infrequently with love as well (5:2-5; 1 Cor. 13:7, 13; Gal. 5:5-6; Col. 1:4-5; 1 Thess. 1:3; 5:8; Heb. 6:10-12; 10:22-24; 1 Pet. 1:21-22). It is distinguished from secular optimism in that it is grounded in what God has done in Christ. In the light of Calvary believers may have confidence that God's purpose will be worked out to the end.[77] Here Paul is saying that Abraham believed *against all hope;*[78] he believed when there was nothing from this world's point of view to justify his faith or his hope.[79] Elsewhere we read of people who were "without hope and without God" (Eph. 2:12). For Paul the two went together. But Abraham was not without God and therefore he was not without hope. His hope was bound up with his faith in God and thus did not depend on human factors. Calvin puts it succinctly: "The meaning is that when he had no grounds for hope, Abraham still relied in hope on the promise of God".[80] In the New Testament there is more of a note of certainty in hope than there is in the way we generally use the term. It is a looking forward to things not present indeed, but whose coming is certain. It is thus akin to faith, and it accords with this that in the present passage Abraham is said to have believed in hope. The result[81] was that he became *the father of*

76. ἐλπίς occurs 53 times in the New Testament, of which no less than 36 are in Paul. Romans has the word most often, 13 times, the next highest being Acts with eight. Paul also has the verb ἐλπίζω most often, 19 times out of 31.

77. Bultmann can say, "Christian hope rests on the divine act of salvation accomplished in Christ, and, since this is eschatological, hope itself is an eschatological blessing, i.e., now is the time when we may have confidence" (TDNT, II, p. 532). He also draws attention to some striking Old Testament passages in which God is said to give hope rather than help, such as Jer. 29:11; 31:17; Hos. 2:17 (2:15, NIV) (*ibid.*, p. 523 n. 34). The point is that the faithful have confidence because they know God, not because they know what God will do.

78. παρ᾽ ἐλπίδα = "beside hope". But Abraham believed ἐπ᾽ ἐλπίδι, "on the basis of hope". Cranfield points out that this may be taken either in the sense "beyond hope" (i.e., "human hope's utmost limit has already been reached and passed"), or, as he prefers, "against hope" ("Abraham's believing ἐπ᾽ ἐλπίδι is a defiance of all human calculations"). Cf. Theodoret, "By 'against hope' he means hope that is consonant with human nature; but 'in hope' refers to the promise of God" (*Commentary*, p. 70). So Chrysostom, "against man's hope, in hope which is of God". There are two different hopes here: a human hope (which failed) and a God-given hope (which did not).

79. Cf. Bultmann, "where we can no longer count on controllable factors, we have to trust in the divine future" (TDNT, II, p. 531).

80. Cf. Barth, "We are able to hear his 'Yes', whilst the world above and below him cries out to him—'No'."

81. For εἰς τό + infinitive see the note on 1:20. In Paul it mostly denotes purpose, and many take it in that sense here. If it is purpose it can scarcely be the purpose of Abraham. Paul is surely not saying that Abraham believed "in order that" he might secure the blessing; that would be a very selfish faith and most unlike the Abraham depicted in Genesis; it must be the purpose of God (so Shedd, Denney, etc.). But Paul is not saying that God did anything εἰς τό. . . . It was Abraham who believed εἰς τό. . . . It is grammatically possible to take the construction as giving the content of Abraham's belief (as Bultmann, TDNT, VI, p. 206; Boylan, and others). But a difficulty in the way of this view is that no example of the construction appears to be cited. It seems, then, that it is best to

many nations (cf. v. 17). This is backed up with a quotation from Scripture in the Pauline manner.[82] The apostle quotes Genesis 15:5 in a form agreeing with both LXX and the Hebrew. The *So*[83] in the Genesis passage refers to the number of the stars and points to the great multitude of Abraham's descendants.

19. In the face of the promise Abraham did not weaken[84] in his faith, unlikely as its fulfilment might be on purely human premises. There is textual uncertainty as to whether we should read "he considered his body as good as dead" or "he considered not his own body now dead" (KJV).[85] It is fascinating that these two readings, the one negating the other, are both well attested and each gives good sense. In the one case Abraham did not consider his body as dead, for God would work his will through it. In the other he took full account of the impotence of his body[86] and held that God would work his will through it. The second is both better attested and gives better sense. Faith does not close its eyes to reality. It is not limited by the best human estimates of what is possible, for it is faith in the God "who gives life to the dead" (v. 17). But it does not overlook the facts either; it recognizes that what is dead is dead and knows that only God can give life where there is no life. Another textual problem is whether or not we should read "already" ("now" in KJV).[87] Not much hangs on this question, but it does seem as though the word is not original, and it is not read in most modern translations. Obviously Abraham's body was not dead, but as far as reproduction went it was in the as-good-as-dead category.[88] The patriarch could not expect a child at his age, *about*[89] *a hundred* (this last word is found here only in the New Testament). The

take it as expressing result. Abraham believed and the result was . . . (so Lagrange, Lenski, etc.).

82. But not with the usual Pauline formula. He introduces the quotation with κατὰ τὸ εἰρημένον (which occurs in Luke 2:24; cf. Acts 2:16; 13:40). Paul uses other tenses of this verb in citing Scripture (as in 9:12; cf. 9:26).

83. οὕτως is an adverb used as an adjective (BDF 434 [1]).

84. Paul uses ἀσθενέω 16 times in all (out of 33 in the New Testament). The word denotes bodily sickness and the like, but it comes to be used of weakness of any kind. In respect of faith Abraham was not weak. Some grammarians give complicated reasons for the use of μή rather than οὐ, but the case seems covered by the general New Testament rule that μή is the negative with participles. Cf. Moule, "The negative with a participle is usually μή, no matter how factual or confident the denial may be" (IBNTG, p. 105; he notes that οὐ is used with a participle about 20 times in the New Testament).

85. The positive is supported by ℵ A B C 81 1739 vg syrᵖ cop, the negative by D G K P Ψ 33 Byz. Metzger agrees that both give a good sense but favors the positive.

86. σῶμα is a definitely Pauline word, occurring 91 times in the apostle's writings out of a New Testament total of 142 (13 in Romans). It is used in a variety of senses, but here plainly of the physical body.

87. The MS evidence seems to favor including ἤδη (ℵ A C Dᵍʳ K P Ψ etc.), but to Metzger's committee the words seems to show some "heightening of the account." It is also hard to find a reason for omitting it if it were original. The committee was divided and in the end put the word in square brackets.

88. This is emphasized by the use of the perfect participle νενεκρωμένον.

89. When used of numbers the enclitic πού, "anywhere", "somewhere", means "about", "approximately" (here only in Paul, four times in the New Testament); it is to be distinguished from ποῦ, "where" (ten times in Paul, 47 times in the New Testament).

participial expression ("being about a hundred") explains why Abraham's body was considered as good as dead.[90] With Abraham's advanced years is linked "the deadness[91] of Sarah's womb". There is a certain lack of life about both. In view of all this deadness it was not possible for the couple to have a child in the normal human fashion, and to believe God's promise under those circumstances was more than a passive acquiescence in a conventional religious posture; it was the active exercise of a profound faith.

20. Yet[92] Abraham *did not waver*[93] *through unbelief*. He had received God's promise (cf. v. 13), and that preserved him from *unbelief*.[94] On the contrary, he *was strengthened in his faith and gave glory to God*. The verb *was strengthened* is in the passive in the New Testament more often than in the active, which accords with the fact that the believer's strength is derivative. I have reservations about translations like "his faith filled him with power" (GNB) or "he grew strong" (RSV). Paul is not saying that faith, so to speak, took a weak Abraham and put strength into him. He is saying that God took a weak Abraham and put strength into him. Abraham was made strong because of his faith indeed, but it was God, not faith, that provided the strength. Faith was no more than the means by which he received it. The Greek may be understood as "he was strengthened in his faith" (his faith grew stronger), or "he was strengthened through his faith". Either way it was God who gave the strength. Throughout this passage Paul is concerned to emphasize the importance of faith. Abraham had nothing going for him except the promise of God. But for the man of faith that was enough. Paul adds that Abraham *gave glory to God*, which is not explicitly said in the Genesis narrative. Paul may be referring to Abraham's general attitude, or to his acceptance of the covenant. At any rate, giving glory to God means ascribing to God what is due to him (in which Abraham stands in contrast to the sinners of 1:21).[95] It is, of course, impossible to increase God's glory; "giving glory to God" means recognizing

---

90. νεϰρόω (only here in Romans; once each in Colossians and Hebrews) means "put to death", but BAGD cite it in the passive with the meaning "be worn out, impotent, as good as dead". This meaning is not given in LSJ, but MM cite a parallel. It is used again for this same situation in Heb. 11:12.

91. νέϰρωσις is found only here in Romans, and again in the New Testament only in 2 Cor. 4:10, with a variant reading at Mark 3:5. It signifies putting to death, and so deadness. GT cites Galen for its use of a dead state, "*utter sluggishness* (of bodily members and organs)". μήτρα is found in the New Testament only in Luke 2:23 and here.

92. δέ is adversative; Abraham took note of the difficulties but did not waver.

93. διαϰρίνω has meanings like "judge", "separate", "dispute", and apparently from this last "be at odds with oneself", "doubt", "waver", a meaning which appears first in the New Testament (BAGD; F. Büchsel, TDNT, III, p. 947), but which is surely plain in the present passage. εἰς before τὴν ἐπαγγελίαν is perhaps unexpected after this verb. It is apparently BAGD's 5: "to denote reference to a person or thing *for, to, with respect* or *reference to*", a meaning it has in 16:19. NIV, *he did not waver . . . regarding the promise* is the sense of it.

94. Turner sees this as a dative of cause and calls it "extraordinary" (M, III, p. 242).

95. There is a good deal of Pauline vocabulary here. ἀπιστία is found five times in Paul (four in Romans) out of 11 in the New Testament; ἐνδυναμόω six out of seven; δίδωμι 72 times out of 416 (only John with 76 has more); δόξα 77 out of 165.

the glory he has and taking the place appropriate to the creature over against the Creator. In Abraham's case perhaps we can say that we see this in his circumcising his household as a sign of the covenant God would establish with Isaac (Gen. 17:21).

21. A further participle carries on the construction, *being fully persuaded*.[96] The verb means "to fill completely" and thus "to convince fully" (see BAGD). A difficulty arises from the fact that Abraham does not seem to have been fully convinced when he was told that Sarah would bear a son, for he laughed at the suggestion and looked to Ishmael as the one through whom God's promise would be fulfilled (Gen. 17:17-18). But this may be taken as part of the way Abraham evaluated the situation; on the human level the suggestion was laughable. Faith, for Abraham, was not automatic or easy. He had his problems just as the rest of us do. But, recognizing the difficulties as he did, Abraham came to a firm faith, as is shown by his circumcising all the males of his household before Isaac was conceived (Gen. 17:21-27). We must not overlook the fact that many years passed between the giving of the promise (Gen. 15:5) and its fulfilment (Gen. 21:2). Abraham must have been sorely tried by the delay, as he saw Sarah and himself growing old and beyond the human capacity of producing a child. Paul is referring to the settled attitude that endured all this, not to Abraham's initial reaction. The unbelief was momentary, the faith constant. Abraham was assured that God could and would do what he had promised.[97] This is the one example of the use of the verb "to promise" in Romans, and it is in the perfect tense (as is the one example in Galatians). There is an air of permanence about this tense that suits the divine promise.

22. It was this[98] constancy in faith that was the reason for Abraham's being reckoned as righteous. Paul quotes once more from Genesis 15:6, a passage he has already quoted in verse 3.

23. The principle found in this verse matters a good deal to Paul. In 15:4 he says that whatever is written in Scripture is written for our instruction (cf. 2 Tim. 3:16), and in writing to the Corinthians he applies to Christian preachers an Old Testament command concerning oxen, rejecting the view that God has animals primarily in mind. He asks, "Is it about oxen that God is concerned?" and answers, "Surely he says this for us, doesn't he?" (1 Cor. 9:9-10). He holds that things that happened during the wilderness wanderings "were written down as warnings for us" (1 Cor. 10:11). So here, while

---

96. πληροφορέω is found in Paul in five of its six New Testament occurrences.

97. This verse is the subject of an article by William Neil, "God's Promises are Sure—Romans iv.21" (ET, LXIX [1957-58], pp. 146-48). He says, "We may feel that Paul's argument in this chapter of Romans smacks at times of the rabbinical schools, but unless we can share his insight into the essential kinship of Abraham with ourselves, it is difficult to see how the Old Testament can become anything more than a treasure house of sacred song and religious inspiration" (p. 148).

98. For διό see the note on 1:24. It is followed by καί in many MSS, such as ℵ A C D Ψ, though not found in B D* F G etc. If it be read, it will signify "that the inference is self-evident" (BAGD).

Abraham's faith was obviously very important for the patriarch and his immediate circle, the words *were not written for him alone*. This means more than that what is written informs and edifies us. Paul is saying that the words laid down an important truth whose application was not limited to Abraham; it is relevant to all the saved. Righteousness will be reckoned to us in the same way it was to Abraham.

24. Paul explicitly applies the words *also for us* to his contemporaries[99]—not, of course, to all, but to *us who believe*. To believers God *will credit righteousness*[100] just as he did to Abraham. The future points to the eschatological aspect of justification. In one sense believers are justified now; they have received right standing with God and this is their present possession. From another point of view the consummation waits till Judgment Day and thus may be referred to as still future. NIV is a trifle more full than Paul, who does not use the word *righteousness* here, but simply says "to whom it will be credited"; but NIV is simply bringing out the sense. This "crediting" is an activity exercised towards *us who believe in him*, where Paul has an unusual construction after the verb *believe*.[101] Notice further that he speaks of faith in God the Father, not, as he more usually does, of faith in Christ. The Father is characterized by his raising Jesus from the dead (cf. 1 Cor. 6:14; 15:15; 2 Cor. 4:14; Gal. 1:1, etc.). Paul uses the human name *Jesus* without adding "Christ", but he goes on to speak of him as *our Lord* (see note on 1:4). Where Paul uses the verb "to raise" in this epistle he is almost invariably speaking of raising the dead (nine times out of ten). Since the resurrection of Jesus is of central importance, it is not surprising that Paul links it with faith in this way. We should also notice that about three out of four of Paul's uses of the term "dead" refer to raising from the dead. His interest is in life even when he uses the terminology of death.

25. Jesus was *delivered over*[102] (there is no *to death* in the Greek; it is the "handing over" of which Paul speaks, though, of course, Jesus' death followed). The verb is not uncommon in Paul (19 times out of 120 in the New Testament), but it is more common elsewhere (Matthew, e.g., uses it 31 times). In the Gospels the word is used frequently of Judas's "betraying" of

---

99. Paul points up the contrast with ἀλλὰ καί. δι' ἡμᾶς will mean "on our account".

100. BAGD speak of μέλλω as "denoting an action that necessarily follows a divine decree *is destined, must, will certainly*" (1.c.δ). They also point out that the verb is rarely followed by the future or aorist infinitive, but 84 times by the present infinitive. It is possible to take μέλλει here as emphasizing the certainty rather than as indicating the future (cf. Cranfield).

101. τοῖς πιστεύουσιν ἐπὶ τὸν ἐγείραντα.... See the note on v. 5. This and v. 5 appear to be Paul's only uses of πιστεύω ἐπί + accusative of person (elsewhere he has the dative), a construction that occurs elsewhere only in Matt. 27:42; Acts 9:42; 11:17; 16:31; 22:19. There will possibly be something more dynamic about it than the dative, together with the thought of faith on the basis of, as resting on. Moule thinks it "possibly retains a sense of movement, metaphorically" (IBNTG, p. 49).

102. The verb is used in LXX in Isa. 53:6, κύριος παρέδωκεν αὐτὸν ταῖς ἁμαρτίαις ἡμῶν, and twice in Isa. 53:12, παρεδόθη εἰς θάνατον ἡ ψυχὴ αὐτοῦ . . . διὰ τὰς ἀνομίας αὐτῶν παρεδόθη.

214

Jesus, but this is scarcely the thought here. Paul is simply saying that Jesus was given over. He will expect his readers to understand "to death", and it is the death rather than the betrayal that is in mind. Here Paul does not say who "delivered him over", but in 8:32 he says that the Father did this.[103] There is a problem with the two occurrences of *for*[104] in this verse: *for our sins* and *for our justification*. If the two are taken in the same sense (as many argue, quite sensibly), the meaning might be "he was delivered up because we had sinned and raised because we had been justified" (NEB mg., "raised to life because we are now justified"), or "he was delivered up to atone for our sins and raised to secure our justification." Cranfield argues that the two "for's" need not have the same meaning, for one refers to what is regrettable (sins) and the other to what is desirable (justification).[105] He takes the first as causal, the second as final. Vincent Taylor maintains that the prospective meaning, "with a view to", is rare; he finds it extremely rarely in the classics and not at all in LXX or in the papyri as reported by MM, while in the New Testament he finds but one possible exception apart from this passage; this should give us pause before we accept the future reference.[106] It is not wise to be dogmatic. We should certainly not take the second clause to mean that the resurrection was the sole cause of our justification. Paul can also say that we are "justified by his blood" (5:9). Perhaps we should go along with Godet: "Our sin had killed Him; our justification raised Him again. . . . His resurrection was the *proof* of our justification only because it was the necessary *effect* of it." Our best procedure is to see the two "for's" as causal but not to try to pin them down too closely (cf. NIV).[107] Many see here a traditional formulation which Paul has taken up, and if this is indeed the case this is an added reason for not insisting too strongly on a rigid grammatical distinction. But clearly Paul is affirming strongly that it was for our sins[108] that Christ died and that he has

103. The "delivering over" of Jesus may be viewed from any one of a number of angles (see the note on 8:32).

104. The word διά generally has a causative sense when used with the accusative, as here. A. Oepke sees it as generally denoting "'for the sake of' with a certain final element" (TDNT, II, p. 70).

105. It is also true that in v. 23 διά + accusative looks back to Abraham; in v. 24 the same construction looks forward to "us".

106. ET, L (1938-39), p. 298. Most commentators ignore Taylor's discussion of this preposition. Apart from 3:25-26 (the passage he is discussing) he holds that "the only possible New Testament example" is the present passage, and he maintains that "in spite of the opinion of Sanday and Headlam, it is extremely doubtful if this is an exception." See the note on 3:25.

107. Cf. Robinson, "Clearly there is no separation or antithesis intended here between the cross and resurrection. It is a characteristic piece of Hebrew poetic parallelism— he died and rose for our justification from sin."

108. The word for sin here is παράπτωμα, "a fall beside", and thus "a false step", "a sin". Paul uses the term 16 times, nine in this letter. W. Michaelis regards it as a synonym of ἁμαρτία, and distinct from παράβασις, which latter "is orientated to the presence of the Law . . . it implies transgression of a commandment . . . παράπτωμα, however, goes further; it refers directly to the disruption of man's relation to God through his fault" (TDNT, VI, p. 172).

perfectly accomplished our justification. His word for *justification*[109] is found only here and in 5:18 in the New Testament. Strictly it signifies the act of justifying, the process rather than the result, but it would be pedantic to insist on this. NIV gives us the meaning.

109. δικαίωσις.

Romans 5

3. The Effects of Justification, 5:1-11

Commentators view this section in a wide variety of ways. Black sees it as a transition from the treatment of justification to that of the spiritual life. Boylan regards it as a study of "the fruits of justification", while others specifically reject this (Godet, e.g., sees it as dealing with the certainty of final salvation for believers). Lloyd-Jones finds in it the key to the understanding of the rest of the letter and speaks of it as teaching that our salvation is "absolute, complete and final"; he entitles his treatment of this chapter "Assurance". Dodd regards 5:1-11 as a summary of the argument to 8:39. Nygren heads it "Free from the Wrath of God", while Cranfield asserts that peace with God gives the section its unity. Similarly, Käsemann heads it "Paradoxical standing in the peace of God".

It is not easy to avoid the impression that some students tend to make the passage more definitely a part of a scheme of their own devising than to try to follow Paul's line of thought. It is not at all obvious that the apostle is following a rigid scheme. But it is clear that he has concluded his basic account of justification and that he is now moving on to the consequences (notice his "Therefore" at the beginning). Justification has results. The justified person has peace and joy, and Paul exults in this. In the process he further emphasizes the importance of the death of the righteous Christ for sinful people. The love of God is behind all this. Paul does not think of God as remote and indifferent but as full of love, and it is from his love that our salvation proceeds.

> [1]Therefore, since we have been justified through faith, we[a] have peace with God through our Lord Jesus Christ, [2]through whom we have gained access by faith into this grace in which we now stand. And we rejoice in the hope of the glory of God. [3]Not only so, but we also rejoice in our sufferings, because we know that suffering produces perseverance; [4]perseverance, character; and character, hope. [5]And hope does not disappoint us, because God has poured out his love into our hearts by the Holy Spirit, whom he has given us.
>
> [6]You see, at just the right time, when we were still powerless, Christ died for the ungodly. [7]Very rarely will anyone die for a righteous man, though for a good man someone might possibly dare to die. [8]But God demonstrates his own love for us in this: While we were still sinners, Christ died for us.
>
> [9]Since we have now been justified by his blood, how much more shall we be saved from God's wrath through him! [10]For if, when we were God's enemies, we

were reconciled to him through the death of his Son, how much more, having been reconciled, shall we be saved through his life! [11]*Not only is this so, but we also rejoice in God through our Lord Jesus Christ, through whom we have now received reconciliation.*

[a]1 Or *let us*; also in verses 2 and 3

1. *Therefore* links what follows to the preceding. It is only because of Christ's work of justification that peace and other blessings follow. For *justified* see Additional Note D. *Through* translates *ek*, which denotes origin. For *peace* see the note on 1:7. Paul speaks of *peace with God*, not "the peace of God" (as Phil. 4:7);[1] he is not referring to a subjective feeling, but to the objective fact that the justified are no longer enemies of God but are at peace with him (cf. v. 10). The inward peace that follows is very important, but it is not the primary thought here. The justified person is no longer tormented by questions of his relationship with God arising from the fact that he is a sinner. Sinner though he is, he is at peace with God because of what God has done for him. A difficult textual problem arises as to whether we should read "we have peace" or "let us have peace".[2] The context favors the former reading, with its indicatives stating facts (there is no exhortation in the entire passage, vv. 1-11, though cf. n. 8). But the MSS favor the second reading. Our decision rests on the relative weights we give to the context and the MSS. Most commentators agree that the indicative is the proper reading; they see Paul as pointing out that the justified have peace with God. "Let us have peace" would seem to imply that the justified have a choice whether to have peace or not, and that is

1. Paul's words are εἰρήνην πρὸς τὸν θεόν (for the construction cf. Josephus, *Ant.* 8.396). Of this construction W. Foerster says, "the reference is to a relationship with God" (TDNT, II, p. 415). Haldane comments, "Through this sense of the pardon of sin, and of friendship with God, the peace of God, which passeth all understanding, keeps his heart and mind through Christ Jesus." This is true, but it is not what Paul is saying. That is rather the force of ἡ εἰρήνη τοῦ θεοῦ (Phil. 4:7).

2. Lagrange says that the subjunctive ἔχωμεν is "the only admissible reading", while Leenhardt states emphatically, "it is impossible to adopt it"! It is strongly attested (א* A B* C D K L 33 etc.), while support for ἔχομεν is definitely weaker (א¹ B³ Gᵍʳ etc.). A majority of Metzger's committee held that the context looks for a statement rather than an exhortation, and therefore favored the indicative. Tasker prefers the subjunctive to "the weakly attested ἔχομεν." He points to the repeated καυχώμεθα (vv. 2 and 3), and sees "three hortative clauses". Most, however, consider the other two to be indicatives. It has been pointed out that in the early church there was a strong tendency to exhort and that this may have led some scribes to change from the indicative. Denney cites a number of passages where critics agree that o should be read, not ω, despite the MSS, and remarks, "they are quite enough to show that in a variation of this kind no degree of MS. authority could support a reading against a solid exegetical reason for changing ω into o." Nygren cites Lietzmann for another important point: "Since, as early as the first century, men no longer made any difference between long and short 'o,' it cannot be proved that there was a long 'o' in the original; and even less can it be shown that Paul so dictated it. He may have said 'echomen,' meaning ἔχομεν, but Tertius wrote ἔχωμεν. This could be the case, even if the ω could be traced back to the original. The meaning here must carry more weight than the letter. Only ἔχομεν gives Paul's real meaning." Cf. 14:19; 1 Cor. 15:49; Gal. 6:10.

un-Pauline. On the whole it seems that there is more to be said for the indicative (if the subjunctive were accepted it would have to be in the sense "Let us enjoy peace"). Justification results in real peace with God, and that for all believers. Gore points out that this involves the destruction of the fancied securities and the false peace that we manufacture, as when we say, "Peace, peace, when there is no peace" (Jer. 6:14; 8:11). Our peace is obtained *through our Lord Jesus Christ.* That it is Christ who brings us the blessing is the emphasis of this part of the letter (vv. 11, 21; 6:23; 7:25; 8:39); this expression thus appears at the end of each section of the argument.

2. Through Christ we approach God. Most translations speak of our having *access,* but the noun seems rather to mean "introduction".[3] "The idea is that of introduction to the presence-chamber of a monarch. The rendering 'access' is inadequate, as it leaves out of sight the fact that we do not come in our own strength but need an 'introducer'—Christ" (SH). The stress is on Christ's activity, not ours. The verb is in the perfect tense,[4] which points to the ongoing result of a past act. Christ's bringing us to God has continuing effect (which may be why so many translations favor "access"). Another interesting textual problem has to do with *by faith* (omitted in RSV), where the evidence for inclusion and exclusion is rather evenly balanced.[5] Since the authorities against the reading are fairly strong, and since it is so natural to slip the words in, perhaps we should regard them as a scribal insertion. The sense is not greatly affected, for Paul has just said that justification is by faith. The introduction is *into this grace,* an uncommon way of using "grace". It is closely connected with God, and indeed Smart says forthrightly, " 'Access to this grace' is access to God. Grace is not something apart from God, but is God giving himself to us in his graciousness" (cf. GNB, "this experience of God's grace").[6] *We stand* translates a perfect tense, used in the sense of the present, and with the thought of a continuing attitude.[7] *Rejoice* translates a verb usually rendered "boast";[8] it carries the thought of giving expression to what is

3. προσαγωγή means "a bringing to" and thus "introduction". The result of this is, of course, access, and it is this that leads many translators to choose it. MM cite evidence that the word can mean "a landing-stage"; if that meaning were acceptable, there would be a nautical metaphor, perhaps with χάριν meaning "haven" and προσαγωγή the "approach" to it. But this is a rare usage, and there seems no reason to adopt it here. "Introduction" is the meaning.

4. ἐστήκαμεν, used intransitively in the sense of the present (cf. John 8:44; 2 Cor. 1:24).

5. The words are included in ℵ A C K P, some OL, boh etc., and absent from B D G, some OL, sah. There is not much support for ἐν, and it should not be read.

6. Cf. BAGD, "this state of grace in which we stand". It is a state brought about by God's grace. Murray sees a reference to justification.

7. James P. Martin remarks, "The justified man is not only freed *from* past guilt . . . but also is freed *for* the new future and consequently for a new present" (*Interpretation,* XXV [1971], p. 315).

8. καυχώμεθα is probably indicative, though the form is identical with the subjunctive and some take it that way. The verb is mostly used of blameworthy speech, but sometimes believers can boast rightly (see on 2:17). The matter for boasting is usually indicated by ἐν, sometimes by ὑπέρ or περί.

felt and not simply the feeling. Perhaps "exult" (NEB) is as good a translation as any; Barrett says that the word "means a triumphant, rejoicing confidence". The exultation is based on *the hope of the glory of God*. Left to ourselves we fall short of God's glory (3:23), but the work of Christ has altered that. Christ prayed that his followers would see his glory (John 17:24), and the dying Stephen did see the glory (Acts 7:55). The glory is closely connected with Christ (cf. "Christ in you, the hope of glory", Col. 1:27). It is ongoing, for we are being transformed "from glory to glory" (2 Cor. 3:18), but the consummation is yet to be revealed (Rom. 8:18). See further on 2:7, and for *hope* on 4:18. On this word Käsemann remarks, it is not "the prospect of what might happen but the prospect of what is already guaranteed" (p. 134). There is a distinctiveness about the Christian hope: "whereas for the English speaker *hope* may imply doubt, for Paul it implied certainty" (TH; cf. Phillips, "happy certainty"). Some take this expression as coordinate with the immediately preceding: "through whom we have gained introduction . . . and exult. . . ." But it seems better to link it with the earlier verb, "we have peace . . . and we exult" (so Murray, Cranfield, and others).[9]

3. *Not only* (see on 1:32) is a mark of Paul's style. It recurs with some frequency when he is piling another argument on to the preceding one. *Rejoice* ("boast" or "exult" again) is a striking word to use of afflictions, but the attitude (with or without this word) is found often throughout the New Testament (cf. Matt. 5:4, 10-12; Acts 5:41; 14:22; 2 Cor. 12:9-10; 2 Thess. 1:5; 1 Pet. 4:13-14). People generally think of troubles as evils to be endured as stoically as possible. Paul thinks of them not as simply to be endured, but to be gloried in. *Sufferings*, or "afflictions" (see on 2:9), is a strong term. It does not refer to minor inconveniences, but to real hardships. No one likes troubles of this kind, but they may be seen as difficulties to be overcome, as ways of opening up new possibilities. One who sees them in this light glories in[10] them. Käsemann sees a reference to "the end-time affliction which comes on the Christian as a follower of the messiah Jesus" (p. 134). But this seems an unnecessary limitation and certainly one the text does not justify. Paul is including all the afflictions that come to the Christian. *We know* is a characteristic appeal to knowledge (see on 2:2). The string of virtues is quite in the Pauline manner (cf. Gal. 5:22-23; Eph. 4:1-3). For *perseverance* see on 2:7 and for *produces* on 1:27 (there translated "committed").

4. *Character* is NIV's translation of a word difficult to put into English.[11]

---

9. Stott points out that Paul gives "a beautiful summary of the Christian life" as it relates to God: "In the word 'peace' we look back to the enmity which is now over. In the word 'grace' we look up to our reconciled Father in whose favour we now continue to stand. In the word 'glory' we look on to our final destiny. . . ."

10. ἐν may mean "in the middle of" or "on the basis of"; here the latter is much more likely (Cranfield, Käsemann, etc.). Turner sees the ἐν as causal, "because of" (M, III, p. 253).

11. δοκιμή is a purely Pauline word in the New Testament (seven times, two in Romans), and no example of it is known before Paul. It connects with δοκιμάζω, "to test", and is the quality of having stood the test.

It indicates the result of being tested, the quality of being approved on the basis of a trial; "the temper of the veteran as opposed to that of the raw recruit" (SH). NEB reads "proof that we have stood the test" (cf. Job 23:10). Steadfast endurance leads to the quality of testedness, and this in turn to hope, for the Christian who has been tested has proved God's faithfulness and will surely hope the more confidently.

5. *Hope* comes last in Paul's list, but it was already present at the beginning (v. 2). Here the apostle goes off in a different direction, saying that *hope does not disappoint us.* He is, of course, speaking of the specifically Christian hope, not human hope in general. His verb is found in Paul in ten of its 13 New Testament occurrences; it usually means "put to shame". Paul is saying that hope, the genuinely Christian hope, never puts those who have it to shame (cf. Ps. 22:5; 25:3, 20; Isa. 28:16, LXX; 2 Tim. 1:12, etc.). This is because God's love is poured into their hearts. Paul's emphasis on *love* is strangely overlooked; the apostle is often seen as somewhat pugnacious and argumentative, while John, by contrast, is "the apostle of love". But the word *love* occurs 75 times in Paul out of a New Testament total of 116 (nine in Romans). For this apostle love is supremely important, and he comes back to it again and again. As he does here, Paul often stresses the fact that it is God's love that motivates believers.[12] While the reference is surely to the love God has for us, we should not overlook the truth that the Spirit's pouring of God's love into our hearts is a creative act. It kindles love in us, and love "becomes the moral principle by which we live" (Dodd). *Poured out* points to abundance (cf. Moffatt, "floods our hearts").[13] This pouring out of God's love is done "through" the Holy Spirit. The thought is that of an action of the Spirit of God on our human spirits. The Spirit is *given* (the aorist indicates a single, decisive act), which reminds us that this is not a human achievement or insight. Paul loves to emphasize the divine initiative.[14]

6. The main thrust of Paul's argument is clear. He is saying that the death of Christ was on behalf of ungodly people. But the exact words in which

12. The genitive ἡ ἀγάπη τοῦ θεοῦ is found again in 8:39; Luke 11:42; John 5:42; 2 Cor. 13:13; 2 Thess. 3:5; 1 John 2:5; 3:17; 4:9; 5:3; Jude 21 (τοῦ Χριστοῦ, 8:35; 2 Cor. 5:14; Eph. 3:19). In some cases it may denote the love of people for God (Luke 11:42[?]), but mostly it is the subjective genitive and means God's love for us. This must be the meaning here (cf. v. 8). Calvin says of Augustine's view that Paul is speaking of our love for God, "This is a devout sentiment, but not what Paul means."

13. For the form of the verb see the note on 3:15. The perfect points to a continuing state after a past action, and Godet finds this the reason for the preposition ἐν ("in") rather than εἰς ("into"). This verb is usually followed by εἰς or ἐπί; this is the sole use of ἐν with it in the New Testament.

14. We expect a verb like "poured out" to be used of the Holy Spirit rather than of love (e.g., Acts 2:17-18, 33; Tit. 3:6), and some think we should see this here. Cf. M. Bouttier, "M. Dibelius proposes to transpose the terms: '"Poured" is said with reference to love, but thought of with reference to the Spirit.' So we should have to interpret thus: 'Hope does not deceive us, because, through the Spirit that has been poured into our hearts, God's love has been pledged to us.' This interpretation slightly changes the emphasis of the last phrase, but it has the advantage of taking better account of the verb ἐκκέχυται" (*Christianity according to Paul* [London, 1966], p. 88 n. 78).

he says it are unclear: the textual problem is all but insoluble.[15] It seems, however, that the apostle is emphasizing[16] that the death of Christ[17] took place, not for good people, but for people still sinners. The emphasis is on our unhappy state. We were weak, ungodly sinners (v. 8), and God's enemies (v. 10). "Weak" (NIV, *powerless*)[18] refers to moral frailty rather than to physical weakness. We were quite powerless to help ourselves (and unable even to understand the things of God, 1 Cor. 2:14, let alone act on them). But God's love triumphed where human power failed. Paul says that God acted *at just the right time*.[19] This agrees with other expressions that refer to Christ as coming at the consummation of the ages and the like (cf. 1 Cor. 10:11; Gal. 4:4; 1 Tim. 2:6; Tit. 1:3; Heb. 1:2; 9:26). The thought here is that there is nothing precipitate or delayed about God's action. Theodoret comments that the phrase means "at the appropriate time" (p. 76). Two ways of looking at the time of Christ's death are combined here: he died at a time when we were still sinners, and at a time that fitted God's purpose. This second way emphasizes that the atonement was no afterthought. This was the way God always intended to deal with sin; he did it when he chose. Christ died for[20] "ungodly

15. There is a variety of readings, such as εἴ γε . . . ἔτι (B sah); εἰ γάρ γε (1852 vg^mss); εἰς τί γάρ (D² F G); ἔτι γὰρ . . . ἔτι (א A C D*). The trouble is that, while the reading with two ἔτι's is best attested, it is grammatically very difficult. Paul may have wished to emphasize that we are *still* sinners, and therefore put ἔτι early in the sentence. When he used it again, he was perhaps not bothered by the repetition owing to the exigencies of dictation or simply trying to give even more emphasis. It is a frequent word of his (15 times, five in Romans). It may be temporal or nontemporal, the former being somewhat more usual.

16. Moule regards this as an "impressive example of bringing the emphatic words near the beginning of the sentence" (IBNTG, p. 166).

17. Barth emphasizes that "the new man lives by the dying of Christ" and proceeds, "Now, the life of Christ is His oboedientia passiva, His death on the Cross. It is completely and solely and exclusively His death on the Cross." He thinks that the traditional view of Christ as Prophet, Priest, and King "obscures and weakens the New Testament concentration upon the death of Christ; for there is no second or third or any other aspect of His life which may be treated independently or set side by side with His death." He goes on to develop the point that "Everything shines in the light of His death, and is illuminated by it."

18. ἀσθενῶν. Paul uses the term 15 times out of 25 in the New Testament, but only here in Romans.

19. κατὰ καιρόν; the expression is not common (elsewhere 9:9; John 5:4; Acts 19:23). Since John 5:4 is not part of the true text, and since the other two have the article, this is the one place in the canonical New Testament where this precise expression occurs. According to Blass, it is a formula from an earlier, anarthrous stage of the language, meaning "at the right time", or possibly "while we were yet in the period of weakness" (BDF 255 [3]). Käsemann rejects the former meaning in favor of "then", i.e., "Christ did his saving work at an unexpected and, morally considered, even inappropriate moment" (p. 137). He cites BAGD in support, but, while this lexicon gives "who at that time were still godless" as a possible meaning, it says that the expression "is more naturally construed with ἀπέθανεν" and includes it under the heading "at the right time" (sub καιρός, 1 and 2a). So Barrett, Cranfield, Michel, and others.

20. ὑπέρ (see on 1:5) generally means "on behalf of", but on occasion it means "in the place of", i.e., the preposition can have a substitutionary meaning. There can be little doubt but that that is its significance here (cf. John 11:50). It occurs four times in vv. 6-8. Moule lists its use in v. 7 as the first of his passages illustrating Winer's point: "In most

people".[21] Despite NIV, there is no article with "ungodly"; Paul is not referring to the ungodly as a class, but to people generally as ungodly. Paul often
uses the verb "to die" (42 times in all). His great interests when he uses the
term are in the death of Christ for sinners, as here, and in our death to sin. The
important references are those to Christ's death and what it has done for
believers.

7. Paul brings out the unexpected aspect of this death. It is unexpected
because no one dies for evil people.[22] *Very rarely* is not quite what Paul is
saying. His expression refers to the difficulty of finding someone to do this
rather than to the number of occasions when it happens.[23] His *righteous man* is
not, of course, a man who has merited his salvation, a man who is righteous
with God. He is one who has done what is required of him here on earth.
Some people are better than others, and Paul is referring to one of the better
ones. It would not be easy to find anyone ready to die[24] for even such a person
(Moffatt, "Why, a man will hardly die for the just"). Yet this is not altogether
impossible. Paul holds out the possibility that *for a good man* someone might[25]
be ready to die. It remains a question whether Paul makes a distinction between the *righteous* man and the *good* one. But he does not seem to regard
them here as synonymous. The *righteous* or "just" man is the one who keeps
the letter of the law; he does what is right. But the *good* person goes beyond
that.[26] There is a warmth of good feeling and a generosity about his actions.

---

cases one who acts on behalf of another takes his place" (IBNTG, p. 64), and Käsemann
sees both meanings. Shedd thinks that the reason ὑπέρ is more frequent in the New
Testament than ἀντί in references to Christ's death is that "ὑπὲρ having two meanings can
teach the two facts that Christ died in the place of, and for the benefit of, the believer,
while ἀντί, having but one signification, can mention but one of them. The more comprehensive of the two prepositions is preferred in the majority of instances."

21. For ἀσεβής see on 4:5.

22. Burton H. Throckmorton, Jr., remarks, "Paul knew about martyrs, who had
given their lives for God, or for a cause, or for people in whom they believed. But self-
renunciation involving excruciating pain and death in torture for the benefit of one's
opponents and *adversaries*—this could be interpreted not as human but only as divine"
(*Adopted in Love* [New York, 1978], p. 34).

23. μόλις (here only in Paul) = "with difficulty, hardly, scarcely" (AS). Cf.
J. Schneider, "it is unlikely that any would give himself for a righteous man" (TDNT, IV,
p. 735).

24. BDF see this as "a *gnomic future*" used "to express that which is to be expected
under certain circumstances (as in classical)" (349 [1]).

25. τάχα, "perhaps, possibly, probably" (BAGD); only in Phlm. 15 again in the
New Testament.

26. Cf. Lightfoot, "Shylock might be δίκαιος, but he was not ἀγαθός." Hodge sees
the distinction as that between the "just" and the "kind"; cf. SH, "The δίκαιος keeps to
the 'letter of his bond'; about the ἀγαθός there is something warmer and more genial such
as may well move to self-sacrifice and devotion" (they cite Irenaeus for the Gnostics who
called the God of the Old Testament δίκαιος and the God of the New ἀγαθός). Others,
however, deny a distinction between the terms here (e.g., Murray, Hendriksen). Some
regard τοῦ ἀγαθοῦ as "his benefactor" (Cranfield, Boylan), but this seems too definite. It is
possible to take ἀγαθοῦ as neuter, "for a good cause", but it is better to understand both
adjectives as masculine. Gifford (in a note) holds that the absence of the article with
δίκαιος is because the proposition is virtually negative and the word is thus indefinite; in

The language is tentative; Paul is not rating highly the possibility of someone dying for the good man. Yet it might happen. Because it would demand courage, he says that the person would *dare* to make this sacrifice.

8. But God's love is greater: Christ did not die for good people, but for *sinners.* The cross is the means by which God *demonstrates*[27] his love. Paul says that the cross shows us God's *own love.* One might expect him to say that the cross shows us the love of Christ. It does that, of course, but *own* puts the emphasis on the love of the Father (cf. 1 John 4:10). "Christ's action is God's action. Christ's love is God's love" (Nygren). It would be easy to see the cross as demonstrating the indifference of God, a God who let the innocent Jesus be taken by wicked men, tortured, and crucified while he did nothing. And that would indeed be the case were it not that "God was in Christ, reconciling the world to himself" (2 Cor. 5:19). Unless there is a sense in which the Father and Christ are one, it is not the love of God that the cross shows. But because Christ is one with God, Paul can speak of the cross as a demonstration of the love of God. There is no opposition between the Father and the Son in the means of our salvation. And it was while we were *still sinners* that Christ died. *Still* points to our state at the time. God did not make some indication that we were ready to amend our lives a precondition of bringing about our salvation. It was for people who had sinned and were still sinners that Christ died.[28] There is a spontaneity about God's love. He loves because of what he is, not because of what we are. There is nothing in sinners to call forth the love of God. But he does love us, as the cross so plainly shows. *Christ died for us* comes at the end with impressive simplicity. It is a succinct statement of the essence of the Christian message.

9. Paul links this statement to the preceding with "therefore" (which NIV omits).[29] Here it is more than a conventional connecting word; it denotes real causal sequence. As in verse 1, *we have been justified* presents our justification as an accomplished fact. Paul takes that as basic and reasons from it. Justification is by grace (3:24), by faith (3:28), and connected with the resurrection (4:25); it is in the name of the Lord Jesus Christ (1 Cor. 6:11), in the Spirit (1 Cor. 6:11), in Christ (Gal. 2:17), and here it is *by his blood.*[30] These are all facets of God's great saving act, and the various ways of expressing it center

---

the affirmative proposition Paul does have the article. Moule sees this article as "deictic", i.e., "as pointing out some familiar type or genus"; here *"for the good type of man . . .* or, as colloquial English might put it, *for your good man"* (IBNTG, p. 111).

27. For συνίστημι see on 3:5; here *demonstrates* is undoubtedly the meaning. εἰς ἡμᾶς might grammatically be taken with the verb, giving the meaning "God demonstrates to us his love". But this is less forceful and less likely. NIV is better. Notice the present tense. The cross is an event of the past but it keeps showing the love of God.

28. For ἁμαρτωλός see on 3:7.

29. οὖν; see the note on 2:21.

30. For δικαιόω ἐν see on 3:4; it refers to justification "by means of". Cf. BAGD, "the means or instrument, a construction that begins w. Homer . . . but whose wide currency in our lit. is partly caused by the infl. of the LXX, and its similarity to the Hebr. constr. w. בְּ" (*sub* ἐν III). BDF see a genitive of price as in 3:25, "at the price of his blood" (219 [3]).

impressively on the truth that it is all of God (8:33). *How much more*[31] introduces an argument from the greater to the less: if Christ has done the great
work of justifying sinners, dying for God's enemies, he will certainly perform
the comparatively simple task of keeping those who are now God's friends.
"We shall be saved" looks to the future, and, indeed, this verb is in the future
tense in seven of its eight occurrences in Romans; in this letter Paul is very
interested in the future aspect of salvation. Here he speaks of salvation from
"the wrath" (see on 1:18; cf. 12:19; 1 Thess. 1:10; NIV inserts *God's* quite
correctly, but for Paul it was enough to say "the wrath"). Clearly Paul is
referring to the wrath to come, the eschatological wrath. Christ's salvation is
effective not only now, but in what lies beyond this life. Believers will not
experience the wrath of God then.

10. The "if" construction implies the truth of the supposition, "if, enemies as we were. . . ." *Enemies* is a strong term; sin had put us completely in
the wrong with God (in 11:28 this term is opposed to "beloved"). An enemy is
not a person who comes a little bit short of being a friend; it means someone in
the opposite camp. Some see the meaning here as man's hostility to God, but
the reference to wrath (v. 9) surely shows that God's hostility to evil is in
view. The wrath and the enmity go together. That sinners are God's enemies
is stated a number of times in the New Testament (11:28; Phil. 3:18; Col. 1:21;
Jas. 4:4; cf. Eph. 2:15-16).[32] But the state of enmity is not the last word; *we were
reconciled to him through the death of his Son.* Reconciliation is a vivid word,
pointing to the making of peace after a quarrel. It is a concept Paul uses a
number of times to bring out the significance of the cross (2 Cor. 5:18-20; Eph.
2:16; Col. 1:20-22). From this point of view the cross meant doing away with
sin, breaking down the barrier that kept God and people apart, and thus the
restoration of good relations.[33] The reconciliation took place *through the death*
of Christ. *Through* is not specific; it simply denotes the instrumentality of the
death in bringing about the result. Paul is the only New Testament writer to
refer in set terms to "the death of Christ" or the like (again in this letter in 6:3,

---

31. πολλῷ μᾶλλον. For πολύς see on 3:2. μᾶλλον is the comparative of the adverb μάλα
("very, exceedingly"), and means "to a greater degree, more". Paul combines it with πολλῷ
on a number of occasions, but the four occurrences in Romans are all in this chapter (vv. 10,
15, 17). It is important for the contrast between Adam and Christ.

32. "Reconciliation took place, Paul says, 'while we were God's enemies.' That is a
troublesome statement for every subjective theory of the atonement which sees in the
atonement only a change in man's attitude to God" (Nygren).

33. See further my *The Apostolic Preaching of the Cross*[3] (London, 1965), ch. VII, and
the literature there cited. Since the New Testament never speaks of God as being reconciled, some conclude that reconciliation means no more than a change in sinful people. But
it is the wrath of God, not of people, that has to be dealt with, the demand of God that we
live uprightly that must be reckoned with. Moreover, v. 11 speaks of receiving reconciliation, which was thus in some sense wrought before we received it. It is also true that the
first change is not in the sinner's feelings, but in his state (Gifford). The death of Christ
puts away our sin, which had aroused not our opposition but God's.

5, 9; for *death* see on 1:32). For him it is important that Christ actually died for us and that it was that *death* of God's *Son* (for *Son* see on 1:3) that dealt with our sins.

But Paul does not dwell on the past. The death and the reconciliation it has brought about are important and he comes back to them often, but he also looks forward to the future. If we have been reconciled, *how much more . . . shall we be saved through his life!* (cf. 8:34). *Saved* is again used with a future reference and with a very full meaning, for it is something that follows from reconciliation. Again there is an eschatological reference. The reconciliation leads to a salvation that never ends. When Christ has done the great work of putting away our sin and bringing about our reconciliation to God, he will certainly go on and bring us salvation through eternity (the thought of the previous verse is repeated). NIV says that we will be saved *through* his life,[34] and this may be the way we should take it. There will then be a reference to the resurrection life. Hodge explains it this way, "If while we were enemies, we were restored to the favour of God by the death of his Son, the fact that he lives will certainly secure our final salvation."[35] But the preposition is often used in the sense "in", and the meaning may be something like "we shall be saved through sharing in his life" (Goodspeed; cf. Gifford, "as partakers thereof"), or "through His *living in us*" (Phillips). Our full salvation is achieved "in" Christ's life, which presumably means that we are in him, and that his life is in us. Certainly our life is bound up with his life (cf. 6:8; John 14:19; Eph. 1:22-23; Heb. 7:25; Rev. 1:18, etc.).

11. With another *not only* (see on 1:32) Paul piles on an additional consideration. He brings out the further riches of the Christian life and reinforces his opening with *but also*. As in verses 2 and 3, his thought is of "boasting" or "exulting", this time exulting in God through whom the reconciliation comes.[36] That we exult in[37] God reminds us of the central place of God in Christian living, and the qualification *through our Lord Jesus Christ* of the significance of the work of our Savior. It is only on account of what he has done

---

34. Cf. Barrett, "it is not probable that Paul means to suggest that Christ's death effects one thing, his (resurrection) life another; that is, the contrast is rhetorical rather than substantial."

35. Bultmann says, "By virtue of his resurrection his death received its decisiveness. Thus instead of 'by his life' one could also say 'by his resurrection' (cf. 4.25 and especially II Cor. 4.14" (W. Klassen and G. F. Snyder, eds., *Current Issues in New Testament Interpretation* [New York, 1962], p. 149). He complains that Barth "emphasizes the resurrection, to which only verse 10 alludes, more strongly than the death, on which the emphasis of the text lies (vss. 6-9 and especially 10)" (*ibid.*, p. 150). Parry finds a reference to "the resurrection life of the Lord as the sustaining environment and inspiration of the new life of the Christian."

36. Instead of the indicative we expect (read by a few MSS, as L 104), we have the participle καυχώμενοι (for this verb see on 2:17). Moulton says, "That the participle can be used for indicative or imperative seems to be fairly established now by the papyri" (M, I, p. 222). Similarly Moule sees it as an example of "the use of the participle where normal Greek would have used a finite verb or imperative" (IBNTG, p. 179).

37. Turner regards ἐν as causal, "because of" (M, III, p. 253).

that we can exult in God. The expression brings out something of the spontaneous exuberance of the Christian life.[38] The final words are important: *through whom we have now received reconciliation*. Denney points out that the Greek term for reconciliation differs from its English and German equivalents, for they both imply that peace with God has actually been achieved, whereas "The work of reconciliation, in the sense of the New Testament, is a work which is *finished*, and which we must conceive to be finished, *before the gospel is preached*."[39] The noun incidentally is confined to Paul in the New Testament (twice each in Romans and 2 Corinthians).[40]

4. Solidarity in Adam and in Christ, 5:12-21

12*Therefore, just as sin entered the world through one man, and death through sin, and in this way death came to all men, because all sinned—* 13*for before the law was given, sin was in the world. But sin is not taken into account when there is no law.* 14*Nevertheless, death reigned from the time of Adam to the time of Moses, even over those who did not sin by breaking a command, as did Adam, who was a pattern of the one to come.*

15*But the gift is not like the trespass. For if the many died by the trespass of the one man, how much more did God's grace and the gift that came by the grace of the one man, Jesus Christ, overflow to the many!* 16*Again, the gift of God is not like the result of the one man's sin: The judgment followed one sin and brought condemnation, but the gift followed many trespasses and brought justification.* 17*For if, by the trespass of the one man, death reigned through that one man, how much more will those who receive God's abundant provision of grace and of the gift of righteousness reign in life through the one man, Jesus Christ.*

18*Consequently, just as the result of one trespass was condemnation for all men, so also the result of one act of righteousness was justification that brings life for all men.* 19*For just as through the disobedience of the one man the many were made sinners, so also through the obedience of the one man the many will be made righteous.*

20*The law was added so that the trespass might increase. But where sin increased, grace increased all the more,* 21*so that, just as sin reigned in death, so also grace might reign through righteousness to bring eternal life through Jesus Christ our Lord.*

Paul enters a detailed (and difficult) comparison of Adam and Christ (cf. 1 Cor. 15:22, 45-49). In dealing with the first man he is concerned not so much

---

38. Cragg sees joy as characteristic of the Christian life, and he differentiates it from pleasure: "Pleasure, when chosen wisely and used in moderation, may do much to mitigate the rigors of experience; but it can never create the atmosphere with which joy surrounds the man who has found it." Joy "is inseparable from a discovery of our proper relationship to God."

39. *The Death of Christ* (London, 1905), pp. 144-45.

40. There is a useful note on reconciliation as mutual and not on the side of man only in SH; so also in Knox.

with the creation of Adam as with his first sin and the calamitous consequences that followed. All mankind is affected by what Adam did. Over
against that Paul sets the saving work of Christ. Just as Adam was the head of
a race of sinners, so Christ is the head of a new race, the redeemed people of
God. The argument is very condensed,[41] and in all translations and comments we must allow for the possibility that Paul's meaning may at some
point be other than we think. But we must not exaggerate this. The main lines
of the argument are clear. It is an important section, and indeed Nygren calls
it "the point where all the lines of (Paul's) thinking converge, both those of
the preceding chapters and those of the chapters that follow."[42] The construction of the whole is not straightforward. Paul begins to compare Adam and
Christ in verse 12, but breaks off his sentence at the end of that verse to
explain the pattern of sin and death (vv. 13-14). He makes it clear that there
are profound dissimilarities between Christ and Adam (vv. 15-17), and in
verse 18 he returns to complete succinctly the thought of the unfinished
sentence of verse 12. To this he adds an explanation (v. 19) and a little section
on the law (vv. 20-21). There is an objectivity to this section that we should not
miss. In verses 1-11 and again in 6:1-9 the pronoun "we" is constant, but in
5:12-21 there is not one "we". Paul is concentrating on objective facts, irrespective of our participation.

   12. This verse begins a new section, linked to the preceding with a
Therefore. Immediately we encounter disagreement. Barrett discovers only "a
loose relation" with the preceding and Käsemann refers to "the break in
thought" (p. 146), whereas Lenski speaks of "a close connection" and Boylan
sees what follows as "an inference from the section, vv. 1-11". Lenski and
Boylan are surely right; we should take Paul's *Therefore* seriously. He is linking
this new section to the preceding. It is because of the reconciliation Christ has
brought about that the evil Adam introduced into the world has been overcome, and more than overcome (cf. v. 20). Had it not been for the pervasive
evil our first father brought into the world, there would have been no need
and no place for reconciliation. It is possible to see *Therefore* as referring to
verse 11, to verses 1-11, or to the whole long passage from 1:18 on. Whichever
way we take it (and there is much to be said for the simpler view that it
depends on v. 11), it is the conclusion of the foregoing argument. A problem
arises from the fact that Paul begins to say something on the basis of the
reconciliation we have received, but he never gets around to completing his
sentence.[43] KJV marks the construction by putting verses 13-17 in brackets;

---

41. Cf. Parry, "This is perhaps the most condensed passage in all S. Paul's writings.
It is consequently almost impossible to give an interpretation with confidence." This is
perhaps too pessimistic, but it is well that we bear in mind the difficulty posed by the
compressed language.
   42. Lloyd-Jones sees it as "the very heart and centre" of the epistle (p. 176), and
Griffith Thomas as "the great central feature and focus of the Epistle".
   43. He begins with ὥσπερ, but there is no corresponding οὕτως (as there is, e.g., in
v. 19). It is generally agreed that οὕτως later in this verse does not correspond to ὥσπερ

this perhaps makes the grammatical construction too complicated; it is probably better to think that Paul simply leaves his sentence unfinished. But, however we take it, it is only in verse 18 that we have the completion of the thought that Paul starts here.

Paul says that *sin entered the world through one man*. He does not name him until verse 14, but there is no doubt that he is referring to Adam.[44] He emphasizes his point by putting "as through one man" first in the clause. This one man, and indeed one evil deed of this one man, is very important and underlies the whole discussion. Twelve times in verses 12-19 we have the word *one*; repeatedly Paul refers to one man Adam (and to one sin of that one man), and opposes to him (and to it) the one man Jesus Christ (and his one work of grace). The one man and his sin and the one Savior and his salvation are critical to the discussion. *Sin entered the world* (which incidentally implies that sin existed before Adam). With the personification we see sin as a mighty force of evil which used Adam as its instrument. *The world* is, of course, the world of people, the human race, not the physical earth. *Death* (see on 1:32; this is one of Paul's characteristic connections of death and sin) is also personified, and seen as using sin as its point of entry. It is sin that brought death. This presents a problem to modern people, for death seems inevitable for bodies constituted like ours, sin or no sin.[45] Some argue accordingly that Paul means spiritual death, not physical death (in vv. 17 and 21 "death" is opposed to eternal life). The warning to Adam ran, "in the day that you eat of it you shall die" (Gen. 2:17, RSV), but in the sense of physical death Adam did not die "in the day" that he ate, nor for many years afterward. It is therefore suggested that a spiritual penalty is meant (cf. 6:23; Eph. 2:1). To this it is

---

(though see BAGD *sub* οὕτως 1a; under ὥσπερ 1, however, this lexicon refers to an anacoluthon here). Many point out that to see this καὶ οὕτως as completing the construction is to confuse καὶ οὕτως with οὕτως καί.

44. Elsewhere Eve is linked with Adam in the first sin (2 Cor. 11:3; 1 Tim. 2:13-14) and her part is emphasized in some Jewish writing (e.g., "From a woman sin had its beginning, and because of her we all die", Sir. 25:24). Paul does not mention her here, probably because he is thinking of Adam and Eve as one in their sin (cf. God "created them male and female . . . and called them Adam", Gen. 5:2).

45. Jewish thinkers in antiquity sometimes thought that Adam would have been immortal had he not sinned; thus "God created man for incorruption, and made him in the image of his own eternity, but through the devil's envy death entered the world . . ." (Wis. 2:23-24; J. Cambier thinks that Paul is here adapting this Wisdom passage [NTS, XI (1964-65), pp. 231-32]). C. S. Lewis has an interesting argument that death was not inevitable for our first parents: "Man, as originally created, was immune from it." At that time his spirit was able to keep the forces of dissolution at bay: "The spirit was once not a garrison, maintaining its post with difficulty in a hostile Nature, but was fully 'at home' with its organism, like a king in his own country or a rider on his own horse—or better still, as the human part of a Centaur was 'at home' with the equine part. Where spirit's power over the organism was complete and unresisted, death would never occur"; "when God created Man he gave him such a constitution that, if the highest part of it rebelled against Himself, it would be bound to lose control over the lower parts: i.e. in the long run to suffer Death" (*Miracles* [London, 1952], pp. 152, 156). A number of writers have thought that if Adam had not sinned he would have ended his earthly course by being "changed" (1 Cor. 15:51), but not by undergoing death.

229

objected that no one would understand from the language used that the writers of Genesis and Romans were referring to anything other than death in the ordinary physical sense (cf. Gifford, "That death must here be understood in its primary sense as the death of the body, is clear from the connexion with *v.* 14, where no other meaning is admissible"). Perhaps the best way to understand both passages is to see a reference to both kinds of death. Physical death is in mind, but not physical death in itself; it is physical death as the sign and symbol of spiritual death.

The consequence of Adam's sin and the death that it brought into the world is that *death came*[46] *to all men.* That the emphasis is on the fact that the whole race is involved is seen partly from the position of *all* (it is first in its clause in the Greek), and partly from the inclusion of *men* (the word *all* would have been sufficient). Adam was one man and he did one act. But the result spread to all his posterity.[47] Paul moves on to the point that *all sinned* (cf. 3:9, 23-24). The Greek construction is difficult.[48] It is not surprising accordingly that interpretations vary. Many have taken Paul to mean that Adam's sin in some way brought the penalty of death not only on himself but on all his posterity. *All sinned* in this case means "all sinned in Adam"; "Adam's sin is the sin of all".[49] Such a view is not wildly popular in our highly individualistic age, but many remind us that we stand in solidarity with the entire race and

46. διέρχομαι (here only in Romans, five times in Paul) seems a curious verb in this context, with its meaning "go through". Perhaps the force has been weakened (BAGD, "come, go"); perhaps, with SH, we should take the διά seriously and hold that the verb "contains the force of distribution; 'made its way to each individual member of the race'".

47. Many statements from Jewish thinkers emphasize the evil Adam brought on his descendants, e.g., "For a grain of evil seed was sown in Adam's heart from the beginning, and how much ungodliness it has produced until now, and will produce until the time of threshing comes!"; "O Adam, what have you done? For though it was you who sinned, the fall was not yours alone, but ours also who are your descendants" (2 Esdr. 4:30; 7:118). Such statements do not show that Paul was repeating a Jewish commonplace, for none of them goes as far as does the apostle. But they do show that his position developed naturally from his Jewish background.

48. There is a problem with the meaning of ἐφ' ᾧ (= ἐπὶ τούτῳ ὅτι, BDF 294 [4]). Many accept the meaning "because" (BDF 235 [2]; BAGD sub ἐπί II.1.b.γ; IBNTG, pp. 50, 132; M, III, p. 272; RSV, NASB, JB, etc.). Some take ᾧ as masculine and find a reference to Adam "in whom all sinned" (the view of Augustine; in modern times cf. Turner, "death passed upon all men through him *in whom* all men sinned" [*Grammatical Insights*, p. 116]). But this gives a strange meaning to ἐπί, and "one man" is a long way away, with nothing to show that they are connected. F. W. Danker argues that ἐφ' ᾧ in both classical and Koine Greek expresses "the formal contractual basis on which reciprocal obligations are met". He sees here the meaning, "on the basis of what (law) they sinned", i.e., "And so death passed to all men, on the legal basis in terms of which all (including the Gentiles) sinned" (NTS, XIV [1967-68], pp. 429-31). Other suggestions include the view of E. Stauffer (and earlier writers) that the pronoun refers to θάνατος (*New Testament Theology* [London, 1955], p. 270 n. 176), or that the meaning is "in view of the fact that" (M, I, p. 107), or "wherefore, from which it follows" (Black, following Lyonnet), or "that is the reason" (John J. Scullion, ABR, XVI [1968], p. 35), or "inasmuch as" (Moffatt).

49. The classic statement is that of Bengel, *omnes peccarunt, Adamo peccante,* "in Adam sinning, all sinned". Cf. Nygren, "Paul's main idea is entirely clear and beyond doubt: it was through one man, Adam, that all men are sinners and are subject to death." Boylan cites the Council of Trent for a view like this and agrees with it himself.

this is something we must keep in view.[50] A second explanation is that of Calvin; he maintains that Adam "corrupted, vitiated, depraved, and ruined our nature. . . . We have, therefore, all sinned, because we are all imbued with natural corruption." Essentially the same point of view may be expressed in terms more acceptable today; we all sin, but our sin is the result of tendencies we inherit.[51] Such views recognize the fact that we are sinful and that we are punished because we are sinful, but they trace the origin of our sinfulness to our human nature. The older forms of this view saw that human nature as changed for the worse by what Adam did (original sin).[52] The main objection to this is that Paul says nothing about a corrupt nature or sinful tendencies; such views read something into the text. A third view puts the emphasis on the unqualified statement, *all sinned*. This must, its adherents maintain, refer to an individual activity; we all follow Adam's example, but our sin is our own. This was put in a memorable phrase by an ancient writer, "each of us has been the Adam of his own soul" (2 Bar. 54:19). Cranfield argues for the meaning "men's sinning in their own persons but as a result of the corrupt nature inherited from Adam", which combines the second and third views. Some variant of the view that we have all actively committed sin of our own and that this is blameworthy is most widely held today.[53] This appeals to modern people and it is, of course, true, but whether it is what Paul means is quite another thing. It ignores the language he uses. The aorist points to one act,[54] the act of Adam; we would expect the present or the

50. Dodd does not, of course, accept the view that all sinned in Adam, but he reminds us that "The isolation of the individual is an abstraction. None of us stands alone. What we are and what we do is largely affected by the forces of heredity and environment, i.e. by the place we occupy in the structure of society as an historical whole." Cf. Hunter, "This passage has much to say about the solidarity of men in evil—a fact which has been ruthlessly forced home on us to-day by the grim logic of history." A. J. M. Wedderburn holds that we must retain the tension between the universal and the individual in Paul's thought: "To obliterate the responsibility of the individual or to make him guilty of that for which he was not responsible may be unethical, but it is equally false to deny that *de facto* it is human to sin and to die and that socially and physically we are thus inevitably involved in a situation from which only Christ can release us" (NTS, XIX [1972-73], p. 354).

51. Barclay says of the view that, "because of his heredity, man is inevitably predisposed to sin" that "To the mind of a modern man (it) is undoubtedly the most acceptable; but equally undoubtedly it is not what Paul meant" (ET, LXX [1958-59], p. 173).

52. Luther argues strongly that Paul means original sin, not actual sin.

53. According to TH, "Paul is saying that death became a universal experience because all men sinned". Not surprisingly these authorities find the next verse "difficult to follow"; once the emphasis is put on the individual sinner and Paul's concentration on "the one" is ignored, of course, the passage is difficult. This view is an interesting illustration of Nygren's point that "More or less consciously interpreters have acted on the assumption that something which is so foreign to today's thought as to seem unreal cannot have been of decisive importance to Paul either." O'Neill points out that "the sentence does not allow us to go to" a view like this. Cf. v. 19.

54. Cf. Barclay, "It means that sin and death entered into the world, not because all men *sin*, as it were habitually, but because all men *sinned*. Further, if we are to give the aorist tense its full value, and in this argument we must do so, the more precise meaning will be that sin and death entered into the world because all men were guilty *of one act of sin*" (ET, LXX [1958-59], p. 192).

imperfect if the apostle were thinking of the continuing sins of all people. Paul says that all sinned in Adam, not in imitating him (cf. Bruce). And it ignores the context with its strong insistence on the sin of *one* man (not all of us) as the cause of the trouble.

Consider the fivefold repetition of this truth: "many died by the trespass of the one" (v. 15), "the judgment followed one sin" (v. 16), "by the trespass of the one man, death reigned" (v. 17), "the result of one trespass was condemnation for all men" (v. 18), "through the disobedience of the one man the many were made sinners" (v. 19; this last statement is especially significant). All this does not mean that we have simply followed Adam's example. The apostle's tremendous emphasis surely forces us to some variant of the first view, that all the race is somehow caught up in Adam's sin.[55] Throughout this whole passage what Adam did and what Christ did are steadily held over against each other. Now salvation in Christ does not mean that we merit salvation by living good lives; rather, what Christ has done is significant. Just so, death in Adam does not mean that we are being punished for our own evil deeds; it is what Adam has done that is significant. This does not mean that our sinful nature or our many actual sins are unimportant to Paul. Nor does it mean that he is indifferent to the importance of individual responsibility.[56] It simply means that these things are not what he is talking about here.[57] He is concerned with what Adam did and its results. He is saying that Adam's sin involved us all in a situation of sin and death from which there is no escape other than in Christ. We should perhaps notice a somewhat similar statement about Christ, "one died for all, and therefore all died" (2 Cor. 5:14). At this point Paul is laying down the opposite of what he says there: Adam's sin meant that he and all his posterity died.

13. Paul breaks off his construction and proceeds in a different direction. But what he says is connected with the preceding, and he links it up with *for*. He can say what he has just said, *for* there was sin even *before*[58] *the law was given:* even before there was any such thing as formal law there was sin. It is usually held that *law* here means the law of Moses (cf. "from Adam to Moses"

55. Lloyd-Jones finds truth in each of two ways of understanding this: "Adam was the totality of human nature" (p. 213) and we are all in him (in much the same way as Levi was in the loins of Abraham and paid tithes, Heb. 7:9-10), and again Adam was the representative, the federal head, of all the race (p. 216). Whether we see the essence in either or both of these, the passage does say that we are all caught up in what Adam did. Olshausen uses an illustration from the army: if a general is defeated, every one of his soldiers is defeated.

56. Paul is not denying human responsibility, for, as Bultmann points out, "He insists that for each man death is the punishment of his own sin" (TDNT, III, p. 15). But the question is, Is this all he is saying?

57. Hodge makes the important point that "Neither the corruption of nature, nor the actual sins of men, and their liability on account of them, is either questioned or denied, but the simple statement is, that on account of the sin of Adam, all men are treated as sinners."

58. The preposition is ἄχρι (BAGD point out that the form is Attic; the Hellenistic ἄχρις is found twice only in the New Testament, both times before vowels). It means "until". "Until law" is a curious expression, but the meaning is clear enough. Despite the NIV, there is no article with *law*.

in v. 14), but NEB makes it general, "before there was law"; this is a possible but unlikely interpretation. Paul puts it in the form *sin was in the world,* keeping up his personification of sin. But before the law there was a difference, for sin is not reckoned or imputed[59] where there is no law. One cannot be a lawbreaker if there is no law to break (cf. 4:15). Despite this sin was indeed present in the world. This has been interpreted in two ways. It is possible to take it (as Hendriksen does) in the sense that it shows that there is a more comprehensive law than that of Moses. There is a law written on people's hearts (2:15). On biblical premises it can scarcely be denied that sin was reckoned to people and punished in the period between Adam and Moses, as the flood narrative, to name no other, plainly shows (Gen. 6:5-7, 12-13). The other is to point out that Paul is emphasizing what Adam did; he may thus mean that it was that one sin that brought death to all.[60] It is objected that this requires the insertion of the words "in Adam"; to leave them out is to leave out what is crucial. Neither view can be said to be proved or to be impossible given our present state of knowledge, but perhaps the context points to the second.

14. *Nevertheless* is a strong adversative.[61] Far from sin not being imputed, death reigned. Death is personified and regarded as supreme over mankind from the time of creation right up to the time of the giving of the law. Death was just as potent in the absence of that law as in its presence. There is an impressive absoluteness about *reigned.* Death's sovereignty was complete. *Even* introduces a clause that shows that there were no exceptions. Those who had not sinned in the way Adam did were yet under death's dominion. *Those who did not*[62] *sin by breaking a command as did Adam* is a trifle free as a translation, for Paul says something like "even over those who did not sin in the likeness of Adam's transgression."[63] There are two possibilities.[64] Paul may mean,

---

59. ἐλλογεῖται; the verb is found only here and in Phlm. 18 in the New Testament. It does not seem to occur before this time, but it is found in the papyri, where it is a technical term for charging to someone's account (MM). H. Preisker remarks, "What is meant is that the sin of man as rejection of the revealed will of God is 'taken into account' or 'charged'" (TDNT, II, p. 517; he thinks that Paul is denying this for the time between Adam and Moses, "but it is the more decisively affirmed of the time after Moses").

60. Murray argues that "the underlying assumption of [Paul's] thought is that the *universal* reign of death cannot be explained except in terms of violation of an expressly revealed commandment of God, a violation that cannot be predicated of each and every member of the race in his own individuality and particularity. The only sin that provides the explanation is the sin of Adam and the participation of all in that sin" (p. 191 n. 23).

61. ἀλλά.

62. μή is absent from a few MSS, 614 1739* 2495* d Ambst and some MSS of Origen. But it is not easy to think that this is the correct text. There may have been an accidental omission or a scribal "correction".

63. παράβασις = "transgression"; see on 4:25. On the time between Adam and Moses J. Schneider remarks, "in this intervening period there was no express statement of God's commandment. Hence ἁμαρτία was present . . . but not παράβασις" (TDNT, V, p. 740).

64. I.e., if we take "in the likeness of Adam's transgression" with "those who did

"they sinned, but their sin was not the same kind of sin as that of Adam. They did not break a direct command of God as he did; they sinned against the law within their hearts (2:15)." Harrisville explains, "the law is not needed to prove that sin is everywhere"; "*law there must have been*, before Sinai". The other possibility may be put this way, "they were not law-breakers, for there was no law to break; they died because of Adam's sin" (cf. NEB, "in the absence of law no reckoning is kept of sin"; Hodge holds that the meaning in verse 12 and here is "men are subject to death on account of the sin of Adam").[65] Either way he is saying that it is not necessary to be an exact imitator of Adam to be a sinner in Adam's likeness (see on 1:23). His sin had effects on the totality of mankind. Adam's successors sinned (see on 2:12). They sinned in their own way certainly, but they still sinned; they were the authentic descendants of Adam. Adam is spoken of[66] as *a pattern* (or "type")[67] *of the one to come*. He was the first man and thus the head of the race. We must not press this to mean that Adam was the decisive person and that Christ conformed to the pattern Adam had laid down. Always for Paul Christ is the decisive one. Paul starts from Christ's saving work and sees a similar pattern in Adam. Christ initiated the new race, the race of the redeemed, just as Adam was the head of the old race, the race of sinners. Christ is here called *the one to come*, which may be a messianic title (so Nygren).[68] But the expression is unusual, and this must remain uncertain.

15. Paul launches into a sustained comparison of the work of Christ with that of Adam. Our first father brought disaster on all his progeny, but Christ procured the supreme blessing.[69] Paul finds many points of direct contrast.

---

not sin", as most exegetes do. Vincent P. Branick has argued that we should take it with "death ruled"; he sees the sense of the passage as "Death rules from Adam to Moses on the basis of the ὁμοιώματι τῆς παραβάσεως Ἀδαμ, the concrete perceptible expression of Adam's transgression" (CBQ, 47 [1985], pp. 258-59).

65. Cf. Shedd, "The relation between their sin and Adam's is not that of resemblance, but of *identity*."

66. RSV and others have "was", but ἐστιν means "is"; the "type" is a present setting forth of the truth.

67. Paul uses τύπος eight times out of 14 in the New Testament, but twice in Romans is his most frequent use (three times in Acts). It meant the impression left by a blow, thence an image or copy, and then a form or pattern. It came to be used "of the *types* given by God as an indication of the future, in the form of persons or things" (BAGD).

68. The expression is ὁ μέλλων, which Nygren sees as equivalent to ὁ ἐρχόμενος. Vincent Taylor discusses this latter as one of Jesus' titles under the heading "Messianic titles", but he does no more than quote Nygren's reference to ὁ μέλλων, "for as ὁ μέλλων He is the head of ὁ αἰὼν ὁ μέλλων" (*The Names of Jesus* [London, 1953], p. 78 n. 2). Edersheim denied that "The Coming One" was a messianic designation (*The Life and Times of Jesus the Messiah*, I [London, 1890], p. 668). More recently Käsemann also denied a messianic reference (p. 151).

69. Käsemann rejects all examples "of the way in which modern exposition tries to avoid apocalyptic. . . . The bearer of eschatological salvation is the only alternative to the first Adam. These two—and basically these two alone—have determined the world as a whole" (pp. 152-53). That Christ is the bearer of "eschatological salvation" is clear enough, but that the whole passage is eschatological is not. Bultmann thinks that here Paul "reach-

He has just said that Adam is a type of Christ, and his *But* is a strong adversative. While Adam foreshadows Christ in many ways, we must also be aware of some significant differences. Indeed, the whole treatment is largely on the basis of contrasts between the two. First comes a firm negative: not as *the trespass*[70] is the grace gift,[71] a term which puts some emphasis on the freeness of the gift. The form of the conditional implies that the condition has been fulfilled, "If, as is the case—." *By the trespass of the one* appears first for emphasis; the significant thing about Adam was his transgression. *The one* (NIV has supplied *man*) clearly means Adam, but he is not named after verse 14. There is not the slightest doubt that he is constantly in mind, but his name is not used. The result of the trespass of that one man was that *the many died*, which states the case with impressive simplicity. *The many* can mean any of a number of things, such as "the majority" or "a great number"; it takes its meaning from its context. Here it signifies the totality of mankind. This way of putting it forms an effective contrast with *the one*. The effect of Adam's sin, then, was disaster. It meant death for everyone.

The work of Christ is introduced with another *how much more* construction. It is far greater than anything with which it can be compared. That work is summed up in the word *grace*, grace which connects in the first instance with God and in the second with Christ.[72] With grace Paul couples *the gift that came by the grace of the one man*. The word *gift*[73] signifies freeness and in the New Testament is used only of God's good gifts to mankind. The freeness is emphasized by the link with *grace*. This gift came from *the one man*, which makes it clear that the saving work was accomplished by Christ alone. *The many* corresponds to the same expression at the beginning of the verse. Just as what Adam did had effects on a great number, so also with Christ. His gift is said to overflow,[74] a word that indicates abundance, a keynote of this chapter. Adam did his descendants a grievous wrong, but Christ gave his people an

---

es for the gnostic myth of the original man, so that he can affirm the presence of life" (W. Klassen and G. F. Snyder, *Current Issues in New Testament Interpretation* [London, 1962], p. 154). Both scholars appear to be reading something into the text.

70. Better, "lapse" (παράπτωμα; see on 4:25). It is not so much the breaking of the law to which the term points as a disruption of the relationship with God. Paul uses this word again in vv. 16, 17, 18, and 20.

71. χάρισμα (see on 1:11). The word is connected with χάρις, "grace". The idea of gift is stressed; it occurs five times in vv. 15-17, with three different Greek terms.

72. Grace is linked with God in 3:24; 15:15; 1 Cor. 1:4; 3:10; 15:10 [ter]; 2 Cor. 1:12; 6:1; 8:1; Gal. 1:15; 2:21; Eph. 1:6; 2:7; 3:2, 7; Col. 1:6; Tit. 2:11, a total of 18 times, 19 with this passage. It is connected with Christ in 16:20; 1 Cor. 16:23; 2 Cor. 8:9; 13:13; Gal. 1:6; 6:18; Eph. 1:7; Phil. 4:23; 1 Thess. 5:28; 2 Thess. 3:18; Phlm. 25, a total of 11 times. It is linked with "Lord" in 2 Cor. 12:9; 1 Tim. 1:14, with both in 2 Thess. 1:12 (or is this with Christ?), and with either in Tit. 3:7. Our familiarity with the formula "The grace of—" inclines us to link grace especially with Christ, but the evidence is that Paul is as apt to connect it with the Father as the Son; outside closing greetings it is more often linked with the Father.

73. δωρεά; the word is found five times in Paul out of 11 in the New Testament.

74. περισσεύω; see on 3:7.

abundant gift. He not only reversed the effects of Adam's sin, but brought an abundance of positive blessings: he brought a whole new life (cf. v. 21).

16. This verse introduces a fourfold contrast: *the gift* is set over against "one having sinned", *judgment* against *the gift, one sin* against *many trespasses,* and *condemnation* against *justification. The one man's sin* is related to Adam by the use of the participle, which draws attention to the sinful activity ("through one man having sinned") rather more than does the noun (as NIV, RSV, etc.). In contrast stands *the gift*[75] (NIV adds *of God,* but Paul does not stay to append any qualification). Sin is not the last word, for *the gift* alters the sinner's entire situation. It points to the freeness of salvation; the believer is not required to strive heroically against Adam's legacy as the price of acceptance with God. The second contrast sets *judgment,* the result of one man's having sinned, over against *the gift.* People (Adam or any other) cannot sin with impunity. Sin always leads to judgment. But over against that[76] stands grace (*the gift* this time is "the grace gift");[77] God is not defeated by sin. Paul's third contrast sets the *one sin*[78] over against *many trespasses.* The one sin was the direct cause of the judgment; it led to disaster. The *many trespasses* were not the direct cause of the blessing, but simply the occasion that called forth the divine mercy (see CBSC).[79] Finally, *condemnation*[80] contrasts with *justification*[81] (see on 1:32). The one sin of Adam had as its end result *condemnation* for all the race, but Christ's act of *justification* was also far-reaching. It was concerned with more than the one sin of Adam. The believer finds pardon not only for the one sin he shares in Adam, but for all his other sins as well.

17. Again we have a conditional clause implying that the condition has been fulfilled, "If, as is the case. . . ." The thought of verse 14 is taken up again, that *death reigned*[82] through what Adam did. Death is supreme—no one escapes its rule ("the world is a place of cemeteries" [Lloyd-Jones,

---

75. The word is δώρημα, an unusual term (it appears again in the New Testament only in Jas. 1:17). Paul may want some variety after using δωρεά (v. 15), and the word puts some stress on free bounty.

76. δέ answers to the preceding μέν.

77. χάρισμα, as in v. 15. We should understand ἐστιν or ἐγένετο.

78. This is probably the way we should take it, but Paul says simply "of one", which could be taken to mean "of one man". But it is the one sin of the one man, so perhaps there is not a great difference.

79. "The starting-point was not one act extending to many; but conversely many acts leading to one" (Lightfoot).

80. κατάκριμα; the word occurs only here, in v. 18, and in 8:1 in the New Testament; *judgment* renders κρίμα (see on 2:2). While κρίμα can mean a negative judgment, a condemnation, κατάκριμα is a stronger term and definitely means "condemnation" or even "punishment" (BAGD). The judgment is "out of" (ἐκ denotes origin) one and "into" (εἰς) condemnation.

81. The word is δικαίωμα (which properly expresses the result of an action), not δικαίωσις (the action itself), which is the term that might have been expected. The reason is probably that just here Paul is using a succession of nouns ending in -μα (there are four in this verse); he conforms this one to the others.

82. The aorist ἐβασίλευσεν is ingressive (Black, Michel): "death gained its sovereignty" (GNB, "began to rule").

p. 261]). Barth comments, "Though the sentence of death was not pronounced at any moment in time, yet, like the sword of Damocles, it is suspended over our heads at every moment." It is linked with Adam in two ways: it is *by the trespass*[83] *of the one man* and it is *through that one man*. Both expressions drive us back to that one sin of that one man. That is Paul's concern throughout this section of his argument. He is not saying that death reigned over us all because we all sinned; he is saying that death reigned over us all because Adam sinned.[84]

Then he moves on to his main interest with another *how much more* construction. The condemnation was according to strict justice; sin got what it deserved—death. But that is not the way it is with grace. You cannot measure grace or work it out in terms of strict justice or equivalence. Grace is superlative generosity. Grace is overflowing abundance. We might have expected the contrast to center on Christ, but instead Paul speaks of what grace and righteousness and life mean to those who receive them. He leaves to the end his statement that all this comes *through the one man, Jesus Christ*. Believers are in the first instance *those who receive God's abundant provision of grace*, where *abundant provision* translates an unusual word,[85] one that emphasizes the generosity of God's provision (cf. Goodspeed, "God's overflowing mercy"). God's grace is never given with niggardly hand (cf. v. 15). Perhaps we should notice that Paul says simply, "the abundance of the grace and of the free gift", but NIV and some other translations insert *God's*. There is no doubt that it is God's grace, but Paul does not stop to say so. JB paraphrases *grace* by translating, "the free gift that he does not deserve".

With *grace* Paul links *the gift of righteousness*.[86] That *righteousness* is a *gift* (for this word see the note on v. 15) shows plainly that Paul is thinking of it as a status, a standing; the term is forensic. We often use the word to denote an ethical quality, but such a quality cannot be given. It must be earned by righteous deeds. What Christ did for sinners was to obtain right standing before God. The result of this gift is that the recipients *reign in life*, a significant expression, for Paul has twice spoken of death as reigning (vv. 14, 17). Lagrange comments on the unexpectedness of this (the slaves of death becoming kings!). Death's reign is certainly part of the story, but it is not the

---

83. Or "lapse"; παράπτωμα, as in vv. 15, 16, 18, and 20.

84. Calvin suggests that one thing Paul omitted because, though important, it is not connected with the argument here is this: "we are condemned by Adam's sin not by imputation alone, as though we were being punished for another's sin; but we suffer his punishment because we too are guilty, since God holds our nature, which has been corrupted in Adam, guilty of iniquity."

85. περισσεία; in the New Testament three times in Paul, once in James. Other words from the root are more frequent (the verb περισσεύω occurs in v. 15); they all stress the idea of abundance.

86. It is possible to take τῆς δωρεᾶς τῆς δικαιοσύνης in the sense "the gift that comes from God's righteousness". But even if we accept this (and not many do), the gift will be that of "right standing", so the sense of NIV is to be accepted. Barrett thinks that in any case each of the two ways of taking the words presupposes the other.

whole story. Ultimately it is believers who will reign, not death. As the opposite of death reigning we might expect Paul to speak of life reigning, but he says that believers will reign,[87] though it is true that they will reign *in life*,[88] the very opposite of all that death stands for.[89] The thought is completed with the reminder that this will take place *through the one man, Jesus Christ*. Again there is the stress on *one*, and again we are reminded that salvation is not our own work, nor is it the work of Jesus Christ assisted from some other source. It is *the one* who brings about this abundant salvation; *the one* referring to salvation is just as significant as the same expression referring to condemnation.

18. Paul returns to the thought he began in v. 12 but broke off, and this time he completes it. He begins with *Consequently*,[90] a term that stresses the logical sequence. Paul does not say *the result* (that is NIV's interpolation), but "just as [cf. v. 12] through one lapse" or "through the lapse of one". Competent support can be found for either of these ways of taking it. Perhaps the former is the more natural, and it is supported by the fact that *one* lacks the article (as in v. 16, though there the construction is somewhat different); it has it in verses 15 and 17. The latter is argued from the context. Throughout this entire section Paul has been opposing the one man Adam to the one man Christ, and he is not yet done with this (see v. 19). In the end it is not possible to produce a convincing reason for preferring one of these ways of taking it to the other. This is not really surprising, for Paul is referring to the one act of the one man in both cases, and he moves easily from the one act to the one man and vice versa.

The construction after this is very difficult. The problem is that Paul has written a verbless sentence, and it is not obvious how (or whether) he wants us to complete it. Most translations supply verbs to make a respectable English sentence (as RSV, "led to", and NIV, *the result . . . was*). But it is possible to take it as a kind of exclamation: "As through one lapse for condemnation for all men, so through one justifying sentence for justification of life for all

---

87. The future tense has been variously understood. Thus Parry holds that "The future is used because of the hypothesis implied in οἱ λαμβάνοντες". Michel sees "an old apocalyptic tradition" in which the saints reign (as in 1 Cor. 6:2). Cranfield speaks of "the eschatological fulfilment".

88. Godet comments, "life does not reign; it has not subjects; it makes kings" (p. 378).

89. Paul does not explain the meaning of "reigning in life", but (with Lloyd-Jones, pp. 263ff.) we may think of the fact that sin has no dominion over the believer (6:14), believers are "more than conquerors" (8:37), and they can do all things through Christ (Phil. 4:13). And, of course, they look forward to a more complete reign (Matt. 25:34; Rev. 1:6; 3:21). Adam's sin brought condemnation, but grace reverses this. And not only does it reverse it, but it does much more.

90. ἄρα is an inferential particle, meaning "so, then, consequently". In the classics it never begins a clause (as it does in Matt. 7:20; Luke 11:48, etc.). Paul is fond of the word and uses it 27 times (out of 49 in the New Testament), 11 being in Romans (the most in any one book). The form ἄρα οὖν (never elided) is peculiar to Paul (eight times in Romans, 12 times in all). The combination indicates a strong, if not strictly grammatical connection, like "wherefore therefore". Like διὰ τοῦτο (v. 12) it refers to the previous discussion, but stresses the logical connection more strongly.

men!" Whichever way we take it, the writer moves from the one man (or the one act) to the result, *condemnation for all men*.[91] *So also* introduces the clause, giving us exact correspondence (and which is lacking in v. 12). There is a problem with the word translated *one act of righteousness*. It is the word that is translated "justification" in verse 16, and it normally refers to a pronouncement of some kind, not an action.[92] But most translators and commentators accept a meaning like that of NIV (e.g., NEB, JB, Murray), largely, it would seem, because they see the word as giving an exact antithesis to *one trespass*, even though in doing so they give the same word two different translations (v. 16 and here). We are faced with a choice between an inexact antithesis and using the word in two different senses in the same passage without explanation (cf. Parry). It seems better to retain consistency both in the way the word is used generally and in the way it is used in verse 16 (so SH, Lenski, and others). "Sentence of justification" or "justificatory sentence" (Godet, Gifford) suits the present context admirably, while the word has the meaning "righteous act" rarely if at all.

Another ambiguity has to do with Paul's use of *one*, which may qualify the word we have been discussing (*one act*, NIV, SH), or mean "of one man" (cf. RSV, Leenhardt). As was the case earlier in the verse, it is not possible to be certain which we should understand. *Justification*[93] is followed in the Greek by the genitive "of life", i.e., it is justification that leads to life.[94] The word is thus not being used in a negative way; it means more than not imputing sin. It is the positive concept of issuing in life. Clearly this is the life that is elsewhere called "eternal life" (as in v. 21); it is the abundant life proper to the age to come, and not merely release from a sentence of death. *For all men* of course means "for all those in Christ".

19. We have seen that Paul quite often does not balance his antitheses

91. For κατάκριμα see the comment on v. 16. εἰς denotes result rather than purpose—the end result was condemnation.

92. For δικαίωμα see the note on 1:32, where AS is cited for the view that the word means an "ordinance" or a "sentence". AS also says that the term may mean "a righteous act", which he finds here and in Rev. 15:4; 19:8. Clearly the word has to do with declarations of various kinds, and it is a question whether it should be taken to signify a deed in the three passages listed. Charles sees the meaning in Rev. 15:4 as "the judicial sentences of God", and we should see a similar meaning or "sentence of justification" in Rev. 19:8 (that we stand in heaven clothed in our own righteous deeds is not a New Testament thought). See further my *The Apostolic Preaching of the Cross*[3] (London, 1965), pp. 287ff. O'Neill thinks we must keep to the same meaning here as in v. 16 (he sees "vindication" in both places). Leenhardt cites a view that to regard the word as an action here would be tautologous with ὑπακοή in v. 19 (though he nevertheless favors "just deed").

93. δικαίωσις occurs elsewhere in the New Testament only in 4:25 (where see note).

94. Other ways of taking the genitive have been suggested, e.g., that it is appositional, "justification which *is* life" (M, III, p. 214). Murray, however, says, "This cannot mean that the justification consists in life"; rather, it is "unto life and issues in life". Leenhardt suggests "the idea of a justification which is here and now realized in a life which concretely practises righteousness". Cranfield sees a genitive of result, and Wuest a "genitive of description . . . describing the quality of the righteousness bestowed upon man".

perfectly; therefore, we should notice that here he does, beautifully. His *just as* (see on v. 12) is balanced by *so also,* and each member of the following clause corresponds to a similar member in the other. This time Adam's sin is called *disobedience,*[95] which brings out a salient feature of the wrong he did. His sin was voluntary. The verb *were made*[96] presents problems. It does not mean that sinless people were compelled to become sinners, but rather that Adam's sin constituted them as sinners. They were born as members of a race already separated from God. *Sinners* (see on 3:7) is in an emphatic position: it is as nothing less than *sinners* that the many are reckoned. *The many* comes last in both clauses, thus standing each time in strong contrast to *one*. Though the words translated *the many* are identical in the two places, the meaning is not the same. The first time *the many* points to the entire human race; all were caught up in the effects of Adam's sin. But Paul does not hold that all are to be saved (2:12); moreover, "his entire presentation of salvation has emphasized the fact that justification is granted only on the basis of faith" (Harrison). The second time he is referring to *the many* who believe. All people insofar as they relate to Adam are sinners and insofar as they relate to Christ are righteous. For *obedience* see the comment on 1:5. Christ's saving work is done in obedience to the Father (Heb. 10:7) and thus stands in stark contrast to Adam's disobedience. Similarly, *righteous* contrasts with *sinners*.[97] Christ's saving work effectively cancels out Adam's destructive sin. We might have expected the aorist tense again, but Paul has the future. He may be thinking of the eschatological aspect of salvation (cf. Gal. 5:5), or, with Murray, "this act of God's grace is being continually exercised and will continue to be exercised throughout future generations of mankind" (cf. Denney, "it is not then [i.e., on Judgment Day], but when they believe in Christ, that men are constituted" as righteous).

20. As we come to the climax, interestingly there is no mention of Adam. Throughout this paragraph Paul has been stressing the contrast between Adam and Christ, and he has offered many points to back up his contention that there is such typology that Adam is to be studied seriously. But his real interest has been in Christ, not Adam. Now he concentrates on his

95. παρακοή = "hearing beside", then hearing amiss, unwillingness to hear, disobedience. It is found three times in the New Testament, twice in Paul. Refusal to hear God is sin (cf. Jer. 11:10; Acts 7:57).

96. καθίστημι. This is not a common Pauline word (twice in Romans, three times in all; 21 times in the New Testament). It means something like "to set down" (AS), and thus has a meaning here like "set down as, show to be, constitute as" (Shedd, "to place in the class of"; Hodge, "were set down in the rank or category of"). Barrett comments, "Adam's disobedience did not mean that all men necessarily and without their consent committed particular acts of sin; it meant that they were born into a race which had separated itself from God." According to Gifford, the word "points to the *formal* essence, to that which *constitutes* men sinners."

97. Bultmann rejects the meaning "they will be regarded as those who are righteous" in favor of "they will be made to be righteous", because righteousness here is not ethical but forensic. "The believing one is the righteous man as one who has been acquitted by the judicial sentence of God" (*Current Issues,* p. 159).

Savior and ceases to refer to Adam. It is somewhat unexpected that he brings in a reference to *law*, but between Adam and Christ stood Moses, revered by the Jews and often seen as the most significant figure among the sons of men because of his giving of the law. This was so important in Jewish religion and in the Old Testament that Christians as well as Jews regarded as Scripture that it had to be seen in its proper place in God's great scheme of salvation.[98] Law,[99] says Paul, *was added*, the verb showing that it held no primary place.[100] Its purpose[101] was *that the trespass might increase*.[102] It was not concerned with preventing sin (it was too late for that). Nor was it concerned with salvation from sin (it was too weak for that). The law can only condemn (4:15). It was concerned with showing sin for what it is, and it certainly showed magnificently that there was much sin (cf. 3:19-20). Notice the singular; Paul does not say that the "trespasses" increased; it is what sin essentially is that the law magnified.[103] JB misses this with its rendering "it was to multiply the opportunities of falling". *Trespass* has been used consistently of Adam's sin (vv. 15, 17, 18), and the word may be chosen as a way of bringing out the continuity between his sin and that of his descendants. The increase of sin, however, is not the last word. *But* is adversative; it sets the following in contrast. Where *sin increased* pretty well equates *trespass* with *sin*. Paul is not concerned with minor distinctions among grades of evil. The important thing is at the end of

---

98. Käsemann puts the point at issue this way: "between Adam and Christ, and the worlds inaugurated by them, there is no third alternative, namely legal piety" (p. 158).

99. There is no article with νόμος (despite NIV). What Paul says is relevant to the law of Moses, but he is not confining sin to the Jews who were born under that law, so he may have in mind law in general. Hodge thinks the term signifies "the whole of the Old Testament economy". But it may well be wider.

100. The verb is παρεισέρχομαι, again in the New Testament only in Gal. 2:4. It means "1. *slip in, come in* as a side issue, of the law, which has no primary place in the Divine Plan" (BAGD; their 2. is "*slip in* w. unworthy motives, *sneak in*"). It points to the subordinate place of the law in God's saving plan. NEB translates "intruded"; Moffatt, "slipped in". Cranfield, however, denies that the sense is pejorative; he thinks that the verb here means that the law was later than Adam's fall. Certainly such a meaning as "sneak in" is impossible here, for the law was given with publicity and splendor. The meaning is that it had a secondary place, not one of prime importance.

101. ἵνα introduces a clause of purpose. We should understand this not in the sense that God designed to produce more and more sin, but rather that he planned that the law should make more and more show sin for what it is. People might not recognize themselves as sinners without the law (v. 13), but after the law had been brought in the fact of sin is plain. This is not the whole purpose of the law; other purposes are given elsewhere (e.g., 3:19; Gal. 3:19-25; 1 Tim. 1:8-11). It is, of course, possible to take ἵνα as indicating result (so Lenski, citing Robertson, p. 998), in which case the whole is simpler. But this is not the usual sense of ἵνα, and we should understand it as purposive.

102. *Increase* translates πλεονάζω, a verb used by Paul in eight of its nine New Testament occurrences (three in Romans). It might be transitive ("to increase the trespass", RSV; "multiplied the offence", Goodspeed) or intransitive ("that the offence might abound", KJV). As in Gal. 3:19, the function of the law is to produce the knowledge and conviction of sin.

103. Hendriksen points out that a magnifying glass does not increase the number of dirty spots, but it does make them stand out more clearly and brings to light some that the naked eye cannot see.

the clause—*grace increased all the more*, or perhaps we should say, "grace superabounded".[104] Paul can never be accused of minimizing the seriousness of sin, but he does not lose an opportunity of stressing the victory of grace. Grace is so much more effective than evil.

21. *So that* introduces a clause of purpose (as in v. 20). The purpose of the superabundant grace was to replace the reign of sin. *Sin reigned*[105] *in death* is an impressive statement of the power of both sin and death. In both cases Paul is saying that sin involves us in a situation where we are not dominant but subordinate. We cannot break free from sin, so sin reigns. We cannot escape death, so death reigns. Death is perhaps more obviously the tyrant, and sin's reign can be said to be *in death* (a rare expression, only here in Paul, though cf. 2 Cor. 11:23). The mention of *eternal life* in the second half of the verse indicates that we should understand *death* here as spiritual as well as physical. *So also* introduces the corresponding thought. The exact antithesis would be ". . . so also righteousness should reign in life". But it is not our righteousness (imputed or imparted) that has the power, but God's grace, and *through righteousness* expresses the means grace employs to overthrow the reign of death. It is God's purpose that not sin but *grace* should be the ruler, and *grace* reigns *through righteousness*. This may mean that grace reigns when God makes people right with himself, when he imputes righteousness to believers, that righteousness which is by faith. Or possibly the thought is that by grace the believer lives righteously here and now and this manifests the triumph of grace over sin. The former is more likely in view of the whole context and particularly because Paul goes on to refer to *eternal life*. Grace triumphs when God imputes righteousness and this leads to eternal life, the end or aim of it all. Paul rounds off the argument by reminding his readers that it all comes about *through Jesus Christ our Lord*. This has been the dominant idea throughout the whole discussion, and it makes a fitting ending. Nygren points out that this last word is no formality: "in this kingdom of God, the reign of life, Jesus is '*Lord*'" (p. 229).

---

104. ὑπερπερισσεύω is an unusual compound, not found before Paul and used by him elsewhere only in 2 Cor. 7:4 (of his overflowing with joy). It points to a more than abundant supply. There was plenty of sin, but much, much more grace. Paul has used περισσεύω in v. 15. That verb means "abound"; with ὑπέρ prefixed we have the thought of "superabound".

105. We might have expected an imperfect, bringing out the thought of continuous happening. The aorist is constative, viewing the reign as a whole, perhaps as a completed whole, for it no longer operates where we are in Christ. For the verb see on v. 17.

Romans 6

IV. THE WAY OF GODLINESS, 6:1–8:39

Having outlined the way God in Christ justifies sinners, Paul goes on to the way the justified should live (cf. 2 Cor. 13:4; Gal. 5:13). His teaching that salvation is a gift of God, that it is the result of Christ's death and not our own achievement, that we obtain it by faith and not by any effort of our own, marked a revolution. And it raised all sorts of questions that could never surface while it was held that law in some form was the gateway to godliness. One question that arose naturally enough was this: "If everything depends on what God has done, then what does it matter how we live?" In one form or another this question has been asked wherever people have come to see salvation as stemming only from God's grace (cf. 3:8). Sometimes it is raised seriously by people who have an imperfect understanding of what grace means and who do not see how it impinges on daily living. Sometimes it is raised merely as an objection to Paul's whole position by people who think he must be wrong because, as they see it, he is removing all incentive to upright living (Earle sees this here). In whatever form it is raised Paul's answer is emphatic: "It matters very much." He proceeds to argue his case.[1] He chooses to make his point by asking a series of four questions. These had probably been put to him at one time or another, and he found them useful for bringing out the main lines of the life of faith. We should not think of this as a completely separate chapter in the life of the Christian, so to speak, as in treatments which see Paul as dealing with justification, then leaving that to go on to a completely unrelated subject, sanctification. As Calvin remarks, those who separate these two doctrines as though Christ might justify without giving newness of life "shamefully rend Christ asunder".[2] Paul is describing

1. How the letter should be divided is a matter of dispute. Käsemann holds that "one should not put ch. 5 in the previous section of the epistle and find the beginning of a new one only with ch. 6". Lloyd-Jones also denies that there is a new beginning here; he sees chs. 6 and 7 as a parenthesis. But they are too important for that. Lagrange, by contrast, sees a new section beginning here, and Murray says, "The transition from one phase of teaching to another at the beginning of this chapter is quite conspicuous." Some such view should surely be held. What impresses those who hold to the former point of view is the close connection between justification and sanctification. That these should not be separated in practice is plain, but that does not mean that they cannot be discussed separately.

2. Cf. Foreman, "God is not a vast forgiving-machine. There is no such thing as justification all by itself . . . justification when it is real always is wedded to sanctification."

one Christian way, the way of grace and faith. Christians reckon themselves as dead to sin and alive to God (v. 11); they do not choose one or the other. The death and the resurrection belong inseparably together.

A. SHALL WE CONTINUE TO SIN THAT GRACE MAY ABOUND? 6:1-14

¹What shall we say, then? Shall we go on sinning so that grace may increase? ²By no means! We died to sin; how can we live in it any longer? ³Or don't you know that all of us who were baptized into Christ Jesus were baptized into his death? ⁴We were therefore buried with him through baptism into death in order that, just as Christ was raised from the dead through the glory of the Father, we too may live a new life.

⁵If we have been united with him in his death, we will certainly also be united with him in his resurrection. ⁶For we know that our old self was crucified with him so that the body of sin might be rendered powerless, that we should no longer be slaves to sin—⁷because anyone who has died has been freed from sin.

⁸Now if we died with Christ, we believe that we will also live with him. ⁹For we know that since Christ was raised from the dead, he cannot die again; death no longer has mastery over him. ¹⁰The death he died, he died to sin once for all; but the life he lives, he lives to God.

¹¹In the same way, count yourselves dead to sin but alive to God in Christ Jesus. ¹²Therefore do not let sin reign in your mortal body so that you obey its evil desires. ¹³Do not offer the parts of your body to sin, as instruments of wickedness, but rather offer yourselves to God, as those who have been brought from death to life; and offer the parts of your body to him as instruments of righteousness. ¹⁴For sin shall not be your master, because you are not under law, but under grace.

An obvious reaction to the thought that we see God's grace in our salvation and that no merit of our own is involved is to reason that the more we sin the more scope there is for God's grace. Has not Paul just said that an increase of sin means a greater increase of grace (5:20)? Sinners might reason, "Let us sin lustily and thus give grace its maximum opportunity!" Paul repudiates all such approaches with decision. He points out that grace liberates us from sin; it does not bring us more firmly under its bondage.

1. *Then* is important. Paul is not going on to some new and quite unrelated subject. Because of what he has said in the previous section, certain things follow. In the light of the fact that we die in Adam and live in Christ he asks, *What shall we say?* (see on 3:5 for the form of the question). The question leads to a suggestion that Paul repudiates strongly.[3] Evidently some had argued

3. Bruce N. Kaye holds that "the rhetorical question in Rom 6.1 does not necessarily imply an objector and thus a digression from the main theme of the letter" (*The Thought Structure of Romans with Special Reference to Chapter 6* [Austin, Texas, 1979], p. 23). Kaye finds 74 rhetorical questions in Romans (p. 14); they are used in a variety of ways, but often to advance the argument.

that since everything depends on grace our part should be to give grace the maximum scope in which to operate. If we *go on sinning*[4] we provide scope for grace to *increase:* should this not be the Christian way? NIV perhaps does not give quite the same emphasis as Paul. His verb is the verb "to remain" ("shall we *remain* in sin?"), not the verb "to sin". He is thinking of sinners staying where they are, declining to budge from their habitual sin. There is method in their projected indolence and evil; it is *so that*[5] there may be more and more *grace* (GNB says "God's grace", but Paul takes it as obvious that grace is God's grace). For *increase* see on 5:20.

2. Paul repudiates this with his vigorous *By no means!* (see on 3:4). This is a strong rejection of a conclusion that he thinks might falsely be drawn from what he has said. He will have none of it. It is quite erroneous. NIV omits an important relative pronoun; cf. RSV, "How can we who died to sin . . . ?" Paul uses the relative of quality,[6] "we who are of such a quality as to. . . ." He is inviting his readers to reflect on what it means to have become Christians (cf. Barrett, "We who in our essential nature, i.e., just because we are Christians, died"). Previously they had been dead *in* sin (Eph. 2:1); now they were dead *to* sin. The aorist in the verb *died* points to an action rather than a state: "we who died" rather than "we are dead" ("we have died", GNB). Becoming a Christian is a decisive step; it is the beginning of faith and it means the end of sin. The emphasis falls on the act rather than the continuing state. There is, of course, a sense in which Christians die to sin every day; they constantly commit themselves to God and become dead to all evil. There is also an eschatological sense; after this life sin will be over; believers will be raised up to live without sin in God's presence. But it is not such senses that Paul's language evokes here. He is referring rather to the death to sin that marks the beginning of the characteristic Christian life. It is the end of the reign of sin and beginning of the reign of grace (5:21). Since we *died to sin*[7] it is a fair

4. ἐπιμένωμεν might be deliberative (as NIV, *Shall we go on sinning. . . ?*) or hortatory ("Shall we say, 'Let us go on sinning in order that grace may increase'?"). Most translations take it in the former sense, but the latter is quite possible. The verb occurs in Paul nine times out of 15 in the New Testament (three in Romans). The ἐπί may strengthen the idea of continuance contained in the uncompounded verb.

5. ἵνα is telic.

6. οἵτινες. Paul uses this relative 44 times, and ὅς 366 times. There is often little difference between the two, but ὅστις can point to the quality, and Moule classes this among passages where a distinction "certainly improves the sense and may have been intended" (IBNTG, p. 124). BAGD also class it with a use "to emphasize a characteristic quality". This is further emphasized by putting the clause first.

7. V. P. Furnish draws attention to an interesting point: "Nowhere does Paul say that sin has, as such, been abolished. It is not *sin* but the *sinner* who has 'died' (vss. 2, 10, 11; cf. 7:4, death to the law) . . . Paul speaks not of the Christian's freedom from *sinning*, but of his freedom from the power of sin" (*Theology and Ethics in Paul* [Nashville, 1968], p. 173). Godet speaks of the "*mirage* of an absolute deliverance, which had been reflected in the eyes of so many souls thirsting for holiness, soon vanishing before the touch of experience." Paul is not setting forth a doctrine of sinless perfection, but of freedom from sin's domination. The Christian may sin, but sinning is out of character. It is a declension from his norm, not his habitual practice.

question, "How shall we still live in it?"[8] Paul is bringing out strongly the truth that acquiescence in sin is incompatible with being a Christian.[9] Knox has a striking translation: "We have died, once for all, to sin; can we breathe its air again?"

3. Paul turns to baptism,[10] which is perhaps surprising. But it helps him make his point emphatically. *Or* points to the alternative to what he has just been saying. If his readers do not understand what it means to die to sin, they do not understand what baptism means, and baptism comes right at the beginning of the Christian life. His question[11] implies that this is something the Roman Christians would be expected to know. Since Paul had not been to Rome he plainly regards this as knowledge common to all Christians. We may perhaps miss something of what he is saying because for us *baptized* evokes liturgical associations;[12] it points to a comforting and inspiring piece of ceremonial. But in the first century, while the verb could denote this ceremony and Paul certainly means that here, to "baptize" evoked associations of violence. It meant "immerse" rather than "dip". It was used, for example, of people being drowned, or of ships being sunk (see LSJ).[13] Josephus used it metaphorically of crowds who flooded into Jerusalem and "wrecked the city" (*Bell.* 4.137; Loeb translation). It is quite in keeping with this that Jesus referred to his death as baptism (Mk. 10:38; Lk. 12:50). When it is applied to

---

8. Moule sees the future here ("how shall we live . . . ?"; NIV inserts *can* in place of the future) as an example of the unusual linear future; the future is normally punctiliar (IBNTG, p. 10).

9. Cf. Denney, "To have died to sin is to be utterly and for ever out of any relation to it." Paul can express this in other ways, e.g., by saying that Christ's people "have crucified the flesh with its passions and desires" (Gal. 5:24).

10. Whether Paul is indebted to the mystery religions for his doctrine of baptism is a matter of dispute. Käsemann argues that baptism was viewed as "a mystery event" in the pre-Pauline community outside Palestine and that Paul develops this. But the considerations adduced by Cranfield make a reference to the mysteries unlikely. Leenhardt also rejects with decision any connection with the mystery cults. A. J. M. Wedderburn, following P. Siber, argues that the "with Christ" terminology originated with Paul. The mystery religions sometimes refer to a dying and rising deity, but "missing in all this is any hint that the initiate died (in the past) with the deity, and if he or she is thought to die *with the deity* in the initiation rite our admittedly scanty sources are completely silent about it" (NTS, 29 [1983], p. 345).

11. The question ἢ ἀγνοεῖτε is repeated in 7:1, and the similar ἢ οὐκ οἴδατε in 11:2. In all three places Paul indicates that he expects any Christian to know these things. In 1 Cor. 15:11, after a summary of Christian teaching, he can say that, whoever may have done the preaching, this is what Christians believed.

12. Brown rejects a reference to the physical act of baptism; the words "cannot be understood of the baptism by water. . . . 'Baptism into Christ' is that of which water baptism is the emblem—that union to Jesus Christ. . . ." Lloyd-Jones also rejects a reference to water baptism in favor of the view that it is "a baptism by the Holy Spirit" (cf. 1 Cor. 12:13). It may readily be conceded that what the Spirit does rather than the physical act of baptism is most important in Christian initiation (cf. Mk. 1:8 and parallels; Acts 1:5; 11:16). But it is quite another matter to say that the language of this verse is such that it does not mean baptism in water.

13. BAGD note the use in non-Christian literature in the sense "plunge, sink, drench, overwhelm". Paul uses the verb only 13 times out of 77 in the New Testament; it cannot be said to be a theme of absorbing interest to him.

Christian initiation we ought not to think in terms of gentleness and inspiration; it means death, death to a whole way of life. It is this that is Paul's point here. Christians are people who have died, and their baptism emphasizes that death. Death runs through this passage and is mentioned in every verse up to v. 13. We should not let the modern associations of baptism blind us to the point Paul is making so strongly. He is saying that it is quite impossible for anyone who understands what baptism means to acquiesce cheerfully in a sinful life. The baptized have died to all that.

Paul goes on to characterize baptism as *into Christ Jesus* ("into union with Christ Jesus", GNB, NEB), an unusual way of describing this sacrament (though cf. Gal. 3:27; and for "into the name", Acts 8:16; 19:5).[14] Baptism, so to speak, incorporates the baptized into Christ; they are baptized "into one body" (1 Cor. 12:13), made part of that body which is the body of Christ (cf. SH, " 'were baptized into union with' [not merely 'obedience to'] 'Christ'. The act of baptism was an act of *incorporation* into Christ"). This can be made a little more precise. Those so baptized *were baptized into his death*, where *into his death* receives some emphasis from its position. It is the death of Christ that makes anyone a Christian, and apart from that death baptism is meaningless. This is a strong affirmation of the centrality of the cross.[15] Leenhardt sees a connection with 2 Corinthians 5:14, "one died for all, and therefore all died."[16] Christ's death alone is the ground of our justification, and when we make that our own by faith we are united with Christ—united with him in his death, united with him in his burial, united with him in his rising again, united with him in life. Paul is affirming strongly that the justified are those united by faith to all that Christ means, and therefore antinomianism is impossible for them. Being united in living out the life is not an option but a necessary part of being saved in Christ.

4. The logical consequence continues *(therefore)*. Not only are we dead, but we are buried with him.[17] Being "with Christ" is an important category

---

14. Baptism is εἰς ἄφεσιν τῶν ἁμαρτιῶν (Acts 2:38) as well as "into Christ" and "into his death" (John's baptism was εἰς μετάνοιαν, Mt. 3:11; cf. εἰς τὸ Ἰωάννου βάπτισμα, Acts 19:3). A. Oepke thinks εἰς τὸ ὄνομα is from the technical term of Hellenistic commerce, "to the account" (TDNT, I, p. 539). Many commentators draw attention to baptism εἰς τὸν Μωϋσῆν (1 Cor. 10:2), a baptism that certainly brought the Israelites under the leadership of Moses (Leenhardt develops the point). But it did not indicate a union nearly as close as that between Christ and the Christian. See TNTC *ad loc.*

15. Cf. Furnish, "Sin's power is not broken by baptism but by Christ's death and resurrection, his 'obedience' and 'righteousness' (5:18-19)" (*Theology and Ethics in Paul*, p. 174). Dodd thinks that Paul could have made his point without reference to baptism. But "here, in this sacrament, is something actually done—a step taken which can never be retraced. Before it a man was not a member of the Church, the people of God: now he is a member. If he should thereafter be unfaithful, that would not simply be a return to his former condition. Something has happened."

16. Leenhardt comments, "God willed that this death should be my own death; when I look at the cross, I see there the victim who represents me objectively, His death includes my own, His death is mine, it is my death which He dies. In the intention of God with regard to myself, I have died."

17. If we take the reference to burial with full seriousness, then baptism is not

for Paul.[18] It is interesting that we are never said to have been born with Christ or to have been baptized with him, as Lagrange points out. But we are crucified with him (v. 6; Gal. 2:20), we died with him (2 Tim. 2:11), were buried with him (here; Col. 2:12), were made alive with him (Eph. 2:5; Col. 2:13), were raised with him and made to sit with him in the heavenlies (Eph. 2:6), we are co-heirs with him (8:17), sharers of his glory (8:17), and we will reign with him (2 Tim. 2:12). The burial has unexpected emphasis in the New Testament (besides the Gospels, see Acts 13:29; 1 Cor. 15:4; Col. 2:12); it even finds a place in the Creed, a short statement which necessarily omits much that is important.[19] Perhaps the point is that the burial emphasizes the completeness and finality of the death. Christ's death was no momentary faint but real death, death followed by the tomb. Jesus really died. And our identification with that death is also complete.[20] When we are baptized we have died. In baptism[21] we are buried with Christ.[22] An old way of life passes away completely.

But that is not the whole story; the death has purpose; it is with a view to something further.[23] The parallel with Christ is followed through. His death was followed by resurrection, and our death to sin and our baptism into his

---

death, but interment: when we believe we die to sin, and when we are baptized the burial is carried out. Gifford sees another thought: "burial, being a sign and seal which attests the reality of death, serves also to attest the reality of the resurrection".

18. Ernest Best discusses this concept in *One Body in Christ* (London, 1955), pp. 44-64. See also W. Grundmann, TDNT, VII, pp. 781-86.

19. Parry comments, "It is remarkable that S. Paul, alone in N.T. outside the Gospels, lays stress on the Burial; he alone was not an eyewitness of the circumstances of the Death, and therefore for him the burial was of high significance, in its evidential value." There may be something in this, but we should bear in mind that it is not only the burial that Paul stresses. He alone speaks in set terms of "the death" of Jesus (others refer to "the blood", "the suffering of death", etc.). Paul alone, with but one exception, speaks of "the cross", other, of course, than in the accounts of the crucifixion. All the circumstances of Jesus' death were of interest to him.

20. συνθάπτω occurs again in the New Testament only in Col. 2:12, also of being buried with Christ in baptism. There the construction is ἐν τῷ βαπτίσματι (or βαπτισμῷ), here διὰ τοῦ βαπτίσματος, but probably there is not much difference.

21. The noun βάπτισμα is not found before the New Testament and seems to be a term coined by the Christians. It is used of Christian baptism again in Eph. 4:5; Col. 2:12; 1 Pet. 3:21, and 13 times of John's baptism. Jewish lustrations are denoted by βαπτισμός. The use of the term seems to indicate that the Christians saw their baptism as different from Jewish and pagan rites, but as having some link with John's baptism. Cf. A. Oepke, "Since the NT either coins or reserves for Christian baptism (and its precursor) a word which is not used elsewhere and has no cultic connections, and since it always uses it in the sing. and never substitutes the term employed elsewhere, we can see that, in spite of all apparent or relative analogies, it understands the Christian action to be something new and unique" (TDNT, I, p. 545). For a detailed discussion see J. Ysebaert, *Greek Baptismal Terminology* (Nijmegen, 1962).

22. We should take εἰς τὸν θάνατον with βαπτίσματος (as Cranfield, Käsemann, etc.). Some are impressed by the lack of the article before εἰς τὸν θάνατον (but see BDF 272), and take it with συνετάφημεν (as Lightfoot does). But this is unconvincing and yields a curious sense, being "buried into death".

23. Again, telic ἵνα, "in order that". This is important. The believer's "death" is with a view to resurrection to new life. It is not an end in itself or a return to the old life (like the raising of Lazarus).

death are followed by our being raised to *new life*. Paul uses aorists in his verbs *were buried* and *was raised*. They give a note of decisiveness to the rising to new life.

Christ was raised, Paul says, *through the glory of the Father*, which is a very unusual expression (cf. Eph. 1:17). For *glory* see on 2:7; it points to the wonder and the greatness of God. We might have expected a reference to "power" or the like, and indeed some take *glory* here to mean "power"; Harrison, for example, says, " 'glory' here has the meaning of power" (cf. Calvin, "That is, by the splendid power by which He declared Himself truly glorious"). But Paul says *glory* (NEB, "the splendour of the Father"); perhaps we could say that the meaning is power manifested and not simply power.[24] Some see in *glory* an eschatological reference (cf. 2:10; 5:2; 8:17-18, 21); Christ's resurrection ushers in the last age. This is true, but it does not seem to be what Paul is saying here. He is talking about the present life of the Christian. Paul, unlike John, does not often speak of "the Father" (though cf. Eph. 2:18; 3:14; Col. 1:12). His use of the term perhaps emphasizes that it was the Father and no other through whom Christ was raised.

We too may live paraphrases a characteristic Pauline locution "we too may walk".[25] Paul invariably uses the verb in a metaphorical sense, as do the Johannine epistles, but this is rare elsewhere. Paul evidently found it a congenial metaphor for the steady, unspectacular progress that should characterize the Christian life. *We too* means "we as well as someone else", and the emphatic *we* underlines the point. Paul clearly means that as the glory of the Father was shown in the raising of Christ from the dead to new life, so it is with us. We walk with Christ. Paul has already said that we died to sin; now he adds that *we too* rise from that death to new life. *Live a new life* is more exactly "walk in newness of life". "Newness"[26] is not what we would have expected. The corresponding adjective "new" was available, and Paul uses it seven times. The unusual expression puts some emphasis on the quality of newness. For *life* see on 2:7. Christ "gave himself for us to redeem us from all wickedness and to purify for himself a people that are his very own, eager to do what is good" (Tit. 2:14).

5. The same truth is put another way. Paul's conditional implies that the condition has been fulfilled, "If (as is the case). . . ." He assumes that this is so and looks at the consequences. *United*[27] *with him* points to a close union.

---

24. The ideas of "power" and "glory" are, of course, closely connected. Thus G. Kittel, commenting on the use of δόξα in LXX, points out that "power and splendour usually bring honour and renown. They are often the outward manifestation and even the cause of being honoured. Thus the meanings often merge into one another" (TDNT, II, p. 243). John 11:40 refers to "glory" at the raising of Lazarus, a work of power.

25. The verb is περιπατέω, which Paul uses 32 times (four in Romans).

26. καινότης (again in the New Testament only in 7:6) means "newness w. the connotation of someth. extraordinary" (BAGD).

27. σύμφυτος is found here only in the New Testament; it means "grown together" (BAGD). It is generally agreed that the word derives from συμφύω, "make to grow together", rather than συμφυτεύω, "plant together", and it signifies a growing together. Cf. Godet, this adjective "denotes the organic union in virtue of which one being shares the life, growth, and phases of existence belonging to another".

According to SH it "exactly expresses the process by which a graft becomes united with the life of a tree" (so Leenhardt, and more cautiously, Barrett; cf. 11:17ff.; Moffatt prefers "we have grown into him"). Cranfield points out that the expression is used much more widely than for grafting; we should not see the expression as a technical term. But we can say that it is appropriate for a graft. Paul's point is that the spiritual life of the believer is not self-originated but is derived from Christ, with whom he is now one. The union is of the closest sort, and life from Christ flows through to him. The verb *have been* might be translated "have become";[28] we are not by nature in this state, but "become" united with Christ. The perfect tense points to something permanent. There is no turning back from death. Paul actually speaks of being united with Christ "in the likeness" of his death (for "likeness" see on 1:23). The word is characteristic of this epistle (four times out of six in the New Testament; Parry thinks that it "implies true assimilation, but of things different"). It is not easy to grasp the force of "likeness" (how does one unite with a "likeness"?), but at least the term brings out the symbolic nature of the death we die when we become united to Christ. Our death "is not the same as Christ's but is similar to it" (Calvin). His death was physical whereas ours is not. JB has "If in union with Christ we have imitated his death", but Paul is not saying this. There is no question of imitation; by faith we become one with Christ and this means a real death to our former life.

In sharp contrast[29] to the death is the resurrection.[30] The death of Jesus was not the end; it led on to his resurrection. And the believer's death to sin points forward to his resurrection (cf. 2 Tim. 2:11). There may be no great significance in that Paul changes his verb "to be",[31] but there is perhaps more significance in the future tense, for it gives an eschatological dimension to what Paul is saying.[32] Paul is primarily concerned with the present moral life of the believer; this is part of his argument that we should not continue in sin so that grace may abound. He is emphasizing that the believer has already risen to new life. But there is another sense in which the consummation will take place only at the future resurrection of the dead. Paul looks forward.

6. Again Paul appeals to knowledge (see on 2:2).[33] He goes over some of the ground again as he hammers home his point that the believer has died to an old way. *Our old self* is really "our old man" (KJV), an expression used twice elsewhere in the Pauline writings (Eph. 4:22; Col. 3:9), in both cases with verbs expressing repudiation. A number of writers in antiquity made the distinction Paul sometimes made between the outer and the inner man (7:22;

28. γεγόναμεν.
29. Gifford sees "the lively turn of the Greek" in ἀλλὰ καί as scarcely possible of reproduction in English. It points up the contrast: "then also of his resurrection we shall be!"
30. ἀναστάσεως depends on ὁμοιώματι, "the likeness of his resurrection".
31. From γίνομαι to εἰμί.
32. Without denying the present aspect Wilckens points to the eschatological significance and finds support in v. 8.
33. His verb is γινώσκω, for which see on 1:21.

Eph. 3:16; cf. 1 Pet. 3:4), but the contrast between the old man and the new man appears to be Paul's own (and incidentally forms a link between Romans on the one hand and Ephesians and Colossians on the other).[34] If his word for "old"[35] is used strictly, it brings out the idea of "wornness", the result of the wear and tear of time, the old as outworn. It is not something to be desired. And this old man, Paul says, *was crucified with*. The verb conveys the thought that the old man was thoroughly destroyed. "The old man" is no longer supreme. This does not mean that the believer lives untroubled by the possibility of sinning. There is a sense in which a death has taken place once and for all in the believer, but there is another in which he dies every day (1 Cor. 15:31). It is believers, not the unregenerate, who are urged to put off the old man (Eph. 4:22; cf. Col. 3:9). But it is another vivid way of saying that the power of sin is broken in the believer. To come to Christ means the complete end of a whole way of life. There may be slips, but they are uncharacteristic (cf. Brunner, "Previously, the ought did not suit us, now sin does not"). The "old man" has been crucified. The verb is a compound, meaning *was crucified with*. In English we must supply an object *(him)*, but the Greek does not have one and the absolute use concentrates attention on the action of the verb. It is used once each in Matthew, Mark, and John of the thieves who were crucified with Jesus, and again in Galatians 2:20 of being crucified with Christ (cf. also Gal. 6:14). But this is the only place where the verb stands alone. The aorist points to a decisive ending of the old, as the believer enters new life.

Further, this crucifixion has a purpose; it is *so that*[36] *the body of sin* might be dealt with. The genitive *of sin* is unusual in such a connection; Paul uses the expression nowhere else. There is a difference of opinion as to whether *the body of sin* means the physical body characterized by sin (cf. Moule, "the sin-possessed body" [IBNTG, p. 38]), or whether it signifies "the sinful self" (NEB). We may reject without hesitation the view that it means that the body is inherently sinful and that it is the source of sin. This is not a New Testament view, and Paul never gives it countenance. But Murray, Lloyd-Jones, and others argue strongly that Paul means that the body is dominated by sin. The body is sin's body; it belongs to sin; sin has made it its own (cf. the following "slaves to sin"). Others think that "body" is here used in the fuller sense of the whole man and hold that Paul is saying that man as a totality is a sinner.[37]

34. Käsemann appears to miss this when he refers to "the obviously pre-Pauline term παλαιὸς ἄνθρωπος, which comes from Adam-Christ typology" (p. 169). Why should we ascribe to others a term which is used only by Paul?

35. παλαιός, "in existence for a long time, oft. w. the connotation of being antiquated or outworn" (BAGD, who see it here as "earlier, unregenerate" man). ἀρχαῖος by contrast signifies "what has existed for a long time, ancient".

36. ἵνα.

37. Thus Dodd understands the body to be "the individual self as an organism (neither flesh nor spirit being individual, and 'soul' being merely the animating principle of the flesh, or physical structure). Thus the sinful 'body' is the self as the organization of the sinful impulses inherent in the flesh." Stott cites and approves NEB, "the sinful self", and contrasts this with "the old man" or "the old self", which is "not my lower self, but my former self". Cf. the dwelling of sin in Paul (7:17, 20).

There is truth in both views, but on the whole it seems that Paul is here referring to the physical body which so easily responds to sinful impulses. As a result of crucifixion with Christ this sinful body is *rendered powerless*, completely nullified.[38] The sinner's terrible situation is completely changed by the work of Christ.

The purpose (or the result)[39] of this crucifixion is that *we should no longer be slaves to sin*. Paul's *no longer* means that until the crucifixion of which he speaks we had been slaves to sin. In our natural state we were unable to resist sin and thus were *slaves*. But *no longer*. Christ has delivered us. But just as Paul thinks of a wholehearted deliverance, so he thinks that the plight from which we were rescued was thoroughgoing. The verb "to be a slave", "to serve as a slave"[40] may be used metaphorically of the service of God (Matt. 6:24; 1 Thess. 1:9, etc.), but it is used only here of the service of sin. As often, Paul personifies sin; he sees it as a master of slaves, assuming full control over those who have not died with Christ. Barrett warns us against the simple interpretation that "the 'old man' is the nature of the unconverted man, which upon conversion and baptism is replaced by a new nature, the 'new man'." His point is that both here and in Colossians 3 Paul is addressing Christians, who are urged in this very context to "count themselves dead to sin" (v. 11). Barrett goes on, "It is much more exact to say that the 'old man' is Adam—or rather, ourselves in union with Adam, and that the 'new man' is Christ—or rather, ourselves in union with Christ".[41]

7. *Because*[42] introduces an explanation of the preceding. Paul drops his "we", and the third person introduces a general statement. Some see a reference accordingly to the general truth which we often find among the rabbis, that death cancels all obligations.[43] But Paul's reference to being justified shows that he is not simply repeating a rabbinic commonplace. His *anyone who has died* is not further defined, but it must be taken to mean "in the way just described" (cf. Harrisville, "death *as such* does not free from sin"). Paul is not referring to physical death but to dying with Christ. Anyone who has died in

---

38. The verb is καταργέω; see on 3:3. It does not mean "destroyed" but "made impotent", "nullified".

39. The construction is τοῦ with the infinitive. Moulton finds it especially characteristic of Luke, who has it 23 times, with 21 more in Acts. Paul has it 13 times, and "there is not one in which purpose is unmistakable". Moulton notes six examples in Matthew, and one each in Hebrews, James, 1 Peter, and Revelation. While he is sceptical about the construction pointing to purpose in Paul as it does in Luke, he sees the present passage, together with Phil. 3:10, as "nearest to pure final force" (M, I, pp. 216-18). Result is possible here, but purpose seems better. Or it may be epexegetic (BDF 400 [8]).

40. δουλεύω is a Pauline word; the apostle uses it 17 times out of 25 in the New Testament, seven being in Romans. The most in any non-Pauline writing is three in Luke.

41. Cf. Godet, "fallen Adam reappearing in every human *ego*".

42. γάρ.

43. E.g., "Once man dies he is free from (all) obligations, and thus R. Joḥanan interpreted: *Among the dead I am free*: once a man is dead he is free from religious duties" (Shabb. 151b).

this way has been "justified (NIV, *freed*) from sin".[44] Robin Scroggs stresses the importance of seeing Jesus' atoning death behind the passage: "The verse refers to the death of Jesus."[45] It may be doubted whether Paul saw Jesus' death as atoning because it was the death of a martyr, as Scroggs suggests, but that he saw it as atoning is beyond doubt. The person who has died with Christ enters into Christ's atonement and is justified from his sin.

It is also possible that the imagery is pointing to a master claiming a slave who proves to be dead. The legal verdict is that the slave is no longer answerable (cf. SH; NEB has "a dead man is no longer answerable for his sin"). But Paul is not speaking only of a cancelling of evil; he refers to a positive act of justification. He has just said that the believer is not enslaved to sin. Why not? Because he has died with Christ and has thus been justified. Our sin deserved death, and we have died (been "crucified with Christ"). Murray speaks of the "judicial aspect from which deliverance from the power of sin is to be viewed". A slave who dies is quit of his master, and those who die with Christ are acquitted from their old master, sin. Sin has no claim on the justified person, just as the law has none on the one who has died.

8. *Now* carries the argument along. Shedd infers "that union with Christ in his atonement involves union with him in spiritual life and sanctification." Certainly the two must not be separated; Paul makes clear what follows if we died (aorist of a decisive act) with Christ. The expression "with Christ" occurs 12 times in Paul[46] and appears to have been coined by him on the pattern of the frequently occurring Greek "with god" or the "gods". He also has a number of compounds that use the preposition "with", some of which occur in this very context ("to bury with", v. 4; "to crucify with", v. 6; "to live with", v. 8).[47] Paul uses "with Christ" of what will happen at the parousia (1 Thess. 4:14, 17), but the concept is not exclusively eschatological. It is grounded in the historical fact of the death of Christ, a death that was not simply a historical fact, but a death for sinners, a death that is the basis of the whole experience of salvation. As W. Grundmann says, "This dying with Christ is grounded in His substitutionary death for us and it takes effect as appropriation in the renunciation of sin."[48]

---

44. The verb is δικαιόω; translations like NIV and RSV obscure the connection with the doctrine of justification on which Paul puts so much emphasis. It is difficult to think that he uses this verb without having in mind the great doctrine to which it so often refers. The verb is not often followed by ἀπό (though cf. Acts 13:38).

45. NTS, 10 (1963-64), p. 107.

46. Rom. 6:8; 8:32; 2 Cor. 4:14; 13:4; Phil. 1:23; Col. 2:13, 20; 3.3, 4; 1 Thess. 4:14, 17; 5:10.

47. W. Grundmann lists 14 such compounds, most of which are found only in the Pauline writings in the New Testament, and quite a few nowhere before Paul (TDNT, VII, pp. 786-87). It is clear that being "with Christ" is an important category for Paul.

48. TDNT, VII, p. 785. Grundmann notices that in LXX God graciously promises to be with his people, but the preposition tends to be μετά. This is used of God's promises both to individuals such as Abraham (Gen. 17:4) or Gideon (Judg. 6:12), and to the people as a

Our death with Christ is not an end in itself; by faith we go on to life with Christ. Paul does not very often speak of "believing that" (again in 10:9; 1 Thess. 4:14), but the truth that genuine trust is based on fact runs through his writings. He strongly emphasizes the reality of Christ's death, which is the basis of faith for the apostle. Here he speaks of the faith that those who died with Christ will also live with him.[49] The Christian way is not negative. There is a death to an old way, it is true, but as the believer identifies with Christ in his death he enters into newness of life. Day by day he lives with Christ.[50] We should probably see an eschatological dimension in the future tense here, but understand it in a way that does not obscure its application to Christian life here and now. The future tense applies from the standpoint of the death we died with Christ. It thus refers to the continuing life of the believer, though it is not confined to the here and now. Paul is saying that the believer lives with Christ now and that this union will be even more wonderful in the life to come.

9. Again Paul appeals to the knowledge believers share (cf. vv. 3, 6). What he is saying is common knowledge for Christians (see on 2:2), so there can be no doubt about the force of his argument. Moule sees a reference to "an admitted foundation-truth. Christian *faith* is always viewed as grounded upon *knowledge*, upon *fact*" (CBSC). Our belief that we will live with Christ is not baseless: it rests upon our knowledge of his resurrection life. As commonly in this epistle, the verb *raised* refers to Christ's resurrection, which Paul here regards as irreversible; it can never be undone. For Christ death is over and done with: *death no longer has mastery over him*.[51] Death is powerful, and it reigned, for example, from Adam to Moses (5:14). But now it is defeated. Christ is supreme. The way Paul puts it *(no longer)* implies that death once did have dominion over him. As Christ trod the lowly path of suffering on behalf of doomed sinners he submitted to the rule of death. But that is all past. There is no more death for him. The resurrection was something very different from the raising of Lazarus. That was an astounding miracle, but it did not deliver

---

whole (Deut. 20:1, 4). People are not often said to be "with God". Grundmann regards Paul's σὺν Χριστῷ as being "linguistically comparable" to the Greek expressions σὺν θεῷ or σὺν θεοῖς (p. 781), but different in that Paul's expression "is not orientated to active life on earth. Its primary reference is to eschatological being with Christ as eternal, non-terrestrial being" (p. 781). This must be understood carefully, for several of Paul's references are to living out life here on earth (e.g., Col. 2:13; 3:3). But the point is that Paul's usage is distinctive and involves a very high view of the person of Christ.

49. The verb συζάω is found three times in the New Testament, all in Paul. It is another example of his stress on being "with Christ".

50. Gore points out that moralists in general agree that there is that in man which must be put to death. "But the novelty in Christianity was the emphasis which it laid rather on the living than on the dying . . . the dying is always made to appear to be in order to a living. The end is always the life."

51. The verb κυριεύω is found in Paul six out of seven times in the New Testament, four being in Romans. It conveys the idea of lordship. It is Jesus Christ who is Lord, not death.

Lazarus permanently from death. In due course he would die. But Jesus rose triumphant and entered into glory (Lagrange makes this point).

10. "For" (which NIV omits) carries on the chain of reasoning. It is because of what follows that Paul can say that death had no mastery over Christ. The clause is elliptical, literally "what he died . . . what he lives. . . ."[52] His death with all that it means had to do with sin, and his life with all that it means has to do with God. That Christ *died to sin* is difficult, especially since the same expression is used of believers (vv. 2, 11; cf. 6, 7). Some see a *dativus commodi*, "with respect to sin"; others, that Jesus died rather than commit sin; still others, that he dealt with the power of sin as well as its guilt. It is best to see Paul as indicating that Jesus' death was related to sin, but that the case does not prescribe in detail what that relationship was. The context makes clear that Christ died for our sins; he had none of his own to which he might die. But dealing with our sins meant coming into this world of sin and then dying the death that put sin away. That death was a death "to sin", for it meant the end of Christ's being in the realm of sin. It was a death to his whole relationship to sin.

Jesus' death to sin was once and for all, "the great New Testament note" (Robinson).[53] Believers face a new contest with sin every day; as long as we are on this earth we are never free from it. But Christ's death was unique, a once-for-all dealing with sin. God made him sin for us (2 Cor. 5:21), and his death dealt decisively with sin, took it out of the way, paid its penalty, removed its sting (1 Cor. 15:55-56), won the victory over it. Look at sin how you will, Christ has effectively dealt with it.

Paul goes on to Jesus' risen life. The construction is the same as in the first part of the verse, and we are to understand it in the sense "what he lives", "his life and all that that life involves". The resurrection marks the victory, the end of the conflict with sin. The life that follows is a life singly devoted to God (for living "to" cf. 14:7-8). This does not mean that on earth Jesus did not live singly devoted to God. He did. But on earth he lived in sin's realm. God's purpose for him was directed to the defeat of sin; it meant that Jesus identified himself with sinners. Now all that is over. His life is beyond the reach of death and every evil. It is a life lived positively in and for the glory of God (cf. Jn. 17:5), no longer with the negative aspect of putting away sin.

11. This has consequences (*In the same way* points to similarity); it leads to the classic "Be what you are" situation (or perhaps, "Don't be what you are

---

52. ὃ γὰρ ἀπέθανεν . . . ὃ δὲ ζῇ. . . . This is not a simple ellipsis, for ὃ is neuter. Moule denies that it is "a strictly cognate relative" and favors "whereas he died . . . whereas he lives . . ." (IBNTG, p. 131). Murray argues for "as regards", and SH see "a kind of cognate accus." Lenski is perhaps best with "his death and all that his death involved".

53. The word is ἐφάπαξ, a strengthened form of ἅπαξ, "once and for all". Stählin considers it "a technical term for the definitiveness and therefore the uniqueness or singularity of the death of Christ and the redemption thereby accomplished" (TDNT, I, p. 383). It occurs twice in Paul and three times in Hebrews.

not").[54] Believers must act in the same way; there is emphasis on *yourselves*,[55] "you, in addition to Christ." Faith means seeing things as Christ sees them and then acting on the vision. *Count* is a favorite Pauline word (see on 2:3); it conveys the idea of reckoning or calculating. Perhaps here "regard" or "recognize" would help us understand that Paul is arguing that his readers should come to see the truth of their situation. Christ's death and resurrection has altered their position, and they should live in accordance with the new reality. The verb might be indicative (so Bengel), but the context demands the imperative here. We should not overlook the fact that this is the first exhortation in the epistle; Paul has laid a strong foundation in doctrine and in the recital of what God has done before he turns to the importance of right conduct. The present tense points to a continuing process; this goes on throughout the Christian life. The believer is to take seriously his death with Christ (v. 8) and Christ's death to sin (v. 10). Since Christ died to sin and since the believer is dead with Christ, the believer is dead to sin and is to recognize the fact of that death. This does not mean that he is immune to sinning. Paul does not say that sin is dead but that the believer is to count himself as dead to it. He feels temptation and sometimes he sins. But the sin of the unbeliever is the natural consequence of the fact that he is a slave to sin, whereas the sin of the believer is quite out of character. He has been set free. Paul tells him that he is to recognize that where sin is concerned he is among the dead. He has been delivered from its dominion. And death is permanent. Once united to Christ he must count himself as dead to the reign of sin forever. He is to reckon also that he is *alive to God*. His life now has a positive orientation; it is directed to the highest there is, the service of God. The Christian way is not just an emotional experience (though, of course, the emotions are involved). It is a life of service.

Paul speaks of all this as being *in Christ Jesus*. This is the first use in Romans of being "in Christ" (3:24 is not quite the same), which is one of Paul's great concepts and one that he keeps on using (the number of occurrences is variously estimated according as "in him" and the like are included, and how one estimates the authorship of certain writings; Deissmann spoke of 164 passages and A. M. Hunter of about 200). Paul never explains what he means by the expression, but clearly it points to the close tie that unites believers to their Lord. Some think it should be taken to mean membership in the body of Christ; others that it is to be understood in terms of corporate

54. Käsemann objects that this slogan "comes from our idealistic legacy and . . . leads necessarily to an intolerable formalizing of the problem." With Bultmann he sees the problem "lifted out of the spheres of mere ethics and a combination with mysticism . . . and set in the dimension of Pauline eschatology"; he argues that the real issue is not freedom from guilt but from the power of sin. We may agree that the slogan must be used carefully and that freedom from the power of sin is important. But guilt is also important, and Paul does not overlook it.

55. καὶ ὑμεῖς. It would be possible to punctuate with a full stop after ὑμεῖς, but it is better to take this with the words that follow.

personality, or of mysticism. Probably we cannot now recover all that Paul understood by the expression, but at least we can say that it emphasizes the closeness of the tie between the saved and the Saviour and that it also indicates something of the unity that binds all Christ's own. The blessings Christians receive they receive because of their contact with Christ. Here we should see that it is only as we are "in Christ" that we live *to God*. And the expression reminds us that God sees us not as we are "in ourselves" but as we are "in Christ."[56]

12. *Therefore* ties this closely in with the preceding. In the light of the truth Paul has been setting forth certain things follow. The apostle is addressing believers, not the general public. Such an exhortation as this would be fruitless addressed to people who did not know the redeeming power of Christ. But it is the duty of those who do know this power to live in the way Paul is suggesting. Godly living is a necessity, not an option. They are no longer sin's slaves. They must *not* (for Paul's negatives see on 1:13) *let sin reign* (cf. 5:21 for sin's reign, and 5:14, 17 for that of death). This of course assumes that sin is still there; believers do not have a serene existence from which sin has been blissfully excluded. They are still "in the flesh" as well as "in Christ". Sin is still a force, but Paul's point is that it is not supreme. Believers are to make sure accordingly that they do not deny their freedom by allowing sin to rule them. They are to enter into the heritage that Christ has won for them. Murray points out that to say to a slave "Do not behave as a slave" is to mock him, but it is a meaningful thing to say to someone who has been set free. He must now give up thinking and living like a slave and start behaving like a free person.

Paul specifically mentions the *body*[57] in connection with this reign (cf. v. 6 for the connection of the body with sin). And the folly of letting sin reign is subtly brought out by characterizing the body as *mortal*. Sin's pleasures take place in a body which is at best mortal and will soon pass away, whereas Paul has been speaking of the life in Christ that brings eternal joy. It is stupid to allow that which will die to have the supreme position. Paul is not arguing that the body is the cause of sin, but that it is the organ through which sin manifests itself, *so that* believers obey it.[58] For *evil desires* ("lusts") see the note on 1:24. The word sometimes means good desires, but here it is clear that evil is in mind. There is a textual problem, with some MSS reading "obey it", some "obey its lusts", and some "obey it in its lusts". This may be an example

---

56. The literature on "in Christ" is enormous, but it may be sufficient to refer to Richard N. Longenecker's discussion in *Paul: Apostle of Liberty* (New York, 1964), pp. 160-70, and the works there cited; cf. C. F. D. Moule, *The Origin of Christology* (Cambridge, 1977), pp. 55-69.

57. σώματι is singular, though ὑμῶν is plural. Together they form a Semitic construction, of a kind that Turner finds "contrary to normal Greek and Latin practice" (M, III, p. 23).

58. In Paul εἰς τό with the infinitive mostly denotes purpose, though sometimes result (cf. M, III, p. 143). Here result seems more likely.

of the longer reading being right, for it is awkward and could be improved by dropping something. But its attestation is primarily late, and it looks like a conflation of the other two readings. The text behind NIV is probably correct.

13. Paul adds another negative command, *Do not offer*.[59] The tense is present, pointing to the cessation of an activity (cf. NEB, "no longer put . . ."). The verb is sometimes used of the sacrifices, with a meaning like "offer", "present" (cf. 12:1). It is such a meaning that it has here.[60] What are to be presented are the "members"[61] of the body, regarded as *instruments*.[62] Once more sin is personified; it is sin that is the potential recipient of the members of the bodies of Paul's readers. If used in this way, these "members" would promote *wickedness*.[63] But *rather*[64] introduces a strong contrast. There is a change of tense and a change from the members to the whole person. The aorist tense signifies a wholehearted and total commitment: "Do not keep on presenting your members to sin . . . but once and for all present yourselves to God." They are to do this *as*[65] "living people from the dead", a striking and vivid way of referring to Christians. They have died to sin with Christ, so death can be used of them as it has been throughout this section of the letter. But they are not dead. They are living and they are separated "from"[66] the dead. With this comprehensive exhortation Paul links another which concerns the members of the body just as did that which began this verse. But now "your members" are to be presented to God *as instruments of righteousness*. Since the believer belongs to God, his body is to be used for God's righteous purposes.

14. *For* introduces the reason. There is a great fact which Paul sees as justification for what he has just said. Again he personifies sin, and views it as a master of slaves. But this time there is a negative: *sin shall not be your master*. Believers are no slaves to sin! In v. 9 Paul has said that death no longer has any

---

59. μηδέ is found 23 times in Paul (four in Romans) out of 57 in the New Testament. Again we find a high proportion in Paul.

60. The verb is παριστάνω, a variant form of παρίστημι. BAGD say it is used as a technical term in the language of sacrifice.

61. μέλος is a thoroughly Pauline word, occurring 29 times in the Pauline writings out of 34 in the New Testament. It is sometimes used of the "limbs", but this is not invariable and here the parts of the body in general are in mind.

62. The word is ὅπλα, another Pauline word (five times out of six in the New Testament). It can denote any tool or implement, and in the plural it is often used of weapons. Many take it in this sense here, but nothing in the context indicates warfare, so perhaps it is better to see it as *instruments* with NIV.

63. Barth has an interesting comment: "By *weapons of unrighteousness* is meant the arrogant behaviour by which, when men identify themselves with God (i.18), this organism is employed as an instrument by which the truth is imprisoned; when, surrendering themselves to this organism as prisoners of sin, they vaunt a supposed freedom and rise up in rebellion."

64. ἀλλά.

65. This is Paul's one use of ὡσεί, a particle of comparison meaning "as", "like", not "as if". Paul is speaking of a reality, not a supposition (so Leenhardt, Michel, and others).

66. ἐκ.

lordship over Christ; now he adds that sin has no lordship over those who are Christ's. Moffatt renders, "Sin must not have any hold over you" (and others see an imperatival future, as O'Neill, TH, etc.), but Paul's statement is stronger. As Parry says, it is "a promise, not a command". Paul has, of course, given commands, and he is never afraid to introduce another. But here he is pointing to the reason why commands like those he has just given can be obeyed. Believers can present their members to God for righteousness precisely because sin has no lordship over them. They are free.

Because introduces the reason. Dunn points out that it is a new thing to have law and grace set over against one another as they are here. He comments, "It is not that anyone said, 'Righteousness is by law and not by grace'; no one posed grace and law as alternatives; rather they saw law as the gift of grace. It was *Paul* who posed them as alternatives".[67] Paul saw clearly that law and grace do not go together. If one is "under"[68] the one, he is not "under" the other. In view of the place Paul's Jewish contemporaries ascribed to the law we must be clear that the apostle saw it as in opposition to the way of grace and thus an impossible way of salvation for the Christian. Paul held that the law was given, not as the way of deliverance, but in order that every mouth might be stopped and all people be held accountable to God (3:19); it gives knowledge of sin (3:20); it makes the offence abound (5:20); it works wrath (4:15); no one will be justified by law (3:20); sin brought about all kinds of lust through the commandment, indeed sin is dead apart from law (7:8); it was "through the commandment" that sin deceived and slew Paul (7:11); people's sinful passions work through the law (7:5); the law is weak through the flesh (8:3). Outside this epistle Paul carries on with much the same teaching. The law never justifies people (Gal. 2:16; 3:11); the law is sin's strength (1 Cor. 15:56); it is there only to lead people to Christ (Gal. 3:24); those under the law were in need of redemption, and Christ came to be under the law in order to redeem those under the law (Gal. 4:5). We should be clear as to the radical novelty and the great importance of Paul's attitude to law. Were Christians "under law" their inability perfectly to keep the law would have left them still subject to sin. "It would be pointless to say to a man who is struggling along under the domination of legalism, 'You will eventually be completely free.' He will always be bound" (Cragg). But Christians are not bound. Their salvation is God's free gift. They are not dependent on their own ability to keep the law. They are free from the tyranny of sin and of law. As Kertelge puts it, "The new rule of grace claims man completely and tolerates no compromise with sin." For grace, see on 1:5.

---

67. ET, 93 (1981-82), p. 260.
68. This use of ὑπό is that which BAGD define as "of power, rule, sovereignty, command, etc."

B. SHALL WE SIN BECAUSE WE ARE UNDER GRACE, NOT LAW?
6:15–7:6

Having established that the Christian cannot take up the position that it is all right to continue in sin with a view to making grace abound, Paul proceeds to his second rhetorical question in this section of his argument. This proceeds from the point the apostle had reached at the end of his answer to the first question, namely that the believer is not under law but under grace. Then does that mean that sin does not matter? His answer divides into two parts. First he establishes that Christians are not slaves to sin but rather to God; then he gives an illustration from marriage.

1. We Are Not Slaves, 6:15-23

> 15*What then? Shall we sin because we are not under law but under grace? By no means!* 16*Don't you know that when you offer yourselves to someone to obey him as slaves, you are slaves to the one whom you obey—whether you are slaves to sin, which leads to death, or to obedience, which leads to righteousness?* 17*But thanks be to God that, though you used to be slaves to sin, you wholeheartedly obeyed the form of teaching to which you were entrusted.* 18*You have been set free from sin and have become slaves to righteousness.*
>
> 19*I put this in human terms because you are weak in your natural selves. Just as you used to offer the parts of your body in slavery to impurity and to ever-increasing wickedness, so now offer them in slavery to righteousness leading to holiness.* 20*When you were slaves to sin, you were free from the control of righteousness.* 21*What benefit did you reap at that time from the things you are now ashamed of? Those things result in death!* 22*But now that you have been set free from sin and have become slaves to God, the benefit you reap leads to holiness, and the result is eternal life.* 23*For the wages of sin is death, but the gift of God is eternal life in[a] Jesus Christ our Lord.*
>
> [a]23 Or *through*

15. *What then?* is similar to the opening of verse 1.[69] Indeed, the whole verse is similar, and some scholars hold that Paul is simply repeating the objection he stated there. There are, however, some differences. In verse 1 the verb is in the present and points to a continuing attitude. The objector there was impressed with Paul's contention that the more sin there is the more grace there is (5:20), and thought he could multiply grace by multiplying sin. This time the verb is in the aorist[70] and points rather to a single act, a particular instance. And the objector is not suggesting that we sin "*so that* grace may abound" but "*because* grace abounds." The thought this time is something

69. Except that there is nothing corresponding to *shall we say*. BDF, however, hold that there is an ellipsis of ἐροῦμεν (299 [3]).

70. ἁμαρτήσωμεν is a late first aorist form of a kind found in LXX. Some MSS have the future, ἁμαρτήσομεν, but most critics accept the aorist.

like this: "It is grace that saves, not the way we live. Therefore the odd sin is neither here nor there. Once we have put our trust in Christ it does not matter whether we slip into sin or not." Paul repudiates this with decision.[71] The Christian can never say, "Sin does not matter. It will all be the same in the end." As Brunner puts it, "Freedom from the Law does not mean freedom from God but freedom for God."

16. A somewhat complicated rhetorical question drives the point home. Once again Paul appeals to knowledge in his readers.[72] They were familiar with slavery, and Paul is reasoning from the well-known fact that a slave was completely at the disposal of his master. No man could serve two masters (Matt. 6:24), for by definition he belonged totally to one and had nothing over for the other.[73] Paul is emphasizing the impossibility of compromise. For all of us in the last resort it is sin or God. It cannot be both. He talks about people offering themselves as slaves, a situation not unknown in the ancient world, when people sometimes became slaves voluntarily in order to secure at least a livelihood. For Paul the basic assumption is that all are slaves before they become believers in Christ; they are not free to do as they will, for they are subject to the bondage of sin. Notice that he is not saying that slaves are required to obey their master. He is looking at it the other way around. The master we obey shows whose slaves we are. Unbelievers are *slaves to sin*, and this leads inevitably to death. But believers are slaves *to obedience*. We might have expected Paul to say "slaves to God", and he does say this in due course (v. 22).[74] He also speaks of belonging to "the form of teaching" (v. 17) and of being slaves of righteousness (vv. 18, 19). The point is that this is a complex situation and Paul does not oversimplify.[75] Obedience was an essential ingredient in slavery: it was the function of the slave to do what he was told. And,

---

71. For μὴ γένοιτο see on 3:4. It is a vigorous rejection of the suggestion.

72. Paul often appeals to his correspondents' knowledge (see on 2:2), but the use of οὐκ οἴδατε ὅτι is frequent in 1 Corinthians and rare elsewhere (cf. οὐκ οἴδατε, 11:2).

73. Legally, of course, ownership could be shared so that there were two owners. This could lead to anomalous situations, e.g., when one owner freed the slave while the other did not. He was then half slave, half free. Jesus is not denying the legal possibility of shared ownership of a slave; he is denying that a slave can give to more than one person the wholeheartedness a slave owed his master. If there are two owners, he will hate one and love the other.

74. We should not miss the point that the Christians had a very unusual attitude to slaves. The term "slave" was everywhere a term of abuse, even among the Jews (cf. K. H. Rengstorf, TDNT, II, pp. 270-71). Slaves were not accepted into societies as they were into the Christian church. Rengstorf sees "a decisive break with Jewish usage" in the fact that "The Rabbis and Pharisees did not think of themselves as the slaves of God" (p. 274 n. 101). They used the expression for the people as a whole or for outstanding servants of God, but not in the way the Christians used it.

75. Nygren points out that Christians "live their life on the border between the two aeons. They live 'in Christ'; but have not thereby ceased to share the fate of the children of Adam." Paul is combating the view that Christians are freed from the pull implied in being children of Adam, but also that which says that they do not belong wholeheartedly to God. He is saying that they are God's and that, though they may slip, their lives show that they belong to God.

of course, a change of owner meant that the slave no longer obeyed his former master. He still obeyed, but his obedience was transferred to his new owner. The obedience he rendered showed whose slave he was. Here Paul insists that obedience is an important part of the life lived in grace (cf. 1:5; 15:18; 16:26). The essence of sin is disobedience to God, while contrariwise to be obedient to God is the hallmark of the slave of God. The quality of our living shows whose we are.

Paul proceeds to set out the alternatives. He sees only two possibilities, being *slaves to sin* with the end result *death*, and *to obedience, which leads to righteousness*.[76] Death here is more than physical death. Its connection with sin shows it to be a horror, greatly to be feared. Sin leads finally to the loss of everything that can really be called life. *Obedience* is a general term, but in this context it probably refers especially to obedience to the gospel call, the obedience of faith. It is this that leads to *righteousness*, which in turn is probably complex. Since Paul has been stressing the importance of upright living, it is impossible to rule this out at this point. On the other hand, to confine it to morality is to overlook the fact that in this epistle righteousness is so often the righteousness that believers attain by faith, and the contrast with death shows that this is in mind here (cf. GNB, "of obedience, which results in being put right with God"). Paul is not distinguishing between the right living that characterizes the servants of God and "the consummated righteousness of the new heavens and the new earth" (Murray).

After the thought that slavery to sin leads to death we expect that obedience will lead to life, but Paul speaks instead of righteousness. A Jewish reader might indeed accept the view that obedience to God, and specifically his own obedience, would lead to life. But Paul is not saying that; he is giving no countenance to any view of salvation by works. So he saves up his references to life until verses 22 and 23.

17. This leads to an outburst of thanksgiving for what has happened to the Roman Christians. Notice that Paul does not praise them for what they have done, but thanks God for what he has done in them. He gives thanks for the past, not, of course, for the Romans' former slavery to sin, but for the fact that that slavery is over; they were then slaves to sin, but are no longer.[77] Simeon points out that, while all were slaves to sin, all were not slaves to the same sin; but whatever the sin, it alienates from God. It is this last point that matters to Paul. All sin alienates from God, and he rejoices that as regards the Roman Christians this is all in the past. They have "obeyed from the heart", where the aorist tense points to the decisive act of obedience when they turned to God. Paul does not elsewhere use the expression "from the

---

76. ἤτοι occurs here only in the New Testament. The construction seems to imply that these are the only alternatives.

77. BDF see this as an example of the use of the imperfect tense where the past is placed in sharp contrast to the present (BDF 327). Olshausen remarks that the former state "is understood as past; for even if sin is not thoroughly removed from the believer, yet it has no *dominion*". Paul has emphasized this in the earlier part of the chapter.

heart";[78] clearly it shows that he is referring to a deeply felt experience, one that is "voluntary and sincere" (Hodge).

He goes on to speak of *the form of teaching*, which means the accepted Christian teaching. Some see a reference to the essential Pauline position, over against, say, the Petrine or the Johannine teaching, but, as Denney points out, this is an anachronism. As far as he knew, Paul preached the same gospel as did the other apostles (1 Cor. 15:1-11). He is referring to the teaching commonly accepted among the Christians.[79] We would expect him to say that the teaching had been delivered to the Romans, but instead he says that they had been delivered to the teaching.[80] The rabbis might view themselves as the masters of their tradition (so Barrett), but the Christians are in subjection to the teaching God has given them. They do not have godliness, but godliness has them. There is no special concentration of the word "teaching" in the New Testament (Paul has it six times out of its 30 occurrences); it is spread widely. It points to the importance of authentic Christian teaching. This is not seen as a series of bright ideas some early believers thought up, but as God-given teaching which grips people.

18. In strikingly bold imagery Paul sets forth the new situation for his readers. They have been set free from sin,[81] liberated permanently from their taskmaster. This will mean freedom from every aspect of sin; "Believers are free from the condemning power of sin, and from its enslaving power" (Shedd). Sin no longer has dominion. Freedom is an important category for Paul, one that he uses more than any other New Testament writer.[82] He can speak of Christians as being free from "the law of sin and death" (8:2), or from sin (v. 22), and of creation as being freed from "its bondage to decay" (8:21), but often he simply speaks of freedom, as when he says, "It is for freedom that Christ has set us free" (Gal. 5:1).[83] People were in the grip of tyrants like sin and death and decay. It mattered immensely to Paul that Christ brought real freedom. He can call on the man caught in the bondage of actual, physical slavery not to let that trouble him, for "in the Lord" he is Christ's freedman (1 Cor. 7:21-22). The freedom there is in Christ is so liberating that slavery to

---

78. ἐκ καρδίας. Cf. 1 Pet. 1:22.

79. Most commentators refer to the tradition, but F. W. Beare denies this. He holds that Paul is speaking of transfer from one owner to another (NTS, 5 [1958-59], p. 207). While it is true that this transfer is an important theme of the passage, it is not easy to remove completely the thought of the tradition from *teaching*.

80. The Greek is εἰς ὃν παρεδόθητε τύπον διδαχῆς, which seems to be equivalent to τύπῳ διδαχῆς εἰς ὃν παρεδόθητε, the antecedent having been attracted into the case of the relative. For τύπος see on 5:14.

81. Deissmann finds here the technical language used for setting slaves free; he points out that ἀπό in passages like this "is also a technical use of language" (LAE, p. 326 n. 1).

82. He has the verb ἐλευθερόω five times out of seven in the New Testament, the noun ἐλευθερία seven out of 11, and the adjective ἐλεύθερος 16 out of 23. He thus uses each of these words more often than all the other New Testament writers put together.

83. This could be understood as "with freedom", but "for freedom" (as Moffatt, NEB, etc.) is much more in accord with Paul's use of the concept.

men matters little beside it. Most religions have a strict set of rules, and even Christianity has often been viewed as something like "the new law". We should not take Paul's great emphasis on freedom too lightly, as though he were pointing out the obvious. Nobody saw the freedom implied in the gospel as clearly as Paul did, or gave it such emphasis.

But Paul does not confuse liberty with license. For him freedom in Christ is not an invitation to splendid self-centeredness. The freed in Christ have become *slaves to righteousness*.[84] They are not aimless, purposeless. They have been freed from sin in order that they may give themselves over wholly to worthwhile causes, boldly expressed here as being enslaved to the right. Elsewhere Paul tells us that, while the slave is Christ's freedman, the free man called to be a Christian is Christ's slave (1 Cor. 7:22). We remember that Jesus said that a good tree "cannot" bear bad fruit (Matt. 7:18). Paul is saying much the same in his own way. Those set free do not wander in a moral vacuum. They are slaves to righteousness.

19. To speak *in human terms* is to speak "as people do in daily life" (BAGD). Paul uses the expression three times in 1 Corinthians and nowhere else (though cf. 3:5). He is not so much apologizing for using an illustration from slavery as explaining why he did it. Slavery was regarded as such a degrading state and it was so firmly repudiated in the contemporary world that it would not normally be regarded as an acceptable metaphor. But it makes things very clear to his readers, and they needed such clarity. "On account of the weakness of your flesh" (NIV, *natural selves*) has been understood as referring to moral weakness, a view strengthened by the words that follow (Gifford points out that "the ancient interpreters" take it in this way). But, while Paul can use the word "flesh" in a pejorative sense, he has not done so in this epistle to this point. Moreover, it is not only the morally weak who need help in understanding Paul's point. Many accordingly think of the term as pointing to intellectual rather than to moral weakness. It is better to decline both alternatives and see it as referring to the weakness proper to this life (Lenski speaks of the "foolish tendency under a false show of logic to draw wrong conclusions from the great spiritual facts"). The natural man lacks spiritual discernment, and Paul evidently fears that some of his readers did not readily comprehend spiritual truths. Because of the weakness that is part and parcel of this life, it is well for him to use an illustration that will make the position perfectly clear.

With his *Just as . . . so now* Paul makes the point that the Roman Chris-

---

84. According to TH "A much more meaningful equivalent may be 'We Are under Obligation to Do What is Right' ". But this draws some of the sting from Paul's powerful paradox. He is not saying that the liberated ought to do right, but that they are the slaves of right. D. Daube comments on Dodd's view that the expression is "sub-Christian" that it is "also 'sub-Jewish'. There is not a single Old Testament or Rabbinic text with the phrase 'slaves of righteousness' or anything like it—say, 'slaves of the Law' or 'slaves of good deeds'. The faithful are 'slaves of God'; they could be slaves to no one and nothing else" (*The New Testament and Rabbinic Judaism* [London, 1956], p. 284). Paul's use is distinctive.

tians are to be just as wholehearted in walking in the ways of God now as they used to be in their bondage to sin. His aorist tenses point to wholehearted commitment. They had given themselves wholeheartedly to sin; let them now give themselves equally wholeheartedly to righteousness. As in verse 13, Paul speaks of offering their "members", not strictly the limbs but every part that goes into making up their person. In verse 13 he spoke of offering them as "implements" of evil, here as "slaves"[85] to *impurity* or "unclean-ness". Sin defiles; it brings about the degradation of the sinner. With this is coupled "lawlessness" (NIV, *wickedness*), which can be regarded as the essence of sin (1 John 3:4); it is "contempt of the standard of right written in the law on every man's conscience (ii.14, 15)" (Godet). Many translations agree with NIV in taking the following expression in the sense *ever-increasing*, but "wickedness for wicked purposes" (GNB) reflects the Greek better.[86] Paul is saying that their lives had proceeded from lawlessness and aimed at (or arrived at) nothing better than lawlessness. Incidentally, this way of putting things is more applicable to Gentiles than to people who had been adherents of the Jewish way prior to conversion. Jews could scarcely be accused of being soft on law.

Now Paul urges them to a different course. Now that Christ has come, now that atonement has been made, now that they are living in a time of eschatological significance, they must act differently. They have given up slavery to evil; they must accept slavery to righteousness (see on v. 18) with all that that means. This is "with a view to sanctification"[87] (CBSC), that is, to becoming holy as befits the slave of God. The lives of the Roman Christians are to reflect the reality of their full commitment to the service of God.

20. Paul looks back to their pre-Christian days. In accordance with his view that a slave belongs to one master he reminds them that, belonging to sin completely as they had been, they had been free with respect to right-eousness.[88] This did not mean that they had never done anything that was right (evil people sometimes do good things). But it meant that they were not subject to the rule of righteousness; they saw no compulsion to do what was right. Their freedom was a grim one.

21. Paul advances his argument with a rhetorical question, but there is

---

85. δοῦλος is normally a noun; indeed, this is the only passage in the New Testament where it is used as an adjective.

86. The point at issue is the meaning of εἰς τὴν ἀνομίαν. In view of the parallel with εἰς ἁγιασμόν later in the verse this must surely be taken in the sense "with a view to", or "leading to".

87. εἰς ἁγιασμόν. The question is whether this refers to the process of becoming holy or the final state. The -μος termination expresses action (Robertson, p. 151), but nouns are not always used in strict accordance with the way they are formed. Murray and others see the state here, but it seems better to take the word in its normal meaning of process, as Cranfield and Moule (CBSC).

88. Moule denies that the dative here is ablatival and regards it rather as comparable to the Latin *dativus commodi*, "free with regard to righteousness", not "free from right-eousness" (IBNTG, p. 46).

considerable doubt as to where his question ends. Many agree with NIV that it goes on to *ashamed* (e.g., Murray, Lenski, Hodge), but others take it as NEB, "what was the gain? Nothing but what now makes you ashamed. . . ." The arguments are so finely balanced that a final decision is perhaps impossible. Perhaps the words after *time* do not naturally follow in the same question, which leads us to accept the shorter form of the question. Interestingly, NIV removes the agricultural metaphor by translating *benefit* where the noun means "fruit" and then inserts it by rendering *reap* where the verb means "have". Godet considers this verb significant; it means "they possess and keep it in themselves." "Fruit" is mostly used by Paul in a good sense and some argue for a good sense here, but F. Hauck is probably right when he comments, "the pre-Christian man is under the power of sin and brings forth the corresponding fruits" (TDNT, III, p. 615). Paul is inquiring what really significant result had followed from their living in those evil ways of which they are now ashamed. The end[89] of those things, he emphasizes, is death. We should not miss the force of his *now*. While they were the slaves of sin they were not ashamed of those things (cf. Jer. 8:12). To be without shame is a mark of the sin-dominated life. But when they became Christians they came to see sin for the evil thing it is and their past deeds for the shameful things they were.

22. *But now* opposes the present state to the past. Being a Christian means that all things are made new (cf. 2 Cor. 5:17). Whereas previously Paul's correspondents had been free with regard to righteousness, now they have been set free (the aorist points to a decisive action) from sin. Then they had been slaves to sin, now they have been enslaved to God. The strong term marks the wholeheartedness involved in Christian commitment. Paul goes on to the consequence of all this. "You have your fruit", he says, "unto sanctification". He does not say what the fruit is, but only what it leads to,[90] the process of becoming holy. Lloyd-Jones emphasizes the importance of "have": " 'you have your fruit.' You have got it! This is true of every Christian. There is no such thing as a Christian who does not bear fruit; you cannot be a Christian without bearing fruit" (p. 296; he goes on to point out that in John 15 Jesus speaks of "fruit", "more fruit", and "much fruit"). The present possession of "fruit" gives assurance that the fulness involved in "eternal life" will in due course be attained. For *eternal life* see on 2:7; it can be viewed as a present possession, and this is not uncommon in the New Testament. But here the future consummation seems to be in mind. As in verse 21, *result* will

---

89. τέλος often denotes the end in the sense of "the aim" or "purpose". But it can mean simply the last in a series (cf. 1 Cor. 15:24; Rev. 21:6, etc.); here it must denote such an end.

90. Some miss this point, as RSV, "the return you get is sanctification", or Barrett, "your fruit proves to be sanctification". But we should surely preserve the distinction between καρπός and ἁγιασμός, especially since the latter is preceded by εἰς. The fruit begins the process of sanctification.

signify the final member of a series rather than the aim (though the latter may not be completely out of sight).

23. *The wages*[91] *of sin is death*, writes Paul, transferring his imagery from sin as a slave owner to that of a general paying his soldiers. But the wage sin pays is death. "Death here is the negation or absence of a life that is truly life. Sin robs life of its meaning, purpose, fulfillment" (Smart, p. 91).[92] As Heidland puts it, sin "promises life and gives death."[93] A sense of equivalence is involved. Sinners get what they have earned. Death is no arbitrary sentence, but the inevitable consequence of their sin.

Over against that Paul sets *the gift of God*, where his word for *gift* stresses the element of freeness, of bounty.[94] Eternal life is not a reward for services rendered. There is no element of pay or requital. Michel and others see a reference to the *donativum*, a gift given by the Emperor to soldiers on special occasions, but this seems unlikely. That might suit the present context, but Paul's word is one he uses quite often and in places where *donativum* would be quite impossible. As Denney puts it, "Paul could hardly use what is almost a technical expression with himself in a technical sense quite remote from his own." His sharp contrast emphasizes that sinners do nothing at all to merit salvation. Eternal life comes as God's free gift or it does not come at all. As in the previous verse, eternal life seems to be used to include both the present possession and the glorious consummation at the end of the age. Paul rounds this off by saying that this life is *in Christ Jesus our Lord* (see on v. 11 for "in Christ"). In 5:21 eternal life is "through" Christ; here it is "in" him. It is doubtful whether we should try to draw too hard a distinction between the two; both insist on the fact that eternal life is bound up with the person and the work of Christ.

---

91. ὀψώνιον is not common in the New Testament, occurring once in each of five books. Derived from ὄψον, "cooked food", and ὠνέομαι, "to buy", it was used of "ration money" paid to soldiers. From this it came to be used of "pay" or "wages" in general, though its most frequent use remained that for the pay of soldiers. LSJ attest a use for an allowance given to a slave, but this was not common. H. W. Heidland says it is used "occasionally" outside the military sphere (TDNT, V, p. 591).

92. This is in sharp contradiction of the Greek understanding. E. Rohde can speak of life as the wages of sin (TDNT, I, p. 309 n. 155). He says, "It is in expiation of a fault that the soul is exiled in the body; the payment for sin is earthly life, which is the death of the soul" (*ibid.*, p. 298).

93. TDNT, V, p. 592.

94. The word is χάρισμα, "a gift (freely and graciously given)" (BAGD).

Romans 7

2. An Illustration from Marriage, 7:1-6

*¹Do you not know, brothers—for I am speaking to men who know the law—
that the law has authority over a man only as long as he lives? ²For example, by
law a married woman is bound to her husband as long as he is alive, but if her
husband dies, she is released from the law of marriage. ³So then, if she marries
another man while her husband is still alive, she is called an adulteress. But if her
husband dies, she is released from that law and is not an adulteress, even though
she marries another man.*

*⁴So, my brothers, you also died to the law through the body of Christ, that you
might belong to another, to him who was raised from the dead, in order that we
might bear fruit to God. ⁵For when we were controlled by the sinful nature,ᵃ the
sinful passions aroused by the law were at work in our bodies, so that we bore
fruit for death. ⁶But now, by dying to what once bound us, we have been released
from the law so that we serve in the new way of the Spirit, and not in the old way
of the written code.*

ᵃ5 Or *the flesh;* also in verse 25

The place of the law in God's scheme of things was a constant bat-
tleground in Paul's controversies with Jewish opponents. For them the law
was the greatest good, the mark of God's kindness to his people in that he had
given it to them. They studied it with the greatest of diligence, regarding even
the minutest detail as important. They took it as central for any pious person
as he sought to live a life of service to God. It seemed to them that Paul was
rejecting this greatest of goods that God had given. Paul found himself in a
difficult position. On the one hand, he could not regard the way of the law as
the way of salvation, and he said this with the utmost firmness. But on the
other hand, it was a good gift of God and, rightly used, was of great importance. In this section of his letter Paul gives serious attention to the place of the
law. Readers often spend a lot of time and energy discussing the question of
whether in this chapter Paul is talking about the regenerate or the unregenerate and, if the latter, whether it is the unregenerate as such or the unregenerate as seen from the perspective of the regenerate. Such questions are not
unimportant, but we should be clear that it is the place of the law that Paul is
discussing.

There are problems with this opening section, such that Barclay could

say, "Seldom did Paul write so difficult and so complicated a passage as this."
Dodd is scathing, holding that Paul's illustration "is confused from the outset" and that in the end we should ignore what he is actually saying "and ask
what it is that Paul is really talking about in the realm of fact and experience."
On the other hand Lenski can say, "Paul's illustration is perfectly chosen."
The main difficulty is that Paul's illustration refers to a wife who is bound to
her husband as long as he lives, but who is free to marry again when he dies as
she could not before the death. This is used to illustrate the truth that the
believer has died to the law and is now given over to Christ. But in the
illustration it is not the wife but the husband who dies, not the husband but
the wife who remarries. We would not use an illustration in this way, so we
find a problem. But it is another question whether we should censure Paul for
using it in his way. Joyce A. Little, who has carefully examined the passage,
finds "a threefold use of analogy. . . . First, Paul is concerned with demonstrating that the law played a necessary role prior to the coming of Christ
(hence the validity of the law governing the first marriage). Second, Paul
wishes to use vv. 2-3 as an analogy demonstrating that death can change
one's relationship to the law. Third, Paul wishes to use the analogy struc-
turally as a means by which to develop his view that our death to the law takes
place for a specific purpose, in order that we might 'serve in the new life of the
Spirit.'"[1]

We should bear in mind that Paul has just argued that the believer is not
under the rule of sin. Now he goes on to the further point that he is not under
the rule of law. It is interesting that there are so many points of resemblance in
the two treatments. Thus the believer has died to sin (6:2) and to law (7:4). He
is free from sin (6:18) and from law (7:3). He is "justified from sin" (6:7) and
discharged "from law" (7:6). He walks in newness of life (6:4) and serves in
newness of Spirit (7:6).

1. Paul begins with "or" (which NIV omits); this next section is linked to
the preceding. It poses alternatives: either his readers must admit the truth of
what Paul has said (most agree that this looks back as far as 6:14, not just to
6:23) or they must be ignorant of the truth to which he proceeds. *Do you not
know* is the construction we saw in 6:3 (where see note). It implies that the
readers do know this and will go along with the argument as it is developed.
Paul has not used the affectionate address *brothers* since 1:13; it perhaps indicates that he is becoming emotionally involved. Certainly it brings out his
affection for those who are with him in Christ. He speaks to knowers of
"law", but what law? Some think he is referring to the Torah (Barrett,
Leenhardt, etc.), but it seems better to see the word as referring to "an obvious axiom of political justice—that death clears all scores, and that a dead
man can no longer be prosecuted or punished" (SH). This is so in Jewish law
and in Roman law, but it is not confined to these systems. All his readers
would recognize this truth. JB speaks of those "who have studied law",

---

1. CBQ, 46 (1984), p. 90. The whole article, "Paul's Use of Analogy: A Structural
Analysis of Romans 7:1-6", should be consulted.

which seems to mean that Paul is appealing to the experts. But he is surely referring to the common knowledge that people in general have rather than to the specialized knowledge of scholars. Everyone knows that the law's authority over a person[2] lasts his entire lifetime.[3] But no more. When life ceases, law ceases to hold sway.

2. Paul proceeds to a specific case, and his *for example* shows that it is an illustration and not a proof. *A married woman*[4] is bound by law to her living husband.[5] *But if*[6] *her husband dies,* the situation is radically altered. This is perhaps the only example in the New Testament of a situation in which death frees some living person who is then able to enter new relationships. It is not only the dead man over whom the law has no authority; this is true of the living woman as well. The man's death alters her obligations. NIV speaks of her as *released,*[7] but this translation is scarcely strong enough for the verb Paul uses. It means to render completely null and void. The apostle is saying that the woman's status as a wife has been abolished, completely done away. She is no longer a wife. And that means, of course, that the obligations proper to a wife have no relevance to her. She is removed from what Paul calls "the law of the husband" (NIV, *the law of marriage*). This is an unusual expression meaning "a husband-type law", a law binding in relation to or binding to a husband. She has no husband, and accordingly a "husband-type law" has no relevance for her.[8]

3. Paul brings out the logical consequence of what he has just said[9] by thinking of her as becoming "another man's".[10] If she does this during the

2. The word is ἄνθρωπος, a member of the human race, including females as well as males. It is a word he uses 126 times out of 548 in the New Testament, which is more than anyone else. In v. 2 he uses ἀνήρ, a male, a term for which he has no special preponderance (59 times out of 216; Acts has it 100 times).

3. ἐφ᾽ ὅσον χρόνον. The subject of ζῇ could grammatically be νόμος. But this is to be rejected since Paul nowhere has the idea that the law dies.

4. ὕπανδρος is found here only in the New Testament. It means "under" or "subject to a man", and thus reflects the Jewish understanding of marriage (an understanding widely accepted in the ancient world). It is used of married women in LXX (see Num. 5:20, 29; Prov. 6:24, 29).

5. The perfect δέδεται puts the continuing nature of the tie at its strongest, and the participle ζῶντι puts some emphasis on the husband as living.

6. ἐὰν δέ introduces the contrary supposition, but the form of the conditional implies nothing as to the fulfilment or otherwise of the condition.

7. κατήργηται (for this verb see on 3:3) is mostly used of things rather than persons, but this use is quite intelligible. The perfect points to a continuing result. The preposition ἀπό is not common with this verb, but BAGD note its use for release "from an association. . . ."

8. Many exegetes take the passage allegorically. Long ago Augustine saw the wife as the soul and the husband as the corrupt nature. This kind of thinking continues, though with different symbolism. O'Neill sees the husband and the wife as the body and the soul. See Little, CBQ, 46, p. 86 for other suggestions. I do not discuss such views because there seems no reason for thinking that Paul had this kind of symbolism in mind. If he did, the variety of views shows that we have little chance of recovering it.

9. For ἄρα οὖν see the note on 5:18.

10. ἐὰν γένηται ἀνδρὶ ἑτέρῳ. BDF see this as an exception to the rule that the genitive is used when possession is recent or the emphasis is on the possessor, the dative when the stress is on the object possessed (189 [2]). Many translations agree with NIV, *if she marries*

lifetime of her husband, she stamps herself as *an adulteress.*[11] If he is dead, she can do it with no stigma. There is a difficulty in that it is the husband who dies, while it is the wife who is free. Paul's point is that death, the death of either partner, dissolves the marriage. *Released* is really "free", Paul's second use of that adjective in this letter (see the note on 6:18 for the importance of freedom in Paul's thinking).[12] Being free from the law that bound her to the husband, she is no adulteress[13] even though she marries once more.

4. *So*[14] leads in to the consequence of the whole of the preceding (vv. 1-4) or perhaps to verse 1 with 2-3 illustrating it. The point is that this verse is not the consequence simply of the marriage illustration, as Cranfield points out. Since the law has no dominion when there has been a death, certain things follow for the Roman Christians. Again Paul uses the affectionate *my brothers* (cf. v. 1), while his *you also*[15] makes what follows personal to his correspondents. Paul is not laying down some abstruse theological point of no great practical significance, but something that applies to the Romans in their own situation. *You died* is rather "You were put to death",[16] and this death is a death to *the law*, where *the law* is used in a comprehensive sense. Some see a reference to the law of Moses, the law that meant so much to the Jews, but Paul is surely speaking of all law. Believers are through with law. It is not for them an option as a way of salvation. They do not seek to be right with God by obeying some form of law, as the adherents of almost all religions have done. There is a finality about death. Paul is pointing to a complete and final break with law. This does not mean antinomianism, as the apostle's whole argument in this part of his letter makes clear. The release "is not from the righteousness which is taught in the law, but from the rigid demands of the law and from the curse which follows from its demands" (Calvin). It is not the law that dies, but the believer. The law still points to the kind of living that is pleasing in the sight of God. But the believer is dead to all forms of legalism. He will engage in upright living as the result but not the cause of his salvation.

---

another man, and this is clearly the sense of it, even though Paul does not use the normal verb "to marry". Kertelge and others render "live with".

11. Paul uses μοιχαλίς twice in this verse and nowhere else. This is his one use of χρηματίζω (nine times in the New Testament). It refers to transacting business. From this there are two lines of development. One refers to answering questions that arise as business is transacted and leads to the meaning "answer as an oracle", "warn", and the like. The other starts from getting a name from one's business activities (many surnames are still those of a trade) and so comes to mean "to name", the meaning we have here.

12. Some adjectives are followed by a genitive, but "to be free from" always takes ἀπό (BDF 182 [3]).

13. The construction τοῦ + infinitive normally denotes purpose, but Paul frequently has it to convey result. Here Gifford sees purpose, BDF find it epexegetic (400 [8]), and Burton thinks it is result (398). Burton seems to be correct; she is free, and the result of that is that she is no adulteress.

14. ὥστε introduces the consequence. Moule says it is "simply an *inferential particle* as if ὥς τε, meaning *and so, accordingly*" (IBNTG, p. 144). The indicative that follows puts some emphasis on the factuality; it really happened.

15. καὶ ὑμεῖς.

16. The verb is θανατόω, not ἀποθνῄσκω. We are probably to see an action of God, not a death from natural causes.

To be put to death *through the body of Christ* is a most unusual expression, though the place of Christ's body is sometimes emphasized (e.g., Col. 1:22; Heb. 10:10; 1 Pet. 2:24). Some see a reference to the church as the body of Christ (e.g., Knox), and this is brought out in some translations. Thus NEB reads, "you . . . have died to the law by becoming identified with the body of Christ" (so GNB). But while that usage appears in some parts of the New Testament, it is difficult to find it here. In any case it raises the further question, "How does church membership put the believer to death?" It is much better to see a reference to the truth Paul emphasized in chapter 6, that we were "buried with him through baptism into death", that "we have been united with him in his death" (6:4, 5). The believer's death with Christ, Paul is now saying, is a death to the law. Salvation by grace, by trusting Christ, means a complete end to trust in the law.

Paul moves to the purpose of all this.[17] It was in order that we might belong to another,[18] described as *him who was raised from the dead*. Paul does not say "to another, even Jesus Christ", but refers to the resurrection. In this place where death is being given such emphasis, it is important to recognize that death is not the end. Christ conquered it. He was "born under law" (Gal. 4:4), and it could be said that all his life he lived "under law", right up to and including his death. But his resurrection finished all that. And Paul is saying that our death with Christ and resurrection to new life finished it for us (cf. Gal. 2:19). Since the construction resembles that which NIV translates "marries" in verse 3, some understand him to mean here that the believer is married to Christ. But whatever the verdict in verse 3, it seems that *belong* is the meaning here. While the New Testament refers to the church as the bride of Christ, this concept is not used of the individual believer, whereas we often get the thought that the believer is the slave of Christ.

Paul goes on to say that our belonging to Christ is not an end in itself. It takes place *in order that* we might have fruitful lives. Those who view the previous clause as referring to marriage with Christ often take *fruit* here to mean "offspring". Against this is the word itself, and also the fact that, though the church is spoken of elsewhere as the bride of Christ, there is never a reference to offspring in such passages. Moreover, the fruit is here borne not to Christ but to God. Paul seems clearly to be saying that believers are united to Christ for the purpose of producing qualities like love, joy, and the rest of "the fruit of the Spirit" (Gal. 5:22-23; cf. 2:19). Notice that Paul changes from "you" to "we" in this last clause. The obligation to produce "fruit" rests on him as much as on his correspondents.

5. *For*[19] relates verses 5-6 to the preceding and explains more fully what is meant. Paul looks back to the past and brings out a contrast with the new

---

17. εἰς τό normally introduces purpose, though Lenski sees it as result here. But purpose fits the context better.

18. γίνεσθαι ἀνδρί is used in v. 3 of being married, and some understand it that way here, as NEB, "you have found another husband in him". This is possible, but it seems more likely that NIV is correct.

19. γάρ.

life. He speaks of being "in the flesh" (NIV, *controlled by the sinful nature*). "Flesh" is a Pauline word (it occurs 91 times in Paul out of 147 in the New Testament; the most in any non-Pauline writing is 13 in John), and the apostle uses it in a variety of ways. It may refer to the soft constituent of the human body (1 Cor. 15:50), and thus to a human being (1 Cor. 1:29). It may mean human nature (Rom. 9:5), or this earthly life (Phil. 1:24), or human attainment (Phil. 3:3), from which it is not a long step to outward appearance (1 Cor. 1:26). But this body of flesh is weak (Rom. 6:19), and the thought of physical weakness leads on to that of moral weakness. It has this meaning here and very often in Paul. When "we were in the flesh" means when "we were characterized by fleshly desires and outlook", a meaning that NIV brings out in its paraphrase. Paul does not mean that the flesh is of itself evil. Indeed, his looking back to the time when we were in the flesh indicates that it is possible to live this life (and therefore to live in this body) without being "in the flesh". But the fact that the flesh is weak means that it is open to temptations of various kinds, and Paul is referring to a way of life that succumbs to those temptations, a life dominated by the lower part of human nature.

At that time the law aroused *the sinful passions*. There is something passive about *passions*,[20] which points to the fact that there is that in our human nature which all too readily leads to evil, those passions that lead to sin.[21] Gore speaks of "those feelings which we experience without any action of our will." These passions are further described as "through the law"; the law in some way brings them about.[22] JB quite misses this with "quite unsubdued by the Law", for Paul is not saying that the law tried unsuccessfully to control these passions. He is saying that the law brings them about. Lloyd-Jones comments that the passions "are actually inflamed even by the Law of God. The very law that prohibits them encourages us to do them, because *we* are impure. So morality teaching can even be a positive danger" (p. 80).[23] Paul is not saying simply that these were passions we had under the law, but that they worked *through* the law (cf. Haldane). The passions then *were at work*[24] in our bodies,[25] and they worked with a view to, or the result was,[26] the

20. πάθημα is explained by BAGD as "that which is suffered or endured"; it is mostly used in the plural, as here. Parry comments that the word denotes "concrete instances of πάθος, the state in which the subject is regarded as not active but receptive of experiences."

21. Cranfield thinks that the plural means "concrete acts of sin" rather than "sin as a condition or principle".

22. διὰ τοῦ νόμου. BAGD think διά here denotes the efficient cause.

23. Cf. Harrisville, "There is no talk here of a transgression of the law. The case is rather that the passions are aroused by the commandment, *whether or not* the commandment is fulfilled. We are thus sinners even when we keep the commandment!"

24. ἐνηργεῖτο is surely to be understood as middle, giving the thought that the passions worked powerfully and inwardly.

25. μέλεσιν means "members". Paul is speaking of the parts of our bodies, where NIV refers to our bodies as a whole.

26. The problem is the meaning of εἰς τό. The construction often signifies purpose, but here it seems better to see result.

bearing of fruit for death. Again Paul personifies death, and this time he sees it as receiving the fruit of sin. All that sin issues in makes for death.

6. The argument moves on with *But now*, where the contrast is "both temporal and logical" (Barrett; Cranfield prefers to see it as temporal), now that we are Christians in contrast to those who are in the flesh. Paul's verb is unexpected[27] and leads to a variety of translations: "discharged" (RSV, NEB), "stand clear of" (Phillips), "are free from" (GNB), "are done with" (Moffatt), "are rid of" (JB). But the basic meaning is tolerably clear. As far as the law is concerned we have been made null and void. There is no link between the believer and the law. Our salvation is not due to the law. We are delivered from the law because we have died to that by which we were held down.[28] The imagery may suggest that we were captives to the law and could not escape (cf. GNB, "held us prisoners").

The result[29] is a new way of service. Paul's verb[30] takes us back to the imagery of slavery which he used so effectively at the end of the previous chapter. He does not forget that, though the Christian is a liberated person, his service to God must be wholehearted, as wholehearted as that of a slave to his master. This is all the more striking since it occurs in a context where Paul is speaking of freedom from the law, a freedom of which he does not speak very often (as Käsemann reminds us, p. 190). To be free from the law is to be free to render more wholehearted service, service done "in newness of Spirit and not oldness of letter." The four nouns give a touch of solemnity to the expression. Paul contrasts letter and spirit elsewhere (2:29; 2 Cor. 3:6-7). It is important for Christians to be clear that the service in which they engage cannot be fulfilled by strict conformity to the letter of any directions whatever.[31] We should not take "letter" as pointing to the essence of the law, for Paul can assure us that the law is "spiritual" (v. 14). But the letter is of no avail[32] in our service of God. That service is a thing of the spirit and of the Spirit. It demands our human spirit, but it cannot be carried out without the

27. κατηργήθημεν. See on 3:3.
28. The verb κατέχω is used in 1:18 of sinners "holding down" the truth, here of sinners being held down by the law. This is one place where KJV misleads; it translates, "that being dead wherein we were held". But it is not the law that dies; it is sinners.
29. The construction is ὥστε + infinitive, which leads some to see a possibility rather than a result; Moffatt, e.g., has "so that we can serve", and Phillips "we are free to serve", whereas NIV renders *so that we serve*. But this construction may be used in the sense of result, and it is best to take it this way here (see BDF 391 [2], Cranfield, Lenski, etc.).
30. δουλεύειν.
31. "Oldness", παλαιότης, is not a common word, being found here only in the New Testament. "Letter" is not so unusual. G. Schrenk comments on the present passage, "Without Christ and the Spirit what is written is absolutely ineffective" (TDNT, I, p. 766). He distinguishes between Paul's use of γράμμα and γραφή: "γράμμα is not used when he speaks of the positive and lasting significance of Scripture. This positive task is always stated in terms of γραφή. When the reference is to γράμμα, Paul is always thinking of the legal authority which has been replaced" (p. 768).
32. Notice the use of οὐ where μή might have been expected. It makes for an emphatic contrast.

help of the Spirit of God. This is not a commonplace of religion, but a new insight which matters very much to Paul. He has a similar thought elsewhere, though he puts it in different words (Gal. 2:19-20).

C. Is the Law Sin? 7:7-12

Enormous controversy has surrounded Paul's exact meaning in the remainder of chapter 7. In particular there has been a great deal of discussion about whether Paul is concerned here with his own spiritual history, or with that of Jews,[33] or of Christians, or of people in general,[34] and, if himself or other Christians, whether he is referring to the experience of the regenerate or the unregenerate.[35] It is probable that such questions will never be answered to the satisfaction of everyone. But it is worth making a few comments.

First, we should be clear that Paul is writing about the law, not trying to answer the questions that modern people ask. This passage is not primarily a piece of personal autobiography or a psychological study of the Christian experience. It is a sustained treatment of the place of the law. For the Jew the law was central, and Paul has denied that the Jew was right. He has said that in any case the Jew has broken the law (2:27). He has denied that anyone is justified by the law (3:20). He has argued that the believer is not under law (6:14), and that he has died to the law (7:4). He has spoken of "the sinful passions aroused by the law" (7:5). Where does that leave the law? Is the Christian to regard it as something evil and discard it? Or is it still God's law? It is with such questions that Paul is concerning himself, and we should not lose sight of where his argument leads in our anxiety to get answers to questions Paul is not asking.

That said, it is still true that our questions are important to us and that Paul's words have some bearing on them. Is he talking about himself or about

33. Cf. J. Christiaan Beker, "Romans 7 is not a description of Christian life or, primarily, an autobiography of Paul's Pharisaic life. Rather, a Christian looks here, in the context of an apology of the law, in hindsight at the plight of the Jews under the law and describes their objective condition of despair . . . a Christian interpretation of Jewish existence under the law is the primary subject matter of Romans 7" (*Paul the Apostle* [Edinburgh, 1980], p. 238; he agrees that there is "an autobiographical element" in this chapter [p. 240]). D. J. Moo can say, "In vv. 7-12, then, it seems best to conclude that Paul describes the experience of Israel at Sinai but uses the first person because he himself, as a Jew, has been affected by that experience" (NTS, 32 [1986], p. 129).

34. Hans Conzelmann says, "Here Paul is describing man in revolt. . . . He is not, however, picturing his feelings before his conversion, but the way in which he later came to know himself through faith. Only faith shows me that without faith I was objectively in despair" (*An Outline of the Theology of the New Testament* [London, 1969], p. 163). He also says that in Rom. 7:7ff. Paul "expounds the history of paradise and the fall as the history of the ego" (*1 Corinthians* [Philadelphia, 1975], p. 45). But this seems to be reading a lot into the text.

35. D. J. W. Milne discusses the possibilities in an article entitled "Romans 7:7-12, Paul's Pre-conversion Experience" (RThR, XLIII [1984], pp. 9-17). He contends strongly for "the autobiographical, pre-Christian view of Romans 7:7-12" (p. 16).

other people? It is surely impossible to deny that Paul is speaking of himself in what he is saying. In this chapter he keeps on using the first person singular pronoun though he has not done this since the opening of his letter.[36] Now he does so consistently, sometimes using the emphatic pronoun. Moreover, words like "What a wretched man I am! Who will rescue me from this body of death?" (v. 24) are impossibly theatrical if they apply to other people, but not to Paul himself. As C. E. Raven put it, "It is a mistaken reverence that explains his cry of bitterness as referring to others. . . . St. Paul does not write at second-hand, but shares with us the intimacy of his own spiritual struggle."[37] The emotional content found throughout the passage points to personal involvement.

But we should also bear in mind that Paul can use "I" when he is referring to people in general. Thus he writes to the Corinthians, "If I speak in the tongues of men and of angels, but have not love . . ." (1 Cor. 13:1), where it is impossible to hold that he means the words to apply to himself only. He is referring to something that is true of everybody, but he makes it more vivid by applying the words to himself. Add to this the fact that it is not easy to apply to Paul, or for that matter to any Jew who had been circumcised on the eighth day, words like "Once I was alive apart from law" (v. 9). Would such an expression be naturally applied to a man who had been brought up as "a Hebrew of Hebrews; in regard to the law, a Pharisee" (Phil. 3:5)? Again, Paul said that in his pre-Christian days he was "as for legalistic righteousness, faultless" (Phil. 3:5). We wonder accordingly whether the words in this passage are words which Paul would naturally use of himself in a piece of personal autobiography. It seems more likely that he is using language that should be given a wider application.

It seems, then, that we cannot exclude Paul from the scope of these words, nor can we exclude others. It is best to see the apostle as identifying himself with the sinner. He is speaking from the standpoint of a convinced Christian and telling us from his own experience what happens to any sinner who is confronted with the law. Throughout verses 7-11 the tense is past; Paul is referring to his preconversion experience.[38]

Paul, then, is describing his confrontation with the law, but doing so representatively. The previous argument might be misunderstood to mean

36. "I am using a human argument" (3:5; 6:19) is not a real exception, and the "I" of 3:7; 4:17 does not refer to Paul.

37. *Jesus and the Gospel of Love* (London, 1931), p. 315. So also Parry, "The personal element is too definite, too sustained and even too passionate, to allow the hypothesis of mere imagination" (p. 217).

38. Cf. Harrisville, "Paul in Romans 7 identifies himself with the sinner, and for this reason uses the 'I-style' in vv 7ff., and the present tense in vv 14ff. What he writes, the sinner would have to say if he could speak of himself. But the text is blunter when hastily treated as the introspection of the Christian, or as the confession of the sinner prior to his coming to faith." Hodge comments, "That he does not speak for himself only; that it is not anything in his own individual experience, peculiar to himself, is obvious from the whole context."

tł:at the law, being linked with sin and with death, is evil like they are. The apostle makes it clear that the law is not sin; rather, the law enables us to recognize sin for the evil thing it is.[39]

> [7]What shall we say, then? Is the law sin? Certainly not! Indeed I would not have known what sin was except through the law. For I would not have known what it was to covet if the law had not said, "Do not covet."[a] [8]But sin, seizing the opportunity afforded by the commandment, produced in me every kind of covetous desire. For apart from law, sin is dead. [9]Once I was alive apart from law; but when the commandment came, sin sprang to life and I died. [10]I found that the very commandment that was intended to bring life actually brought death. [11]For sin, seizing the opportunity afforded by the commandment, deceived me, and through the commandment put me to death. [12]So then, the law is holy, and the commandment is holy, righteous and good.

> [a]7 Exodus 20:17; Deut 5:21

7. The argument advances with a couple of rhetorical questions. *What shall we say, then?* is a deliberative device Paul has used before (6:1; cf. 9:14). *Is the law sin?* puts the question somewhat more sharply than "Is the law sinful?" Clearly, that the law is evil is a conclusion he thinks some may have erroneously drawn from some of the things he has been saying (cf. 5:20; 6:14). But this is far from his thinking, and he repudiates it with the vigorous *Certainly not!*[40] On the contrary,[41] he would not have come to know[42] sin had it not been for the law. We could translate "I did not know sin, except through law."[43] Paul does not mean that people without the law do not know sin at all; he has said the opposite (2:14-15; 5:12-14). All people have some idea of right and wrong; a moral code of some sort is almost universal. People who do not have the law may well know that they have done wrong. But people without God's law do not see wrongdoing as it really is, as sin against God. There is a

39. From very early times Paul's "I" has been taken to refer to Adam. Käsemann holds that "the event depicted can refer strictly only to Adam. . . . There is nothing in the passage which does not fit Adam, and everything fits Adam alone" (p. 196). This last statement is certainly exaggerated, for in the Adam story there is nothing about the command not to covet, of which Paul makes so much (Gen. 3:6 is sometimes urged, but this is not a command not to covet). Cranfield cites a number of writers who hold that Paul is speaking in the name of Adam, but he finds this view "forced". His own view is "that Paul is using the first person singular in a generalizing way without intending a specific reference to any particular individual or clearly defined group, in order to depict vividly the situation of man in the absence of law and in its presence."

40. For μὴ γένοιτο see on 3:4.

41. This is the force of the strong adversative ἀλλά.

42. The aorist is inceptive. Paul uses two verbs for "know" in this verse, ἔγνων and ᾔδειν. Some see a difference in meaning, but this is not apparent. The difference in tense may be more significant, with the aorist meaning "come to know" and the pluperfect used as an imperfect, "keep on knowing".

43. The usual translation assumes that in his onward rush Paul has omitted ἄν. Strictly this should have been inserted, but it is sometimes omitted (see BDF 360 [1]), so the conditional translation is quite in order. But some prefer to take the words exactly as they stand: "I did not know sin. . . ."

great difference between the breaching of a human moral code and sin, that evil thing which God forbids. It takes the law to show wrongdoing to be sin. And to see my misdeeds as sin against God inevitably means that I am troubled and begin to see my need of a Savior. There is a healing function in the law's work of convicting the sinner.

Paul appends an example.[44] The tenth commandment is particularly well suited to his purpose, for it is the only one that explicitly goes beyond the outward action to the inner root of the action, though as we see from the way Jesus handled some of the other commandments, this is the way they should all be interpreted (Matt. 5:21ff.). The noun NIV renders as *what it was to covet*[45] denotes strong desire in general and is occasionally used in the New Testament of good desires (e.g., Luke 22:15). But in the overwhelming number of cases the strong desire is a lust for evil things, and "covet" is a good way of bringing this out. The command is cited from LXX (Exod. 20:17; Deut. 5:21), though without the objects there specified. GNB misses Paul's concentration on the inwardness by adding an object: "Do not desire what belongs to someone else." It is, of course, wrong to desire other people's property, but Paul's point is that behind the desire for specific objects is a desire that is blameworthy in itself. As Barrett says, it is desire that is guilty "independently of its object, and sinful though quite possibly respectable. Desire means precisely that exaltation of the *ego* which we have seen to be of the essence of sin". It means putting the sinner in the supreme place. Paul elsewhere links this evil desire with idolatry (Col. 3:5). He says that love is the fulfilling of the law (13:10), but this is the love of the self that takes the place of the love for God and man that the believer should manifest.[46] It is possible that translations like RSV, "I should not have known what it is to covet" (NIV is similar), are missing something of Paul's meaning. He is not saying that he did not know the meaning of the word. He is saying that he did not know the thing. The law brought home to him coveting, his coveting. In the light of the law he came to know his sin.

8. Paul pictures sin in vigorous action. He uses a picturesque term[47]

---

44. τε indicates a close connection (BDF 443 [3]; they suggest that we supply here "as well as the ἁμαρτία mentioned above"). Cf. Parry, "This isolated τε introduces a particular example of the effect of law from the 10th Commandment: almost = even, or in particular".

45. ἐπιθυμία. The corresponding verb follows in *Do not covet*. LB brings out the inwardness by translating "I would never have known the sin in my heart. . . ." As earlier in the verse, we have the indicative without ἄν, but this time it is not as easy to take it to mean "I did not know" because of the following εἰ μή with finite verb. BDF regard this as an example of the omission of ἄν in the apodosis of contrary-to-fact conditions (360 [1]); μή is the negative with the unreal indicative (428 [2]).

46. "The essential point in ἐπιθυμία is that it is desire as impulse, as a motion of the will. It is, in fact, lust, since the thought of satisfaction gives pleasure and that of non-satisfaction pain. ἐπιθυμία is anxious self-seeking" (F. Büchsel, TDNT, III, p. 171).

47. ἀφορμή (ἀφ᾽ ὁρμή) is that from which an attack is launched, a starting point, or a base of operations. NIV has *opportunity*. Paul has the word in all six of its New Testament occurrences.

which depicts sin as engaging in a military operation. Sin made the commandment[48] its base of operations and from that vantage point *produced in me every kind of covetous desire*.[49] It is a distressing fact about human nature that any prohibition tends to awake in us a desire to transgress that prohibition. The standard illustration is the passage in Augustine's *Confessions* in which he speaks of the time as a boy when he joined his companions in stealing pears, not because they wanted them (they fed them to pigs), but because they wanted the pleasure of disobeying the law. Foreman cites a most unlikely theologian in Mark Twain. "This plain-spoken American said that most idealists overlooked one feature of the human make-up which is very prominent, namely, plain mulishness or perverseness. Mark Twain said that if a mule thinks he knows what you want him to do he will do just the opposite, and Twain admitted he was like that himself—often mean for the sake of meanness. But the fault lies not in the ideal but in the man who reacts against it." The point of it all is that until the command not to do an evil thing comes we may not feel much urge to do it, but when we hear the command our native mulishness takes over. But the fault is not in the command. It is in the mulishness, in the sinner.

Paul explains by saying that *apart from law*[50] *sin is dead* (cf. 5:13).[51] If there is no law, clearly there is no transgression of law. Without a commandment there can be no disobedience. Paul is establishing the point that the law does not in practice function as a means of salvation. Rather, it is a means of establishing people's guilt. It gives them something to sin against and in this way is an ally of sin. The commandment is aimed at our good, but it is quite possible for us to view it as a limitation on our freedom. Seen in that light it becomes a cause of resentment and opposition. Without something to rebel against there could be no rebels.

9. Paul starts this verse with an emphatic *I*, perhaps because he wants to differentiate himself from the sin of which he has just been speaking, perhaps because he wants to make it clear that he is involved, that he knows what he is talking about, perhaps because he wants to convey a universal sense.[51a] He is

48. In this passage Paul uses both νόμος and ἐντολή without much difference of meaning. G. Schrenk comments, "the ἐντολή is both the concrete Mosaic Law and the characteristic mark of the Law, i.e. its character as command" (TDNT, II, p. 552).

49. Most translations agree with NIV in taking διὰ τῆς ἐντολῆς with ἀφορμὴν δὲ λαβοῦσα. But it is better to take it with κατειργάσατο, "produced in me through the commandment. . . ." This is favored by the word order (cf. v. 13) and the use of διά (the commandment is not that "through" which sin obtained its base of operations, but is that base).

50. νόμος lacks the article, but Paul can scarcely mean law in general. He is speaking about the law of God, the law we see in the Old Testament.

51. The Greek does not supply a verb here. If we understand the words as referring to Paul alone, we should read "was"; if we hold them to have a general reference, then "is" is correct.

51a. Cf. TH, "He begins by interpreting his own experience in the light of the account in Genesis 3. But he also assumes that every other man's experience is similar to his own, and so what he says has relevance for all men in all periods of history."

referring to Paul, but he is also referring to Everyman.[52] His *once*[53] makes it clear that he is talking about a past experience, not a present reality. There has been a good deal of discussion of the meaning of *I was alive apart from*[54] *law*. It is difficult to see how a Jewish boy from a pious family could ever be *apart from law*, for from his earliest days he would have some instruction in the way to serve God.[55] But he may mean *apart from law*, in the sense that there had been a time in his experience when he had not realized the force of the law's demands, a time when he was "under no conviction of sin" (Hendriksen). Elsewhere he himself refers to a time when he had been "blameless" as regards the righteousness of the law (Phil. 3:6). This will be not unlike the rich young ruler who, confronted with the law's demands, said, "All these I have kept since I was a boy" (Luke 18:21). Paul is referring to the life of the natural man, the happy pagan, the person who lives cheerfully with no reference to law and with an untroubled conscience.[56] He is not alive with the life that the New Testament writers so often speak about. He is alive in the sense that he has never been put to death as a result of a confrontation with the law of God. His lack of remorse and his enjoyment of the evil he does make up a sorry imitation of that life which is life indeed. But Paul is emphasizing that the law puts the sinner to death. The person of whom he is writing has not died as a result of a confrontation with the law. In that sense he is alive.

But then *the commandment came*. The commandment may mean the law of God in general, or it may point particularly to the commandment of which Paul has been speaking, the commandment not to covet. Whichever way we take it, the commandment of course had been in existence long before Paul appeared. His meaning is not that it had its origin in Paul's day, but as Moffatt translates, "the command came home to me" (cf. Calvin, "when it has begun to be truly understood"). Hunter remarks, "there is no period in life to which a man can look back as the time when he had no conscience. Still, there comes a day when we come rudely up against the demands of the moral law".[57] It is that day of which Paul is speaking, a day we can recognize, for we too have

52. BDF 281 see the use of the first person in this passage, like the use of the second person in a number of other passages, as a way of referring to any third person in order to illustrate something universal in a vivid manner.

53. ποτέ, "of time *at some time or other* of the past" (BAGD).

54. χωρίς, "apart from", is found in Paul 16 times out of its 41 New Testament occurrences.

55. Cf. Harrison, "there was actually no time in his life before his conversion when he was unrelated to the law."

56. Cragg refers to "The Problem of the Happy Pagan" and speaks of people who take it as perfectly natural to engage in dishonest practices and the like. "For them in any real sense the commandment has not come."

57. Cf. Simeon, "None are so blind as to think they have never sinned; but the generality suppose that they have never sinned in any great degree." Not appreciating the seriousness of their sin, they are at ease. Cf. Scott, "The savage who has never learned anything of moral restraint is happy; misery begins when you know better, and are still enslaved by desires and impulses which are destroying your soul" (p. 47).

come to see God's demand for what it is and to see that alongside that demand our lives don't measure up.

Then, Paul says, *sin sprang to life and I died*. Sin was there but dormant. When the commandment came home to him, it was no longer possible to overlook its existence. Paul puts this vividly with sin *sprang to life*.[58] Now he could not but see himself as a sinner, condemned before God. The result was death. LB translates ". . . a sinner, doomed to die." But Paul does not say "I was doomed to die", but "I died" (cf. v. 24). When the commandment "came" it killed forever the proud Pharisee thanking God that he was not as other men and sure of his merits before God. It killed off the happy sinner, for it showed him the seriousness, not so much of sin in general as of his own sin. The "coming" of the law in that sense always kills off our cheerful assumption of innocence. We see ourselves for what we really are, sinners, and we die. This is not the death "to sin" of which Paul wrote earlier (6:2, etc.). That is a saving death, a death we die in our union with Christ, a death that frees us from our bondage to sin. Here the thought is rather that to realize that we are not good and decent people in God's sight is a death. It marks the end of self-confidence, self-satisfaction, self-reliance. It is death.[59]

10. The commandment, Paul goes on, was "unto life" (NIV, *was intended to bring life*).[60] If kept faithfully it would have brought life, as Jesus assured a lawyer who asked about eternal life (Luke 10:28; cf. Lev. 18:5; Ps. 19:7-10; Ezek. 20:11; Rom. 10:5). The law was not designed to bring death; it directed people in the way of righteousness and peace and thus was meant to promote life. But Paul did not keep it faithfully any more than anybody else did, and the result was death. Paul says the commandment "was found to me";[61] the passive indicates that he did not find it as a result of vigorous search. Rather, it was disclosed without any initiative of his own. He puts some emphasis on the fact that *the very commandment* that was meant to produce life brought death to him.[62]

11. Again Paul uses the imagery of the base of operations (as in v. 8), and again it is sin that made the commandment its base. This time he has the new thought that sin *deceived* him. It may well be that the language is sug-

---

58. The verb ἀναζάω strictly means "come to life again", but BAGD see its use here as "*spring into life* with loss of the force of ἀνά". NIV well brings out the force of the aorist with *sprang to life*.

59. Barclay comments, "No man ever took a forbidden thing without thinking that it would make him happy, and no man ever found that it did." Nonsense. There are and always have been happy thieves. But in them honesty has died. Sin always means death of some sort.

60. εἰς before ζωήν signifies purpose or intended result, while that before θάνατον means actual result.

61. Chrysostom comments: "He does not say, 'it was made,' or 'it brought forth' death, but 'was found,' so explaining the novel and unusual kind of discrepancy, and making the whole fall upon their own pate . . . the fault is with them that received the commandment, and not of this, which was leading them to life."

62. Notice his word order in the Greek and the use of the emphatic αὕτη.

gested by Genesis 3:13,[63] where Eve says that the serpent deceived her (for the deceiving of Eve cf. 2 Cor. 11:3; 1 Tim. 2:14). The deceit took various forms. The tempter had said, "You will not surely die" (Gen. 3:4; this shows that he was a liar, for they did die), he had concentrated on the negative (they should not eat from this one tree; he ignored the positive, they could eat from every other tree), he had implied that the commandment raised doubts about God's good will. Some element of deceit is always involved in temptation, for it makes the evil alluring and obscures the fact that it means death in the end. We should not, however, press the connection with Genesis too hard, for it is Paul's thought that we sinned in Adam, not Eve. Here he apparently means that sin took advantage of the fact that one does not expect God's commandment to be the occasion of death and it thus used that commandment to bring about death. We should be clear that it was not the commandment that slew Paul. God's commandment is always directed towards life. It was sin that killed the apostle. Sin took advantage of the situation and used the commandment to bring about Paul's death.

12. *So then*[64] introduces the consequence, the conclusion to which this reasoning leads up. The expression is elliptical,[65] and its terseness highlights Paul's point—the law is not sin as was suggested (v. 7). The law may have been used by sin, but that does not make sin and law identical or even put them in the same class. *The law is holy* (JB, "sacred"), which puts it as far away from sin as possible. The law is God's law, and it takes its character from him. He is holy ("Holy, holy, holy is the LORD Almighty", Isa. 6:3), and his law accordingly is holy. It is possible that we should see no significant difference between *the law* and *the commandment* (though Godet finds in the law "the Mosaic system in its entirety" and in the commandment "each article of the code in particular"). But the commandment not to covet has been given special emphasis in the preceding argument, and it may be that Paul has it particularly in mind here. Whichever way we take it, the commandment, he says, is *holy*, a quality he has just assigned to the law. It is also *righteous* or "just". It makes no unfair demands; it is equitable; it is not unjust in condemning sinners. And it is *good*. It has our welfare in mind, not our hurt. It is beneficent in its outlook and aim. Paul leaves the reader in no doubt about the high place he assigns to the law even if he emphatically rejects it as a way of salvation. He is just as firm in his acceptance of it for right purposes as in his rejection of it for wrong ones.

---

63. Paul's verb is ἐξηπάτησεν, a strengthened form of ἀπατάω, the verb used in LXX of Gen. 3:13. ἐξαπατάω is found six times in Paul and nowhere else in the New Testament.

64. ὥστε, inferential; see Moule's comment on v. 4.

65. There is no verb in the sentence, and ὁ μέν looks for an answering ὁ δέ, which, however, does not come. Cranfield sees "an implicit contrast between the law and sin".

D. Did the Good Law Cause Death? 7:13-25

It is important to keep in mind throughout this section that Paul is basically concerned with the law. The question of whether he is talking about the regenerate or the unregenerate is at the center of much modern discussion (and it is a question we cannot avoid). But this is not Paul's subject. He is dealing with the law and following up certain things he has already said. Christians are not "under law" but "under grace" (6:14). Like the woman whose husband has died, they are free from the law (v. 3), they have died to it (v. 4), have been made quite unresponsive to it (v. 6). Paul has denied that the law is sin, but he has said that it is the law that gives knowledge of sin (v. 7). Apart from the law sin is dead (v. 8). Sin made God's commandment its base of operations and slew Paul (v. 11). In the light of all this it is easy to ask, "Where does that leave the law? Is it an evil thing that keeps killing people?" Paul cannot leave the subject with this as a deduction people are likely to make. In the latter part of chapter 7, he is basically concerned with the question he poses in verse 13; he is demonstrating that the law does not bring death. He has just said that it is holy, and he carries on from there. Nine times he uses the word "law" in verses 14-25, not always with the same meaning. But there can be no doubt that law is his concern in this part of his letter.[66]

There is autobiography here, but the passage is not basically Paul's account of his spiritual experience. He is not saying, "I will tell you what happened to me. You can profit from my example." Rather he is saying, "This is how the law confronts people. Let me illustrate it from my own experience."[67] Had it been simply a piece of autobiography it would doubtless have been clearer whether we should see the regenerate or the unregenerate here. But Paul is talking about the law and its demands and showing the reader what the law cannot do.[68]

In the early church most people thought that Paul was here referring to the unregenerate state. Augustine held this at first, but more mature reflection caused him to affirm that what Paul said was true of the regenerate, too. This view came to be widely accepted, and throughout the Middle Ages most exegetes saw the passage this way. There was a variety of opinion at the Reformation, with thinkers like Erasmus favoring the reference to the unregenerate and Luther, Calvin, and others seeing Paul as speaking of the regenerate. Subsequently Arminians and Pietists have tended to take the

66. "It is important to remember that the whole section is an analysis of man's state under law" (CGT on v. 25). Krister Stendahl says, "Paul is here involved in an interpretation of the Law, a defense for the holiness and goodness of the Law" (*Paul Among Jews and Gentiles* [Philadelphia, 1976], p. 92). Stendahl perhaps minimizes the autobiographical element in what Paul is saying, but he is right in emphasizing the place of the law in Paul's argument.

67. Cf. Manson, "In 14-20 man's predicament is more closely analysed. He is no free agent to say Yes or No to the law's demands."

68. Lloyd-Jones comments, "sanctification by the Law is as impossible as was justification by the Law" (on v. 7 [p. 110]).

passage of the unregenerate, while those in the Calvinist tradition have argued that the regenerate are in mind. In recent times Kümmel, Bultmann, and Althaus are cited as leading holders of the view that sees the unregenerate in the passage, with Nygren and Cranfield stoutly contending for the regenerate. It cannot be said that there is anything like a consensus.[69]

With such a long-lasting and sometimes bitter division it is clear that the problem is a difficult one. Strong arguments are brought forward for both points of view. It is important to approach the subject bearing this in mind and with a sympathetic understanding of those who view things differently. We proceed to notice some of the arguments that are brought forward for each of the two viewpoints. First, those that favor the regenerate.

1. *The present tense* is used throughout this section, which contrasts with the past tenses throughout the preceding section. It is argued that it would be unnatural and artificial to take this to mean something that was completely in the past. It is countered that no attention is drawn to this, so that Paul is not making a clear contrast with his former way of life. There is something in this, but it is still true that the string of present tenses is impressive and difficult to refer to something that lies wholly in the past. It is also pointed out that Paul uses the emphatic *egō* six times in this passage, which more naturally refers to Paul as he is than to Paul as he was. Paul's language, the way he chooses to express himself, points more naturally to his present experience than to his recollection of the past.[70]

2. *Paul's view of the unbeliever* is given in 1:18–3:20. It is very different from this. But we must bear in mind that Paul can speak of those not regenerate as having conflicting thoughts (2:15).

3. *Paul's view of himself before conversion* is very different from this. He was a persecutor, advancing in Judaism and very zealous for the traditions (Gal. 1:13-14). It is clear that he prided himself on his achievements and that he was not deeply grieved by his inability to keep all the law. He speaks of himself then as "faultless" (Phil. 3:6). Robinson says of his account of himself in this latter passage: "All these he regards as valuable assets he was prepared to write off, not as a way of life which was by then paying no dividends anyhow."[71] Leenhardt also reminds us that "The conversion of Paul was not that of a heart burdened by remorse for its acts of disobedience, but rather that of a proud soul exalting itself before God because of its obedience to the law" (p. 181).

4. *The Christian life* is the theme of chapters 5–8, not that of the un-

---

69. There are many discussions of the problem. Perhaps it will be sufficient to refer to the useful account in Robinson, pp. 81-95.

70. In discussing the contention that Paul is dealing with his inner situation before he became a Christian Knox says, "the only basis for such a judgment lies in this supposed impossibility; there is nothing in Paul's *language* to suggest that he is remembering the past rather than describing the present."

71. Robinson, p. 83. Cf. E. Stauffer, "The Damascus event is hardly the conversion of a despairing sinner but the calling and overthrow of a self-righteous Pharisee" (TDNT, II, p. 358).

believer. If Paul now turns to the unbeliever, it is contended, we are justified in looking for some indication. But against that verses 7-8 speak of coming to know sin and thus of the pre-Christian experience; so the point is not decisive.

5. *The will is directed towards the good* throughout this passage. That cannot be said of the unregenerate. The subject agrees with the law (v. 16); he desires the good (vv. 18, 19, 21). It is "no longer" he that does evil (vv. 17, 20), which implies that formerly he did and thus points to a new, regenerate status. He hates sin (v. 15). It is pointed out that Job could be described as "blameless and upright" but that he could still say, "I despise myself and repent in dust and ashes" (Job 1:1; 42:6). Other such scriptural statements could be cited. Paul speaks of himself here as "unspiritual" (v. 14; better, "carnal" or "fleshy"), but this does not mean that he has "the sinful mind" (8:7; "the mind of the flesh"), for with his mind he serves God's law (v. 25). This is not a description of the unregenerate (Murray develops this).

6. *Paul's view of life apart from Christ* is not the meaning when he says things like "I myself in my mind am a slave to God's law" (v. 25), or "if I do what I do not want to do, it is no longer I who do it" (v. 20).

7. *The tension* between will and action agrees with Paul's view of the Christian experience.[72] It is pointed out that in 8:23 Paul says we "groan inwardly as we wait eagerly . . .", but nobody doubts that this is the experience of the regenerate. Similarly Paul speaks of beating his body (1 Cor. 9:27), which points to some form of division in the regenerate. He is the chief of sinners (1 Tim. 1:15). He speaks of the flesh and the Spirit as in conflict (Gal. 5:17), though it should be pointed out that this is in a context where he exhorts his readers to live by the Spirit so that "you will not gratify the desires of the sinful nature" (Gal. 5:16). While Paul clearly holds that the Christian life is a victorious life, he does not see the victory as unclouded and without conflict. The flesh is to be reckoned with even in the life of the regenerate.

8. *Verse 25*, where "I myself in my mind am a slave to God's law, but in the sinful nature a slave to the law of sin" follows "Thanks be to God— through Jesus Christ our Lord", is difficult to assign to an unbeliever. There are difficulties regarding this verse on any view, but "Thanks be to God" is certainly the cry of the believer.

But those who feel that the passage refers to the unregenerate draw attention to other considerations.

1. *Sin is not defeated* in this section, and it is asked, "Does Paul really hold that Christ cannot overcome sin in the believer?" This is a strong point. Elsewhere Paul insists that sin is not supreme: "sin shall not be your master" (6:14). The struggle of which Paul writes here, it is suggested, is the experience of the unregenerate, not necessarily as the unregenerate would describe it but as the believer would regard it when he looked back on it.

---

72. "He has in mind the tension which exists, in the Christian life, between will and action, between intention and performance" (Nygren, p. 293).

2. *The Christian life* is one of peace, not inner conflict (cf. ch. 8).

3. *Jesus Christ* is not mentioned until verse 25 (apart from v. 4), and *the Holy Spirit* is not mentioned in the passage at all. But the presence of the Spirit is a distinctive mark of the Christian. This cannot be the believer speaking, it is said.

4. *"I know that nothing good lives in me"* (v. 18) is not the verdict of the believer.

5. *"What a wretched man I am! Who will rescue me from this body of death?"* (v. 24) is an impossible cry from the one who has been already rescued by Christ. The same could be said of other parts of this passage, such as "a slave to sin" (v. 14) and "a prisoner of the law of sin at work within my members" (v. 23).

6. *The unregenerate as seen by the regenerate*, not as seen by themselves, is said to be the natural understanding of the words. Paul is speaking of the commencement of the Christian life.

7. *Now* in 8:1 marks a contrast with the preceding. Chapter 8 with its description of the victorious Christian life is thus set over against chapter 7. Therefore Paul is not here describing the believer.

Thus a good deal can be said on both sides. There have been some variants. C. Leslie Mitton, for example, in a series of articles in the *Expository Times* argues that a simple reference to either the regenerate or the unregenerate is not good enough. He prefers to see a reference to man under the law or to a Christian who has lapsed.[73] Ronald Y.-K. Fung thinks of the legalistic or immature Christian.[74] Griffith Thomas thinks "a Jew under the Mosaic law" is primarily in mind, but he holds also that "The one point of the passage is that it describes a man who is trying to be good and holy by his own efforts and is beaten back every time by the power of indwelling sin"; it thus refers to anyone, "regenerate or unregenerate".

Such views have not convinced many, though a good deal can be said for the view that it applies to everyone trying to overcome evil in his own strength. But with every respect to those who take the opposite opinion I do not see how it can be denied that what Paul says refers to the regenerate. This is not the whole story: Romans 7 leads right on into Romans 8. But it is part of the story and an important part.[75] Paul is not talking here about the whole of his experience but what happens when the believer sins. It is not true to Christian life to say, "This cannot be the experience of the believer, which is found rather in chapter 8."

For surely this *is* the experience of the believer. No believer is com-

73. ET, LXV (1953-54), pp. 78-81, 99-103, 132-35.

74. *Scripture, Tradition, and Interpretation*, ed. W. Ward Gasque and William Sanford LaSor (Grand Rapids, 1978), pp. 34-48.

75. J. I. Packer argues that the passage "reproduces Paul's present theological self-knowledge as a Christian: not all of it, but just that part of it which is germane to the subject in hand—namely, the function of the law in giving knowledge of sin" (*Studia Evangelica*, II [Berlin, 1964], p. 626).

pletely sinless. He is still a sinner, no matter how much out of character his sin is. What happens when he does sin? He feels dreadful about it. Then why does he do it? He simply does not understand (v. 15). In view of all that Christ has done for him and the resources Christ makes available for him, surely he should have resisted the temptation? He does not want to sin. He knows that. He knows that he ought not sin. But he is weak ("in the flesh"). Because he does not want to sin he can say with Paul, "I do what I do not want to do" (v. 16). When he reflects on that sin he is apt to say, "nothing good lives in me" (v. 18). But he cannot deny his responsibility; his sin proceeds from what he is. He knows that he did it himself. But his regret is deep and genuine, and he cries, "O wretched man that I am!" The sin is not the product of regeneration; it takes place despite regeneration. There is that within the believer (the old Adam?) which leads him to sin even when he does not want to. And when he sins he cannot but see that there is a power of evil that is too strong for him; thus he is enslaved to sin (v. 14), a prisoner (v. 23). But his inability to explain how he, a regenerate and redeemed person, falls into sin does not give him license to deny either the fact of his sin or the fact of his regeneration. On the wider view this is not the whole story. Most of the time and characteristically the believer is on top, victorious over evil and at peace. But at the moment he realizes that he has sinned it *is* the whole of the story for the person with a sensitive conscience (cf. Ps. 38:3-5, and notice what the vision of the Lord did to the prophet, Isa. 6:5). Paul is giving expression to the horror of sin committed. It matters little that the sin is occasional. This is the way the sensitive believer views it when it happens.

It is worth bearing in mind that the great saints through the ages do not commonly say, "How good I am!" Rather, they are apt to bewail their sinfulness. "Go away from me, Lord; I am a sinful man" (Luke 5:8) is the authentic cry not of someone who does not believe, but of someone who does. Jesus said, "No one is good—except God alone" (Mark 10:18), and it is this recognition of evil even in the regenerate of which Paul writes.[76]

> [13]*Did that which is good, then, become death to me? By no means! But in order that sin might be recognized as sin, it produced death in me through what was good, so that through the commandment sin might become utterly sinful.*
> [14]*We know that the law is spiritual; but I am unspiritual, sold as a slave to*

---

76. Brown comments, "as he has proved from his own *past* experience that law cannot make a bad man good, he now proves from his *present* experience that law cannot make a good man better" (p. 158). He also says that the law "can tell us what we ought to be and do, and what we ought not to be and do: it can tell us what will be the consequences of obedience and of disobedience; but it cannot make us what it requires us to be" (p. 150). Barth points out that the great in all manner of disciplines recognize their shortcomings: "Take the case of any respectable and serious-minded philosopher, poet, statesman, or artist. Does he ever suppose his actual achievement to be identical with what he wished to achieve?" (p. 261).

sin. *15I do not understand what I do. For what I want to do I do not do, but what I hate I do. 16And if I do what I do not want to do, I agree that the law is good. 17As it is, it is no longer I myself who do it, but it is sin living in me. 18I know that nothing good lives in me, that is, in my sinful nature. For I have the desire to do what is good, but I cannot carry it out. 19For what I do is not the good I want to do; no, the evil I do not want to do—this I keep on doing. 20Now if I do what I do not want to do, it is no longer I who do it, but it is sin living in me that does it.*

21So I find this law at work: When I want to do good, evil is right there with me. 22For in my inner being I delight in God's law; 23but I see another law at work in the members of my body, waging war against the law of my mind and making me a prisoner of the law of sin at work within my members. 24What a wretched man I am! Who will rescue me from this body of death? 25Thanks be to God—through Jesus Christ our Lord!

So then, I myself in my mind am a slave to God's law, but in the sinful nature a slave to the law of sin.

13. Once again Paul advances his argument with a question. Some see this question as much the same as the one in verse 7, but there is a difference. There he was concerned with whether the law was an evil thing. The way he repudiated that view might perhaps lead some to infer that it was the commandment that brought death to him. Indeed, he came rather close to saying this (v. 10). But it is not his intention to cast a slur on any part of God's law. That law he calls *that which is good*, and his question here is whether that good law caused his death. He immediately rejects the idea with his vigorous *By no means!* (see on 3:4). The law did not cause death. Right through this passage sin is the villain. It is sin that killed him, sin using the law as its base, it is true, but sin. His *But* introduces something quite different.[77] His clause of purpose, *in order that sin might be recognized as sin*, sums up much of the relationship between sin and the law. The law was given in order that sin might be seen for what it is.[78] Without the law we would not recognize sin in its deepest evil; we would not see it as rebellion against the command of God. *Through what was good* repeats Paul's essential point about the goodness of the law. Sin did the harm but did it through the law; it made use of what is good to bring about something evil. A second clause of purpose goes a little further than the first. Paul has said that the law's working of death in the sinner was to show sin to be evil. Now he says that it was *so that through the commandment*

---

77. He uses the strong adversative ἀλλά. RSV ignores this emphatic word with its "It was sin". The Greek sentence is elliptical, but the meaning is reasonably clear. We could supply ἐμοὶ ἐγένετο θάνατος after ἁμαρτία or alternatively take ἐγένετο with κατεργαζομένη.

78. Cf. Harrison, "the law, which seemed to be victimized by being taken over by sin, emerges as having gained an important objective. It has exposed sin for the evil thing it is."

sin might become utterly sinful. This is somewhat more than making sin appear to be evil; now it "becomes" utterly evil.[79]

14. This verse marks the change from the past tense so common in the previous section to the present, which is equally characteristic of the verses to which we now come. As we have already noticed, the most natural way of understanding this is to see it as pointing to Paul's present experience. He begins with *We know*, an appeal to knowledge shared with his correspondents.[80] He does have a "for"[81] (which NIV omits), which gives a reason for the foregoing (cf. 8:22). He proceeds to characterize the law as *spiritual*,[82] a term which clearly signifies a highly desirable quality, but one not easy to define with precision. It seems best to connect it with the Holy Spirit rather than the human spirit and to understand the expression to refer to the law's "divine origin and character" (Murray). It certainly sets the law with God over against man, as the following words show. Paul contrasts himself with the law.[83] *I am unspiritual* is better rendered as "I am carnal" (presumably NIV avoided the old-fashioned word; the term certainly does not mean "unspiritual").[84] It draws attention to the physical life, though it is not confined to the physical (though Goodspeed translates "I am physical"). As Robinson puts it, "Man *qua sarx* is man viewed in his difference and distance from God, man left to his own weakness and mortality" (p. 90). Paul is not saying that there is a problem with his body as though differentiating the body from the essential self. He is referring to his "own unaided human nature", to quote Robinson again. The expression points to the weakness of mankind and to the

---

79. Sin "in the supreme sense" (G. Delling, TDNT, VIII, p. 521). ὑπερβολή is a Pauline word (eight times out of eight in the New Testament). W. Grundmann explains the passage in this way: "the function which we assert the Law to have in the divine plan for the world is finally achieved when sin is unmasked in its demonic character as utter enmity against God. The state of the world and each individual since Adam has a demonic character as directed against God" (TDNT, I, p. 311).

80. Instead of reading οἴδαμεν Lenski and others prefer to divide into οἶδα μέν, which would accord with the singular throughout the passage. But there is nothing to elicit a μέν, and it is characteristic of Paul to use "we" in an appeal to "a commonly acknowledged truth" (Metzger) (see on 2:2).

81. γάρ.

82. πνευματικός, an adjective Paul uses 24 times out of its 26 New Testament occurrences. BAGD note that it may be used of Jesus, but "as a rule it is used of impersonal things: the law given by God Ro 7:14".

83. He uses the emphatic ἐγώ six times in vv. 14-25. Käsemann says that here it "means mankind under the shadow of Adam" (p. 200), and thus does not refer to the Christian. But the emphatic pronoun seems rather to draw attention to Paul himself, the Christian.

84. σάρκινος means "made of flesh", "fleshly", though it is not always distinguished from σαρκικός, "characterized by flesh". Paul uses it three times out of its four New Testament occurrences. It can certainly be applied to believers (as in 1 Cor. 3:1), though indicating their weakness and imperfection. Which, of course, is its point here.

sin we so easily commit because we are weak.[85] Paul recognizes the divine origin and the excellence of the law, he knows that constant obedience to the law is the way he should live, but he also knows that owing to the weakness of his fallen human nature he does not always do what he should.

He brings that out by saying that he is *sold as a slave to sin*. The imagery is that of a slave market. Paul regards himself as sold "under" sin,[86] which is more than NIV's *sold to*. It means that he is "under" sin's control. This is a vivid way of bringing out the truth that Paul sins, though he does not want to. It does not mean that he never does the right, but is a strong expression for his inability to do the right as he would like to. Calvin brings out the paradox: "It would not be sin if it were not voluntary. We are, however, so addicted to sin, that we can do nothing of our own accord but sin." The passive means that Paul is carried off by sin, not that he sold himself to sin, as Ahab did (1 Kings 21:20). He still desires to do the right, which is not true of the person who abandons himself to evil. Every earnest Christian advances in goodness, but he cannot arrive at perfection. Why not? Because he is sold under sin. There is that about him (he is "carnal") which prevents him from being the perfect being he would like to be.[87]

15. Once again Paul uses "for" (which NIV omits) to advance his argument. It indicates that what follows is related to the preceding; it explains something of what it means to be sold under sin. Paul says, *I do not understand what I do*. The verb translated *understand*[88] may point to Paul's perplexity as to why he does evil though he earnestly wants to do good.[89] Or the word may be used in the sense "acknowledge" or "approve" (cf. "the LORD knows the way of the righteous", Ps. 1:6, RSV). Or he may be carrying on the imagery of slavery. The slave does what he is told to do. He does not know the reason for it or where the action leads, or even what the action means in itself. This is the

---

85. Luther comments on "I am carnal": "Because it is characteristic of a spiritual and wise man that he knows that he is carnal, that he is dissatisfied with himself and hates himself, and that he praises the law of God because it is spiritual. Conversely, it is characteristic of a foolish and carnal man that he thinks he is spiritual or that he is satisfied with himself and that he loves his life here in this world."

86. πεπραμένος ὑπὸ τὴν ἁμαρτίαν. The perfect participle points to the continuing state. This is the only New Testament passage where this verb is followed by ὑπό.

87. Cf Packer, "'I am carnal, sold under sin', is stated categorically and without qualification, not because this is the whole truth about Paul the Christian, but because it is the only part of the truth about himself that the law can tell him" (*Studia Evangelica*, II, p. 627).

88. γινώσκω.

89. It is usual to draw attention to pagan parallels such as Ovid, "I see and approve the better course, but I follow the worse." Closer to Paul is Epictetus, ὃ θέλει οὐ ποιεῖ καὶ ὃ μὴ θέλει ποιεῖ (ii.26.4). These are interesting, but we must bear in mind that Paul is not discussing an interesting psychological phenomenon. He is rebelling against indwelling sin, which he considers an alien intruder. He is discussing the problem in the light of God's law. There are differences.

case of Paul vis-à-vis sin.[90] He goes on to affirm that it is not what he wills that he does but[91] what he hates. He does not say that he is not responsible; he himself does it. That is the problem. It is not that he never does good or that his doing of evil is habitual. But there is no reason for concern over a good action, whereas sin is always a problem for the servant of God. Paul is concentrating on the problem area.[92] Slavery helps him bring out what is involved. He is not completely free, and the sin he commits shows that he is in some sense a slave. He finds sin too powerful and too much in control to resist at all times. "Only the hypothesis of slavery explains his acts" (Denney).[93]

16. Consequences flow from Paul's good intentions. His *if* construction implies that the condition has been fulfilled—"if, as is the case".[94] The fact that he is doing what he does not want to do shows that he is not in theory opposing the law. He is for it. He agrees[95] with it. The construction is elliptical, and we should supply something like "and thus I testify" that it is good. Barclay translates "fair", but this is not the meaning. Paul's word[96] can mean "beautiful"; it "suggests the moral beauty or nobility of the law" (Denney). The law is fair, certainly. But that is not what Paul is saying. He is asserting that it is fundamentally good; it is morally beautiful. Paul's very good intentions tell us something about the goodness of the law.

17. *As it is* paraphrases Paul's "But now", where his "now" is logical rather than temporal; "Now, in the light of my endorsement of the law. . . ." The fact that it is his view that the law is good shows that it is not the real Paul

---

90. Käsemann comments, "What a person wants is salvation. What he creates is disaster" (p. 203). He also reminds us that "we constantly show ourselves to be the captives of our own arrogance, passions, caprice, and stupidity." Paul, he says, "affirms, not just the contradictoriness of existence even in the pious, but the entanglement of a fallen creation in all its expressions in the power of sin" (p. 204).

91. ἀλλ', "on the contrary".

92. Krister Stendahl may perhaps not be giving sufficient attention to this when he says of Rom. 7, "The possibility of a distinction between the good Law and the bad Sin is based on the rather trivial observation that every man knows that there is a difference between what he ought to do and what he does"; "what to him and his contemporaries was a common sense observation appeared to later interpreters to be a most penetrating insight into the nature of man and into the nature of sin" (*Paul Among Jews and Gentiles* [Philadelphia, 1976], p. 93). Whatever be the truth of Stendahl's view on "the introspective conscience of the West", he seems to have missed some at any rate of what Paul is saying in this chapter. The apostle is not making "a rather trivial observation" and not repeating a first-century commonplace, but dealing with the truth that it is the law *of God* that people have broken.

93. SH distinguish between κατεργάζομαι, "put into execution", πράσσω, "act as a moral and responsible being", and ποιέω, "produce a certain result without reference to its moral character." Barrett doubts whether Paul is distinguishing between "practise" and "do". Cranfield points out that κατεργάζομαι and ποιέω are used of effective action, and πράσσω of action disapproved (it is never used of God or Christ). C. Maurer agrees in distancing πράσσω from the other two verbs. He sees it used here of a "doing" "which is not orientated to fulfilment" (TDNT, VI, p. 636). Shedd sees the present as pointing to intermittent action, not invariable action.

94. εἰ with the indicative.

95. σύμφημι is found here only in the New Testament.

96. καλός.

who does it. He does not define *it*, but in the context he is undoubtedly referring to the sin that the law forbids, the "what I do not want to do" of verse 16. On the contrary,[97] "the dwelling in me sin" does it.[98] Sin is pictured as having taken up residence in Paul. This is not the honored guest, nor the paying tenant, but the "squatter", not legitimately there, but very difficult to eject. Paul is personifying sin again; it is in some sense a separate entity, even though it is within him.[99] But it is not external to him. This sin that lives in him, though it is not the real Paul, is what produces the acts which the real Paul hates so much. Sin is out of character for the believer, even though it is so difficult to be rid of it entirely.

18. Verses 18-20 repeat verses 14-17, more or less. Certainly the vocabulary and the thoughts are much the same. But in the earlier section Paul is saying basically that he cannot stop doing things of which he disapproves, whereas in these verses he cannot carry into action things of which he approves. He has just said that sin lives in him, and now he carries this further with *I know that nothing good lives in me*. This requires qualification, for he has been saying that he approves the law (v. 16). So he explains it as "in my flesh" (NIV, *in my sinful nature*). We should not understand this of "the lower self" in contrast with "the higher self" or "the mind", etc. It is rather man as fallen. Brunner sees "on the one side an irrational flesh, on the other an ineffectual law of reason." Reason is no match for desire. Flesh is not inherently sinful, but it is weak and thus not able to do the good Paul approves. Käsemann considers it "the workshop of sin" (p. 205). Some see Paul's view as akin to the Jewish view of the good and the evil inclination (*yetser*).[100] There is, of course, something in this, but with the important difference that for Paul "It is 'sin' which is the enemy, not the 'evil impulse' " (Black). He is not repeating a commonplace of Judaism. To will, he says, is present[101] with him, but to do the good, No.[102] What he does is never completely what he wants to do.

19. Paul states again the dilemma of the man who wants to do good and cannot. "For not what I will, I do, a good thing, but on the contrary, what I do not will, a bad thing, this I do." The first negative precedes the entire clause and negates the whole, whereas the second is in the normal place before the verb and negates the verb only. This probably has no profound effect. But

97. ἀλλά, the strong adversative.

98. οἰκέω (eight times in the New Testament, all in Paul) and ἐνοικέω (six times, also all in Paul) have similar meanings— "live in", "inhabit", or the like. They derive from οἶκος, "to live in as in a house". Most accept ἐνοικέω here. Both verbs are used in the New Testament largely of God or of spiritual qualities (good or bad) dwelling in people.

99. Cf. O. Michel, "The dwelling of sin in man denotes its dominion over him, its lasting connection with his flesh, and yet also a certain distinction from it" (TDNT, V, p. 135). The rabbis could say of sin, "At first it is like a (passing) visitor, then like a guest (who stays longer), and finally like the master of the house" (Genesis Rabbah xx.6).

100. See, e.g., the discussion in W. D. Davies, *Paul and Rabbinic Judaism* (London, 1948), pp. 25ff.

101. παράκειταί μοι, "lies to my hand" (SH). The verb occurs only here and in v. 21 in the New Testament.

102. Accented οὔ is the firm negative "No", and not simply "not".

Paul is saying emphatically that he wills to do good but does not do it, while he does not will to do evil but in fact does it.[103] Luther borrows an illustration from horseback riding: "It is as with a rider: When his horse does not trot exactly as he wishes, it is he and yet not he that causes it to trot as it does. For the horse is not without him nor he without the horse."

20. The thought of verse 17 is repeated. Paul's *if* clause implies that the condition has been fulfilled—"if, as is the case".[104] There is no doubt about his doing what he does not want to do. Again, his *no longer* implies that formerly he had done this. But things being what they are, it is the indwelling sin that brings about the evil action. Paul's will is not behind it. He is not saying that he is not responsible; after all, it is his action. He is saying that he is no careless or audacious sinner. His will is firmly in opposition to evil, and that is to be borne in mind in assessing the situation.

21. *So* leads us to the logical consequence.[105] Paul sums up with a "law" which has caused some difference of opinion. Most take it in the sense "principle" (NEB) or "rule" (JB), but others think the law of Moses is meant, as Moffatt, "So this is my experience of the Law . . ." (cf. RV mg. "I find then in regard of the law . . ."). Either is possible, but it seems more likely that Paul has in mind the law which he later calls "the law of sin" (v. 23). This is more than simply an observed sequence, as in the way we might speak of "a law of nature". Throughout this passage Paul has in mind the compulsion to do evil, and that will be his meaning also when he speaks of the "law" he has now found (Hodge speaks of a "controlling principle", and SH of "the coercion of the will"). His nature, so to speak, obeys this "law". *I find* puts this as a discovery. It is not something that Paul lays down as his presupposition, but a conclusion he has reached from a study of the facts. There is some emphasis on the fact that the self-same "I" has both these opposite experiences.[106] Paul insists that he has the will to do good. But the trouble is that *evil is right there with me*.[107] He cannot escape it.

22. *For* introduces an explanation. He is happy inwardly with the law of God. *I delight* is a stronger expression than "agree" (v. 16).[108] This rejoicing is *in my inner being*.[109] Leenhardt regards the expression as "certainly of

---

103. Michel sees the use of "the 'good' (ἀγαθόν, καλόν) of the fulfilling of God's demand, the 'evil' (κακόν) of the performance of men which corresponds to lust." Maurer comments on the use of πράσσω: "Life is lived . . . in the stupid doing of the evil which is not willed, and this is expressed by πράσσειν" (TDNT, VI, p. 637).

104. εἰ with the indicative.

105. For ἄρα see on 5:18. This is the first example without οὖν in this epistle; there does not seem to be much difference in meaning.

106. Note the repeated ἐμοί, in each case early in its clause (cf. Gifford's note).

107. Paul has used the verb παράκειμαι of the presence of the good will within him (v. 18), and now of the evil, τὸ κακόν.

108. His verb is συνήδομαι (here only in the New Testament), "rejoice with someone"; here it is "I (joyfully) agree with the law" (BAGD). The thought is of agreement with the law, but not in the sense of a grudging assent. Rather, it is a joyful acceptance of all God has given in the law (cf. the many expressions of joy in the law in Ps. 119).

109. κατὰ τὸν ἔσω ἄνθρωπον. ἔσω is found here only in Romans, but in Paul four times out of nine in the New Testament.

Hellenistic origin," and he finds evidence in Plato, Philo, and the hermetical literature. It is a question whether Paul is using the expression here in much the same way as his Hellenistic contemporaries or whether he is referring to the person who has been regenerated. In favor of the former view is the fact that the Holy Spirit is not mentioned in this chapter. Paul is certainly not speaking explicitly of the Spirit's regenerating work. Further, the apostle goes on to say that he sees "another law" at work warring against "the law of my mind", and it may well be that we are meant to see this as equivalent to "the inner man". The objection is that the expression elsewhere refers to the essential being of the believer, the inner life that Christ has brought (2 Cor. 4:16; Eph. 3:16). Paul may not be making our distinction here. He doubtless knows that the expression was widely used in the world of his day and that it has a special meaning for Christians. But he may not be referring with precision to either way of using the term. He is contrasting the real Paul, the Paul who is known only in the deep recesses of the man, and who delights in the law of God, with that other Paul who so readily does the sin of which the real Paul does not approve. It is true that the regenerate Paul would abhor that evil, and it is also true that the respectable and intellectual Paul would abominate it. But would the unregenerate *delight* in the law of God? I doubt it. This leads to the conclusion that if the distinction is in Paul's mind, then he is referring to the man enlightened by the working of the Spirit of God within him.[110]

23. The real Paul rejoiced in God's law. He recognized it for what it was and rejoiced accordingly. But obeying it is another thing altogether, and to that he now turns. He sees *another law* at work within him, which may well signify "a law of a different kind".[111] This law should be seen as the same as *the law of sin*, for it is highly unlikely that Paul thinks of two different hostile laws at work within his being. *Law* will be used in the sense "principle" or "rule of action", though with the nuance that there is some element of compulsion (he is made prisoner). The law is *in*, not "of", my members (NIV supplies *at work*; it is not in the Greek). Consistently Paul proceeds from his basic position that the body is not evil, though the forces of evil work through it. The "other law" makes war[112] against *the law of my mind*. The thought of conflict is important. Paul is still fighting. He has not surrendered to the powers of evil. The *mind* emphasizes the intellectual side of the struggle.[113]

---

110. Cf. Barrett, "The 'inward man' belongs to the Age to Come, just as the 'outward man' belongs to the present age." There is certainly a reference here to the present age, but there may well also be an eschatological reference (see on v. 25).

111. ἕτερος is probably used here in the sense "of a different kind" (so BAGD). The word strictly means "*other* of two, contrasting a definite person or thing w. another" (*ibid.*); it is used also where more than two are in question and sometimes as more or less equivalent to ἄλλος. But where two are contrasted they are different, and it is this that we apparently have here.

112. ἀντιστρατεύομαι, "make war against", occurs only here in the New Testament. It is another example of Paul's love of military metaphors.

113. BAGD define νοῦς as "*the mind, intellect* as the side of life contrasted w. physical existence, the higher, mental part of the natural man which initiates his thoughts and plans". J. Behm says, "This is the moral consciousness as it concretely determines will and

Paul is referring to the principle that is operative in his rational nature. But this principle is not victorious. Paul anticipates our modern psychologists in their recognition that there are limits to what reason can do. Paul finds himself made captive[114] by what he has called *another law* and now proceeds to speak of *the law of sin* ("the evil principle", Bruce). This will be the way sin works, but there is also the thought that it exercises sway (Cranfield sees "the power, the authority, the control exercised over us by sin"). Again there is a reference to *my members* (cf. 6:13, 19; 7:5); the body is that through which sin makes its suggestions.

24. Paul's deep emotion explodes in the exclamation "Wretched man that I am!"[115] Some object that this is not Paul's view of himself.[116] But the language of this verse is impossibly theatrical if used of someone other than the speaker. The more we advance spiritually the more clearly we see the high standards God sets for his people and the more deeply we deplore the extent of our shortcoming. Paul is surely referring to his own experience. As Robinson well remarks, "One" could not be substituted here for "I" without loss (p. 82). Paul is expressing in forceful terms his dismay at what sin does to him. It is, moreover, important that we understand this as applying to the regenerate. It is all too easy to take our Christian status for granted. We so readily remember our victories and gloss over our defeats. We slip into a routine and refuse to allow ourselves to be disturbed by what we see as occasional and minor slips.[117] But a sensitive conscience and a genuine sorrow for every sin are the prerequisites of spiritual depth.

The apostle goes on to ask who will deliver him. The verb denotes deliverance generally, without specifying the mode. In the New Testament it is mostly used by Paul.[118] Paul asks who will deliver him *from this body of death*, an expression which may also be translated "the body of this death"

---

action. . . . The 'I' of R. 7 realises that it is bound by the νόμος of God according to the ἔσω ἄνθρωπος (v. 22)" (TDNT, IV, p. 958).

114. αἰχμαλωτίζω (from αἰχμή, "spear", and ἁλίσκομαι, "capture", AS) is another piece of military imagery. Paul uses it in three of its four New Testament occurrences. He likes military terminology.

115. The nominative will be the nominative of address (Shedd). Cf. BDF 147. It is typical of Paul's terse, forceful style that there is no verb.

116. Thus Denney says, "The words are not those of the Apostle's heart as he writes; they are the words which he knows are wrung from the heart of the man who realises in himself the state just described." Over against such views Stott can say, "The unbeliever is characterized by self-righteousness, and would never acknowledge himself a 'miserable creature', which is the NEB version of 'wretched man'. The immature believer is characterized by self-confidence, and does not ask who is going to deliver him. Only the mature believer reaches the place both of self-disgust and of self-despair."

117. "Let us cease to know that we are 'carnal, sold under sin,' sinners enmeshed in a sinful world, desperately in need of redemption—and all too quickly we shall be anchored in complacency" (Smart, p. 100).

118. ῥύομαι is found in Paul in 11 of its 16 New Testament occurrences. It is sometimes followed by ἀπό, and sometimes, as here, by ἐκ. In the New Testament it is used of God as he saves people. W. Kasch points out that the term often has an eschatological content in the New Testament (TDNT, VI, p. 1003).

(NASB).[119] Some insist on taking *this* with *death* (e.g., SH, Murray); some, indeed, suggest that the emphasis is on "this death" (e.g., Gifford). But it is more likely that "the body of death" is the basic expression, perhaps with something of a Semitic flavor (where there tends to be a multiplication of nouns rather than the use of adjectives). The whole expression is then marked out with "this".[120] Some exegetes take *body* figuratively; Hodge, for example, translates "the burden of this death" (so Shedd). But in the context it is better to see the word as referring to the physical body, which is characterized by death (cf. 6:12; 8:11). It is itself mortal, and it is that in which sin operates and so brings death to us.

25. The question in verse 24 appears to be a rhetorical one, with the answer "Nobody can" all too apparent. But Paul answers it with the joyful shout *Thanks be to God—through Jesus Christ our Lord!*[121] The victory is God's, and he gives it through Christ. It is Paul's consistent teaching that God in Christ has supplied all our need and will continue to do so (cf. Phil. 4:19). Clearly Paul's words express gratitude for a present deliverance, but it is likely that they also have eschatological significance. The deliverance we have today is wonderful, but it is partial and incomplete. It is but a first instalment of greater things to come, and Paul looks forward to that great day with his burst of thanksgiving.[122]

So then[123] introduces a logical summary of what Paul has been saying. This, then, is what it all adds up to. There is disagreement about this, it is true. Some exegetes feel that the outburst of thanksgiving cannot have been followed by a reference to being *a slave to the law of sin.* Moffatt accordingly transfers this part of the verse to the end of verse 23, a rearrangement that is accepted by Dodd and others. There is no support for this in the MSS, but Dodd says, "we cannot avoid trusting our own judgment against their evidence". But it is hazardous to set our view of what Paul ought to have said against all the evidence.[124] It is better to view the second half of verse 25 as a summary of the preceding argument before going on to the triumph of chap-

119. ἐκ τοῦ σώματος τοῦ θανάτου τούτου. The problem is whether to take τούτου with the whole expression or with θανάτου.

120. This view is taken by Turner, M, III, p. 214. Lenski accepts it and cites Zahn in support. Zahn's point is that the genitive θανάτου is attributive like an adjective (cf. BDF 165), and "such genitives never have a pronoun or some other modifier that make them definite, for they would then cease to be adjectival."

121. There is a textual problem here. Most critics accept χάρις δὲ τῷ θεῷ with אa C² Ψ 33 81 etc. ἡ χάρις τοῦ θεοῦ is read by D and some MSS of OL, ἡ χάρις κυρίου by G with OL support, εὐχαριστῶ τῷ θεῷ by א* A K etc. The first reading has respectable support and explains the other readings, so it should be adopted.

122. Robert Banks, in his article "Romans 7:25A: An Eschatological Thanksgiving?" ABR, XXVI (1978), pp. 34-42, draws attention to other exclamations in Paul involving χάρις, especially 1 Cor. 15:57. He argues convincingly that the expression must be understood eschatologically.

123. ἄρα οὖν; see the note on 5:18.

124. Cf. Bruce, "it is precarious to rearrange the words of Paul in the interests of a smoother logical sequence."

ter 8. As Cranfield puts it, "it sums up with clear-sighted honesty . . . the tension, with all its real anguish and also all its real hopefulness, in which the Christian never ceases to be involved so long as he is living this present life." Notice that Paul does not shrug off his responsibility; he does not say that his mind serves God while his flesh serves sin. He uses the emphatic pronoun "I".[125] It is what he has been saying all along. While there is that in him which approves God's way there is that in him also which follows the paths of sin.

125. He uses the emphatic αὐτὸς ἐγώ, which Parry explains as "I by myself and apart from any new or other power which may be available to change the balance of contending powers." Hodge warns against putting too much stress on the expression as though it meant "I alone, without the aid of Christ": "Paul had not been teaching what his unrenewed, unaided nature could accomplish, but what was the operation of the law, even on the renewed man." Parry, it is true, does go on to speak of the situation under the law. It is the emphasis on αὐτὸς ἐγώ that is in question.

Romans 8

E. The Holy Spirit in the Believer, 8:1-39

This is one of the great chapters in the Bible, and its teaching about the way the Holy Spirit operates in enabling the believer to defeat the forces of evil has always been recognized as of the utmost importance. There are problems in detail, but the main thrust is clear. Paul is saying that a new and wonderful life opens out before those who put their trust in Christ and that this depends heavily on the work of the Spirit of God. An interesting feature of the chapter which is not always noticed is that there is not a single imperative.[1] Paul is talking about life in the Spirit, life in which the Spirit guides so constantly that there is no need for a string of commandments. Griffith Thomas sums it up with some negatives: "as Godet says, the chapter begins with 'no condemnation,' and ends with 'no separation,' while in between, as C. A. Fox remarks, there is 'no defeat.'"

1. The Opposition of Flesh and Spirit, 8:1-11

¹*Therefore, there is now no condemnation for those who are in Christ Jesus,ᵃ* ²*because through Christ Jesus the law of the Spirit of life set me free from the law of sin and death.* ³*For what the law was powerless to do in that it was weakened by the sinful nature,ᵇ God did by sending his own Son in the likeness of sinful man to be a sin offering.ᶜ And so he condemned sin in sinful man,* ⁴*in order that the righteous requirements of the law might be fully met in us, who do not live according to the sinful nature but according to the Spirit.*

⁵*Those who live according to the sinful nature have their minds set on what that nature desires; but those who live in accordance with the Spirit have their minds set on what the Spirit desires.* ⁶*The mind of sinful man is death, but the mind controlled by the Spirit is life and peace,* ⁷*because the sinful mind is hostile to God. It does not submit to God's law, nor can it do so.* ⁸*Those controlled by the sinful nature cannot please God.*

⁹*You, however, are controlled not by the sinful nature but by the Spirit, if the Spirit of God lives in you. And if anyone does not have the Spirit of Christ, he does not belong to Christ.* ¹⁰*But if Christ is in you, your body is dead because of sin, yet your spirit is alive because of righteousness.* ¹¹*And if the Spirit of him*

---

1. But see Günther Bornkamm, *Paul* (London, 1971), p. 156.

*who raised Jesus from the dead is living in you, he who raised Christ from the
dead will also give life to your mortal bodies through his Spirit, who lives in you.*

[a]1 Some later manuscripts *Jesus, who do not live according to the sinful nature but according
to the Spirit*   [b]3 Or *the flesh;* also in verses 4, 5, 8, 9, 12 and 13   [c]3Or *man, for sin*

In this opening section we find ourselves in a different atmosphere from
that in chapter 7. There is still the opposition between good and evil, but the
dominant note is that of victory.

1. *Therefore* links the great chapter on life in the Spirit logically to the
preceding. NEB brings out something of the force of it with "the conclusion of
the matter is this". It is possible to take *therefore* to refer to the immediately
preceding words, but most agree that this is not the primary context. It is
much more likely that Paul is referring to the whole of the preceding argument. He has taken several chapters to bring out the way God saves us in
Christ, and in the light of the whole of that massive argument he can say *there
is now no condemnation.* His *now* is surely temporal, now in contrast to times
gone by before we had entered into the justification Christ brought. It is
possibly also in contrast to the time to come. He has a strong eschatological
thrust in many places, and he may be hinting that, though we do not as yet
experience all the fulness of what salvation in Christ means, we do enjoy all
that *no condemnation* means. *Now* believers have a wonderful gift of salvation
from God in Christ. *Condemnation*[2] is a forensic term which here includes both
the sentence and the execution of the sentence. But for believers there is no
condemnation at all.[3]

2. *Because*[4] is important; it gives the reason for what Paul has just said.
There is no condemnation because of what Christ has done in freeing people
from the law that condemns. *The law of the Spirit of life* is an unusual expression. We have seen that sometimes Paul uses the term "law" in the sense
"principle", though usually with the added idea that there is some element of
coercion (cf. AS, "Of a force or influence impelling to action"). Thus "the law
of sin" is the rule that governed his conduct, and it made him a prisoner
(7:23). The *law* here then is the principle on which the Holy Spirit works, a

2. κατάκριμα occurs elsewhere in the New Testament only in 5:16, 18; the corresponding verb κατακρίνω is found 16 times. F. Büchsel points to the fact that with human
judgment there is a distinction between condemnation and its execution (e.g., Mark
14:64), whereas with the divine judgment the two "can be seen as one." This passage, he
thinks, "refers not merely to the divine sentence but also to its actual results" (TDNT, III,
pp. 951, 952). Deissmann points out that it is a rare word and argues that it means the
punishment following sentence (*Bible Studies* [Edinburgh, 1901], pp. 264-65), as does MM.
3. οὐδέν is given special emphasis by its position at the head of the sentence and its
separation from its noun. It signifies " 'not a single one' of any kind" (Lenski). But this is
not a blanket exemption, applying to all people. Paul is speaking of those who are *in Christ
Jesus* (for this expression see on 6:11).
4. γάρ.

principle that operates in power. *Spirit* here is surely the Holy Spirit,[5] who is characterized as *the Spirit of life*, that is, the life-giving Spirit. The presence of the Spirit is the distinguishing mark of the Christian, and this presence means the defeat of the power of sin. Gifford rejects such ideas as that the the law of the Spirit means the gospel (so Hodge) or the plan of salvation, and says it is "the life-giving power of the Holy Ghost, ruling as a law within the heart." Paul is saying that when the Holy Spirit comes into a person that person is liberated from bondage to evil and finds a new power within, a power that causes the defeat of sin and leads the liberated person into ways of goodness and love. Manson has an interesting summary of Paul's teaching on various laws: "Moses' law has right but not might; Sin's law has might but not right; the law of the Spirit has both right and might."

It is not completely clear with what we should take "in Christ Jesus". In the Greek the expression occurs between "the life" and "freed", and it could be taken with either. We could thus understand it as "the law of the Spirit of life in Christ Jesus freed . . ." or as "the law of the Spirit of life freed in Christ Jesus. . . ." The former understanding is accepted by Nygren, Boylan, and others. Leenhardt agrees and sees this as meaning "the life-giving Spirit in Christ Jesus" (cf. Haldane). The latter view is favored by Cranfield, Shedd, and others. Either view is a possible understanding of the Greek (so Murray).[6] Whichever way we take it, the believer was freed (the aorist points to a decisive act) from *the law of sin* (cf. 7:23, 25) *and death* (cf. 7:10-11, 13). The last word is not with sin or with death. While believers are not sinless, they have real liberation in Christ (cf. 6:18, 22). There is a textual problem as to what we should read after "freed", the manuscripts being divided between "me" and "you". While certainty is not attainable, it seems best to accept "you".[7] Not much depends on the point because either way Paul clearly means the term to apply to any believer.[8]

3. *For*[9] introduces the reason for the preceding statement. It is what God

5. Until now Paul has used πνεῦμα five times only, and some of these do not refer to the Holy Spirit. But in this chapter the term occurs 20 times, the most in any one chapter in the New Testament. By contrast the "I" which occurred more than 30 times in chapter 7 is almost absent from this chapter. Lenski says that the Holy Spirit and his work appears here for the first time in the letter, but this ignores 1:4; 5:5.

6. The words ἐν Χριστῷ could be taken with ὁ νόμος or with τῆς ζωῆς, though to make this clear they should be preceded by ὁ or τῆς. The absence of either favors a link with ἠλευθέρωσεν. But this rule is not invariable in the New Testament, so either of the former two is possible.

7. σε is read by ℵ B G some OL Tert etc., and με by A C² D K etc. ἡμᾶς has slight support (Ψ boh etc.), but it seems secondary, a way of making the words applicable to all (cf. v. 4). Barrett omits any object on the basis of "slight evidence (mainly from Origen)" and the fact that it is the harder reading. σε has the better attestation and is a harder reading than με, though it is objected that it could have arisen by the accidental repetition of the end of the preceding word.

8. It is an example of the use of the first or second person singular to represent any third person (BDF 281; cf. M, III, p. 39).

9. γάρ.

did in Christ that brings about the liberation of which Paul has just been speaking. Paul begins this part of his argument with a very difficult Greek expression rendered *what the law was powerless to do*.[10] Fortunately the obscurity of the Greek grammar does not extend to the sense. Paul is saying that there is something that the law of Moses (or for that matter, any law) simply could not do, and that God has now done that thing. The reason[11] for the law's failure is that it was "weak through the flesh". Consistently Paul sees "the flesh" not as evil, but as weak—so weak, he is saying here, that the law could not bring about salvation. The fault is not in the law, but in the flesh. Previously he praised the law as good (7:12), and the same view underlies this passage.

Paul proceeds to inform his readers that God condemned sin, and did so by sending his own[12] Son. *Own* is important, pointing as it does to the close relationship between the Father and the Son. It was no remote messenger that God sent, but the Son who stood in a unique relationship to him. As Hunter says, he is "the Son by nature, as we are sons by grace." Paul does not often use the concept of God's sending of his Son, but the idea is clear here. He says further that God sent him "in the likeness of sinful flesh", an expression that has caused a great deal of discussion.[13] On the one hand there are those who emphasize "sinful flesh", and consider this expression important if we are to see Jesus as really "one of us". Unless this is taken realistically, it is contended, Christ did not really become man, for humanity's flesh is invariably "sinful flesh".[14] On the other hand it is pointed out that unless Christ was sinless he could not be our Savior; he would need to be saved himself. So our passage is something of a minefield where it is necessary to tread carefully. We cannot take the view that Jesus was no more than just another man, sinful as we are. Paul certainly held that Jesus was sinless (2 Cor. 5:21). Nor can we see him (as the Docetists did) as of a different order from us. He came right where we are.

---

10. τὸ ἀδύνατον τοῦ νόμου seems to have no grammatical connections. There is difference of opinion as to whether it is nominative or accusative and whether we should take the verbal adjective as active, with the meaning "the inability of the law (was overcome)", or passive, signifying "what was impossible for the law (was accomplished)". In the end both possibilities of taking the words must be left open. Turner holds that the article τὸ ἀ. means "the one thing the Law could not do" (M, III, p. 13).

11. ἐν ᾧ, "because" (Cranfield, BDF 219 [2]). But it may be a relative, "in which", i.e., denoting the point at which the law is weak (so Denney, Boylan).

12. ἑαυτοῦ. Cf. ἰδίου, v. 32. Paul uses υἱός of Christ rather sparingly, there being only eight examples in Romans, three of which are in the opening.

13. ὁμοίωμα in Greek generally has the idea of a "copy" rather than the abstract notion of "likeness", but its meaning in the New Testament is "likeness". When used of Christ here and in Phil. 2:7, the idea is of being exactly like rather than a somewhat similar copy. J. Schneider says that in this passage the term "indicates two things, first the likeness in appearance, and secondly the distinction in essence" (TDNT, V, p. 196).

14. Barth speaks of "the likeness of sin-controlled flesh" and refers to Jesus' "impenetrable incognito". "Judged by the record of what He did and omitted to do, His sinlessness can be as easily denied as ours can, more easily, in fact, than can the sinlessness of those good and pure and pious people who move about in our midst. . . . The sinlessness of Jesus is guaranteed only by God. . . ."

Stott comments on the expression, "Not 'in sinful flesh', because the flesh of Jesus was sinless. Nor 'in the likeness of flesh', because the flesh of Jesus was real. But 'in the likeness of sinful flesh', because the flesh of Jesus was both sinless and real." We must bear in mind that Paul is not giving us a full explanation of his understanding of the incarnation; he is talking about the way Christ saved us in his death.[15]

God sent him, further, *to be a sin offering*. This translation of NIV depends on the fact that the expression Paul uses here[16] is the regular translation in LXX of the Hebrew expression for "sin offering". NIV may well be correct, but we find nothing in the context that prepares us for anything as specific as this, or indeed for a reference to the sacrificial system at all. Would the Roman Christians have been expected to detect the allusion? It seems more likely that we should take the words as they are: "for sin", that is, to deal with sin, whatever that involved. We know that Christ's sacrifice may fittingly be called a "sin offering", but that does not mean that that is what Paul is calling it here. When God sent his Son in this way, Paul says, he "condemned sin in the flesh". We should take "in the flesh" with "condemned" rather than with "sin"; we are not to think that "sin in the flesh" is condemned and other sin is not. It was what Jesus did "in the flesh" that condemned all sin. Paul is now picturing sin as a litigant in a law court; the verdict goes against sin and thus sin is condemned. "Condemned" here means more than that a form of words goes against it. There is the thought that the condemnation is brought into effect (as when a derelict building is "condemned"; it is used no more, and demolition follows).[17]

4. *In order that*[18] introduces the divine purpose, and since that purpose never fails of fulfilment, it points us to the result as well. How *the righteous requirements*[19] *of the law are fully met in us* should be interpreted is a matter of dispute. Shedd is typical of many when he sees the fulfilment as "*vicarious, and not a personal performance*" (so Calvin, Hodge, and others). The thought is that only Christ perfectly met the law's requirements and that accordingly the reference here must be to him and not to anything the believer does. Justification, not sanctification, is in view. Others, however, argue that Paul is here referring to what happens to the person who is in Christ. Bruce

---

15. Cf. Olshausen, Paul is bringing forward "the *affinity* of Christ's nature with ours; he is silent, therefore, on the *difference* between them."

16. περὶ ἁμαρτίας.

17. T. C. G. Thornton argues that καί should be taken as "even" and περὶ ἁμαρτίας as "on a charge of sinfulness" or "because of sin", citing patristic support. Thus he gets the meaning, "condemned sin in the flesh, on the very grounds of its sinfulness" (JTS, N.S. XXII [1971], pp. 515-17). But this view has won little support and does not seem very probable.

18. ἵνα.

19. The word is δικαίωμα. Despite NIV it is singular. It signifies "regulation, requirement, commandment" (BAGD), and is often used in LXX for the requirements of the law. There, however, it is plural unless a single requirement is in mind. But Paul uses the term in a way that indicates not a series of different commandments, but one harmonious divine will.

puts it this way: "God's commands have now become God's enablings" (so Hendriksen, Lloyd-Jones, Denney, and others). Reformed theologians have stressed that justification and sanctification are not to be separated, and it seems that this is what Paul is saying here. In the full sense only Christ has fulfilled all the law's requirements, but when we are in him we in our measure begin to live the kind of life that God would have us live. Notice that Paul does not say "we fulfil the law's righteous requirement", but that "the righteous requirement of the law is fulfilled in us", surely pointing to the work of the Holy Spirit in the believer. Before we came to know Christ we were continually defeated by sin. When we came to know him and to receive the indwelling Holy Spirit we were able to attain a standard we could never reach in our own strength. In interpreting these words the emphasis on the way the Christian life is lived that is so stressed in this part of the letter is important. Earlier Paul spoke of establishing the law (3:31). There is something like that here, too.

The fulfilment in question is *in us*, not in all people, and this is further defined as "who walk, not according to the flesh, but according to the Spirit." Paul finds the metaphor of walking congenial as a way of bringing out the steady if unspectacular progress that characterizes the Christian way (cf. 6:4; 1 Cor. 7:17; 2 Cor. 5:7, etc.). The believer does not walk "according to the flesh".[20] There is, of course, a sense in which he is "in the flesh" (cf. 2 Cor. 10:3), and Paul can go so far as to speak of "Christ, according to the flesh" (9:5). But to live with our horizons bounded by the requirements of this fleshly life is quite another thing, and it is this that Paul has in mind here. The person outside Christ sees nothing beyond the here and now and, however altruistic he may be, in the end is wrapped up in the things he wants or on which he has set his seal of approval.[21]

Not so the Christian. The believer walks *according to the Spirit*. Some take this to mean "the principle of holiness in the regenerate" (Shedd; so Chrysostom, Bengel; cf. Lenski, "As flesh is the old nature, so spirit is the new"). But all such views founder on the fact that through this whole chapter runs the thought that believers are not left to live the Christian life in their own strength. The Holy Spirit dwells in them and enables them to live on a standard they could never attain left to themselves. It is this life, lived in accordance with all that the Holy Spirit means, of which Paul writes.

5. Verses 5-8 form a closely knit section, with a series of conjunctions tying the various members together. "For"[22] (which NIV omits) connects it with the previous words; Paul is now about to cite evidence to support what he has just said. In verse 4 Paul had spoken of walking "according to the flesh"; there is a slight change now when he refers to those who "are accord-

---

20. κατὰ σάρκα. BAGD class this use of κατὰ as "according to, in accordance with, in conformity with, corresponding to".

21. "To live *kata sarka* is to accept the fact of the flesh as one's sole horizon and criterion" (Robinson).

22. γάρ. NIV omits another γάρ at the beginning of v. 6.

ing to the flesh", but there is not much difference in meaning. The expression he uses here perhaps conveys a hint at what these people are rather than what they do, but we should not press this. Paul still has in mind that those whose lives are dominated by "flesh" are strongly opposed to the things of God. His list of "the works of the flesh" in Galatians 5:19-21 shows that we must not think only of gross sensuality, for Paul includes such things as enmity, jealousy, and anger. There are many ways of manifesting a disposition that is confined to the flesh. Those in the flesh, he now says, *have their minds set on*[23] the things of the flesh. They are preoccupied with the flesh; they concentrate on the flesh to the exclusion of all else. It is this verb that Jesus uses of Peter when that apostle rebuked him at Caesarea Philippi, "your mind is not set on the things of God but the things of men" (Matt. 16:23). Peter was not being desperately wicked, but he was looking at things from a completely worldly point of view. Paul is saying something of the sort about fleshly people. They may have good intentions, but their horizon is bounded by the things of this life. The flesh is the focus of their whole life. And because they are concentrating on this fleshly life, they cut themselves off from the blessings Christ offers.

Paul has a corresponding saying about those who "are according to the Spirit."[24] Such people are not intermittently interested in the things of the Spirit; their whole being centers on them. What the Spirit does is their absorbing interest. We should not understand this as a self-centered concentration on the piece of Christian work in which they are engaged. It is rather a delighted contemplation of what the Spirit does wherever the Spirit chooses to move. It is the very opposite of a concentration on oneself, even on the service one renders to God.

6. The significance of Paul's "For" here is not as obvious as that of the one at the head of the previous verse (Lagrange and Boylan find it difficult). Probably, as Cranfield puts it, "it is intended as explanation of the opposition between the Spirit and the flesh presupposed in v. 5." The apostle changes his form of expression slightly when he speaks of *the mind*[25] of the flesh. The thought is of a thoroughgoing concentration on the flesh, the things that pertain to this life. This, Paul says starkly, *is death* (so RSV). There is no verb in the Greek, but NIV seems to have the meaning with *is*. GNB reads "results in death", NEB "spells death", and Moffatt "mean death". But Paul does not

---

23. Paul's verb is φρονέω, a word that he uses often (23 times out of 26 in the New Testament). It derives from φρήν, "the midriff", "the diaphragm", regarded by the Greeks as "the seat of intellectual and spiritual activity" (G. Bertram, TDNT, IX, p. 220). Here BAGD understand the verb to mean "set one's mind on, be intent on".

24. There is no participle ὄντες here, but it is clearly to be understood from the first clause.

25. From the verb φρονέω to the cognate noun φρόνημα, which occurs in vv. 6, 7, and 27 only in the New Testament. It means the "mind" and is generally taken as equivalent to the expressions with the verb in the previous verse. Cranfield, however, objects, holding that it signifies the "outlook, assumptions, values, desires and purposes, which those who take the side of the flesh share", and correspondingly with "the Spirit's mind".

seem to be referring to the consequences of having the mind of the flesh. He is saying that to be bounded by the flesh is itself death. It is a cutting off of oneself from the life that is life indeed.

The opposite of the mind that is death is "the mind of the Spirit", which, Paul says, "is life and peace." Again the thought is of thoroughgoing concentration. When the things of God dominate one's outlook, when one is constantly responsive to the direction of the Spirit, then there is life. This is the opposite of the death that concentration on the flesh means. Just as the flesh brings death, so the Spirit brings life. But Paul does not leave the antithesis there. The believer has peace as well as life. Paul spoke earlier of peace with God (5:1), but there is general agreement that this is not what he has in mind here. It will be the basis of the peace he now deals with, for without peace with God there could not be the life and peace which the Spirit brings. This peace will mean the enjoyment of all that reconciliation with God means, a peace that pervades the whole of life and cannot be dispelled by the conflicts life brings.[26] We are reminded of the way Paul so constantly links peace with grace in his salutations.

7. Again this verse is linked to the preceding, this time with *because*.[27] We have been told that "the mind of the flesh is death" (v. 6), and now we find that it is "enmity" towards God.[28] It is not simply being slightly uncooperative; it is downright hostility. It means being in the opposite camp, refusing to be subject to God's law. "In withdrawing from God," Brunner writes, "I eliminate him so far as I am concerned. I am hostile to him." Paul explains the hostility in that this "mind" *does not submit to God's law*. The implication is that it ought to do this. That is the common lot of man. God has given his law so that people may know what is right and submit to it. But the person whose general bent is towards the things of this earth, fleshly things, the person dominated by his fallenness, is by that very fact rebellious against God's law.[29] Indeed, Paul says, such a mind cannot submit to God. By definition it is set on a contrary course. There is no possibility that anyone will at the same time set the course of his life on the merely fleshly and be obedient to God. This does not mean being horribly and blatantly wicked. Bowen quotes Bernard of Clairvaux: "So far from being able to answer for my sins, I cannot even answer for my righteousness!" People may do good with completely wrong motives; they may try to "gain control over God by paying Him His

---

26. Gifford speaks of "the holy calm breathed over the soul by the Holy Ghost pouring forth God's love upon the heart." Dodd sees "the condition of inward harmony when all elements of the personality are organized about a single centre, and division and conflict are at an end." W. Foerster discerns an eschatological significance in the term; it is the equivalent of salvation and "is the state of final fulfilment, the normal state of the new creation" (TDNT, II, p. 414).

27. διότι; see the note on 1:19. It means "on this account" and introduces an explanation of what precedes.

28. Paul's word is ἔχθρα, a strong term which must not be watered down.

29. "All the meditations of the flesh are at war with the will of God, for the will of God can be sought only where He has revealed it" (Calvin).

fee." Bernard was concerned lest his good deeds be tainted by self-seeking motives, a danger to which we are all subject.

8. There is disagreement on the way we should understand the link with the previous verse.[30] AV has "so then", Godet suggests "and on the other hand", Barrett "It follows that", Cranfield simply "and"; many, like NIV, simply omit the connective. It seems that Paul is just carrying on the argument, so that "and" is as good an understanding as any. This verse rounds off this section of the argument with the flat statement: "those who are in the flesh cannot please God." This repeats what Paul has just said with some small alterations.[31] The apostle is still concerned that those whose interests are earth-bound cut themselves off from fellowship with God and from the blessings that follow. To be wholly involved in this life is to make it impossible to please God.[32]

9. You, however,[33] points a sharp contrast. Paul has been speaking of the fleshly minded; now he turns away from the worldly to the life of believers. He expresses his confidence in the Romans by his use of the emphatic you; whatever be the case with others, they do not come under the condemnation of being "in the flesh".[34] There is, of course, a sense in which they are "in the flesh". They live this bodily life as all people do. But they are not bound to it, not characterized by it. They do not belong to it. On the contrary, they are "in the Spirit".[35] Parry sees a reference to the human spirit. In contrast to those who live according to the flesh the Roman Christians have set their minds on higher things, on the things that concern their spirits. But Paul is surely referring rather to the Spirit of God. Their life as Christians is "in the Spirit". Earlier he has spoken of believers as being "in Christ" (v. 1). Here he goes on to speak of the Spirit as "in" believers. He can also speak of Christ as "in" his people (v. 10; Gal. 2:20), and of the Spirit as likewise "in" them (here). Paul clearly has the thought of a mutual indwelling; he simply varies the terminology in which he expresses it. His habit, however, is to speak of believers as

---

30. οἱ δέ.

31. In v. 5 he had οἱ κατὰ σάρκα ὄντες, in vv. 6 and 7 τὸ φρόνημα τῆς σαρκός, now οἱ ἐν σαρκὶ ὄντες. These are all ways of bringing out the attitude that Paul opposes, that of being bounded by the concerns of this life. He is not using ἐν σαρκί here in the way he uses it in 2 Cor. 10:3, where it refers to the life we all live in the body; there he contrasts it with κατὰ σάρκα.

32. W. Foerster points out that ἀρέσκω originally meant "to make peace with", "to reconcile", from which it comes to mean "to please". He sees it here as denoting an attitude (TDNT, I, p. 455).

33. ὑμεῖς δέ.

34. James D. G. Dunn regards this as one of the passages where "σάρξ, as not only mortal but defective, disqualifying, and destructive, is set against the life-giving πνεῦμα" (JTS, n.s. XXIV [1973], p. 46).

35. ἐν πνεύματι. BDF 219 (4) note a fluctuation between the local and instrumental meanings of ἐν in this passage. Leenhardt sees ἐν here as instrumental, not locative; the Holy Spirit is not "a quasi-material atmosphere in which the believer had his being". He sees a reference to "communion with God" and goes on, "The Spirit is at one and the same time the author of this communion, the essence of this communion, and the consummation of this communion."

in Christ (rather than Christ in them) and of the Spirit as in believers (rather than they in him).[36] Whichever way he puts it, believers live very close to God and the constant presence of God is important.

If the Spirit of God lives in you is not a way of throwing doubt on the divine indwelling. Paul's *if*[37] means "if (as is the case)". Over against the life in the flesh of which he has been speaking Paul sets life in the Spirit, life of a different quality, life made possible only because the Spirit of God has come to live in believers. *Lives*[38] is important. The Spirit is not an occasional visitor; he takes up residence in God's people.

Paul proceeds to consider another possibility. *If anyone does not have the Spirit of Christ, he does not belong to Christ.* Notice the "characteristic delicacy of expression" (SH); Paul used "you" when speaking of those who are not in the flesh, but now "anyone" as he refers to those who do not have the Spirit. *The Spirit of Christ* is not a common expression (but cf. Acts 16:7; Phil. 1:19; 1 Pet. 1:11). *Spirit*, of course, is to be spelled with a capital, for the word refers to the Holy Spirit (though Schonfield has "spirit of Christ"; this would mean "if anyone does not live in the same way, in the same spirit as Christ"). *The Spirit of Christ* is another way of referring to *the Spirit of God*. The doctrine of the Trinity had not yet been formulated, but it is this kind of expression that led Christians in due time to speak of God as triune.[39] Paul sees the Spirit as integrally related to Christ as well as to the Father. We receive him on the basis of Christ's saving work, and without that there would be no activity of the Spirit in the specifically Christian sense (cf. John 7:39).[40] The verb *have*, like *lives* earlier in the verse, points to more than a passing contact. There is the thought of continuity. Of anyone who lacks the Spirit Paul says, "he is no Christian" (NEB). He does not belong. The presence of the Spirit in believers is not an interesting extra to be seen in a few unusual people (as in the case of the "pneumatic" men of some ancient religions). It is the normal and necessary feature of being a Christian at all.

10. As Paul returns to the positive he returns to direct address *(you)*. His

36. See further C. F. D. Moule, *The Origin of Christology* (Cambridge, 1977), pp. 54-69. John has the thought of the mutual indwelling of believers in Christ (John 15:4) and in the Father (1 John 4:15), but Paul prefers to speak of our being "in Christ" and of the Spirit being in us.

37. εἴπερ, "if indeed, if after all, since" (BAGD). JB translates "since" here, and Hendriksen "seeing that".

38. For οἰκέω see the note on 7:17.

39. A number of commentators point out also that it is such expressions as "the Spirit of Christ" that justify the Western church in speaking of the Spirit as proceeding "from the Father and the Son" (whereas the Eastern church insists that he proceeds "from the Father" only). To have the Father strengthen us through the Spirit in the inner man is to have Christ dwell in us (Eph. 3:16-17). It is interesting that the letters to the seven churches (Rev. 2 and 3) all begin with some expression indicating that they come from Christ and end with an injunction to hear what the Spirit says to the churches.

40. Simeon gives three reasons for the expression "the Spirit of Christ": the Spirit's "peculiar agency in reference to Christ himself" (as in the conception, Luke 1:35; the coming of the Spirit at Jesus' baptism, etc.), "his subserviency to Christ in the economy of redemption", and "its being his special office to glorify Christ."

But makes a contrast with what has gone before; he is speaking now of the believer, the one in whom Christ is. There seems little difference between the indwelling of Christ and that of the Holy Spirit. The indwelling of the Spirit is mentioned both before and after this verse, and there is no indication of a change of subject. Paul is not identifying Christ with the Spirit, but he is saying that in the indwelling of the Spirit none less than Christ is present. " 'Spirit in you' is impossible apart from 'Christ in you'. Union with Christ is the only way into the life of the Age to Come, of which the distinguishing mark is the Spirit" (Barrett). Dodd agrees that Paul is not identifying Christ with the Spirit, but "his virtual identification of the experience of the Spirit with the experience of the indwelling Christ is of the utmost value. It saved Christian thought from falling into a non-moral, half-magical conception of the supernatural in human experience, and it brought all 'spiritual' experience to the test of the historical revelation of God in Jesus Christ."[41]

When Christ is in you, says Paul, *your body is dead because of sin.*[42] This is a difficult expression. We should probably take it as a subordinate clause, "though the body . . ." (as RSV, NEB, Moffatt, etc.). But the big question is the meaning of *dead*. The body has been characterized as the body of sin (6:6), the body in which sin reigns (6:12), this body of death from which Paul longs to be delivered (7:24), and he will go on to speak of it as the body whose deeds are to be mortified by the Spirit (v. 13). When anyone is in Christ this body is not supreme, and it is possible to take the words here to mean that this body is dead, utterly overcome. The difficulty with this exegesis is the following *because of sin*. We are delivered from sin, not because of it. We should accordingly take death to be physical death. Because we have sinned we will die, but this is not the really significant thing.[43] That is rather that "the Spirit is life because of righteousness." The question here is whether Paul is referring to the human spirit (as NIV, Hodge, Hunter, and others) or to the Holy Spirit (with Calvin, Murray, Barrett, etc.). The contrast with "body" leads many to affirm that the human spirit must be in view here, and that would make a fine antithesis. Against this is the fact that in verses 9-11 every other use of *pneuma* refers to the Holy Spirit. Further, Paul does not say "is alive" but "is life". This is something that can be said of the Holy Spirit, but the human spirit is not "life".[44]

---

41. Cf. Käsemann, "The Pauline doctrine of the Spirit is constitutively shaped by the fact that the apostle, so far as we can see, is the first to relate it indissolubly to christology. In the Spirit the risen Lord manifests his presence and lordship on earth" (p. 213). This "risen Lord" is the same Lord Jesus who walked this earth.

42. Barth comments paradoxically that "Christ in us" is "both the place where we are deprived of our liberty and the place where we receive it".

43. Haldane comments that there are three deaths: "one is in this life, the other at the end of this life, and the third after this life." Believers, he thinks, are delivered from the first and the third, but undergo the second.

44. R. Bultmann sees a reference to "the divine *pneuma*, which has become the subject-self, so to say, of the Christian; the contrast of *pneuma* to *soma* ('the *soma* of sin') requires this understanding" (*Theology of the New Testament*, I [London, 1952], pp. 208-9).

There is some discussion as to the meaning of *righteousness* here. It may be the righteousness that is imputed to believers when they become Christians (so, e.g., Lenski). It may be the righteousness believers demonstrate in daily life (Lagrange). Or this may be asking the wrong question. It is possible that Paul is not distinguishing between one form of righteousness and another. A good deal of his argument in the previous chapters depends on the fact that justification and sanctification are not to be separated. The believer is credited with "the righteousness of God"; it is this that brings him into the sphere of salvation. But then he is required to live a life that is in conformity with this salvation; he cannot be indifferent to the importance of righteousness in his daily living. At this point it may well be that Paul has in mind neither the process that brings salvation, nor the life that follows, but both.[45]

11. Once again Paul's *if* has the meaning "if (as is the case)".[46] He goes on to relate the Spirit to the Father (cf. 1 Cor. 2:11; 12:3, etc.), as in verse 9 he related him to Christ. The Father is characterized by his raising of Jesus. It is usual in the New Testament to ascribe the resurrection to the Father, though we should not overlook the fact that Jesus said he had power to lay down his life and take it up again (John 10:17-18), nor that on occasion it is said that he rose (14:9; Acts 10:41; 1 Thess. 4:14). The Spirit, then, of the resurrecting Father "lives" in the Roman Christians. He does not pay a fleeting visit, but "has its home" (Way) in them.

Paul goes on to the further point that the Father (again characterized as having raised Christ)[47] will in due course raise believers too (for this link, cf. 1 Cor. 6:14; 2 Cor. 4:14; 1 Thess. 4:14). But where he speaks of God as "raising" Jesus, he speaks of him as "giving life" to believers. We stand in a relation to death different from that of "the Prince of life" (Acts 3:15); we need not only to be raised, but to be given life.[48] God will give life, Paul says, to our *mortal bodies*, where the adjective may be significant. At the resurrection our bodies will not only cease to be dead but to be liable to death.

The Spirit is not usually linked with resurrection, but here he seems to

---

45. Cf. SH, the expression "includes all the senses in which righteousness is brought home to man, first imputed, then imparted, then practised." Denney says, "It is probably not real to distinguish here between 'justification' and 'moral righteousness of life,' and to say that the word means either to the exclusion of the other. The whole argument of chaps. vi.- viii. is that neither can exist without the other."

46. This is the sixth time since v. 8 that he has used δέ. This term is not a strong adversative, but it can set things over against one another. Throughout this section of the letter Paul is setting forth some important contrasts, here the contrast between life here and now and the eschatological consummation.

47. Bengel finds significance in the change from "Jesus" to "Christ": "The name *Jesus* has respect to Himself; the name *Christ* has reference to us. The former appellation, as a proper name, belongs to the person; the latter, as an appellative, belongs to the office."

48. Bowen speaks of the present activity of the Spirit as assuring believers of the fulfilment of God's promise. He illustrates this by referring to a young woman who looks at the engagement ring on her finger; the ring "which she has already received, 'belongs' to her marriage which has not yet taken place; and so the Spirit belongs to the new age which our bodies have not yet entered, but will enter in the future."

be. It is not clear whether Paul is saying that the Spirit is to be the agent in raising us or the guarantee that we will be raised.[49] Both are true, and it does not seem to matter greatly which way we resolve the textual problem.

2. The Family of God, 8:12-17

> [12]Therefore, brothers, we have an obligation—but it is not to the sinful nature, to live according to it. [13]For if you live according to the sinful nature, you will die; but if by the Spirit you put to death the misdeeds of the body, you will live, [14]because those who are led by the Spirit of God are sons of God. [15]For you did not receive a spirit that makes you a slave again to fear, but you received the Spirit of sonship.[a] And by him we cry, "Abba,[b] Father." [16]The Spirit himself testifies with our spirit that we are God's children. [17]Now if we are children, then we are heirs—heirs of God and co-heirs with Christ, if indeed we share in his sufferings in order that we may also share in his glory.
>
> [a]15 Or adoption   [b]15 Aramaic for Father

Having made it clear that Christ gives life to believers, Paul goes on to bring out some of the implications of all this. It is important that those who are Christ's live as those who are Christ's. Paul reminds us of the obligations that rest upon us and of the place of mortification in the Christian life. And that brings us to the Holy Spirit, for it is what the Spirit does in us that enables us to render the service to which we are called.

12. Paul's "wherefore therefore" (see on 5:18) introduces the logical consequences. This paragraph is closely connected with the preceding. His "we" links Paul with his readers, whom he addresses with the affectionate *brothers* (see on 1:13). Then he moves to the thought of *obligation*, though the word would better be rendered "debtors".[50] The justification for NIV is that no monetary debt is in question. But certainly the note of obligation is strong. Paul is laying it down firmly that for Christians the flesh has no rights; as Earle says, "we owe the flesh nothing". The way Paul puts it, "we are debtors, not to the flesh—", leads us to look for "but to the Spirit" or for some other expression to indicate where our debt lies, "but this is elegantly left to be understood" (Bengel). The characteristic life of the Christian owes nothing to the flesh, though we should not ignore the force of this warning about "the flesh" in a letter to Christians. "The flesh" is not eradicated but is an ever-present reality. Paul goes on to explain that to be indebted to the flesh means "to live according to the flesh". This is not an option for the believer.[51]

---

49. There is a textual problem here. τοῦ ἐνοικοῦντος αὐτοῦ πνεύματος is read by ℵ A C etc., and τὸ ἐνοικοῦν αὐτοῦ πνεῦμα by B D etc. There seems no compelling reason for choosing either.

50. ὀφειλέται.

51. τοῦ with the infinitive often means "in order that" (which Hodge sees as the meaning here). But in Paul this sense is often weakened, and this passage may be one in which there is "a very loose relationship between the substantive and the infinitive" and which "tend[s] toward the consecutive sense" (BDF 400 [2]). Moulton regards it as epexegetic (M, I, p. 217). We should probably understand the present infinitive ζῆν to indicate the continuing attitude, the bent of the life.

13. There is a change from "we" to "you" as Paul turns to the link between living the fleshly life and death. This does not mean that he saw the Romans as living the unregenerate life; Lloyd-Jones sees "a general statement comparable to the form of speech which we use when we say to a person, 'If you put your finger into that fire you will be burned'" (p. 109). But there is certainly a strong note of warning. To live "according to the flesh"[52] is to live with one's horizon bounded by the flesh, that is, by the concerns of this life. To live like this is death (cf. 1 Tim. 5:6). There is certainty in *you will die*,[53] "a sure effect from the given cause" (CBSC).

The contrary supposition is made with equal definiteness. If you mortify ("put to death", GNB)[54] the body's deeds you will live. The verb may be used of literally putting a person to death (Luke 21:16 etc.), or of undergoing the danger of death (v. 36). Mortifying deeds means killing them off, getting rid of them altogether. But the tense is present, which indicates a continuing activity. It is not something that we can do once and for all and be done with. It is a daily duty. What is to be killed is "the deeds of the body". NIV has *misdeeds*, a translation that can be defended, for the word is sometimes used of evil actions (as in Luke 23:51).[55] Such actions are the objects of decisive and hostile action as far as the believer is concerned. There is to be no life in the deeds in question. They are not living options. And this is to take place through an action of the believer ("you put to death"), though not an unaided action, for the mortification is to be done "by the Spirit". It is the energy of the divine Spirit, not the energy of the flesh, that enables the believer to put the body's deeds to death.[56] Paul speaks of the *body*, not the "flesh"; he probably has in mind the fact that the body is "this body of death" (7:24, where see note; it is this body that he buffets and keeps under control, 1 Cor. 9:27). If you do this, Paul says, *you will live*. Real life is not a possibility when we choose to luxuriate in the body's deeds. We must renounce all such deeds if we are to experience life in the Spirit. This is not because some meritorious achievement is required of us as a way of earning such life. It is because the two are incompatible. The one excludes the other. There is a living that is death and there is a putting to death that is life.

14. *Because*[57] carries on the logical sequence; it introduces the basis for saying, "you will live". *Those* translates a comprehensive term[58] which is

52. κατὰ σάρκα; see the note on 1:3.

53. μέλλετε ἀποθνῄσκειν, μέλλετε here "denoting an action that necessarily follows a divine decree *is destined, must, will certainly*" (BAGD). Cf. Burton, 72.

54. θανατόω, "to put to death", points to an activity on our part; we actively mortify the deeds of the body. There are passives of what is done to us in 7:4, 6, etc., but this is something we do, not something done to us.

55. LSJ note its use in Polybius for "trickery, treachery".

56. SH take the words to refer to the human spirit, being impressed by the antithesis to σάρξ, but they add, "but it is the human πνεῦμα in direct contact with the Divine." That is the point. Paul is not referring to an unaided human action, just as he is not speaking of a purely divine intervention.

57. γάρ.

58. ὅσοι; BAGD comment that even without πάντες it has the meaning "all that".

better rendered "all who" (NEB) or "Everyone" (JB). Paul admits of no exception. The people he is describing are *led by the Spirit of God*.[59] Most commentators agree that we should understand Paul to mean that the Spirit "leads" people, but Käsemann argues for "drives": "The phrase 'driven by the Spirit' in v. 14 is taken from the vocabulary of the enthusiasts according to 1 Cor 12:2. It therefore should not be weakened to 'be led by'" (p. 226). But it is not easy to see why this verse should be interpreted by the very difficult 1 Corinthians 12:2. Käsemann gives no reason for thinking that the "enthusiasts" of Corinth should not only be understood to be in Rome but also to be so important there that they became the objects of Paul's writing. The vocabulary is against him, too.[60] We can say with Haldane, "we are naturally so indisposed to go to Jesus Christ, that it is necessary that God, by His Spirit, draw us to Him", but this is a long way from "driven". Paul is saying that what this verb conveys is true of all believers and, while we may fairly apply "driven" to a few ecstatics, it is not an accurate description of the typical Christian experience. Elsewhere Paul says, "if you are led by the Spirit, you are not under law" (Gal. 5:18), where the note is freedom rather than compulsion. With a different verb we read in the discourse in the Upper Room of the Spirit leading believers in (or into) all the truth (John 16:13). Such passages emphasize that it is the Spirit who shows us the way. We are not left to our own wisdom (or the lack of it). It is these people, then, those led by the Spirit, who *are sons of God*. NASB has, "these are sons of God", retaining a pronoun which puts some emphasis on the fact that they really are God's sons. We should understand the leading of the Spirit as a distinguishing sign of God's sons, but not as making us sons. It is "Because you are sons" that "God sent the Spirit of his Son into our hearts" (Gal. 4:6). As in verse 9, the work of the Spirit is not an option or an extra for the advanced Christian. Being led by the Spirit is a mark of all God's people. Earle sees the result in their conduct: "They not only belong to the family but act like it!" We should not miss the note of the great dignity attaching to believers. From verse 13 we learn that they do not die. But being Christians is more than a negative, the fact that they do not die. It is a wonderful positive, being admitted into the family of God. Paul does not often call believers "sons of God" (but cf. v. 19; 9:26; 2 Cor. 6:18; Gal. 3:26).

15. This is the third verse in succession to be introduced by "for".[61] As Paul elaborates on sonship to God, he uses a closely knit argument. He speaks

---

59. πνεύματι looks like a dative of agent, but grammarians are reluctant to describe it that way. They prefer to see it as the dative of instrument (e.g., IBNTG, p. 44), which seems a curious way to view the Spirit of God. Perhaps this is no more than semantics, for Robertson says of the use of the dative, "no usage of this case is more common than that of means. With things we call it means, with persons agent, though more often the agent is expressed by ὑπό with genitive-ablative" (p. 532).

60. BAGD nowhere include "drive" as a possible meaning for the verb ἄγω; it has this passage under "be led, allow oneself to be led", which is a long way from "be driven".

61. γάρ.

of receiving, where his aorist tense points to a definite time, probably that of conversion. But there are problems with his use of "spirit", and commentators are divided. We could use a small "s" in both instances in this verse and understand the apostle to mean "a temper, mood or state" (the "spirit of slavery", NBCR), or translate "the spirit of slaves . . . the spirit of sons" (as JB; NASB is similar). Or we could take the first with a small "s" and the second with a capital, as Moffatt, "You have received no slavish spirit . . . you have received the Spirit of sonship" (so NIV). Or we could use the capital both times, as Murray: "Ye did not receive the Holy Spirit as a Spirit of bondage but as the Spirit of adoption" (so TH). Any of these must remain a possibility. But throughout this whole passage the emphasis is on the work of the Holy Spirit, and it seems that Paul is here saying two things about the Spirit: first, negatively, that the Spirit believers received is not one of bondage; second, positively, he is a Spirit of sonship (for the Spirit believers receive cf. 1 Cor. 2:12; 2 Tim. 1:7). The Spirit does not make people slaves but sons.

Slavery would have meant a good deal more to Paul's readers, who were in daily contact with it, than it does to us. Paul has been arguing that they have been given a wonderful freedom in Christ, a freedom they may enjoy to the full even if in their physical existence they were in fact slaves. We might not have expected him to say *again*, but the word is apparently being used in the sense of "back" and refers to a reversion to the state from which they had been delivered.[62] Christ had freed them from their bondage to sin; they must not think that the Spirit would lead them back to it. Paul has, of course, used slavery as a way of describing the wholeheartedness of Christian service (1:1; 6:19; 7:6). Paradoxically this is real freedom, as Käsemann points out: "Radical obedience is pointedly defined as slavery. But insofar as this is offered to the gracious Lord as a joyful sacrifice (1 Cor 9:17), it also denotes genuine freedom and sonship" (p. 227). It is not this that Paul has in mind when he refers to "a spirit of slavery". Rather, he is thinking of what sin does to a person. This state is further described as *to fear*, for slavery to sin inevitably leads to fear. John tells us that there is no fear in love and that perfect love casts fear out (1 John 4:18). Paul is saying that the leading of the Spirit delivers from fear and does not take us back to it again.

On the contrary,[63] believers received "the Spirit of adoption". The word for "adoption" is used only by Paul in the New Testament (five times, three being in Romans), and it does not occur in LXX, for the Jews did not practise adoption. Some Old Testament examples are suggested,[64] but most

---

62. BAGD say that πάλιν may be used in "expressions that denote a falling back into a previous state or a return to a previous activity."

63. ἀλλά, the strong adversative, has this force.

64. Most involve people with a foreign background, such as Moses (Exod. 2:10) or Esther (Esth. 2:7). Provisions such as polygamy, the giving of a concubine to provide children, and levirate marriage took care of most situations. This probably accounts for the fact that there are no laws on adoption in the Old Testament and that even the word is lacking. Despite this, F. H. Palmer denies a Roman background to the New Testament concept, seeing only "Jewish custom, which conferred the benefits of the family on the adoptee" (IBD, I, p. 17).

scholars agree that Paul took the concept from Roman or Greek law in both of which adoption was important. Francis Lyall argues convincingly that Paul's concept is taken from Roman, not Jewish law.[65] Most agree, though some think rather of Greek law. SH cite E. L. Hicks for the information that "No word is more common in Greek inscriptions of the Hellenistic time: the idea, like the word, is native Greek".[66] It is a useful word for Paul, for it signifies being granted the full rights and privileges of sonship in a family to which one does not belong by nature. This is a good illustration of one aspect of Paul's understanding of what it means to become a Christian. The believer is admitted to the heavenly family, to which he has no rights of his own. But he is now admitted and can call God "Father".

Paul goes on, *by him*[67] *we cry,* "Abba, *Father"* (an expression found again in Mark 14:36; Gal. 4:6). There has been some discussion of the verb *cry*, which is perhaps not what we would have expected. It may well point to the emotion involved in the uttering of the cry in question. It is also true that the verb is used a number of times of crying to God in prayer (Ps. 3:4; 4:3, etc.), and it would make a lot of sense if we were to think of Paul as referring to the fervent prayer of the believer (cf. Denney's comment, "We have not only the status, but the heart of sons"). Paul certainly has prayer in mind, for who else would Christians address in this way? But there seems no reason to think of ecstatic utterance, as some have suggested.[68] It is the fervent utterance of the devout believer that he has in mind.

The word *Abba* is an Aramaic word meaning "Father".[69] The word is from the babbling of a little child (like "papa") and is the familiar term used in the home. But before we assume that it was used much like our "Papa" or

---

65. "Roman Law in the Writings of Paul—Adoption", JBL, LXXXVIII (1969), pp. 458-66. His conclusion is "that Paul's use of the term 'adoption' in Romans, Ephesians, and Galatians was a deliberate, considered, and appropriate reference to Roman law" (p. 466). In this process, "The adoptee is taken out of his previous state and is placed in a new relationship with his new *paterfamilias*. All his old debts are canceled, and in effect he starts a new life. From that time the *paterfamilias* owns all the property and acquisitions of the adoptee, controls his personal relationships, and has rights of discipline. On the other hand he is involved in liability by the actions of the adoptee and owes reciprocal duties of support and maintenance" (*ibid.*).

66. W. von Martitz outlines Greek forms of adoption (TDNT, VIII, pp. 397-98). He says, "The continuity of the family and the family cultus was maintained by adoption. . . . The adopted son entered at once into the rights of the parent and undertook out of the assigned income to keep the testator and his family to the end of their lives" (p. 398).

67. ἐν ᾧ may mean "by whom" or "in the time which" (TH). Most agree that "by whom" is the meaning, but some (e.g., Hunter) agree with RSV in putting a full stop after "sonship" and going on, "When we cry 'Abba! Father!' it is the Spirit himself bearing witness. . . ." But it seems better to reject it (with Cranfield, Knox, and others). "By whom" is surely the meaning. SBk find no place in rabbinic literature in which the Holy Spirit is mentioned in connection with an Israelite's prayer; this is a specifically Christian teaching.

68. Cf. Käsemann, "In it the congregation is uttering an ecstatic cry in response to the message of salvation" (p. 228). But he gives no satisfactory reason for understanding it this way.

69. It is a vocative rather than the emphatic state (BAGD), the exact equivalent of ὁ πατήρ which follows.

"Daddy", we should reflect that the head of a family was an august figure in first-century society (the Roman *paterfamilias* still had the right to put members of his household to death, even if the right was used rarely; cf. Gen. 38:24). But the word certainly points to love and to intimacy. The Jews would not address God in this familiar way, but when they prayed to him as "Father" they always added something like "in heaven" to avoid any impression of undue presumption. In the Gospels Jesus constantly addresses God as "Father", and in Gethsemane he has this doubled form, "Abba, Father" (Mark 14:36). It is probable that the opening of the Lord's Prayer in the language Jesus spoke would be this "Abba"; if so, Jesus was giving his followers the privilege of being in the heavenly family and of addressing God in this warm and familiar way.[70] As G. Schrenk says, "an everyday infant sound is applied without inhibition to God. . . . This basic word tells us that God is not a distant Ruler in transcendence but One who is intimately close. Unconditional faith in the Father is thus taken seriously."[71] We should not overlook the fact that in this passage Paul puts the Father at the center. The Spirit does not cause us to cry "I am God's son", but "God is my Father." The believer looks at God rather than contemplating himself. The repetition of the word, once in Aramaic and once in Greek, is probably not to be seen as a translation, for translation is out of place in prayer. Rather, the word was repeated. We need not be surprised at the use of an Aramaic term by Greek-speaking people, for we do much the same when we say "Amen", or "Hallelujah".

16. This time there is no connecting word, and the asyndeton perhaps gives added weight to what is being said. Paul proceeds to say that the Spirit *himself* bears witness, where the pronoun puts emphasis on the truth that it is none less than the Spirit. There is a problem as to whether we should understand him to say that the Spirit bears witness "to" our spirit or that he bears witness "with" our spirit. The form of the verb might be held to favor the latter, but this is not conclusive.[72] Great names can be urged in favor of "with our spirit" (as Hunter, Haldane, Murray, and others; cf. NEB, JB, Moffatt). But the thought that the Spirit bears witness to our spirit and thus enables us

---

70. Cf. J. Jeremias: "In the Lord's Prayer Jesus gives His disciples a share in this privilege to address God as *abba*, a share in His position as the only begotten. He empowers them to speak to their Heavenly Father literally as the small child speaks to his father, in the same confident and childlike manner. This one word *abba*, if it is understood in its full sense, comprehends the whole message of the gospel" (ET, LXXI [1959-60], p. 144). At the same time Paul's use is not confined to the Lord's Prayer or any other liturgical form. It is, as G. Schrenk puts it, "an experience of fundamental significance. . . . Paul views it as the working of the Spirit of adoption given in the heart" (TDNT, V, p. 1006).

71. TDNT, V, p. 985.

72. συμμαρτυρέω means strictly "bear witness along with another", though in usage this is weakened to "agree" (cf. 2:15). But if we take it strictly in this place, we are saying "that the spiritual ego of the man in Christ already declares him to be a child of God". This leads us to see the simple sense "bear witness" (H. Strathmann, TDNT, IV, p. 509).

to cry "Abba, Father" is the view of Luther, Calvin, Hodge, Leenhardt, and others. We cannot stand alongside the Holy Spirit and give testimony. Perhaps the decisive point is that put forward by Cranfield, who asks, "what standing has our spirit in *this* matter?" Unaided, we cannot testify to the reality of our standing before God. But we are not unaided; the Spirit of God testifies to our Spirit and gives us the assurance of our membership in the heavenly family. There is a direct operation of the Holy Spirit on our spirit. The content of that testimony is *that we are God's children*. The change from "sons" (v. 14) to *children* is probably not significant, though, as Black points out, "children" includes daughters as well as sons. As we saw on verse 14, Paul uses the expression "sons of God" five times. He has "children of God" four times (8:16, 21; 9:8; Phil. 2:15; it also occurs twice in John and four times in 1 John). Neither expression can be said to be very common. Though membership in the heavenly family is real and important, the New Testament writers prefer to express it otherwise than by calling believers either "sons" or "children" of God.

17. Paul proceeds to unfold some of the implications of being members of God's family. If we are *children*, he says, we are also[73] *heirs*. The word properly denotes those who receive property as a result of the death of someone else, but F. J. A. Hort points out that in the Old Testament the concept of inheritance "apparently contains no implication of hereditary succession, as it does usually in classical Greek. The sense is rather 'sanctioned and settled possession.'"[74] The concept of inheritance is an important one in the Old Testament, and it carries over into the New Testament. SH point out that it originally meant "simple possession of the Holy Land", but later came to mean "Its permanent and assured possession" (Ps. 25:13; 37:9, 11, etc.). It especially denoted "the secure possession won by the Messiah" (Isa. 60:21; 61:7), and thus it became "a symbol of all Messianic blessings" (Matt. 5:5; 19:29; 25:34, etc.). Paul uses the term here to denote full possession of all that sonship means in the new age, but it is not so much ownership as relationship that he has in mind. He speaks of being *heirs of God,* a bold piece of imagery, found here only in the New Testament (though cf. Gal. 4:7). Since God does not die, there is no question of inheritance in the strict sense of the term. But the heir is in a position of privilege as a result of his place in the family. Paul has been speaking of "sons" and of "children"; we are in a privileged position because of our membership in the family of none less than God. We are also *co-heirs with Christ*. It is difficult to see what possessions we share as fellow heirs with Christ; the title is surely one of dignity, assuring us of our place in the heavenly family where he is the Son (he also spoke of himself in a parable as heir, Matt. 21:38).

But to this picture of privilege Paul immediately adds another consid-

---

73. Turner points out that the original meaning of καί, before it became merely a coordinating particle, was "also", and cites this as an example (M, III, p. 335).

74. *The First Epistle of St Peter* (London, 1898), p. 35.

eration: *if indeed we share in his sufferings.*[75] Neither Paul nor any other New Testament writer lets us forget that believers have no easy path. Their Master suffered, and they are called to suffering, too. This is not some perverse accident but an integral part of discipleship. But this suffering is in some way linked to the sufferings of Christ (2 Cor. 1:5; Phil. 3:10; Col. 1:24; 2 Tim. 2:11-12; cf. Mark 10:39). It is interesting that, when Saul of Tarsus was persecuting the church, the Christ who met him on the Damascus road asked him, "why do you persecute me?" (Acts 9:4). He is one with us in our sufferings. But also "we died with Christ" (6:8). We are one with him in his death. But our sufferings are not meaningless. We suffer *in order that*[76] *we may also share in his glory.* The path of suffering is the path to glory.

3. The Glorious Future, 8:18-25

> [18]I consider that our present sufferings are not worth comparing with the glory that will be revealed in us. [19]The creation waits in eager expectation for the sons of God to be revealed. [20]For the creation was subjected to frustration, not by its own choice, but by the will of the one who subjected it, in hope [21]that the creation itself will be liberated from its bondage to decay and brought into the glorious freedom of the children of God.
>
> [22]We know that the whole creation has been groaning as in the pains of childbirth right up to the present time. [23]Not only so, but we ourselves, who have the firstfruits of the Spirit, groan inwardly as we wait eagerly for our adoption as sons, the redemption of our bodies. [24]For in this hope we were saved. But hope that is seen is no hope at all. Who hopes for what he already has? [25]But if we hope for what we do not yet have, we wait for it patiently.

It is a wonderful thing to belong to God's family, to be "heirs of God and co-heirs with Christ" (v. 17). Paul might well have gone from this thought to the magnificent vista that it opens out before us, and so he does in due course. But he was not unmindful that our heavenly destiny does not blot out the fact of our earthly existence and that that earthly existence is in a troubled world. There is pain and misery in this world, and they are not confined to human existence. Paul recognizes that there is pain throughout creation, and he writes movingly about it: "here we have, as nowhere else in the Bible— perhaps nowhere in ancient literature—a man who feels with the pain of creation" (Gore). But for Paul the great thing is that this is not meaningless pain, and he could look forward with confidence to the final unfolding of the

75. εἴπερ does not introduce a doubt about what follows; it "is a rather emphatic term and implies that Paul assumes that his statement represents the circumstances as they do in fact exist" (TH). The verb συμπάσχομεν (used again in the New Testament only in 1 Cor. 12:26) lacks a complement, but there is no doubt that we should supply "with him", not "with one another". The same is true of συνδοξασθῶμεν (used here only in the New Testament). Paul has nine different compounds with σύν in vv. 16-29; he is not writing about a religion of solitude.

76. "The ἵνα indicates the necessary connection between our suffering with Christ, and our sharing in His glory" (Boylan).

purpose of God. He is sure of this, despite the pains of the present. Denney cites R. A. Lipsius for the "threefold testimony to the future transfiguration" that he discerns here, in verses 19-22 "the sighing of creation", 23-25 "the yearning hope of Christians themselves", and in 26-27 "the intercession of the Spirit".

18. Contemplation of the future privileges of the believer leads Paul to think of the contrast this makes with the present state. He shows that suffering is the path we tread as we move to blessing and to glory. Since the early Christians led a somewhat precarious existence, it may well be that the contemplation of the future glory was very precious to them. Paul links this to the preceding with a conjunction giving the reason for the foregoing.[77] *I consider* should not be taken as a mere matter of personal opinion. There is, to be sure, the thought of a calculation, a mental weighing of the evidence, but the word here "expresses strong assurance and not doubt" (TH).[78] Paul speaks of *our present sufferings*, which means the sufferings characteristic of this present age[79] rather than the present moment. There is no reason to think that the circumstances in which he wrote were especially significant, but this age is in marked contrast to the age to come. Paul holds that the believer must expect sufferings in this present age. There is suffering that is the direct result of our sinning and there is suffering that we endure for Christ's sake, suffering that arises directly from our Christian profession in a world that rejects Christ. But beyond that, there is suffering that arises simply because we are in this imperfect world. Paul is realistic; there is no reason to think that Christians will be free from troubles in this present life. It is important, therefore, that they learn how to bear them.

Paul sets these sufferings over against the coming *glory*, saying that they are *not worth*[80] *comparing* with it.[81] Troublesome as they are to us who experience them, they are of no weight when set over against the glory that awaits God's people. Paul also has this idea elsewhere; he speaks of "our light and momentary troubles" as "achieving for us an eternal glory that far outweighs them all" (2 Cor. 4:17). So here he looks forward to *the glory that will be revealed*. There is a touch of certainty about *will*, which is not simply the future but a

---

77. γάϱ. See on 1:9 for NIV's omission of this word. Dana and Mantey say that here and "in several succeeding verses it introduces reasons" (DM, p. 243). TH, however, sees not so much a "logical conclusion" as Paul "making a theological declaration in light of his own faith and hope." It is possible, however, to recognize the theological importance of these words without missing the logical connection.

78. The word is λογίζομαι, of which Boylan says, "it indicates certain knowledge".

79. τοῦ νῦν καιϱοῦ.

80. ἄξιος is connected with ἄγω. W. Foerster says of it, "Properly, 'bringing up the other beam of the scales,' 'bringing into equilibrium,' and therefore 'equivalent'" (TDNT, I, p. 379; cf. GT).

81. BDF note this use of πϱός with the accusative as "'In comparison with' (classical)" (239 [8]). It is not common in the New Testament.

separate verb.[82] The glory will be *revealed*,[83] not created. The implication is that it is already existent, but not apparent. The Jews had some very materialistic ideas of what life would be like in the coming age, and there are some striking sayings which emphasize unusual fruitfulness in vines and the like. Paul is just as certain of the glory, but he does not see it in any materialistic way. The glory, he says, will be revealed *in us*, where his preposition is not the one we might have expected.[84] He may mean that in the coming age all that is involved in our being "sons of God" will become apparent and that this will be a revelation in us as well as to us.

19. Another "for" (again omitted by NIV) carries on the chain of reasoning. There is much to be said for the view that the whole of verses 19-30 supports what has been said in verse 18. Paul uses a most unusual word[85] to convey the thought of persistent and eager expectation. This expectation he ascribes to *the creation*,[86] a term which has caused a good deal of discussion. It is broad enough to include everything that God has created, but not many see such a wide meaning here. Thus it is hard to envisage good angels as being included, for they were not subjected to the "frustration" of verse 20. Evil angels are surely not eagerly anticipating the revelation of the sons of God. It can scarcely be a reference to believers, for they are distinguished from "the whole creation" (vv. 22-23), nor to unbelievers, for they are not looking for the revelation of the sons of God. This makes it probable that Paul means the whole of subpersonal creation.[87] He personifies it and pictures it as looking

82. His expression is τὴν μέλλουσαν δόξαν ἀποκαλυφθῆναι. BAGD include μέλλω here under "be on the point of", but it seems rather to belong to their classification "*be destined, inevitable* (acc. to God's will) ἀποκαλυφθῆναι *that is destined to be revealed* Gal 3:23." Moule draws attention to the unusual word order and notes a similar order with the same two verbs in Gal. 3:23; he wonders whether there is "any other evidence in κοινή Greek for μέλλω exercising a disturbing influence" (IBNTG, pp. 169-70). Turner points out that, whereas μέλλω takes the future infinitive in classical Greek, in the New Testament it has the present 84 times and the aorist only five times (as here). Paul's construction is unusual, but there is no problem with his meaning.

83. Paul uses the verb ἀποκαλύπτω in half its New Testament occurrences (13 out of 26). He is very interested in revelation.

84. εἰς (cf. 1 Pet. 1:3-4). NEB sees it as meaning "for us", NASB as "to us"; cf. Godet, "at once *for* us and *in* us".

85. ἀποκαραδοκία appears to derive from κάρα, "head", and Ionic δέκομαι, "perhaps origin. 'to stretch'", thus "stretching the head forward" (G. Delling, TDNT, I, p. 393; Delling says, "There are no instances of the term except in Christian literature"). The ἀπό may be intensive, or have the thought of stretching the head "away from" the body. Paul uses the word again in Phil. 1:20. Wilckens speaks of creation as "in eager longing" for the future revelation (he sees the idea of eager, anxious waiting in the corresponding verb as well).

86. κτίσις, which may refer to the activity of creating or to what is created; clearly it is the latter meaning here.

87. Many scholars apparently find the idea of a cosmic fall difficult and opt for a view which confines it in one way or another to mankind. Thus Leenhardt sees the meaning as "the world in so far as it is distinct from the church", while John G. Gager cites approvingly H. Hommel's view that in Paul the "primary reference has become the nonbelieving, human world" (JBL, LXXXIX [1970], p. 329). Käsemann similarly holds that

for the consummation of all things (which should not surprise us too much;
the Old Testament also contains passages which speak of nature as rejoicing,
such as Ps. 96:12; 98:8; Isa. 35:1; 55:12). Paul uses two unusual double compounds (NIV, *waits* and *eager expectation*) which together give a vivid picture of
the hushed expectancy with which the whole creation awaits the disclosure of
the coming glory. Creation waits for[88] "the revelation[89] of the sons of God."
Sonship to God is a reality. There is such a thing as membership in the
heavenly family, even though creation as a whole does not know the sons as
such. Paul is saying that in due time all will be made plain.

20. The third *For* in as many verses (this time translated in NIV) carries
the argument on in logical sequence. We know that the creation waits for the
revelation because it has been *subjected to frustration* (or "futility", NASB).[90]
Of itself and without any thought of divine purpose the whole creation is
futile. Paul is saying that sin, which affected the divine purpose in man,
affected also the entire nonhuman creation. Lacking the purpose for which it
was designed, it has no purpose. As Bruce puts it, "Man is part of 'nature',
and the whole 'nature' of which he forms part was created good, has been
involved in frustration and futility by sin, and will ultimately be redeemed."
The creation, Paul says, *was subjected* to this futility, and that *not by its own
choice*. The aorist tense of the verb looks to a single occasion, which is not
likely to be creation. Rather it is the fall, which Paul sees as cosmic in its
effects. This subjection was not by creation's own choice but *by the will of the
one who subjected it*.[91] Who is it that subjected it? Most agree that Paul means
God, but some see a reference to Adam (Robinson, O'Neill), whose act was
responsible, to Satan, or to Adam or Satan (Godet). But Scripture never assigns to Adam or to Satan the power to bring about such a far-reaching
change. We must think of God (cf. Gen. 3:17). And this accords with the note
of hope on which the verse ends. There is no reason to think of Adam or of
Satan acting in hope for the future of the race, but hope is characteristic of

---

"There can be no doubt that non-Christians are included" (p. 233). Manson finds a problem in seeing how the material world can "obtain the glorious liberty of the children of
God" and settles for "mankind".

88. ἀπεκδέχεται is a double compound with the meaning "await eagerly" (BAGD).
W. Grundmann sees "a distinctive Pauline usage" in its use for the "expectation of the
end" (TDNT, II, p. 56).

89. ἀποκάλυψις points to an uncovering, a revealing. It may be used of the second
coming (1 Cor. 1:7).

90. The word ματαιότης is found three times only in the New Testament, but 37 times
in LXX of Ecclesiastes. Its meaning is "emptiness, futility, purposelessness, transitoriness"
(BAGD). In LXX it usually translates הבל, which Brown, Driver, and Briggs define as
"vapour, breath," and go on to say is used "fig. of what is evanescent, unsubstantial,
worthless". μάταιος is the very opposite of τέλειος.

91. διὰ τὸν ὑποτάξαντα. BDF regard this use of διά as classical (222). BAGD include
this under the heading "to denote the efficient cause" and translate it with "by". NIV has
inserted *the will*; it is absent from the Greek.

God, who may indeed be called "the God of hope" (15:13). The cosmic fall is not the last word; the last word is with hope.[92]

There is an ambiguity about the end of this verse and the beginning of the next, brought about partly by the possibilities in punctuation and partly by the conjunction at the beginning of verse 21, which may be translated either "that" or "because". Thus we may go along with NIV, *in hope that* (so Bruce, Lenski, etc.), or with RSV, ". . . subjected it in hope; because the creation . . ." (so Cranfield, Boylan, etc.). There is no convincing reason for preferring either understanding of the text.[93]

21. If we take the conjunction to mean "because" (see the previous note), the logical sequence is maintained; otherwise the content of the hope is brought out. *Itself* puts some emphasis on *creation*, for Paul looks forward to a time when the total effect of sin will be done away and creation will stand forth in all its glory as God intends it to be. It will be set free from "the slavery of corruption"[94] which is so characteristic of the physical world: "Change and decay in all around I see". But Paul does not regard this as permanent. Creation will in due course be freed from this bondage to decay. It will share to some extent in "the liberty of the glory of God's children". Many modern translations agree with NIV in rendering *the glorious freedom*, but this over-looks the fact that throughout this section the emphasis falls on the coming glory.[95] The creation will be liberated into the glory that then will be (for the coming glory of creation cf. Isa. 11:6; 32:15-16; 35:1-2, 6ff.; Col. 1:20; 2 Pet. 3:13; Rev. 21, 22).[96]

22. Once again with *We know* (see the note on 2:2) Paul appeals to knowledge accepted among Christians, and again he carries on his logical sequence with "for" (which again NIV omits). What is a matter of common knowledge among believers here is that creation is in trouble. *The whole creation* is involved; Paul is not referring to some tiny segment, though "Not only

92. Cf. Cranfield, "And, if the question is asked, 'What sense can there be in saying that the sub-human creation—the Jungfrau, for example, or the Matterhorn, or the planet Venus—suffers frustration by being prevented from properly fulfilling the purpose of its existence?', the answer must surely be that the whole magnificent theatre of the universe, together with all its splendid properties and all the varied chorus of sub-human life, created for God's glory, is cheated of its true fulfilment so long as man, the chief actor in the great drama of God's praise, fails to contribute his rational part" (*Reconciliation and Hope*, ed. Robert Banks [Grand Rapids and Exeter, 1974], p. 227).

93. Unless we accept the reading διότι with א D* G etc.; ὅτι is the reading of P[46] A B C etc. and is probably to be preferred. διότι means "because", not "that".

94. The genitive is a genitive of quality (M, III, p. 213); Moule points out that it is not a Semitic construction with the meaning "corrupting bondage" (IBNTG, p. 175). "Corruption" may be used with an ethical meaning, but here physical corruption more likely is meant. Death and decay set their mark on all creation (cf. Col. 2:22)

95. Cf. SH, "δόξα, 'the glorified state,' is the leading fact, not a subordinate fact".

96. For the dignity of creation, cf. Cranfield, "If the sub-human creation is part of God's creation, if to it also he is faithful, and if he is going to bring it also (as well as believing men) to a goal which is worthy of himself, then it too has a dignity of its own and an inalienable, since divinely-appointed, right to be treated by us with reverence and sensitiveness" (*Reconciliation and Hope*, pp. 229-30).

so" at the beginning of the next verse shows that believers are not included. Paul uses the words "groans together and travails together",[97] a vivid expression for the troubled state of nature (cf. Moffatt, "the entire creation sighs and throbs with pain"). But Paul sees not only an expression of pain, but of meaningful pain like the pain of childbirth. Creation is not undergoing death pangs, but, as Calvin pointed out, birth pangs. Some remind us of the Jewish idea of "the birth pangs of Messiah" and suggest that Paul is referring to pain as the precursor of the coming again of Christ. This is probably too specific. Paul's thought is rather that God will produce something completely new ("the freedom of the glory of the children of God"), not that what happens will be an inevitable outcome of the world's troubles. *Right up to the present time* brings this right up to date. The world's anguish is a continuing phenomenon.

23. "And that is not all!"[98] Paul proceeds to add believers to the creation that is groaning, and indeed he puts strong emphasis on "we ourselves".[99] We Christians have wonderful privileges, but we groan too. Perhaps Paul's thought is that we groan partly because of those privileges, for they enable us to understand that there must be something much better than we now see, and we long for it to come. So he speaks of having *the firstfruits of the Spirit*. The *firstfruits* refers to the Jewish custom of bringing the first of the harvest to the temple and offering it to God (Lev. 23:10-11). This consecrated the whole harvest, and it carries with it the thought that there will be later fruits (otherwise there is no point in "first"). The concept is mainly Pauline in the New Testament.[100] Whereas in the Old Testament the word normally refers to what we give to God, Paul usually has it for what God gives to us, with the thought that more is in store. Paul is saying here either that the measure of the Holy Spirit that we now have is but a foretaste of the greater measure there will be in the age to come, or that the gift of the Spirit now is a foretaste of the many other blessings we will have in due course.[101] Interestingly, when he is talking about the resurrection Paul says that Christ is the firstfruits (1 Cor. 15:20), but now, from another point of view, he says that the Spirit is the firstfruits. The same term may be used of God's pledge to us that we will rise from the dead, and also that we will receive abundant blessings after we rise.

97. συστενάζει καὶ συνωδίνει. It is agreed that we should not understand the σύν as meaning "with Christ" or "with believers"; rather, it means "with one another", "together"; "in all its parts" (as NEB). Both verbs are found here only in the New Testament.

98. οὐ μόνον δέ, "But not only—", lacks a modifier. But there is no difficulty in understanding "creation" from the preceding expression. δέ will have adversative force, which is strengthened by the following ἀλλά: not only creation, but also believers!

99. There is textual uncertainty, but καὶ αὐτοί seems to be repeated and the emphatic ἡμεῖς is read by important MSS. Paul is clearly emphasizing the truth that none less than believers join in the groaning.

100. ἀπαρχή is found in Paul in seven of its nine New Testament occurrences.

101. The genitive τοῦ πνεύματος is seen by some as partitive, by others as in apposition. The consideration that it is hard to think of us as having some of the Spirit leads us to see it as apposition. But it would be possible to see the work of the Spirit in us now as partial, a foretaste of the greater things he will do later.

323

Paul uses the participle "having", and this may be understood either in the sense "though we have the Spirit we groan" (as Gifford) or "because we have the Spirit we groan" (Denney). Both are true, and there is no way of deciding between them.

Paul emphasizes that we Christians are caught up in the groaning that is characteristic of all creation. *Groan* expresses something of our deep[102] sorrow at the circumstances in which we find ourselves (cf. 2 Cor. 5:2-4) as we *wait eagerly* (the same emphatic compound as in v. 19, where see note) *for our adoption*. Paul has spoken of believers as having already received "the Spirit of sonship" (v. 15). It would be a quibble to say that that does not mean our adoption (but only the Spirit who brings about adoption). The reconciliation with what Paul is saying here is that there is more to adoption into the heavenly family than we now experience. What we have now is real, but it is not the whole (cf. 1 John 3:2), and our foretaste leads us to look forward with eager longing to the completion of what God has already begun in us (cf. v. 19).

Paul speaks of this future blessing as *the redemption of our bodies*.[103] Redemption (cf. 3:24) is used of the process whereby the sinner is purchased for freedom, purchased to be God's own. It is not generally used in the New Testament of what is physical, and its use here of the body shows that in the process of salvation the values of the body are not overlooked. This does not mean that the body will be resurrected to continue in its present state (see 1 Cor. 15). Rather, it will be what Paul there calls "a spiritual body" (1 Cor. 15:44; cf. v. 51; Phil. 3:21). The apostle is sure that bodily values will not be lost. In the end there will be not the survival of the immortal soul but the resurrection of the body.

24. "For in hope were we saved", Paul says, linking this to the preceding as the reason for it. There has been a good deal of discussion of the expression rendered "in hope".[104] The problem is the significance of the dative. KJV rendered it "by hope" (so Phillips, Barclay, etc.). But it is Paul's habit to speak of being saved "by faith", and hope certainly does not have the same place as does faith, though the two are closely connected.[105] It is better to render "in hope" (with RSV, NEB, etc.). There is little to be said for "for hope" (SH note this among some German writers; cf. O'Neill). Paul says "we

---

102. ἐν ἑαυτοῖς points to what is deep-seated within us and is not to be understood as "among ourselves". Turner draws attention to the use of the third person reflexive in place of second or first, as in LXX "and illiterate papyri" (M, III, p. 42).

103. This is a further example of the use of the singular, σῶμα, of something that is true of each member of a group—a Semitic use, as Turner points out (M, III, p. 24).

104. τῇ ἐλπίδι. The article probably signifies "the hope in question", "the hope just mentioned", which is the justification for NIV's *this hope*.

105. Cf. F. J. A. Hort, "a faith without hope, without a glad outlook into the future, would not be such a faith as the Gospel inspired" (*The First Epistle of St Peter* [London, 1898], p. 86). Cf. also B. F. Westcott, "Faith reposes completely in the love of God: Hope vividly anticipates that God will fulfil His promises in a particular way" (*The Epistle to the Hebrews* [London, 1892], p. 323).

were saved", not, as JB puts it, "we must be content to hope that we shall be saved" (that is a misunderstanding of what Paul is saying). Salvation is often seen in the New Testament as future (5:9), and sometimes as present (1 Cor. 1:18). But it is also past. It was effected by Christ's death in the past, and our appropriation of that death by faith is also past. So the aorist tense brings out an aspect of salvation which the other tenses do not. But while Paul is appreciating what we have already experienced, he recognizes that there is more, and thus he speaks of our having been saved "in hope". We look forward in hope to the full realization of what Christ has done for us. Paul goes on to bring out something of the meaning of hope by telling us what it is not: *hope that is seen is no hope at all.* The word "hope" may be used for the thing hoped for as well as for hope itself (cf. Col. 1:5; Heb. 6:18), and there is some of that meaning here. Why should anyone hope for what is a present reality? The very existence of Christian hope shows that the full extent and the full riches of the Christian salvation have yet to appear.[106]

25. Now Paul sets forth the opposite position. *If we hope for what we do not yet have,* the case is different. This is not really an exact complement to the preceding, but the meaning is plain enough. If we do not yet see something we very much want, then hoping for it is a meaningful expression. Characteristically Paul does not leave it at that. He could have said that if we hope in this way, "then we have real hope" or something like that. Instead he says, *we wait for it patiently,* though NIV's *patiently* may not be the best way of putting it, despite the fact that several translations have something like this. But Paul's word[107] denotes not so much a quiet acceptance as a positive endurance (cf. NASB, "perseverance"). It is the attitude of the soldier who in the thick of the battle is not dismayed but fights on stoutly whatever the difficulties. And once again he uses the rare double compound for *wait* (earlier in vv. 19 and 23), a word which combines the thoughts of eagerness and endurance. W. Grundmann considers Paul's use of this word as distinctive, and here "In virtue of the reception of the Spirit the Christian attitude is one of burning expectation in conformity with the divine plans".[108]

4. The Spirit's Intercession, 8:26-27

26In the same way, the Spirit helps us in our weakness. We do not know what[a] we ought to pray, but the Spirit himself intercedes for us with groans that words cannot express. 27And he who searches our hearts knows the mind of the Spirit, because the Spirit intercedes for the saints in accordance with God's will.

a26 Or how

106. There are textual variants at the end of this verse, turning on τίς, τί. But there is no real difference in meaning. Again, while some MSS read ὑπομένει there seems little doubt that we should read ἐλπίζει (see Metzger).

107. ὑπομονή.

108. TDNT, II, p. 56.

Believers ought not to be unduly perturbed by the difficulties of life. Paul has pointed out that the frustrations and futility inherent in this life are not proof against the Christian hope. He now goes on to add to that. Just as the Spirit is with us as the firstfruits while we await the consummation (v. 23), so he is with us in the difficult business of prayer. It is easy to become discouraged in our praying, for we are conscious that we do it so badly. But here, too, we are not left to our own devices. The Spirit intercedes for us.

26. *In the same way* links this to the foregoing. Believers are helped in their earthly troubles (in which they "groan inwardly", v. 23). Likewise[109] they are helped in their weakness, specifically in their weakness in prayer. Perhaps we should see a reference also to the hope of which Paul has just been speaking. The Spirit's help preserves and enlarges the hope in which we live. The Spirit *helps us,* says Paul, using a most uncommon verb.[110] His *us* shows that he does not set himself on some pedestal, as though his prayers were not subject to the limitations he finds in those of the Romans. He, too, needs the Spirit's help. We should notice further that Paul does not say that the Spirit removes our weakness; it is still there, and we live our whole life in conditions of weakness. What the Spirit does is to help; he gives us the aid we need to see us through. *Weakness* is not sin, nor is it suffering (though the sufferings of which he has been speaking will not be out of mind). Paul is simply referring to the fact that we who are Christians are not the spiritual giants we would like to be (and sometimes imagine we are). We are weak, and left to ourselves we will always be in trouble. The later MSS often have the plural (cf. KJV, "our infirmities"), but Paul is referring to the overall weakness of human nature rather than to particular manifestations of that weakness.

One such manifestation is our ignorance about prayer.[111] *We do not know what we ought to pray* is often taken to mean that we do not know how to pray (NEB, Moffatt). That is true, but it does not seem to be what Paul is saying.[112] He is rather referring to the words we use (so NIV), and perhaps the objects for which we pray (cf. NEB mg., "what it is right to pray for"). There is nothing in the Greek to correspond to "for", but "what we should pray" is

---

109. ὡσαύτως (here only in Romans, but eight times in Paul out of 17 in the New Testament). It points to a correspondence. It is possible to take this in the sense, "Just as hope sustains them, so also does the Spirit". But as the Spirit is at work in the time of hope, it is better to see the meaning as joining one work of the Spirit to another. δέ may, as Lenski thinks, indicate that what is added is of a somewhat different nature.

110. συναντιλαμβάνομαι is found again in the New Testament only in Luke 10:40. Robertson brings out the meaning of the picturesque double compound: "The Holy Spirit lays hold of our weakness along with (σύν) us and carries his part of the burden facing us (ἀντί) as if two men were carrying a log, one at each end" (p. 573). We should, however, not press this, for Paul speaks of a divine work, not of one half-divine and half-human.

111. Paul's τό turns the following into the equivalent of a noun and the object of οἴδαμεν. Moule thinks that this "may have been a sheer idiosyncrasy of Paul's" (IBNTG, p. 111), but this scarcely takes notice of Gifford's point that the construction is found ten times in Luke and five times in Paul. Turner finds no significant difference in meaning (M, III, p. 182).

112. "How" would surely require πῶς.

surely broad enough to include the object. The two go together. It is not only that we do not pray very well;[113] it is also the case that, while we often think we know what we need, we are not always good judges of that either. Thus Paul tells us that three times he asked God to take away his "thorn in the flesh", only to be told that God's strength "is made perfect in weakness" (2 Cor. 12:7-9). Or we might think of Moses' prayer to enter the Promised Land (Deut. 3:25-26), or Jeremiah's for the Jews (Jer. 15:1). So difficult is it to know what it is best to pray for that some of the heathen philosophers advised their followers not to pray at all! Our horizon is always limited, and we do not know what is best. As Knox puts it, "our needs go far beyond the power of our speech to express them"; he goes on to point out that it is only as the Holy Spirit is at work within us that we can cry, "Abba, Father" (v. 15).

But we cannot hide behind a plea of ignorance and give up prayer. Prayer is part of the Christian life. Paul's expression is somewhat stronger than NIV's *what we ought to pray*[114] and points to what is absolutely necessary. We must pray aright, and since we cannot do that, the Spirit comes to our aid (cf. Eph. 2:18 for access to the Father in (or by) the Spirit; Lagrange draws attention also to Matt. 10:20).[115] He himself (the pronoun puts some emphasis on the fact that it is the Spirit, he and none else) *intercedes*[116] *for us*. Christ prays for us (v. 34; Heb. 7:25; 1 John 2:1), but it has been said that his prayer is concerned with atonement whereas that of the Spirit is concerned with "sanctifying and perfecting" (Olshausen). Christ's intercession is in heaven (Heb. 7:25-26; 9:24), whereas that of the Holy Spirit is within believers.

The Spirit's intercession is *with groans that words cannot express*. There is some discussion about the latter part of this saying, and some hold that "unspoken" is a better understanding than "inexpressible".[117] The word is found here only in the New Testament, so there are no other passages with which to compare this one. Both possibilities must be kept open, though "inexpressible" does seem more likely. A second difficult question is whether the *groans* are those of the believer or not. Phillips translates, "His Spirit

---

113. Bowen aptly quotes John Bunyan: "I find that my heart is slow to go to God; and when it does go to Him it does not seem to want to stay with Him; so that very often I am forced in my prayers, first to beg of God that He would take my heart and set it on Himself, and then when it is there, that He would keep it there."

114. He says καθὸ δεῖ, "according to what is necessary" (Chamberlain, p. 175). Michel thinks this should be connected with κατὰ θεόν in v. 27. So Leenhardt, "we must pray according to the will of God".

115. The strong adversative ἀλλά introduces the activity of the Spirit in contrast to our weakness.

116. Another double compound, ὑπερεντυγχάνω, found only here in the New Testament and not attested anywhere before this. ἐντυγχάνω has the meaning "meet, turn to, approach, appeal, petition" (BAGD), which readily yields the idea of intercession. The preposition ὑπέρ is used to give the thought of petition "on behalf of" (just as κατά that of "against", as in 11:2).

117. ἀλάλητος. Lloyd-Jones says, "The phrase means 'without words', 'not formulated in words'" (p. 134). He points out that the word is different from that in 2 Cor. 9:15; 12:4. But this is not decisive, and many see the word as "unutterable" (Denney, Shedd, Lenski, etc.).

within us is actually praying for us in those agonising longings which never find words", and NEB, "through our inarticulate groans", while O'Neill regards the passage as "a defence of inarticulate prayer in Christian worship". This is understood in the sense that the Spirit produces these groanings within us; Paul is not describing what happens to the natural man. But others insist that the *groans* are metaphorical. They point out that the believer is not said to groan and hold that Paul is speaking of an activity of the Spirit only. They also notice that creation is said to groan (v. 22) without this meaning a literally audible sound. So here they understand a figurative way of referring to an activity of the Spirit. Thus George W. MacRae says, "The 'groans' of the Spirit are of course likewise metaphorical; they do not imply any kind of human prayer."[118] Such a view is taken up by Hendriksen, TH, and others. There is no way of deciding the question with finality, but perhaps there is a little more to be said for the view that the groans are uttered by the believer. The Spirit is not said to groan, but to intercede "with" or "in" groans, and these may well be those of the believer. Paul seems to be saying that when we cannot find words in which to express our prayer and can do no better than make inarticulate sounds, the Spirit takes those sounds and makes them into effective intercession.[118a] It is an encouragement to all of us who find praying difficult. The natural man does not groan over his weakness in prayer. Believers do, and this groaning is the work of the Spirit in them.

Some exegetes regard this as a form of praying in "tongues". Thus Käsemann thinks it makes good sense if "what is at issue is the praying in tongues of 1 Cor 14:15" (p. 241).[119] But there seems little reason to hold such a view. Charismatic praying may well be included, but Paul's words are wide enough to cover "all praying of Christian men" (Cranfield). Are we to say that only the charismatics have the Spirit's help? A better position is that of Leenhardt: "These 'sighs' are a form of the 'sigh' of creation. Hence they cannot be assimilated to glossolaly. Moreover Paul is speaking here of the prayer of every Christian, whereas glossolaly is a special charismatic gift." Charismatic prayer is usually seen as a form of praise, whereas Paul seems here to be referring to intercession.[120]

118. *Interpretation*, XXXIV (1980), p. 291.
118a. E. A. Obeng points to the Jewish idea that heavenly intercessors are specially effective, and to the fact that Jesus is seen by Christians as a heavenly intercessor. He holds that Paul's teaching on the Spirit's intercession is to be understood in the light of such teaching (NTS, 32 [1986], pp. 621-32).
119. Such a view seems to be supported by Hunter, "The 'sighs' are no doubt those uttered at church meetings under stress of deep religious emotion". Cf. G. Delling, "Here the pneuma is not thought of as *tertia persona* but as having become one with man. It has entered into union with the human καρδία and there fashions prayers which cannot be grasped by the human understanding and are not immediately adequate before God, but must first be searched out by Him. This pneumatic prayer is a charismatic dealing with God like speaking with tongues, whether with or without the corresponding forms" (TDNT, I, p. 376). Althaus also favors a charismatic reference.
120. Leenhardt sees encouragement for the humble believer: "let him look to God instead of regretting that he is not a virtuoso of prayer like the Pharisee of Lk. 18:10"; again, Jesus warned "against pious chatter". To know that the Spirit makes intercession

27. And[121] *he who searches our hearts* is not named, but God is the only one who can be thus described (cf. Ps. 7:9; Prov. 17:3; Acts 1:24; 1 Thess. 2:4; Christ, Rev. 2:23).[122] He is now said to know *the mind of the Spirit*. Since God knows the hearts he certainly knows what the Spirit is doing in those hearts; thus some take the reference to be to the human spirit (e.g., Olshausen). The identical expression is found in verse 6, where it refers to the general bent of thought and motive set on the Spirit. If it has the same meaning here, the thought will be that the all-knowing Spirit (cf. 1 Cor. 2:10) knows who are spiritually minded, for he makes intercession on behalf of saints. But it is generally agreed that it makes much better sense here to see a reference to the Holy Spirit. God knows the Holy Spirit's mind and thus takes full account of the Spirit's intercession for saints. Perhaps we should say that as God searches the hearts he finds the "unutterable groanings" which are the intercession of the Spirit. He knows the Spirit's mind, and the implication is that he answers the prayers so offered.

There is some dispute as to whether we should introduce the second part of the sentence with *because* (as NIV) or "that" (as JB). The Greek could mean either.[123] If we take it to mean "because", Paul is telling us why it is that God knows the Spirit's mind; if "that", he is giving us the content of the Spirit's thought. Those who favor "because" maintain that Paul is clearly giving us the reason and further that "that" would tell us very little ("God knows that the Spirit intercedes"; how could it be otherwise?). Those who argue for "that" hold that the following is insufficient as a reason; God cannot be said to know the mind of the Spirit only because he intercedes. There seems no way of deciding the point, and both possibilities must be kept open.

The Spirit then *intercedes*[124] *for the saints*, and this intercession is *in accordance with God's will*.[125] *Saints* lacks the article, the force of which will be that they are being prayed for because of their quality as "saints", not because they belong to "the" saints as a group. Paul is giving encouragement to the humblest of God's people. They may be dissatisfied with their praying, but they have a powerful intercessor and one who prays for them in accordance with the will of God himself.

---

through even our groanings is to be delivered from bondage to human achievement in prayer.

121. Godet thinks that δέ here means "but"; it "contrasts the knowledge of God, which thoroughly understands the object of this groaning, with the ignorance of the heart from which it proceeds."

122. The verb ἐραυνάω is mostly used of human searching. But it is used of the glorious Christ's searching of the kidneys and the hearts (Rev. 2:23) and of the Holy Spirit's search of "all things, even the deep things of God" (1 Cor. 2:10).

123. ὅτι.

124. The simple ἐντυγχάνω scarcely differs in meaning from the compound in v. 26, especially since it is followed by ὑπέρ.

125. κατὰ θεόν does not mention the "will", but it is generally agreed that some such translation as that of NIV is correct (so SH; IBNTG, p. 59).

5. *The Purpose of God, 8:28-30*

> [28]*And we know that in all things God works for the good of those who love him,[a] who have been called according to his purpose. [29]For those God foreknew he also predestined to be conformed to the likeness of his Son, that he might be the firstborn among many brothers. [30]And those he predestined, he also called; those he called, he also justified; those he justified, he also glorified.*

> [a] Some manuscripts *And we know that all things work together for good to those who love God*

Paul turns to the way the purpose of God is worked out in believers. They may be depressed at the harsh conditions of their lives, but they should bear in mind that through it all God is working out a great purpose. No matter what the circumstances that purpose will not be overthrown, and it culminates in final glory.

28. There are different views about the opening of this verse.[126] Some favor "and", seeing not a contrast with the preceding but a transition to a further thought of much the same kind (e.g., Murray). Others perceive a contrast between the groanings of the previous section and God's working in this one (e.g., Godet). Either is possible, and many solve the problem by leaving out the connective (e.g., JB). A more important question is how we should take the words translated as *in all things God works for the good. . . .* Traditionally this has been taken as "all things work together for good" (as KJV), but this has come under criticism (Dodd calls it "a serious mistranslation"). It is not difficult to cite sayings from the ancient world of the "In the end everything will turn out all right" type, and it is urged that Paul is not simply repeating a commonplace, and moreover one that leaves God out. Nor is it likely in the sense in which we find this thought in the Old Testament and Jewish writings (cf. Gen. 50:20; Eccl. 8:12; Sir. 39:24-27), in the first instance because they do not say what Paul is saying and in the second because of necessity they omit what Christ is doing and that is central in Paul's present argument as it moves on to the way of salvation. Mere "things" do not work together (for good or ill). TH points out that no modern translation has this as its first choice (though it is a possible understanding of the Greek and is often put as an alternative). But it has this going for it, that it is the most natural way of taking the Greek and is accepted by Barrett, Cranfield, Hendriksen, and others.[127]

A few MSS read "God works all things. . . ."[128] This gives an excellent sense and is accepted by RSV. But it is hard to understand why it is read by so

---

126. δέ may mean "and" or "but".

127. A useful note accepting this view is found in W. L. Knox, *St Paul and the Church of the Gentiles* (Cambridge, 1939), p. 105 n. 2.

128. ὁ θεός is read by P[46] A B 81 sah etc. This is impressive support, but it is not easy to see how the words could have been omitted by so many MSS, whereas they are the kind of explanation that a scribe may well have inserted.

few MSS if it is correct and involves us in a problem with the Greek construction.[129]

Luther commented, "the Spirit makes all things, even though they are evil, work together for good", and in recent times a number of scholars have taken up this view. They understand the "he" that is the subject of the verb "works together" to mean the Holy Spirit and take the sense of the passage to be, "He makes intercession for the saints according to the will of God and he makes all things work together. . . ." This is an attractive solution and is adopted, for example, by NEB.[130] The principal objection to it is that, while the transition from verse 27 to 28 is easy, that from 28 to 29 is harsh and involves an unexpected change of subject. On the whole it seems best to take "he" as the subject and to understand the passage of the working of God in some such sense as "he that searches the hearts knows . . . he works all things for good . . . them he foreknew. . . ."[131] In any case it is certain that Paul is ascribing the working of everything for good not to some "evolutionary optimism" (Dodd) but to God, and that however we translate.

Paul does not explain what he means by *the good*, but we must clearly understand it in the sense "final good" or "true good"; it certainly does not mean in all the things we count for good, such as our pleasures. And it is good for "those who love God", words which are in an emphatic position. Paul is not writing about the general public but about believers, here described in terms of their love for God. This is a most unusual way of referring to Christians;[132] it is much more common to find references to God's love for them. But there are many exhortations to believers to love, usually to love one another, but sometimes to love God (Matt. 22:37). Paul speaks of believers loving God in a couple of other places (1 Cor. 2:9; 8:3; cf. Eph. 6:24). It is a very impressive way of characterizing them; love is central in the life of the Christian.

Those who love God are also *those who*[133] *have been called according to his purpose*. For *called* see on 1:1; the idea of the divine call is very important for

129. The verb συνεργέω is intransitive and means "to work together with"; we would take it here to mean "God works together with all things. . . ." But God is sovereign, not a partner, working "with" the things he has made. It helps to view the verb as an example of the process whereby some intransitive verbs were beginning to take a direct object in Hellenistic times (M, I, p. 65; BDF 148 [1]). But Godet points out that there are no examples of the use of this verb in the sense "makes things work together". Perhaps it is better to take the accusative as an "accusative of respect" meaning "in all things".

130. It is argued by James P. Wilson in his article "Romans viii.28: Text and Interpretation" (ET, LX [1948-49], pp. 110-11). The view is adopted (not necessarily in the same form) by NBCR, Robinson, and others.

131. Cf. G. Bertram, "God must be supplied as the subject of συνεργεῖ. . . . God is a helper for good in all things. He turns all for good for the righteous" (TDNT, VII, p. 875). In an excellent discussion of the subject Carroll D. Osborn comes to much the same conclusion; see "The Interpretation of Romans 8:28" (WTJ, XLIV [1982], pp. 99-109).

132. Cf. Nygren, "one cannot point out a single place in his writings where the noun 'love,' ἀγάπη, clearly means love to God".

133. τοῖς . . . οὖσιν; the participle is used in such contexts only when there are further defining words in the clause (M, III, p. 151; BDF 413 [3]).

Paul. In the Gospels we sometimes read "many are called, but few chosen", but Paul is not using the term "call" in that sense. He means "effectual call"; he is speaking of those who have not only heard the call but have responded. He goes on to link this with God's *purpose*, which means God's saving purpose. It is that purpose which we see in the sending of Jesus, in his life, death, resurrection, and ascension, and in the preaching of the gospel whereby people are brought out of their darkness into God's marvellous light.[134]

29. *For*[135] links this closely to the preceding. NIV has introduced the word *God* to make the passage plain, but Paul simply says "those he foreknew". The verb[136] means "know beforehand" and is the first of a series of five verbs outlining what God has done in fulfilment of his saving purpose. Many scholars feel that we cannot take the verb in this place to refer to no more than knowledge. They point out that in the Old Testament the equivalent means something like "choose in advance" (as in Jer. 1:5; Amos 3:2). This must surely be borne in mind, but we must also remember that Paul's next verb is *predestined* and we must be on our guard against making the two say the same thing.[137] Moreover, Paul is describing the saved, and God's foreknowledge of them is not the same as his foreknowledge of all mankind. Perhaps "chose beforehand" is as good as we can do, viewing this as a reference to election.

Paul goes on to predestination.[138] This is an important New Testament concept and one which some people find difficult because they are so sure that we have free wills. This is not the place to go into a discussion of the relative places of the two; it must suffice to notice that the meaning of the word is plain. We must not allow ourselves to be sidetracked by modern notions of what is or is not possible for God. Paul is saying that God is the author of our salvation, and that from beginning to end. We are not to think that God can take action only when we graciously give him permission. Paul is saying that God initiates the whole process. As Barrett puts it: "The history and personal make-up of the Church are not due to chance or to arbitrary human choices, but represent the working out of God's plan. . . . Our own intentions, like our own virtues, are far too insecure to stand the tests of time and judgement." He sees it as "the most comfortable of all Christian doc-

---

134. Cf. C. Maurer, "Paul adopts πρόθεσις in a wholly new sense when he uses it for the primal decision of God whereby the saving event in Christ and the resultant way of the community to eschatological glorifying are established and set in motion." Here the words "are not a lame appendix but point to the sustaining ground of the hope of the community" (TDNT, VIII, p. 166).

135. ὅτι is perhaps explicatory or introduces a reason: we know that God works all for good for us, *for. . . .*

136. προγινώσκω is found twice in Romans, the only Pauline writing that has the word.

137. To avoid this a number of suggestions are made: "whom he foreloved" (Murray); "already chosen" (GNB); "foreknown as His *by faith*" (Godet).

138. προορίζω means "set the boundary (ὅρος) beforehand" and clearly points to what we mean by predestination.

trines, if men will accept it in its biblical form, and not attempt to pry into it with questions which it does not set out to answer. It is . . . the final statement of the truth that justification, and, in the end, salvation also, are by grace alone, and through faith alone."

God predestined his people *to be conformed*[139] *to the likeness*[140] *of his Son.* We are to become like Christ (cf. 1 John 3:1), which, as Hendriksen points out, means sanctification. It is God's plan that his people become like his Son, not that they should muddle along in a modest respectability. We should be in no doubt as to the high standard that Paul sets for Christian people. We have been admitted to the heavenly family; we are *brothers* in that family and we call God "Father". We are accordingly to live as members of the family, and that means being made like our elder Brother. This is all part of God's predestination; he predestined us not only to be released from an unpleasant predicament, but in order that we might become like his Son.

This is further explained: *that he might be the firstborn among many brothers.*[141] The firstborn is, of course, the most important of the children. He is the heir and the one singled out for special honor.[142] But firstborn implies "later born"; the term points to others who will in due course be members of the family. Paul is saying that it was always in God's plan that there might be many in his family, children who look to Christ as the firstborn and rejoice that they are children of the same Father (cf. v. 17).[143]

30. The sequence is resumed. Those he predestined God also *called* (again the call is an effectual call, for it is preceded by predestination). Those he called God also *justified* (see Additional Note D). This is an important concept for Paul and receives special emphasis in this epistle. It leads on to glorification, for those whom God justified *he also glorified.* The aorist tense here is unexpected (though Paul sometimes speaks of a present glory; e.g., 2 Cor. 3:18; 4:11). Some think the verb has been attracted into the tense of the other verbs in the sequence, but it is more likely that it is used of set purpose to bring out the truth that our glorification is certain. So certain is it that it can be

---

139. σύμμορφος. In the New Testament it is found again only in Phil. 3:21, where it is followed by the dative. The genitive here is "ablatival" (M, III, p. 215); it means "taking part" etc., here "participating in the form of his image" (BDF 182 [1]). And, of course, Christ is in the μορφή of God (Phil. 2:6).

140. εἰκών may denote a literal image or likeness (like the head of the Emperor on a coin), or more generally may mean the form or appearance. Christ is the εἰκὼν τοῦ θεοῦ (2 Cor. 4:4; Col. 1:15) where "all the emphasis is on the equality of the εἰκών with the original" (G. Kittel, TDNT, II, p. 395).

141. εἰς τό with the infinitive surely denotes purpose (Burton, 409). Note the dignity of the church; the church is in God's foreordaining plan "in order that Christ might be the firstborn".

142. J. B. Lightfoot has an important note on πρωτότοκος in *St Paul's Epistles to the Colossians and to Philemon* (London, 1876), pp. 146-50.

143. G. Kittel reminds us that this has eschatological consequences: "Like all the gifts in which Christians share, the εἰκών is an ἀπαρχή. . . . This means that it now is, and yet that it is still to be. It is enjoyed, but not yet enjoyed. Its eschatology is even now at work, and its presence has an eschatological basis" (TDNT, II, p. 397).

spoken of as already accomplished. It is in the plan of God, and that means that it is as good as here. It is "certain in the Divine counsels. To God there is neither 'before nor after'" (SH).[144]

6. The Christian's Triumph Song, 8:31-39

[31]What, then, shall we say in response to this? If God is for us, who can be against us? [32]He who did not spare his own Son, but gave him up for us all—how will he not also, along with him, graciously give us all things? [33]Who will bring any charge against those whom God has chosen? It is God who justifies. [34]Who is he that condemns? Christ Jesus, who died—more than that, who was raised to life—is at the right hand of God and is also interceding for us. [35]Who shall separate us from the love of Christ? Shall trouble or hardship or persecution or famine or nakedness or danger or sword? [36]As it is written:

"For your sake we face death all day long;
    we are considered as sheep to be slaughtered."[a]

[37]No, in all these things we are more than conquerors through him who loved us. [38]For I am convinced that neither death nor life, neither angels nor demons,[b] neither the present nor the future, nor any powers, [39]neither height nor depth, nor anything else in all creation, will be able to separate us from the love of God that is in Christ Jesus our Lord.

[a]36 Psalm 44:22   [b]38 Or nor heavenly rulers

Paul rounds off the first half of his letter with a passage which Christians have always regarded as one of the most wonderful parts of a wonderful epistle. There have been widely differing estimates of the literary form of this section, and, for example, Dodd regards it as "Paul's poetry" while Käsemann maintains that "The style of the whole is thoroughly prosaic" (p. 247). I prefer to go along with Wilckens, who sees it as the Christian's "triumph song". Some think there is a careful division into subsections, others that it is a fine rhapsody, paying little attention to the sequence of thought. Be that as it may, it will suffice to notice that in the first half Paul is concerned with the impossibility of any charge against the believer being sustained before God (vv. 31-34), and in the second with the impossibility of anything separating us from God's love (vv. 35-39). The whole should be seen as the conclusion and summing up not of the immediately preceding section, but of the whole of the letter up to this point.

31. Paul's "therefore"[145] introduces the following paragraph as a logical inference from what he has been saying; this will refer to the whole letter, not

144. Cf. Denney, "the tense in the last word is amazing. It is the most daring anticipation of faith that even the N.T. contains". Nygren cites Zahn for glory as "a renewing of life effected by the reception of the Spirit"; he rejects any idea that Paul is writing "as if" the glory had come: "He speaks of a reality which both *has* come and *is to* come."

145. οὖν; NIV, "then".

just verses 29-30. For "What shall we say?", so characteristic of this letter and so rare elsewhere, see the note on 3:5. The argument proceeds with a series of rhetorical questions, the first being Paul's characteristic appeal to what the reader's response will be.[146] The second is introduced with an "If" which implies no doubt about what follows: it signifies "If (as is the case). . . ." We must bear in mind that it is dangerous to say confidently *God is for us*, as religious fanatics have shown all too plainly through the centuries in their perpetration of innumerable horrors out of an arrogant conviction that they are completely right and others are completely wrong. But it is dangerous also to avoid it. Paul has been writing about a God who, in order to bring salvation to sinners, works all things for good, foreknows them, predestines them, calls them, justifies them, and glorifies them. It would be wrong to say anything less than that that God is "for" the sinners who are the objects of such love. When Paul goes on to ask, *who can be against us?* he does not mean that the Christian has no opponents. His entire correspondence is eloquent of the foes the Christian encounters constantly. He means that with God "for us" it makes not the slightest particle of difference who is against us. No foe can prevail against people who are supported by a God like that. The Christian's confidence is in God, not in anything he himself does, and for all eternity he can rely on God's gift. Paul is not speaking out of grim desperation, but in "joyous elation" (BDF 496 [2]).

32. Paul's third rhetorical question directs attention to God's gift of his Son for us.[147] God *did not spare his own Son,* where the language is reminiscent of that used of Abraham's readiness to sacrifice Isaac (Gen. 22:16).[148] But Abraham was praised only for his readiness to sacrifice Isaac, for in fact the boy was not offered. God, however, did not spare *his own Son,* where *own* points to a special relationship.[149] Rather, *he gave him up for us all,* the supreme

---

146. πρὸς ταῦτα is perhaps unexpected. Moule thinks πρός is used in the transferred sense of "tending towards, leading to, concerning, against, in view of", thus "what then shall we say in view of this?" (IBNTG, p. 53).

147. The grammarians have a good deal to say about the unusual use of γε with the relative pronoun. BDF point out that it is nearly always used with another conjunction and often becomes "a meaningless appendage"; here without another particle it means "he who" (439 [3]). Turner agrees that it can become a meaningless appendage, but it can also lend emphasis to another word (M, III, p. 331). Lagrange sees a reference to "the same God who . . ." (cf. Cranfield, Barclay, etc.). A. W. Argyle holds that we have here a "clear instance of the causal usage of the relative pronoun in the occurrence of *hos ge*", and he translates, "seeing that he spared not . . ." (JTS, N.S. IV [1953], pp. 214-15).

148. The same verb φείδομαι is used here and in Gen. 22:16. Jewish thinking paid a good deal of attention to this incident. The rabbis were clear that Isaac was not a small boy but a husky youth and that the aged Abraham could not have bound him on the altar had he resisted. So they made much of the "Binding of Isaac". H. J. Schoeps thinks that this was in Paul's mind (*Paul* [London, 1961], pp. 141-49). But, of course, in Jewish thinking it was important that the sacrifice was not completed, in Paul's that it was.

149. ἰδίου distinguishes Christ's sonship from ours. The same adjective is used of Jesus making God "his own Father" (John 5:18).

act of love.[150] *For us* indicates that he stood in our place,[151] while *us all* adds a touch of completeness; none is missed. This is not universalism, for *us* means "us Christians", "us of whom we have been speaking".

The rhetorical question brings out the certainty that God will continue his blessings for the redeemed. He has done the greater thing in giving up his Son; how can he not now do the less?[152] The gift is given *along with him*; in other words, it is to be understood in terms of our union with the crucified Christ (v. 17; so Wilckens, Michel). The gift is *graciously* given, where the verb stresses the freeness of the giving.[153] When God gives, both to his Son and to his sons, he does so with no grudging hand. Indeed, Paul speaks of our being given *all things!* This may be understood in terms of our being "co-heirs with Christ" (v. 17), or perhaps better in the sense "all things connected with salvation".

33. There is a punctuation problem arising from the fact that there were practically no punctuation marks in antiquity. All are agreed that Paul is asking some rhetorical questions, but how many? NIV has a question followed by a statement in this verse and the next, but some prefer to see questions throughout (e.g., Barrett, Moffatt). However, it would be strange to have such a long series of questions without an answer anywhere, and we should accept the position of NIV. The passage is reminiscent of Isaiah 50:8-9, and the alternation of question and answer there may favor a similar construction here. Paul first asks, *Who will bring any charge against those whom God has chosen?* where the language is that of the law court.[154] *Those whom God has chosen* is more exactly "God's elect". This, as Black points out, is "an old name

---

150. Murray cites Octavius Winslow: "Who delivered up Jesus to die? Not Judas, for money; not Pilate, for fear; not the Jews, for envy;—but the Father, for love!" This is a moving statement and expresses an important truth, but it is worth bearing in mind that the verb used here is used also of Judas delivering up Jesus (John 18:5), of the chief priests and elders (Matt. 27:2), of the people of Jerusalem (Acts 3:13), and of Pilate (Mark 15:15). More importantly, we had a part in it, for Jesus was delivered up for our transgressions (Rom. 4:25). Here we read that God gave him up, and in possibly the most moving statement of all Jesus gave himself up (Gal. 2:20).

151. *For* is ὑπέρ, which Shedd says "is equivalent to ἀντί, by reason of its connection with παρέδωκεν" (for this preposition see my note in *The Apostolic Preaching of the Cross*[3] [London, 1965], pp. 62-64). It certainly can mean "in the stead of", and that seems to be its meaning here. Cf. Lenski, "Substitution is included because only by being delivered up 'in our stead' could the Son have been delivered up 'in our behalf.' Remove substitution, and nothing of saving value 'in our behalf' is left."

152. πῶς οὐχί makes for an awkward question. Either could have been used on its own, but the combination is strange; οὐχί is necessary for the sense; it is πῶς that is the problem. BAGD consider it under the heading "in rhetorical questions that call an assumption into question or reject it altogether *how* (could or should)? = *by no means, it is impossible that*". But accompanied by οὐχί "the 'impossible' becomes *most surely, most certainly*". Cf. 2 Cor. 3:8. Moffatt translates here, "surely He will give us everything besides!"

153. The verb is χαρίζομαι, and we should not miss the connection with "grace". It is sometimes used in the sense "forgive", but it is difficult to find that meaning here, especially since what we are given we are given "with" Christ.

154. ἐγκαλέω is the legal technical term for presenting an accusation in a law court (BAGD; cf. Acts 19:38; 23:28-29).

for Israel (1 Chr. 16:13; Ps. 105:6, 43), but specially used in the later apoc-
alypses and inter-Testamental writings for the 'Elect Israel', or 'Remnant',
and its members". Paul uses the expression rarely, despite his insistence on
God's electing activity (only in Col. 3:12; Tit. 3:5; but cf. 16:13). He may have
been deterred by the use to which it was put in contemporary Judaism.[155] He
does not have the definite article with "elect", which indicates that he is
thinking not so much of "the" elect as a class as of people whose characteristic
is to be elect. The emphasis is on the quality. When he asks who will bring a
charge against such people, he does not imply that no one will do this. The
very name "Satan" means "accuser" (cf. Zech. 3:1), and there has never been
a shortage of enemies to make accusations against God's people. He means
that no accusation will stand for a moment, for it is none less than God[156] *who
justifies.*[157] God will surely justify his own. The believer might well be concerned about his sins and wonder whether in the end they might prevail
against him. Paul is sure that they will not. Since it is God who justifies, the
believer's justification can never be overthrown.[158]

34. *Who is he that condemns?*[159] The immediate reference to Christ may in
part at least arise from the fact that at the last great day it is Christ who is to be
the judge and who will condemn those who are to be condemned (2 Cor.
5:10). If he then is for us, how can we possibly be condemned? Our heart may
condemn us (1 John 3:20-21), but it is Christ, not our heart, that matters in the
final resort. The impossibility of condemnation is shown by the fact that it is
Christ *who died.* His death removes the possibility of condemnation for those
who are in him. *More than that* introduces a preferable statement. The death is
important, and indeed central. But it does not stand on its own, and Paul
proceeds to the thought that Christ *was raised.* It is usual in the New Testament to ascribe the resurrection to the Father, and the passive agrees with
this.[160] Christ *is at the right hand*[161] *of God,* an important part of New Testament

155. Cf. Leenhardt, "The term articulated the sentiments of pride fostered by religious nationalism. Perhaps the apostle tended to avoid it for this reason."
156. There is some emphasis on θεός from its being adjacent to θεοῦ; God will
surely justify his own! Cf. GNB, "God himself declares them not guilty!"
157. The legal term δικαιῶν answers the legal term ἐγκαλέσει. This incidentally is
the last occurrence of δικαιόω in this epistle, a verb which has been so prominent in the
argument.
158. Dodd thinks a "sense of sin" a hindrance. He does not distinguish between a
religiously healthy recognition of one's shortcomings and that morbid dwelling on one's
inadequacies which, as he says, "daunts our courage, saps our confidence, and frustrates
our effort." He goes on, "What is the cure for it? Not to repress it, or to sophisticate
ourselves out of it. The only cure is 'justification by faith'—the faith that the infinite love of
God in Christ takes charge of our whole life, sins and all." This conclusion makes a
valuable point. When God justifies us, we have nothing to fear.
159. There is considerable support for the view that we should accent κατακρινῶν,
in which case it is a future: "Who shall condemn?" (Moffatt; cf. BDF 351 [2]). It is possible
to accent it as κατακρίνων, making the tense present, and it could be argued that this
brings it into line with δικαιῶν. But the future corresponds to ἐγκαλέσει. The future
should be accepted.
160. It is possible, however, to see the participle as having middle force and understand it as "rose" (cf. JB, Moffatt).
161. *Hand* is omitted, but this is usual (M, III, p. 17). In the New Testament it is

teaching (Acts 2:33; 5:31; 7:55-56; Eph. 1:20; Col. 3:1; Heb. 1:3; 8:1; 10:12; 12:2; 1 Pet. 3:22). It means that he is in the place of highest honor in heaven. The posture of sitting (Eph. 1:20; Col. 3:1; Heb. 1:3, etc.) signifies "the finished work of Christ", as the older theologians delighted to put it. This means that we should take *is also interceding for us* with some care (cf. Heb. 7:25; 1 John 2:1). We should interpret the intercession passages in the light of frequent references to sitting at the right hand of God. His presence at God's right hand in his capacity as the one who died for sinners and rose again is itself an intercession.[162] Barclay makes another point regarding the intercession. He states that "the earliest creed of the Church" makes four points: Christ died, he rose, he is at the right hand of God, and he will come again to judge the living and the dead. Paul has the first three, but he thinks of Christ's interces-sion rather than of judgment. Both are true, but it is interesting to note Paul's emphasis.

35. *Who shall separate*[163] *us from the love of Christ?* continues the rhetorical questions. It is of interest that Paul says *who* rather than "what", especially when we look at the candidates he lists. But perhaps this is no more than a recognition of the fact that the nouns he lists are all masculine or feminine; there are no neuters. Cranfield notes that there is a slight emphasis on *us* from its position in the Greek; *us* for whom Christ died. *The love of Christ* might mean "our love for Christ" or "Christ's love for us", depending on whether we see the genitive as subjective or objective. But it is generally agreed that it is Christ's love of which Paul writes.[164] To say that we will never be separated from our love for Christ gives us no great confidence (we know ourselves only too well!). But it is a wonderful assurance that Christ's love for us will always be there. It is perhaps a little surprising that Paul speaks of the love of Christ rather than the love of God (cf. 5:5). But there is not much difference between the two (cf. v. 39), and the apostle has just been referring to Christ's death for us.

This launches him on to a rhetorical passage in which he suggests a

---

usual to have the singular with ἐν and the plural with ἐκ, but there appears to be no difference in meaning.

162. In some modern writing great emphasis is placed on Christ's perpetual plead-ing in heaven. We should bear in mind B. F. Westcott's note in which he says: "The modern conception of Christ pleading in heaven His Passion, 'offering His blood,' on behalf of men, has no foundation in the Epistle (i.e. Hebrews). His glorified humanity is the eternal pledge of the absolute efficacy of His accomplished work. He pleads, as older writers truly expressed the thought, by His Presence on the Father's Throne" (*The Epistle to the Hebrews* [London, 1892], p. 230).

163. Paul uses the verb χωρίζω again in Romans only in v. 39. It signifies "to make a space (χώρα)" and so "to separate".

164. Though for different reasons. Thus Boylan looks outward and says, "There are many things, it is true, that might interfere with our love for Christ", while Haldane looks inward and holds that "A person could not be said to be separated from his own feelings." They agree that Paul cannot be saying, "Who shall separate Christ from our love?" but must mean, "Who shall separate us from the love of Christ?"

number of possible candidates. *Trouble*[165] is a word for strong pressure; it is a general term and does not define the nature of the pressure. *Hardship*[166] is also a general word, though Hendriksen holds that the combination of the two words means outward affliction plus inward distress. *Persecution* brings before us an ever-present possibility for the early church. *Famine* (the word may mean no more than "hunger") reminds us of the precariousness of food supplies in the world in which Paul's readers lived. Earle has a good comment on *nakedness:* "This term today suggests indecency on parade. Then it meant a lack of clothes simply because one had no ways or means of getting any" (cf. Goodspeed, "destitution"). *Danger*[167] reminds us of the many risks the early Christians ran; it was not a comfortable world in which to profess the faith. *Sword,* of course, means execution; it is the only item in the list that Paul had not undergone, and in due time he would experience this also.[168]

36. A quotation from Psalm 44:22 (cf. 2 Cor. 4:11) reinforces what Paul has been saying in the last few words rather than in the thought of the all-embracing reach of the love of Christ. The words in the original psalm express the perplexity of the people of God in the face of inexplicable suffering. But Paul cites them to bring out the truth that for God's people there is real risk and a call for real devotion. Christians might be tempted to think that because the love of Christ is so real and so unshakable they need not fear that they will run into trouble. Scripture shows that, while the love is sure, so are troubles. For the sake of God *we face death all day long.* Actually Paul says something stronger than this: "We are being killed all day long". It is real and not imaginary peril that Christians face. *We are considered* is an aorist, which is somewhat unexpected. Probably we should see it as pointing to an accomplished fact. *As*[169] *sheep to be slaughtered*[170] points to the very real risks believers ran. Barrett comments, "Suffering and persecution are not mere evils which Christians must expect and endure as best they can; they are the scene of the overwhelming victory which Christians are winning through Christ."

37. Paul begins with "But",[171] introducing something contrary to all

---

165. θλῖψις means "pressing", "pressure" (BAGD); it is used, e.g., of the treading of grapes, the pressure that bursts.

166. στενοχωρία, from στενός, "narrow", and χῶρος, "space", means "straits" and thus "difficulties". Paul is the only New Testament writer to use it (four times).

167. κίνδυνος means peril of any sort. In the New Testament it is used by Paul only (nine times, eight of them in 2 Cor. 11:26).

168. Käsemann's preoccupation with apocalyptic comes out in his comment at the end of this list: "Like all that God does, the love of Christ also manifests itself in time under its opposite. Apocalyptic alone can express this and preserve us from the usual edifying interpretation of the text" (p. 250). But Paul is surely referring to real and actual experiences of himself and other Christians, not indulging in apocalyptic speculation.

169. BDF 157 (5) sees ὡς + accusative as used for the predicate accusative and equivalent to the Hebrew כ.

170. πρόβατα σφαγῆς will be sheep destined for slaughter (cf. Zech. 11:4-7); Shedd comments, "not the sacrificial slaughter . . . but that of the market. The Roman regarded the Christian as a cheap and common victim."

171. The strong adversative ἀλλά.

that might have been expected and which NIV renders with *No* (as do KJV, RSV, Phillips, Moffatt, etc.). *In all these things* shows that Paul is overlooking nothing.[172] *We are more than conquerors* is an inspired piece of translation which KJV took over from the Genevan version and which a number of modern translations retain. It emphasizes the totality of the victory that God gives his beloved.[173] The ability to triumph over all adversity does not arise from any inherent superiority of believers. It is *through him who loved us*, which may refer to the Father (Bengel) or to the Son (Shedd). Perhaps Paul is not distinguishing sharply between them. The tense of the verb is aorist, which is not quite what we expect of a love that goes on and on. It may be that Paul wants us to think of the love as focused on the cross; there we see what love really is (cf. Murray, Lenski, etc.).

38. Paul comes to the end of this eloquent section on a very personal note with his *I am convinced*.[174] The verb expresses certainty; Paul sees no possible shadow of doubt. And the perfect points to a permanent state. This is no passing whim. The apostle proceeds to make his point by listing potential candidates for separating us from God's love. If none of these can effect a separation, then why should believers fear? They are assured that God will always keep them secure in his great love.[175]

Paul has ten items in his list. The manuscripts vary a little, but he seems to arrange them in four pairs, along with two single items. The first pair is *death* and *life*. Death is an obvious antagonist, for people have always feared it. It is so certain and so final. It is obvious that no one can escape it, and it is easy to be scared of what lies on the other side. "God is there in all his love", Paul is reasoning. He could say "I die daily" (1 Cor. 15:31). He could say "to die is gain", and he looked forward to dying and being with Christ (Phil. 1:21, 23). For him death might be a grim tyrant, but there is no reason why the believer should fear it. We may be puzzled at *life* occurring in this list, but it forms a natural opposite to death and it is true that, just as many fear death, so many are afraid of life. Life has persecutions and trials on the one hand and it has tranquillity and pleasures on the other, and any of these could be the means of

172. ἐν τούτοις πᾶσιν is not what might have been expected. Moule thinks that it means "perhaps *in the midst*, or *in spite*, *of all these things*" (IBNTG, p. 78), while Turner says that it is one of a group that "elude classification" and here may mean "with regard to" (M, III, p. 265). Bruce sees "possibly a Hebraism, meaning 'despite all these things', 'for all that'".

173. Brunner regards ὑπερνικῶμεν as untranslatable but tries with we are "excessively victorious". W. B. J. Martin says, "Hate can make a man a conqueror, can fill him with furious energy, but only love can make him more-than-conqueror" (ET, LXXXIV [1972-73], p. 276). J. G. McKenzie brings out another aspect of Paul's meaning with "The true Christian way of living, the true Christian joy in living, comes to us not in spite of tribulation, disappointment, or even sin, but because of them. . . . We have something left over when life and death have done their worst" (ET, LXXI [1959-60], 319).

174. πέπεισμαι. Brown regards this as "not a matter of opinion, but of assured fact" (p. 275).

175. Each item in the list is introduced with οὔτε, which is thus repeated ten times in this sequence; it is a way of continuing a negative. Paul uses it 33 times, but this sequence is the only place where it occurs in Romans.

seducing us from the path of service. But nothing in life can stop God from loving us.

So it is with *angels* and *demons*. We may be surprised to find *angels* in such a list, but good angels seem to have been the objects of worship in some circles (Col. 2:18; cf. Rev. 22:8-9) and thus might conceivably be obstacles in the way of the believer. Perhaps we should bear in mind also that the word "angel" means "messenger" and, though in the New Testament this normally means a messenger from God, occasionally it may be an evil being (cf. Rev. 12:7). It is also possible that angels are here thought of as serving spirits over against spirits who rule (cf. BAGD). The word NIV renders *demons*[176] refers to rulers, sometimes earthly and sometimes in the spiritual realm. It is the word KJV, RSV, and others render "principalities". The problem here is that it might denote either heavenly beings or earthly rulers. NIV uses it for the realm of spirits, whereas Phillips translates "neither messenger of heaven nor monarch of earth". Paul may have had earthly monarchs or demons exclusively in mind, but if so we have no way of knowing which. But we can be sure that he could not imagine any ruler in heaven or earth, of good character or bad, hindering the outreach of the love of God.

He moves on to *the present* and *the future*. Harrison well remarks that time is powerless against believers, "whether it be the present with its temptations and sufferings or the future with its uncertainties." This may be what Paul had in mind, or he may be thinking of what is involved in the two ages, this present age and the age to come. But whatever time brings, the love of God triumphs. It is not quite clear what he means when he goes on to *powers*.[177] The word is often used for "mighty works" or "miracles", and such a meaning is possible here. No powerful magician can interfere with God's love. But the word is also used of heavenly "powers" (Eph. 1:21; 1 Pet. 3:22), and it seems probable that this is what Paul has in mind, though it is not easy to know precisely what such a being could be apart from angels and authorities.[178] But perhaps in such a lyrical passage as this we should not push our distinctions too hard. Paul is saying that no angelic power of any sort can separate from God.

39. *Neither height nor depth* may negate the immensity of the physical universe. We can feel very small in such a vast environment, and Paul may well be assuring us that God's love is greater still (cf. Ps. 139:8). But the terms were often used in astrology, and many scholars see some such reference here.[179] GNB retains something of the ambiguity with "neither the world

176. ἀρχαί.

177. δυνάμεις. There is nothing in the Greek to correspond to NIV's *any*.

178. Leenhardt has another suggestion, "Perhaps the forces of nature which form the physical framework of the Christian life?" But this does not seem probable.

179. ὕψωμα was a technical term in astronomy for the space above the horizon, and of course βάθος was the opposite. The former is used in 2 Cor. 10:5 of every high thing that exalts itself against the knowledge of God, and nowhere else in the New Testament. The latter is used eight times, but mostly in the sense "depth". MM cite ὕψωμα from a

above nor the world below". If the terms are being used with an astrological reference, Paul will be saying that neither the height (when a star is at its zenith) nor the depth (with all its unknown potential) is strong enough to separate from God's love.

With *anything else in all creation* Paul abandons specifics and settles for a sweeping generalization wide enough to cover everything else that exists.[180] He does not say "will separate" but *will be able to separate;* he is talking about power, and no created being is powerful alongside the Creator. *The love of God* is, of course, God's love for us and not ours for him. And this love is explained as *in Christ Jesus our Lord.*[181] We cannot know the love of God apart from Christ. The cross, and only the cross, shows what real, divine love is (cf. 5:8).[182]

---

horoscope of A.D. 138 referring to the height (and exaltation) of Ἡλ(ίου). BAGD say of both terms, "since they are said to be creatures and the context speaks apparently only of supernatural forces, are prob. astral spirits; they are both astronomical t.t. and β. means the celestial space below the horizon fr. which the stars arise".

180. The use of ἑτέρα rather than ἄλλη may signify "any other kind of creature" (cf. SH, "'any other mode of being,' besides those just enumerated and differing from the familiar world as we see it"). But this cannot be insisted on.

181. BDF 269 (2) see the article repeated "for emphasis". Of the whole expression Parry says, "The full phrase sums up the whole argument from i.16" (CGT), which is in strong contrast to TH, which holds that it "conveys little, if any, meaning to the English reader in this form". This is an idiosyncratic opinion and more scholars will be found agreeing with Käsemann: "the conclusion, which emphatically at the end of v. 39 again refers to true salvation in liturgical predication of Christ, provides us not only with a summary of the preceding chapter but also with the sum of Paul's theology" (p. 252).

182. It is often said that "Paul is no theologian" or the like. Dodd comments on such views: "no one can go honestly through the labour of following the strong and coherent, though complicated, thread of argument, from Rom. i.17 to viii.39, without knowing that he is in the presence of a first-rate thinker, as well as a man of the deepest religious insight."

Romans 9

V. THE PLACE OF ISRAEL, 9:1–11:36

These difficult chapters have been the subject of much discussion.[1] K. Stendahl, for example, holds that that they are "the climax of Romans"; everything before leads up to this critical discussion.[2] D. M. Lloyd-Jones, on the other hand, regards chapter 8 as the completion of Paul's statement of the doctrine of salvation and chapters 9–11 as "a kind of postscript".[3] As we saw in the Introduction, some scholars hold that the basic aim of the letter is to deal with the problem of the relationship of Jews and Gentiles in the church at Rome. Those who hold such views naturally find in these chapters that to which everything leads up. But there are strong objections to this view of the letter, and it is better not to see these difficult chapters as the heart and the essence of what Paul is saying to the Romans.

On the other hand it is not easy to see them either as no more than an appendix to what has gone before. Granted that Paul has completed a massive argument by the end of chapter 8, important considerations remain to be treated. In the "thesis" of this letter Paul not only spoke of the gospel as "the power of God for salvation" but also said it was "to the Jew first" (1:16-17). He has not yet shown what this means. Again, for his doctrine of justification and sanctification Paul has consistently appealed to the Old Testament as sacred Scripture (his opening sentence speaks of the gospel as promised "in holy scriptures", 1:1-2), and in that Scripture the Jews appear as God's chosen people. How can he establish a system of salvation for Gentiles on the basis of the Scripture that gives a special place to Jews? If the place of the Jews as set forth in the Old Testament does not agree with the justification Paul sees in the Old Testament, then his position can scarcely stand.

Paul's whole argument demands an examination of the Jewish question. Chapter 8 ends on a note of assurance. Those saved in the way of which Paul is writing have been foreknown and predestined by God, and they are

---

1. Foreman holds that Paul is "thinking out loud as it were" at this point and that he gives no less than eight different answers to his problem. This is perhaps unnecessarily sceptical, but the passage certainly is far from easy, and nothing approaching agreement has been reached.

2. *Paul Among Jews and Gentiles* (Philadelphia, 1976), p. 4. He also says chs. 9–11 are "the climax of the letter" (p. 85), "The real center of gravity" (p. 28).

3. *Romans 8:17-39*, p. 367.

assured that this brings them to glory and that nothing can separate them from the love of God. Then what about the Jews? Did not the same God give the same assurance to the Jews as his "elect"? But the Jews for the most part were outside the church. Paul must face squarely the fact that, as a whole, Israel had rejected its Messiah. What does this say about the purposes of God? If God cannot bring his ancient people into salvation, how do Christians know that he can save them? Will the Christian salvation also be superseded one day? If Paul's position was a valid one, he had to show that "believers of today are the heirs of a valid promise" (Leenhardt).[4] The first eleven chapters of Romans are a unity, and this is important. Paul is not here proceeding to a new and unrelated subject. These three chapters are part of the way he makes plain how God in fact saves people.[5]

The passage must be approached with care. We often find expressions like "The problem of Israel's rejection", but we should bear in mind that Paul does not exactly say this. Indeed, he asks "Did God reject his people?" and answers "By no means!" (11:1). There is a tendency to recognize this and, for example, Lloyd Gaston says, "Romans 9 is not about the unbelief of Israel nor the rejection of Israel." He holds that Paul "really does not, in Rom. 9–11 or elsewhere, charge Israel with a lack of faith or a concept of works-righteousness."[6]

It is true that the idea that Israel has been rejected has often been stated too strongly. But it is also the case that the idea that Israel has not been rejected can be stated too strongly. If Paul is not writing about Israel's rejection he says things that look suspiciously like Israel's defection. He asserts that "they pursued it not by faith" (9:32) and "they did not know the righteousness that comes from God" (10:3), and he even refers to "their rejection" (11:15). If Paul's "heart's desire and prayer to God for the Israelites is that they may be saved" (10:1), then clearly he does not regard them as already saved. It is easy to take up a simplistic position.[7] It will be necessary to exercise care and to pay close attention to what Paul actually says as we examine this part of his argument.

---

4. We seem to need something like Manson's understanding: "The first eleven chapters are devoted to a full-dress debate on the question which lay at the root of most of the troubles of the Ephesian ministry, the question, Can one be a good Christian without embracing Judaism? To this Paul's answer is that the real question, and the only question for Jews, is, Can one be a good Jew without embracing Christianity?" (Donfried, p. 2).

5. Barrett sees a much closer connection between chs. 1–8 and 9–11 than is sometimes maintained. The first part "is concerned with the character and deeds of God who is the source of salvation", and chs. 9–11 with "the character and deeds of God who elected the Jews and now calls the Gentiles." James P. Martin sees a sense in which chs. 9–11 "recapitulate the argument" of chs. 1–8: "God has consigned all men to disobedience in order that he may have mercy upon all" (*Interpretation*, XXV [1971], p. 308).

6. NTS, 28 (1982), p. 418.

7. G. B. Caird points out that some have found a doctrine of double predestination in these chapters, some the view that Paul is talking about a free response to God's grace, and some the doctrine of universalism. He thinks that Paul holds all three simultaneously (ET, LXVIII [1956-57], pp. 324-27).

We should bear in mind that Paul is here dealing with the community rather than with individuals. Of course, there is an application to the individual, but basically the apostle is thinking of the place of Israel as a whole.[8]

Some linguistic phenomena are of value as we approach these chapters. Paul speaks of God 26 times in chapters 9–11, but of Christ only seven times and the Spirit once. The emphasis falls on God in his sovereignty rather than on Christ in his saving activity.[9] "Jew" is mentioned twice, but "Israel" 11 times (and not elsewhere in this letter). Paul is referring to the nation in its capacity as the covenant people, the people of God.[10] There is continuity with the rest of the letter in the use of terms like righteousness (nine times), believe (eight times), and faith (six times). Particularly important is the concept of mercy (the verb "to have mercy" occurs seven times in these chapters and once in the rest of Romans and is supported by the noun, which occurs twice in this part and once elsewhere in the letter); Cranfield well says that this is the "keyword" of these chapters.

A. THE TRAGEDY OF ISRAEL, 9:1-5

> [1]*I speak the truth in Christ —I am not lying, my conscience confirms it in the Holy Spirit—*[2]*I have great sorrow and unceasing anguish in my heart.* [3]*For I could wish that I myself were cursed and cut off from Christ for the sake of my brothers, those of my own race,* [4]*the people of Israel. Theirs is the adoption as sons; theirs the divine glory, the covenants, the receiving of the law, the temple worship and the promises.* [5]*Theirs are the patriarchs, and from them is traced the human ancestry of Christ, who is God over all, forever praised![a] Amen.*

> [a]5 Or *Christ, who is over all. God be forever praised!* Or *Christ. God who is over all be forever praised!*

Paul begins his treatment of the problem with a section in which he affirms his deep sorrow at what had happened to Israel. It may well be that there were some who held that he was nothing but a bitter renegade, lashing out against his own nation. He makes it clear that Israel's failure to accept his doctrine of salvation by God in Christ was a cause of unceasing sorrow to him.

8. Cf. Gore, "the argument as a whole and its conclusion make it quite certain that what he is speaking of is the election of men in nations or churches (only subordinately of individuals) to a position of special spiritual privilege and responsibility in this world, such as the Jews had formerly occupied, and the Christians were occupying now."

9. John Piper's "exegetical and theological study of Romans 9:1-23" is significantly entitled *The Justification of God* (Grand Rapids, 1983). This section of the epistle is taken up with the divine sovereignty.

10. W. Gutbrod sees the issue here as "one which arises out of the character of the Jews as the people of God. Can the new community trust God's Word when it seems to have failed the Jews (9:6)? The answer is complete only when it is given with reference to the Jews as Israel, because this is the name which implies that they are God's people" (TDNT, III, p. 386).

He also makes it clear that, no matter what people of his own nation had done to him, he still regarded himself as a faithful Jew.

1. There is no connective to link this with the preceding passage, and chapter 12 would follow on quite acceptably. This has led to the view that we have here a completely independent section. Dodd thinks it may have been a sermon Paul had often preached on the subject. We may well doubt whether Paul would have written out his sermons, and feel that it is unlikely that he would have carried a pile of sermon manuscripts with him on his travels. But in any case the hypothesis of an insertion is unlikely for reasons outlined above: this section is important for the argument of the epistle as a whole and must be regarded as an important part of the original. The lack of a conjunction is not as significant as the continuity of the argument. It indicates that a new subject is being introduced but no more. Godet sees it as evidence of "a lively emotion" and speaks of "the profound relation of feeling which unites this piece to the preceding."

Paul begins by asserting strongly that he is speaking the truth. *Truth* is his first word, and this gives it strong emphasis. He goes on to say that he speaks *in Christ*, which means more than "as a Christian"; it is unthinkable that a believer would tell a lie in the very presence of Christ, and Paul's "in Christ" means that he is indeed in that presence (cf. JB, "in union with Christ"). It is not an oath, but it is a firm indication that what he says is not to be doubted. It is not uncommon for the New Testament writers to follow a positive statement with a negative one *(I am not lying)*, as Paul does here (cf. 2 Cor. 11:31; Gal. 1:20; 1 Tim. 2:7). He completes an unusually solemn affirmation that he is telling the truth with *my conscience confirms it in the Holy Spirit*. He means that he speaks "with a good conscience", but that is not all. The reference to the Holy Spirit brings another divine Person into the process. The Spirit witnesses with the spirit of believers (8:16), and now we find that Paul's conscience is illuminated by the Spirit. Paul does the speaking, but in one way or another Christ, the Holy Spirit, and Paul's conscience are all involved. It forms a most emphatic protestation that he is speaking the truth.

2. Paul was not an uncommitted bystander; he identified with Israel. So he says that he has *great sorrow and unceasing anguish,* though interestingly he never says what causes this. However, there is no reasonable doubt that he is giving his reaction to his nation's failure to accept the Messiah. It is not easy to distinguish between *sorrow* and *anguish*[11] in this context, but *unceasing* may indicate the endless duration of the pain. But the combination certainly emphasizes Paul's discomfort at the plight of his nation. The *heart*[12] often stands for the whole of the inner life, but here it is clearly connected with the emotions.

11. λύπη and ὀδύνη. The latter seems often to have been used of physical pain, and SH think it "never quite loses its physical associations" (Leenhardt is similar).
12. Lenski remarks that the use of the dative means "my heart has" rather than "in my heart". But the difference is small.

3. *For* does not introduce the reason for his grief but an explanation of what it is. *I could wish* is Paul's way of expressing his deep desire to do something for Israel and the impossibility of action along the lines he mentions.[13] It is "an impossible wish" (Harrison); it could not happen, and a true believer could not really wish to be estranged from Christ. But the expression brings out Paul's deep concern for his fellow-Jews. His *I myself*[14] emphasizes his personal involvement; he is not talking in neutral fashion about someone else. *Cursed*[15] means "bearing the curse of God" and is not to be softened to excommunication, as some suggest. It is impossible for a believer to suffer this fate, but Paul's readiness to undergo it on behalf of his nation is vivid evidence of his feeling for his people. NIV speaks of being *cut off from Christ*, but nothing in the Greek corresponds to *cut off*. This helps us understand the meaning, but Paul simply says "accursed from Christ".[16] But of course anyone who was accursed would be separated from Christ.

Paul speaks of this action as *for the sake of my brothers*, where his preposition may denote substitution.[17] He longed to be able to take their place so that they might be in Christ. The parallel with Moses (Exod. 32:32) is often pointed out, sometimes with the addition that, whereas Moses preferred to perish with his people rather than to be saved alone, Paul wants to take their place, to be lost so that they may be saved. But the parallel seems to be closer, for Moses said to the people, "perhaps I can make atonement for your sin" (v. 30). Then when he spoke to God he said, "please forgive their sin—but if not, then blot me out of the book you have written." It seems that being blotted out of the book was the way Moses sought atonement. Be that as it may, Paul was certainly speaking of taking the place of his sinful people. He describes the Jews first as *my brothers*, a term he generally uses of Christians (indeed, this is the only place where he uses the term of the Jews). But he is still within the same community as other Jews, and we should note that he is speaking here of what is true "according to the flesh". He prefaces this ex-

---

13. The imperfect ηὐχόμην without ἄν is what Moule calls the "*Desiderative Imperfect*, because it is chiefly used in expressing a wish"; he translates "I could almost pray to be accursed", adding "the Imperfect softening the shock of the daring statement or expressing awe at the terrible thought" (IBNTG, p. 9). The verb means "to pray" as well as "to wish", and some see here a past prayer of Paul's. But this is very difficult to accept (when did he pray such a prayer?).

14. αὐτὸς ἐγώ. It is nominative though going with the infinitive because the subject is the same as that of the main verb (see M, I, p. 212).

15. From the idea of "laid up" (i.e., in a temple) ἀνάθεμα came to mean what is devoted to deity, and then either consecrated or, since what is thus given to deity is permanently lost to the giver and may be completely destroyed, accursed (see BAGD). J. Behm says, "The controlling thought here is that of the delivering up to the judicial wrath of God of one who ought to be ἀνάθεμα because of his sin" (TDNT, I, p. 354). The word is a dialectal variant of ἀνάθημα and was used along with it in LXX.

16. He uses the preposition ἀπό, which here clearly denotes separation, an unclassical use which denotes alienation (BDF 211).

17. He uses ὑπέρ, but this is one of the places where it is hard to distinguish it from ἀντί. Cf. IBNTG, p. 64.

pression with "my kinsmen", a way of referring to his fellow-countrymen.[18] There were ties that bound Paul to his nation, and while he came to see his relationships in Christ as much more significant than these, that did not give him license to forget the race to which he belonged.

4. *The people of Israel* is more literally "who[19] are Israelites", a term which means that they are not simply members of a national or racial group, but members of the people of God. Paul proceeds to list some of the great blessings that this entails.

He speaks first of their *adoption as sons*. This expression is applied to the Jews only here in the New Testament (it is normally used of Christians; see the note on 8:15). It is not used in the Old Testament, though the idea is found expressed in other terms (e.g., Exod. 4:22; Deut. 14:1; 32:6; Jer. 31:9; Hos. 1:10; 11:1). It means that Israel did not naturally belong in the heavenly family, but that God was gracious enough to admit them. Paul adds "the glory",[20] which is not an obvious choice of word and is not explained. But the word denotes not only outward splendor but true glory, the glory of God. It is used in the Old Testament of "the visible presence of God among His people" (SH; cf. Exod. 16:10; 33:22; 40:34; 1 Kings 8:10-11). God was manifestly present among the people Israel in a special way, a way not granted to other peoples.

The covenants is perhaps surprising, for we might have expected the emphasis to be on the great covenant of Exodus 24.[21] But there was a Jewish habit of distinguishing within the Exodus covenant three covenants, those at Horeb, in the plains of Moab, and at Gerizim and Ebal.[22] Irenaeus points out four covenants, those with Adam, with Noah, with Moses, and the gospel covenant (iii.11.8). A number of commentators see a reference to the old covenant at Sinai and the new covenant prophesied by Jeremiah and fulfilled in Christ, but this could scarcely be said to belong to the Jews. It is more likely that the reference is to the several covenants in the Old Testament, as with Noah (Gen. 9:9), with Abraham (Gen. 17:2), with Moses (Exod. 24:8), with Joshua (Josh. 8:30ff.), and with David (2 Sam. 23:5). The concept of covenant is very important for Old Testament religion, and God repeatedly entered covenantal relations with his people.

---

18. W. Michaelis thinks that συγγενής "had now a primary Christian orientation for Paul" and that it is the addition "according to the flesh" that shows that he is referring to the Jews (TDNT, VII, p. 741).

19. The relative pronoun οἵτινες often scarcely differs from οἱ but is often the relative of quality, "who are of such quality as to". Moule points out that here the distinction "certainly improves the sense and may have been intended" (IBNTG, p. 124; cf. also M, I, pp. 91-92).

20. The expression is linked to the previous one with καί, which is used six times in this sequence. "The glory" without qualification is unusual and appears to be without parallel in the rabbinic literature (SBk, III, p. 262).

21. Some MSS, such as P[46] B D[gr] etc., have the singular, but it is generally agreed that the plural is the harder reading and is to be preferred.

22. See SBk, III, p. 262.

Paul thinks next of *the receiving of the law*.[23] Both the fact that God gave the law and that the law remained as an abiding possession of God's people mattered greatly to the Jews, and Paul considers it one of their high privileges. NIV explains "the worship" by inserting *temple*, but Paul does not use the word. While, of course, worship in the temple was the high point of Jewish worship, Paul may also be glancing at the worship in the tabernacle that preceded it and possibly also at what went on in the synagogues. But certainly temple worship was the great and central thing for the Jews.[24] *The promises* will refer to the many promises God gave his people, but especially to the messianic promises. The promises in the Old Testament are not always limited to Israel, but they are addressed to that nation and are preserved in its literature.[25]

5. The Israelites were justly proud of *the patriarchs*, the great men of long ago. The term was applied especially to Abraham, Isaac, and Jacob, but was not limited to them. Paul brings his catalogue of outstanding blessings to its climax[26] with the reminder that from them also was "the Christ" (this is the title, not the name) as regards "the flesh".[27] The qualification suggests that there is more to be said about the Christ than his human ancestry. Paul stresses the privilege of his nation while leaving open the source of the essential Christ.

The meaning of the rest of the verse is one of the most hotly disputed questions of the New Testament.[28] The basic problem is whether Paul is saying that Christ is God (as NIV text) or moving on from his reference to Christ to a doxology to the Father (as NIV mg.). The problem is compounded by the fact that there is practically no punctuation in the ancient manuscripts and we must decide for ourselves whether it is better to put a comma or a full stop after "flesh"; the former ascribes deity to Christ, the latter makes for a doxology to the Father. The grammatical arguments almost all favor the first position, but most recent scholars accept the second on the grounds that Paul nowhere else says explicitly that Christ is God; he may come near it, but, they say, he always stops short of it.

---

23. νομοθεσία has about it some of the ambiguity of our word "legislation"; it may denote the making of the laws or the body of the laws. The word is found only here in the New Testament.

24. According to the Mishnah Simeon the Just used to say: "By three things is the world sustained: by the Law, by the (Temple-) service, and by deeds of loving-kindness" (Aboth 1:2).

25. Paul is interested in the concept of "promise" and uses the term 26 times (52 in the New Testament).

26. Cragg remarks about the failure of the Jews to recognize this: "It is disastrous to be blind, but to be blind to the crowning glory of one's own heritage is a tragedy which words alone cannot convey."

27. ἐξ ὧν ὁ Χριστὸς τὸ κατὰ σάρκα, "where the addition of the art. strongly emphasizes the limitation ('insofar as the physical is concerned')" (BDF 266 [2]).

28. This is illustrated by the fact that SH have a note on it covering more than five pages of small type.

The view that the passage refers to Christ is supported by a number of considerations. (1) The word order favors it: "of whom is the Christ as far as flesh is concerned, who is over all, God blessed forever." To understand it as "God, who is over all . . ." is to do violence to the word order; the relative pronoun does not precede the noun to which it refers (cf. 2 Cor. 11:31, a passage similar to this and where there can be no doubt that "who is" refers to a preceding noun).[29] (2) A doxology begins "Blessed be . . . ,"[30] whereas here "God" precedes "blessed". (3) A joyful doxology is out of place. Why should Paul bless God that Christ was born a Jew in a passage where he is expressing his grief over the Jewish rejection of Jesus? To take the words to refer to Christ is understandable; Paul speaks of him as being of the Jewish nation according to the flesh and goes on to bring out his greatness. (4) The reference to Christ "according to the flesh" looks for an antithesis. It would be very unexpected to have this as all that is said of him. (5) To have the doxology apply to God requires a very abrupt change of subject. (6) The early Fathers, including many whose native language was Greek, usually take the words to refer to Christ.

The one strong argument against the ascription of deity to Christ is that Paul does not do this elsewhere. Dodd says, "Even though he ascribes to Christ functions and dignities which are consistent with nothing less than deity, yet he pointedly avoids calling Him 'God'". So convincing is this line that Denney, though he fully accepts the deity of Christ and regards the arguments for seeing it here as forceful, refers the words to the Father. But Dodd's "pointedly" may be going too far. After all, those who today whole-heartedly accept the deity of Christ do not often call him "God", but this does not invalidate those few occasions when they do just that. We should also notice that it is not certain that Paul does not elsewhere call Christ "God". Nygren sees him doing this in Philippians 2:9-11 where Paul says that God has given Christ "the name which belongs only to God—the name LORD, Kyrios" (what else does he mean by the name "above every name"?).[31] But in the last resort this is an argument from outside the passage, and it suffers from the objection that because Paul does not say something elsewhere he cannot say it here.[32]

29. SH note a further grammatical point: "no instance seems to occur, at any rate in the N.T., of the participle ὤν being used with a prepositional phrase and the noun which the prepositional phrase qualifies. If the noun is mentioned the substantive verb becomes unnecessary" (p. 236).

30. Hodge says there is no known exception to this (so Denney and others). Lagrange says that this is true not only of the Bible but of Semitic inscriptions as well.

31. Among relevant passages we should notice Eph. 1:20-22; Col. 2:9; 2 Thess. 1:12; Tit. 1:3-4; 2:13. In some at least of these the argument against seeing Paul call Christ "God" is mainly that he does not do this elsewhere. How far can this argument be extended?

32. So difficult is the passage that some favor emending the text so as to read ὧν ὁ for ὁ ὤν, "theirs is the God. . . ." But emendation should be resorted to only if we cannot get good sense out of the words as we have them. That is not the case here. There are many good discussions of the passage, but perhaps we should mention that of B. M.

Amen is normally the response by a congregation to something uttered on its behalf by a leader. It is thus strange to have Paul append it to his own words. However, this is done often in this kind of construction. It may be that people were so used to the *Amen* at the close of doxologies that they automatically put it in.[33]

B. God's Sovereign Freedom, 9:6-29

As he moves from his expression of sorrow to the development of his argument Paul begins with a powerful statement about the sovereignty of God. His God is no petty deity, unable to effect his purpose in the universe he has created, but a mighty God who is doing what he has planned. There is a strong emphasis on mercy, for Paul is not talking about a mighty and arbitrary tyrant, but about a God who loves all that he has made and specifically the people he has chosen. In this section of his argument he first makes the point that God has always worked on the principle of election, of choosing out people through whom he would work his purpose, then he goes on to make it clear that that purpose is mercy, and thirdly he looks at the question, "Why then does he find fault?"

1. God Works by Election, 9:6-13

> [6]*It is not as though God's word had failed. For not all who are descended from Israel are Israel.* [7]*Nor because they are his descendants are they all Abraham's children. On the contrary, "It is through Isaac that your offspring will be reckoned."[a]* [8]*In other words, it is not the natural children who are God's children, but it is the children of the promise who are regarded as Abraham's offspring.* [9]*For this is how the promise was stated: "At the appointed time I will return, and Sarah will have a Son."[b]*
> [10]*Not only that, but Rebecca's children had one and the same father, our father Isaac.* [11]*Yet, before the twins were born or had done anything good or bad—in order that God's purpose in election might stand:* [12]*not by works but by him who calls— she was told, "The older will serve the younger."[c]* [13]*Just as it is written: "Jacob I loved, but Esau I hated."[d]*

a7 Gen. 21:12   b9 Gen. 18:10, 14   c12 Gen. 25:23   d13 Mal. 1:2, 3

Paul begins by demolishing the position that the whole Jewish nation

---

Metzger in Barnabas Lindars and Stephen S. Smalley, eds., *Christ and Spirit in the New Testament* (Cambridge, 1973), pp. 95-112; Nigel Turner, *Grammatical Insights into the New Testament* (Edinburgh, 1965), pp. 13-17; O. Cullmann, *The Christology of the New Testament* (London, 1959), pp. 312-13; C. F. D. Moule, *The Origin of Christology* (Cambridge, 1977), p. 137.

33. Cf. H. Schlier, "This does not mean, however, the self-confirmation of the one who prays. It expresses the fact that in divine service prayer and doxology have their place before the people whose response they evoke or anticipate" (TDNT, I, p. 337).

would be saved, a view held by many (Jews tended to say things like "All Israelites have a share in the world to come", Sanh. 10:1). He says in effect, "Look at the way God has acted in the past in working out the fulfilment of his promise. You will see that from the very beginning there have been descendants of Abraham who were not among the elect." It was an error to assume (as many Jews of his day did) that descent from Abraham gave them total security and a favored position before God. The purpose of God was fulfilled in Isaac, not Ishmael; in Jacob, not Esau. The significance of what God had done should be pondered by those who put such emphasis on God's choice of Israel. Throughout this section of his letter Paul seems to have Israel as a whole primarily in mind, not individuals, and to be dealing with election to service rather than eternal salvation. God is working out a great purpose in history, and we can discern something of it by looking at Abraham's descendants, by bearing in mind what happened to those who claim as ancestors Isaac or Ishmael, Jacob or Esau.

We should bear in mind also that this is not merely a piece of antiquarianism, of no great importance for us. Paul is looking at a problem that is a mystery still: Why do some people have so much going for them in this life, while for so many others there is nothing but hardship and difficulty? Are we to put it all down to chance? Godless people of the twentieth century might well do this, but a religious man like Paul could not rest in such a conclusion.[34]

6. Paul begins by denying[35] that God's purpose has failed.[36] *God's word* here means all God's promises to Israel. It is not often used in this sense in the New Testament (being more commonly a way of referring to the gospel), but there can be no doubt as to the meaning here. Paul has earlier said that "the promise" is by faith and that it is sure to all Abraham's seed, not only those "of the law" but also those "of the faith of Abraham" (4:16). He has something of the same thought here. God's *word* has not failed because those to whom that *word* was directed were not simply physical Israel. "Not all those who are of[37] Israel, these are Israel." His compatriots were in error in holding that the promise of God applied to the whole of physical Israel.[38] Paul is

---

34. Cf. Scott, Paul was "facing, quite honestly, one of the mysterious facts of life, perhaps the most mysterious. Why is it that some men, for no fault of their own, are doomed from their very birth to misery, while others have all good things heaped on them without their asking? . . . Paul is a religious man, and cannot rest in the easy solution that life is all a lottery" (p. 57).

35. οὐχ οἷον δὲ ὅτι seems to be a mixture of two constructions, οὐχ οἷον and οὐχ ὅτι (BDF 304; M, III, p. 47, etc.). It is an unusual construction (SH find it "unique"; and Olshausen says, "a precisely parallel idiom is nowhere found"). The meaning appears to be "it is not as though" rather than "It is impossible that" (NEB; Cranfield rejects this as a mistranslation). οἷος is a Pauline word (ten times out of 14 in the New Testament), but he uses it here only in Romans.

36. His verb is ἐκπίπτω, "fall off, or from". Figuratively it comes to mean "fail", a meaning attested outside the Bible but not in LXX (TDNT, VI, p. 169), and found again in 1 Cor. 13:8.

37. ἐκ is used of origin, and may be used of family, town, race, people, etc. (BAGD).

38. "As the Puritan John Flavel put it, 'If Abraham's faith be not in your hearts, it will be no advantage that Abraham's blood runs in your veins'" (cited in Wilson on v. 7).

denying that it was ever intended to apply in this fashion. If descent from Abraham was what mattered, then the Ishmaelites and Edom were in the same position as Israel. But "Israel" was not ethnic Israel. Whatever might happen to ethnic Israel, the promise to "Israel" stood; the falling away of some, who were not true Israelites, had no bearing on the issue. "Israel is not a term like Ammon, Moab, Greece, or Rome. 'Israel' cannot be defined in terms of physical descent, or understood simply 'on the human side' (v. 5); it is created not by blood and soil, but by the promise of God, and therefore exists within the limits of God's freedom. If he were bound by physical descent, he would be unfree, and no longer God" (Barrett). This was clear in Old Testament days, with the emergence of the concept of the "remnant"; it had long been obvious that the nation as a whole was not responding to God's leading. It was a smaller group within the nation that was really God's "people". It was stupid to think that, since the whole nation had not entered the blessing, the promise of God had failed. The promise had not been made to the whole nation and had never been intended to apply to the whole nation.[39]

7. Paul develops his argument with reference to the immediate descendants of Abraham. Not all who are Abraham's "seed"[40] are true descendants, the recipients of the promises.[41] Paul is showing that more than physical descent from Abraham is required if one would inherit the promises. Every Jew must agree with this, else he would be admitting Ishmael and the sons of Keturah to the same status as the Jew. It is possible to have impeccable outward descent from Abraham and yet not to belong to Abraham's "children." *On the contrary*[42] Paul can cite Genesis 21:12 to show that it is only the descendants through Isaac that constitute the "seed" (here used of the true successors of Abraham). It would perhaps be true to say that the Jews would have regarded this as meaning that God was bound, bound to Isaac's descendants, whereas Paul understood it to signify that God is free, free to choose Isaac and reject Esau. This does not mean that Ishmael and Esau were necessarily excluded from the covenant; it was God's command that they receive circumcision, the sign of the covenant (Gen. 17:9-13; cf. vv. 23, 26).[43] They were not excluded from the mercy of God and both received blessing. It was said of Ishmael, "I will surely bless him. . . . I will make him into a great

---

39. Käsemann points out that the problem was faced by others than Paul. The Qumran community had its own radical solution (they alone were the covenant people). "Paul does not adopt the Jewish answer, which could consist only in the demand for closer keeping of the Torah" (pp. 262-63).

40. σπέρμα. It is used in 4:16, 18 of the true successors of Abraham (cf. Gal. 3:29), but here of physical descent (cf. 11:1), while the true descendants are τέκνα. In Gen. 21:12-13 σπέρμα is used in both senses.

41. πάντες τέκνα will refer to children of Abraham, not, as some suggest, to children of God.

42. NIV's translation of ἀλλ', the strong adversative.

43. Cf. Calvin, "Since it was the will of the Lord that His covenant should be sealed, as much in Ishmael and Esau as in Isaac and Jacob, it appears that they were not altogether estranged from Him, unless perhaps one disregards the circumcision, which was communicated to them by God's command" (on v. 6).

353

nation" (Gen. 17:20). Esau was so important that Scripture includes a significant account of his descendants (Gen. 36) as well as many references to the
nation Edom (e.g., Num. 20:14; Jer. 49:7). But the nations they represented
were not the people to whom God would give his revelation, to whom he
would send his Son, the Messiah, and who would be his covenant people.
Reckoned is more exactly "called",[44] an unexpected choice of word. BAGD
class it with passages where "the emphasis is to be placed less on the fact that
the name is such and such, than on the fact that the bearer of the name
actually is what the name says about him". Paul uses this verb for the divine
call, and that may influence his choice of the quotation here (cf. v. 25). The
seed through Isaac (and that alone) is the true seed.

8. "That is"[45] introduces an explanation. "Not the children of the flesh"
(NIV, *the natural children*) are *God's children*. This may well refer to the birth of
Ishmael. When Abraham could not have children by Sarah, he took Sarah's
maidservant Hagar and had a son by her. This looks very much like a human
expedient adopted in an attempt to bring about the desired result when the
divine promise did not look as if it were being fulfilled (and thus aptly described as "of the flesh"). Paul is saying that it is not children like this that are
the children of God. On the contrary (the strong adversative again), it is *the
children of the promise*, an unusual expression, conveying the idea of children
born as a result of a promise and pointing to the fact that Isaac was born as a
result of God's promise to Abraham. He could not have been born without
divine intervention.[46] His descendants may thus realistically be characterized
in terms of promise. They are *regarded as Abraham's offspring* ("will count as the
true descendants", JB).[47] It is only the fact that God so reckons them that
makes them significant. Physical descent from Abraham is not enough.

9. *For* carries the argument along. Now we are told in what the promise
consisted. The word *promise* comes first for emphasis: "Of promise was this
word"; it is important that God gave a promise, for God always keeps his
promises. The promise is quoted from Genesis 18:10, 14. *At*[48] *the appointed time*
may be understood in more ways than one.[49] In Genesis it means "this time
next year" (Gen. 18:10, 14), but Paul's abbreviated quotation could be understood as "the time between conception and birth". Nothing much hinges on

---

44. κληθήσεται.

45. τοῦτ᾽ ἔστιν.

46. Cf. Chrysostom, "In what way was Isaac born then? Not according to the law of
nature, not according to the power of the flesh, but according to the power of the
promise."

47. The verb λογίζομαι is a favorite word of Paul's (see on 2:3). It brings out the
point that there is no absolute reason for including them. But in his sovereign freedom
God chooses to reckon them as the "seed". Howard considers λογίζομαι εἰς σπέρμα a
Semitism (M, II, p. 463).

48. κατά can have a variety of meanings, but there seems little doubt that "at" is
correct here.

49. NEB has "At the time fixed", and JB "at such and such a time", where the
former apparently sees a fixed time and the latter an indeterminate one.

the answer; the important thing is that it will all happen at the time God has fixed. "I will come" (NIV, *return*) points to the coming in power of the God who can do all things; it is his coming and not any human initiative that determines the fulfilment of the promise. "God promises, God fulfils" (Leenhardt). The promise is that Sarah (not someone else such as Hagar or Keturah) would have a son.

10. *Not only that*[50] introduces a reinforcement of the argument. In verse 6 Paul spoke of differences in Israel, and in verse 7 of differences in Abraham's descendants; now he sees differences in Isaac's posterity. Nothing human binds God. A case could be made for justifying the choice of Isaac and not Ishmael, for Isaac was the son of Abraham's wife, Ishmael the son of a slave girl. But Jacob and Esau had the same father and mother and were of the same pregnancy. The only possible difference was that Esau was born a little before Jacob (which would give him a certain priority according to human measurement). But it was Jacob whom God chose. The grammar of the sentence is difficult,[51] but the meaning is not in doubt. "One" has some emphasis as though to bring out the fact that in this matter there was no difference between the two sons.[52] We should notice two things in regard to the expression *our father Isaac*. One is that the use of *our* includes Paul with Israel; he is not separating himself from his fellow-Jews. The other is that it is usually Abraham who is called "our father", not Isaac. But the line ran from Abraham through Isaac; thus the expression, though unusual, presents no problems.

11. To emphasize the divine purpose Paul goes back to the time before the children were born[53] (he does not say who "they" were but assumes that the Romans would know this; clearly Christians were expected to know at least some parts of the Old Testament). At that time there is no question of merit or good works. The case of Ishmael had showed that birth from Abraham does not ensure acceptance; now that of Esau shows that works do not. As Hunter puts it, "claims as of right on God, whether based on birth or on works, are futile."[54] *Anything*, which is quite general, is spelled out with the addition *good or bad*. It is not human merit of which the apostle is speaking,

---

50. οὐ μόνον δὲ ἀλλά is an elliptical construction which Paul uses from time to time (as 5:3, 11; 8:23; 2 Cor. 8:19), but only here "are the words to be supplied not definitely given in the context" (BDF 479 [1]).

51. Ῥεβέκκα has no grammatical connection. Paul seems to have begun a parenthesis and not returned to his original construction. Or perhaps, "not only Sarah received a promise, but Rebecca also".

52. κοίτη meant "bed", then "marriage bed" and thus "intercourse", and finally "seminal emission" (see BAGD). It signifies here "having seed from one".

53. μήπω is rare (only in Heb. 9:8 in the New Testament), but MM cite it in the papyri. It means "not yet". γεννηθέντων is a genitive absolute but without the subject being expressed.

54. Cf. Burton H. Throckmorton, Jr., "Lineage cannot guarantee election; nor does election presuppose righteousness; but God's election is, rather, a free act of mercy. If either lineal descent or ethical performance could guarantee election, then God's choice would not be *free* and would not be an act of *mercy*" (*Adopted in Love* [New York, 1978], p. 81).

and he firmly excludes anything, anything at all, that the children did as the basis for the divine choice.

Paul stresses *purpose*[55] and *election*.[56] There is a strong emphasis on the divine act. It is not that Jacob could be said in any way to merit selection. God had a purpose, and he worked it out in his own way. Paul says that God did what he did so that his purpose in election *might stand*.[57] This is a somewhat unusual use of the verb, but a perfectly intelligible one. God's purpose will remain, no matter what.

12. *Not by works* further stresses the divine initiative. *Works* is broad enough to cover all kinds of human activity; it is not circumscribed in any way as, for example, "law works" would be. That God's purpose is not dependent on what people do is implicit in the preceding argument but is explicit here. It is God's call that counts. *Works* and *calls* are set in sharp antithesis.[58] The one excludes the other. Paul clinches the point by quoting the words, *"The older will serve the younger."*[59] It is election to privilege that is in mind, not eternal salvation. Moreover, it seems clear that Paul intends a reference to nations rather than individuals (though Murray strongly defends a reference to individuals as well as to nations). The words quoted say specifically that the elder will *serve* the younger, but Esau did not in fact serve Jacob, though the Edomites in time came to serve the Israelites. We must also bear in mind that the oracle Paul quotes has earlier said, "Two nations are in your womb, and two peoples from within you will be separated" (Gen. 25:23). The argument concerns Israel as a whole and its place in the purpose of God.

13. Characteristically Paul backs up his argument with a quotation from Scripture, this one from Malachi 1:2-3: *"Jacob I loved, but Esau I hated."*[60] Two questions are important here: Is Paul referring to nations or individuals? and What is meant by *hated*? As to the first, we have just seen that the Genesis passage refers primarily to nations and we would expect that to continue here. That this is the case seems clear from what Malachi writes about Esau: "Esau I have hated, and I have turned his mountains into a wasteland and left

---

55. This is involved in the telic ἵνα, which is dependent on the later ἐρρέθη (see BDF 478 for moving a final clause forward). SH comment on Paul's use of πρόθεσις whereas βουλή was the normal term for "purpose": "no previous instance of the word πρόθεσις in this sense seems to be quoted. The conception is worked out by the Apostle with greater force and originality than by any previous writer, and hence he needs a new word to express it." Cf. C. Maurer, cited in the note on 8:28.

56. This is Paul's first use of ἐκλογή in Romans; he will use it four times in this letter and five times in all (out of seven times in the New Testament). G. Schrenk sees the word here as denoting the "electing divine will" and as referring "not to salvation, but to position and historical task"; the word "lays emphasis on the free decision of God" (TDNT, IV, p. 179).

57. The verb is μένω, which is not nearly as common in Paul as in John (17 times; John has it 40 times and the Johannine epistles 27). It is the opposite of ἐκπέπτωκεν in v. 6.

58. οὐκ ἐξ ἔργων ἀλλ᾽ ἐκ τοῦ καλοῦντος.

59. An exact quotation from Gen. 25:23 LXX, which is an exact translation of the Hebrew. The use of "greater" and "less" for "older" and "younger" is more common in Hebrew than in Greek generally, but Cranfield shows that it is found in Greek writers.

60. The aorists in the two verbs seem to refer to the act of choice in the womb.

his inheritance to the desert jackals" (Mal. 1:3). Both in Genesis and Malachi the reference is clearly to nations, and we should accept this as Paul's meaning accordingly.

The meaning of *hated* is a different kind of problem. There is a difficulty in that Scripture speaks of a love of God for the whole world (John 3:16) and the meaning of "God is love" (1 John 4:8, 16) is surely that God loves, quite irrespective of merit or demerit in the beloved. Specifically he is said to love sinners (Rom. 5:8). It is also true that in Scripture there are cases where "hate" seems clearly to mean "love less" (e.g., Gen. 29:31, 33; Deut. 21:15; Matt. 6:24; Luke 14:26; John 12:25). Many find this an acceptable solution here: God loved Esau (and the nation Edom) less than he loved Jacob (and Israel). But it is perhaps more likely that like Calvin we should understand the expression in the sense "reject" over against "accept". He explains the passage thus: "I chose Jacob and rejected Esau, induced to this course by my mercy alone, and not by any worthiness in his works. . . . I had rejected the Edomites. . . ."[61] This accords with the stress throughout this passage on the thought of election for service. God chose Israel for this role; he did not so choose Edom.

2. God's Purpose Is Mercy, 9:14-18

14What then shall we say? Is God unjust? Not at all! 15For he says to Moses,

"I will have mercy on whom I have mercy,
and I will have compassion on whom I have compassion."[a]

16It does not, therefore, depend on man's desire or effort, but on God's mercy. 17For the Scripture says to Pharaoh: "I raised you up for this very purpose, that I might display my power in you and that my name might be proclaimed in all the earth."[b] 18Therefore God has mercy on whom he wants to have mercy, and he hardens whom he wants to harden.

[a]15 Exodus 33:19   [b]17 Exodus 9:16

Throughout these chapters we must bear in mind what Paul is doing

61. This is the only passage in the New Testament where God is said to hate any person. He hates the deeds of evildoers (cf. Rev. 2:6), but that is quite another matter. In the Old Testament God is more often said to hate, but mostly this means that he hates evil things (Deut. 12:31; Prov. 6:16, etc.), especially idolatrous practices (Jer. 44:4; Amos 5:21, etc.). A few times he is said to hate people, but, apart from the Malachi passage, this seems to refer to "bloodthirsty and deceitful men" (Ps. 5:6) and the like (cf. Ps. 11:5; Jer. 12:8). It cannot be said that hate is at all characteristic of God. Some commentators, however, view God as having "a holy hatred" of evil people. Thus Murray says that the present passage "is not satisfactorily interpreted as meaning simply 'not loved' or 'loved less' but in the sense that an attitude of positive disfavour is expressed thereby" (p. 23). Wilson says, "Both were hateful on account of Adam's sin, so that it is in fact easier to explain God's hatred of Esau than his love for Jacob." Harrison objects that "Hatred in the ordinary sense will not fit the situation, since God bestowed many blessings on Esau and his descendants." There is an emotional content in hatred which is not easy to apply to God.

and not complain because he is not answering the questions we would like him to answer. He is arguing that his doctrine of justification is not in contradiction of the Old Testament position that marks out the Jews as God's chosen people. He is saying that the Jews of his day were in error in seeing themselves as the only people acceptable before God. In the previous section he made the point that God always works by the method of election. At this point he shows that the Jew cannot argue that Paul must be wrong because if his view were accepted God would be unjust. Sometimes his argument is regarded as not particularly convincing, but that is because we look at it from a modern Western standpoint. Paul, however, was arguing with first-century Jews, not modern Westerners.

This will account for the omission of some things that we would like to see dealt with. Thus Paul argues for God's absolute freedom and does not address himself to the measure in which we have freedom or how our freedom relates to God's freedom. If God is free to do what he wills and if all who are saved are saved because God predestined them, then modern people are apt to ask, "Are we not reduced to the level of puppets?" But Paul is not discussing our freedom at all. We would like to have his thoughts on the matter, but that is not the question before him. He neither affirms nor denies that we are free. He simply does not discuss the question at all.[62] His big point here is that the relationship between God and sinners cannot be thought of simply in terms of justice. We have no claim on God, no rights before him. We are dependent on his mercy.

14. Once again Paul begins with *What then shall we say?* (see the note on 3:5), and suggests a possible question, *Is God unjust?* This he rejects with the vigorous *Not at all!*[63] To say that God is unjust is for Paul self-contradictory. A powerful but unjust being might be "god" in the sense of one of the gods of the Gentiles. But he would not be God, the perfect being who reveals himself in Scripture. It is simply not possible for that God to act unjustly.[64] "Will not the Judge of all the earth do right?" (Gen. 18:25). A Jew might well object: "Paul, you must be wrong because if what you say is true, God cannot be just." Paul's reply is to argue from the Jew's own Scripture. He says in effect, "It is the very Scripture that you accept and that shows God to be perfectly

---

62. Cf. Robinson, Paul has brought his analogy in "for one purpose only, to show that the Creator has absolute freedom over his creatures: he is not concerned at this point to find one which will also safeguard *their* freedom." Nygren makes a slightly different point: "Men think that if everything rests in God's hand and depends on His will, there is then nothing that rests with men; so there can no longer be talk of his responsibility and guilt. Paul does not admit that alternative. He can affirm both points at the same time" (p. 368). And in the present argument he is not concerned with how the two points relate to one another.

63. μὴ γένοιτο, for which see the note on 3:4.

64. Cf. Lenski, "Righteousness (justice) belongs to the very nature of God"; on v. 17 he says, "The fact that God is righteous is axiomatic and is settled as being axiomatic in v. 13. To prove it is like trying to prove that whiteness is white, that the sun is light, that God does not sin."

just that tells us that God did these things." Denney points out that a Jew might reply to Paul, but to Scripture he can make no reply (on vv. 17-18). So Paul's argument from Scripture is convincing. He shows that God is out to secure mercy, not condemnation. God is not unjustly condemning some, but in mercy saving some. We sinners have no claim on God whatever. If we are saved, that is due to God's mercy, not the justice of our cause. To say that God is not just in his treatment of Jacob and Esau misses the point that neither has a claim on God and that in both cases he acts in mercy.[65]

15. *For* will give grounds for Paul's strong "Not at all!" There is another relevant passage from Scripture which he proceeds to quote (Exod. 33:19). Paul introduces it with *he says to Moses*.[66] The quotation does not mention justice but speaks of God's will to do mercy. His exercise of *mercy* and *compassion* is as he himself chooses. There is probably no great difference in meaning between *mercy* and *compassion*, but the combination puts emphasis on the truth that God acts in a compassionate and merciful manner and further that he does this freely towards anyone he chooses.[67] Leenhardt points out that if God's reaction depended on man he would have had to punish Israel. "Instead of that He gave to this rebellious people a new revelation of His grace." God's freedom to have mercy is not limited as though he could show mercy only on certain classes, such as people with works or piety or rights. Paul is saying that God's freedom is absolute. It is important to be clear that before God we have no rights. That is why mercy is so important for sinners.

16. From the example he has cited Paul reasons to the principle behind it; notice his *therefore*.[68] He has three genitives, two preceded by negatives, but he does not say what the "it" to which he is referring is. It may be salvation, or perhaps mercy. This is not dependent on human volition; the sinner may desperately will that God will have mercy, but he cannot bring it about. Nor is it a matter of "him that runs" (NIV, *man's . . . effort*). The Psalmist can say "I run in the path of your commands," but this he sees not as a merit of his own, "for you have set my heart free" (Ps. 119:32). Like Paul, he is saying that it is not what people do that determines God's grace, and further that it is God's grace that enables him to "run" as he should. BAGD class the use of the verb here as "using the foot-races in the stadium as a basis . . . *exert oneself to the limit of one's powers in an attempt to go forward, strive to advance*" (cf. 1 Cor. 9:24, 26; Gal. 2:2; 5:7; Phil. 2:16). Paul is saying that all

---

65. The use of παρά is interesting: μὴ ἀδικία παρὰ τῷ θεῷ; BAGD class its use here with those where the term means "someth. is (not) with or in someone, someone has someth. (nothing) to do w. someth." Cf. 2:11; Eph. 6:9. Perhaps this way of putting it is due to motives of reverence: Paul asks, "Is there injustice with God?" rather than "Is God unjust?"

66. The word order τῷ Μωϋσεῖ γάρ (not τῷ γὰρ Μωϋσεῖ) puts some emphasis on "Moses"; it was to the great lawgiver that God spoke.

67. Wuest sees ὃν ἄν as meaning "whoever" and explains the passage in these terms: "'I will have mercy on anyone, whoever he is, that I will show mercy to in the future.' This emphasizes the absolute sovereignty of God in the disposition of His mercy."

68. For ἄρα οὖν ("wherefore therefore") see the note on 5:10.

human effort leaves us in condemnation. We cannot clear ourselves of sin.[69] If we are saved it is because God chooses to show mercy on us.

Barrett argues that this is critical to Paul's argument: "If the fundamental fact . . . that Christ is the seed of Abraham, and that men are elected in him, is lost sight of, the assertions of *vv.* 6-13 are open to objection." Unless we realize that in his dealings with Abraham, with Isaac and Ishmael, and with Jacob and Esau, God was acting in mercy, we cannot understand Paul. It is possible to look at those actions and find something that we would not classify as justice, but if we concentrate on those things and overlook God's mercy we miss the thrust of it all. Paul sees clearly that if salvation were to rest on human willing and human striving we would all be in difficulties. But it does not. It depends on the will and the mercy of God. That is clear in Christ's atoning work. And it is clear, as Paul is showing, when we look again at what God did among the patriarchs in days of old.

17. *For* should probably be seen as parallel to the "for" of verse 15; this verse, like that, carries on the logical sequence from verse 14. Moses corresponds to Jacob and Pharaoh to Esau. *The Scripture says to Pharaoh* is an unexpected way of introducing Paul's quotation, for the Scripture had not been written at that time. The meaning, of course, is that God spoke the words in question (Exod. 9:16), but the way Paul puts it brings out the truth that these words would be embodied for all time in Scripture (cf. Gal. 3:8, 22).[70] This is the only time that Paul mentions Pharaoh. His quotation differs in some respects from LXX. *For this very purpose*[71] makes it clear that God's plan was being advanced through what Pharaoh was doing. Indeed, God says *I raised you up*, where the divine activity is stressed rather more than in the usual LXX text.[72] The meaning here appears to be to raise to one's place in history,[73] though some prefer the thought that he was preserved (through the plagues?), raised from sickness, or spared from being killed for his sins. None of these fits the context or the meaning of the verb as well as the first-mentioned view. Paul is speaking not just of Pharaoh's survival, but of his whole place in history (cf. Cranfield).

The purpose, then, of Pharaoh's appearance in history was that God

---

69. A very different position is advocated in the Jewish *Psalms of Solomon:* "for thou art a just Judge over all the peoples of the earth. For there will not be hidden from thy knowledge any one who doeth wickedness: and the righteousness of thy upright ones, O Lord, is before thee . . . we work by free-will and the choice of our own souls to do either good or evil by the work of our hands" (Ps. Sol. 9:4-7). Paul is writing in opposition to views such as this.

70. Michel suggests that Paul uses "Scripture says" perhaps because this stresses the distance between God and the heathen ruler. But we have a similar locution with Abraham (Gal. 3:8).

71. εἰς αὐτὸ τοῦτο (again in 13:6; 2 Cor. 5:5; Eph. 6:22; Col. 4:8) means "just this (and nothing else)" (BDF 290 [4]). It seems to stress the idea of purpose.

72. LXX has διετηρήθης, "you have been preserved"; Paul may have felt that ἐξήγειρα was nearer the Hebrew הֶעֱמַדְתִּיךָ. Whether that was so or not, "I raised you" is more dynamic than "you were preserved" (cf. LXX of Jer. 27:41; Hab. 1:6; Zech. 11:16).

73. Cf. Wilckens, "Auftreten-Lassens in der Geschichte".

might *display* his *power* in him,[74] and further that God's *name might be proclaimed in all the earth*. What God did in the plagues that preceded the Exodus and then in bringing his people out of Egypt certainly showed power and was widely spoken of (cf. Exod. 15:14-15; Josh. 2:9-10; 9:9). What emerged was not the setting forth of Pharaoh's purposes but those of God. Paul surely means his reader to see that what will emerge from the current situation will likewise not be the triumph of the self-will of his Jewish opponents, but the glory of God.

18. *Therefore*[75] introduces a statement of the principle on which the foregoing depends. The will of God is the important thing. We must bear in mind that this is an occasional writing and that Paul is dealing with a specific Jewish type of opposition. We must not think that he is giving us his full mind on the question. But what is relevant for those contemplating the bearing of the situation of Israel on the truth of justification by faith is that God does what he wills.[76] He wills to have mercy, and it is this on which the emphasis falls. Mercy is the keyword throughout this discussion.

But Paul also says, *he hardens whom he wants to harden*. This statement is a difficult one for modern readers. Let us notice first that neither here nor anywhere else is God said to harden anyone who had not first hardened himself. We must bear in mind that, while God is repeatedly said to have hardened Pharaoh (Exod. 9:12; 10:1, 20, 27; 11:10; 14:8; there are also prophecies that he will do this [Exod. 4:21; 7:3]), it is also true that Pharaoh is repeatedly said to have hardened himself (Exod. 7:13, 14, 22; 8:15, 19, 32; 9:7, 34, 35; I have included here some passives of the form "Pharaoh's heart was hardened" on the ground that they come at the end of one or other of the plagues and represent Pharaoh's reaction to what God has done; cf. also Exod. 13:15). God's hardening follows on what Pharaoh himself did. His hardening always presupposes sin and is always part of the punishment of sin. God could kill the sinner immediately when he sinned, but he usually does not. But he shuts him up to the effect of his sin, so that the person who hardens himself is condemned to live as a hardened person. God does not harden people who do not go astray first (cf. Jas. 1:13).

This is a much bigger question than that of Pharaoh. God is in all of life. The sinner could not do any sin unless God permitted it (and what God permits Scripture often says that he does, as in 2 Sam. 12:11; 16:10; 1 Kings 11:23; Ps. 105:25; Isa. 63:17). And somehow even the sins of those who vigorously oppose God are seen in the end to be part of the way God's plan works out. RSV seems to be right in translating Psalm 76:10 as "Surely the

---

74. Paul uses ἐνδείκνυμι in nine of its 11 New Testament occurrences (three in Romans). *Power* quite often means something like "saving power" (e.g., 1:16; 1 Cor. 1:18), a meaning which would be very appropriate here.

75. "Wherefore therefore" as in v. 16; see the note on 5:10.

76. Burton comments on the present tense here and classes it among those in which "it is possible that a particular imagined instance in the present or future is before the mind as an illustration of the general class of cases" (MT, 313).

wrath of men shall praise thee"—even that which is opposed to God in some way serves his purpose. An interesting example is seen in David's census. Looked at in one way, it is God punishing the king's sin (2 Sam. 24:1); looked at in another, it is Satan at work (1 Chron. 21:1). God uses the evil to bring about his purpose. So the hardening of Pharaoh, whether we look at it from God's standpoint or that of Pharaoh, resulted in a display of power and in God's name being widely proclaimed. But the fact that God works through it does not make the hardening any the less Pharaoh's act.[77]

God's action is not arbitrary. When Pharaoh (or anyone else) chooses to reject the right, he will be hardened in the wrong, whether we think of God or of Pharaoh as at work.[78] It is true that God used Pharaoh, but the monarch was not a mere puppet. He did what he willed to do. Nor must we think that hardening is necessarily permanent. That God does not bring about the immediate death of the sinner but endures his sin means that he is giving that sinner the opportunity to repent (2:4).[79]

3. God's Wrath and God's Mercy, 9:19-29

[19]One of you will say to me: "Then why does God still blame us? For who resists his will?" [20]But who are you, O man, to talk back to God? "Shall what is formed say to him who formed it, 'Why did you make me like this?'"[a] [21]Does not the potter have the right to make out of the same lump of clay some pottery for noble purposes and some for common use?

[22]What if God, choosing to show his wrath and make his power known, bore with great patience the objects of his wrath—prepared for destruction? [23]What if he did this to make the riches of his glory known to the objects of his mercy, whom he prepared in advance for glory— [24]even us, whom he also called, not only from the Jews but also from the Gentiles? [25]As he says in Hosea:

> "I will call them 'my people' who are not my people;
>   and I will call her 'my loved one' who is not my loved one,"[b]

[26]and,

> "It will happen that in the very place where it was said to them,
>   'You are not my people,'
>   they will be called 'sons of the living God.'"[c]

---

77. Cf. H. H. Rowley, "His act was none the less his own because God could use it. But for Pharaoh's oppression Israel would never have perceived that the God who elected her was a gracious and saving God" (*The Biblical Doctrine of Election* [London, 1952], p. 133).

78. "God punishes by delivering up to sin" (K. L. and M. A. Schmidt, TDNT, V, p. 1030; they also speak of "The self-hardening of man as his hardening by God, the guilt and responsibility of man as self-judgment and yet also God's judgment" [p. 1024]).

79. Brevard S. Childs discusses the hardening of Pharaoh and minimizes the theological interest in the Exodus account; he thinks the terminology describes rather Pharaoh's resistance to the signs God did in Egypt (*Exodus* [London, 1974], pp. 170-75).

27*Isaiah cries out concerning Israel:*

"*Though the number of the Israelites be like the sand by the sea,*
    only the remnant will be saved.
28 *For the Lord will carry out*
    his sentence on earth with speed and finality."*d*

29*It is just as Isaiah said previously:*

"*Unless the Lord Almighty*
    had left us descendants,
we would have become like Sodom,
    and we would have been like Gomorrah."*e*

*a*20 Isaiah 29:16; 45:9   *b*25 Hosea 2:23   *c*26 Hosea 1:10   *d*28 Isaiah 10:22,
23   *e*29 Isaiah 1:9

Paul has made it clear that God does what he wills in both showing mercy and hardening (v. 18). But to human ways of thinking that presents some problems. Paul proceeds to look at them, and he advances his argument by showing that what God has done has been to extend his mercy to the Gentiles.

19. Paul regards a retort as certain; he pictures his reader as asking questions (he says "You", not *One of you* as NIV). The first question is, *Then why does God still blame us?* If God is Lord of history, if mercy and hardening alike cause his name to be proclaimed throughout the earth, if he shows mercy where he wills and hardens where he wills, then how can anyone possibly be blamed for what he does. *Still,* after God has hardened him? But he has simply done what God moved him to do. *For who resists his will?*[80] It is not the usual word for "will", and it appears to have been chosen as "implying more definitely the deliberate purpose of God" (SH). The verb *resists*[81] means "set oneself against" (see BAGD); it signifies the setting of the will of puny man against the all-powerful will of God. The question implies that this does not happen if what Paul has been saying is true. We tend to approach this in a different way from Paul, for we tend to think of the eternal destiny of the individual. We must bear in mind throughout this section that Paul is not dealing with that subject. He is dealing with the failure of Israel as a whole to respond to the Messiah over against the fact that the church was largely Gentile. He is saying that God works his purpose out by such means as choosing Isaac and rejecting Ishmael, choosing Jacob and rejecting Esau, or hardening Pharaoh. He is arguing that Israel's present hardening does not

80. βούλημα is not a common word. G. Schrenk shows that it means here "the purposeful intention of God" (TDNT, I, p. 637). We perhaps see something of the stress on purpose in the fact that it was sometimes used of a last will and testament (see MM).
81. ἀνθέστηκεν is perfect tense. NIV takes it as equivalent to a present (as Cranfield, Lagrange, and others). It could be taken as "hath resisted" (KJV), but NIV is probably correct. A number of translations have "Who can resist?" but this does not appear to be the meaning.

defeat God's purpose, but rather that it is God's means of bringing the gospel to the Gentiles. This may have an application to individuals, but Paul does not spell it out. He makes his point that God has always worked out his purpose. It is a purpose of mercy, though it may be attained by hardening some people.

20. Paul anticipates the questions his reader will ask, but he does not answer them. He argues that they are illegitimate questions, questions that the creature has no right to ask of the Creator. The creature is demanding that God give answers on the basis of the creature's ideas. But, as Parry puts it, "the question cannot be properly raised by man as against GOD, because man has to accept the conditions of his creation" (on v. 19). The whole of man's thinking and living are on the basis of his being a created being who as such cannot call the Creator to account (and could not understand him if he were to oblige).[82] Smart points out that "A Pilate, a Judas, and a Jerusalem council can nail the Savior of the world to a cross but it is God who decides what that cross is to mean in the subsequent history of mankind" (p. 136). Paul is saying that the questions we ask are illegitimate questions, and he lets it go at that.

He addresses his reader as *O man*,[83] which comes first in the sentence and is balanced by placing the word *God* last in emphatic contrast. "Little, impotent, ignorant man" (Wesley) is set over against the great God whose purpose runs through the whole creation and who moves people and nations.[84] Cranfield well brings out the thrust of Paul's argument with his comment: "It is because, whether one is Moses or Pharaoh, member of the believing Church or member of still unbelieving Israel, one is this man, the object of God's mercy, that one has no right to answer God back." Paul is not saying that there is no answer to the question; he is saying that the question is illegitimate. Man is not in a position to ask it.[85] The use of the emphatic pronoun for *you* strengthens the contrast. Paul is leaving no doubt that man is in sharp contrast with God. The verb *talk back*[86] is not one we expect to be used of an action directed towards God. The activity is not proper for a creature.

Paul moves to a further question that *what is formed* might ask of *him who*

---

82. As Job found out, with the result that he repented in dust and ashes (Job 42:6). But there is a difference between the honest searching of a Job or a Jeremiah and the objector of whom Paul writes and whose objection is characterized by "insolence rather than anguish" (Lagrange).

83. A very unusual form of address in the New Testament; see the note on 2:1. BDF 146 (1b) discerns "some emotion" in the use of the expression here, but Turner sees "no great emotion" (M, III, p. 33). It seems wiser not to insist on it.

84. Translations like "my friend" (GNB) or "sir" (NEB) reduce this to an ordinary form of address and miss the contrast.

85. μενοῦνγε (which is not frequent in the New Testament) is "used esp. in answers, to emphasize or correct . . . even—contrary to class. usage—at the beginning of a clause . . . *rather, on the contrary*" (BAGD). Moule sees it here as adversative, "But who are you. . . ?" (IBNTG, p. 163).

86. ἀνταποκρίνομαι means "answer in turn" and thus "answer back" ("answer by contradicting" [Chamberlain, p. 133]). "The language is startling" (Earle) and thus underlines the incongruity of the question.

formed it.[87] The expression does not specifically refer to the potter and the clay, but there is no doubt that he has this in mind here. Paul is quoting from Isaiah 29:16 or 45:9-10, the thought in both passages being that God formed Israel into a nation. "The rhetorical questions in both contexts reflect incredulity that the Artist should be thought of as inferior to his material" (Harrisville). We are not of such stature that we can query God's doings. The very fact that we stand in the relation of creature to Creator precludes this.[88]

21. NIV omits Paul's "Or",[89] which introduces a necessary alternative. If it is not as he has just said, the alternative he is about to introduce must be accepted. Unless the reader admits that man has no right to ask the kind of question he has suggested, he must conclude that the potter does not have the complete right[90] to make out of his clay[91] anything that suits his purpose. The Old Testament makes use of the potter-clay motif several times (e.g., Isa. 29:15-16; 45:8-10; 64:8-9; Jer. 18:1-6; it is seen also in Wis. 15:7-8, a passage with many resemblances to the present one). Sometimes the thought is that the potter has complete authority to do what he wants with his clay, often that a marred vessel can be remade with the same clay into a satisfactory utensil, and sometimes, as here, that the clay has no right to answer back to the potter. That is not the function of clay.

Sometimes Paul's argument is criticized unfairly, as when O'Neill says, "The objection is entirely warranted, and the reply does nothing to answer it." Dodd regards this as "the weakest point in the whole epistle", and says further, "But the trouble is that man is not a pot; he *will* ask, 'Why did you make me like this?' and he will not be bludgeoned into silence." Such positions imply that the creature is in a position to call God to account and to judge him by human standards and by the limited insight humans can bring to a complex problem. They overlook the fact that the sinner is out of his league when he takes on God (to use very human language). Again, they ignore the fact that the Creator constantly does things which the creature does not and cannot understand. And they overlook the main point that Paul is making, that God, like the potter, is alone responsible for the final purpose.[92] We may

---

87. The verb πλάσσω means "to form or fashion out of a soft mass", while the noun πλάσμα "is commonly used for the product of the artisan or artist" (H. Braun, TDNT, VI, pp. 254, 255). Braun finds a reference here to Old Testament passages speaking of the potter and the clay, though there God's "sovereignty is orientated to the bringing of salvation" while here "man is set before the *tremendum* of a demonstration of judgment by the God who exercises both mercy and hardening. Man, as God's product and creature, is absolutely dependent on the deity. He is thus delivered up to God's judgment and referred to His mercy" (pp. 260-61).

88. *Like this* reflects οὕτως, an unusual construction: "An adverb in place of a predicate acc. is found only in R 9:20" (BDF 434 [2]).

89. ἤ.

90. Some translations have "power", but ἐξουσία means "right". The potter does not have to ask permission before he can go to work. He is entitled to do what he wants with his clay.

91. πηλός can mean "mud" as well as the potter's clay. But no doubt "clay" is the meaning here.

92. Cf. Barrett on Dodd: "To stress this point, however, is to emphasize a detail in

agree that it would not be right for God to create sinners simply in order to punish them. But that is not what Paul is saying. He is saying that God created people, that people became sinners, and that God then dealt with them as sinners.[93] If it is a question of the "rights" people have, we must bear in mind that, whatever we may be in our own eyes, in God's sight we are sinners. If we demand that we be treated in strict justice (and not like so many clay pots), we must bear in mind that justice will go hard with sinners.[94]

Paul makes the point that the potter is quite entitled to make out of the one batch of clay[95] some vessels *for*[96] *noble purposes and some for common use* (cf. 2 Tim. 2:20). It is not unjust for the potter to make a vessel for what we call "dishonorable" or menial use. And it is not unjust for God to make a man (e.g., Pharaoh) for dishonorable or menial use. In both cases the right is absolute. Paul will go on from there to show that in any case God's purpose is mercy; he does not speak of any of the vessels as being destroyed (a potter makes some pots for menial use, but never makes pots simply in order to destroy them) but only of being put to different uses. Here he simply says that God is "within his rights", so to speak. The accusation of unfairness is unjustified.[97]

It is worth bearing in mind that it is the use to which the pots are put that differs, not the material of which they are made. They are all made of the same clay. And it is also the case that Isaac and Ishmael, Jacob and Esau, Moses and Pharaoh, believing Christians and unbelieving Jews, were all of the same clay. It is their function in the working out of the divine purpose that differs. The Jews were inclined to think that God could not make them anything other than vessels of honor. Paul rejects this view and points out that God does what he wills.

22. "Only a few passages in Paul are more obscure than this one (i.e. vv. 22-23), and no certainty is possible as to how it ought to be translated" (Knox).

---

the analogy instead of the major comparison, which is between the final responsibility of the potter for what he produces, and the final responsibility of God for what he does in history."

93. Cf. Hodge, "It is not the right of God to create sinful beings in order to punish them, but his right to deal with sinful beings according to his good pleasure, that is here asserted." Similarly Murray, "Paul is not now dealing with God's sovereign rights over men as men but over men as sinners."

94. Cf. Bruce, "all are guilty before God; no-one has a claim on his grace. If he chooses to extend his grace to some, the others have no ground for arguing that he is unjust because he does not extend it to them. If it is justice they demand, they can have it".

95. φύραμα means *"that which is mixed"* (fr. φυράω) or *kneaded, (a lump or batch of) dough"* (BAGD). It is applicable to the doughlike stuff on which the potter works.

96. ὁ μὲν . . . ὁ δέ is apparently an example of the use of ὅς as a demonstrative pronoun (BAGD). εἰς is used to convey the idea of purpose.

97. Robinson comments, "God, Paul has just said, is not to be charged with injustice *even if* no principle can be seen in his dealings. *But* in fact, so far from being unjust, his record with men reveals precisely the opposite quality. There *is* a principle and it is one of quite unmerited mercy."

We must bear this warning in mind as we deal with a very difficult passage. It begins with an *if*, which is not followed up with the appropriate apodosis.[98] Perhaps we should supply one: "But if God . . . what will you say?" or the like. NIV favors *What if*, and this is acceptable to many (Barrett, e.g., takes this view and points to John 6:62 as another example of the same construction).[99] This seems the best way of taking it. Paul also has a "but", which is not easy to fit into our translation but which gives a certain adversative force: "But if God has shown mercy why complain about injustice?" *Choosing* translates a participle usually understood as "willing". Commentators are divided as to whether we should understand this to mean "although he willed" (Black, Denney, etc.) or "because he willed" (Robinson, Cranfield, etc.). The former way of taking it will signify that, although he willed to show wrath, God endured the vessels of wrath with much longsuffering. The latter will mean that, because he willed to show both wrath and mercy, God endured the vessels. . . . Either way of understanding the words is quite possible, but perhaps there is more to be said for the second, for in this passage Paul seems to be saying that God is working out a single purpose of mercy and this is to be discerned in his wrath as well as his longsuffering.[100] God willed to reveal his mercy, but also his wrath; he lets sinners be in no doubt as to the consequences of sin. "The wrath" (see the note on 1:18) is here unqualified (NIV's *his* is inserted to show whose wrath it is); for Paul "the" wrath is so significant that there is no need to say whose it is. With this he links *make his power*[101] *known*. It is part of the revelation that God is opposed to evil and part also that he is powerful enough to do what he wills about it. So he *bore*[102] *with great*

---

98 BDF have a note on the anacoluthon, which, they say, is avoided if the καί of v. 23 is dropped with B Or vg etc. (BDF 467). But this attestation is not sufficient to counter the suspicion that the reading arose as an attempt to smooth away the difficulty.

99. C. Maurer accepts the "What if" solution and paraphrases the passage in these terms: "What if God in fulfilment of His will, to demonstrate His wrath and reveal His power, endured with much patience vessels of wrath appointed for destruction, and did so for the one purpose that He might reveal the riches of His glory, which He works on the vessels of mercy which He prepared beforehand to His glory and to which He has called us not only from among the Jews but also from among the Gentiles, how much the more then should defiant obstinacy turn into humble praise?" (TDNT, VII, p. 363).

100. G. Stählin, who sees God's longsuffering as having "the same enigmatic dual operation as all God's tokens of grace", paraphrases this verse in these terms: "But if God tolerated in great longsuffering the vessels of wrath which were made for destruction, because He willed to manifest His wrath and declare His power in them, (he did it) also in order that he might make known the riches of his glory in the vessels of mercy, which he had prepared long before for glory" (TDNT, V, p. 426).

101. δυνατόν; the neuter of the adjective used as an abstract noun, a use which is apparently peculiar to Paul (BDF 263 [2]). Moule lists this among passages where "there seems to be no implied noun, or at least it is hard to conceive of one" (IBNTG, p. 96).

102. Notice the aorist ἤνεγκεν. Paul does not use the present, which would emphasize God's continual practice, but the tense that tells us that he bore with people like Pharaoh. That he bore with Pharaoh rather than destroyed him shows that even in wrath God remembers mercy.

patience[103] *the objects of his wrath* ("vessels of wrath"; the absence of an article with "vessels" perhaps points to the class). The genitive "of wrath" will mean "characterized by wrath",[104] the recipients and not the instruments of God's wrath (cf. BDF 165, "figuratively, as if 'bearers of wrath, mercy'").[105]

These "vessels of wrath", Paul says, are *prepared*[106] *for destruction*, but he does not say how they became so fitted and widely differing views are held. Thus some think the people fitted themselves for this fate (Wesley; Griffith Thomas; some think that the participle is middle and that it has this force); some think God fitted them for it (Murray; so Hodge, though he rejects a supralapsarian view); some see Satan as responsible (Lenski; Hendriksen, "themselves—in cooperation with Satan!"). The difference in construction from the next verse (the passive over against the active, the participle against the indicative, the absence here of anything equivalent to the prefix for "before") makes it probable that we should not think of God as doing this. Rather the people did it themselves, perhaps, as Hendriksen thinks, with some help from Satan. Paul does not describe *destruction*, but clearly it stands for the ultimate loss.[107]

23. The opening to this verse is awkward,[108] and it is not clear precisely how we should translate it. But the meaning is tolerably clear. The verse counterbalances the reference to wrath and the lost with one to mercy and the saved. God has willed to demonstrate his wrath and make known his power; he has also purposed to make known his glory in what he does to "vessels of mercy". *Make . . . known* is a Pauline word.[109] *Riches* is a somewhat unusual word applied to *glory* (though cf. Eph. 3:16), but it brings out the point that there is no lack in God's glory. God is an exceedingly glorious God, and we

103. μακροθυμία, "longsuffering"; see the note on 2:4. J. Horst says that this passage rules out the possibility of "irresolution on the part of God, as though He could decide only after a period of waiting." He further says, "God's patience does not overlook anything. It simply sees further than man. It has the end in view" (TDNT, IV, p. 382).

104. Note the change from εἰς τιμήν and εἰς ἀτιμίαν of v. 21. These people are "characterized by wrath", not "destined for wrath".

105. Käsemann comments, "Naturally an impersonal process of wrath, carried forward by the σκεύη (*contra* A. T. Hanson . . .) is not in view" (p. 270).

106. κατηρτισμένα. The verb means "*to render* ἄρτιος, i.e. *fit, complete*" (AS). The perfect tense conveys the idea of completely fitted for destruction (cf. Moffatt, "ripe and ready to be destroyed"). Paul does not use προκαταρτίζω as in 2 Cor. 9:5.

107. Gifford remarks that "vessels of wrath fitted for destruction" is a description "eminently applicable to the mass of the Jewish nation in St. Paul's day" (cf. 2 Thess. 2:15-16). There is a reference to people now Christians who had once been "children of wrath" (Eph. 2:3). Would Paul have regarded such a transposition as possible for "vessels of wrath"?

108. καὶ ἵνα. It is not suprising that καί is omitted in some MSS (B cop vg Or etc.), for this gives an easier sense. But the word should surely be retained both because of its attestation and because it is the harder reading. ἵνα indicates purpose, but it is not clear whether it depends on ἤνεγκεν ("bore the vessels of wrath in order to make known . . .") or κατηρτισμένα ("prepared for destruction in order that he might make known . . ."), or whether it may be equivalent to an infinitive ("to manifest his wrath . . . and to make known his mercy").

109. γνωρίζω is found in Paul in 18 of its 26 New Testament occurrences.

see this especially in the way he shows mercy. *The objects of his mercy* is more exactly "vessels of mercy", and these vessels, Paul says, *he prepared in advance for glory.*[110] This is usually understood of God's electing activity, but Parry sees a reference to "the training through history and life, not to 'election' ". It is unlikely that Paul is not speaking of election, but he may also have in mind that God does prepare his people through all the experiences of their lives. We should also notice that, while Paul makes it clear that some (like Pharaoh) are prepared for destruction, the emphasis is on the positive, on preparing those who receive mercy for glory.

24. The grammatical connection of this verse with the preceding is not clear. There are several possibilities. (1) It would be possible to see verse 23 as ending with a question, so that a new beginning is made here. (2) Or *us* could be seen as in apposition with "vessels of mercy", as NIV. (3) Verse 24 begins with the relative pronoun *whom* in the Greek, and we could take what follows as a relative clause.[111] Any of these is possible, but the last-mentioned is simplest and should probably be accepted. *Called* brings in the notion of an effectual call once more, a very important concept for Paul. God calls whom he wills to call. *Us* sheets this home; Paul is not talking in generalities but referring to himself and his readers who have all been called in this way. He points out that they together include people *from*[112] *the Jews but also from the Gentiles.* The Jews could not claim that the only way into the people of God was through their community (cf. Bengel, the Jew is not called on the ground that he is a Jew, "but he is called *from* the Jews"). And the Gentiles could not claim that God had rejected the Jews so that the only way was by being a Gentile. God had called his "vessels of mercy" "out from" both groups. It is the "vessels of mercy" in whom Paul is interested; he does not explain "vessels of wrath" any further.

25. Paul launches into a series of quotations from Scripture to establish his point. He begins with some passages from Hosea to establish the acceptability of the Gentiles, then goes on to some from Isaiah to show that the call does not include all Israel. The multiplicity of citations from Scripture shows clearly that this is not a Pauline idiosyncrasy—God says it.[113] He begins with a rather free quotation from Hosea 2:23 (LXX 2:25).[114] The prophet is referring

---

110. προετιμάζω is used only of God in the New Testament (again in Eph. 2:10; BAGD note its use in other literature). εἰς indicates the purpose of the preparation.

111. There is no antecedent for οὕς other than σκεύη, but there is no real difficulty in seeing an *ad sensum* construction. Moule sees a displacement from ἡμᾶς, οὕς καὶ κτλ. (IBNTG, p. 168).

112. ἐκ means "out from", and its repetition makes it clear that the call applies to both Jews and Gentiles. But it does not apply to all of either group, only to those "called out from" the number. The church is neither a Jewish nor a Gentile community.

113. "Paul is able to show from Scripture itself that even under the Old Covenant God's saving action already envisaged a new creation of Israel" (Kertelge).

114. He introduces it with ὡς καὶ ἐν τῷ Ὡσηὲ λέγει, which is an unusual way of citing Scripture. It is found again in Mark 1:2, on which SBk comment that an exact parallel is not found in rabbinic literature.

369

to the ten tribes of Israel, but Paul applies the words to the Gentiles (as is also the case in 1 Pet. 2:10). The point apparently is that the sin of the ten tribes had been such as to place them outside the people of God. If there was hope for people who had been put there as a punishment, then much more was there hope for people who were there naturally. Apostate Israel, God says, was *not my people;*[115] they had lived as heathens and now they had become as heathens. But that was not God's last word. Rather, *I will call*[116] them *'my people'*. Those whom God wills to restore will be restored. Further, *I will call her 'my loved one' who is not my loved one*.[117] Hosea has this before the "not my people" clause, and his verb here seems to mean "my pitied one"; Paul has reversed the order of the clauses and has "love" rather than "pity".[118] He is saying that in Scripture it is the call of God and the love of God that make the people of God, and this quite irrespective of Jewish or Gentile origin. There is, of course, a sense in which all the people of the world are the objects of God's love (John 3:16). God loves because it is his nature to love. But there is also a sense in which those who are his people are specially beloved, and this is the theme of the present passage.[119]

26. This reads like a continuation of the preceding, but Paul has simply placed one quotation after another, this one from Hosea 1:10 (exactly as LXX). The addition further emphasizes the divine call that makes the *not my people* into *sons of the living God*. There is a division of opinion on the significance of *in the very place*. Some hold that it means no more than "instead of" (so JB, "Instead of being told . . ."). But against this is the reinforcement of this expression with the later "there"[120] (which NIV omits). It seems that Paul understands Hosea to be saying that it is the same people, who occupy the same place (be it Palestine, or, more probably, the place of the Gentiles), to whom the word of God comes. *You are not my people* is an emphatic rejection,[121] but "there they will be called . . ." is an emphatic reversal. Again there is the thought of God's effectual call, this time directed to people in the

---

115. Turner regards οὐ λαόν μου as one of the passages "where the negative expressions form a single idea" (M, III, p. 282); it "serves as a proper name" in Hosea (BDF 426).

116. LXX has ἔρω but Paul καλέσω; it is characteristic of the apostle to emphasize the divine call. Some think that καλέω with a double accusative means "name" (e.g., SH). But it is impossible to limit the meaning in this way when Paul uses the verb. If it does mean "name", it means "name effectually", name in such a way as to make them what the name signifies.

117. Here we have οὐ with the participle, not μή. Chamberlain finds about 20 examples of this construction in the New Testament and says, "It is always used for a definite denial" (p. 159). That meaning is appropriate here. BDF point out that LXX translates the Hebrew אֹל with οὐ plus an articular participle (430 [3]).

118. Rahlfs reads ἐλεήσω but notices ἀγαπήσω in some MSS, notably B.

119. The perfect ἠγαπημένην indicates a continuing state; the love of God is no transitory phenomenon.

120. ἐκεῖ. It is often said that Paul has inserted this word into the text of LXX. He may have done so, for there are MSS which do not have it. But Rahlfs accepts the word, so it may be the right reading. For Paul's meaning the word is important.

121. Note the emphatic pronoun ὑμεῖς.

situation of Gentiles. It is not the situation that prevails, but the divine call. And the call is to membership in the heavenly family. The substantives have no articles, which puts the stress on the quality. The people who were not God's people will be called nothing less than *sons* (with all the rights and privileges that that implies) of One who is none less than *God*, and *living God* at that.

27. From the inclusion of Gentiles in the people of God Paul turns to passages which speak of the exclusion of all but a remnant of Israel. Most of the Jews of the day did not believe in Christ, and they might well feel that this of itself showed that Paul must be wrong. "If Jesus were the Christ, would not the people of God accept him?" would have been their reasoning. So Paul goes on to show them from their own Scriptures that in other days this had been much the situation. The prophets speak of a "remnant" only as being saved, and that necessarily means that most of the Jews to whom the message was directed had failed to respond. The situation in Paul's day was typical rather than novel. NIV omits a connective which NASB renders "and" and NEB "but."[122] NEB is to be preferred, for Paul is contrasting the inclusion of Gentiles with the exclusion of many Jews. Isaiah, Paul says, *cries out*,[123] and his verb may bring out the thought of urgency rather than loudness (so BAGD, who cite Josephus, *Ant.* x.117 for a similar use). Godet thinks the verb has a "threatening tone", but perhaps Käsemann is better in seeing it as suited to "inspired, proclamatory speech" (p. 275). NIV may be right in rendering *concerning*.[124]

Paul moves from the situation of the Gentiles to that of Israel with a quotation from Isaiah 10:22-23. His quotation implies nothing about the fulfilment or otherwise of the condition,[125] but it points to the possibility that the Israelites would be very numerous. "As numerous as the sand by the seashore" is a proverbial expression for a very large number; in the Old Testament it is usually employed, as here, for the number of the Israelites.[126] But a large number of Israelites does not mean that the saved will be correspondingly numerous: *only the remnant will be saved*. The promise of God never meant that all, or even most, Israelites would be saved. The doctrine of *the remnant* is important. We should not miss the force of the article: *the* remnant, not "a" remnant. It is the scriptural remnant, "not some accidental leftover" (Lenski), that is Paul's concern. Some exegetes make a good deal out of the

---

122. δέ. The former translation sees a transition from the previous section to this one, whereas "but" marks a contrast.

123. κράζει.

124. ὑπέρ, according to Moule, means here "concerning, about" (IBNTG, p. 65). O'Neill, however, thinks of it as "for the sake of", and BAGD think the sense might be "in the interest of". H. Moule suggests "over": "with the thought of a *lament over* the ruined ones." But "concerning" is simpler.

125. ἐάν with the subjunctive. Burton sees it as "referring to a future possibility, or what is rhetorically conceived to be possible" (MT, 285 [b]).

126. The language of the quotation is not Pauline. This is his one use of ἀριθμός (18 times in the New Testament) and of ἄμμος (five times in the New Testament).

fact that the Hebrew text says only that a remnant "will return" and not that they will be saved. The suggestion is that Isaiah is referring to return from exile and no more. But we should not miss the fact that in Isaiah we read, "A remnant will return, a remnant of Jacob will return to the Mighty God" (Isa. 10:21). The thought of returning to God is there from the beginning.

28. There are problems with the second part of Paul's quotation. There is a textual uncertainty, but this is not serious.[127] LXX differs from the Hebrew is some respects, and Paul is abbreviating its text. But in general it seems that, despite the problems, both Paul and LXX give the sense of the Hebrew, though the exact meaning of the quotation is not clear. Some of the vocabulary is unusual in Paul,[128] and there are several possibilities. It is obvious that the main idea is that of bringing to an end, of shortening, but this might mean a shortening of the promise (i.e., fulfilling it only to a limited degree; Leenhardt puts it this way, "He shortens it in its execution, by cutting out something"), a shortening of the nation (no more than a remnant will be saved; Murray, "so widespread will be the destruction that only a remnant will escape"), or a shortening of the time, combined with the completeness with which God will do his work ("the Lord will quickly settle his full account with the world", GNB). Most modern translations and commentators accept the third view in some form, and it certainly seems probable.

29. Paul has another quotation from Isaiah (1:9), this one introduced with *Isaiah said previously*.[129] This is unlikely to mean that Isaiah spoke before Hosea. It might mean "a long time ago" (as NIV) or "foretold" (as NASB, JB), probably the latter. The construction is that of a condition contrary to fact.[130] This passage goes further than the preceding one. Paul has been saying that, though the number of the Israelites be large, no more than a small number will be delivered. Now he cites Scripture to show that the nation would have been totally destroyed had it not been for the Lord's saving intervention. It would have been like Sodom and Gomorrah, whose fate was proverbial for total destruction. It is a strong statement of the unworthiness of the nation and leaves no grounds for complacency. God is spoken of as "the Lord of hosts",[131] which may mean "Lord of the hosts of heaven" and thus "Lord of all"; cf. Hodge, "of the universe as a marshalled host . . . Lord of hosts being equivalent to Lord of the universe." The expression brings out the greatness of God (hence NIV, *the Lord Almighty*). He *had left*[132] "a seed".[133] Paul has

127. In some MSS the words ἐν δικαιοσύνῃ ὅτι λόγον συντετμημένον occur after συντέμνων, but most agree that this is an attempt to assimilate the text to that of LXX. The words should be rejected.

128. συντελέω, which means "1. bring to an end, complete. . . . 2. carry out, fulfill, accomplish" (BAGD), is found here only in Paul (six times in the New Testament), while συντέμνω, "cut short, shorten, limit", is found nowhere else in the New Testament.

129. προείρηκεν, used here only in Romans.

130. εἰ with past tenses of the indicative: "If he had not left us (as he has) . . . we would have been like Sodom (as we are not). . . ."

131. κύριος Σαβαώθ.

132. The verb is ἐγκαταλείπω, a double compound with the meaning "leave behind" (BAGD).

133. σπέρμα.

used this term in an earlier part of his discussion (vv. 7-8), but in a different sense. There it denoted the true descendants of Abraham. Here the thought is rather that there are few survivors, and that, few though they be, they have the potential for new growth (this is apparently the only New Testament passage where "seed" is used with this meaning). The seed gives hope for the future. It is only stylistic variation that refers to "becoming" *like Sodom* and being "likened" to *Gomorrah*. The destruction of the Cities of the Plain was apparently total: we hear of no survivors other than Lot and his band. So far from Israel being in a position complacently to rely on divine protection no matter what, it was only due to a miracle of grace that any of them survived.

Paul has made it clear that the sinner is lost because of his sin. Now God is not the author of sin (cf. Jas. 1:13). We should not think that God hardens people in sin and that therefore they are lost. Rather, sinners harden themselves. There comes a time in the odyssey of the hardened sinner when the question arises, "What is God to do with him?" That happened with Israel. The thrust of Paul's argument is that the Old Testament, on which those who taught the eternal security of all Israel relied, in fact bears clear witness to the truth that God's purpose is concerned only with the remnant of the nation. God fulfils his promise by saving the remnant together with some from the Gentiles. The promise has not failed, even if it was fulfilled in a way that many of the nation did not expect.

C. HUMAN RESPONSIBILITY, 9:30–10:21

Paul has made a strong argument that God works out his purposes. He has been putting emphasis on the divine initiative, on predestination and election, on God's calling people like Abraham and his hardening of people like Pharaoh. He has made it clear that God calls people and nations, that he chooses an Isaac but not an Ishmael, a Jacob but not an Esau. Does that mean that people are no more than puppets? That the lost are lost because God decided this and quite irrespective of anything in them? Paul does not quite answer the questions we would like him to have answered, but he does proceed to stress the importance of human responsibility.[134] That will occupy us throughout this section.

1. The "Stumbling Stone", 9:30-33

> 30What then shall we say? That the Gentiles, who did not pursue right-eousness, have obtained it, a righteousness that is by faith; 31but Israel, who pursued a law of righteousness, has not attained it. 32Why not? Because they pursued it not by faith but as if it were by works. They stumbled over the "stumbling stone." 33As it is written:

134. Cf. Murray, "The emphasis upon the sovereign will of God in the preceding verses does not eliminate human responsibility, nor is the one incompatible with the other."

"See, I lay in Zion a stone that causes men to stumble
and a rock that makes them fall,
and the one who trusts in him will never be put to shame."[a]

[a]33 Isaiah 8:14; 28:16

This paragraph could be taken as part of the preceding section, concluding it and summing it up. But it seems better to see it as introducing the new section, stressing the importance of human responsibility, more especially that of Israel. Paul emphasizes the fact that Israel's position is the result of the nation's unbelief, not a refusal on God's part to accept them.

30. Again we have Paul's *What then shall we say?* (see the note on 3:5). But where he often uses it to introduce a refutation of an inference that might falsely be drawn from what he has said, here it leads in to a summary of his argument up to this point. Some suggest that *That* leads into a question (as often with this construction), but that seems unlikely and it would lead to some very awkward Greek. Paul is far from stereotyped in his use of grammatical constructions, and we should see this as a statement (as NIV). The discussion of *righteousness* and *faith* shows that he is still concerned with his great topic of justification by faith; he has not completed it and then gone on to the Jewish problem. There is no article with *Gentiles;* it is people who possess the character of being Gentiles rather than the Gentiles as a definite group that Paul has in mind. As Gentiles they *did not pursue*[135] *righteousness.* This is not to deny that there were people with serious moral purpose among the Gentiles. But typically the Gentile nations did not show the same concern for being right before the one God that Israel did. A "right standing" with God was not their major concern. Paul puts some emphasis on *righteousness* here, using the term four times in two verses (NIV renders one of them by *it*). It is an important concept in his theology.[136] Some exegetes think that the meaning of the word varies, but it is better to see the thought of a right standing with God in all four, though clearly the Jews did not understand the word in quite the same way as Paul did.[137] This right standing, Paul says, Gentiles *obtained,*[138] and he goes on to explain that it was a *righteousness that is by faith.*[139] The Jews might have been expected to have attained this, but characteristically it was

135. The verb διώκω, "pursue", may here convey the imagery of a footrace (as in Phil. 3:12; so Shedd, Leenhardt, and others); Wilckens thinks it corresponds to τρέχειν in v. 16. The idea is of an earnest striving.

136. Denney finds the repetition "striking: it is the one fundamental conception on which Paul's gospel rests."

137. Cf. Cragg, righteousness "may stand either for a certain pattern of behavior or for a certain kind of relationship with God. The Jews were apt to use it in the former sense; Paul insists that it must be used in the latter."

138. καταλαμβάνω means "seize, win, attain, make one's own" (BAGD). The meaning here is something like "attain."

139. δέ introduces "an explanation or an intensification" (BDF 447 [8]). ἐκ πίστεως does not mean that the righteousness originated with faith, but that the faith of the believer is the means whereby he receives the righteousness in question.

Gentiles who did so. The Jews failed to profit from their possession of the law.[140]

31. *But* is adversative; Paul sets Israel over against Gentile believers as they *pursued a law of righteousness.* The verb conveys the idea of earnest effort, which was, of course, characteristic of many Jews. Neither noun has the article, which puts some stress on the quality in each case. *Law* is sometimes understood as "a rule of life which would produce righteousness" (SH; Brown likens the expression to the "law of the mind" etc. earlier in the letter [p. 359]). But there seems no good reason for taking it in any way other than the law of Moses which the Jews pursued so zealously with the idea that thereby they were attaining righteousness before God. Paul approved of their pursuit of the law. As he makes clear in the next verse, it was not the pursuit of the law itself but the way the Jews pursued it that he saw as wrong. Paul consistently saw the law as meant to lead people to Christ and therefore to right standing with God. Properly understood, that was its function, and it could thus be called *a law of righteousness.* There were, of course, people who followed that way (e.g., Zacharias and Elizabeth, Luke 1:6), though most Jews did not.[141]

32. Again there is an argumentative question *Why not?* which leads to the answer, *Because they pursued it not by faith but as if it were by works.* Actually, in Paul's rush forward there is no verb and we must supply one. Two possibilities have won support. One supplies *pursued* as NIV and goes on to take *They stumbled* as beginning a new sentence. The other way is to supply the participle as Gifford does: "because seeking it not from faith, but as from works, they stumbled . . ." (so also Godet). This is certainly possible, but most agree with NIV. Paul is again affirming the impossibility of salvation other than by justification by faith.[142] Righteousness is *by faith*,[143] but the Jews did not come in faith. They sought the right goal indeed, though they did it in the wrong way: "but as of works",[144] where "as" is important. Paul does not say that righteousness could be attained in this way, but only that the Jews thought so and therefore acted "as" though it could.

Paul moves on to the thought of stumbling. He finds in Isaiah 8:14 a reference to God as "a stone that causes men to stumble and a rock that makes them fall" and applies this to Christ. The Jews' lack of faith prevented them

---

140. Cf. Tom Wright, "the law was actually intended to evoke faith. When, therefore, Gentiles come to believe in Jesus Christ, they are in fact fulfilling the law, whether or not they have even heard of it" (Gavin Reid, ed., *The Great Acquittal* [London, 1980], p. 25).

141. Calvin comments, "The whole verse, therefore, means that although Israel depends on the righteousness of the law, it has not obtained the true method of justification, viz. that which is prescribed in the law."

142. "The paradoxical state of affairs exhibited in the Christian Church is absolutely inexplicable except by the inscrutable fiat of God, *unless* the principle of justification by grace through faith is accepted" (Dodd).

143. ἐκ πίστεως.

144. ἀλλ᾽ ὡς ἐξ ἔργων. The ἀλλ᾽ makes a strong contrast, while ὡς "stresses the contrast between the true way, viz. faith, and the false way, viz. works" (Leenhardt).

from recognizing their Messiah when he came. He should have been the cause of rich blessing to them, but instead became the "stumbling stone".[145]

33. Characteristically Paul rounds off this section of his argument with a quotation from Scripture, this time one in which he combines words from Isaiah 28:16 with some from Isaiah 8:14. The former passage has the stone motif, but there it is "a precious cornerstone for a sure foundation". This Paul replaces with words from the latter passage about the stumbling stone. He could have used the original words, for Christ is the sure foundation on which Israel might well have built. But at this point he is more concerned to bring out Israel's stumbling, so he concentrates on the words that make this clear. Israel failed to recognize the "stone" God laid in Zion,[146] and she bears responsibility accordingly. The stone motif is found in a number of Old Testament passages (Gen. 49:24; Ps. 118:22; Isa. 8:14; 28:16; Dan. 2:34-35, 44-45) and is taken up in the New (Matt. 21:42; Luke 20:17-18; Acts 4:11; 1 Cor. 3:11; Eph. 2:20; 1 Pet. 2:4-8). It does not always have the same significance, but the New Testament writers see Christ as the stone. The 1 Peter passage combines the two Isaiah passages as Paul does here (it adds Ps. 118:22), and this has led a number of scholars to think that the early church was in the habit of taking these passages together.[147] They enabled believers to see Christ as a sure foundation on which they could build, but while he was a source of help to them he was equally a stumbling block to those who refused to believe (cf. 1 Cor. 1:23; 3:11).

The stone is not only a "stumbling stone" but also *a rock that makes them fall*.[148] But over against this is the assurance that the believer[149] *will never be put to shame*.[150] Paul ends not with despair but with hope and confidence. He who builds on the sure foundation of Christ is delivered from the situation in which contemporary Jews found themselves, and which meant that they would be ashamed when they stood before God. Not so the believer.

---

145. Cranfield comments: "The christological content of Israel's disobedience is now laid bare—and the intimate and essentially positive relation between the law and Christ" (*Interpretation*, XXXIV [1980], p. 71).

146. "Regardless of how the synagogue may have read the latter verse (i.e. Isa. 28:16)—of Zion, Messiah, faith, the remnant, or simply of 'him who believes'—Paul interpreted either 'stone' as referring to 'the Lord of hosts,' to the Christ, 'set' for the Jews' stumbling" (Harrisville). G. Stählin holds that this passage was taken messianically by the Jews in pre-Christian times (TDNT, VI, p. 755 n. 56).

147. Dodd appeals to Rendel Harris for the view that the combination was made "in a very early collection of proof-texts from the Old Testament"; Dodd also discusses these passages in *According to the Scriptures* (London, 1957), pp. 41-43.

148. πέτραν σκανδάλου. This second word properly denotes the bait stick of a trap, the stick that triggers off the trapping mechanism when dislodged by a bird or beast. This obviously means trouble for the trapped, and the word is used generally for trouble.

149. ὁ πιστεύων ἐπ᾽ αὐτῷ. The masculine seems to mean that Paul is speaking of faith in Christ; otherwise we would have needed a feminine to agree with πέτραν. The construction of πιστεύω with ἐπί and the dative is found in quotations from LXX in 10:11; 1 Pet. 2:6 (also in Matt. 27:42; Luke 24:25).

150. Bultmann points out that in the Old Testament the "shame" words are often linked with judgment (TDNT, I, p. 189) and that in this passage we have the Old Testament sense (p. 190).

Romans 10

3. Two Ways of Righteousness, 10:1-13

¹Brothers, my heart's desire and prayer to God for the Israelites is that they may be saved. ²For I can testify about them that they are zealous for God, but their zeal is not based on knowledge. ³Since they did not know the righteousness that comes from God and sought to establish their own, they did not submit to God's righteousness. ⁴Christ is the end of the law so that there may be righteousness for everyone who believes.

⁵Moses describes in this way the righteousness that is by the law: "The man who does these things will live by them."ᵃ ⁶But the righteousness that is by faith says: "Do not say in your heart, 'Who will ascend into heaven?'ᵇ" (that is, to bring Christ down) ⁷or 'Who will descend into the deep?'ᶜ" (that is, to bring Christ up from the dead). ⁸But what does it say? "The word is near you; it is in your mouth and in your heart,"ᵈ that is, the word of faith we are proclaiming: ⁹That if you confess with your mouth, "Jesus is Lord," and believe in your heart that God raised him from the dead, you will be saved. ¹⁰For it is with your heart that you believe and are justified, and it is with your mouth that you confess and are saved. ¹¹As the Scripture says, "Everyone who trusts in him will never be put to shame."ᵉ ¹²For there is no difference between Jew and Gentile—the same Lord is Lord of all and richly blesses all who call on him, ¹³for, "Everyone who calls on the name of the Lord will be saved."ᶠ

ᵃ5 Lev. 18:5   ᵇ6 Deut. 30:12   ᶜ7 Deut. 30:13   ᵈ8 Deut. 30:14   ᵉ11 Isaiah 28:16   ᶠ13 Joel 2:32

Paul is deeply concerned about his own nation (he begins each of these three chapters [9, 10, and 11] with strong statements proceeding from this concern). Here his concern has to do with Jewish error about the righteousness that meant so much to them; they put tremendous effort into securing righteousness before God but went about it the wrong way. The one way is through Christ, and Paul speaks of him as "the end of the law".

1. The friendly address *Brothers* (emphatic from its position) refers of course to "brothers in Christ", not "brothers in Israel". But it introduces a warm statement about the Israelites (Paul does not mention them specifically; he says "them", but the context makes it clear to whom he is referring; NIV reads *the Israelites*, but this is not in the Greek). He is about to give some teaching that Jewish readers may find harsh, but he first makes clear the depth of his feeling for his nation. There is no grammatical link with the preceding, and the asyndeton may well arise out of the writer's emotion (so BDF 463). Moffatt tries to bring out something of Paul's attitude with "Oh for their salvation, brothers!" There has been a good deal of discussion about the term NIV renders *desire*.[1] The word is not classical and appears to have originated in LXX.[2] It is practically confined to Jewish and Christian literature. Many take it in the sense "desire", but it is hard to see this in the word. Goodspeed seems to have the sense of it with "my heart is full of good will toward them" (cf. its use in Phil. 1:15; 2 Thess. 1:11). The word "heart" is often used in the New Testament as a kind of shorthand for all the inner states; it is used on occasion to stress the intellectual faculties, but here it is rather the emotions to which it points. Paul is emphasizing his warm affection for his own people. With this affectionate goodwill he links his *prayer*[3] *to God*. He not only has goodwill for them, but he does what he can for them—he prays. Prayer is, of course, always addressed to God, but by saying this specifically Paul emphasizes his concern for his fellow countrymen before the highest tribunal. His use of the third person ("for them") seems to indicate that he is writing to a church that is predominantly Gentile. His prayer is "for salvation", which probably indicates his purpose (though some see result as in mind).[4]

2. *I can testify* is not quite what Paul says; we should translate rather "I testify". Paul is actually giving his testimony, not affirming that he could do so if necessary. He does not often use this verb (eight times out of a New Testament total of 76). Here, as H. Strathmann says, it is used "for the declaration or confirmation, on the basis of first-hand knowledge, of individual acts or general facts of experience" (TDNT, IV, p. 496). He knew the Jewish zeal from firsthand experience and indeed at one time had been as zealous as any of them and in the same way. His testimony is that the Jews "have a zeal for God".[5] His word "zeal" can be used in a good or a bad sense; here it will be in the good sense, with a meaning something like our "enthusiasm". The Jews were certainly zealous, for "No nation had given itself to God with such devoted and courageous zeal as Israel" (Barrett). But unfortunately this zeal had to be qualified with *not based on knowledge* (cf. John 16:2; Acts 22:3; 26:9-11;

---

1. εὐδοκία. It is preceded by a μέν, which has no answering δέ. BDF note that this is "excusable or even good classical usage" and give the meaning as "so far as it depends on my desire" (447 [4]). Lagrange sees it as meaning "certainly".

2. As a translation for רָצוֹן, "goodwill, favour, acceptance, will" (BDB). See G. Schrenk, TDNT, II, pp. 742ff. He favors the meaning here as "the will of the heart which becomes petition to God" (p. 746).

3. Paul uses δέησις here only in Romans, but 12 times out of its 18 New Testament occurrences. He is very interested in prayer.

4. Moule says of εἰς σωτηρίαν, "has their salvation as its purpose" (IBNTG, p. 70).

5. His expression is ζῆλον θεοῦ, which is best taken as an objective genitive with the meaning "zeal for God" (the same expression is used in a different sense in 2 Cor. 11:2). The expression could mean "a very great zeal" ("a divine zeal", as Olshausen puts it), but this does not suit the context as well.

Gal. 1:14).[6] Enthusiasm is good, but enthusiasm run riot can lead to disastrous results. Calvin reminds us that "It is better, as Augustine says, to limp in the right way than to run with all our might out of the way."

3. *Since*[7] introduces the reason for the foregoing statement. The Jews were ignorant of something of first-rate importance, *the righteousness that comes from God*. Here Paul says no more than that they did not know; later he will make the point that their ignorance was culpable: they should have known. Luther quips that zeal according to knowledge is "to know that one does not know". It was this that the Jews characteristically lacked. They did not understand that they could not establish their own righteousness by their own efforts, so they *sought to establish* it themselves.[8] Sincerity is not enough. If we are in the wrong, no matter how sincerely we believe we are doing right, we are going astray. The Jews were doing that, Paul says, because they were in the wrong about God's righteousness. "The righteousness of God" is the righteousness, the right standing, that comes from God (see the note on 1:17). Paul has made it clear that this is something that Christ has accomplished for us in his death and that all that we sinners need do is accept it by faith (cf. Phil. 3:9).[9] Paul is saying that the Jews were ignorant of this (or perhaps that their lives gave no evidence of it, but this is less likely). Their activism meant that they *did not submit*[10] *to God's righteousness*; they were sure they could do it themselves. Their attempt to be righteous as their own achievement was a refusal to submit to God's way.

4. "For" (which NIV omits)[11] gives a reason for what was implied in the previous verse even if not stated explicitly—they were wrong in the way they looked for righteousness (cf. SH). There is uncertainty about how we should take the Greek: it might be understood as "Christ ends the law and brings righteousness for everyone who has faith" (NEB) or as "Christ is the end of the law as a way to righteousness for everyone who has faith" (NEB mg.).

6. Commentators often take ἐπίγνωσις to mean a fuller and more comprehensive knowledge than γνῶσις, but J. Armitage Robinson's examination of the word makes that difficult to hold (*St Paul's Epistle to the Ephesians* [London, 1907], pp. 248-54). His conclusion is that "γνῶσις is the wider word and expresses 'knowledge' in the fullest sense: ἐπίγνωσις is knowledge directed towards a particular object" (p. 254). In the present passage he thinks that "the word may perhaps suggest the idea of discernment" (p. 252). Bultmann sees here "the sense of obedient recognition and insight into the will of God" (TDNT, I, p. 707).

7. Or "For", γάρ.

8. Shedd finds KJV, "going about to establish" their righteousness, "felicitous, implying the toilsomeness and futility of the attempt." Paul has used ἱστάνω, a variant of ἵστημι, of establishing the law (3:31), and in Hebrews we find ἵστημι of establishing a covenant (Heb. 10:9); there is the idea of "making it stand". The Jews were trying to make their righteousness stand, that is, stand in the judgment.

9. Once again Käsemann thinks that righteousness is to be understood as power (p. 281). But this is not what Paul says and it is reading something into the passage.

10. The verb ὑπετάγησαν is sometimes taken as middle (SH), but it is probably better to see it as passive though used in the sense of the middle, "they did not subject themselves".

11. γάρ.

Either is possible, and whichever we adopt Paul is speaking of the decisiveness and the finality of the work of Christ. There has been a good deal of discussion of the word translated *end*,[12] which may be understood as "termination" or "fulfilment" or "goal" (it has other meanings, but they do not concern us here). Most scholars these days take it in the sense "end", "termination" and understand Paul to be saying that the work of Christ means the end of the law. But others argue for "goal"[13] or for a combination (BAGD see goal + termination, as does Barrett; Shedd argues for all three meanings). Karl Barth argues for something like "fulfilment" as the meaning: "It is with Him and Him alone that the Law is concerned as the order of life under the promise. It is He who interprets this order and fulfils it."[14] Cf. Calvin, "This remarkable passage declares that the law in all its parts has reference to Christ, and therefore no one will be able to understand it correctly who does not constantly strive to attain this mark." Not many have seen "fulfilment" here; it would fit in with Paul's theology, but it is not the usual meaning of the word he uses.[15]

There is also division as to the meaning of "law". Some see a reference to the law of Moses (e.g., Cranfield), others to law in general (SH, Denney). We should probably understand this as the law of Moses in the first instance, but what Paul says about that law rules out any other law. He is saying that Christ's atoning work has made a way whereby those who believe receive a right standing before God. This means an end to the law of Moses considered as a way of attaining righteousness (of course Paul also thinks that the law of Moses pointed people to Christ and this function is not altered; it is the end of the law "for righteousness"[16] of which he is speaking). But equally it means an end to all other law as a way of attaining righteousness. Once we grasp the decisive nature of Christ's saving work we see the irrelevance of all legalism.[17]

---

12. τέλος.

13. See, e.g., C. Thomas Rhyne, CBQ, 47 (1985), pp. 486-99. Cranfield also accepts this view and argues strongly against the usual understanding, "end". George E. Howard sees the meaning as "goal", but in the sense that the aim and goal of the law "was the ultimate unification of all nations under the God of Abraham according to the promise. In this sense Christ is the *telos* of the law; he was its *goal to everyone who believes*" (JBL, LXXXVIII [1969], p. 336).

14. *Church Dogmatics*, II/2 (Edinburgh, 1957), p. 245. He sees τέλος νόμου (like the rabbinic *kelal*) "as a comprehensive formula for the manifold content of the Law, as a designation of the common denominator, the sum of all its demands, or ontically as the substance, the be all and end all of the Law, or practically, as its meaning in virtue of which it has authority as law and which is immediately also the way to its fulfilment" (*ibid.*).

15. Paul uses τέλος, but "fulfilment" is rather τελείωσις (see, e.g., the entries in BAGD).

16. εἰς might be understood as "with reference to", or it may express result (TH accepts this) or purpose ("for the attainment of righteousness, as a means to righteousness" [IBNTG, p. 70]). On the whole, purpose seems most likely.

17. Denney argues that while it is true and Pauline that Christ is the consummation and the goal of the law, "these ideas are irrelevant here, where Paul is insisting, not on the connection, but on the incompatibility, of law and faith." F. W. Danker in his review of Cranfield's commentary says forthrightly that "end" is the meaning: "Those who seek

It is true that Christ is the fulfilment of the law. It is true that Christ is the goal of the law. But here Paul is saying that Christ is the end of the law; he "writes *'finis'* to the sorry spectacle of man's vain attempt to achieve life through works of law."[18] We may certainly say that Christ is the goal of the law[18a] and that he is its fulfilment. But here Paul is saying rather that Christ is the end to law as a way of attaining righteousness. This does not mean the abolishing of the law, for Paul claims that he is establishing it (3:31), and he claims value for it (e.g., 7:7). What Paul is emphasizing is the decisive end to all such claims as those of the Jews (cf. 6:14; 7:4, 6; Eph. 2:15). The saving work of Christ has brought to a close any attempt to attain righteousness by way of law.

We should not overlook the importance of *for everyone who believes*. This is not a way for the Jews only or for the Gentiles only; it applies to *everyone*. But we are not to interpret this as meaning that everyone without exception attains the righteousness in question; it is everyone *who believes*. Faith is absolutely necessary, and without it no one obtains the righteousness of which Paul writes.

5. Paul insists that his view of justification by faith is scriptural. It is important for him that it is not some new-fangled idea, but that God has always accepted people on this basis. So now he assembles a group of passages from Scripture to show that God has always accepted people through grace. All that has been required on their part is faith.

"For"[19] (which NIV omits) gives grounds for what Paul has just said. How could the Jews be expected to know the truth of what he has been saying? Because it is the teaching of the law and the prophets. Paul begins with Leviticus 18:5, a passage which evidently meant a good deal to him (cf. 2:13; Gal. 3:12). There is a textual problem[20] which RSV solves by reading "Moses writes that . . ." (so NASB), but most recent translations, "Moses describes in this way: . . . 'The man. . . .' " (so NIV). RSV also sees "that" as introducing indirect speech, but the Greek word can introduce a direct quotation (as NIV). We should follow NIV, for Paul is surely quoting from Scripture (it is his point throughout this paragraph that Scripture supports his position and this is best done by quoting it). He starts, then, by saying that Moses writes about[21] the righteousness that is of the law and proceeds to quote

---

refuge in Torah promote a coterie; Christ aims to terminate the Balkanization of humanity, for he makes righteousness a reality for *anyone* who believes, and without reference to Torah" (*Interpretation*, XXXV [1981], p. 191).

18. V. P. Furnish, *Theology and Ethics in Paul* (Nashville, 1968), p. 161. He also says, "in Christ, the law's true function is for the first time accurately appraised and its true 'goal' achieved."

18a. Robert Jewett argues for the meaning "Christ is the goal of the law" (*Interpretation*, XXXIX [1985], p. 354).

19. γάρ.

20. Whether we should place ὅτι after γράφει (with ℵ* D* 33* etc.) or after νόμου (with P46 ℵc B etc.). The weight of MS evidence favors the second, and this should be accepted.

21. γράφω can take an accusative of the person or thing written about (see BAGD 2.c).

Scripture to that effect. There are further textual problems here,[22] but they do not greatly affect the meaning.

There are two ways of taking the words. We may understand them as meaning that the Jews did not take the law in which they delighted seriously enough. The law pronounces a curse on anyone who does not keep all its requirements (Deut. 27:26). Salvation by works meant doing all (and not just most) of the things the law teaches. If they had really taken notice of the law and compared their lives with its teaching, they would have seen that they did not and could not keep all of the law. Since they were not meeting its demands, they needed a Savior. The other way is to understand Paul to be saying that the law really pointed people to Christ. If it had been properly observed, it would have taught the Jews that God's way is grace. As we have seen, Paul certainly taught that. It was basic to his understanding of the law. Denney comments, "the law was not a collection of statutes, but a revelation of God's character and will, and he who sought to keep it did so not alone, but in conscious dependence on God whose grace was shown above all things else by His gift of such a revelation." Both these ways of taking the words then are true, and both are found in Paul. There seems no reason for choosing between them.

6. But[23] introduces a contrast: over against "the righteousness that is by the law" Paul sets *the righteousness that is by faith*.[24] This does not, of course, mean that faith creates the righteousness of which Paul writes, but that faith is the means by which it is received. He goes on to speak of it in words found in Deuteronomy 30:12-14, but what he says does not agree exactly with either the Hebrew or LXX. This raises the question of whether he is quoting from one or more of these verses or whether he is using scriptural words in which to convey his thought. He does not introduce the words with "Moses says" or the like, but personifies righteousness: it is *the righteousness that is by faith* that *says* the words in question. Perhaps it is best to see him as making an *ad sensum* quotation (Shedd); he is giving the essential thought of the passages but not in the exact words of the original. Some scholars criticize Paul here, maintaining that the passages to which he is referring teach that the law can be attained, whereas Paul is using them for a very different purpose. But, while Moses is certainly encouraging the Israelites to obey the law ("what I am commanding you today is not too difficult for you or beyond your reach", Deut. 30:11), we should not overlook the fact that he says, "Do not say to yourself, 'The LORD has brought me here . . . because of my righteousness. . . . It is not because of your righteousness . . .'" (Deut. 9:4-5; cf. 8:17-18); "The LORD your God

---

22. αὐτά and ἐν αὐτοῖς are read by most MSS, but the former is omitted in some and the latter is replaced by ἐν αὐτῇ in some. Certainty is impossible (Cranfield regards αὐτά and ἐν αὐτοῖς as assimilation to the text of LXX, while Metzger sees the omission of αὐτά and the use of ἐν αὐτοῖς as "scribal emendations"), but we should probably take the first-mentioned position.

23. δέ.

24. ἐκ πίστεως, as in 9:30; Gal. 5:5.

will circumcise your hearts . . . so that you may love him" (Deut. 30:6). Paul read these passages as witnesses to the grace of God, and they fitted his argument accordingly.[25] Leenhardt can say, "In writing the words which he here borrows from Deuteronomy Paul knows that they revolve around a thought which is completely in conformity with the doctrine of 'justification by faith', which consists essentially in not claiming before God 'a right-eousness of one's own' [v. 3]; in other words, in not trusting to the power and might of one's hand."

There are two courses of action which one is not to advocate in one's heart (i.e., deep down inside one; the expression means "to think" in passages like Matt. 24:48; Luke 12:45; Rev. 18:7). The first is put in the question *"Who will ascend into heaven?"*, explained as[26] *to bring Christ down.*[27] The implication of this question, Paul seems to be saying, is that the incarnation had not taken place, and the speaker plans to remedy that (though some see it as an attempt to establish contact with Christ; Käsemann, "one wishes to bring Christ back to earth" [p. 288]). This, of course, is quite impossible. The verb *ascend*[28] is used of going up to something physically higher like an upper room (Acts 1:13) or going up to Jerusalem (Gal. 2:1). It is used a number of times of ascending to heaven (Acts 2:34; Rev. 11:12). This is beyond the ability of mankind (John 3:13).

7. *Or* introduces the suggested alternative. There is a small problem with *descend*[29] *into the deep* (more exactly, "into the abyss"), for the passage Paul is quoting has "Who will cross the sea. . . ?" (Deut. 30:13). But it may be that "the sea" here is being used as the opposite of "heaven" and that Paul's "abyss" is simply emphasizing the thought.[30] The abyss was seen as the abode of the dead (see BAGD), and to go there, Paul explains, is with a view to bringing about the resurrection of Christ. Mankind cannot do this, and in any case Christ has already risen. In these two verses Paul is using expressions that had become proverbial for what is impossible.[31] "The righteousness of faith" does not demand that we be supermen; it does not set some impossible

25. Cf. Murray, "It would be a complete misconstruction of Deuteronomy to interpret it legalistically. The whole thrust is the opposite (*cf.* Deut. 7:7ff.; 9:6ff.; 10:15ff.; 14:2ff.; 15:15f.; 29:9f., 29; 32:9; 33:29)."

26. *That is* is like the *pesher* formula of the Qumran scrolls in which the commentator introduces an application of the words of the Bible to events in his own day. Cranfield does not consider Paul arbitrary in using this method, for "Christ is the goal, the essential meaning, the real substance of the law."

27. Turner sees this as a "simple infinitive of purpose" (M, III, p. 135); it is the purpose of the suggested ascent to bring Christ down.

28. ἀναβαίνω is found in Paul seven times out of its 81 New Testament occurrences (here only in Romans), and κατάγω once out of nine. Neither verb is part of the apostle's characteristic vocabulary.

29. καταβαίνω, like the verbs in the previous verse, is unusual in Paul, being found four times only out of 81 times in the New Testament.

30. "The abyss" is used for "the sea" in LXX of Ps. 107:26 (106:26, LXX). Paul's use is thus not unprecedented. This is Paul's one use of the word.

31. They are used in this way, e.g., in the Talmud: B.M. 94a; Git. 84a.

task before us.[32] God has done all that is necessary, and we receive his gift of righteousness by faith.

8. Paul cites another passage from Scripture (Deut. 30:14), though without any such formula as "it is written" or "Moses said". The quotation is not exact, but it gives the sense well enough. It carries on the thought of the previous verses that God does not set his people too difficult a task. They have no such problem as how to attain heaven or descend into the abyss, for *the word* is near them.[33] For Paul the *word*[34] is not a series of commandments, but *the word of faith*, "the message that calls for faith" (TH) as he immediately explains.[35] This means the whole way of faith that was the burden of his preaching, the word that tells of faith and that invites to faith.[36] The verb *we are proclaiming*[37] is in the present tense, denoting the habitual act. Paul and his companions constantly proclaim *the word of faith*.

9. If we accept *That*, with which NIV opens this verse, Paul is giving us the content of "the word of faith" (as Murray, TH, Käsemann [p. 291], and others). But the word is identical with that for "because" (accepted by Cranfield, Lenski, and others; cf. Wilson, "'because' it has Christ himself for its content"). It is impossible to dismiss either of these views as impossible, but perhaps there is more to be said for "that"; the context looks for the content of the preaching rather than the reason for it.

Paul proceeds to speak of confessing and believing. We would have expected the reverse order, but we should probably not make too much of this. The two are in the order of "mouth" and "heart" in the passage Paul has just quoted, and he goes on to put them in the order we would expect (v. 10). In any case we should understand them to be closely related as the outward and the inward aspects of the same thing (Paul is not referring to the kind of confession that is unaccompanied by faith, as in Matt. 7:22-23; Tit. 1:10). Both the outward and the inward are important. No one is saved by the merely outward; the state of the heart is important. But Paul does not contemplate an inner state that is not reflected in outward conduct. If anyone really believes he will confess Christ, so it is natural to link the two.

The verb translated *confess* has a wide variety of meanings,[38] but con-

---

32. Cf. Leenhardt, "Paul has recognized the real bearing of the Deuteronomic text, whereas his modern detractors have failed to see it."

33. Cf. Barth, "The Word is nigh unto us. Wherever we cast our eye, the dynamite is prepared and ready to explode."

34. ῥῆμα, which is not common in Paul; he has it eight times whereas he uses λόγος 84 times.

35. Nygren comments, "In its literal meaning this passage refers to the law, but in the deeper sense, intended by God beforehand, it refers to 'the word of faith.'"

36. τῆς πίστεως could be understood in the sense "the faith", the body of Christian teaching. But it is more in keeping with the way the word is used in the rest of this chapter to see it as used in the sense "trust".

37. The verb is κηρύσσω, for which see the note on 2:21. It points to the derivative nature of the message; the herald does not deliver an oration of his own composing, but passes on the message that has been given him.

38. ὁμολογέω means basically "to say the same thing", so one of its meanings is "to

fessing Christ is clearly a solemn religious act. It is a public declaration of commitment to Christ and of faith in him. Some see in this the confession that was made at baptism (e.g., Michel), but this is going beyond what Paul says. We need not doubt that such a confession was made at baptism, but it cannot have been confined to it and there is nothing here to indicate a baptismal context.[39]

The content of the confession is *"Jesus is Lord"* (cf. 2 Cor. 4:5; for the word "Lord" see on 1:4). It points to the deity of Christ (the word "Lord" is used over 6,000 times in LXX for the name of God [so Cranfield] and is used frequently among the Gentiles for a deity or for the Emperor [worshipped as "god"]).[40] Some scholars have held that the use of this term in the Gentile world generally shows that its use for Christ must have originated outside Palestine and that it cannot have been a primitive designation of Jesus. But the survival of the Aramaic *Marana tha,* which probably means "Our Lord, come" (1 Cor. 16:22), shows that the equivalent was used in Palestine. While initially this may have been in some such sense as "Teacher", the prayer we have just noticed shows that Christians "were addressing not a Rabbi but a heavenly being" (Barrett). This confession is important,[41] for Paul tells us elsewhere that "no one can say, 'Jesus is Lord,' except by the Holy Spirit" (1 Cor. 12:3; cf. Phil. 2:11). Anyone can, of course, utter the words. What Paul is saying is that to know that Jesus is the Lord is not a human discovery; it is something revealed by the Holy Spirit.

With that confession Paul links believing[42] in the heart. The reference to the heart points to the inwardness of faith; Paul is not referring to a superficial confession, accompanied by no more than a token faith. He is referring to a faith that takes hold of the whole of the inner man. Notice further that he speaks of believing that —. This construction is not frequent in Paul (though cf. 6:8), but what it signifies means a good deal to him. It means that faith has content; Paul is not advocating a fideism in which all that matters is to believe. To Paul it matters that we believe, but it also matters what we believe. Here he

---

agree". It is used of making a legal confession (cf. Acts 24:14), but also in a religious sense, as for confessing sins (1 John 1:9). It may refer to a public declaration (Matt. 7:23), to which confessing Christ is a similar usage (see BAGD). Paul uses it four times.

39. The succession of second person singular pronouns is not to be overlooked. This is another example of the "1st and 2nd person sing., used to represent any third person in order to illustrate something universal in a vivid manner by reference to a single individual, as though present" (BDF 281). Paul is describing "something universal"; there is but one way for both Jew and Gentile.

40. Deissmann points out that the word was used very frequently of Nero, the Emperor at the time: "the statistics are quite striking; everywhere, down to the remotest village, the officials called Nero *Kurios*" (LAE, p. 353). A little later this title became a religious test, as when the officials tried to get Polycarp to say "Lord Caesar" and to offer sacrifice, both of which he steadfastly refused to do (Martyrdom of Polycarp 8:2) and which led to his execution.

41. Olshausen remarks that "A dumb faith is no faith" and draws attention to 2 Cor. 4:13.

42. The aorist πιστεύσῃς may well point to the initial act of believing, as Parry thinks.

speaks of believing *that God raised him from the dead*. The resurrection is of critical importance. It is at the cross that God did his saving work, but Paul does not believe in a dead martyr but in a living Savior. Not only did Jesus die for our sins but God raised him, triumphant over all the forces of evil. If Christ is not raised, Paul holds, our faith is futile and we are yet in our sins (1 Cor. 15:17). But where we have the confession and the faith of which he has been speaking, we *will be saved* (for salvation see the note on 1:16). As usual, salvation is envisaged as future. Paul is looking to the end of this age and the coming of eternal salvation, the life of the world to come.

10. *For* introduces a reason, or more precisely a further explanation of the preceding. We should not treat the two clauses as though they were detailing separate happenings. They belong together and are "two modes of the same thing: viz., the new divine life in the soul. Christian confession is as truly a gracious and holy act, as Christian faith" (Shedd). We now have them in the natural order—faith first, then confession. NIV has *it is with your heart that you believe,* but in fact the verb is an impersonal passive.[43] It may be used, as Shedd thinks, "for the sake of abstract universality." Certainly we should not overlook the fact that Paul's argument throughout this whole section is that Jews and Gentiles are saved in the same way. He speaks of believing "unto righteousness".[44] Once again we have this leading idea of Paul's that righteousness is not a matter of law works; we attain it by faith. All that we can do is to believe. Here it is linked to confession (again the impersonal passive) which issues in salvation. As in the preceding verse we should not think of faith as leading to righteousness and confession as a different act that leads to salvation (for this noun see the note on 1:16). These are but two parts of the same saving experience.

11. Once again Paul cites a scriptural passage that witnesses to the importance of faith (Isa. 28:16). He has already quoted these words in 9:33 (where see the notes). "For the Scripture says" is a more usual way of introducing Scripture than in the quotations he has just made, though it makes no difference to the authority Paul sees inherent in all the sacred writings. "For" gives the ground for what the apostle has just said, but significantly the quotation is concerned with faith, not confession. It is in faith that Paul's deep interest lies, and it is on faith that he constantly places his emphasis. In 9:33 the passage was quoted in the form "the one who trusts", whereas here Paul has *everyone who trusts.* The word *everyone* is not found in the Hebrew or LXX, and it seems that Paul has inserted it. But we may fairly say that he is doing no more than bringing out a truth that is implicit in the original. Isaiah speaks of salvation as through faith (and not anything else), and this means that it is

---

43. πιστεύεται. Moule speaks of "apparently impersonal Passives, where in reality the noun cognate to the verb can in most cases be supplied as subject". This passage, he says, "is in a different class, and is striking" (IBNTG, p. 27), but unfortunately he does not say what this class is.

44. εἰς δικαιοσύνην, where εἰς may express either purpose or result (cf. 1:16).

open to all. Paul is simply leaving no doubt that every believer enjoys this promise. None will be put to shame.[45]

12. *For* carries the argument along in logical sequence (as in the other two affirmations in vv. 12-13). Paul has been emphasizing the importance of faith as the one way to God. This in itself implies that Jews and Gentiles are saved in exactly the same way, but the apostle now becomes explicit on this point. *There is no difference,* he says. Earlier he made the point that there is no difference in sin (3:22); now he says there is no difference in salvation. Once again Paul links Jew and Greek, the fifth time he has done so in this epistle (1:16; 2:9, 10; 3:9; see further the note on 1:16). These two, Cragg says, "were divided at every significant point. Racially, culturally, and religiously there were distinctions between the two. Moreover, both were proud races. . . ." But for Paul these divisions have been overcome. There is but one God, who saves people by the way of the cross, that is to say, by grace and through faith, and that means that distinctions like those between Jew and Greek are irrelevant. God is not bound to the Jews (or for that matter to the Gentiles). SH see both a warning and a consolation to the Jews: a warning if they seek salvation in their own way, but a consolation if they realize that they are free from the law.

A second "for" (which NIV omits) carries the argument a stage further. The expression is elliptical (Paul says "for the same Lord of all"), and NIV rightly supplies the words that are to be understood "the same Lord (is Lord) of all" (cf. 3:29; 1 Cor. 12:5). Jews and Greeks must have the one way of salvation because there is but one Lord over both. *Lord* could refer to God or to Christ; Paul more commonly uses the term of Christ, but it often refers to the Father, and this is just possible here. But Paul has just spoken of confessing that "Jesus is Lord" (v. 9), and that seems decisive. At this point he is speaking of Christ whose "unsearchable riches" (Eph. 3:8) bring salvation to all, Jew and Gentile alike. This Lord has the riches to bring blessing to all; the Jew need not fear that there will not be enough to go around.[46] Chrysostom comments, "He who considereth it as riches to Himself to save us, will not cease to be rich. Since even this is riches, the fact of the gift being shed forth unto all" (p. 474).[47] The Lord's generosity is extended to *all who call*[48] *on him,*

---

45. For Paul's frequent use of πᾶς see the note on 1:5.

46. πλουτέω usually signifies "to be rich" in the sense of possessing riches for oneself, though it is sometimes used figuratively of being rich in good works and the like, which points to being outgoing. But BAGD cite no other passage in the New Testament for the sense of being generous, of giving riches away (though they note one in Philostratus).

47. Similarly Calvin notes that the riches of God are not "diminished by His liberality", and he draws the lesson that Christians should not "envy the blessings of others, as if they lost anything thereby."

48. ἐπικαλέω means "to call, call upon" and is used of giving a name. In the middle it is used of calling on someone for aid, sometimes in a legal context (where it is a technical term; cf. Acts 25:11 etc. of Paul's appeal to Caesar), sometimes in calling on a deity (see BAGD).

and it is significant that Paul uses this verb of calling on Christ. It is the language of the suppliant to deity.[49]

13. Yet another *for* carries the argument along, and once again this is done by citing Scripture. Paul quotes Joel 2:32 for the thought that *Everyone who calls on the name of the Lord will be saved* (cf. Acts 2:21). This is comprehensive; there is no exception.[50] We must understand *calls on* in no mere formal sense; it is a calling on the Lord out of a sense of inadequacy and need and proceeds from a genuine conviction that the Lord can be relied on. It is significant that once again Paul takes words which in the Old Testament are used of Yahweh and uses them of Christ. Characteristically we have the future of the verb "to save"; it is salvation in the final state of affairs that Paul has in mind. The salvation Christ brings is adequate through eternity as well as in the here and now.

3. Worldwide Proclamation, 10:14-21

> [14]How, then, can they call on the one they have not believed in? And how can they believe in the one of whom they have not heard? And how can they hear without someone preaching to them? [15]And how can they preach unless they are sent? As it is written, "How beautiful are the feet of those who bring good news!"[a]
>
> [16]But not all the Israelites accepted the good news. For Isaiah says, "Lord, who has believed our message?"[b] [17]Consequently, faith comes from hearing the message, and the message is heard through the word of Christ. [18]But I ask, Did they not hear? Of course they did:
>
> > "Their voice has gone out into all the earth,
> > their words to the ends of the world."[c]
>
> [19]Again I ask, did Israel not understand? First, Moses says,
>
> > "I will make you envious by those who are not a nation;
> > I will make you angry by a nation that has no understanding."[d]
>
> [20]And Isaiah boldly says,
>
> > "I was found by those who did not seek me;
> > I revealed myself to those who did not ask for me."[e]

49. SH draw attention to its use in LXX for calling on Yahweh and they consider it significant that it is here applied to Christ.

50. πᾶς . . . ὃς ἄν. For Paul's fondness for πᾶς see the note on 1:5. Cf. Bengel, "This monosyllable, πᾶς (all), more precious than the whole world. . . ." Moule sees a latent conditional clause here: "*whoever invokes*, is close in sense to *if anybody invokes*" (IBNTG, p. 151). But this still implies universality.

21*But concerning Israel he says,*

"All day long I have held out my hands
to a disobedient and obstinate people."f

a15 Isaiah 52:7 b16 Isaiah 53:1 c18 Psalm 19:4 d19 Deut. 32:21 e20 Isaiah 65:1 f21 Isaiah 65:2

There is division of opinion as to whether we should take verses 14-15 with the preceding or the following, and great names can be cited for either view. Both make sense, but on the whole it seems best to tie in closely the verses which speak so forcefully of the preaching with the attitude of the Jews who rejected the preaching. Paul has been at pains to show that God's way is not that of legalism. He saves people by grace, as the Gentiles who have come into the church show so clearly. But perhaps the Jews have not had a fair deal? Perhaps the way has never been made clear to them? Paul proceeds to make it plain from the Bible that God has dealt fairly with the Jews. Grace is clear throughout Scripture, and if they did not know it, that was because they had not taken sufficient notice of what God had said to them. It was all there, in Scripture. This is an important part of Paul's argument.[51]

14. Paul now launches into a series of rhetorical questions.[52] The first is *How, then,*[53] *can they call*[54] *on the one they have not believed in?*[55] Paul does not define his *they*. Obviously this is a term with wide application and may be seen as equivalent to "all people". But the apostle may have the Jews especially in view. Throughout these chapters he is discussing the plight of his own nation, and they will be prominently in mind, whatever other application we may fairly discern. Paul advances to *And how can they believe in the one of whom they have not heard?* It is possible to cavil at NIV's rendering *of whom* they have not heard, a rendering shared by several recent translations. But NASB

51. Scott remarks, "This passage might seem to be only a digression, but it is central to the whole Epistle. More plainly than anywhere else Paul here discloses his purpose in writing as he does to the Roman church. He is coming to Rome in order to make it his starting-point for a new mission, and he needs the co-operation of the Christians in the capital" (p. 59).

52. BDF see this as an example of climax, which "consists in taking up the key word of the preceding member in the following one" (493 [3]; cf. 5:3ff.).

53. οὖν may do no more than play its part in introducing the rhetorical question, but it may possibly have adversative force (BAGD 4). A number of commentators point out that in this part of the letter several paragraphs have οὖν at the beginning, and this strengthens the view that a new paragraph begins with v. 14.

54. The series of subjunctives beginning with ἐπικαλέσωνται shows that the questions are deliberative (Burton classes them as "rhetorical deliberative" [MT, 169]) and not only rhetorical. Such questions are concerned with possibility, desirability, and the like. It is this idea of possibility in the subjunctive that is the justification for NIV's *can* throughout (there is no verb "can"). BDF translate here "how should they, can they. . . ?" (366 [1]), while Burton has "how shall they. . . ?" (MT, 169).

55. εἰς ὅν follows ἐπίστευσαν, not ἐπικαλέσωνται (cf. BAGD πιστεύω 2αβ). The whole clause will be the object of ἐπικαλέσωνται. πιστεύειν εἰς is not common in Paul (Gal. 2:16; Phil. 1:29; cf. Col. 2:5).

has it right with "How shall they believe in Him whom they have not heard?"[56] The point is that Christ is present in the preachers; to hear them is to hear him (cf. Luke 10:16), and people ought to believe when they hear him. Paul's third question is *And how can they hear without*[57] *someone preaching to them?* It is important to see the impossibility of hearing without someone preaching. "Hearing" is a reflection of first-century life. Paul does not raise the possibility of the message being read. While there were people who could read, the ordinary first-century citizen depended rather on being able to hear something. If the message of God was going to be effective in biblical times, it had to be heard. And for this a preacher was needed.[58]

15. The climax to which Paul builds up is *And how can they preach unless they are sent?* We should not confuse *preach* here with the modern Sunday morning sermon (that, too, may be included in Paul's meaning, but it is not the kind of thing he has primarily in mind). His verb properly denotes the action of a herald, someone who was given a message and told to proclaim it. The notion of a higher authority is implicit in the concept: a self-appointed herald is a contradiction in terms.[59] Paul is saying that the preaching of the Christian message is impossible without the divine commission. A herald can have nothing to say unless it be given him. The gospel is derivative. It does not originate with preachers, and the other side of that coin is that nobody can operate as a preacher in the sense in which Paul is using the term here unless God has sent him. The words also point to a certain confidence. Paul is sure that those who proclaimed the gospel did so because God had sent them.

Typically he hammers home the point with a quotation from Scripture (Isa. 52:7; cf. Nah. 1:15; the rabbis understood the former passage in a messianic sense see [SBk]). *How*[60] *beautiful*[61] *are the feet of those who bring good news!* It is interesting to have the feet selected as the beautiful parts of the body. But, of course, the messengers normally travelled on foot and the feet were the

---

56. The genitive οὗ is the normal construction after ἀκούω of persons; it means "whom", not "about whom" (which, as Cranfield points out, would be very unusual Greek). Lenski rightly points out that οὗ should not be taken as "where".

57. χωρίς is occasionally used as an adverb (John 20:7), but in the New Testament it is mostly a preposition. Paul uses it 16 times (six being in Romans).

58. It is perhaps a little strange that Paul uses the participle κηρύσσοντος when the noun κῆρυξ was available. But this noun is comparatively rare (three times in the New Testament, of which two are in Paul), whereas the verb is frequent (61 times, of which Paul has 19). The participle will be somewhat more dynamic than the noun. It indicates an activity and not merely a person.

59. Cf. G. Friedrich, "This statement is decisive for our understanding of the preaching office. The fact that ἀποστέλλειν is linked with κηρύσσειν elsewhere in the NT is no accident. It belongs to the very nature of things. Without commissioning and sending there are no preachers, and without preachers there is no proclamation" (TDNT, III, p. 712).

60. ὡς is used occasionally in exclamations with the meaning "How!" BAGD cite only this passage in the New Testament for this meaning but add, "Cf. 11:33" (IV.6). The word is common in Paul (158 times).

61. ὡραῖος connects with ὥρα and points to what is timely or seasonable; from that it is but a step to ripe, beautiful. Paul uses the word only here.

significant members. They might be dirty and smelly after a long, hot journey, but to those who eagerly awaited good news they were beautiful. Those who *bring good news* are always welcome.[62]

16. *But* (contrary to what might have been expected)[63] *not all the Israelites accepted the good news*. NIV makes Paul a little more definite with *the Israelites;* the apostle simply says "all". Some take this to mean the Gentiles while others think it refers to both Jews and Gentiles. The language is broad enough to include both, but the thrust of the argument is such that we should see a reference to the Jews. Since the whole of the argument in chapters 9–11 has to do with the problem of the Jewish failure to accept Christ as the Messiah, we would need strong reasons for seeing a general term applying to others here. That is not to say that the words do not suit Gentiles as well as Jews. They do. But Paul's argument here concerns Jews, and we should understand him to be writing about the Jews accordingly. *Not all* is a masterly understatement (cf. 3:3). *Accepted* is rather "obeyed"; it is not the verb we expect (and clearly the translators of NIV did not expect it). But we must not overlook the fact that the gospel contains an implicit demand for obedience (cf. 1:5). To decline the gospel invitation is to disobey God.[64]

Characteristically Paul hammers home a point by quoting Scripture (Isa. 53:1), this time introducing it with *Isaiah says*. His *for* shows that this is logical: that all who hear the gospel do not respond "should not seem strange to any acquainted with prophecy: it is the very testimony of Isaiah" (Haldane). Scripture shows that a message from God himself is not always received as it should be, nor does it necessarily result in faith.[65] *Lord* is not in the Hebrew, but it is in LXX. The question *who has believed our message?* implies that not many have believed it.[66] Paul implies that they ought to have believed but did not.[67]

17. This verse has caused some difference of opinion. Some think it out of place and transfer it to another position, others think it a scribal gloss. It is better to regard it as a "summarizing conclusion" to the argument so far (Hendriksen). Verse 16 has introduced the thought of "hearing", a concept

---

62. εὐαγγελίζομαι is quite often followed by what is proclaimed, but ἀγαθά is somewhat unusual. It emphasizes the goodness of the good news. Paul is not thinking of some run-of-the-mill good tidings, but of something really outstanding, the gospel.

63. ἀλλ᾽, the strong adversative, used "with a stronger reference to the difference than δέ would have provided" (BDF 448 [3]). Lenski renders, "But (alas!)".

64. ὑπακούω is used of the gospel in 2 Thess. 1:8, of "the faith" (Acts 6:7), and of "the word" of the preachers (2 Thess. 3:14). Paul uses the verb 11 times; obedience is important to him.

65. Wilson points out that the words Paul quotes are "at the head of the clearest prediction of Christ's sufferings in the whole of Scripture".

66. ἀκοή can mean that by which one hears (the ear, the sense of hearing), the act of hearing, or the thing one hears (which might be a report or rumor or, as here, what is preached). The dative after πιστεύω means "give credence to".

67. Dodd comments, "The proof is complete: Israel has been rejected, not because God did not give them the opportunity of salvation, but because they refused it when it was given."

that Paul will develop further. He therefore inserts here an appropriate remark about hearing which arises out of what he has said and leads on to the
next stage of his argument.[68] His statement here is very succinct and, for
example, there is no verb. English versions usually supply "comes" or the
like, and this gives the sense of it (NIV supplies both *comes* and *is heard*). NIV's
hearing the message translates one word (which it rendered "message" in v. 16
[where see note] and goes on to render "message" when it occurs a second
time in this verse). Here it may mean "the act of hearing" (cf. v. 14) or "the
message". And if "the message", is it the message heard or the message
preached? These last two come to much the same, however, when we reflect
that it may be viewed either from the standpoint of the preacher or from that
of the hearer.[69] Whichever way we may prefer to translate, Paul is speaking of
the derivative nature of the Christian gospel. It is not something that wise
men have made up; it comes from hearing the message given by those sent
from God. This is further brought out with "hearing through the word of
Christ." Whether we take this to mean "the word about Christ" or "the word
from Christ", it locates the content of the preaching in what God has given,
not in what the preacher has thought up. It is possible to understand this
expression either as referring to the teaching of the historical Jesus passed on
in the church or to the teaching of the exalted Lord, the Lord of the church.
Probably it is both, for there seems no reason for separating the two.[70]

   18. Paul proceeds to an objection that might be raised, or perhaps it is an
excuse that might be offered. He introduces it with the strong adversative
"*But* (in contradiction)",[71] and proceeds to an interesting double negative
construction.[72] The effect is to rule out entirely the possibility that "they did
not hear".[73] "They" is not defined, but as throughout this passage it means

   68. ἄρα is inferential, "so then".
   69. Cf. Boylan, "what is κήρυγμα from the preacher's standpoint is ἀκοή from that
of his audience" (on v. 16).
   70. Käsemann points out that there is nothing in the context about the command of
the historical Jesus sending the disciples; "Mission is now traced back to the exalted Lord,
which was not possible prior to the quotation" (p. 295). But it is scarcely justified to di-
vorce the exalted Lord from the historical Jesus. G. Kittel has a better perspective when he
says this passage "certainly has in view the recorded ῥήματα; nevertheless, as the Χριστοῦ
shows, it refers also to the Word of the present Lord as this is at work in the ἀκοή" (TDNT,
IV, p. 109). Both are involved. The change of preposition is interesting: faith arises "out
of" (ἐκ) hearing, and hearing is "through" (διά) the word of Christ. A. Oepke finds in this
usage of διά "a tendency for the instrumental to become causal" (TDNT, II, p. 68). He also
remarks, "Paul surely saw an inseparable unity between the pneumatic Christ and the
historical" (p. 67).
   71. ἀλλά.
   72. μή introduces a question expecting the answer "No", but the question itself
contains the negative οὐ. Burton holds that each of the negatives has its proper force, "οὐ
making the verb negative, and μή implying that a negative answer is expected to the
question thus made negative" (MT, 468). The result is that a positive answer is anticipated.
Gifford says the meaning is "Nay verily" rather than "Yes verily"; it corrects the suggestion that they did not hear. Cf. Parry, "μή can it be pleaded that. . . ?"
   73. TH advises translators that they should make of this "a strong statement: 'but it
is certainly true that they did indeed hear. . . .'"

"the Jews". Paul quotes from Scripture but without a formula of quotation. He introduces it with an expression NIV translates *Of course they did*.[74] Some reason from the absence of a recognized quotation formula that Paul is not so much quoting as giving his own thought in biblical language. But since he has the exact words of Psalm 19:4, this is very improbable; he is surely invoking the authority of Scripture for the point he is making. This Psalm deals with nature, with the heavens declaring the glory of God and the skies his handiwork, with day and night playing their part. In all the earth God is revealed in the processes of nature. The second line in parallelism repeats the essential thought of the first.[75] "The ends of the world"[76] means that the message has penetrated to the remotest part of the inhabited earth. This raises questions. Does Paul really mean that every person in all the earth had heard the gospel? Or even every Jew? The answer in either case can scarcely be "Yes". In this very letter Paul is envisaging a missionary trip to Spain which implies that there were people there who had not heard the gospel. His meaning is rather what Bruce calls "representative universalism"; the gospel had been widely enough preached for it to be said that representatives of Judaism throughout the known world had heard it (for this way of speaking cf. Col. 1:5-6, 23). Those who did not respond to the gospel "had at any rate as a body had the opportunities of hearing it" (SH).

19. "But"[77] perhaps the trouble was that Israel did not understand? "Knowing" was not included in the series of questions in verses 14-15, and some may have felt that, though the Jews heard all right with their physical ears, this was of little importance because they did not understand what the words meant. The question, like that in verse 18, has two negatives which add up to the fact that a negative answer is anticipated.[78] Paul does not say what it was that Israel did not know. Most think that he means the gospel (the message about the Messiah [SH and others]). Others think it is the fact that the Gentiles would be saved (Hodge), or that the promise to Abraham was universal in its scope (Shedd). In the end there is not a world of difference between these views; they all add up to the thought that Israel went serenely

---

74. μενοῦνγε, which Moule sees as adversative, "On the contrary, 'Into all the earth . . .'" (IBNTG, p. 163). Turner comments on the unclassical position of the expression (M, III, p. 338).

75. φθόγγος is used of "any clear, distinct sound" (LSJ) and sometimes refers to the sound of musical instruments. But it is used also of speech. In the second line we have ῥήματα, which certainly means coherent speech, often words or sayings.

76. οἰκουμένη means "the world" in the sense of "the inhabited earth". Paul does not use the word elsewhere.

77. Again the strong adversative ἀλλά introduces something contrary to what might have been expected.

78. μή introduces the question, but οὐ is found with the verb: the question negates the suggestion that Israel did not know. It is not certain where the question ends, and some put the question mark after πρῶτος: "Was not Israel the first to know the gospel?" (cf. Scott). But, as Leenhardt points out, though the grammar will allow this, "the meaning loses". We should end the question at "know". Paul is surely saying that Moses said this first and that Isaiah made the same point later (cf. CBSC, Michel, etc.).

on its own way not realizing that the gospel of God's grace meant that the way of faith was open to the Gentiles and always had been. The point is of critical importance to Paul's doctrine of justification by faith, so he cites both the law and the prophets to show that this was in God's plan.

First comes a quotation from the law (Deut. 32:21). God says *I will make you envious,* where *I* renders the emphatic pronoun: it is none less than God who does this. The verb is usually rendered "provoke":[79] when Israel sees what is happening among the Gentiles she will be provoked into securing some of that blessing for herself, an argument Paul will take up and expand in chapter 11. It is interesting that he does not appeal to the success of his Gentile mission to make his point, but to Scripture. Quoting from LXX, he substitutes "you" for "them" in both lines. This make the words personal to Israel. The passage does not refer explicitly to "Gentiles", but to "a not-nation". Bruce points out that "To one acquainted with the Hebrew Bible, as Paul was, the comparison between Moses' 'no-people' (*lo'*-'am) and Hosea's 'not my people' (*lo'*-'ammi) suggested itself readily". In the second line the quotation replaces "provoke" with "make angry",[80] a verb which makes clear the divine attitude to the nation's sinful rejection of what God had revealed. The Gentiles are characterized as "senseless".[81] On this point Manson comments, "The Gentiles were not very bright theologically—'a foolish nation'. They did not know how or where to seek. Yet *they* have found. Therefore mere ignorance is no obstacle."[82] If Gentiles could know the way, Israel could too.

20. Now comes a quotation from Isaiah 65:1,[83] introduced in an unusual fashion with *boldly says.*[84] Haldane sees the reason as "If Moses predicted, somewhat obscurely, the calling of the Gentiles, Isaiah had foretold it very plainly, and placed it in a light most offensive to the Jews." For some reason Paul reverses the order of the lines. In the quotation the words are from God, who speaks of being found by people who had not looked for him.[85] The

---

79. παραζηλόω is used four times in the New Testament, three in Romans and all in Paul.

80. παροργίζω. Both verbs are followed by ἐπί, which BAGD class here under the heading "of that upon which a state of being, an action, or a result is based" and specifically "w. verbs that denote aroused feelings" (ἐπί, II.1.b.γ).

81. ἀσύνετος, "*senseless, foolish,* implying also a lack of high moral quality" (BAGD).

82. Cf. Earle, "used of those who fail to understand the clear, simple things of God, who do not have sense enough to know the truth."

83. The connective is δέ, which Shedd sees as having here "a somewhat adversative sense".

84. ἀποτολμᾷ καὶ λέγει. The construction is paratactic where we might have expected a participle; perhaps this puts a little more emphasis on "dares". The verb occurs only here in the Greek Bible.

85. ἐμέ is emphatic in both lines. It is none less than God for whom they were not looking or asking. There is a problem with the ἐν before τοῖς in some MSS. It may have arisen, as Cranfield thinks, because the dative is not an easy construction after εὑρέθην. BDF see only one genuine dative of object in the whole New Testament (in Luke 23:15); this one they regard as "related to 'to appear'" (cf. Acts 1:3) (191 [3]). If ἐν is read, it "appears to stand for the customary dat. proper", as in Gal. 1:16 (220 [1]; see also Turner, M, III, pp. 58, 264). Fortunately the sense is clear, whichever reading is adopted.

parallel statement refers to his becoming visible.[86] The Gentiles did not consciously look for God as the Jews did. But in the end they found him, because he revealed himself to people of faith. It is a mark of God's sovereignty, on which Paul is insisting throughout this whole argument.[87]

21. But a continuation of the words quoted in verse 20 brings out the point that Israel reacted very differently from the Gentiles.[88] The speaker continues to be God, and the words bring out the depth of his concern for his wayward people. *All day long* brings out the continuing nature of the Lord's entreaty, while the stretching out[89] of the hands is a bold anthropomorphism to bring out the tender concern of God.[90] The *people*[91] are described as *disobedient*[92] and *obstinate*.[93] Israel point-blank refused the gracious invitation. God's call went unheeded.[94]

One more comment should be made. Paul has made some strong statements about predestination in earlier passages such as chapter 9. In this chapter he has insisted on Israel's responsibility. This does not cancel out what has been said previously. As Käsemann says, "The predestinarian statements in ch. 9 are not revoked in our entire chapter. They are unflinchingly adopted in the appeal to Scripture" (p. 297). If we are to understand what Paul is saying in Romans we must hold both truths at the same time, no matter how hard we find it to reconcile them to one another.

86. ἐμφανής, found only here and in Acts 10:40 in the New Testament.

87. It is usually held that Paul takes words meant for Israel and applies them to the Gentiles. But Calvin points out that Isa. 65:1 goes on to refer to "a nation that was not called by my name" and thus to the Gentiles. Most accept "a nation that did not call on my name", which, of course, could apply to Israel but also to the Gentiles. SBk cite rabbinic support for the view that the words refer to Rahab and Ruth. Whatever Isaiah had in mind originally, Paul sees in the words a reference to the Gentiles.

88. πρός seems not to mean "to" (though Godet accepts this). The words are not an address to Israel but a statement about the nation. The preposition can come close to the meaning "against" (Luke 20:19), but it is better to see it as "concerning", "with respect to" (as in Luke 19:9; Heb. 1:8).

89. ἐκπετάννυμι is found only here in the New Testament. It means here "*spread* or *hold out the hands* in an imploring gesture" (BAGD).

90. Cf. Denney, "The arms outstretched all the day long are the symbol of that incessant pleading love which Israel through all its history has consistently despised. It is not want of knowledge, then, nor want of intelligence, but wilful and stubborn disobedience, that explains the exclusion of Israel (meanwhile) from the Kingdom of Christ and all its blessings."

91. λαός is normally used of Israel, just as ἔθνος (v. 19) is the word for the Gentile peoples.

92. ἀπειθοῦντα normally means "disobedient", but it is sometimes used of those lacking faith; Paul may see something of this meaning here. At any rate both are involved.

93. ἀντιλέγοντα means "speak against" and thus "oppose, refuse".

94. Barth comments, "Guilt is not innocence. Guilt means that we can, but we will not. . . . Characteristic of men is a tenacious, profitless opposition to God." Cf. Hendriksen, "The passage indicates that Israel was fully responsible for the divine judgment that was pronounced upon it."

Romans 11

D. GOD'S PROMISES WILL BE FULFILLED, 11:1-36

Paul has made it clear that God is working out a great purpose and insisted on divine predestination and election; the will of God is done. He has also insisted that human responsibility is real and important, and he has made it plain that this must be borne in mind when considering the fact that Israel has not entered the blessing as Gentile believers have. What then does it matter to belong to the chosen people? At first sight, it may seem, not very much, for Gentiles may be saved as well as Jews. But it is far from Paul's thought that being a Jew matters little. He goes on to show that, while in the providence of God Israel's sin and unbelief have been used to open up the way for the Gentiles, now the conversion of Gentiles will lead to the conversion of the Jews. The Jews still have a place in God's plan. Even the hardness of the Jews furthered that plan, but hardness is not God's last word for his chosen people. Paul looks forward to that great day when "all Israel will be saved" (v. 26).[1]

1. The Remnant of Israel, 11:1-10

> ¹*I ask then, Did God reject his people? By no means! I am an Israelite myself, a descendant of Abraham, from the tribe of Benjamin.* ²*God did not reject his people, whom he foreknew. Don't you know what the Scripture says in the passage about Elijah—how he appealed to God against Israel:* ³*"Lord, they have killed your prophets and torn down your altars; I am the only one left, and they are trying to kill me"ᵃ?* ⁴*And what was God's answer to him? "I have reserved for myself seven thousand who have not bowed the knee to Baal."ᵇ* ⁵*So too, at the present time there is a remnant chosen by grace.* ⁶*And if by grace, then it is no longer by works; if it were, grace would no longer be grace.ᶜ*
> ⁷*What then? What Israel sought so earnestly it did not obtain, but the elect did. The others were hardened,* ⁸*as it is written:*
>
> > *"God gave them a spirit of stupor,*
> > *eyes so that they could not see*

1. Achtemeier sees this chapter as the climax of the discussion begun in the first chapter. "Fittingly enough, since the story of the rescue of God's creation began with Israel, the chosen people, it will also conclude with them, with this difference however— their belonging to the chosen people is now on the same basis as the gentiles: on the basis of trust in Jesus Christ."

and ears so that they could not hear,
to this very day."[d]

[9]*And David says:*

"May their table become a snare and a trap,
  a stumbling block and a retribution for them.
[10] *May their eyes be darkened so they cannot see,*
  and their backs be bent forever."[e]

[a]3 1 Kings 19:10, 14   [b]4 1 Kings 19:18   [c]6 Some manuscripts *by grace. But if by*
works, then it is no longer grace; if it were, work would no longer be work.   [d]8 Deut. 29:4;
Isaiah 29:10   [e]10 Psalm 69:22, 23

1. *Then*[2] carries on the argument, but there is uncertainty about the
connection. Some think that Paul is looking back to the reprobation of the
Jews in chapter 9 (Shedd), others that it follows on 9:6 (CGT), still others that it
follows on 10:14-21 (Barrett) or on 10:21 (Hendriksen). Probably Paul is not
attaching it closely to any particular point in his argument, but what he is
about to say is the consequence of what he has already said. In the light of his
argument he asks, *Did God reject his people?*[3] a suggestion that he immediately
repudiates with the vigorous *By no means!*[4] The suggestion is unthinkable. To
some it may seem the logical result of what Paul has been saying, but to the
apostle it is an utter impossibility. God is thoroughly reliable, and it is impossible to think of him first choosing and then rejecting a people.

Paul goes on to say that he himself is an Israelite, the precise point of
which has been understood in various ways. Luther suggested that Paul had
opposed God with all his might so that if anyone would be cast off it would be
he; his existence as a Christian shows that God had not rejected his people.
Others think that the fact that Paul is both a Jew and a Christian proves that
Christian Jews may exist (he did not teach his own rejection!). Or he may
mean that since he is an Israelite he finds the suggestion just as blasphemous
as other Jews did. Or that he, a Jew, is God's apostle to the Gentiles and thus
through him Israel's missionary vocation is on the way to fulfilment. None of
these is impossible, and Paul may not be intending to exclude any of them.

He underlines his Jewishness with three statements: he is an Israelite, of
the seed of Abraham, of the tribe of Benjamin (cf. Phil. 3:5). The Jews venerated Abraham as the great forbear of their race; Paul will have this in mind,
but also the fact that the patriarch had special significance for him as the great
exemplar of faith. Benjamin was the only son of Jacob born in the land of
Israel. It was the tribe in whose territory was the holy city Jerusalem; it was the

2. οὖν.
3. The question introduced by μή looks for the answer "No." The verb ἀπωθέω
expresses vigorous action, "push aside", as when the Israelite pushed Moses away (Acts
7:27); its position gives it a certain emphasis. The juxtaposition of ὁ θεός and τὸν λαόν
should not be overlooked; they belong together.
4. μὴ γένοιτο.

one tribe that remained faithful to Judah. And it may not be out of mind that the first king of Israel came from this tribe and that his name was that of the apostle (Michel stresses the importance of the connection with Benjamin).[5]

2. Again a quotation from Scripture (1 Sam. 12:22; Ps. 94:14; cf. Judg. 6:13), and one that uses the exact words of Paul's question with the addition of *whom he foreknew*. This puts further emphasis on the impossibility of God's rejection of his people. The precise meaning of *people* and *foreknew* has caused discussion. One view is that foreknowledge means something like predestination and that this applies to the remnant rather than to the nation as a whole (cf. Hodge). But Paul is referring to "the people he foreknew", not "those of his people whom he foreknew", and to most the use of *his people*, the same expression as in verse 1 (where it is plainly the nation), is significant. It is the nation that is being discussed.

But did God foreordain the whole nation to be saved? That is not implied. Paul appears to have in mind that God chose Israel to be his people, the people in whom his purpose would be worked out in a special way. They would be the recipients of the revelation and of many blessings (cf. 9:4-5). God would never go back on that. But none of this has ever meant that the entire nation would be saved. We see something of the way Paul's mind is working in that he immediately goes on to refer to the believing remnant in the time of Elijah; it is clearly this that he has in mind when he speaks of the people as foreknown. Godet speaks of "the indestructible existence of a believing remnant at all periods of their history" (on v. 5), and this fits Paul's argument.[6]

"Or" (which NIV omits) introduces the alternative if what he has been saying is not accepted. In that case his readers must be ignorant of what happened in the case of Elijah. Again Paul appeals to *the Scripture*,[7] this time referring to a trying experience that befell Elijah. In his loneliness and isolation that prophet on one occasion prayed "against" Israel.[8]

3. Paul quotes Elijah's prayer (1 Kings 19:10, 14) in words differing a little from LXX. *Prophets* and *altars* come first in their respective clauses for

---

5. ἐκ denotes origin, and the one ἐκ refers to both the seed of Abraham and the tribe of Benjamin. φυλή may denote a nation or people (Matt. 24:30; Rev. 1:7), but it is used more characteristically of the 12 tribes of Israel.

6. Barrett sees the existence of Jewish Christians as evidence that God had not in fact rejected his ancient people. But there was only a small number of Jewish Christians. "This very fact, however, suggests a line for advance. There are important Old Testament precedents for the presence of such a minority within an apostate people."

7. He refers to what the Scripture says ἐν Ἠλίᾳ, "in the passage called 'Elijah'" (Moffatt). People did not refer to chapter and verse in those days; they located passages by their content. We see a similar usage in Jesus' ἐπὶ τοῦ βάτου (Mark 12:26). SBk find the usage in the rabbinic writings, and Turner says "there are class. exx." (M, III, p. 261).

8. ἐντυγχάνω has meanings like "meet", "turn to", "appeal to", "petition", and thus "pray". It is used of praying ὑπέρ, "on behalf of" someone (8:27, 34), but here κατά, "against", a meaning not found elsewhere in Scripture but attested in the apocrypha (e.g., 1 Macc. 8:32; 11:25). This is an indictment of evildoers and a plea that God take action against them.

emphasis. It was holy people and holy objects that the Israelites abused. The aorist tenses point to decisive action and the verbs show that strong action was taken. They killed the prophets and destroyed[9] the altars. There was, of course, to be only one altar in Israel (Deut. 12:13-14), but it seems that from time to time other altars were regarded as acceptable (Exod. 20:24; Judg. 6:24-26), and particularly would this be the case in the northern kingdom when it would often be difficult for people to go to Jerusalem to worship (cf. 1 Kings 18:30). Elijah is speaking about people who have rejected wholeheartedly the worship of the God of Israel and whose actions leave no doubt about their repudiation of all that was connected with that God.

I am the only one left does not mean "I am the only prophet left", for the 7,000 were not 7,000 prophets but 7,000 people who honored God. But Elijah had found himself so isolated that he thought there was no other worshipper of Yahweh left in the kingdom (did Paul feel some kinship with Elijah in the way his nation declined to walk in God's way and thus left him isolated?), and the final desolation is brought out with *they are trying to kill me.* "It is the classic example of the folly of a pessimism which rests on judgments based upon appearances" (Cragg).

4. But Elijah's estimate of the situation was not the final one.[10] Paul asks, *what was God's answer to him?* Lagrange points out that the answer is to an implied petition, something in the depths of the prophet's soul, rather than to any express request. This use of *answer* for a divine response is unusual,[11] but it does make clear that what follows is a word of God, not the best human thought on the matter. Paul proceeds to quote 1 Kings 19:18 in a form agreeing exactly with neither the Hebrew nor LXX. God says, *I have reserved*[12] *for myself seven thousand.* Paul seems to have inserted *for myself,* for the expression is in neither the Hebrew nor the Greek. It serves to emphasize the divine action; it was God and no one else who saw to it that the 7,000 remained. Luther remarks, "He does not say: When they were all cast away, seven thousand men were left over, or: When Nebuchadnezzar or the devil took them away, he left me seven thousand men, but: I myself kept them back, I who took them, i.e., the others, away." Paul is making it plain that it was

---

9. κατασκάπτω means "tear down, raze to the ground" (BAGD). It is found here only in the New Testament (but see Acts 15:16).

10. ἀλλά introduces a contrary position, this time in the form of a question.

11. LSJ include "oracular response, divine injunction" among the meanings of the word χρηματισμός, but Anthony Hanson sees its use here as unusual and refers to "this remarkable use of 'oracle'". He concludes his examination of the use of the term in this passage with "The oracle in Romans xi.4 then points to a revelation of God's nature, but suggests that what was indirectly revealed in the old dispensation has been directly revealed in Christ in the new" (NTS, XIX [1972-73], pp. 300, 302). Bo Reicke notices the use of the word in a variety of contexts such as money-making, healing, and official response, but here "Elijah is thought of, not as an attorney submitting written petitions, nor as a mantic practising incubation, but as a man of God receiving revelations" (TDNT, IX, p. 482).

12. καταλείπω usually has a meaning like "leave (someone or something) behind"; BAGD cite only this passage in the New Testament for the meaning *"leave over; see to it that someth. is left"* (cf. Sir. 24:33). But clearly this is the meaning here.

God's action that made the 7,000 stand out. They were in a special relationship to him; they were his people. The number may be symbolical, as often in the Bible with seven and the multiples of seven.[13] In that case it indicates the completeness, the perfect number of those God chose to be his own.[14] Even in a time of national declension God had chosen out his remnant, which showed among other things that he had not cast off the whole people.

The 7,000 are characterized as people who[15] have not bowed the knee to Baal. Bowing the knee is, of course, a symbol of submission, a recognition of a spiritual lord. Baal is used here only in the New Testament, but it is frequent in the Old Testament for the Canaanite deities whose worship was such a temptation for the Israelites. The noun is masculine, but here Paul has a feminine article. When Scripture containing this word was read, apparently the reader substituted the noun for "shame", "shameful thing", and this is feminine. It indicates contempt for this deity.[16] That the 7,000 had given no allegiance to shameful heathen deities was an indication of their commitment to the true God.

5. So too is reinforced by at the present time:[17] as in the days of Elijah, so now. At both times the nation as a whole was not obedient to God, but in both also a minority did obey. And in both the minority was a standing witness to the truth that God has not cast away his people. Paul goes on to speak of a remnant,[18] which in this context is a symbol of hope.[19] It is not simply an assorted group of individuals who happen not to have been caught up in apostasy; it is a group chosen by God in which Paul finds assurance of God's continuing mercies which will in due course lead to the salvation of "all Israel" (cf. Nygren, the remnant "is Israel in nuce").

Paul proceeds to bring out an important feature of the remnant; it is chosen by grace.[20] Both chosen and grace speak of the priority of the divine and of the love of God which is exercised in both. God's loving purposes are not defeated by people's hard hearts.[21] Lagrange points out that it was not the

13. So Cranfield. Cf. Calvin, "we may take the definite for an indefinite number."
14. Bengel points out that it is not a small number. He also notices that in an adjoining chapter it is the number of the Israelites in Ahab's victory over Ben-Hadad (1 Kings 20:15); it is a significant number, though of course still a remnant.
15. The relative is not οἵ but οἵτινες, "who were of such a character that. . . ."
16. Hodge thinks it is not so much contempt as that Baal was regarded as both masculine and feminine. But in 1 Sam. 7:4 where we read of Baals and Ashtoreths (this latter meaning feminine deities) both nouns are feminine. See also Hos. 2:8; Zeph. 1:4. See IBNTG, p. 183.
17. οὕτως οὖν with its inferential force introduces the application to the current situation of what had happened so long before. For ἐν τῷ νῦν καιρῷ cf. 3:26.
18. λεῖμμα, here only in the New Testament, is cognate with κατέλιπον in v. 4. There was a reference to ὑπόλειμμα in 9:27. See further the note in TDNT, IV, pp. 194-214.
19. Dan G. Johnson points out that the concept of remnant may be understood in terms of judgment or of hope; in ch. 9 it pointed to judgment; "But for Paul the remnant motif is now a sign of hope that all Israel will be saved" (CBQ, 46 [1984], p. 96).
20. κατ' ἐκλογὴν χάριτος. For ἐκλογή see the note on 9:11; here it signifies the choosing out of some from a larger group.
21. "It is God's free generosity, not their own deserts, which preserves the remnant" (CGT).

number so much as the permanence of God's plan for Israel that mattered in the time of Elijah, and it is this that mattered for Paul too. He put his trust in God's grace, not in numbers. The final word in the Greek text is that translated *is*,[22] with its suggestion of continuity. The election of which Paul speaks will not speedily fade away. It is permanent.[23]

6. The apostle proceeds to an antithesis between grace and works. The Greek construction he uses implies the meaning "If it is by grace (as is the case). . . ."[24] The construction is elliptical, and Paul does not say what is by grace. It will be something like membership in the people of God, which is conferred by God in his grace, not merited by good works of any kind. *No longer by works* does not mean that it was once by works but it has ceased to have that character. Rather, Paul is saying that once we have come to see that salvation is by grace there is no longer any place for works. *If it were* is better "for otherwise" (BDF 456 [3]); Paul is introducing something completely different. If works have any place at all, he is saying, then there is no point in speaking about grace. If we do so speak we have changed the meaning of "grace": *grace would no longer be grace* (JB, "grace would not be grace at all"). If *works* come into salvation at all, and the end result is called *grace*, then Paul has misunderstood what grace is; the meaning of the term would have been drastically altered. Barrett points out that God's choices are eternal "and the election is therefore antecedent to all works. That is why it is by grace." This rules out the idea that God foreknows what people will do and chooses the elect on the basis of this foreknowledge of their works. If works of any kind, retrospective or prospective, come into it, then we *no longer* have grace.[25] It is important to take grace seriously and not to let works creep in by some back door.[26]

7. In his insistence on God's grace Paul does not forget the reality of widespread unbelief among the Jews. He proceeds to bring out some of its consequences. *What then?* looks for the result of what he has been saying. With the word *what* we have an indefinite construction rather like that in the previous verse, for Paul does not explain to what it refers. We should understand something like "righteousness". Israel kept looking for it without ob-

---

22. γέγονεν, where the perfect carries the note of permanence: "there has come to be and there remains".

23. Turner sees in this passage (vv. 5-8) Paul's equivalent of the "messianic secret" in Mark: "St. Paul saw the secret as due to God's deliberate act, but in his view it was achieved not so much by the parabolic method as by a process of making dull the spiritual faculties of the Jews" (*Grammatical Insights*, p. 49).

24. There is no verb in the clause and we must supply one, but Burton points out that the use of εἰ plus the nature of the sentence shows the class of conditional even without the verb (MT, 243). In the previous sentence Paul has used the genitive χάριτος; the change to the dative χάριτι does not mean a change of meaning.

25. Leenhardt points out that "the works of Israel are of no avail either to establish the covenant, or to maintain it, or to annul it."

26. NIV mg. includes some words found mostly in the later MSS. It is impossible to understand why they would have been deleted if they had been in the original, and most agree that the reading should be rejected. See the note in Metzger.

taining it. NIV's *sought so earnestly* renders a strengthened form of the verb *sought;*[27] the search was no perfunctory effort, but serious and sustained. But for all that Israel did not *obtain*[28] what it sought. By contrast, *the elect did.*[29] *The others*[30] evidently means all the nonelect, and this includes Israelites as well as Gentiles (indeed, Dodd takes it to mean the others "of Israel" only; he specifically rejects the view that it means "the rest of men"). These nonelect people, Paul says, *were hardened.*[31] The passive may well ascribe the hardening to God (the passive was often used as a reverent way of avoiding the name of God). But, while it is certainly true that God did the hardening in verse 8, it is the people who do the stumbling in verse 11 and it is possible that the passive here is a neutral expression which may be taken either way. In either case we must remember that those who failed God did not do so because they had been hardened, but they were hardened because they had failed him (so SH).[32]

8. Paul supports his contention with an appeal to Scripture (he combines words from Deut. 29:4 and Isa. 29:10). God gave to certain people *a spirit of stupor,*[33] an attitude of deadness towards spiritual things. They make no response to the things of God (any more than a stupefied body does to physical stimuli). This is not seen as an excuse; as Earle points out, "A drunkard may claim that he is not responsible for what he does. But he is accountable for getting into that state. So with those whose hearts are dulled by disobedience." Paul is not making excuses for those who reject God; he is bringing out the seriousness of their plight and the fact that God is at work in their punishment. He spells this out with references to eyes that do not see and

27. He uses ἐπιζητέω, which Abbott-Smith calls the "'directive' of ζητέω", with the meaning "to inquire for, seek after, wish for".
28. ἐπιτυγχάνω means "1. to light upon. 2. to obtain, attain to" (AS). In late Greek it is followed by the accusative (as here) more often than the genitive (as in Heb. 6:15; 11:33). BDF point out that of the use with the genitive "there are vestiges only in the better educated authors" (171 [2]).
29. This appears to be the only place in the New Testament where ἡ ἐκλογή is used for οἱ ἐκλεκτοί. The use of the term may put some stress on the idea of election rather than the individuals elected (SH).
30. δέ has adversative force and puts *the others* in contrast with the elect.
31. Paul's verb is not the one he used for hardening in 9:18, but πωρόω, which means "*cause a stone or callus to form*" (LSJ). It is used of the uniting of fractured bones; thus it can denote a very hard deposit. NEB and some other translations have "were made blind", a rendering Bruce justifies since in modern English "blindness" is commonly used for moral or spiritual insensitiveness. But it is better to retain Paul's imagery.
32. Cf. Leenhardt, "If the creature refuses to be carried along by the current of divine grace, his very refusal drives him toward nothingness, for one cannot refuse the call of God except by positively opposing Him."
33. πνεῦμα κατανύξεως. The latter word is apparently derived from κατανύσσω, which means "1. *to strike* or *prick violently.* 2. *to stun*" (AS). There may be some confusion with κατανυστάζω, "to fall asleep"; at any rate, in LXX κατάνυξις can translate הַרְדֵּמָה "deep sleep" (it does in Isa. 29:10). Possibly also there is the thought of repeated blows bringing about a state of insensibility. Whatever the reason, in passages like this the meaning is something like "torpor of mind, stupefaction". This is the only New Testament occurrence of the word.

ears that do not hear.[34] That part of them that ought to be most sensitive to the divine leading is not operative, not functioning as it was intended to function. *To this very day*[35] points to a continuing attitude. Paul is not talking about ancient history, but about an attitude, known in the past indeed, but persisting right up to the time of writing.

9-10. A further quotation backs up what Paul has been saying (Ps. 69:22-23, but with words from Ps. 35:8; 38:4). Psalm 69 is cited a number of times in the New Testament, mostly in prophecies of Christ's passion. Initially the reference was to the troubles that the Psalmist was having when persecuted by his own people,[36] which makes it relevant to the situation of the apostle confronted with a similar situation. The *table* is the place of food, of sustenance, and it is most unexpected when this source of nourishment becomes a source of trouble.[37] Or the thought may be that of a person sitting at a low table on which are decorative cloths in which he gets entangled when he springs up suddenly in response to some emergency. Perhaps Paul is thinking that the Scriptures, which should have been a source of spiritual nourishment to the Jews, are in fact the very thing that brings about their downfall, for they use them wrongly. He speaks of *a snare*[38] *and a trap.*[39] NIV's *a stumbling block* is a usual translation for the Greek word Paul uses,[40] but it properly means the bait stick of a trap, the stick which triggers off the trapping mechanism when a bird or animal makes contact. Obviously it means trouble, though not necessarily in the way of stumbling. To this is added *a retribution,*[41] where the thought is that those who have sinned should receive a suitable recompense for the wrong they have done. The piling up of expressions indicates an intensity of desire that the Psalmist's enemies should not go scatheless. And it shows Paul's deep conviction that unbelieving Jews will not escape.

The Psalmist's petition continues with *May their eyes be darkened.*[42] In the

---

34. τοῦ with the infinitive is a construction that ordinarily denotes purpose and sometimes result, but neither suits this passage very well. BDF find this "a peculiar use of the inf." and translate "such ears that they . . ." (393 [6]; cf. also M, III, p. 141).

35. ἕως τῆς σήμερον ἡμέρας (cf. Acts 20:26; 2 Cor. 3:14) is a curious expression, but it is found a number of times in LXX. The meaning is not in doubt.

36. Cf. Parry, "The justification of this use of the passage is that to the Psalmist also the persecutors were his own people. The punishment is inevitably found in the very privileges and faculties which they had misused" (CGT).

37. Some see a cultic reference. Käsemann (p. 302), e.g., thinks there is a reference to Jewish piety which causes the blinding and fall of the nation. But this is not a natural understanding of *table.*

38. παγίς means a "trap", but in the New Testament it is always used figuratively "of things that bring danger or death, suddenly and unexpectedly" (BAGD).

39. θήρα in this context does not differ greatly from παγίς. It does not occur in either the Hebrew or the Greek of the passage Paul is quoting. Nor is it found elsewhere in the New Testament.

40. σκάνδαλον.

41. ἀνταπόδομα, "repayment", may be used in a good sense (Luke 14:12) or a bad sense (as here).

42. The verb σκοτίζω is always in the passive in the New Testament, "be darkened". In 1:21, as here, it refers to the mind. τοῦ with the infinitive might indicate purpose here, but result is equally possible.

final petition the Psalmist changes from the third person ("May . . .") to the second person as he makes a direct address to God (NEB, "Bow down their backs . . ."; NIV does not follow the Greek construction at this point). The petition has reference to the *backs*[43] of his enemies, but it is not quite certain what the force of it is. It may be a request that "their backs bend forever under their burden!" (Goodspeed; so Wilckens), or that they be bent under a burden of grief and terror. Denney thinks it means "keep them continually in spiritual bondage, stooping under a load too heavy to be borne." Whatever the precise significance, it is clear that Paul sees catastrophe as inevitable for unbelieving Jews as they continue to reject the gospel.[44]

2. The Restoration of Israel, 11:11-24

> [11]*Again I ask, Did they stumble so as to fall beyond recovery? Not at all! Rather, because of their transgression, salvation has come to the Gentiles to make Israel envious.* [12]*But if their transgression means riches for the world, and their loss means riches for the Gentiles, how much greater riches will their fullness bring!*
>
> [13]*I am talking to you Gentiles. Inasmuch as I am the apostle to the Gentiles, I make much of my ministry* [14]*in the hope that I may somehow arouse my own people to envy and save some of them.* [15]*For if their rejection is the reconciliation of the world, what will their acceptance be but life from the dead?* [16]*If the part of the dough offered as firstfruits is holy, then the whole batch is holy; if the root is holy, so are the branches.*
>
> [17]*If some of the branches have been broken off, and you, though a wild olive shoot, have been grafted in among the others and now share in the nourishing sap from the olive root,* [18]*do not boast over those branches. If you do, consider this: You do not support the root, but the root supports you.* [19]*You will say then, "Branches were broken off so that I could be grafted in."* [20]*Granted. But they were broken off because of unbelief, and you stand by faith. Do not be arrogant, but be afraid.* [21]*For if God did not spare the natural branches, he will not spare you either.*
>
> [22]*Consider therefore the kindness and sternness of God: sternness to those who fell, but kindness to you, provided that you continue in his kindness. Otherwise, you also will be cut off.* [23]*And if they do not persist in unbelief, they will be grafted in, for God is able to graft them in again.* [24]*After all, if you were cut out of an olive tree that is wild by nature, and contrary to nature were grafted into a cultivated olive tree, how much more readily will these, the natural branches, be grafted into their own olive tree?*

Paul has been arguing that a remnant of Israel will be saved, but only a remnant. What about the sinning majority? Are they lost forever? That is not

---

43. νῶτος is used here only in the New Testament.
44. Cragg has an apposite comment: "Judgment is inseparable from the rule of law in a moral world; to ignore it is not a proof of our emancipation, but merely an indication that indifference is bordering on folly."

v. hat Paul is saying. He proceeds now to make three points: (1) Israel has indeed "stumbled" but their stumble is not final, (2) God uses this "stumble" to bring salvation to the Gentiles, and (3) in the end the Jews will be brought in. He sees the purpose of God as worked out through what has happened to the Jews, and precisely because it is the purpose *of God* that is worked out he is fundamentally optimistic. The God who has done so much for his people will see them through to the end.

11. Paul carries his argument a stage further with a question. NIV has *Again I ask,* but this is not quite what Paul is saying. His word is "Therefore".[45] He has just been quoting Scripture to show the horrible fate of the mass of the Israelites. Since they have "a spirit of stupor" and other unpleasant characteristics (vv. 8-10), it seems that they face a very grim prospect. Therefore Paul asks his question: *Did they stumble so as to fall beyond recovery?* That they stumbled is clear, and Paul has already said that they did (9:32-33; his verb is different, but the meaning is essentially the same).[46] This is a surprisingly mild way of expressing what has happened to Israel in view of what Paul has said in the immediately preceding verses. But he is doubtless using it to bring out his point that there was nothing final in what had happened to Israel thus far. The result of it all was the salvation of the Gentiles, not the loss of the Jews. There is a contrast between stumbling and falling. "One may recover from a stumble" (Black); the man who stumbles may regain his feet. K. L. Schmidt sees perhaps "a certain crescendo from stumbling to falling, for the one who stumbles may get up again, pull himself together and stand on his feet, or he may fall and lie on the ground. Falling as a possible result of stumbling is perhaps a figure for the eternal ruin which threatens to overtake the Jews through their stumbling."[47] There is a question about whether we should take the fall here as the purpose or the result of the stumble.[48] Certainly the divine purpose was worked out in what Israel did, and that divine purpose was the salvation of the Gentiles, not the "complete downfall" (NEB) of the Jews. But the grammatical construction does not favor the view that that is what Paul is saying here. It is true, and he says it elsewhere, but here it seems that result is what he has in mind. The apostle repudiates the idea of Israel's being lost permanently in two ways. He frames his question in such a way that it looks for the answer "No",[49] and he follows it with the emphatic *Not at all!* For Paul the idea is preposterous.

45. οὖν.

46. In 9:32 the verb is προσκόπτω; here it is πταίω. This latter is always intransitive in the New Testament (five times; Paul has it only here).

47. TDNT, VI, p. 884. W. Michaelis comments, "Falling does not mean becoming guilty; it refers to the possibility that Israel will persist in its guilt, or rather that it will be abandoned by God in its guilt, that it will be excluded from salvation" (*ibid.*, p. 164).

48. ἵνα usually denotes purpose, "in order that", but if that is the meaning here it ought to be the purpose of the subject of the verb ἔπταισαν, i.e., of the Jews. But obviously it was not their purpose that they would fall. There is a good note in SH in which it is made clear that ἵνα can denote result. This should be accepted here. Chamberlain argues that "It is hardly conceivable that Israel stumbled in order to fall, but it is quite in keeping with Israel's history to say that she stumbled so (seriously) that she fell" (p. 185).

49. The question is introduced by μή.

The strong adversative[50] introduces the contrary and true idea. It was not Israel's downfall but the salvation of the Gentiles that their *transgression*[51] brought about. The construction is elliptical, but NIV seems correct in supplying the verb *has come*. The alternative is to see the meaning as "but in order that by their transgression salvation might come to the Gentiles", but we have already seen that purpose is not the probable meaning here. The idea of purpose comes in at the end of the verse with *to make Israel jealous*.[52] This verb is a strong one (cf. Deut. 32:21). Paul is saying that the salvation of the Gentiles was intended in the divine providence to arouse in Israel a passionate desire for the same good gift. When they saw the wonder of the messianic salvation, the Jews would want it for themselves. It is a matter for profound regret that just as Israel refused to accept this salvation when it was offered to them, so the Gentiles have all too often refused to *make Israel envious*. Instead of showing to God's ancient people the attractiveness of the Christian way Christians have characteristically treated the Jews with hatred, prejudice, persecution, malice, and all uncharitableness. Christians should not take this passage calmly.[53]

12. Paul gives the argument another twist, or rather drops it for the time (he takes it up again in v. 14) and substitutes another. He begins with *But if*, and his elliptical construction signifies "if, as is the case. . . ."[54] He speaks of their *transgression* again (the same word as in v. 11), and says it means *riches for the world*. Parallel to this is the statement that their *loss*[55] means *riches for the Gentiles*. Their rejection of the Messiah is both a sin and a defeat for them. But it results in *riches* for others. The word *riches* is repeated, the first time being linked with *the world* and the second time with *the Gentiles*. There is probably

---

50. ἀλλά.

51. παράπτωμα. It is a question whether we should see this as a continuation of the metaphor of stumbling (as Moffatt, "by their lapse . . ."). But Paul's habitual use of this word is for a sin, and it is better to see his normal use here. The word is cognate with πίπτω, not πταίω.

52. The expression is introduced with εἰς τό, which normally indicates purpose. For the verb παραζηλόω see the note on 10:19.

53. H. Moule has a long note in which he brings this out. Haldane draws attention to another point arising from the admission of the Gentiles: "We ought to remember that the Lord may have infinitely wise and gracious motives for His most severe and terrible judgments. Thus did the fall of the Jews become the occasion of the Gentiles being enriched with the inexhaustible treasures that are in Christ. . . ."

54. Notice that εἰ begins vv. 12, 14, 15, 16, 17, and 21, a noteworthy succession of "if" clauses. Lenski points out that here "The condition is one of reality. Only in such conditions can the verb be left out."

55. ἥττημα is a very rare word (apparently cited again only in Isa. 31:8; 1 Cor. 6:7, in both of which it means "defeat"). Scholars who consider this meaning unsuitable in this passage point to the use of πλήρωμα later in the verse. They suggest that since that word has numerical force, "the full number", ἥττημα must mean the opposite, it must signify a diminution of the number. Thus Barrett, "whatever be the witness of etymology, Paul is not here speaking of a defeat of Israel but of a diminution of their numbers." But it is not only etymology; the use in other passages is also important. Thus Leenhardt, "the only known meaning of ἥττημα is relative to quality (inferiority, degeneration . . .)". It seems that we should not understand the word of a numerical reduction, but rather in some such sense as "defeat" (as Murray, Cranfield, etc.).

no great difference between these two; the first use regards the recipients comprehensively as the world's population, while the second characterizes them religiously, as Gentiles. *Riches* is used in an unusual way here. Normally the word denotes a wealth of possessions, which may be physical or metaphorical, and which are the property of him to whom they belong. But here the meaning is rather an abundance of blessings available for other people.[56] Israel's loss was the Gentiles' gain. Paul now suggests that if instead of a defeat Israel had a victory, if instead of a loss a gain, then that would mean much more. The meaning of *fullness* is not clear.[57] Either the fulfilling of God's will or the bringing in of the full number of the Jews gives good sense and marks a contrast with the situation in which Paul found himself. The salvation will mean no diminution of the blessing that had come to the Gentiles, but rather an enrichment. "To Paul it would be paradise if the Jews could come in" (Barclay).[58]

13. There is a diversity of opinion on the connection of this verse with the preceding. Some consider verses 13-14 "somewhat parenthetical" (Knox, SH; cf. Denney), while others see a close connection with verse 12 (Leenhardt; no new paragraph, Lenski). The connection is probably more important than the break; Paul is still speaking about making Israel jealous (vv. 11, 14), and it is just the way he is tackling it that is different. He addresses his readers as *Gentiles*, which to most seems to indicate that the majority of the Roman church was Gentile. Others take this in the sense "those of you who are Gentiles" (though if that was what he meant there seems no reason why he should not have said it). *To you* comes first with emphasis. It is important that Paul address the Gentile section of the church. They may well have been reasoning that all this about the Jews had little to do with them. They may have wondered why the apostle to the Gentiles should be spending so much time worrying about the Jews. Lagrange thinks that the Gentile majority at Rome may well have been surprised that Paul should attach such importance to the conversion of the Jews. Whichever be the rights of it, Paul now gives attention to the question of why he should be so concerned about the Jews. Basically he says that this is the case because he wants to see them provoked into following the example of the Gentiles. This would mean blessing for them and blessing, too, for the Gentiles.

56. For the normal genitive after πλοῦτος cf. the riches of God's kindness (2:4), of his glory (9:23), of his wisdom and knowledge (11:33), of his grace (Eph. 1:7), and so on. The list could be extended. But πλοῦτος κόσμου, meaning riches "for" the world rather than "of" the world, is unusual. Turner remarks that κόσμος is anarthrous in the genitive after another noun (M, III, p. 175) and that ἔθνη is especially liable to be anarthrous (p. 181). But this does not affect the meaning.

57. πλήρωμα has a variety of meanings, the most favored being "that which is brought to fulness" (full number) and "fulfilment". The former is seen by many as the meaning in v. 25 and is accepted here by Black, SH, and others. "Fulfilment" in the sense of fulfilling the divine demand is favored by BAGD, fulness of salvation by Lenski, and there are other views.

58. Parry points out that in chs. 1–3 Paul had made it clear that Israel and the Gentiles failed in the same way; now he is clear that they are saved in the same way.

Inasmuch as[59] *I am the apostle to the Gentiles*[60] expresses Paul's deep conviction that God had given him a special responsibility to bring the gospel to Gentile people. It has a full meaning here. It is Paul and no other (his *I* is emphatic) who has this special task, and his readers should be in no doubt but that he is deeply concerned for the Gentiles. The word *Gentiles* is given some prominence and stands in immediate juxtaposition to *I*. Paul's particular calling in life was to bring the gospel to Gentiles rather than Jews (cf. Acts 22:21; Gal. 1:16; 2:7, 9; 1 Tim. 2:7). This he saw not as an arduous and repellent task which he must bring himself to face as well as possible. It was something he gloried in.

I make much of my ministry is more exactly "I glorify my ministry". This has been understood in any one of several ways. It may mean "I will take pride in my work" (GNB) or "I endeavour to render my office glorious by bringing as many Gentiles as possible into the Redeemer's kingdom" (Hodge). Or it may mean that to provoke the Jews to envy by the conversion of the Gentiles and thus to bring them in, too, is a bigger work than simply the conversion of the Gentiles. Paul speaks of his *ministry*,[61] his service of others. He could insist on the dignity of his office, but he saw it also as lowly service.

14. *In the hope that* is a somewhat free translation of an expression that does not occur very often.[62] NASB has "if somehow", which is a little closer to the Greek. NIV brings out the fact that the words are an expression of Paul's hope that his activities among the Gentiles will in the end stir[63] the Israelites into following the example of the Gentile believers in accepting the gospel. *My own people* is more literally "my own flesh", a very unusual way of referring to Israel (though cf. 1 Cor. 10:18) but one that brings out Paul's sense of identification with his own nation. With all his deep conviction that the Jews of his day had for the most part gone hopelessly astray, Paul never forgets that he, too, is an Israelite.

His deep longing is that he might *save some of them*. *Save* is the general term for the deliverance Christ brings (where forgiveness, redemption, and

---

59. The expression is ἐφ᾽ ὅσον. Olshausen points out that we should supply with it τρόπον, not χρόνον, "in so far as", not "so long as". This is followed by a μέν which lacks an answering δέ but which is accompanied by οὖν to mean something like "Contrary to what you may be inclined to think" (Cranfield). BAGD do not connect μέν with οὖν but take the former to indicate a contrast.

60. ἐθνῶν ἀπόστολος with the attributive genitive coming first (BDF 474 [4]); ἔθνη is especially liable to be anarthrous in such expressions (M, III, p. 181).

61. His word is διακονία. Originally it meant the service of a table waiter and later it came to mean lowly service in general. It is not without importance that this term came to be the typical term for Christian ministry. Christian ministers (even apostles) are not lords of the flock, but servants.

62. εἴ πως (see 1:10; Phil. 3:11). πως is the enclitic, meaning "somehow, in some way, perhaps" (BAGD), not the interrogative πῶς, "how?" Burton comments on this use of εἰ: "An omitted apodosis is sometimes virtually contained in the protasis, and the latter expresses a possibility which is an object of hope or desire, and hence has nearly the force of a final clause" (MT, 276).

63. *Arouse . . . to envy* translates the verb παραζηλόω, used here as in v. 11.

the like draw attention to specific aspects). It is generally used in the passive (this is the only use of the active in eight occurrences of the verb in Romans). When it occurs in the active God is usually the subject (e.g., 1 Cor. 1:21; 2 Tim. 1:9; Tit. 3:5), and, of course, this is implied when the passive is used.[64] Paul makes no exaggerated claims for himself. His aim is to save *some of them.* He looks for "all Israel" to be saved ultimately (v. 26), but he is not claiming, as some exegetes have suggested, that he will initiate the process that brings about the End. Some take it as axiomatic that Paul expected the End during his own lifetime and that his own labors would usher in the last happenings. But there is evidence that Paul expected that he would die in due course (1 Cor. 6:14; 2 Cor. 4:14), and the present passage shows that he thought of his own work as making no more than a modest contribution. As Harrison puts it, "The word 'some' is important. It is a clear indication that he does not expect his efforts to bring about the eschatological turning of the nation to the crucified, risen Son of God, when 'all Israel will be saved' (cf. v. 26). This belongs to the indefinite future."[65]

15. *For* links the argument to the preceding, but it is not clear just how. Some see a close connection with the immediately preceding, others think it links up with the end of verse 12. Paul is simply moving forward logically but without tying this next point closely to the preceding. His *if* means "if, as is the case" (see the note on v. 12). He speaks of Israel's *rejection*[66] as *the reconciliation of the world,*[67] another thoroughgoing statement. The general thrust of this is clear enough, though there are problems in detail. Reconciliation is one of the striking expressions Paul uses to interpret Christ's saving work (5:10-11; 2 Cor. 5:18-20; Eph. 2:16; Col. 1:20-22); indeed, he can speak of his whole ministry as one of reconciliation (2 Cor. 5:18-19). But it is not clear whether he means here the reconciliation of Jew and Gentile in one people of God (as in Eph. 2:11-18) or the reconciliation of the Gentiles to God through the fall of the Jews or the reconciliation of the whole world through Christ's atoning work (in which case *rejection* will refer to the cross). All are possible, and perhaps the general expression does not rule out any of them. Since there

---

64. Paul uses the active of husband and wife saving each other (1 Cor. 7:16), of Timothy (1 Tim. 4:16), and, of course, of Christ (1 Tim. 1:15; 2 Tim. 4:18). The active is more common outside Paul and, e.g., James always has it.

65. Käsemann comments, "nowhere is it more evident that apocalyptic is the driving force in Paul's theology and practice" (p. 306). This perhaps shows the weakness of that scholar's position, for there is nothing here about apocalyptic (unless we say that the verb "save" can be used in no sense other than an apocalyptic one and insist that "fullness" and "life" are apocalyptic terms). The whole context is concerned with the problem of Israel's failure to accept the gospel while the Gentiles responded to it. If apocalyptic is no more evident elsewhere in Paul than it is here, we must conclude that it is not a significant concept for the apostle.

66. ἀποβολή is a comprehensive word and can be used of loss by death (BAGD). In its only other New Testament occurrence it refers to the loss of a ship (Acts 27:22).

67. Note anarthrous κόσμος in the genitive after the noun on which it depends, as in v. 12 (M, III, p. 175).

is no verb in either clause of this sentence, Paul leaves us to work out whether we should supply "is" (NIV) or "has meant" (NEB) or something else.

Whatever we decide on in the first clause should probably be taken over to the second. There Paul refers to *their acceptance*,[68] which clearly means acceptance by God. This he sees as *life from the dead*. As things stood, Israel was dead spiritually. Paul's eager compassion looks for a giving of life. There are two ways of understanding this expression, depending on whether one takes it literally or figuratively. If it is understood literally, then it will be the resurrection of the dead, the general resurrection that ushers in the messianic age (so SH and others). This would give a good sense, but the words Paul uses here are not used elsewhere for the general resurrection.[69] It seems much more likely that he has in mind the powerful spiritual impetus that will be given by a change in Israel; this will be "the greatest blessing imaginable" (TH). This may, of course, take place at the end time, but the point is that Paul does not say so and he does not use words that commonly point to the end time. It is much more likely that he is referring to a great spiritual movement without locating it specifically in time.[70]

16. Paul proceeds to bring out the certainty that Israel will in due course enter salvation by using a couple of illustrations from the Old Testament. NIV is a trifle more definite than the apostle with its rendering *If the part of the dough offered as firstfruits*, for Paul says no more than "And if the firstfruits (are) holy"; NIV has reasoned from the "lump" (*whole batch*) at the end of the clause that Paul must be referring to dough, and this may well be right. There are several references to firstfruits in the Old Testament (as Exod. 23:19; 34:22; Lev. 2:12, 14; 23:10, 17, 20; Num. 15:20-21; 18:12; 28:26; Deut. 26:2, 10). Most commentators agree that Paul's reference is to the firstfruits in Numbers 15, for this passage refers to "the first of your ground meal" from which a cake is to be presented as an offering to the Lord.[71] The firstfruits are holy and so, reasons Paul, is the cake made from the firstfruits.

He goes on to the similar thought that if *the root is holy, so are the branches*. Ancient religions had the concept of a holy tree. The tree might put forth new branches, but these too were holy; they came from the same root. There is little doubt that Paul is here appealing to the fact that the patriarchs (perhaps he means only Abraham) were holy people and this has consequences for their descendants. It means that God will not discard them wholly, and thus in due course the fact that the root of Israel is holy will have its effect in the latest branches. Is he teaching the same thing with his reference to the first-

---

68. πρόσλημψις, here only in the New Testament.

69. Paul has ζωὴ ἐκ νεκρῶν, but the final resurrection is spoken of as ἀνάστασις νεκρῶν (1 Cor. 15:12 etc.).

70. Murray has a powerful argument for the figurative interpretation. "It must be accorded its full force as that which brings 'the reconciliation of the world' to climactic realization"; he refers to "an unprecedented quickening for the world".

71. In LXX we read of ἀπαρχὴν φυράματος, the same language Paul uses here.

fruits and the lump? Some think not, and they see the firstfruits as Jewish Christians who sanctify the nation so that from it there will come more believers (see Harrisville). This must remain as a possible understanding of the text, but it seems more likely that Paul is making parallel statements. In both he is viewing the patriarchs as "holy" and is considering the effect of this on their descendants.

17. Paul proceeds to a warning to Gentile Christians not to presume on their position. He plunges into an illustration from processes of grafting which seems rather improbable horticulturally. The normal process was to take a shoot from an olive that bears good fruit though it does not grow vigorously and graft it onto a wild olive stock, whose fruit is poor but which grows strongly. The result is a tree with vigorous growth which bears good olives. Paul, however, talks of the reverse process, of grafting a wild olive onto the stock of a good olive and later even of grafting back some of the good olive branches that have been cut out. All this has led to some caustic comments on Paul's knowledge of what went on in olive orchards.[72] To this two things may be said. One is that Paul is well aware that what he is talking about is "contrary to nature" (v. 24); he is not referring to something that went on every day in the olive orchards he passed. The other is that there is evidence that the grafting of a wild olive into a good olive tree is not as daft as many commentators have assumed. When an old olive tree had lost its vigor, it seems that one remedy in antiquity was to cut away the failing branches and graft in some wild olive shoots.[73] The result was said to be the invigoration of the failing tree. W. Ramsay says that early in this century the same process continued to be used in Palestine.[74]

Whether the process was widely practised and widely known or not, some Jewish writings use pretty much the same illustration as Paul. Thus Philo speaks of sinful Israelites and contrasts them with good proselytes, saying: "that God welcomes the virtue which springs from ignoble birth, that He takes no account of the roots but accepts the full-grown stem, because it has been changed from a weed into fruitfulness" (De praemiis et poenis 152). In the Talmud we read of Ruth the Moabitess and Naamah the Ammonitess (the mother of Rehoboam, 1 Kings 14:31) as "two goodly shoots" engrafted into Israel (Yeb. 63a; the Midrash on Numbers viii.9 cites "thy children like olive plants" and proceeds to praise "the sons of the proselytes", which may mean the same thing). It thus appears that Paul's illustration would not have seemed as bizarre to first-century readers as it does to some modern commentators. And we should bear in mind that it is an illustration. Paul does not say,

---

72. Cf. Dodd, "A truly remarkable horticultural experiment! Paul had the limitations of the town-bred man . . . he had not the curiosity to inquire what went on in the olive-yards which fringed every road he walked."
73. The passages cited to attest this are Columella, De re rustica v.9.16 and Palladius, De insitione xiv.53-54. Michel, Cranfield, and others draw attention to these passages.
74. Pauline and Other Studies (London, 1906), p. 223.

"This is what happens constantly in olive yards"; he simply uses the illustration in the same way as Philo and the Talmud do.

If carries on the sequence of "if" clauses (see the note on v. 12), implying that the condition has been fulfilled.[75] With another considerable understatement Paul speaks of *some* of the branches as broken off (he has just said that only a "remnant" is faithful, v. 5). His *some* reminds the reader that not all were faithless, and his passive will be another instance of referring to what God does without explicitly using his name. The olive tree is a symbol of Israel in a number of Old Testament passages. Thus we read, "The Lord called you a thriving olive tree with fruit beautiful in form" (Jer. 11:16; the prophet has to go on, "But with the roar of a mighty storm he will set it on fire, and its branches will be broken"; see also Hos. 14:6). Paul envisages some olive branches removed from the good olive tree.

And you[76] puts the Gentile believer in emphatic contrast; he has not been cut out but grafted in. He is called *a wild olive*,[77] which by nature bears small fruit and not much of that. This wild olive is *grafted in among the others*. Actually Paul says "among them" (NIV has added *the others*), and strictly this should refer to the branches just mentioned, those broken off.[78] But Paul does not always pay attention to grammatical niceties, and clearly his meaning is that the wild olive is grafted in among the branches that remain. It becomes a "sharer",[79] a partner with the branches that remain.

The text at the end of the verse is uncertain,[80] but Paul seems to be saying that the Gentile graft has become a sharer in "the root of the fatness of the olive". "Fatness" seems a curious word to apply to a root, but other examples are cited for its use of plants, so evidently it did not appear as strange to the ancients as it does to us. The genitive "of the fatness" may be a genitive of quality, "the fat (or rich) root" (cf. GNB, "the strong spiritual life of the Jews"); or it may be in apposition, "the root, that is, the fatness". The reference to the root points to "the patriarchal base established by God's covenant" (Harrison).[81]

75. εἰ with the aorist indicative. δέ is better understood as "now" than as "but".
76. σύ is emphatic. The passage is another example of the use of the pronoun in what Robertson calls "the representative sense" (Robertson, p. 678). Cf. BDF 281.
77. ἀγριέλαιος. The word refers to a tree; *shoot* is NIV's addition. It is generally held that the word is used here as an adjective (though BAGD think "it may also be taken as a subst., as we say 'oak' of a piece of furniture").
78. Some try to apply their grammar strictly and see the meaning as "in the place the branches occupied", but, as Godet says, this is "rather forced".
79. συγκοινωνός may be used of sharing in any one of a variety of things (cf. 1 Cor. 9:23; Phil. 1:7; BAGD note its use for business partners). Denney comments, "there is an argument in σύν. At the best, the Gentile only *shares* with Jews in the virtue of a root which is not Gentile, but Jewish."
80. The most probable text is τῆς ῥίζης τῆς πιότητος (א* B C Ψ); some MSS have τῆς ῥίζης καὶ τῆς πιότητος (אᶜ A Dᵇ·ᶜ P33), and some omit τῆς ῥίζης (P46 D* G). But these latter two appear to be scribal attempts to improve on the first (Metzger says they "are suspicious as ameliorating emendations").
81. Dodd makes an important point: "The illustration shows clearly how complete,

18. Evidently some of the Gentile converts were impressed by their new standing. Paul tells them to stop boasting (present imperative with the negative) against the branches. The verb means "boast against, exult over" (BAGD cite its use by a gladiator boasting over his defeated foe). It is not clear whether by "the branches" Paul means the branches that were broken off or those that remained in the tree or both. Perhaps we should not try to separate these too narrowly, for pride tends to be indiscriminate. Chrysostom points out that Paul does not say "Boast not", but "Boast not against": it is not so much an attitude of "I am wonderful" of which Paul is complaining as "I am more wonderful than you." Such a practice may have been helped by the widespread Roman contempt for the Jews. We have no evidence that Roman Christians engaged in anti-Semitism, but there would have been a temptation for imperfectly instructed Gentile Christians to see themselves as superior to Jews—had not Jewish branches been removed so that they could be grafted in? But pride is never in place for the Christian. Particularly is this the case when, as Barrett points out, "the privilege he has acquired is—that of being an Israelite." Paul reminds his hypothetical Gentile believer who so boasts that it is not he who bears the root, but the root that bears him.[82] The graft, and more especially the graft from a wild olive tree into a good olive, has no cause for feelings of superiority.[83]

19. In typical argumentative style Paul puts a retort into the mouth of an imaginary opponent: *Branches were broken off so that I could be grafted in.* There is no article with *branches;* it means some branches rather than all the branches and it puts some emphasis on the fact that those broken off have the character of being branches, no less. *I* is emphatic and, taken with *so that* (which expresses the divine purpose), expresses "the egoism and vainglory of this boasting" (Murray). The objector is arrogant as he sees that he, no less, is intended by God to replace Israel.[84]

20. *Granted* concedes the point, though with some irony. Manson suggests that it be translated "Well, well!" rather than "That is true." It suggests that that is not the whole story. *Because of unbelief* renders an unusual dative,[85] but this translation is surely correct. The lack of faith means that they could not possibly stay within the tree. *And you* sets the Gentile in strong contrast to

---

in Paul's thought, was the continuity between the Christian Church and the Israel of the Old Testament. The Church is not a new society; it is 'the Israel of God'".

82. The οὐ before the emphatic σύ, the τὴν ῥίζαν preceding its verb, and the strong adversative ἀλλά all make for an emphatic declaration.

83. Cf. Wesley, "Had the graft been nobler than the stock, yet its dependence on it for life and nourishment would leave it no room to boast against it. How much less, when, contrary to what is practised among men, the wild olive tree is engrafted on the good!"

84. Gifford reminds us that "it would be arrogant and selfish to assume, as in this supposed reply, that the advantage of the Gentiles was the direct and sole cause of God's casting away of His people."

85. τῇ ἀπιστίᾳ. Turner classes this as "cause" and remarks, "This dat. is extraordinary" (M, III, p. 242). BDF 196 also class it as "dative of cause", while Moule sees it as "virtually instrumental" (IBNTG, p. 44). A preposition might have been expected.

the branches that were broken off.[86] The Gentile believer has no natural superiority over the Jew. He stands in place of the Jew, indeed, but this is only because of the mercy of God and of God's saving action in Christ.[87] The Jew's rejection arose from the fact that he did not appropriate this salvation by faith. The Gentile is accepted only because he did so appropriate it. In himself he is nothing; he cannot stand at all. He should not be complacent as he contemplates his salvation and the loss of the Jews. "We should never think of the rejection of the Jews without being struck with dread and terror" (Calvin on v. 21).

This leads on to another warning about pride. *Do not be arrogant* goes to the heart of being a Christian. Barrett puts it this way: "The moment he begins to grow boastful he ceases to have faith (humble dependence upon God), and therefore himself becomes a candidate for 'cutting off'." To trust in God and to be proud of one's spiritual achievement are mutually exclusive. Instead of being arrogant Paul counsels the reader to *be afraid*. This translation might give a wrong impression, and some modern translations use the concept of awe, as RSV, "stand in awe", or Moffatt, "You should feel awed instead of being uplifted". Thomas helpfully points out that "There are two kinds of fear, that of the slave and that of the son. The one implies fright, the other awe and reverence." It is the latter that Paul is counselling here. Without a proper reverence no one can stand before God.

21. The fate of the Jews is now drawn into a warning for the Gentiles. *For* gives a reason for the foregoing statement; there is good reason for the awe Paul enjoins. For *if* see the note on verse 12.[88] God, Paul says, *did not spare the natural branches,*[89] those that we might expect to find on the tree. They were cut out of the tree. Now if God did that to the branches we expect to find on the tree, let those we do not expect to find there be duly warned. The fate of the natural branches could so easily become that of the grafted-in branches.

There is good reason for NIV's going straight on with *he will not spare you either*, but there is a textual problem of some magnitude.[90] However we solve it, Paul is giving a strong and unmistakable warning to his readers not to presume on God's mercy.

---

86. οὐ δέ, where the pronoun emphasizes the subject and δέ may be adversative, "but you" (RSV).

87. There is no ἵνα, as in v. 19; the branches were not broken off "in order that you might stand. . . ." For this use of *stand* cf. 1 Cor. 10:12.

88. εἰ with the aorist tense is a condition of reality, "if (as is the case). . . ."

89. φείδομαι is a Pauline word (seven times out of ten in the New Testament, three being in Romans). *Natural* renders κατὰ φύσιν, where the noun means "*nature*", a word that may in turn mean "the *nature* (natural powers or constitution) of a person or thing" (AS).

90. The text behind NIV (and most modern translations) is supported by א A B C P etc., but the insertion of μή πως before οὐδέ is found in our oldest witness P46 and MSS like D G Ψ etc. Gifford thinks that μή πως was inserted by scribes "to soften the stern note of warning." Metzger holds that "copyists may have taken offence at its presence here because of its apparent unrelatedness", so his committee put it into the text but within square brackets. It is impossible to be certain of the original.

22. *Consider* is not used in the sense "think about" but rather "Notice" (GNB, "Here we see"). *Therefore*[91] draws a conclusion from the whole previous argument. Arising from it all Paul calls on his Gentile to look at the *kindness* and the *sternness* of God (a combination found in the Old Testament; e.g., Ps. 125:4-5). For *kindness*[92] see the note on 2:4; the word combines the thoughts of goodness and kindness. It is a goodness which is not so much austere as kind, a kindness that is not indifferent to moral values. *Sternness*[93] points to God's inflexible moral purpose. While he is certainly kind to us sinners, kind beyond all our deserving, Paul sees his opposition to evil as unyielding. The combination draws attention to a fascinating contrast of attitudes, held simultaneously.

Paul proceeds to differentiate the application of the two qualities. *Sternness* is exercised *to*[94] *those who fell*. In verse 11 Paul denied that Israel's stumbling was in order that they might fall, and he has the same verb here. But there he was denying that ultimate disaster was the fate of God's Israel; here he is affirming that it is the fate of those branches that were cut off on account of unbelief (v. 20). Those who shut themselves up to unbelief can look forward to nothing but severity. Over against this[95] there is *kindness to you*, the Gentile believer.

To this Paul appends a warning, *provided that you continue*[96] *in his kindness*. The Greek here has "the kindness", but NIV has correctly interpreted this with *his*; Paul is not saying that the believer is to persist in doing deeds of kindness (though that, too, is part of being Christian), but that he is to continue in "the" kindness just mentioned, the kindness of God. We should not understand this to mean that the believer can stop himself from falling away from grace by his own unaided effort. Paul is not saying, "if you continue to merit his kindness" (TH). He is warning "against a false and unevangelical sense of security" (Cranfield).[97] There is a humble security that leans constantly on the kindness of God, and there is a proud self-dependence that scorns any need of help. It is the latter against which Paul is warning.

91. οὖν.
92. χρηστότης.
93. ἀποτομία, twice in this verse and here only in the New Testament, derives from ἀποτέμνω, "to cut off". AS sees it as meaning "steepness, sharpness", and thus "severity". Olshausen says the word "is equivalent to ὀργή, but is preferred on account of the figure of the cut-off branches."
94. *To* renders ἐπί, used here of "feelings, actions, etc. directed toward a pers. or thing. . . . Esp. also if the feelings or their expressions are of a hostile nature *toward*, *against*" (BAGD III.b.ϵ).
95. μὲν . . . δέ marks a contrast.
96. ἐπιμένω means much the same as μένω, though perhaps with some strengthening of the idea of persistence.
97. Calvin comments that it is "improper to say in particular of any of the godly that God had mercy on him when he chose him, on condition that he should continue in His mercy. The perseverance of faith, which perfects the effect of God's grace in us, flows from election itself." In any case Paul "is not discussing here the special election of each individual, but is setting the Gentiles and Jews in opposition to one another." Cf. Bruce, "The perseverance of the saints is a doctrine firmly grounded in New Testament (and not least in Pauline) teaching; but its corollary is that it is the saints who persevere."

Otherwise,[98] *you also will be cut off.* Paul's *you* is emphatic. His hypothetical Gentile has no mortgage on the blessing. Jewish branches were cut off on account of unbelief; why should he think he is immune? There is no place for smug complacency.

23. Now comes a note of hope for Israel. *And* might perhaps be better "but",[99] while *they* of course refers back to the Israelites. Paul opens up the possibility that they will *not persist*[100] *in unbelief.* Some Jews had already believed, and Paul could not think that there would be no more. So he thinks of unbelievers becoming believers, and in that case *God is able to graft them in again.* It is pointed out that this is a most unlikely piece of horticulture, and so, of course, it is. If the orchardist wanted certain branches in his tree he would never have cut them off in the first place. But Paul is not talking about orchardists; he is talking about God, and the orchard is no more than an illustration. He is talking about a miracle of grace and assuring his readers that God *is able* to perform that miracle. In the sphere of salvation he is able to do something that the orchardist would never do in his orchard.

24. "For if you" continues Paul's emphatic mode of speaking as he addresses his Gentile.[101] That Gentile was cut out of[102] *an olive tree that is wild by nature.* It was *contrary to nature*[103] that it was grafted into *a cultivated olive tree.*[104] God is not bound by the limits of what people see as natural. Paul has spoken of God as grafting the wild olive onto the good olive; now he proceeds with "How much more. . . ?"[105] as he goes on to the grafting of the natural branches back into the olive tree from which they had been broken off. This could be a question (as NIV and others), but it may be seen as a statement (RSV) or an exclamation (NEB). Any of these is possible.[106]

---

98. ἐπεί is a causal conjunction, "because, since". Here there is an ellipsis, "since (if it were different). . . ." NIV gives the sense of it.

99. δέ can, of course, mean "and", but it seems that here it has adversative force. Paul is contrasting his hypothetical Jew with his hypothetical Gentile.

100. The verb is ἐπιμένω, which was translated "continue" in v. 22.

101. NIV renders γάρ *after all,* but "for" is the meaning. εἰ is yet another conditional, meaning "if (as is the case). . . ." σύ is the emphatic pronoun.

102. Notice that ἐξεκόπης is followed by its own preposition ἐκ, but later in this verse ἐνεκεντρίσθης by εἰς.

103. παρὰ φύσιν. This receives emphasis from its prominent position. It is a significant point.

104. καλλιέλαιος, "good olive tree"; it contrasts with ἀγριέλαιος, "field olive tree", i.e., one that grows unaided in the fields. The good olive tree is one that has been cultivated.

105. NIV has *how much more readily,* but the Greek is simply πόσῳ μᾶλλον. Boylan remarks that this means "How much more certainly!" rather than "How much more easily!" We are not to think of one thing as more easy than another for omnipotence. Paul is talking about what is fitting, not about what is easy.

106. Barrett sees this passage as pointing to processes that go on in every age: "Paul's picture is of the religious and the irreligious man. The former lives in an atmosphere which should constantly remind him that God is in heaven and he upon earth (Ecclus. v.2); but in this atmosphere he makes himself at home and domesticates his God. The irreligious man stumbles by accident (as he may think) upon the terror and the grace of God, and supplants his brother, because he knows he has no virtue and no piety to offer to his Maker, but trusts the grace he has glimpsed in Christ. And the religious man, or

3. The Conversion of Israel, 11:25-32

> 25I do not want you to be ignorant of this mystery, brothers, so that you may not be conceited: Israel has experienced a hardening in part until the full number of the Gentiles has come in. 26And so all Israel will be saved, as it is written:
>
> > "The deliverer will come from Zion;
> > he will turn godlessness away from Jacob.
> > 27 And this isª my covenant with them
> > when I take away their sins."ᵇ
>
> 28As far as the gospel is concerned, they are enemies on your account; but as far as election is concerned, they are loved on account of the patriarchs, 29for God's gifts and his call are irrevocable. 30Just as you who were at one time disobedient to God have now received mercy as a result of their disobedience, 31so they too have now become disobedient in order that they too may nowᶜ receive mercy as a result of God's mercy to you. 32For God has bound all men over to disobedience so that he may have mercy on them all.

ª27 or will be   ᵇ27 Isaiah 59:20, 21; 27:9   ᶜ31 Some manuscripts do not have now.

Until now Paul has spoken of a "remnant" of Israel that is saved while the bulk of the nation has been "hardened". As he brings his discussion of justification to a close, he looks forward to the time when "all Israel" will be saved. Some commentators see in this a vision of the time at the end of the age when the whole nation of Israel will turn to Christ and enter the salvation for which he died. They point out that throughout this section of the epistle Paul is concerned with the nation, and specifically they see no good reason for seeing a difference of meaning in "Israel" in verses 25 and 26. So they see Paul as looking forward to a glorious time when the Jews, as a nation, will turn to Christ. There may be some individuals who will not respond to the gospel, but the nation as a whole will become Christian. Others insist that Paul has been giving special attention to the "remnant" throughout the discussion until now, and they ask on what grounds we should hold that Paul thought that the last generation on earth before Christ comes again would be treated differently from all the others. They also hold firmly that "all Israel" is a curious way of referring to most of the last generation, after many, many generations have died outside Christ. Should not "all Israel" have something to say about these generations? They see in "Israel" accordingly a reference to the true people of God and thus to elect Jews in all generations including the last. While both positions are held very firmly, it cannot be said that either

---

Pharisee, learns with painful inward struggle that he must divest himself of his pride, count his gains loss and his boasts dung, in order to be found in Christ, with a right-eousness not of his own fabrication but from God (Phil. iii.8f.)." We should beware of treating Paul's argument as an academic exercise.

418

has been able to bring forward an argument so decisive that it makes the position of the other untenable. It is clear that we must examine what Paul says with great care.

25. "For" is omitted by NIV, but it is important; it links this verse closely with verse 24 and indeed with the whole of the argument leading up to this point. What has preceded is no idle conjecture, "for" Paul has a revelation which assures him of its truth. *I do not want you to be ignorant* is an opening Paul uses a number of times (see the note on 1:13). This opening always leads into something Paul regards as important, and he always follows it with *brothers*, which joins him with his readers in the bonds of Christ and removes any impression that he is taking up a position of superiority. He has been using the singular pronoun in addressing a hypothetical reader, but he switches now to the plural, and he retains the plural throughout the subsequent discussion.

He speaks of a *mystery*,[107] a term the Christians used in the sense of something that people could not possibly know of themselves, but which has now been revealed to them. It was not incomprehensible, not "mysterious" in our sense of the term; it was something beyond us to discover, though we can understand it all right when God has made it known to us. It is an important term: in this discussion of the place of Israel Paul is not referring to the obvious, but to something that required a revelation before Christians could understand it. Paul uses it to refer to a number of facets of the Christian message (e.g., 1 Cor. 2:7; 15:51; Eph. 3:4), but especially to the gospel (e.g., Eph. 6:19). Here his thought is that the place of Israel could not be worked out by the unaided human mind; if we are to understand it, it has to be made known by God. This revelation is *so that*[108] *you may not be conceited*, "wise in yourselves".[109] In other words, you may not think that your own intellect or merit has brought this knowledge.[110] Evidently some Gentile believers were tempted to think that there was no future for Israel. She had rejected the gospel and it had now passed to the Gentiles; Israel was finished, rejected, cast off. God had chosen them instead. It is this kind of pride that Paul is opposing.

That about which Paul does not want his readers ignorant is that *Israel*

---

107. μυστήριον is used by Paul 20 (or 21; see 1 Cor. 2:1) times out of 27 (28) in the New Testament; again in Romans only in 16·25 (which "virtually furnishes a definition" of the term, Murray). In the "mystery religions", a well-known feature of the Hellenistic world of the time, the mystery stood for a secret that was made known only to the initiates, a meaning we can see also among the Jewish apocalyptists.

108. ἵνα expresses purpose.

109. It is uncertain whether we should read the dative ἑαυτοῖς or whether it should be preceded by παρ' (which, however, may be due to assimilation to 12:16; Prov. 3:7) or by ἐν (which could come from Isa. 5:21). Cf. BDF 188 (2), "both prepositions following references in the LXX". Fortunately the sense is not greatly affected.

110. Black comments on "wise in your own conceits" (KJV), "a matchless translation capturing exactly the nuance of Pauline thought and emotion." He thinks that the Greek expression "clever in oneself" "may have been an idiomatic one for 'too clever by far in his own esteem'".

has experienced[111] *a hardening in part.*[112] Goodspeed translates "only partial insensibility", but most agree that it is not partial hardening but part of Israel that is meant (cf. RSV, "a hardening has come upon part of Israel"; Chrysostom says, "not the whole people"). This is a temporary hardening, taking place while God's purpose is worked out among the Gentiles or, as Paul puts it, *until*[113] *the full number of the Gentiles*[114] *has come in.* The word NIV renders *full number* is that rendered "fullness" in verse 12. NIV may well be right in seeing a reference to number. In that case a certain number of Gentiles are to be saved, and God is waiting until that number has been reached before taking action for Israel. Another possibility is that here, as perhaps also in verse 12, something like "fullness" is meant. It is also possible to understand the expression as the fullness of the blessing of the Gentiles[115] or the full contribution of the Gentiles, or the Gentiles as a whole. Whichever way we take it, the fullness is regarded as active and as entering the scene (it "comes in"). This verb is sometimes used of entering the kingdom or life (as in Matt. 7:21; 18:8; Mark 9:43-47), and absolutely in much the same sense (Matt. 7:13; 23:13; Luke 13:24), as SH point out. We should probably see a reference to the fulfilment of God's purpose in bringing Gentiles into his kingdom, however we understand the individual words.

26. *And so,* Paul says, *all Israel will be saved.* This expression has caused unending disputation among expositors. Paul's *so*[116] is usually taken to refer to what precedes, in which case it surely means "in this way", that is, through the divinely appointed process whereby the hardening of part of Israel brought salvation to the Gentiles, a temporary hardening effective only until "the fullness of the Gentiles" has come in. But *so* can also refer to what follows (e.g., 10:6; 1 Cor. 3:15, etc.). If that is the case here, we should put a full stop at the end of verse 25 and see a new thought in verse 26, namely that all Israel will be saved when the Redeemer comes to Zion. This second suggestion is not impossible, but on the whole the former way seems more likely to be correct. The end result of this process will be the salvation of *all Israel,* an expression that exegetes have found notoriously difficult. There is considerable agreement that *all Israel* does not mean "each and every Israelite without exception"; the term refers to the nation as a whole. It is used in this way in the Old Testament (1 Sam. 12:1; 2 Chron. 12:1; Dan. 9:11).[117] Particularly

---

111. The verb is γέγονεν and its subject is "hardening"; RSV renders it "has come". The perfect tense denotes a continuing state.

112. πώρωσις (elsewhere in the New Testament only in Mark 3:5; Eph. 4:18) means *"a covering with a callus, a hardening:* metaph. of dulled spiritual perception" (AS).

113. ἄχρις οὗ "can be regarded strictly as prepositional = ἄχρις ἐκείνου χρόνου ἐν ᾧ" (IBNTG, p. 82). This adds to the point that the hardening is partial (vv. 5, 7, 17), the thought that it is temporary. It is limited in time as well as extent.

114. τὸ πλήρωμα τῶν ἐθνῶν.

115. So Murray, "blessing for the Gentiles that is parallel and similar to the expansion of blessing for Israel denoted by their 'fulness' (vs. 12) and the 'receiving' (vs. 15)."

116. οὕτως.

117. It is probably this that allows BDF to see the expression as Hebraizing with the meaning "the whole of Israel" (275 [4]).

instructive is a passage in the Mishnah which assures the reader that "All Israelites have a share in the world to come" (Sanh. 10:1) and then goes on to give a considerable list of Israelites who "have no share in the world to come", sometimes mentioning classes such as those who deny the resurrection of the dead and sometimes individuals such as Jeroboam and Balaam. Clearly *all Israel* indicates the people as a whole, but it leaves open the possibility that there may be exceptions. So much is clear.

But some exegetes understand *Israel* here of the nation while others see it as referring to spiritual Israel, the people of God whether Jewish or Gentile (so Calvin). Lenski has a strong argument for the elect Jews. But what seems decisive is the fact that "Israel" in verse 25 plainly means the nation (it is physical Israel, not spiritual Israel, that is hardened in part), and it is not easy to understand why in the next line it should have a different meaning (Hodge has a strong argument for this position). A further strong argument is that Paul has just said that this is a "mystery". Now it is no "mystery" that all the elect, Jews as well as Gentiles, will be saved. Nor is the conversion of a few Jews in each generation such as has happened until now the kind of thing that needs to be the subject of a special revelation. That looks for a very different kind of happening. It may also be argued that Paul is looking for the restoration of the Jews in the sense in which they had been rejected, that is, the nation generally. Paul then is affirming that the nation of Israel as a whole will ultimately have its place in God's salvation.[118] This may well be located in the end time and be part of the eschatological program that Paul anticipates then.[119] But if "all Israel" means more than one generation, it will take place earlier.

Paul proceeds to quote Isaiah 59:20-21 along with a line from Isaiah 27:9.[120] *The deliverer* is surely a reference to Christ, but whether Paul sees a reference to the incarnation with its messianic salvation coming out of Zion (Lenski), or the parousia with the Savior coming to Zion in glory (Parry, Cranfield) is not clear. Denney finds it impossible to say whether the apostle is referring "to the first or to the second advent: the distinction is not present to Paul's mind as he writes". Zion may be the earthly city or it may stand for the heavenly city, in which case the deliverer is thought of as coming from the very presence of God (cf. Isa. 2:3). His function is given in terms of turning

---

118. Parry puts it this way, "The idea is that Israel as a nation will have its part fully in the consummated kingdom of Christ (cf. 1 Cor. xv.) and in this final reconciliation S. Paul sees the fulfilment of the promises. What fate awaits those Israelites who fell away, he does not consider . . . this question of the ultimate salvation of individuals is as completely ignored at this point, as it has been throughout these chapters."

119. Thus James P. Martin argues that the expression *all Israel will be saved* "belongs to the language of faith and apocalyptic mystery, not the language of historical necessity" (*Interpretation*, XXV [1971], p. 307). Käsemann sees "the apocalyptic expectation of the restitution of Israel and the associated pilgrimage of the nations to Zion" (p. 312).

120. The quotation is mostly as LXX except that ἕνεκεν Σιών ("for the sake of Zion") has become ἐκ Σιών ("out of Zion"), which may derive from Ps. 14:7 (LXX 13:7), 53:6 (LXX 52:7); MT has "to Zion". Paul may also have in mind Jer. 31:34.

godlessness[121] *away from Jacob*. He is to remove their sin, more particularly as it is seen as sin against God. The nation is more commonly called Israel than Jacob, but there seems no real significance in the choice of name.

27. Paul's quotation moves on to the thought of the covenant, the covenant that originates with God.[122] The particular aspect of the covenant to which attention is drawn is that which has to do with the forgiveness of sins (cf. Jer. 31:34). This does not mean that the covenant is concerned only with forgiveness; in fact a good deal more is involved. But Paul's subject throughout these chapters is justification by faith and how what happened and will happen to Israel fits into that great doctrine. So he concentrates on the sins aspect. *When* is indefinite;[123] the prophet leaves the time unspecified. *Take away* is a verb with a wide range of meaning,[124] but basically it signifies "take from, take away"; in the context it clearly means the complete removal of sins. When the covenant is put into force, God will take such action as will remove sins from the scene. An important feature of God's salvation is that sin will no longer be there to disrupt relationships. The saved will live in unbroken fellowship with God.

28. There is no connective to link this with the preceding; Paul moves abruptly to a new aspect of his subject. He sees the Jews in two relationships to God—one linked to the gospel, the other to the fathers. *As far as*[125] *the gospel* (see the note on 1:1) *is concerned,* the Jews are *enemies.* There has been some discussion as to whether we should understand this term passively (i.e., the Jews are the objects of God's hostility), or actively (the Jews are hostile to God). What turns the scale is probably the fact that *enemies* stands over against *loved,* and *loved* must mean "loved by God". In such a context Paul must be saying that in connection with the gospel the Jews are the objects of divine hostility. They have refused to believe in Christ, they have turned their backs on the divinely appointed way of forgiveness, so what else could the situation be? This does not mean that the gospel makes them God's enemies, a suggestion that is immediately negatived by the fact that Jews like Paul himself had responded to the gospel and entered into salvation. It is "with reference to" (not "because of") the gospel that they are enemies. As a whole they did not receive it, and this opened the way for it to be preached to the Gentiles so that a large Gentile church emerged. It is in order to bring about this spread of the gospel that they are enemies. They are enemies *on your account;* in the providence of God their rejection of the gospel was not aimless. It was the means of bringing salvation to others. God's purpose was carried on through it. This carries with it the possibility that when the gospel has had its effect

---

121. ἀσέβεια means "*godlessness, impiety,* in thought and act" (BAGD).

122. ἡ παρ' ἐμοῦ διαθήκη. Chamberlain thinks παρά is used here of authorship, "the covenant from me" (p. 126).

123. ὅταν, "whenever".

124. ἀφαιρέω in LXX translates 35 words in all (AS), so that plainly it is not easy to tie down narrowly.

125. κατά here means "with reference to", "in relation to".

among the Gentiles they will come back, and that is precisely the point that Paul is making.

So he goes on to refer to a different set of relationships, *as far as election is concerned*. For *as far as* see the note on the opening to this verse (the construction is identical), and for *election* see that on 9:11. Paul is emphasizing the divine plan; though Israel had been faithless and thus the object of God's hostility, God had nevertheless worked through this faithlessness to bring about his will. And he had not forgotten that Israel was his people; their refusal to accept the gospel did not alter the fact that he had chosen them to be in a special relationship to him, the people through whom he would make his revelation and to whom he would send his Son. Election is an important concept even when the nation had not lived up to all that is involved in its calling. And election means that *they are loved on account of the patriarchs*. It does not mean that they are all elected to eternal salvation; Paul is talking about the place of the nation in God's plan, not the fate of individuals. The reference is to the nation (as in v. 2), not to the remnant (as in v. 7). The nation is *loved* (cf. 9:25), and Paul links this with *the patriarchs* (he says "the fathers"). We should not understand this in the sense of the rabbinic doctrine of the merits of the fathers that won all sorts of benefits for their descendants. Rather, Paul is appealing to the covenant God had made with Abraham and the promises he had made again and again to Abraham's descendants. God will carry his purposes out (as Paul will insist in v. 29).

Käsemann makes an important point when he says of verses 28-32 "The justification of the ungodly, which is announced in various places in our chapters, emerges now as the dominant theme of the whole portion" (p. 314). We must bear in mind that chapters 9–11 are part of Paul's treatment of justification, not a historical essay or an exercise in Jewish patriotism. Paul is showing that the doctrine he has been expounding in the earlier part of the epistle is not vitiated by what had happened to Israel. God had made promises to Israel, and these promises would be kept. Israel's refusal to accept the gospel did not mean either that the gospel was a failure or that God would not perform all he had promised to his ancient people. But we make sense neither of the Old Testament Scripture nor of the history of Israel nor of the place of the Christian church unless we see that justification by faith is central. Here the point is that God justifies Israelites who believe just as he justifies Gentiles who believe, and the whole history of Israel is to be seen in the light of that fact.

29. *For* introduces a reason for what Paul has just said; there is a logical basis for his position. In the Greek the first word of this verse is *irrevocable*;[126] God does not change his mind after he has made gifts or issued calls. He does not take them back. What God has done and said stands. Paul speaks specifi-

---

126. ἀμεταμέλητος is found in the New Testament again only in 2 Cor. 7:10, and it does not occur in LXX. It means "not to be regretted, without regret" and hence "irrevocable", used "of someth. one does not take back" (BAGD).

cally of God's *gifts*,[127] a very general term. Godet sees the word as denoting "the moral and intellectual aptitudes with which God endows a man with a view to the task committed to him." He thinks that Greeks, Romans, and others had their own gifts while Israel had "singular qualities for their mission as the salvation-people." There may be something in "singular qualities", but Paul is not referring to natural endowments of any kind. He is speaking rather of the gifts he has listed in 9:4-5. Israel was a special people and had special gifts accordingly, gifts like covenants, adoption, and the like which are not to be thought of as individual or racial endowments. With this Paul links God's *call*. Some consider this as more or less equivalent to *gifts*, but the two words are distinct. As Cranfield points out, aspects of call like commission, function, and task are not gifts. God gives gifts, then, and calls people and nations. And he does not go back on either. God can be relied on.[128]

30. Verses 30-31 form one carefully constructed sentence marked by a series of correspondences which may be set out as follows:[129]

verse 30	*verse 31*
you	*they*
at one time	*now (the first now)*
were disobedient	*become disobedient*
now	*now (the second now)*
received mercy	*receive mercy*
their disobedience	*mercy to you*

Clearly Paul saw justification as working out for both groups and in such a manner that each in some way assisted the other. There is a consistent divine purpose. *Just as* leads on to a "so too" in the second part of the sentence. Paul's *you* sets his Gentile readers over against the Jews. *At one time*[130] is indefinite, "formerly". It refers to the past generally, the time when the Gentiles were *disobedient*.[131] The whole pre-Christian experience of Paul's readers is summed up as disobedience (cf. ch. 1). "But now" (NIV omits "but") puts the present situation in contrast. Interestingly and significantly the apostle does not say "you have become obedient", but "you have ob-

---

127. χαρίσματα, the term employed (mostly by Paul) of the special gifts of the Spirit (1 Cor. 12:4, 9, 28, etc.). But here it does not seem to be used of the gifts in the technical sense; rather, it is wide enough to cover all God's good gifts of grace.

128. Barrett points out that there is no contradiction with 9:6-13: "The underlying truth which connects the two apparently contradictory lines of thought is that, for God, freedom is freedom to act in grace, and that since he is ever the same he never regrets or revokes the acts of grace which he performs".

129. Cranfield sets these forth in Greek.

130. ποτέ.

131. ἠπειθήσατε. The verb means "disobey", but for the Christians the worst disobedience was the refusal to believe; thus there is some reason to hold that it can mean "disbelieve" (see the note on 2:8). That meaning is possible here, but we should probably take it as "disobey".

tained mercy". It is no human achievement of which he speaks, but a divine gift. *As a result of their disobedience* renders a dative which is variously interpreted.[132] But NIV seems to have the sense of it, even if *as a result of* may be going further than the Greek. Paul is saying that it was the disobedience of the Jews that God used to bring the gospel to the Gentiles (cf. Acts 18:6). In these two verses he is emphasizing the divine mercy and saying that both Jew and Gentile were disobedient before God's mercy saved them.[133]

31. There is similarity and difference in the experiences of the Gentiles and Jews. There is similarity in that both are characterized by disobedience. There is difference in that it was through the Jews' disobedience that the Gentiles came to experience God's mercy but it will be through the mercy God has shown to the Gentiles that he will bring mercy to the Jews. There are two ways of taking the main part of this verse, depending on where we place *God's mercy to you*. GNB puts it in the first clause, "because of the mercy that you have received, the Jews now disobey God, in order that they also may now receive God's mercy." But RSV has it in the second clause, "they have now been disobedient in order that by the mercy shown to you they also may receive mercy." The point is that the words in question precede the conjunction *in order that* and this would fit easily into the first clause; indeed, some scholars think this rules out the possibility of including them in the final clause.[134] But this opinion is not well grounded, and to take the words as in RSV and NIV yields a better sense. Paul is putting some emphasis on the expression *God's mercy to you* and thus puts it in an especially prominent place. It would be the very mercy God showed the Gentiles that would in due course ensure mercy for the Jews. There is a textual problem regarding the second *now*, which is not found in some MSS[135] (it is not read by RSV and O'Neill). But its attestation in the MSS and transcriptional probability show that we should accept it, even though it presents us with what Barth calls an "an almost intolerable eschatological tension" (p. 417 n.). Is Paul speaking of the End? Or something that is to happen in this present age? *Now* locates it in this age, though, of course, Paul may well mean towards the end of that age.

32. Another *for* links this verse to the preceding; what follows is not a general statement about the way God treats mankind, but the conclusion to

---

132. τῇ τούτων ἀπειθείᾳ, which is probably a dative of cause as in v. 20 (so BDF 196). Turner thinks it is temporal, "at the time of their disbelief" (M, III, p. 243), but this is less likely.

133. Barrett sees more than either temporality or instrumentality and says of these two verses, "In each case, behind disobedience and mercy, stands the same sovereign divine activity"; he further says, "For Jew and Gentile alike, the end of the road is God's mercy; and for each the road leads through disobedience."

134. τῷ ὑμετέρῳ ἐλέει precedes ἵνα. But words may precede ἵνα and thus receive emphasis, as in 2 Cor. 2:4; Gal. 2:10. It seems that that is the way we should take the sentence here.

135. It is read by ℵ B D^{gr*} boh etc. but is not found in P[46vid] A^{b,c} G etc. The decision is not easy, but the word should probably be read. A scribe would more likely omit it than insert it.

what Paul has been saying in verses 30-31. God, says Paul, *has bound all men over to disobedience*. But we may well question NIV's translation of the verb rendered *bound over*.[136] BAGD translate "has imprisoned them all in disobedience" and then explains this: "i.e. put them under compulsion to be disobedient or given them over to disobedience". The second suggestion is better than the first: Paul is not saying that God predetermined that all should sin, but rather that he has so ordered things that all people, Jew and Gentile alike, being disobedient, show themselves to be sinners (cf. 1:24, 26, 28) and have no other escape than through his mercy. Cf. JB, "God has imprisoned all men in their disobedience". There has been a good deal of argument about the meaning of *all men*,[137] which some have understood to mean "all of the elect",[138] while others see a reference to universal salvation.[139] But such positions are reached by detaching the words from their context. Paul is dealing with Jews and Gentiles in their disobedience, and it is "the" all in question, both these groups, who are shut up in this way (cf. BDF 275 [7]). He is not dealing with the salvation of the individual, but with what happens alike to Jews and Gentiles. And God's final purpose[140] is that he may have mercy on them all. That purpose is not condemnation or the like. It is always mercy.[141]

136. συγκλείω means "shut together, enclose, shut in on all sides" (AS). It is used, e.g., of catching fish in a net (Luke 5:6) and of people confined to certain consequences (Ps. 31:8; 78:50; LXX 30:9; 77:50). Denney holds that σύν means "together" rather than "on all sides", while Lenski takes the reverse position. Chamberlain sees it as perfective (p. 146). Such arguments are inconclusive, but usage indicates that we should think of something like imprisonment (cf. GNB, "prisoners of disobedience"). Michel remarks, "Paul seems quite clearly to have the figure of prison before him" (TDNT, VII, p. 746). Turner sees εἰς as causal and translates "because of disobedience" (M, III, p. 266).

137. τοὺς πάντας. τὰ πάντα has interesting, but perhaps not decisive attestation (principally P[46vid] D*); Cranfield thinks there may be assimilation to Gal. 3:22. The article should not be overooked.

138. Cf. A. Schweitzer, "by 'all' is meant nothing more nor less than all the Elect" (*The Mysticism of Paul the Apostle* [New York, 1931], p. 185).

139. Cf. O'Neill, "God leaves no one outside his love and care and eventually all— or all who believe in one God—will be saved (11:25-32)"; he later says, the meaning is "God's mercy would extend to all the Gentile members of the Church and all Jews." Dodd says, "Whether or not . . . Paul himself drew the 'universalist' conclusion, it seems that we must draw it from his premisses."

140. ἵνα means "in order that".

141. Barclay finds back of all this "*a philosophy of history. To Paul, God was in control.* There was nothing which moved with aimless feet." Scott concludes his treatment of this part of the letter this way: "Paul thus speaks the final word on what must always be the most baffling of all problems. He did not in some wilful mood invent the harsh doctrine of predestination, which now, in our more enlightened day, we can set aside. He was confronted with a fact, which we may call by various names, but which forces itself upon us in ever more terrible forms as we understand more of that mechanism of necessity in which man's earthly life is involved. Questions arise to which there can be no other answer than this one which is offered by Paul. The ways of God are inscrutable, but we can trust His purpose, and since He is God, whose will is revealed to us in Christ, His purpose must be one of love" (p. 65).

4. The Mercy of God, 11:33-36

33 Oh, the depth of the riches of the wisdom and*a*
knowledge of God!
> How unsearchable his judgments,
> and his paths beyond tracing out!
34 "Who has known the mind of the Lord?
> Or who has been his counselor?"*b*
35 "Who has ever given to God,
> that God should repay him?"*c*
36 For from him and through him and to him are all things.
> To him be the glory forever! Amen.

*a*33 Or riches and the wisdom and the   *b*34 Isaiah 40:13   *c*35 Job 41:11

Paul rounds off this discussion of a very difficult subject with an expression of adoring wonder and praise. Black notes that Michel speaks of it as a hymn but he prefers to see it as a doxology, and rightly. It is elicited immediately by what was said in verse 32, but it is a fitting conclusion to the whole of the preceding argument. It is interesting that it is prompted by what we do not know about God (even what he has revealed we do not fully comprehend) rather than by what we do know (cf. Murray). Paul is not breaking into praise because he has been able to give a final and complete solution to some very difficult problems. He has certainly given some of the answers, but to some very important questions the answer is still not revealed. But it is Paul's conviction that there is a solution and that that solution is in God's hands. Therefore he breaks out into this doxology.

33. Oh,[142] the depth of the riches of the wisdom and knowledge of God may be understood in more ways than one. The *depth* points to the inexhaustibility of the following quality (BAGD; Paul uses it of "the deep things of God", 1 Cor. 2:10).[143] But it is not clear whether we should understand the depth as referring to three qualities—riches, wisdom, and knowledge (as NEB, Barrett, and others) or to two—the depth of the riches of both wisdom and knowledge (as Moffatt, Lenski, and others). The Greek is capable of either interpretation. It may be urged that "riches" is different in quality from "wisdom" and "knowledge"; this favors the second interpretation. But it is countered that we should understand "riches" to refer to God's riches in mercy and grace, which fittingly stand with wisdom and knowledge. In the end either in-

---

142. ὦ here introduces an exclamation (ὤ) rather than an address (ὦ; Paul is not addressing *the depth*), the only place in the New Testament where the term is used in this way. It "leads up to the rhetorical questions in the quotation *vv.* 34f., and ends in the solemn ascription *v.* 36, introduces an act of adoration, thus excluding the possibility that an abstract quantity is being addressed" (BDF 146 [2]).

143. *Depth* is used in Prov. 18:3 (βάθος κακῶν) of "troubles to which there is no bottom". Philo refers to "the depths of knowledge" (*On the Posterity and Exile of Cain* 130), another metaphorical usage. Clearly the term conveys the idea of impressive magnitude.

terpretation is allowable. It is possible to distinguish between *wisdom* and *knowledge* as, for example, Bengel does: *"Wisdom* directs all things to the best end; *knowledge* knows that end and issue."[144] However we understand the two terms, Paul is saying that God has both in fullest excellence. He goes on to speak of God's *judgments* as *unsearchable,* and his *paths* as *beyond tracing out.*[145] *Judgments* ("decisions", GNB) is normally a legal term and is often used of adverse judgments passed on offenders (which would be appropriate in a context dealing with the disobedient). However, it is not confined to the adverse, and in this context where it is in parallel with *paths* or "ways", we should not insist on the meaning "negative judgments". Paul is simply pronouncing on the impossibility of our ever understanding fully what God is doing.

34. Now comes a characteristic quotation from Scripture which seems to have elements from several passages (see Isa. 40:13; Job 15:8; Jer. 23:18; cf. 1 Cor. 2:16). The question "is equivalent to a strong negative" (Brown, p. 425), and it reinforces what Paul has just been saying about the impossibility of created beings fathoming the mind of the Creator. In his reference to *the mind of the Lord* neither noun has the article, and this gives a crisp quality to the question. The impossibility thus disclosed is brought out further with *who has been his counselor?*[146] The term implies great wisdom, perhaps even superior wisdom, on the part of the adviser (who takes advice from one who is clearly inferior?). From another angle Paul is showing the impossibility of our understanding fully all that God is doing.

35. The third rhetorical question changes ground by referring to resources other than intellectual: *Who has ever given to God, that God should repay him?*[147] This is the point made by David in his prayer, "Everything comes from you, and we have given you only what comes from your hand" (1 Chron. 29:14). We have nothing else to give. We cannot place God under obligation; he owes us nothing (cf. Manson, "He can finance his own undertakings").[148] The idea of making an advance to God is completed with *that*

144. Trench notes that there have been "various attempts to divide to each its own proper sphere of meaning." Though differing, they "have this in common, that in all σοφία is recognized as expressing the highest and noblest" (*Synonyms,* p. 281).

145. ἀνεξεραύνητος, here only in the New Testament, derives from alpha-privative, the preposition ἐκ, and ἐραυνάω, "that cannot be searched out", "unsearchable". ἀνεξιχνίαστος (again in the New Testament only in Eph. 3:8) similarly reflects alpha-privative, the preposition ἐξ, and ἴχνος, "a track", "a footstep", and thus points to what cannot be tracked. "The first of these terms describes something that cannot be found by searching for it, while the other suggests footprints that cannot be tracked down" (TH). The combination points to the complete impossibility of any of the human race penetrating the mind of God.

146. σύμβουλος, here only in the New Testament.

147. This is one of the passages in which LXX has apparently misunderstood the Hebrew (or read a different text). Paul cites the words in a form closer to the Hebrew than is LXX; he may have made his own translation.

148. The verb προδίδωμι is found here only in the New Testament (and as a reading in some MSS of Mark 14:10). Its meaning here is "give before", "give in advance".

God should repay him, where the verb has the notion of making a just repayment. No person can ever be in a position where God is required to make a fair requital. That would require an element of equality that is infinitely beyond the capacity of the greatest of the race.

36. Paul closes this paragraph on a note of praise and adoration. His *for* links it up with the preceding and gives a reason for the foregoing. He has a triple prepositional expression that has caused much discussion: *from him and through him and to him.* In the early church this was often taken as a reference to the Trinity, and this has sometimes been accepted in more modern times (as Olshausen). But it is very difficult to see this in the words used (Hendriksen finds the notion "about as unreasonable as anything can be"). *From him* could reasonably be said of the Father and *through him* of the Son (cf. 1 Cor. 8:6), but there is no scriptural justification for seeing *to him* as a reference to the Spirit. In any case Paul seems simply to be speaking of the Godhead without trying to differentiate the Persons. The meaning is nicely expressed in Moffatt's translation "All comes from him, all lives by him, all ends in him." Paul is speaking of God as the Originator, the Sustainer, and the Goal of all creation.[149] *All things*[150] means the totality. It may refer to the universe, the whole of creation, or Paul may be thinking of all things concerning salvation. Either way, the totality belongs to God. He ascribes to God not simply "glory", but "the glory". Supreme glory belongs to God. Paul does not have a verb, but NIV's *be* is probably correct. It would be possible to understand "is", but this is not as suitable in a doxology. *Forever*[151] employs a plural form, "into the ages", which is especially common in doxologies. It emphasizes the idea of eternity. *Amen* is normally the response of a congregation to prayer or praise uttered by a leader and which the congregation thus makes its own. Strictly perhaps it should not be used in a place where a writer is making a point with no congregation to affirm it. But it is so much a part of a doxology (it seems that whenever a speaker uttered a doxology in the early church he could rely on those who heard it to affirm it with their "Amen") that it follows almost automatically.

Cranfield finds a doxology the "natural and fitting conclusion" to the argument. "Paul has certainly not provided neat answers to the baffling questions which arise in connexion with the subject matter of these three chapters. He has certainly not swept away all the difficulties. But, if we have followed him through these chapters with serious and open-minded attentiveness, we may well feel that he has given us enough to enable us to repeat

---

149. Many commentators point out resemblances between these words and statements made by Hellenistic writers and think Paul has picked the expression up from one of them. We should bear in mind Barth's point that Paul is "so much more original" than the postulated source. He says, "Whatever the truth may be about the method of his borrowing, Paul could not have provided the chapter with a more appropriate conclusion."

150. τὰ πάντα.

151. εἰς τοὺς αἰῶνας.

the 'Amen' of his doxology in joyful confidence that the deep mystery which surrounds us is neither a nightmare mystery of meaninglessness nor a dark mystery of arbitrary omnipotence but the mystery which will never turn out to be anything other than the mystery of the altogether good and merciful and faithful God.''

Romans 12

VI. CHRISTIAN LIVING, 12:1–15:13

It is something of a pattern with Paul to begin a letter with a strong doctrinal section and follow this with an exhortation to live out the Christian faith (see Galatians, Colossians, and 1 and 2 Thessalonians; the pattern is not so apparent in Corinthians or Philippians). This is a Pauline distinctive; SH point out that it does not occur in Peter or John. When he uses this pattern Paul is saying that the Christian life is dependent on the great Christian doctrines. Because these things are true, this is the kind of person you should be, is the line of reasoning. In a way we can say that here Paul is still concerned with justification by faith, for it is fundamental to him that the justified man does not live in the same way as the unrepentant sinner. "Faith expressing itself through love" (Gal. 5:6) is the kind of faith of which he has been writing, and he now turns to what he earlier called "the obedience that comes from faith" (1:5). The legalist says something like "Do these things and you will live", but Paul is saying "Live and you will do these things." Only when the power of sin is broken by what God did in Christ can ethical admonitions be effective (and not simply increase sin; Achtemeier makes this point).

This does not mean that Paul makes this a hard-and-fast rule, so that all the doctrine comes in chapters 1–11 and all the ethical teaching from this point on. He has a not inconsiderable amount of such teaching in the earlier part of the letter: "do not let sin reign in your mortal body" (6:12); "we serve in the new way of the Spirit" (7:6); "You . . . are controlled not by the sinful nature but by the Spirit" (8:9), and much more. But there can be no doubt that in these concluding chapters the way Christians live preoccupies the apostle to a far greater extent than in his earlier argument. There is little that is specific to Rome in most of what Paul says in this section, but since he had never been to Rome this is not surprising. He evidently assumes that what applied to Christians generally applied to Roman Christians specifically.[1] Many commentators have pointed out that there is much in these chapters that reminds us of the teachings of Jesus; Paul was carrying on the kind of teaching that

---

1. Foreman points out that Paul had not been to Rome and goes on, "But he knew that in Rome Christians met the same essential problems which they meet everywhere. That is one reason this chapter 12 appeals so strongly to all Christians; just because it is general it speaks to all sorts and conditions of men."

Jesus had committed to his followers. What he says is very practical. As Handley Moule put it, in this part of the epistle the Christian "is told how not to dream, but to serve."

A. THE CHRISTIAN ATTITUDE TO GOD, 12:1-2

> ¹*Therefore, I urge you, brothers, in view of God's mercy, to offer your bodies as living sacrifices, holy and pleasing to God—which is your spiritual worship. ²Do not conform any longer to the pattern of this world, but be transformed by the renewing of your mind. Then you will be able to test and approve what God's will is—his good, pleasing and perfect will.*

Paul begins by making it clear that in view of the wonderful salvation of which he has been writing believers must respond with wholehearted commitment. Being the servants of a God who loves like that means that the whole of life is to be lived in service to God.

1. *Therefore*[2] is an important word. Paul is not writing an essay in abstract ethics, but telling the Romans what their conduct must be in the light of what God has done. We should probably not tie it in too closely to the immediately preceding words (though there is a good sequence of thought), but take it as referring to the whole massive argument that has preceded it.

I urge you is variously understood. The verb[3] can mean "to call alongside, summon" and thus "exhort" or "beseech" or "encourage", and it has other meanings (see BAGD). Some commentators see the word as meaning "implore" (NEB) or the like, to which Cranfield objects that there is a note of authority and we should understand the word in the sense "exhort". Lenski goes so far as to urge "admonish". But Bengel has the succinct comment: "Moses commands: the apostle exhorts." The question is whether there is a decided note of authority or whether Paul is taking a lower profile and simply commending what he regards as desirable modes of conduct. There can be no doubt that Paul is quite capable of taking a strong line and delivering firm instructions when that is called for. But there is no doubt either that he prefers to have people see for themselves what is desirable and do it. It thus seems that something less than a command is what is needed: "beseech" or "urge" is the meaning.[4] The decision is to be that of the Romans; the surrender to God must be completely willing.

---

2. οὖν. Curiously O'Neill says that the conjunction "is certainly not an indication that the saying follows on logically from the previous chapter". But this is an isolated opinion. There is a similar οὖν in Eph. 4:1; Col. 3:1; 1 Thess. 4:1, and a similar break in Gal. 5:1; 2 Thess. 3:6.

3. παρακαλῶ.

4. Griffith Thomas, arguing for "beseech", says, "It is noteworthy that not once in the writings of St Paul do we find him 'commanding' his converts." This will scarcely stand up, for Paul does issue commands; Meinert H. Grumm finds "about thirty-five" of them in this section of the epistle, though only five in chs. 1–11. Grumm extends "imperative" a little, for he finds, e.g., 22 participles with imperatival force. But even so it is clear that Paul does issue commands. Grumm's point is that Paul grounds "all his 'guideline'

Paul adds a note of warmth with his address, *brothers*, and proceeds to appeal to *God's mercy*, though it is not clear how he makes the connection. NIV has *in view of* where KJV has "by".[5] We should probably accept "by". It is on the grounds of the mercies of God that Paul makes his appeal. NIV has *mercy*, though the Greek is plural.[6] An appeal on the basis of mercy comes fittingly after the conclusion of chapter 11, and indeed after the whole of the argument up to this point.[7]

The appeal is that the readers *offer* their *bodies* as *sacrifices*, a suggestion whose force would be more obvious to Paul's first readers than to most modern students. First-century people were familiar with the offering of sacrifices whereas we are not. They had stood by their altar and watched as an animal was identified as their own, as it was slain in the ritual manner, its blood manipulated, and the whole or part of the victim burned on the altar and ascended in the flames to the deity they worshipped. To suggest that they themselves should be sacrifices was a striking piece of imagery. Paul's verb *offer*[8] could be used of offerings of various kinds (it is used, e.g., in 6:13, 16, 19), but it was a technical term for the offering of a sacrifice.

The use of the term *bodies* is interesting, for Paul surely expected Christians to offer to God not only their bodies but their whole selves. Indeed, Leenhardt takes it here to mean "the human person in the concrete manifestation of his life". Many others take up a similar position (NEB, "your very selves"). But we should bear in mind that the body is very important in the Christian understanding of things.[9] Our bodies may be "implements of righteousness" (6:13) and "members of Christ" (1 Cor. 6:15). The body is a temple of the Holy Spirit (1 Cor. 6:19); Paul can speak of being "holy both in body and in spirit" (1 Cor. 7:34). He knows that there are possibilities of evil in the body but that in the believer "the body of sin" has been brought to nothing (6:6); sin

---

imperatives in the impelling indicative of who and what they are in Christ by the act of God" (ET, 93 [1981-82], pp. 239-42).

5. διὰ τῶν οἰκτιρμῶν τοῦ θεοῦ. διά with the genitive commonly denotes "means, instrument, agency", but here BAGD class it "in urgent requests" and translate "by the mercy of God". Moule says "the dividing line between 'accompaniment' and 'instrumentality' is thin", and suggests "in God's mercies' name" (IBNTG, pp. 57, 58). BDF say "Idiomatically with urgent questions = 'by'" (223 [4]), and Turner also sees the meaning as "by" (M, III, p. 267).

6. οἰκτιρμῶν. In the New Testament the word is in the plural in four of its five occurrences, which may be meant to express the thought of many acts of mercy or may be due to nothing more than assimilation to the Hebrew רַחֲמִים. Paul has it four times, but no more than once in any one epistle.

7. Cf. Barrett, "'the mercies of God' forms a not inadequate summary of what is contained in chs. i–xi, and especially in chs. ix–xi".

8. παρίστημι. The aorist infinitive points to decisive action.

9. Does any other religion put such an emphasis on the body? Cf. NBCR, "The Christian view of the body as sacred and as the servant of the soul is unique among the religions of the world, Judaism excepted." Certainly the Greeks of the first century stressed the importance of the soul and regarded the body lightly. We see something of the same attitude in modern times when the excuse is offered for someone who has sinned with his body: "But his heart is in the right place!"

does not reign in the believer's body (6:12). Grace affects the whole of life and is not some remote, ethereal affair.

Many translators do as NIV and speak of *living sacrifices*, qualifying this with *holy and pleasing to God*, but the Greek speaks of a sacrifice and follows the word with three qualifiers; in other words, *living* is not separated from *holy* and *pleasing to God*. *Living* marks a difference from the general run of sacrifices. It is true that animal victims were living when they were brought to the altar (a dead animal could not be brought for sacrifice), but as offered they were dead. Paul can speak of believers as dying to sin (6:2), but his emphasis is on the glorious life they now live with Christ (6:8); they are "alive from the dead" (6:13). As offered they are alive. The sacrifice of which Paul writes demands not the destruction but the full energy of life. It is positive and dynamic. This sacrifice is also *holy*, which we understand as "consecrated" (Moffatt) or "dedicated" (NEB). It is given over entirely to God; the believer is his alone. Further, it is *pleasing to God*.[10]

This, Paul says, *is your spiritual worship*, an expression that could be understood as KJV, "your reasonable service." There are problems relating to both adjective and noun.[11] Today most interpreters understand the adjective as *spiritual*, which makes good sense and is certainly in mind. But it is hard to think that the connection with "reason" has been completely lost, and there is something to be said for "intelligent worship" (Phillips) or JB's "that is worthy of thinking beings". In any case it is a striking word to use in connection with the offering of the body. The noun may be understood of service in general or of the particular service rendered in the act of worship. Harrison sees "service" as having the advantage that it "covers the entire range of the Christian's life and activity." But in the end we are left with the fact that Paul has used two words, both of which are ambiguous. We cannot feel confident that either "spiritual" or "rational" is absent from the adjective or that "worship" or "service" is lacking in the noun. There is a "rich complexity" (Leenhardt) in the expression.[12]

2. With this positive attitude toward God Paul links a negative attitude to *the pattern of this world* (he has negatives also in vv. 3, 14, 16, 19, and 21; there are things the Christian must avoid as well as things to do). Cranfield argues

---

10. εὐάρεστος is used by Paul in eight of its nine New Testament occurrences. It always refers to what is pleasing to God (except in Tit. 2:9). Luther comments here: "He says this by way of criticizing the vainglory and pride that commonly undermine the good. For just as envy doggedly pursues somebody else's happiness, so pride and vainglory dog one's own."

11. λογικός (again in the New Testament only in 1 Pet. 2:2) derives from λόγος and frequently has the meaning "rational", "reasonable". But Michel points out that it was often used in Hellenistic literature for the spiritual thanksgiving that replaced animal sacrifices. Bruce holds that there is a contrast here with "the externalities of Israel's temple cult." λατρεία may mean either "service" or "worship"; both are appropriate in response to the deity. It may be distinguished from δουλεία in that it is voluntary.

12. On the accusative case Moule comments, "When a word or phrase is flung loosely into apposition with a whole sentence it is (or, where the form is ambiguous, may be assumed to be) in the Accusative" (IBNTG, pp. 35-36).

strongly that there is no great difference in meaning between the two verbs NIV translates *conform* and *be transformed*, though he notes that many commentators do see a difference. Hendriksen has a long note in opposition to Cranfield's position.[13] There can be little doubt that the two verbs are not synonyms and that there is a basic difference between outward conformity and inward transformation.[14] Those who object to making the difference too sharp have this going for them, that "conformity to this age is no superficial matter" (Barrett). But while this should be granted, it is still the case that Paul is looking for a transformation at the deepest level that is infinitely more significant than the conformity to the world's pattern that is distinctive of so many lives. The word for *world* is often translated "age";[15] there is a temporal force to it, and Leenhardt can say, "what madness it is to join in this puppet show which is displayed on a tottering stage".[16] Christians have been introduced into the life of the world to come; what a tragedy, then, if they conform to the perishing world they have left.

The transformation is to take place *by the renewing of your mind*.[17] The believer, whose life is that of the new age, does not think like an unbeliever. The reference to the mind is important. Paul does not envisage a mindless emotionalism, but a deeply intelligent approach to life, as characteristic of the Christian who has been renewed by the Holy Spirit. The term *mind* is not confined to intellectual pursuits (it includes an important moral element), but it certainly embraces them.[18] The force of the present tense should not be overlooked; Paul envisages a continuing process of renewal.[19]

---

13. *Conform* renders συσχηματίζεσθε and *be transformed* μεταμορφοῦσθε. The former is said to concern the σχῆμα, the outward form, and μορφή the essential being. Harrisville sees the difference this way: "'Conform' refers to a posture or attitude which may be changed at will, whereas 'form' at the heart of 'transformed' refers to what grows out of necessity from an inward condition." Käsemann puts it neatly: "συσχηματίζεσθε is the adaptation while μεταμορφοῦσθαι . . . is the transformation" (p. 329). There is some textual evidence for the infinitive rather than the imperative, but both the MS evidence and the sense of the passage favor the imperative.

14. The strong adversative ἀλλά points to a real contrast.

15. αἰών. Parry comments on τῷ αἰῶνι τούτῳ, "The phrase always implies contrast to ὁ αἰὼν ὁ μέλλων, even when the latter is not expressed" (CGT). It is the present age in contrast with that to come.

16. Cf. J. Behm, "Redeemed by Christ, Christians no longer stand in this aeon but in the coming aeon (Gl. 1:4). In conduct, then, they must not follow the forms of life in this aeon but the very different form of life in the coming aeon" (TDNT, IV, p. 759).

17. ἀνακαίνωσις is "not quotable outside Christian lit." (BAGD). In the New Testament it occurs again only in Tit. 3:5, referring to "the renewal of the Holy Spirit". It may be significant that the word relates to καινός rather than νέος. AS speaks of νέος as "the new primarily in reference to time, the young, recent; κ . . . the new primarily in reference to quality, the fresh, unworn". Moule takes the dative as instrumental (IBNTG, p. 44).

18. Cf. J. Behm, νοῦς "expresses the inner orientation or moral attitude, whether of the natural man or of the Christian. . . . In the νοῦς of Christians, i.e., in the inner direction of their thought and will and the orientation of their moral consciousness, there should be constant renewal, R. 12:2" (TDNT, IV, p. 958).

19. Parry contrasts the early Christians with their contemporaries: "The youthful joy and vigour of Christians was the constant wonder of observers. The word brings out

The purpose (Cranfield) or the result (Lenski)[20] of this is not so much that *you will be able to test* (as NIV) as that "you will test"; the renewal gives more than a possibility. NIV has rendered the one Greek verb by *test and approve*, which is a good solution of a difficult translation problem.[21] The word here will include *test*, for Paul is not advocating an uncritical approval, but it will also include *approve*, for more than the process of testing is in mind. Indeed, there is probably more than approving, for Paul is really saying not only that the Romans would find out that God's will is good, but that having found out, they should put it into practice. He is arguing for the spiritual discernment that ascertains what God wants us to do and then sets itself to do it.

NIV takes three adjectives that Paul uses and applies them directly to God's will, speaking of *his good, pleasing and perfect will*. But this may not be the best way of taking the Greek.[22] It is tautology to say that God's will is pleasing to God. We should rather see the three adjectives preceded by the article as meaning "the thing that is good and pleasing and perfect." It is that which is the will of God. "The Christian has received the ability to prove what God's will is in the concrete situation" (Nygren). The renewal of the mind enables the believer to discern what is good, what is pleasing to God, and what is perfect.[23] And having discerned it, that same renewal sets him to the task of performing what is seen as the will of God.

B. THE CHRISTIAN ATTITUDE TO OTHER CHRISTIANS, 12:3-16

Paul turns to the kind of conduct that should characterize Christians in their relations with other believers. It was just as easy for them as it has been for Christians through the centuries to have wrong ideas about themselves and those they meet and to fail in their Christian performance accordingly. The apostle proceeds to some considerations that Christians should always have in mind. He refers to the way believers should act towards other Christians, then somewhere along the way goes on to the way they should behave towards those outside. I have made the break at the end of verse 16, but others prefer to make it at the end of verse 13. That is quite possible, and indeed the whole section is somewhat loosely structured as Paul moves from one topic to another. As long as we do not insist too rigidly on our way of following the apostle's thought, not much hinges on where we end our section.

---

vividly the contrast with the prevailing pessimism of contemporary thought. The effect of the Spirit is fresh vitality and a true direction of the mind" (CGT).

20. εἰς τό with infinitive; for this construction see the note on 1:20.

21. δοκιμάζω means first "test", "prove", but then "approve as a result of testing".

22. τὸ θέλημα τοῦ θεοῦ, τὸ ἀγαθὸν καὶ εὐάρεστον καὶ τέλειον. It is better to see the three adjectives as forming an appositional expression than as directly qualifying θέλημα.

23. Cranfield reminds us that it does not necessarily mean "something manageable and achievable".

1. *Humility, 12:3*

>[3] *For by the grace given me I say to every one of you: Do not think of yourself more highly than you ought, but rather think of yourself with sober judgment, in accordance with the measure of faith God has given you.*

3. There is a tendency to make this and the following verses refer to people holding official positions in the church (thus Brown regards vv. 3-8 as "a directory to the gifted office-bearers of the Church" [p. 429]). This is probably misguided, for we know little about what offices existed in the church at the time Paul wrote, and in any case he puts what he says in very general terms. Since a good deal of it applies to all believers, there is no reason to think that he was referring to office-bearers as such.[24]

For[25] . . . *I say* leads into a series of directives that spell out the implications of what Paul has just said.[26] He is an apostle and therefore a teacher. So he exhorts *by the grace given* him (cf. 1:5; Eph. 3:8).[27] It is interesting that at the beginning of the chapter he made an appeal, whereas now he enjoins by virtue of his apostolic authority. *Grace* will refer to the grace of apostleship, but it should probably not be confined to that. Paul had many gifts of grace, and he is surely including them all as justifying him in the line he is now taking. He addresses his words solemnly to *every one of you*. Each of the Roman Christians has a gift and therefore a responsibility. With a complex play on words[28] Paul makes a powerful exhortation to humility. His first infinitive (the verb occurs here only in the New Testament) conveys the idea of thinking of oneself *more highly than* one *ought*.[29] This is a natural human tendency. As Denney puts it, "To himself, every man is in a sense the most important person in the world, and it always needs much grace to see what other people are, and to keep a sense of moral proportion." Rather, it is important to think of oneself *with sober judgment*[30] (Moffatt, "take a sane view of himself").

24. Cf. Hunter, "N.B. There is nothing 'official' here: all ministry is a function of membership in the Body, and each Christian has the function of ministry in some degree."

25. γάρ links this to the preceding section as its consequence.

26. BAGD note the use of λέγω with dative of person and with a following infinitive in the sense "*order, command, direct, enjoin, recommend* more or less emphatically" (II.1.c).

27. διά is used in a different sense from that in v. 1, though we may still translate "by": the meaning here is "by virtue of" (BDF 223 [4]). The aorist δοθείσης seems to point to a definite, decisive gift rather than the continuing manifestation (though that, too, is a reality).

28. ὑπερφρονεῖν . . . φρονεῖν . . . φρονεῖν . . . σωφρονεῖν, "which might almost be called flowery" (BDF 488 [1b]).

29. Actually he says something a little stronger; it is more highly than one *must* (δεῖ). Paul sees humility not merely as desirable but as necessary for the true Christian. Shedd points out that "The pagan ethic is vitiated, even in its best form as seen in the Platonic philosophy, and still more in the Stoic, by egotism, or the disposition ὑπερφρονεῖν παρ' ὃ δεῖ φρονεῖν."

30. εἰς τὸ σωφρονεῖν, where εἰς τό may be used to convey the idea of purpose (M, III, p. 143) or of result (MT, 411). Moule says, "perhaps *to adopt an outlook which tends to*

Paul proceeds to the thought that this is to be done *in accordance with the measure of faith God has given*. NIV omits "to each" with which this clause starts, but it is important. Paul is not speaking only about great leaders, but about all the Romans. "To each" God has given faith as the measure.[31] Without faith none of the gifts can be exercised, and faith is the standard whereby they are to be estimated. If we take this with full seriousness, seeing God as the sole author of the gifts and ourselves as totally dependent on him for them all, it is unlikely that we will be arrogant. Humility proceeds from genuine faith. There is another thought here. When we see that God is the giver of all the gifts and that faith is the measure, we will not deny our own gifts either. Being sober-minded means recognizing what God has given us and being zealous in its use as well as humble.

2. Difference of Function, 12:4-8

4Just as each of us has one body with many members, and these members do not all have the same function, 5so in Christ we who are many form one body, and each member belongs to all the others. 6We have different gifts, according to the grace given us. If a man's gift is prophesying, let him use it in proportion to his faith. 7If it is serving, let him serve; if it is teaching, let him teach; 8if it is encouraging, let him encourage; if it is contributing to the needs of others, let him give generously; if it is leadership, let him govern diligently; if it is showing mercy, let him do it cheerfully.

The church is likened to one body with its multiplicity of members a number of times (e.g., 1 Cor. 10:17; 12:12-30; Eph. 1:23; 4:4-16; 5:23-30; Col. 1:18, 24; 2:19; 3:15). Evidently the thought of the basic unity underlying considerable diversity made a deep appeal. Paul also has lists of "gifts" in the church in other places (1 Cor. 12:4-11, 28-30; Eph. 4:7-11; cf. also 1 Cor. 14). Here his point is that different members of the church have different gifts, all of which have their place. Each should use whatever gift he has to the full.

4. That there be unity of Christians in the church *just as*[32] there is unity in the members of the physical body matters a great deal to Paul. Clearly he found the illustration of the human body a very useful and convenient one. Here his point is that it takes many members to make up the body, but they do

---

sobriety" (IBNTG, p. 70). σωφρονέω means "be of sound mind", which may refer to mental health (Mark 5:15) or to being sensible. U. Luck says that here Paul "is using the term in its classical sense: 'to observe the proper measure,' 'not to transgress the set laws'. . . . But Paul defines this measure as the μέτρον πίστεως which God gives and which is exhibited in integration into the community and concrete service within it" (TDNT, VII, p. 1102).

31. μέτρον means a measuring instrument or standard, not a measured quantity as many translations have it. Cranfield has a detailed examination of this passage (NTS, VIII [1961-62], pp. 345-51). He concludes that it means "a standard (by which to measure himself), namely (his) Christian faith" (p. 351).

32. καθάπερ. See the note on 4:6.

not all have the same function.[33] Our physical body is certainly a unit, with all the members contributing to the good of the whole. But equally certainly a wide variety of function goes into making up that one body.

5. In the same way[34] we the many are one body in Christ. Paul does not speak of "the body of Christ" as in Ephesians and Colossians, but of "one body in Christ" ("one body in union with Christ", GNB).[35] There the point is the headship of Christ, here that of the unity of the members of the body for all their diversity, a unity brought about by the fact that they are all in Christ, a unity that does not reduce them all to a drab uniformity. And there is interdependence, for *each member belongs to all the others.*[36] The interrelatedness of Christians is important; Paul does not say "members of one body" but "members of one another" (cf. Eph. 4:25). We should also bear in mind that "members" has no meaning apart from the body; one cannot be a "member" of nothing.[37]

6. We now come up against another of Paul's difficult pieces of grammar. It is possible to take the opening of this verse as a continuation of the sentence in the previous verses, for *we have* is really a participle, "having", and there is no main verb following. But it is generally agreed that it is more likely that we have a new sentence here[38] and that Paul wants us to supply the verb. This may be in the indicative (*We have different gifts,* NIV), but it is more usual to see an imperative as needed ("Having gifts, let us . . .", RSV etc.). *Gifts* introduces a characteristic Pauline concept.[39] It may refer to special gifts of the Spirit like tongues, or it may be used of divine endowments generally,

---

33. πρᾶξις, from πράσσω = "do". Paul uses the word three times (it is the word used in the title of "The Acts of the Apostles").

34. οὕτως.

35. "The meaning of 'we are one body in Christ' appears to be that Christians owe their organic unity with one another to the fact that they are 'in Christ'—incorporated in him. Thus, it is not, strictly speaking, that Christ is here identified with the body. Rather, Paul is saying that, if the congregation finds itself to be an organic unity like a well coordinated living body, this is because of its connexion with Christ" (C. F. D. Moule, *The Origin of Christology* [Cambridge, 1977], p. 72).

36. τὸ δὲ καθ᾽ εἷς is a curious expression. τὸ δέ (not ὁ δέ) "may be taken as an adverbial phrase: *relatively to,* or better, as a pronoun, in the sense: '*and that,* as members of of one another'" (Godet). κατά appears to be an adverb rather than a preposition governing the nominative εἷς. It may be that καθ᾽ εἷς comes from the distributive use of κατά and that the expression καθ᾽ ἕνα ἕκαστον became fixed as καθένα ἕκαστον, from which a corresponding nominative developed. "Yet not many examples of this vulgarism are found in the N.T." (BDF 305; they give the meaning as "individually, with relation to each individual"). On the similar expression in Mark 14:10 Moule asks, "Is (this) an *adverbial* use, or sheer bad grammar?" (IBNTG, p. 60). See also M, I, p. 105; III, p. 198.

37. Käsemann makes the further point that "The gift is a charisma only as service to the brother" (p. 339).

38. This is supported (though not proved) by the use of δέ, which may well be the transition to a new sentence (so SH, Shedd).

39. The word χάρισμα is used in Paul in 16 of its 17 New Testament occurrences. It is "a rare and late word" (H. Conzelmann, TDNT, IX, p. 402), and Paul may well have been the first to use it in the sense of the special gifts the Spirit gave to the church. See further the note on 1:11.

which appears to be the meaning here. *Different*[40] brings out the truth that God does not make Christians into a collection of uniform automata. They differ from one another both in their native endowments and also in the gifts that God gives them through the Spirit. The differences are not arbitrary but *according to the grace given us*. The thought of grace persists. The apostle is not writing about some human excellence. And *given* is important.[41] It is not a matter of the believer making an earnest effort in order to produce some spectacular result in Christian character or achievement, but something God has given.

The first of the gifts Paul considers is prophecy,[42] which accords with the high esteem in which it was held in the early church generally. It is second only to the apostolate in lists which rank gifts in order of importance (e.g., 1 Cor. 12:28), and the church is built on the foundation of the apostles and prophets (Eph. 2:20). Nobody in the New Testament explains precisely what this gift was, but it appears to mean that there were people who had the gift of passing on direct words from God. They were people who could say "Thus says the Lord."[43] There is an extended treatment of prophecy in 1 Corinthians 14, still without a definition. It is common to supply an imperative here ("whether prophecy, let us prophesy . . .", KJV), though some prefer an indicative ("we should do it", GNB).[44]

The prophet is to do this *in proportion to his faith,* an expression that has been variously interpreted.[45] It looks as though the prophet, a man or woman of faith, is to speak in accordance with that faith; personal faith which puts the prophet into immediate touch with God dictates what is to be said. The warning, on this view, is against continuing to speak "when he has nothing further to say that is inspired by the Spirit" (Leenhardt). But against allowing the prophet to "judge himself by his own faith" it is urged that this "would open the gates to every abuse and even false teaching" (Käsemann, p. 341). It is pointed out that *faith* here has the article, "the faith", and the suggestion accordingly is made that the prophet is to prophesy in accordance with the

---

40. διάφορος can have the meaning "excelling, excellent", but here it has rather the primary meaning of "different".

41. The aorist δοθεῖσαν properly signifies a gift made at a point of time, perhaps at conversion.

42. εἴτε . . . εἴτε, "if . . . if", or "whether . . . or", is used by Paul without a verb again in 1 Cor. 3:22; 2 Cor. 5:10, etc. BDF see the sense of it as much the same as καὶ . . . καί (454 [3]).

43. Goodspeed translates "preaching", but the term seems to mean more than that. Wilckens suggests "the gift of inspired preaching", and alluding to 1 Cor. 14:3 he sees it as οἰκοδομή, παράκλησις, and παραμυθία.

44. Cf. Cranfield, "These verses indicate the unselfconscious, business-like, sober way in which Christians who do measure themselves by the standard which God has given them in their faith will give themselves to the fulfilment of the tasks apportioned to them by the χαρίσματα they have received".

45. ἀναλογία, here only in the New Testament, means primarily "mathematical proportion" (LSJ). G. Kittel sees ἀνάλογος as "corresponding to λόγος. . . . Hence ἀναλογία, the 'correspondence of a right relationship,' or 'proportion'" (TDNT, I, p. 347).

faith, the general Christian position. Advocates of both positions argue their case with some fierceness. On the one hand are those who maintain that it is nonsense to speak of an official check on a charismatic gift; a "charisma" by definition needs no "official" authorization. On the other are those who say that if there is no check the way is wide open for any heresy to be introduced; all a man has to do is claim that he is a prophet. Perhaps what decides the point is the way prophecy was in fact practised. Paul tells us that two or three would prophesy and "the others should weigh carefully what is said" (1 Cor. 14:29). It is clear that the early church was well aware of the danger of false prophets (Matt. 24:11, 24); there must be a testing of the spirits (1 John 4:1-6). It is some such process of which Paul appears to be speaking here.

7. Paul moves to *serving*, a very general term[46] which became the normal New Testament word for the service Christians perform, but which was also used of the service of the deacon. Some see an official function here; Wilson, for example, says, " 'Ministry' may refer either to the ministry of the word or to the office of a deacon." But this is surely to make too specific a very general word. The same criticism should be made of translations like "administration" (JB); as far as our information goes, the early church had very little administration, and in any case a "charismatic administration" is pretty close to a contradiction in terms. Chrysostom has a wiser comment, "every spiritual work is a ministry." Elsewhere Paul tells us that there are "different kinds of service" (1 Cor. 12:5; the same Greek word), which should put us on our guard against a too precise identification of the gift. It seems that Paul is simply moving on from prophecy. It is not given to all to prophesy. If anyone is not given that great gift but is given the more humdrum gift of being able to serve in a lowly place, then he should not sigh for what he does not have but use the gift God has given him. And the ability to do lowly service well is a gift. Many quite brilliant people seem constitutionally unable to perform lowly service well. There is a lot of lowly service to be done, and anyone who has the gift of doing it should rejoice at the wonder of divine grace.

Next we come to *teaching*.[47] The teacher is to be about his work. In the early church with its fewness of books and with most of its members having little or no education the place of the teacher must have been very important. There was no question of the ordinary church member learning about the faith by reading many books at home. He learned from what the teachers had to say. We do not wonder that Paul makes much of this gift.

8. Paul continues with his participles, going on to *encouraging*.[48] The exact meaning of this verb is uncertain (see on v. 1). It may mean "exhorting" (as many think) or "consoling", but there is a good deal to be said for NIV.

---

46. διακονία was originally the service of a table waiter, but came to mean lowly service of any kind.

47. Paul changes his construction from the nouns "prophecy" and "serving" to the participle "the teaching one", "he who teaches". SH suggest that "teaching" might refer to the one receiving instruction; the change in construction removes ambiguity.

48. ὁ παρακαλῶν.

Luther comments, "The teacher transmits knowledge; the exhorter stimulates", and however we translate, something like this is in mind. For many people in the early church life was a pretty grim affair; there must have been a continuing need for people who could encourage others, and it is interesting to find that there were people who had a gift for this sort of thing.

Contributing to the needs of others says a little more than the Greek does. Paul's participle means no more than "he who imparts", and there are those who think that the apostle is referring to "the deacons who are charged with the distribution of the public property of the Church" (Calvin). But this is probably to make the gift more of an office in the church and, as we have seen, this is an unlikely reading of the list. NIV is probably correct. There must have been many poor people in the church of the time, and Paul is speaking to those who had the gift of coming to the assistance of the poor. They should do this, he says, *generously*.[49] NIV may be correct (many favor the meaning "generously"), but perhaps something like "single-mindedly" is the idea. The giver should not have other motives, like the desire to be well thought of. Giving is concerned with the need of the other person only.

Leadership is a general term which neatly reflects Paul's word.[50] As elsewhere in this list, some have made the term specific and understood it to mean "elder" or "president". The term comes between one that refers to giving and another that refers to being merciful, which leads some to the idea that what is meant is the administrator of the congregation's charitable work. All such suggestions seem to be going beyond what the term implies in this context. It is better to let it remain general, "he who leads".[51] Leadership is to be exercised "with diligence" or "eagerness".[52] The leader must not be slack, but do his work well. If he does not, then all the followers are affected. The leader's work is very important.

So is that of *showing mercy*.[53] The general thrust of the participle is clear, but the precise application is not so plain. Since mercy is necessarily shown to those in difficulty of some sort, we may well assume that Paul is referring to the sick, the suffering, the indigent, and the like. And he says that mercy should be shown *cheerfully*.[54] The word clearly points to something far from a grim determination to get through an unpleasant task. The person who has

49. ἐν ἁπλότητι, where the noun means "singleness", "simplicity". Cranfield approves the view of Althaus, "the simplicity, which without ulterior motives is wholly directed toward the other person's need". Notice that from this point on the nouns following the participles lack the article "in a perhaps *adverbial* use" (IBNTG, p. 114).

50. ὁ προϊστάμενος, a verb which is used of leadership of many kinds.

51. RSV has "he who gives aid", but this is surely the wrong sense.

52. σπουδή has the meanings "1. haste, 2. zeal, diligence, earnestness" (so AS). "Haste" is not suitable here, but any of the other meanings is possible.

53. The verb ἐλεέω occurs nine times in Romans, the most in any one book in the New Testament. Paul uses it 14 times altogether.

54. ἐν ἱλαρότητι, a noun found here only in the New Testament. We get our word "hilarity" from it.

this gift is to be "radiant with joy" (Lyonnet, quoted in Leenhardt). Mercy is not a grim duty but a joy and a delight.

3. Love of the Brothers, 12:9-10

9Love must be sincere. Hate what is evil; cling to what is good. 10Be devoted to one another in brotherly love. Honor one another above yourselves.

9. At this point Paul moves from the charismatic gifts, functions exercised by individuals, to virtues he expects to see in all believers. Characteristically he begins with love. At the beginning of 1 Corinthians 13 he passes from the topic of "spiritual gifts" to that of love, and in Galatians 5:22 he puts "love" first in his list of the fruit of the Spirit. In similar strain he passes here from the "gifts" to the love that should characterize Christians. Perhaps we can say that what follows is little more than a spelling out of what love means. Wilckens sees Paul as saying that in all the conduct of the Christian, "inside and outside the church, the one foundation and criterion is: love."[55] It is clear from the emphasis Paul gives to love throughout his writings that he saw it as particularly important, both the love of God in Christ that brought our salvation (5:8) and the loving response that sinners make when they become believers.[56] Since he has no verb here, we could understand him to say "Love is without hypocrisy". This would be a worthwhile affirmation about love, but it is not easy to fit into what follows. It is better to understand an imperative, as throughout this section: "Let love be without hypocrisy."[57] There must have been a temptation for imperfectly instructed Christians to claim virtues they did not have. But the New Testament writers consistently look for sincerity, especially when it is a question of love. Love was the basis of their salvation as well as in the forefront of the life they were expected to live.[58]

Yet another change of construction brings us the participle, best under-

---

55. Käsemann denies that vv. 9-21 should be "put under the theme of love" (p. 343); he thinks that rather "the manifold charismatic ministry of Christians is also described in vv. 9-21" (p. 344). This is an interesting view, but he fails to substantiate it. In contrast to the preceding nouns, ἀγάπη and the following nouns have the definite article "as virtues assumed to be well known" (BDF 258 [1]). Moule detects "a remarkable series of articles" in vv. 10-13, but compares Heb. 12:18-24 for "an equally striking series of omissions" (IBNTG, p. 114).

56. For a fuller treatment of the Christian view of love may I refer to my *Testaments of Love* (Grand Rapids, 1981).

57. ἀνυπόκριτος. The word is used of love again in 2 Cor. 6:6, of brotherly love in 1 Pet. 1:22, of faith in 1 Tim. 1:5; 2 Tim. 1:5, and of wisdom in Jas. 3:17. Wilckens says, "In the NT ἀνυπόκριτος is a fixed attribute of ἀγάπη in the hortatory tradition of Hellenistic Christianity" (TDNT, VIII, p. 570). The word is not found often before the New Testament, and it appears very rarely in profane writers.

58. It is perhaps worth noticing that Ignatius, writing to the Roman church early in the second century, greeted the Romans as "preeminent in love"; the seed Paul sowed fell into good ground.

stood as used in the sense of the imperative.[59] *Hate what is evil*, writes Paul, where his verb is a strong one, expressing utter abhorrence of the evil thing (cf. KJV, "abhor").[60] We should be clear that love is quite different from sentimentality. True love involves a deep hatred for all that is evil, for evil can never benefit the beloved. There will be a special hatred for the evil in the beloved and the evil that touches the beloved, but Paul's expression is general. He is saying that the person who really loves with the deep fervor of Christian *agapē* will have a holy hatred for every evil thing.

With this is joined *cling to what is good*, where there is another picturesque verb.[61] It can mean "to glue", though this use does not occur in the New Testament. But it indicates that the tie it denotes is of the closest sort. The Christian's attachment to the good is a very firm tie, and not a casual approval. The Christian is committed to the way of goodness; his whole life is wrapped up in it ("glued" to it).

10. Paul proceeds to use two compound words to convey the idea of the love that unites Christian people. The first is that rendered *brotherly love*,[62] a concept that appears to be unique to the Christians. The Jews had the idea that they were all brothers, a concept that the Christians took over and applied to themselves, as we have seen. It might also be used by such groups as the Essenes, and there are examples of its use for fellow countrymen, for members of a religious society, and even for friends (see TDNT, I, p. 146). But the idea of *brotherly love* in such groups is not found anywhere but among the Christians.[63] They saw themselves as a family in a special sense. God was their Father and they were all brothers and sisters. Therefore they were united in a love that other people saw only in those of a natural family.

59. Moulton speaks of the papyri as establishing "beyond question" the use of the participle among "substitutes for the imperative"; he sees us as "absolved from inventing an anacoluthon, or some other grammatical device when we come to such a passage as Rom. 12:9-19" (M, I, p. 180). Moule also takes the construction as an imperative use of the participle and regards the construction as Semitic (IBNTG, p. 179). So also BDF, "Paul considered the descriptive ptcp. to be the equivalent of the impera." (468 [2]). Turner, however, says, "as ἐστέ (imperat.) never occurs in NT we must presume that it is understood as a copula with all these ptcs., which therefore do not constitute an anacoluthon" (M, III, p. 343). Robertson affirms that "the participle in itself is never imperative nor indicative" (p. 1133). In view of Semitic usage, however, it seems that we should regard this as an imperative construction. In vv. 10-21 Parry notes "the remarkable coordination of participles, adjectives, infinitives (15), and imperatives. All should be translated by the imperative. . . . The participles are all durative in action, implying habits" (CGT).

60. ἀποστυγοῦντες. Chrysostom points out that the ἀπό is intensive, and SH comment, "the word expresses a strong feeling of horror; the ἀπο- by farther emphasizing the idea of separation gives an intensive force, which is heightened by contrast with κολλώμενοι."

61. κολλάω.

62. φιλαδελφία. This is the first of nine datives, each of which comes first in its clause with some emphasis, and has a meaning like "as regards", "with respect to".

63. "There are no examples of this more general use of φιλαδελφία and φιλάδελφος outside Christian writings" (H. F. von Soden, TDNT, I, p. 146). In other writings it refers to the love of physical brothers and sisters.

This is further brought out with the adjective NIV renders *Be devoted*.[64] The adjective is used with imperatival force, as are other terms in this sequence (as most translations render it).[65] KJV has "Be kindly affectioned", where "kindly" is used in its original sense, "referring to kin". It is a family word. Paul is underlining the truth that Christians are members of one family and that accordingly they should have a warm and fervent love for one another. They should be a family not only in a formal sense, but in a sense that is marked by a love not seen elsewhere. Paul has spoken of a love for all that should be characteristic of Christians (v. 9), but that does not preclude special affection for those within the family.

NIV translates a very difficult expression *Honor one another above yourselves*. The trouble here is that the verb is used in a way that is difficult to find elsewhere, which makes us uncertain of the precise meaning.[66] The alternatives appear to be "be eager to show respect for one another" (GNB) and "let each man consider the other worthy of more honor than himself" (TH). Following on the references to love within the Christian family there can be no doubt that Paul is telling the Romans not to push for first place for themselves; they are to seek honor for one another rather than for themselves. At the same time we must bear in mind that he has just condemned the love that is hypocritical (v. 9), so we must beware of interpretations which imply that the gifted believer affirms that the less gifted are superior to himself. Paul is not advocating hypocrisy but humility, and that love which eagerly seeks out and rejoices in and honors the good qualities in other believers.[67]

---

64. φιλόστοργοι. The word is a compound of φιλο-, "love", and στοργή, "natural affection", "family love". It means the love that unites members of a family. It occurs here only in the New Testament.

65. It would be possible to understand ἐστέ here, but Moule notes "how simple adjectives are sometimes imperatively used". He cites Ignatius *Eph.* 10:2 as well as *Rom.* 12:10, 11, and proceeds, "This is a usage closely akin to the use of the participle just illustrated" (IBNTG, p. 180). He thinks this may be a Semitism.

66. προηγέομαι means "*go before* and show the way τινός (*to someone*)"; the versions have the meaning "*try to outdo one another in showing respect*", while another possibility is "*as far as honor is concerned, let each one esteem the other more highly* than himself" (BAGD). The difficulty is that while the first meaning suits the context here, the case is accusative, not genitive, whereas "esteeming the other more highly" is a meaning that does not seem well attested. BDF include the verb among those which "otherwise intransitive may be rendered transitive by a preposition in composition"; they see the meaning as "'preferring' (not 'outdoing')" (150).

67. Hendriksen finds grounds for humility in the fact that "A Christian knows that his own motives are not always pure and holy (I Cor. 11:28, 31)." He goes on, "This is a kind of knowledge which at times causes him to utter the prayer, 'O Lord, forgive my good deeds.' On the other hand, the Christian has no right to regard as evil the motives of his brothers and sisters in the Lord." The only other place in the New Testament where the word occurs is in several MSS of Phil. 2:3 where again Paul is counselling humility and esteem for fellow believers.

4. Some Practical Advice, 12:11-16

> 11Never be lacking in zeal, but keep your spiritual fervor, serving the Lord. 12Be joyful in hope, patient in affliction, faithful in prayer. 13Share with God's people who are in need. Practice hospitality.
>
> 14Bless those who persecute you; bless and do not curse. 15Rejoice with those who rejoice; mourn with those who mourn. 16Live in harmony with one another. Do not be proud, but be willing to associate with people of low position.a Do not be conceited.

a16 Or willing to do menial work

11. Zeal translates a word that combines the ideas of haste and diligence.68 It is an important aspect of the Christian's commitment. Never be lacking is another use of the adjective in the sense of an imperative,69 but be lacking does not give the sense as well as "do not be lazy" (GNB). The word signifies "indolent" or "lazy", and Paul is telling the Romans that where zeal is needed they must not be lazy people.

But keep your spiritual fervor is perhaps not the best translation. There is nothing in the Greek corresponding to NIV's but; Paul has a long series of these injunctions with no connective, and we lose something of the flavor with such insertions. And his imperative is something like "with respect to the spirit, boiling." It is not easy to determine whether we should spell the noun with a capital letter (to refer to the Holy Spirit) or with a small letter (to refer to the human spirit). Great names can be cited to support either view, and it is difficult to see a convincing reason for excluding either. There is much to be said for the view of Leenhardt: "the spirit of man, of course, when filled and aglow with the Spirit of God" (cf. Käsemann, "according to Rev 3:15 lukewarmness is the worst offence. If nothing burns, there can be no light" [p. 346]). It is important that the human spirit be on fire, but Paul is not referring to something that occurs by some natural process but as a result of the indwelling Spirit of God.70

---

68. σπουδή. We see haste in its use in Luke 1:39, diligence in v. 8 (where see note). Here G. Harder says, "What is meant is the 'holy zeal' which demands full dedication to serving the community" (TDNT, VII, p. 566).

69. The negative is μή, not οὐ. Moule compares a construction of which he says, "it is virtually participial since μὴ ὄντα κ.τ.λ. would give the meaning" (IBNTG, p. 156). Robertson comments, "in Ro. 12:11 μὴ ὀκνηροί is in the midst of participles used in an imperative sense" (p. 1172).

70. The verb ζέω means "to boil", though Oepke regards this as a secondary meaning, the basic sense being "to well up," "to bubble". Oepke also says, "The combination τῷ πνεύματι ζέειν seems to be peculiar to the NT and was perhaps coined by Paul." He sees here the meaning "that it is their duty fully to develop their energy as Christians. In the first instance this is human energy. But then attention is drawn to the impelling power of God, i.e., to the Spirit" (TDNT, II, p. 876). The expression is used of Apollos (Acts 18:25).

The verse is rounded off with *serving the Lord*, where the verb[71] points to thoroughgoing devotion, service like that of a slave. There is nothing half-hearted about it. There is a textual problem in this part of the verse, with some MSS reading "the time".[72] If we adopt this reading, the meaning will be "meet the demands of the hour" (NEB mg.) or "Seize your opportunities" (Barclay). It might also be understood in an eschatological sense; the children of the new age should accept the challenges of that age. All these give a good sense, but we should probably accept the reading as "the Lord".[73]

12. The first of three more clauses is *Be joyful in hope*. Both joy and hope are characteristic New Testament concepts. The early Christians often had little to be joyful about or to hope for in this world, but they rejoiced in the Lord always (Phil. 4:4) and they knew Christ in them, "the hope of glory" (Col. 1:27).[74] It is not that hope is itself the object of the Christian's joy; rather, it is that which, being what it is, inevitably leads the Christian to rejoice. Hope lifts him out of his present difficult circumstances, and rejoicing is the inevitable result.

Patient in affliction is another characteristic New Testament attitude. *Patient* may give a wrong impression; Paul's word denotes not a passive putting up with things but an active, steadfast endurance.[75] And something like that is needed, for *affliction* denotes not some minor pinprick, but deep and serious trouble (see the note on 2:9).

Faithful in prayer brings us to another characteristic of New Testament Christianity. Paul has a great deal to say about prayer,[76] and it is clear that he himself was constant in his praying. It is a very important part of the Pauline understanding of Christianity. *Faithful* is perhaps not forceful enough for the word Paul uses.[77] "The strong word suggests not only the constancy with

---

71. δουλεύοντες.

72. Most MSS read κυρίῳ (as P46 ℵ A B Db.c), but some have καιρῷ (D* F G Or). There is no doubt that the weight of MSS evidence favors the first reading, but the second has transcriptional probability (why would a scribe alter "the Lord" to "the time"?), and some accept it as the more difficult reading. Its attestation is chiefly Western and seems insufficient to outweigh that of the other MSS.

73. Though Barth says it is "insipid" and regards it as "a quite intolerable generalization." Luther accepts "serving the Lord" and acutely points out that people can be very busy in what they consider as a good work but "not ready to do whatever God wills unless they can choose what it shall be . . . among people of this kind there must also be numbered the princes who are constantly in church and the higher clergy who cannot absent themselves from court."

74. BDF see the dative as meaning " 'by virtue of hope, in hope', not 'over hope' " (196).

75. ὑπομένω has the meaning "*remain* instead of fleeing . . . *stand one's ground, hold out, endure* in trouble, affliction, persecution" (BAGD). This is Paul's one use of the verb in Romans (he has it four times altogether). He uses the corresponding noun often (16 times out of 32 in the New Testament).

76. He uses προσευχή 14 times out of its 36 New Testament occurrences (three in Romans).

77. προσκαρτεροῦντες. It can mean "busy oneself with, be busily engaged in, be devoted to" (BAGD). It points to persistence in prayer, not the offering of an occasional petition.

which they are to pray, but the effort that is needed to maintain a habit so much above nature" (Denney). We are left in no doubt but that persistent prayer is a necessary part of the Christian life.

13. The participial construction continues with imperatival force. There is a textual problem as to whether we should read "needs" or "remembrances".[78] Most scholars accept "needs", but some cite Zahn for the view that Paul is referring to the contributions to his collection for the poor saints in Jerusalem (cf. 15:25; Cranfield finds no evidence for this meaning for the word). Another idea is that the readers are being invited to remember the saints as a way of gaining encouragement. But this involves the use of "saints" as outstanding Christians, a later usage than that of the New Testament, where the word means all believers. We should reject "remembrances" and understand the word to mean "needs". There is further discussion about the meaning of the verb.[79] Some hold that Paul is urging the Roman Christians to make themselves one with the needy, to share in their predicament. It seems more likely that he is calling on them to come to the aid of such people, but this will certainly be in no condescending manner but as being one with them. The early church took a deep interest in the poor, whose lot in the first century was often desperate. Calvin commented, "It generally happens that those who are more weighed down by poverty than others and stand in need of help are treated with greatest contempt." Whatever the situation in Reformation Europe, Paul wanted there to be no doubt about Christian concern in first-century Rome. The needy were not to be a class apart, for the more well-to-do were to share in their needs.

With this he links *Practice hospitality*. The exercise of hospitality was of great importance to the church of that day. It was not always possible or desirable to stay in inns, and in any case inns were not always available. But Christians like Paul travelled widely in the exercise of their ministry, and it mattered very greatly that wherever they went they found hospitality among the believers. They were all one family, and they readily welcomed as guests even believers whom they had never met (cf. 3 John 5). The verb for *practice* is unexpected[80] and points to vigorous effort. Leenhardt reflects that "Christian hospitality must inconvenience us more than that of the world; we do not choose our time or our guests". Paul is not advocating a pleasant social exercise among friends, but the use of one's home to help even people we do not know, if that will advance God's cause.

---

78. Most MSS read χρείαις, but μνείαις is found in D* F G. This is usually taken as a variant that arose at a time subsequent to New Testament days when the invocation of the saints came into vogue in some places.

79. κοινωνέω means "1. *share, have a share*. . . . 2. *give* or *contribute a share*" (BAGD). This looks like an example of 2, but the lexicon classes it under a subdivision of 1: "Participation in someth. can reach such a degree that one claims a part in it for oneself *take an interest in, share*".

80. διώκω has meanings like "pursue", "persecute". It certainly is a strong term and one that looks for the expenditure of considerable effort in being hospitable. The accusative φιλοξενίαν after the verb replaces the datives that Paul has used so extensively up to this point.

14. It is possible that we move now to Paul's instructions about Christian behavior toward outsiders; this is surely the meaning of the first injunction in this verse. But the following words seem to apply better to what Christians should do among themselves. In any case Paul is not dividing up his instructions to conform to a neat pattern, and it should not surprise us if he moves from believers to non-Christians. His construction changes, and he now uses the imperative instead of the participles that have been so characteristic of this chapter. This leaves the readers in no doubt that they have a firm instruction as to how to behave toward the persecutors.

Bless can be used in various senses, all good. Here it will be used in the sense "ask God to bless" (GNB). Paul takes the verb he has just used for pursuing hospitality and enjoins his readers to call down God's blessing on people who pursue, who persecute. This seems to be a reminiscence of the teaching of Jesus (cf. Matt. 5:44; Luke 6:28); it is certainly in harmony with his general approach. It sets a very high standard for Christians. Paul is not saying simply that they should refrain from retaliating against persecutors or that they should forgive them. He is saying that they should actively seek their good as they pray for God's blessing on them.[81] His own practice agrees with this (1 Cor. 4:12-13). Most MSS refer to those who persecute *you*, but it is omitted in some of them. If it is omitted, it is persecutors in general, not only those who persecute the believers, who are to be the objects of blessing.

Bless is emphasized by being repeated, and it is reinforced with the prohibition of the opposite: *do not curse*. This is Paul's only use of the term (it occurs five times in the New Testament). The present imperative may imply that it has already started and have the meaning "Stop cursing". But perhaps this is reading too much into a tense. It is, however, the natural thing among the ungodly. Paul makes it clear that it has no place among those whom Christ has saved.

15. The commands continue, but they are now continued with infinitives[82] as Paul enjoins his readers to *Rejoice with those who rejoice* and to *mourn with those who mourn*. Sympathy is an important Christian virtue. Chrysostom points out that it "requires more of a high Christian temper, to rejoice with

---

81. Cf. Calvin, "Although there is hardly any who has made such advance in the law of the Lord that he fulfils this precept, no one can boast that he is the child of God, or glory in the name of a Christian, who has not partially undertaken this course, and does not struggle daily to resist the will to do the opposite."

82. Moulton says that the infinitive used as an imperative "was familiar in Greek, especially in laws and in maxims." He finds it in the papyri, and "We have therefore every reason to expect it in the NT, and its rarity there is the only matter for surprise" (M, I, pp. 179, 180). He finds an English parallel in the hymn

So now to watch, to work, to war,

And then to rest for ever! (*ibid.*, p. 203).

BDF say, "The imperatival infinitive is extremely old and is especially common in Homer", less frequent in Attic. They think a governing verb (of saying or χρή or δεῖ) can readily be supplied (389). Turner also thinks that such a verb "may perhaps be assumed" (M, III, p. 78), but Moule says, "At least a few passages in the N.T. exhibit Infinitives so independent of any verb of commanding or the like that one can only class them as Infinitives used in an imperatival sense" (IBNTG, p. 126).

them that do rejoice, than to weep with them that weep. For this nature itself fulfils perfectly: and there is none so hard-hearted as not to weep over him that is in calamity: but the other requires a very noble soul, so as not only to keep from envying, but even to feel pleasure with the person who is in esteem." Cranfield cites Origen, who points out that people sometimes rejoice and weep at the wrong things and suggests that we rejoice "in those experiences in which he is most truly himself". This is true, but it does not appear to be what Paul is saying. The apostle is not trying to cover every case, but simply calling for sympathy. The Christian is not to be indifferent to the joys and sorrows of others.[83]

16. Paul now reverts to his participial construction, still with imperatival force. NIV's *Live in harmony with one another* is a defensible translation, but so is GNB's "Have the same concern for everyone". Paul's Greek has a meaning like "thinking the same thing to one another".[84] There is no question but that Paul is advocating genuine unity, and his words probably are to be taken in the sense "Be of the same mind".

He goes on to a negative which NIV renders *Do not be proud* and which might be more literally rendered "not thinking high things".[85] The true Christian is genuinely humble and is not given to thinking high things about himself.

On the contrary,[86] he is to *be willing to associate with people of low position*. There is a difficulty here in that the Greek rendered *people of low position* is ambiguous; those same words may be translated "willing to do menial work" (mg.).[87] Those who take the term as neuter point out that the preceding adjective is certainly neuter ("high things") and argue that we should take this one as neuter to agree. Those who favor the masculine point out that elsewhere in the New Testament this word is always masculine and argue that the masculine gives a better meaning. Both are possible and both are true. It may be that the ambiguity is intentional and that we should accept both meanings.[88] The verb translated *associate with* has the meaning "lead away"

83. David Daube thinks that Paul here is probably "dealing with relations between Christians and outsiders" (*The New Testament and Rabbinic Judaism* [London, 1956], p. 341). It seems more likely that Paul is applying this first of all to relations among Christians, though a further application to outsiders is not unlikely.

84. τὸ αὐτὸ εἰς ἀλλήλους φρονοῦντες (cf. 15:5; 2 Cor. 13:11; Phil. 2:2; 4:2). The present participle will point to the habitual bent.

85. μὴ τὰ ὑψηλὰ φρονοῦντες. ὑψηλός may be used of what is physically high, such as a mountain (Matt. 4:8), or of what is proud (11:20). BAGD give the meaning here as "strive after things that are (too) high, be too ambitious".

86. ἀλλά is the strong adversative.

87. τοῖς ταπεινοῖς might be masculine or neuter. The adjective has meanings like "*low:* 1. of Place *low-lying* . . . 2. of persons, *humbled, abased in power* . . . 3. of the spirits, *downcast, dejected* . . . 4. in moral sense, either bad, *mean, base, abject* . . . or good, *lowly, humble* [most examples are from the New Testament] . . . 5. of things, *mean, low, poor*" (LSJ). It is clear that the word was habitually used of unattractive qualities. It is another example of a term that Christianity ennobled, as it saw humility as a virtue. See further Turner, *Christian Words*, pp. 216-18.

88. Cf. Barrett, "it is impossible to feel confident that either translation is correct to

or "carry off with" (BAGD); here it is in the passive, "be led away",[89] which thus may mean "be accommodated to humble people" or "to humble ways".

A final command enjoins the readers, *Do not be conceited*, or "do not be wise in your own sight".[90] The person who is wise in his own eyes is rarely so in the eyes of other people. Haldane says caustically, "Self-conceit is an evidence of weakness of mind and of ignorance."

C. The Christian Attitude to Non-Christians, 12:17-21

This should not be regarded as a hard-and-fast division. Some of what we saw in the previous section applies to the way Christians should behave towards outsiders and some in this section to their treatment of fellow believers. But there is a difference of emphasis, and predominantly here Paul is concerned with how Christians should behave towards those who do not profess the faith (Lagrange makes the division at this point).

> [17]*Do not repay anyone evil for evil. Be careful to do what is right in the eyes of everybody.* [18]*If it is possible, as far as it depends on you, live at peace with everyone.* [19]*Do not take revenge, my friends, but leave room for God's wrath, for it is written: "It is mine to avenge; I will repay,"[a] says the Lord.* [20]*On the contrary:*
>
> "*If your enemy is hungry, feed him;*
>   *if he is thirsty, give him something to drink.*
> *In doing this, you will heap burning coals on his head.*"[b]
>
> [21]*Do not be overcome by evil, but overcome evil with good.*
>
> [a]19 Deut. 32:35   [b]20 Prov. 25:21, 22

17. A further participial construction enjoins the readers to repay evil to "no one".[91] Paul has the word in an emphatic position: Christians should repay evil to no one at all, Gentile or Jew, Christian or pagan. It is a universal duty for believers, a duty which is brought out in a variety of ways in the New Testament (cf. Matt. 5:39ff., 43-44; 1 Cor. 13:5-6; Gal. 6:10; 1 Thess. 5:15; 1 Pet. 2:23; 3:9). Clearly it is an important part of Christian living. There is a

---

the exclusion of the other. It is well to remember that Greek occasionally allows an ambiguity impossible in English; Paul may have been aware, and may have approved, of both ways of taking his words."

89. συναπαγόμενοι.

90. φρόνιμος means "sensible", "wise", and this use of παρά is classed by BAGD under the heading *"in the sight* or *judgment of someone"*. Moule says the commonest use of παρά with the dative is the metaphorical sense "in the sight of", here "wise in their own eyes" (IBNTG, p. 52). Cf. Prov. 3:7.

91. μηδενί.

sense of equivalence about both *repay* and *for*;[92] Paul is dealing with a natural human tendency to get "even".

Be careful to do is NIV's rendering of a verb meaning "think beforehand, take care" and thus "1. care for, provide for. . . . 2. take thought for, take into consideration, have regard for" (BAGD, who class this passage under 2).[93] *What is right* translates one word which is more usually taken to mean "good",[94] and this not of a hidden, interior goodness only (though the deeds in question must have this characteristic as well), but of a goodness that is manifest to all.[95] NIV agrees with GNB, "Try to do what everyone considers to be good", and other translations, but this does not seem to be what Paul is saying. He is not appealing to his readers to fall in with generally accepted moral maxims (people's minds are darkened, 1:21, and they will not always approve what is right in the sight of God). He is calling on them to live out the implications of the gospel.[96] Their lives are to be lived on such a high plane that even the heathen will recognize the fact.[97] They will always be living in the sight of non-Christians, and the way they live should be such as to commend the essential Christian message (cf. Prov. 3:4; Matt. 5:16; Luke 2:52; 2 Cor. 4:2; 8:21; Tit. 2:10).

18. Attention shifts to the importance of living peaceably; the opening *If it is possible* shows that this cannot always be done.[98] It is qualified with *as far as it depends on you*.[99] The Christian is never to take the initiative in disturbing the peace. Regrettably it may be disturbed, for the Christian lives among evil people and they will sometimes refuse to let peace remain. But that is their responsibility. As far as the Christian is concerned, there is to be no breach of the peace. This must also be qualified by the fact that the Christian is to bear witness to the truth and to live by Christian principles. Peace at the price of the sacrifice of truth or the compromise of principle is not asked for. The Christian, because he is a Christian, cannot do such things. "As far as it depends on you" includes the thought "you, being who you are, someone

---

92. ἀποδίδωμι and ἀντί. Paul uses this verb eight times (out of 47 in the New Testament) and the preposition five times (out of 22), so neither can be said to be a favorite term.

93. προνοέω. Leenhardt thinks it "suggests foresight, providential careful thought; thought which precedes and controls action. Cf. 1 Tim. 5:8."

94. καλά. The word "properly refers to goodliness as manifested in form" (AS *sub* ἀγαθός); it is "the outward expression of an inward goodness" (Wuest).

95. Bengel brings this out: "A precious stone should not merely be a precious stone, but it should also be properly set in a ring, so that its splendour may meet the eye."

96. Cf. Cranfield, "Christians are to take thought for, aim at, seek, in the sight of all men those things which (whether they recognize it or not) are good, the arbiter of what is good being not a moral *communis sensus* of mankind, but the gospel."

97. Tertullian speaks of the heathen as saying, "A good man is Gaius Seius, only that he is a Christian" (Apol. iii). That is the kind of thing at which Paul is aiming.

98. For εἰ δυνατόν cf. Matt. 24:24; Mark 14:35; Acts 20:16; Gal. 4:15, etc.

99. τὸ ἐξ ὑμῶν. Moule sees this as an accusative of respect or reference "denoting that in respect of which some statement is made", here "for your part, so far as it is in your power" (IBNTG, pp. 33-34; he also includes this among "striking and idiomatic" uses of nouns or neuter adjectives "employed as adverbs" [p. 160]).

redeemed by Christ and called to live in his service."[100] We must bear in mind that Paul often uses military metaphors, as when he speaks of the Christian's armor (Eph. 6:11ff.) or of fighting the good fight (2 Tim. 4:7).[101] We need such metaphors as well as the exhortation to peace if we are to be true to Paul's thinking. Brown has a significant comment: "To 'live peaceably,' is descriptive of that state, in which a man does not disturb others, and is not disturbed by them. The first is always in our own power, the second is not" (Brown, p. 474). Paul is urging his readers to do all that is in their power to bring about and to preserve peace; but that does not remove the possibility that others will make this laudable endeavor impossible.

Barth has a comment about a further aspect of our subject. He says, "Our fellow men have no right to peace. Everything they do irritates us. Unattractive, crotchety, impenitent. . . ." We do not live in an ideal world, but a world peopled by sinners. The command to live peaceably is meant, not for an ideal environment, but for this sinful world, a world inhabited by people like us! The command should cause us to do some self-examination before we blame other people too quickly for the difficulties in which we find ourselves. And it is a command meant to be obeyed, not the occasion for a crop of plausible excuses as to why we did not obey it.

19. One last participle with imperatival force gives us the injunction *Do not take revenge.*[102] Even when someone has done us harm we are not to seek retribution; that is not our function.[103] Paul slips in the address "beloved" (NIV, *my friends*), which is particularly appropriate in a place where he is urging the Roman Christians to a line of conduct which runs counter to a strong natural urge. He is making it clear that the command does not arise because he is indifferent to them, for he loves them. "The believers are entreated by the voice of love to walk in love" (CBSC).

But, he says, using the strong adversative[104] to set what follows in sharp contrast to the thought of taking revenge. Rather, we should *leave room for God's wrath,* or, more exactly, "Give place to the wrath".[105] Some have taken "the wrath" to be the wrath of the injured person, who is then counselled not to bottle up his anger but to find some outlet for it. Others have thought of the wrath of the opponent and suggested that the injured person should keep out

---

100. Cf. Calvin, "We are not to strive to attain the favour of men in such a way that we refuse to incur the hatred of any for the sake of Christ, as often as this may be necessary. . . . The soldiers of Christ cannot have lasting peace with the world, which is ruled by Satan."

101. Cf. Hodge, "Paul's own example shows that he was far from thinking that either truth or principle was to be sacrificed for the preservation of peace."

102. ἐκδικέω means "to avenge"; there is the implication that a wrong has been done for which vengeance is now exacted.

103. Cragg comments that if we do try to take the law into our own hands, "We are inept bunglers in a region where we do not belong".

104. ἀλλά.

105. δότε τόπον, where δότε is the one aorist imperative in this list (cf. Eph. 4:27). Leenhardt gives the meaning as "give scope for an action by leaving the field free."

of the way ("leave the place, and let wrath occupy it; or give place, as a man would do if attacked by a wild beast, stepping aside to let it rush by", Haldane). But NIV is surely right in seeing a reference to "the wrath of God" (cf. 5:9; 1 Thess. 2:16). The force of the article is that "we must think of it as *the well-known wrath*" (M, III, p. 173), that is, the divine wrath.

Paul backs up his injunction with a quotation from Deuteronomy 32:35 in a form identical to that in Hebrews 10:30 but differing from LXX (it is like that in the Targum of Onkelos; see SBk). Perhaps both Paul and the writer to the Hebrews used a translation that has not survived.[106] The passage makes it clear that God has taken to himself the task of avenging those wronged. They are not to take things into their own hands, but leave it to him. In the light of 13:4, it is possible that on occasion this may take place through the secular power, but Paul will not be thinking of that exclusively or even mainly. The eschatological wrath of God is that which in the end will punish all evildoers. The translation of NEB, "Justice is mine", reminds us that we should not think of God as vindictive. Whenever his wrath is seen in punishment, this is an activity in which justice is done.

20. The apostle makes his meaning clear by citing examples of acceptable behavior. *On the contrary* sets what follows in sharp contrast with taking vengeance into our own hands.[107] The quotation, taken from Proverbs 25:21-22 (basically LXX), urges the reader to give food and drink to an enemy who is in need.[108] The implication is that we should give any help that is needed (and not confine our help to these two articles of diet). This is no piece of lofty, ethereal advice without application to the practicalities of daily life, but something very down-to-earth. Cragg comments, "spiritual fare is poor sustenance for an empty stomach. . . . To a hungry person blessing means bread".

The quotation goes on to refer to this as heaping *burning coals on his head*, a most unlikely procedure if taken literally. It is clearly a metaphorical expression whose meaning is not obvious. From early times some have drawn attention to Old Testament passages expressing the idea of punishment (e.g., 2 Sam. 22:9, 13 = Ps. 18:8, 12; Ps. 11:6; 120:4; 140:10). The thought then would be that by doing your enemy kindness you were increasing his guilt and magnifying his punishment.[109] But to most commentators this seems an im-

---

106. G. Schrenk thinks of "a Gk. transl. not identical with the LXX" (TDNT, II, p. 446 n. 4). We may perhaps not be correct in speaking of "the" LXX. May there not have been a number of translations of which our LXX is for the most part the only one to have survived?

107. It translates ἀλλά, the strong adversative. This should probably be read (with ℵ A B P etc.), though some MSS have ἐὰν οὖν, and some simply ἐάν.

108. ψωμίζω connects with ψωμίον, "a morsel", and means *"feed by putting little bits into the mouth*, as nurses do to children" (LSJ). But clearly here there is no question of the manner in which food is given; it is simply a matter of feeding a hungry foe.

109. C. Spicq thinks that in Prov. 25 by heaping coals of fire "you will increase his culpability. In the Old Testament, live coals are invariably a symbol of divine anger, of punishment for the wicked, or of an evil passion. It would be very strange if St. Paul were

possible way of understanding the passage. The context is dominated by thoughts of love, and indeed the whole paragraph (vv. 9-21) is an expression of what Christian love means in practice.[110] For reasons like this most agree that something like Moffatt's translation gives the sense of it: "for in this way you will make him feel a burning sense of shame". William Klassen, however, has made a detailed examination of the problem and rejects such solutions. "The interpretation so widely accepted by interpreters that the coals of fire refer to shame, remorse, or punishment lacks all support in the text." He points to a custom attested in Egyptian literature whereby a penitent person carried coals of fire in a bowl on his head and to contacts between Proverbs and Egyptian writings and says, "In the Egyptian literature and in Proverbs the 'coals of fire' is a dynamic symbol of change of mind which takes place as a result of a deed of love."[111] Whether we prefer to go along with Moffatt or with Klassen, there can be no doubt that Paul is referring to the change in the enemy which deeds of love effect. As Barrett, Bruce, and Barclay all say in one form or another, we should use deeds of love to turn the enemy into a friend.

21. Paul rounds off the section with an exhortation to defeat evil: *Do not be overcome*[112] *by evil.*[113] Paul does not spell it out, but the context and his whole argument show that to be overcome by evil means to respond to evil with evil. When we do this we simply increase the amount of evil in the situation. The command not to do this is an important negative; evil must not be allowed to triumph.

Then Paul goes on to the positive: *but overcome evil with good.* Evil cannot stand against good. This is a very different attitude from that of the dying Mattathias who commanded his sons, "avenge the wrong done to your people. Pay back the Gentiles in full . . ." (1 Macc. 2:67-68). Such an attitude is

---

to use the phrase in a favorable sense. Moreover, all the Greek fathers, as well as Estius, taking into consideration the way the words are ordinarily used, their context here, and their relation to 'vengeance' in verse 19, understand that kindnesses poured out on an enemy are so many glowing coals heaped over him, so many titles to divine punishment" (*Agape in the New Testament*, II [St. Louis and London, 1965], p. 208). Cf. Haldane, "The conduct recommended will have the effect of increasing the punishment of the enemies of God's people". Chrysostom is cited for this view.

110. V. P. Furnish draws attention to a number of writers including K. Stendahl who think that Paul, like the men of Qumran, sees leaving vengeance to God as a covert way of expressing hatred for one's enemies. Furnish dissents, pointing out that these exhortations "stand under the general one to 'let love be genuine,' and the immediately preceding counsels (vss. 14-18) are clearly intended to show how love should treat outsiders and enemies" (*The Love Command in the New Testament* [Nashville and New York, 1972], p. 108).

111. NTS, IX (1962-63), p. 349.

112. μὴ νικῶ. The negated present may be understood to mean "Stop being overcome", but this should probably not be pressed. Turner classes it as a "Perfective Present" and says, "class. *be a conqueror*" (M, III, p. 62). His verb is in the singular, whereas he has mostly used the plural in this section. The singular will arise partly because it is used in the quotation and partly because it individualizes what Paul is saying. Each must take it as personal.

113. It is possible to take τοῦ κακοῦ as masculine, "the evil one" (so Spencer Robertson, ET, LX [1948-49], p. 322). In either case Paul is urging the defeat of wrong.

very common, but it overlooks the fact that to retaliate is to be overcome, not to win, for the enemy has then succeeded in bringing us down to his own level.[114] We should be clear that Paul is not laying down some useful ethical precepts for the edification of the general public. He has spent a lot of time in this letter on the subject of justification by faith, and it is the justified person of whom he continues to write. Those who know what it is to be justified by God's grace, know also what it is to have the love of God poured into their hearts through the Holy Spirit (5:5). They know the new power that comes from the love the Spirit brings. That is why and that is the way they overcome evil with good. The way of love lifts them above all vindictiveness.

114. Cf. Luther, "Men commonly regard as the victor the one who has the last word and can deal the last blow, whereas, as a matter of fact, he who is the last to inflict pain is the one who is worse off, for the evil remains with him while the other is done with it." Boylan comments, "Evil only grows through being requited."

Romans 13

D. The Christian Attitude to Civil Rulers, 13:1-7

1Everyone must submit himself to the governing authorities, for there is no authority except that which God has established. The authorities that exist have been established by God. 2Consequently, he who rebels against the authority is rebelling against what God has instituted, and those who do so will bring judgment on themselves. 3For rulers hold no terror for those who do right, but for those who do wrong. Do you want to be free from fear of the one in authority? Then do what is right and he will commend you. 4For he is God's servant to do you good. But if you do wrong, be afraid, for he does not bear the sword for nothing. He is God's servant, an agent of wrath to bring punishment on the wrongdoer. 5Therefore, it is necessary to submit to the authorities, not only because of possible punishment but also because of conscience.

6This is also why you pay taxes, for the authorities are God's servants, who give their full time to governing. 7Give everyone what you owe him: If you owe taxes, pay taxes; if revenue, then revenue; if respect, then respect; if honor, then honor.

There has been a very wide divergence of opinion about the way this passage is to be understood. Since it forms a unit without formal grammatical connection to what precedes or follows and since verse 8 would follow quite naturally on 12:21, some see it as an interpolation into a letter that originally lacked it. This is strengthened by the fact that there is nothing quite like it anywhere else in Paul (though attention may be drawn to 2 Thess. 2:6-7). Nor is there any mention of Christ in these verses. All this leads O'Neill to the view that they are not only non-Pauline, but non-Christian (he thinks they come from a Stoic source).[1]

Others find the passage an integral part of the epistle ("There is no reason to dispute the authenticity of the text" [Käsemann, p. 351]). After his words forbidding private vengeance it was necessary, it is argued, for Paul to point out that this does not mean that the state may not take punitive action. It has been pointed out that the apostle is writing to people in Rome, the capital

---

1. O'Neill says of the passage: "These seven verses have caused more unhappiness and misery in the Christian East and West than any other seven verses in the New Testament." James Kallas is not so severe, but he finds the passage alien to the thought of Paul and argues that it is an interpolation (NTS, XI [1964-65], pp. 365-74).

of the world, the seat of empire, and it would be suitable to say something to them about the role of the state. Again, there were Jews who took strong exception to acknowledging any heathen king (cf. Deut. 17:15) and who objected to paying taxes to support a heathen state.[2] Sometimes it is argued that the Jews in Rome may well have been restive (cf. the rioting about "Chrestus" of which Suetonius wrote and Claudius's expulsion of the Jews from that city, Acts 18:2; it is conjectured that some of them may have had ideas akin to those of the Palestinian Zealots who recognized no king but God and would pay taxes to no one but God); Paul may have wanted to dissuade Christian Jews in the capital from taking part in revolutionary movements.[3]

Such considerations seem to show that we must take this passage seriously in its present context. It is part of what Paul is saying to the Romans and it has abiding significance for Christian readers in all ages. Jesus taught his followers that they must "Give to Caesar what is Caesar's and to God what is God's" (Mark 12:17), and several other passages urge the believer to obey the authorities (1 Tim. 2:1-3; Tit. 3:1; 1 Pet. 2:13-17; cf. Prov. 8:15; Jer. 29:7; Dan. 2:21, 37-38, etc.). This passage seems accordingly to be Paul's considered treatment of a theme that was important for the early Christians. Many of them were Jews, with Jewish reluctance to be ruled by a foreigner. Christians were in an ambiguous position vis-à-vis the authorities. If they were regarded as a variety of Judaism, they came under the umbrella protection afforded people of that nation (cf. Gallio's refusal to take action in what he saw as a dispute among Jews, Acts 18:12-16). But if they were seen as a distinct religion, they had no protection. What attitude should they adopt to people who might at any time persecute them?

Paul's view is distinctive.[4] He is firmly convinced that God is in control and that nobody secures a position of rulership unless God permits. Ordered government is not a human device, but something of divine origin. The servants of God must accordingly submit to its laws. Paul regards rulers not as autonomous, but as "established by God" (v. 1); the ruler is "God's servant" (v. 4). This gives the ruler a special dignity but at the same time stresses that his position is a subordinate one. He is to do, not whatever he wishes, but what the will of God is for him in his situation.

---

2. This attitude persisted, and we see something of it in Wis. 6:1-5, though that passage concerns the duties of rulers rather than those of subjects.

3. Marcus Borg argues along these lines (NTS, XIX [1972-73], pp. 205-18). He says of this passage that "it not only fits into its immediate context, but that it also has an intimate connection to Romans as a whole" (p. 214).

4. A. Schweitzer finds no parallel to these verses except among "the great Stoic Emperors, who felt themselves to be truly the servants of the State for the realisation of good" (The Mysticism of Paul the Apostle [New York, 1931], p. 315). These emperors, of course, were later and viewed the matter from the perspective of the ruler. "But from the point of view of the subject this ethical valuation of rulership was expressed by no other writer of antiquity, except the Jew, Paul. Neither Socrates, Plato, nor Aristotle carry the idea of obedience to authority so far. Not even Reitzenstein can discover any parallels in Hellenistic literature to Rom. xiii.1-7" (ibid.).

This understanding of the state has been strongly criticized on the grounds that it justifies every tyrant and compels the believer to obey him.[5] It is this that is behind O'Neill's remark cited above that no passage has caused more unhappiness and misery than this one. But it must be borne in mind that Paul is writing in general terms to meet the need of the Romans and not legislating for every conceivable situation in which the Christian might find himself. He does not face, let alone resolve, the problem of when it is right to rebel against unjust tyranny (it has well been remarked that the first-century Romans had no experience of a successful revolt), or what to do when there are rival claimants to the crown or conflicts between civil and religious authorities. He does not distinguish between legitimate and usurped authority, nor go into the question of when a successful rebel may be held to have become the legitimate ruler. He does not speak of the situation in which the state asks the citizen to do something against the law of God. All the New Testament writers were clear that they must obey God rather than men (Acts 5:29),[6] and Paul's whole manner of life shows that he accepted this wholeheartedly. He does not say what the Christian should do when the state fails in its duty. He is not trying to cover every situation. His concern is authority, however it has come to be possessed. He is writing out of a settled order where there is no doubt as to who the ruler is, and he is telling his readers something of the duty of a citizen in such a situation.

Paul owed a good deal to the protection the Romans had afforded him, but he was not unaware of the fact that the state could be unjust. No Christian could, for the atoning death of Jesus lay at the very heart of the faith and that death had been brought about on the human level by evil and unjust people (though even here the early Christians saw God at work even in the deeds of evil men, Acts 4:24-28). The man who had been often in prisons in the Roman empire and had frequently been flogged (2 Cor. 11:23) was not unaware that the authorities can be unjust. For that matter he knew that he himself had been unjust when he was one of the authorities that persecuted the church. But here he is writing about the state's essential nature, about what it should be and in some measure at least is. Rulers may misuse the authority God has given them, but Paul's point is that that does not alter the fact that it was God who gave it to them. People are often tempted to evade their civic responsibilities (and not only in the first century); Paul reminds them of the significance of those responsibilities. Order is important, and the state embodies order.

We should be clear that Paul is writing about the existing state, not some

---

5. Haldane argues that the passage demands unconditional obedience; rebellion is not lawful (p. 585). But Hunter seems closer to the mark when he says, "what Paul condemns in these verses is rebellion in the name of Christian freedom."

6. This is clear in the Old Testament also. The king was "the Lord's anointed" and as such to be treated with respect (1 Sam. 24:6 etc.). But the prophet Ahijah, speaking in the name of God, said that the bulk of the kingdom would be taken away from Rehoboam and given to the rebel Jeroboam (1 Kings 11:29-31).

ideal state that he hoped would appear. Every state has its faults, and first-century Rome had many. But it still had to be treated as the ruling authority and as such as the servant of God.[7]

Mention should be made of the view that Paul has in mind angelic beings of the kind designated "principalities and powers" (8:38; Eph. 6:12, etc.). This was argued by M. Dibelius and taken up by O. Cullmann (*The State in the New Testament* [London, 1957]; *Christ and Time* [London, 1951], pp. 191ff.); Clinton D. Morrison (*The Powers That Be* [London, 1960]), and others. It is clear that the state is in mind in, for example, verse 4, so the position is stated in terms of angelic beings behind the state. But there are strong reasons for rejecting this view. The angelic beings in the New Testament are never regarded as the servants of God, but as enemies defeated by Christ (Col. 2:15). Again, references in this chapter to "God's servants", to "the sword", and to taxes surely point to humans, not spirit beings. The difficulties are too great, and not many hold this view in recent times.[8]

1. There is no connecting particle, but this paragraph follows naturally on 12:19-21; the Christian is not to seek private vengeance, so what are we to say of the state when it punishes wrongdoers? *Everyone* is more exactly "every soul", a Hebraism with the meaning given by NIV (the Hebrews said "every *soul*" where we say "every *body*", but the meanings are the same). Paul is referring to a universal duty. He makes no distinction between Christians and non-Christians; this is a duty incumbent on people simply as people.[9] *Authorities*[10] means those who exercise authority, and is here defined as *govern-*

---

7. Geoffrey W. Bromiley points out that civil authorities are "means by which God exercises his authority. Outside the sphere of revelation, rulers have only an indistinct and perverted apprehension of this truth. They thus tend to think in terms of absolute or inherent power or to confuse divine authorization with a transferred right to do all things at will. This can raise acute problems for the Church and can produce the clash of authority that brings tension, persecution, or compromise. Even where rulers are Christians and know clearly the source of their authority, they may still fail to see that this authority can be properly exercised only according to the Word of God and within the sovereign authority that God always reserves for himself" (W. Ward Gasque and William Sanford LaSor, eds., *Scripture, Tradition, and Interpretation* [Grand Rapids, 1978], p. 25).

8. See the detailed criticisms in Murray, Appendix C (pp. 252ff.), and Hendriksen, pp. 430-31.

9. πᾶσα allows of no exceptions. ψυχή is used by Paul 13 times out of its 101 occurrences, so it cannot be said to be a favorite word of his. It means "soul" but is sometimes used in the sense "living creature" as here.

10. ἐξουσίαις. This word first of all means "authority", from which it easily comes to mean those who exercise authority. In the plural it often refers to "spirit authorities", spirits exercising power in heavenly places (Eph. 3:10; 6:12; Col. 1:13, 16), but it is not easy to see the singular here as having that meaning. Cf. Morrison, "The *linguistic* aspect of the problem illustrates the general frustration of the argument. The strong point of the affirmative, that the plural of *exousia* is *consistently* used by Paul to indicate the spiritual powers, is countered by the negative observation that everywhere *except in Romans 13* the context supports the spiritual interpretation of the word. In Romans 13, however, the word appears to be defined by its singular meaning in a context which has to do only with civil government" (*The Powers That Be*, p. 57). Josephus uses the plural of the Roman authorities in Judea (*Bell.* ii.350).

ing[11] authorities. Paul says everyone is to *submit himself* to these rulers. GNB, Moffatt, and others render the verb "obey", but this does not seem to be the meaning; NIV is correct with *submit*.[12] Submission may well include obedience, at least on some occasions, but we should observe what Paul says. Wilckens reminds us that, while the word may be used of the reaction to authoritative commands, it is used also of Christians being subject to one another (1 Cor. 16:16), where, of course, it is not easy to think of obedience. Even less so is this the case with "Submit to one another" (Eph. 5:21); consistently taking the lowly place over against one another is understandable, but obeying one another consistently is not. There is nothing servile about the attitude to authority that Paul is advocating. He simply looks for a due recognition of the subordinate place that is part of the Christian understanding of life. The Christian is subordinate because he recognizes that the brother is Christ's representative to him, and in a different way the ruler, who is "God's servant" (v. 4), is Christ's representative too.[13]

For introduces a reason for this. All authority comes in the end from God. This means that "the authority of the state is a delegated, and not an absolute authority" (Wilson), that authority must always be respected, and that an uncritical obedience is impossible. Anything in the directions given by authority that is manifestly not from God shows that the authority has exceeded its lawful function. That, however, is a deduction from what Paul is saying and not his point here. That point is simply that all human authority comes ultimately from God. Paul first puts it negatively, there is no authority except from God, then positively, the existing authorities are from God.[14] There are problems with this statement, but clearly *de facto* government is to be respected (even if we think it is not *de jure*). Order in the state and the authorities that enforce that order are of divine origin; they would not be there without that. On what Paul says the Christian is not justified in refusing obedience to the state because he has his doubts about the legal standing of the government. The Christian is to recognize that order is important in any state.[15] But if the state exceeds its lawful function, if it plainly directs subjects

11. ὑπερέχω is literally "to have over", "to rise above", sometimes "to excel". Turner cites this as an example of the Hellenistic use of a transitive verb in an intransitive sense (M, III, p. 52). It may be used of "the higher ones", i.e., the authorities (BAGD). NEB translates "the supreme authorities", but the word does not mean "supreme". "The higher authorities" is the meaning.

12. The verb is ὑποτάσσω, which Paul uses 23 times out of its 38 New Testament occurrences. BAGD give the meaning as "subject, subordinate". There may be occasions when this comes close to "obey", but in the New Testament that idea is expressed by ὑπακούω, πειθαρχέω, or πείθομαι; there seems no reason why ὑποτάσσω should be used for this significance.

13. Calvin well comments that even kings and governors "rule that they may serve" (on Gal. 5:21).

14. With αἱ δὲ οὖσαι we must understand ἐξουσίαι, "the existent powers", "the authorities that are".

15. The perfect τεταγμέναι adds a touch of permanence. The state is to be marked by stability.

to actions that are wrong, then that is another matter. Jesus said that we are to render to Caesar only the things that are Caesar's, for we are to render to God what is God's (Mark 12:17), and Christians have always understood that "We must obey God rather than men!" (Acts 5:29). Paul does not say this in set terms, but that is a legitimate deduction from his view of the state's delegated authority, which is all that it has.[16]

2. *Consequently*[17] introduces "a conclusion based on the judgment in the previous verse" (TH). Because God has willed that there be orderly states, anyone who sets himself in opposition rebels against what God has ordered. NIV's *rebels* and *is rebelling* translate two different words (cf. NEB, "rebel . . . resist"; Moffatt, "resist . . . oppose").[18] They are different ways of expressing the thought of asserting oneself in the face of authority. Paul is making it clear that the believer is to respect the state and not make himself the final arbiter. *What God has instituted* is better "a divine institution" (NEB), for Paul is using a noun, not a verb.[19] Clearly he is giving the ordinances of the Roman authorities a very exalted place and expecting that his readers will obey them. "Resistance to legitimate authority legitimately exercised is wrong" (Manson). To resist the authorities God has set in place is to resist what God has commanded, and such resisters *will bring judgment on themselves*.[20] The *judgment* may be the punishment inflicted by the authorities or the divine judgment; more probably it is both: the punishment carried out on the order of the authorities is itself the way the divine judgment works out.

3. It is possible to take the *For* that begins this verse as referring to what immediately precedes, but it is better to see it as giving an additional reason for being subject to the authorities. Paul changes from "authorities" to *rulers*,[21] but the change is probably stylistic. Rulers, he adds, are not a *terror*[22]

---

16. Cf. Bruce, "the state not only may but must be resisted when it demands the allegiance due to God alone" (on v. 2).

17. ὥστε is followed here by the indicative, a construction found three times in Matthew, twice in Mark, once in John, and 15 times in Paul (three in Romans, four in 1 Corinthians, three in 2 Corinthians, and five in Galatians). It is thus much more typical of Paul than of the other writers. Moule lists this among "certain contexts" where ὥστε is "simply an *inferential particle* as if ὥς τε, meaning *and so, accordingly*, etc." (IBNTG, p. 144).

18. ἀντιτάσσω is the opposite of ὑποτάσσω in v. 1; over against "be in subjection" it sets the idea of "oppose, resist". This is Paul's one use of the verb. ἀνθίστημι, "to set against", in the New Testament always has the middle sense, "to set oneself against"; Paul has it eight times out of 14 in the New Testament.

19. διαταγή, which means "ordinance, direction" (BAGD). Deissmann cites a second-century inscription which he thinks read τῶν θείων δια[ταγ]ῶν and meant "imperial ordinances", "a most exact parallel to the celebrated passage in the Epistle to the Romans, which also refers to the Roman authorities" (LAE, pp. 90-91).

20. ἑαυτοῖς is not strictly needed after "will receive judgment", but it puts some emphasis on the recipients.

21. ἄρχοντες, which Paul uses here only in Romans and four times in all out of 37 in the New Testament. It does not differ significantly in meaning from ἐξουσίαι in vv. 1 and 2.

22. φόβος may mean "*the causing of fear*. . . . Also concrete *that which arouses fear, a terror*" (BAGD). The word brings out the truth that a secular state operates with compulsion, the use of the police force, etc.

to people who *do right*,[23] but only to wrongdoers, a statement which presents
a problem in view of, say, the persecuting emperors. But, of course, Paul is
not directing himself to such problems. He is presenting the norm, laying
down conditions for living in a state in normal times, not covering every
eventuality. And, of course, no ruler ever favors what he sees as wrong and
punishes what he regards as right. Paul's point is that Christians are not to see
themselves as free to obey duly constituted authority or not, just as they
please. Submission to duly constituted authority is a divinely instituted good,
not an evil to be endured with as good a grace as can be mustered. NIV makes
the next part of the verse a question, *Do you want. . . ?* which is certainly
possible. But the words might be taken as a statement. Turner sees this as an
example of an independent clause serving as the protasis of a condition, and
translates "If you wish to be fearless of." He adds, "Such interpretation lends
point to the context and is good Greek" (M, III, p. 319).[24] The change to a
direct address to the reader using the second person singular makes the
exhortation more vivid, but it is still general. Whether we take the construction as a question or a condition, it leads in to the command *do what is right*.
Paul wants his readers to be law-abiding citizens, assuring them that then
they will be commended.

  4. In the Greek the word *God's* comes first for emphasis. The ruler is
God's servant, no less. And *servant* reminds us that he is no more; he is not
God even if some rulers have had very exalted views of themselves and their
functions. The word *servant*[25] originally signified the service of a table waiter
and denotes lowly service in general. However exalted he may be among
people, the ruler is nothing more than a lowly servant before God. And he is a
servant "to you",[26] an expression that adds a personal touch. The ruler's
function concerns the individual subject. And this function is "for good".[27]
The authority is God's servant to bring about good and not something else,
but this "good" can be understood in more ways than one. Some hold it to
mean the good of the individual, his prosperity. Or, bearing in mind 8:28
where God works everything for good, it is possible to see the words as
meaning that what the ruler does will in the end promote God's purpose for
the blessing of his people, that is, their salvation. Another possibility is that
the ruler is to bring about conditions for a tranquil and quiet life in which
God's people can serve him effectively (cf. 1 Tim. 2:2). Or again, the good
may be the good that subjects do; authority may be exercised not so much in
the interest of the person as that the person may be led to do the good. This is

---

23. τῷ ἀγαθῷ ἔργῳ, which Turner takes as a generic singular (M, III, p. 22). Moffatt
translates "an honest man", which presupposes τῷ ἀγαθοεργῳ. For an argument that this
should be accepted as the right reading despite its slight attestation in the MSS see W. L.
Lorimer, NTS, XII (1965-66), pp. 389-90.
24. BDF 471 (3) see parataxis "in place of conditional subordination".
25. διάκονος.
26. σοί, the dative of advantage (SH).
27. εἰς τὸ ἀγαθόν, where εἰς introduces intended result.

supported by the fact that the passage immediately goes on to deal with the opposite: *But if you do wrong.* None of these suggestions is impossible, and Paul may possibly have more than one of them in mind. But perhaps there is most to be said for the last mentioned. The ruler is God's servant to enable God's other servants to get on with the job of doing God's will. We should not overlook the point that the ruler is to act responsibly.[28]

But if the subject does wrong he is in trouble.[29] *Be afraid,* says Paul, and the present points to a continuing process, "fear continually". There is something to be very much afraid of: *he does not bear the sword for nothing.*[30] This certainly means that the government is armed and can use force, but whether it means more than this is far from certain. Many see a reference to the Roman *ius gladii,* the right to inflict the death penalty. But Paul does not use this expression or a translation of it. Further, the *ius gladii* is sometimes misunderstood as though at this time it meant the right of any magistrate to inflict the death penalty. But A. S. Sherwin-White has shown that "For the first two centuries of the Empire the term referred only to the power given to provincial governors who had Roman citizen troops under their command, to enable them to maintain military discipline without being hampered by the provisions of laws of *provocatio.*"[31] Others point to the carrying of a sword before higher magistrates or to the Emperor's wearing of a sword. Whatever there may be in such suggestions, Paul's point is that it is folly for subjects to do what displeases government, for the authorities have great punitive capacity.

A second time Paul refers to the ruler as *God's servant,* and a second time he has *God's* first for emphasis. The Emperor on his throne, and for that matter any petty local bureaucrat, might well see his power as something to be exercised as he chose. But Paul is clear that everyone in any position of responsibility is first and foremost God's servant and that it is to God that he will one day be forced to render account. The authority is not an independent operator, but *an agent of wrath to bring punishment on the wrongdoer.*[32] *Wrath* means "God's wrath". Paul has spoken of the eschatological wrath (2:5) and of God's wrath in the present (1:18). Now he adds the thought that civil government can be an agent of the divine wrath when it punishes wrongdoing.[33] It is as the punisher of evil that the authority is viewed as God's servant.

28. "In one fell swoop government is torn from its pedestal and made the servant of God for the Christian" (Harrisville). Calvin says of rulers, "Nor do they have unbridled power, but power that is restricted to the welfare of their subjects."
29. ἐάν with the subjunctive makes the condition very general; there is no implication as to the fulfilment of the condition or otherwise.
30. εἰκῇ is Pauline in all five of its New Testament occurrences. It means "without cause, in vain"; here "to no purpose" (BAGD). φορέω means *"bear* (in contrast to φέρω) *for a considerable time* or *regularly,* hence *wear"* (BAGD).
31. See his *Roman Society and Roman Law in the New Testament* (Oxford, 1963), pp. 8-11; the quotation is from p. 10.
32. *Agent* translates ἔκδικος, which more properly means "avenger"; the authority is there to bring appropriate punishment on those who do wrong. εἰς is rather "for" than "of"; it indicates purpose.
33. The present participle πράσσοντι points to habitual practice. Dodd accepts ret-

5. *Therefore*[34] draws a conclusion. Because the authority is God's servant and is there to punish wrongdoing, therefore the Christian must *submit*.[35] It is necessary to be subject to state authorities, and that not only[36] because we are in trouble if we do not. That in itself is a valid reason, and we should notice that *possible punishment* is not really what Paul is saying but "on account of the wrath". Again he is referring to the wrath of God manifested in the punishment inflicted by civil authorities. RSV has "God's wrath". This makes the reference to God specific and brings out the meaning of what Paul is saying.

To this Paul adds *but also because of conscience*—a most significant addition. Christians obey the authorities not only because of what will happen to them if they do not but because it is right. They give positive and enthusiastic cooperation to promoting the right things the state does. "It is only such conscientious approbation which will make of our obedience a vital participation in the mission with which the civil authority is entrusted" (Leenhardt). The failure to do one's duty to the state is to violate one's conscience as well as to invite punishment.[37] Conscience is a powerful reinforcement of the outward directions to submit to the state. But once conscience is brought in, there is a limit: what is against conscience cannot be done. The believer may have to refuse obedience on the grounds of conscience. This is what members of the early church did (cf. Acts 5:29).[38] Conscience at one and the same time obliges us to be obedient and sets a limit to that obedience.[39]

6. Paul proceeds to relate the paying of taxes to this fact.[40] Taxes are not

---

ribution as the meaning; he thinks that Paul sees civil government as "part of the natural moral order, of divine appointment, but lying outside the order of grace revealed in Christ."

34. διό.

35. ἀνάγκη means "*necessity, compulsion* of any kind, outer or inner, brought about by the nature of things, a divine dispensation, some hoped-for advantage, custom, duty etc." (BAGD). Turner points out with respect to ὑποτάσσεσθαι that the infinitive is often used where classical Greek would have the accusative and infinitive (M, III, p. 148).

36. Burton points out that in the New Testament οὐ (not μή) μόνον is regularly used with the infinitive (MT, 481).

37. C. A. Pierce gives the meaning of the verse as "It is your duty to God to be subject to the power: to rebel is not only illegal therefore: it is also morally wrong. It is not simply punishment by society that awaits the rebel, and the fear of which should deter him: it is also, for the law can be broken on occasion with impunity, the more terrible and less avoidable—for it is within him—pain of conscience." He goes on to say that this is the "internal counterpart" of the wrath of God (*Conscience in the New Testament* [London, 1955], p. 71).

38. Cf. C. Maurer, "συνείδησις is responsible awareness that the ultimate foundations both of one's own being and also of the state are in God. Members of the community are to have neither a higher nor a lower estimation of the state than as a specific servant of God" (TDNT, VII, p. 916).

39. Cf. Käsemann, "There can then, here or elsewhere, be no question of interpreting Christian obedience in action as slavish passive obedience. Christian obedience is never blind; and, indeed, open-eyed obedience, directed by συνείδησις, must even be critical" (*New Testament Questions of Today* [London, 1969], p. 213).

40. διὰ τοῦτο establishes a causal relationship which is then strengthened by γάρ. The verb τελεῖτε is taken by NIV as an indicative, probably correctly. The form could be imperative, but it is not easy to relate this to the causal opening.

just an arbitrary impost. They are the means of carrying on responsible government—the state could not exist without them.[41] It is because the authorities are *God's servants* and because they *give their full time to governing* that taxes must be paid.[42] The word for *servants*[43] differs from that used twice in verse 4.[44] Paul follows this with an expression not easy to put into English and which most translations omit (though cf. KJV, "upon this very thing").[45] It points to a concentration on the collecting of taxes. The authorities make this their business.

7. Paul calls on his readers to pay what is due to *everyone*. NEB takes this to mean "to all men", while GNB has simply "them", meaning the collectors of taxes. The Greek could mean either, but in this context it surely refers to payment to the authorities, for Paul goes on to spell out what is to be paid.[46] NIV distinguishes between two Greek words with *taxes* and *revenue*. The first word is one we have already seen in verse 6. Strictly it means "tribute",[47] whereas the other term refers to customs duties and the like.[48] It is probable that Paul is not distinguishing sharply between the two but saying in effect, "Whatever taxes you owe". *Respect*[49] moves away from the realm of taxes and indicates a proper regard for those in high places, as does *honor*. It is not easy to grasp the distinction Paul makes between them. Cranfield takes seriously

---

41. Paul's word for "tax" here (φόρος) strictly means "tribute". It was the tax a subject people paid to its conqueror (it is the word used in Luke 20:22) and was usually hated in consequence. Paul is probably using the word in a general sense for any kind of tax, but his choice of this word is interesting.

42. Cf. Bowen, "Rulers have a *right* to demand taxes from their subjects; but they also have a *responsibility* to use these taxes for the good of the whole country, and not to spend them on luxury living for themselves or on special privileges for certain groups." Calvin also remarks, "all that they receive from the people is public property, and not a means of satisfying private lust and luxury."

43. λειτουργός (it is from this root that we get our word "liturgy") is not confined to priestly service, but in the New Testament, with the possible exception of Phil. 2:25, is always used of the service of God. It indicates service of a serious nature, even if we cannot say that it points to anything "liturgical".

44. H. Strathmann says, "It may be that Paul, who does not use the term often, is conscious of an aura of solemnity deriving from the LXX, but one can hardly say that he intends it sacrally" (TDNT, IV, p. 231). In nonbiblical contexts the word is often used of public service, especially service carried out by wealthy citizens at their own expense.

45. εἰς αὐτὸ τοῦτο. On this BDF 290 (4) comment, "Paul frequently has αὐτὸ τοῦτο 'just this (and nothing else)' ". Denney holds that we must take this with the preceding because προσκαρτερέω elsewhere is used with the dative. This verb is then used absolutely, emphasizing the thought that they do this continually.

46. The verb NIV renders as *Give* is ἀποδίδωμι; it has about it the idea of payment of what is due. Deissmann says that in the papyri borrowers used this verb in the "stereotyped formula" "I will repay" what has been borrowed (LAE, p. 331). It is the verb in Jesus' words "Render to Caesar . . ." (Mark 12:17). The idea of what is due comes out also in ὀφειλάς, "debts".

47. Denney comments that τῷ τὸν φόρον τὸν φόρον "is quite intelligible, but nothing can make it grammatical". SH essays this task by understanding ἀπαιτοῦντι.

48. Michel cites Origen for the view that φόρος was tax on land and τέλος was tax on trade. Cranfield takes the two to refer to direct and indirect taxes.

49. The word is φόβος, "fear", though "respect" is probably correct here.

the idea that *respect* is to be paid to God (as in 1 Pet. 2:17), but this seems to be introducing something into the text that is not there. While Paul would have agreed that people should respect God, he is here talking about the attitude they should have to the authorities, not their whole duty to God and man. He is saying that Christians should have a respectful attitude to those in high places, not for secular reasons such as that they are important or wealthy or powerful, but because God has made them his ministers. Their work confers on them a dignity that Christians should observe.

E. THE CHRISTIAN ATTITUDE TO PEOPLE IN GENERAL, 13:8-10

> *8Let no debt remain outstanding, except the continuing debt to love one another, for he who loves his fellow man has fulfilled the law. 9The commandments, "Do not commit adultery," "Do not murder," "Do not steal," "Do not covet,"ᵃ and whatever other commandment there may be, are summed up in this one rule: "Love your neighbor as yourself."ᵇ 10Love does no harm to its neighbor. Therefore love is the fulfillment of the law.*

a9 Exodus 20:13-15, 17; Deut. 5:17-19, 21   b9 Lev. 19:18

From the attitude to the ruling authorities he expects to see in believers Paul turns to that to people in general. The Christian should be characterized by love, love to other Christians but also to people in general. In short, the Christian is to be a loving person.

8. *Let no debt remain outstanding* is more exactly rendered "Owe no one anything" (RSV), but NIV makes it plain (as RSV perhaps does not) that Paul is not forbidding borrowing. Jesus permitted this (Matt. 5:42), and circumstances may well arise in anyone's life in which a debt is permissible. But Paul is saying that the believer should not leave debts unpaid; they should be settled promptly. The present imperative[50] will have a continuous force: "Don't continue owing. Pay your debts."

He has just said that they should pay what they owe to officialdom; now he moves the same obligation into private life. But he goes beyond the payment of debts in the ordinary sense to the thought of a debt that can never be discharged, the debt of love.[51] We may pay our taxes and be quit. We may give respect and honor where they are due and have no further obligation. But we can never say, "I have done all the loving I need do." Love is a

---

50. The form ὀφείλετε could be indicative (Brown understands it as a statement, "Ye owe no man anything . . ." (p. 494). But the negatives μηδενί, μηδέν point to the imperative, and in any case "Pay your taxes. . . . You owe no man anything" would be a strange sequence. The double negative adds emphasis to the command. ὀφείλετε is striking after ὀφειλάς (v. 7).

51. εἰ μή introduces an exception. Some think the expression means "but" (e.g., Barrett, "Owe no man anything—but remember the debt of love . . ."), but "except" is a more usual meaning of the expression and is very suitable here.

permanent obligation, a debt impossible to discharge.[52] As Origen put it long ago, "The debt of charity is permanent, and we are never quit of it; for we must pay it daily and yet always owe it" (cited in Dodd). Notice that Paul does not refer to this as a work of supererogation, an outstanding achievement that we look for only in the greatest of saints. He sees it as a duty resting on the humblest believer. Whatever else we do or do not do, we are to love.[53]

One another is sometimes taken as meaning "fellow Christians", but it is difficult to hold that in this context Paul is limiting love. This is all the more the case in that he goes on to refer to loving "the other" (NIV, *his fellow man*),[54] on which GT says "*the other*, when the relation of conduct to others is under consideration is often put by way of example for *any other person whatever*, and stands for 'the other affected by the action in question'". It is "the other person" in the sense "any other person with whom I have to do."

The believer who loves like this *has fulfilled the law*, where it is surely the law of Moses that is in view, though, of course, this is true of any law (the absence of an article with *law* may be meant to help us understand this). Paul is repeating what Jesus said about the law being summed up in the commandments to love (Matt. 22:37-40). There is an air of completeness about the use of the perfect tense of the verb (Phillips translates "has obeyed the whole Law"). But we ought not to think that love is a legal requirement. As Bengel puts it, "To love is liberty", and Brunner, "the commandment of love can be neither correctly understood nor rightly fulfilled as law." Love is something poured into our hearts by the Holy Spirit (5:5).

9. "For" (which NIV omits) brings out the logical connection. Paul proceeds to cite four of the ten commandments to show that if one loves, these commandments will be fulfilled.[55] He omits the commandments that refer to God, presumably because he is dealing with the duty to one's neighbor, and he omits the commandment not to bear false witness but he is not

52. Cf. Robinson, "Love may satisfy every claim of the law, but nothing can satisfy the claims of love." Haldane has a different thought: "The more they pay of this debt, the richer they will be in the thing that is paid."

53. BDF 399 (1) see the nominative and accusative of the substantivized infinitive (which occurs sporadically in Matthew and Mark, somewhat more frequently in Paul, and rarely elsewhere) as usually anaphoric—referring to something previously mentioned or otherwise well known. Here it means "the well-known command."

54. τὸν ἕτερον. Since this is immediately followed by νόμον, some think we should understand it as "the other law" (e.g., Leenhardt, who sees a reference to the law of Moses as well as Roman law). But, while grammmatically possible, this is most unlikely (Lenski considers it an "exegetical curiosity"). Parry points out that "the phrase would be strained, and the context (ἀλλήλους—τὸν πλησίον) is against it" (CGT). It is also true that there is no reference to "law" in the context, and in fact we must go back to 10:5 for the last mention of it.

55. The τό with which he begins is classical (M, III, p. 182); it is the equivalent of our quotation marks. The order in which he cites the commandments differs from the Hebrew and LXX of Exod. 20:13ff.; Deut. 5:17ff., but agrees with that in the text of codex B in Deut. 5:17 (also in Luke 18:20; Jas. 2:11; Philo *On the Decalogue* 121ff.; Clement Alex. *Strom.* 6.16; not all have four commandments).

giving a complete list and this is surely to be included in *whatever other*[56] *commandment there may be*. He is citing some typical requirements of the law simply to show that love fulfils all that they lay down. He speaks of the commandments as being *summed up*[57] "in this word" (NIV has *rule*)[58] and goes on to quote Leviticus 19:18, *Love your neighbor*[59] *as yourself*. This is sometimes taken as justification for self-love, but neither the commandment nor Paul says as much. The fact is that people do love themselves, and "God addresses His command to us as the men that we actually are, the sinners who do, as a matter of fact, love ourselves, and claims us as such for love to our neighbours" (Cranfield).[60] Paul is saying in strong terms that believers must love the people they do in fact encounter. It is easy to "love" in an abstract way, but Paul wants his readers to love the people they actually meet day by day (with all their faults). Love is something that takes effect in the home, in the marketplace, in the workshop, on the village green, wherever people are met.[61]

10. In a neat chiastic sentence that begins and ends with *love* Paul proceeds to personify this virtue and goes on to tell us that love *does no harm to its neighbor*. The negative way of stating it is perhaps due to the fact that law is mostly concerned with things people must not do; certainly over Paul's writings as a whole love is much more than a negative virtue, an abstaining from harm. But where the law is concerned, it is this that is important.

Therefore introduces a consequence of this function of love; it fulfils all that law requires. Lagrange comments that love is not only the fulfilling of a precept "but something that includes the plenitude of all the precepts and all the works." Nygren reminds us that love is the fruit of the Spirit and that against such there is no law (Gal. 5:22-23). Law is against sin, not against love. "To live 'in Christ,' to walk 'in love,' is something entirely different from living under the law and striving to fulfill all its requirements; and yet the law

---

56. Turner points out that ἕτερος has lost the sense of duality (M, III, p. 197). It sometimes has the meaning "another of a different kind"; whether this is its meaning here or not, it excludes the possibility that any commandment not cited will not be covered by love. Love is all-embracing.

57. ἀνακεφαλαιόω is "rare in secular Gk. and unknown outside literary sources." It means "to bring something to a κεφάλειον," "to sum up" (H. Schlier, TDNT, III, p. 681). It is found in the New Testament again only in Eph. 1:10.

58. λόγος is used of the ten commandments, as in Exod. 34:28.

59. πλησίον is the neuter of the adjective πλησίος (which is not used in the New Testament), used as an adverb meaning "near". With the article ὁ πλησίον (ὤν) it means "the person who is near" and thus "the neighbor". It is used widely of any other person than oneself.

60. Cf. Luther, "because of the defect of his nature, man loves himself above everything else". Hendriksen remarks, "it is a certain thing that a person will love himself, and it is also certain that he will do so in spite of the fact that the self he loves has many faults."

61. "Those who love humanity can be 'horrid' to the men and women whom they actually meet, while those who love their families and their friends can be quite deaf to the cry of those beyond their circle" (Cragg).

is fulfilled in it." Love is all-important in the servant of God; without genuine love service will always be defective.[62]

F. Living in the Light, 13:11-14

> [11]And do this, understanding the present time. The hour has come for you to wake up from your slumber, because our salvation is nearer now than when we first believed. [12]The night is nearly over; the day is almost here. So let us put aside the deeds of darkness and put on the armor of light. [13]Let us behave decently, as in the daytime, not in orgies and drunkenness, not in sexual immorality and debauchery, not in dissension and jealousy. [14]Rather, clothe yourselves with the Lord Jesus Christ, and do not think about how to gratify the desires of the sinful nature.[a]

[a]14 Or *the flesh*

Paul adds a section drawing attention to the urgency of getting on with the business of living as Christians should. In view of the coming of "the day" they should live wholeheartedly for Christ.

11. "And this", says Paul (into which NIV inserts *do*; Moulton also favors understanding an imperative [M, I, p. 182]; the expression is found again in 1 Cor. 6:6, 8; Eph. 2:8; Heb. 11:12). It adds something that heightens what has just been said. Godet gives the force of it as "And all that (we fulfil) knowing. . . ." *Understanding* renders a participle[63] which might conceivably renew the imperative of earlier verses or might be taken as an indicative (as RSV, "you know") but is probably better taken as NIV. "Knowing the time", Paul says (NIV has inserted *present*), certain conduct is appropriate. His word for *time*[64] points to the character of the age in which he found himself, a time in which Christ had come and made all things new and which pointed forward to the consummation of all things. So he goes on to say that already[65]

---

62. Cf. Manson, "some of the worst mischief in the world can be caused by people who set out to do good to their neighbours but do not love them." Bowen reminds us that love can take many forms: "Sometimes people are unwilling to receive gifts or teaching from people of another race or tribal group, but this is a wrong attitude, based on pride, which can only be broken down by love. Love is needed both by the 'giver', so that he may not adopt a superior or patronizing attitude, and by the 'receiver', so that he may be ready to take the lowly position which involves saying 'Thank you'".

63. εἰδότες.

64. καιρός (which Paul uses 30 times out of 85 in the New Testament) has sometimes been sharply differentiated from χρόνος (as by J. A. T. Robinson, *In the End God* [London, 1950]; J. Marsh, *The Fulness of Time* [London, 1952]). χρόνος on this view is merely chronological time, whereas καιρός is meaningful time, the right time. J. Barr has sharply criticized such views (*The Semantics of Biblical Language* [Oxford, 1961]; *Biblical Words for Time* [London, 1962]). It seems clear that too much has been made of the difference between the two words, but it may be that Barr has made too much of their similarity. In a context like the present one καιρός is the appropriate word; it is time as a significant era.

65. ἤδη.

The hour has come[66] for you[67] to wake up[68] from your slumber. "Already" gives a touch of urgency to his exhortation; he is not speaking of some remote period for which they could make leisurely preparation but of imperative action now. Many understand him to mean that the second coming was to take place in the very near future, but we should be clear that that is an interpretation; it is not what Paul says. There are many places where the New Testament writers make it clear that they did not know when the Lord would come again (e.g., Matt. 24:36; Mark 13:32; Luke 21:8-9; Acts 1:6-7; Rom. 11:25; 1 Thess. 5:1-2; 2 Thess. 2:1-3, 5). But that he would come and that they should be ready for him gave a note of urgency to all that they said (cf. 1 Pet. 4:17; Rev. 1:3; 22:10). Brunner remarks that "Faith is indeed nothing but living in the light of what is to come." It is that kind of living which Paul calls for. *Slumber* will denote a lethargic Christian life; it "suggests the thought of forgetfulness of God" (Thomas).

Paul gives a reason in the nearness of *salvation*. This will point to the consummation of all that is implied in being saved. Salvation may be spoken of as something accomplished in the past (Eph. 2:8), in the present (1 Cor. 1:18), or in the future (5:9). Here the future is in mind: Paul is saying that it is nearer to us[69] than at the time when we first believed.[70] Paul writes elsewhere, "We eagerly await a Savior from there (i.e., heaven)" (Phil. 3:20), and it is something like that that he is saying here. There is the thought of eager expectation and the thought that the fulness of all that salvation means is yet to come.

12. There is no connective. Paul does not explain what the *night* is, but clearly he is referring to this present life as in some sense lived in darkness. But the consummation of which he has just spoken indicates that the *night* will not last forever; indeed, in view of what Christ has done in bringing light and salvation it is far advanced.[71] "The day has drawn near"[72] does not mean that the parousia is imminent but that after Christ all history "must be of the nature of an epilogue" (Cranfield). Christ's coming to save us is the decisive event.

---

66. There is no verb here, and NIV has inserted *has come*. BDF note the omission of ἐστίν in "impersonal constructions, especially those expressing possibility or necessity" (127 [2]). It is the necessity of the hour that is in mind here; there is no escaping it.

67. There is some MS support for ἡμᾶς (P⁴⁶ᵛⁱᵈ ℵᶜ D). But ὑμᾶς is more likely (with ℵ* A B etc.). ἡμᾶς was perhaps suggested by the end of the verse.

68. The infinitive ἐγερθῆναι is used, as in classical Greek (M, III, p. 139), after ὥρα to indicate the time to do something. The construction "implies a necessity" (MT, 378).

69. NIV takes ἡμῶν with σωτηρία, but there seems more point in taking it with ἐγγύτερον (as Lagrange, Barrett, and Cranfield).

70. ἐπιστεύσαμεν is an ingressive aorist, "when we began to believe", "became believers".

71. προκόπτω means "to lengthen by hammering" (as a smith in forging metals) and thus "to forward," "to go forward," "advance" (GT). It is another example of a transitive verb used intransitively in Hellenistic Greek (M, III, p. 52). The aorist is unexpected, but it will give the idea of an accomplished fact.

72. The perfect ἤγγικεν, which NIV renders *is almost here*.

It is because[73] of this near approach of the day that Paul calls on his correspondents to put off *the deeds of darkness* and put on *the armor of light*. The verbs "put off" and "put on"[74] are often used of clothing (see, e.g., Acts 7:58 for the former and Mark 15:20 for the latter), but Paul uses them often in metaphorical senses. *Deeds* (or "works")[75] is a word used in many combinations, such as "works of God", "good works", and "works of faith". Here we must see that darkness is the natural habitat of evil, so that "works of darkness" are wicked works and as such are to be decisively "put off" by the believer. They are no part of his equipment. Instead he is to "put on"[76] the equipment[77] suitable for his life as a Christian (Denney comments, "the Christian's life is not a sleep, but a battle"). Paul is fond of the metaphor of the Christian's armor (2 Cor. 6:7; Eph. 6:13-17; 1 Thess. 5:8; perhaps Rom. 6:13). He does not consistently locate any particular Christian attribute with any one piece of armor and, for example, the breastplate is righteousness in Ephesians 6:14 and it is faith and love in 1 Thessalonians 5:8. It is the general idea that appeals to the apostle. It is interesting that here he speaks of putting off the "works" of darkness, but of putting on not the "works" of light, but its "armor". That life is a battle was highly important to Paul.[78]

13. As[79] in "the day" (RSV has *daytime*, but the word is identical with that in v. 12) starts the verse with an insistence that Christians belong with Christ, not with the powers of darkness. Accordingly they are exhorted to "walk becomingly" (NIV, *behave decently*). Paul often uses the metaphor of walking for the steady if unspectacular progress that should characterize the Christian. His use of the aorist imperative sets the direction of the life rather than emphasizing continuity.[80] Barclay renders "in loveliness of life".[81]

73. οὖν, "therefore".
74. ἀποτίθημι and ἐνδύω.
75. ἔργα.
76. Both "put off" and "put on" are aorist imperatives and point to decisive action.
77. ὅπλον means a tool or implement, but in the New Testament it is always plural and seems mostly to mean "arms", "weapons". Godet thinks that the meaning here is the garments of a workman, but most agree that it is more likely that the usual meaning of weapons should be understood, weapons which the light itself both demands and supplies (Althaus).
78. Some hold that Paul is thinking of people who, on getting up in the morning, put off their night clothes and put on their day garments, but it is countered that in the first-century Roman empire people did not have night clothes; they simply took off some of their outer clothing and slept in the rest (so Michel, p. 330 n. 2; Jerome Carcopino, *Daily Life in Ancient Rome* [Harmondsworth, 1962], pp. 171ff.). Chrysostom brings out the urgency of the coming day with a reminder of getting up at dawn that characterized most of the ancients: "as soon as it (night) is actually departing, we hasten one another, and say, It is day now! and we all set about the works of the day, dressing, and leaving our dreams, and shaking our sleep thoroughly off, that the day may find us ready, and we may not have to begin getting up, and stretching ourselves, when the sunlight is up."
79. ὡς, used here with ellipsis of the participle (M, III, p. 158 n. 1; BDF 425 [4] suggest ὡς ἡμέρας οὔσης). Käsemann sees the meaning as "as is actually the case" (p. 363).
80. BDF 337 (1) take the aorist as ingressive: "with reference to the commencement of this way of life".
81. This brings out something of the force of εὐσχημόνως (εὐ + σχῆμα).

Paul contrasts this way of life with the way acceptable to the world with a series of negatives arranged in three pairs, such that the members of each pair signify somewhat similar qualities. His first pair is *not in orgies and drunkenness*,[82] pointing to the abuse of strong drink. Next comes a pair of sexual sins, *sexual immorality*[83] *and debauchery*, this last denoting licentiousness, unrestrained lust. Both these words are plural, so again it would seem that Paul has in mind many examples of these vices. Both items of his third pair, *dissension and jealousy*, are in the singular, and point to attitudes of the spirit of man. Both indicate a determination to have one's own way, a self-willed readiness to quarrel. All six of these vices stem from self-will; they are all the outreach of a determined selfishness that seeks only one's own pleasure. As Barrett puts it, "All these practices constitute a failure in love, which 'works no harm to the neighbour' (*v.* 10)." It is not without its interest that Paul is writing these words to "all in Rome who are loved by God and called to be saints" (1:7). We should not think that first-century Christians came from the most upright and honorable sections of society (cf. 1 Cor. 6:9-11 with its "that is what some of you were"). Rather, the gospel took up and transformed many who were the dregs of society. Paul is mindful of this and warns against relapse.[84]

14. *Rather*[85] introduces the contrary position. *Clothe yourselves* translates the verb rendered "put on" in verse 12;[86] it signifies not that which is merely external but habitual association and identification with Christ. "Putting on Christ" is a strong and vivid metaphor. It means more than "put on the character of the Lord Jesus Christ", signifying rather "Let Christ Jesus himself be the armor that you wear" (NEB). Wesley sees this as "a strong and beautiful expression for the most intimate union with Him, and being clothed with all the graces which were in Him." There is a sense in which this takes place in baptism (Gal. 3:27; cf. Rom. 6:3). But it is necessary to put off the old and put on the new throughout the Christian life (cf. Eph. 4:22-24; Col. 3:12), and it is this of which Paul writes here.

KJV captures the sense of the rest of the verse with "make not provision[87] for the flesh, to fulfil the lusts thereof." As often, Paul has the thought

---

82. κῶμος was "prop. a nocturnal and riotous procession of half-drunken and frolicsome fellows who after supper parade through the streets with torches and music in honor of Bacchus or some other deity, and sing and play before the houses of their male and female friends; hence used generally, of *feasts and drinking-parties that are protracted till late at night and indulge in revelry*" (GT). Clearly Paul is referring to a far from respectable practice. μέθαις is plural, indicating many examples of the practice.

83. κοίτη originally meant a place for lying down, a bed. It came to mean specifically a marriage bed, then sexual intercourse lawful or unlawful. Here it is clearly the latter.

84. Lagrange thinks the expressions too strong to be applied to the Roman Christians and holds that Paul is contrasting Christianity with the immoral life of pagans. If so, it is to warn them to hold such practices in horror.

85. This translates the strong adversative ἀλλά.

86. ἐνδύσασθε, where Paul "turns to the peremptory aorist imperative which is incisive and strong" (Lenski).

87. πρόνοια means "foresight"; when it is used with ποιέω the thought is of making provision for something. LB has "don't make plans".

that the flesh all too easily leads to sin, and he counsels his readers to make no provision at all for the lower desires. Foreman puts it somewhat colloquially: "Put into very simple English, Paul is saying: Do not plan for sin; give it no welcome; offer it no opportunity. Kick the sin off your doorstep and you won't have it in the house." Olshausen thinks that Paul writes "not to censure the care of the body as such, but only in the excess," but this is probably reading something into the passage. Paul is not here concerned with the right way of using the body; he is warning against the wrong way. It is this that came home to Augustine in the most famous conversion associated with this passage. Augustine was a highly intellectual person, but found it completely impossible to break away from his sexual sins. But one day when he heard a child at play calling out "Take up and read", he took up a copy of Romans and his eye fell upon this passage. God used that to bring home to Augustine both the reality of his sin and the reality of salvation in Christ. It can do so still.

Romans 14

G. Love and Liberty, 14:1–15:13

Exactly what the problem was with which Paul is dealing in this section is not clear. There has been interminable discussion about it, and nothing like a consensus has been attained.[1] Paul is discussing the relations between those he calls "weak" and those he calls "strong", but he never explains in detail who they were and what teachings they held. Quite clearly the Roman Christians knew, so there was no need to go into the question. Some hold that these were parties in the Roman church, others that they were individuals and not sufficiently organized to be called "parties". Still others think that Paul was not referring specifically to people at Rome but to tendencies he found in the church everywhere, and thus his advice was as relevant to Rome as to any other place. Some think the weak were Jewish Christians and the strong were Gentile believers. They point to the somewhat similar situation at Corinth where some believers refrained from eating meat that had been offered to idols and argued that this would be typical of Jewish believers. Jews living in the Gentile world might well abstain from meat because they could never be sure it had not been contaminated by associations with idol worship. Against this it is argued that in a city like Rome with a large Jewish population *kosher* meat was sure to be available. It is urged that it is illegitimate to bring in the case of Corinth because nothing is said here about idols and we have no reason to hold that the two situations were at all similar. It is further pointed out that some Gentile groups like the Orphics and Pythagoreans were vegetarian, so that the practice might well have originated in Gentile circles. Moreover, the abstention from wine is not known among the Jews except for the Nazirites and for the priests when engaged in their ministry.

The arguments are endless, but no one has been able to come up with convincing evidence for any one position. It is best to accept the fact that we are ignorant of the precise situation and simply to consider what Paul says. The apostle sides with neither the weak nor the strong; clearly he thought that unity was more important than holding either position. The situation is not like that in Galatians where he contended vigorously against legalists; here both groups were evidently clear about the centrality of justification by faith; it was the way that was put into practice that was at stake.

1. For an outline of the principal views see the Introduction, pp. 12ff. Cranfield outlines six possible ways of understanding the points at issue.

1. Christian Liberty, 14:1-12

[1]Accept him whose faith is weak, without passing judgment on disputable matters. [2]One man's faith allows him to eat everything, but another man, whose faith is weak, eats only vegetables. [3]The man who eats everything must not look down on him who does not, and the man who does not eat everything must not condemn the man who does, for God has accepted him. [4]Who are you to judge someone else's servant? To his own master he stands or falls. And he will stand, for the Lord is able to make him stand.

[5]One man considers one day more sacred than another; another man considers every day alike. Each one should be fully convinced in his own mind. [6]He who regards one day as special, does so to the Lord. He who eats meat, eats to the Lord, for he gives thanks to God; and he who abstains, does so to the Lord and gives thanks to God. [7]For none of us lives to himself alone and none of us dies to himself alone. [8]If we live, we live to the Lord; and if we die, we die to the Lord. So, whether we live or die, we belong to the Lord.

[9]For this very reason, Christ died and returned to life so that he might be the Lord of both the dead and the living. [10]You, then, why do you judge your brother? Or why do you look down on your brother? For we will all stand before God's judgment seat. [11]It is written:

> *" 'As surely as I live,' says the Lord,*
> *'Every knee will bow before me;*
> *   every tongue will confess to God.' "[a]*

[12]So then, each of us will give an account of himself to God.

[a]11 Isaiah 49:18; 45:23

The church was never meant to be a cozy club of like-minded people of one race or social position or intellectual calibre. Christians are not clones, identical in all respects. One of the difficulties the church has always faced is that included in its membership are the rich and the poor, the powerful and the powerless, those from every stratum of society, the old and the young, adults and children, the conservatives and the radicals. People from a great number of nations are Christians, and people of every temperament. This is a wonderful thing about the church, and most of us have thrilled at some time at the contemplation of the rich variety in our brothers and sisters in Christ. But this very variety puts strains on us all. How are we to coexist within one church? Other groupings in the societies we know are more limited in their membership. This takes away from the richness they might otherwise know, but it makes it easier for them to get along with one another. There are bound to be tensions in the Christian society,[2] and this part of Romans shows that

2. "There are always brethren in every church who entertain imperfect conceptions of Christian truth combined usually with a certain doggedness for their defective creed" (NBCR).

those tensions have been there from the first. It is easier to put our trust in Christ for salvation than to solve the hard problems that confront us when we try to live out the implications of our faith in a society that is not Christian. Paul gives us advice as to how we are to live with others who love the Lord but who do not see what we are doing as the ideal way of living out the Christian faith.

1. Paul begins with "But him that is weak",[3] or what TH calls "the emphatic element in the Greek sentence." The weak may not matter greatly in the sight of the congregation as a whole, but they are important and Paul emphasizes them. NIV has *whose faith is weak*, but Paul says rather, "him that is weak in faith", "in respect of faith".[4] As the discussion shows, he does not mean a person who trusts Christ but little, the man of feeble faith. Rather, the person he has in mind is the one who does not understand the conduct implied by faith; perhaps he is the person whose faith is ineffective. His faith is weak in that it cannot sustain him in certain kinds of conduct. He does not understand that when the meaning of justification by faith is grasped questions like the use of meat and wine and special days become irrelevant. Paul is not referring to basic trust in Christ. He assumes that that is present, for this weak person is a member of the church, not an outsider who it is hoped will be converted. What is being discussed is the way the believer should live, the actions that are permissible or required.

Those converted to Christianity in the first century did not come with minds like empty slates. They had had years of living in Judaism or in some pagan situation and in the process had acquired deeply rooted habits and attitudes. They did some things but avoided others. When they became Christians, all this did not drop away from them in a moment. For example, some pagans were so repelled by the self-indulgence they saw as an integral part of the world in which they lived that they turned from it all and lived ascetic lives, sometimes giving up the eating of meat altogether (Olshausen cites Seneca as one who did this). Jewish converts had kept the law of Moses, and specifically they had observed the Sabbath. When such people became Christians they often maintained such habits. They did not see that justification by faith made them irrelevant. It is people who brought from their previous life such habits of thinking and living of whom Paul is speaking.

Throughout the centuries of the Christian church there have been people like that, people who for reasons good or bad have seen certain actions as things they must do and others as things they must not do. And there have

---

3. NIV in common with most recent translations omits any equivalent of δέ, though NASB has "Now". There is probably a weak adversative force. Paul has been speaking of the importance of being strong in the Lord; now he adds that this does not forbid a certain gentleness. The singular is, of course, generic (M, III, p. 22). The verb ἀσθενέω may be used of bodily weakness, but here, of course, it is more intellectual and spiritual.

4. τὸν ἀσθενοῦντα τῇ πίστει. The similar expression in 4:19 refers to one whose faith is feeble (and cf. the weak conscience of 1 Cor. 8:7 etc.).

been others who have felt no compulsion either way; their faith has made them strong. It is this division (which is still with us) of which Paul writes.⁵

Accept him, says the apostle, and the fact that he is addressing the church at large is surely an indication that the weak were in a minority among the strong. The verb means more than "allow to remain in the membership"; it has the notion of welcome, of taking to oneself and so taking into friendship.⁶ The weak are not to be made to feel that they are barely tolerated and seen as second-class members. They are to be received with warmth and true fellowship. Christian love demands no less.

Paul adds, *without passing judgment on disputable matters,* a passage not without its obscurities⁷ but which makes clear that the weak brother's scruples are not to hinder the warmth of Christian fellowship. The Greek may mean "without attempting to settle doubtful points" (NEB), or "without starting an argument" (JB), or "not to.pass judgment upon his scruples" (Moffatt). Whichever way we take it, Paul is dissuading the strong from any activity that will discourage the weak. "The weak man should be accepted as the Christian brother he claims to be. One should not judge the thoughts which underlie his conduct. This is for God alone to do, cf. v. 22" (F. Büchsel, TDNT, III, p. 950).

2. Paul gives an example of the kind of thing he has in mind, contrasting two people⁸ one of whom eats *everything* while the other eats only *vegetables.*⁹ The vegetarian has taken over into his Christianity some scruple about eating meat that he has retained from his pre-Christian experience. In Corinth some

---

5. Barth reminds us of the important contribution of the "weak" (among whom he includes people like the devotees of Orpheus and Dionysus, the monks of the Middle Ages, the Baptists of the Reformation era, and modern total abstainers and vegetarians): "We cannot be blind to the deep earnestness which has brought and still brings into being such human endeavours. We are not ignorant of the great personal perplexity and disintegration, of the great courage and sacrifice, which lie behind them. We remember with genuine reverence the long succession of heroes and saints, martyrs and prophets. Without doubt, the noblest figures in history are marshalled behind the Roman eaters of vegetables." People whose trust in Christ is strong but whose understanding of what that means in terms of liberty in daily living is weak have often been driven to do great things for Christ. Let us not despise the weak.

6. On προσλαμβάνω here G. Delling says, "As God (or Christ) has taken every member of the Church into fellowship with Himself, so incorporate each other into your Christian circle with no inner reservations" (TDNT, IV, p. 15).

7. διακρίσεις διαλογισμῶν is difficult, for both words have more than one meaning. διάκρισις may mean "distinguishing, differentiation" or "dispute, quarrel" (see BAGD), while διαλογισμός may be used for "thought, opinion" or for "doubt, dispute" (BAGD). In the New Testament it is often used of evil thoughts.

8. There is a change in the construction ὃς μὲν . . . ὁ δὲ ἀσθενῶν ("one man . . . but he that is weak"). Turner thinks the article is used with demonstrative force (M, III, p. 36). We should also notice the unusual πιστεύει φαγεῖν, on which Leenhardt comments, "a curious expression which may mean: he has the faith to eat . . . or else: 'he believes he may eat' (Lagrange)." πιστεύω + infinitive occurs also in Acts 15:11. On the construction BDF remark, "it does not mean 'believe' here, but 'to have confidence to risk, to feel equal to'" (397 [2]).

9. λάχανον derives from λαχαίνω, "to dig", and thus means what is grown on land that has been dug, garden plants as distinguished from wild plants, and thus vegetables.

Christians could with a good conscience eat meat part of which had been offered to an idol, for they held that an idol is nothing (1 Cor. 8:4). For others conscience made this impossible (1 Cor. 8:7). Paul is not saying that the Corinthian situation was a problem in Rome also (nothing in this passage indicates this, and the idea that the Roman problem was identical with the Corinthian problem must be rejected). But he was writing from Corinth, where he would certainly be mindful of local problems. And the Corinthian dilemma shows us the kind of thing that could arise in the Roman world of the day. Paul is referring to someone who had conscientious scruples about eating meat, and thus confined his diet to vegetables. This is certainly not part of authentic Christian teaching (cf. Mark 7:19), but the scruples were very real and Paul is saying that they must be respected.[10]

3. In a situation like this where different Christians had different practices tolerance was important. Each must maintain a right attitude to the other. The eater must not despise[11] the non-eater, and the non-eater must not pass judgment on the eater. The strong often have a tendency to look down on the weak and regard them as inferior Christians, while the weak, knowing that it would be wrong for them (thinking as they do) to do something that the strong do, all too easily hold that the strong are sinning and slip into condemning them. Not infrequently the weak is the greater tyrant. Ironically both are falling into much the same error. The weak are clearly in danger of letting works obscure the centrality of justification by faith, and the same is true of the strong, for their attitude implies "My faith is better than yours", and that turns us to what we do rather than to what Christ has done for us. It is important for each to realize that *God has accepted*[12] the other. The weak is not to judge the strong because God has welcomed him. And it is just as true that the weak, with all his scruples, is not to be despised, for God has welcomed him, too.

4. Paul begins this sentence with an emphatic *you*,[13] which sets his imaginary conversationalist over against God, "Who are *you* that judge. . . ?" Both strong and weak should realize that it is God, not they and those who think like them, whose verdict counts. Paul speaks of judging "another's", not "another man's"; his illustration is taken from human affairs, but he has in mind the divine Master. The possessive means that the servant in question belongs to and therefore is accountable to that Other. If a servant is acceptable to his master, it does not matter what his fellow servants think. The word for *servant*[14] means a household slave. There may be little significance in the use

---

10. For ἐσθίει some MSS read ἐσθιέτω (P46 D F G etc.), but the imperative should probably be rejected. Apart from the attestation Paul seems to be "stating the facts of the situation rather than recommending a course of action" (Barrett).

11. ἐξουθενέω is from οὐθέν, "nothing", with the perfective prefix ἐξ, "to make absolutely nothing of".

12. The verb is προσλαμβάνω (see on v. 1), which has the notion "welcome" (so Moffatt).

13. See the note on 2:1 for this construction.

14. οἰκέτης, here only in Paul.

of this word rather than the ordinary word for "slave" which Paul uses elsewhere, but it is possible that he is reminding his readers that a household slave would be especially close to the master. He says that it is with respect to the master (and no one else) that he *stands or falls*.[15] This may mean either that whether he stands or falls is to his master's advantage or disadvantage or that it is his master's business whether he stands or falls.

And he will stand, the apostle goes on. He is surely thinking now of the weak and the strong rather than of his illustration. Neither can disenfranchise the other. It is God, not the strong/weak brother, who makes him stand. Paul finishes with the reminder that *the Lord*[16] *is able to make him stand* (Gifford quotes Wiclif, "the Lord is mighty . . ."). In the last resort it is the power of God that matters. The Lord is able to make his servant stand, and he will.

5. Food was not the only matter in dispute; there was also the question of the observance or nonobservance of certain days.[17] One person *considers one day more sacred than another*,[18] whereas another person makes no such distinction. This has often been taken to mean that the weak brother observes the Jewish Sabbath.[19] But Paul does not say this, and it is equally possible that he is referring to feast days and fast days, either those laid down in the Jewish law or those derived from other sources. Some refer to lucky and unlucky days deriving from pagan life (so Käsemann [p. 370], O'Neill, and others). The absence of any words of condemnation makes this last unlikely; it is hard to imagine that Paul would have accepted an appeal to luck as an acceptable Christian lifestyle. There is no indication as to which of the other possibilities is to be preferred, but we should bear in mind Paul's strong words about those who observed "special days and months and seasons and years", of whom he said, "I fear for you, that somehow I have wasted my efforts on you" (Gal. 4:10-11; cf. Col. 2:16ff.). It seems that some regarded the keeping of sacred times as of the essence of the Christian way. Paul rejected all such views with

---

15. The dative will be a dative of advantage or disadvantage and refer to the master in an earthly house; Paul is not here speaking of final judgment but using an illustration. For πίπτω in a moral sense cf. 11:11, 22, and for στήκω 1 Cor. 16:13; Phil. 1:27. They are contrasted in 1 Cor. 10:12. στήκω is a present formed from the perfect ἕστηκα; it is not found before the New Testament (BAGD) and is used by Paul in seven of its ten New Testament occurrences.

16. This reading should be accepted with P46 א A B C etc. rather than ὁ θεός with D F G etc.; the latter reading may well have been imported from v. 3.

17. The sentence begins with ὃς μέν, which this time has an answering ὃς δέ, giving the meaning "one . . . another". The pronouns are used as demonstratives (IBNTG, p. 125). γάρ is read by some MSS (א* A P etc.) but is probably to be omitted (as P46 אc B D F etc.).

18. There is an interesting change of meaning in Paul's use of κρίνω. He used it in the sense "condemn" in v. 4 whereas he uses it to mean something like "esteem" here. He follows it with παρ' ἡμέραν, where παρά has the meaning "'passing by' and so 'in preference to'" (SH). NIV understands this as *more sacred than*, but Paul says only "esteems one day more than a(nother) day."

19. And other days. A pious Jew could ask, "Why is any day better than another, when all the daylight in the year is from the sun?" and answer, "By the Lord's decision they were distinguished, and he appointed the different seasons and feasts" (Sir. 33:9).

decision. But where the centrality of justification by faith was clear and the observance of a certain day (or days) was no more than a practice some believer found helpful, it was another matter.

In this situation it is important that each individual *be fully convinced*[20] *in his own mind.*[21] To go along with what others do simply because they do it and without being convinced for oneself can be a dangerous practice. Specifically the weak brother can hurt his conscience by following the strong brother's practice without holding the strong brother's convictions.[22]

6. Paul proceeds to relate the practice of both the strong and the weak to the Master they both serve. His emphasis is on *the Lord* (mentioned three times in this verse). He speaks first of the person who "sets his mind on the day",[23] and says that he does this *to the Lord.*[24] It is not a device of the weak brother, brought about for his own comfort, convenience, or edification. He really is seeking to serve his Lord. The observance of the day, then, is in order to honor the Lord. Paul makes a similar statement about eating. The eater eats "to the Lord" (Paul does not say what is eaten, but the context makes it clear that it is *meat*, as NIV), and this is demonstrated by the fact that he *gives thanks to God.* But the person who does not eat "does not eat to the Lord", and he, too, gives thanks (contrast 1:21). In other words, both "say grace" over their meal, whatever it is. Both equally have a religious attitude, and neither is simply conforming to worldly practice or social custom. Paul is not referring to religious indifferentism or to ritualism. He is referring to genuinely held religious conviction, and action that springs from that conviction.

7-8. Paul substantiates this[25] by pointing out that none of us lives or dies to himself;[26] "we neither live nor die as self-contained units" (Phillips). There is a sense in which "no man is an island", for all our actions affect our fellowmen. But that is not what Paul is saying here. His thought is rather that neither in life nor in death can we escape the fact that what we do and are we do and are before God. Neither in life nor in death are we quite alone; we do both before God. No one lives or dies "for himself" (GNB). It is God, not self,

20. πληροφορέω means "fill (completely), fulfill" and is a synonym of πληρόω. But it can also mean "convince fully" (BAGD). Cf. its use of Abraham (4:21).

21. ἴδιος is important; the person must act according to *his own* mind, not that of someone else. And νοῦς is important; his intellect should be fully involved and he should not depend on some opinion (cf. Bengel).

22. Harrisville draws attention to another aspect: for Paul " 'indifferent things' remain indifferent, but never the disputes they occasion."

23. φρονέω means "to think" and is used in a variety of ways. One is "to set one's mind on, be intent on"—here on "a particular day rather than others" (BAGD).

24. This is an unusual construction. BDF take it as the "dative of advantage and disadvantage" with the meaning "in honor of the Lord" (188 [2]; so M, III, p. 238).

25. Note his use of γάρ, *for*. Kertelge finds the hymnlike style of vv. 7-9 and the introduction of "we" in place of the third person to be possible indications of a liturgical text. Käsemann sees the passage as rather having the characteristics of a diatribe.

26. The dative is the dative of advantage and disadvantage, though BDF think that it here "expresses more the possessor" (188 [2]), pointing out that the series ends with τοῦ κυρίου ἐσμέν.

that is important ultimately; to concentrate on self is to neglect our Maker and to sin against him (Black quotes D. M. Baillie, "the very essence of sin is self-centredness").[27] The reference to death is important in more ways than one. The first-century Stoic might seek to choose both the time and the manner of his death, but this is not a Christian option: our death is in the hands of God and in the purpose of God. Death is an enemy (1 Cor. 15:26), but it cannot separate us from the love of God in Christ (8:38-39). When Paul says that *we die to the Lord*, he is not saying that we die in any such sense as ceasing to have fellowship with him but rather that we pass from one form of service to God to another form of service to God. He is, of course, talking about Christians, not mankind at large. Alive or dead, we are the Lord's, and Paul's threefold use of *the Lord* in verse 8 puts emphasis on his supreme place.[28]

9. The death and resurrection of Jesus are now related to his lordship.[29] There is textual variation here, but there seems little doubt that we should accept the Greek underlying NIV's *died and returned to life*.[30] Not appreciating that the aorist is ingressive, some have taken the verb to refer to Jesus' earthly life (so Olshausen; cf. Phillips, "Christ lived and died"). But the aorist, coming as it does after the reference to the death of Jesus, signifies the entrance to a new state of life (IBNTG, p. 10); he died and subsequently sprang to life. Denney sees the purpose of this[31] as the purpose of God, and Murray as the purpose of Christ. However, we should probably not make a distinction between the two. Paul is simply referring to the divine purpose. This was that Jesus might *be the Lord of both the dead and the living*. Again we have an ingressive aorist,[32] giving the sense "became Lord". There is of course a sense in which Jesus was always Lord; that follows from his essential nature. Being who and what he is, he is necessarily Lord of all. But Paul is not talking about that. He is referring to what happened as a result of Jesus' atoning work; that brought about "the lordship of redemptive relationship" (Murray). In a very special sense Christ is Lord of those to whom he brought salvation through his atoning death. Paul sees *both the dead and the living* as under the scope of this lordship. The unusual order (we mostly speak of "the living and the

---

27. V. P. Furnish sums up this section of the epistle by saying, "All these expressions refer to man's release from the tyranny of a life turned in upon itself, preoccupied with its own ambitions and accomplishments, and thus alienated from its true destiny"; he cites 2 Cor. 5:15 (*Theology and Ethics in Paul* [Nashville, 1968], p. 181).

28. There is some textual uncertainty here, but it seems that we should read ἀποθνήσκωμεν on the first and third occasion, but the indicative ἀποθνήσκομεν on the second. The introduction of the substantive here is doubtless "a touch of edifying exhortation" (Cranfield).

29. εἰς τοῦτο signifies "to this end", and γάρ gives the reason for the foregoing. The atoning work of Jesus was to establish his lordship.

30. ἀπέθανεν καὶ ἔζησεν is read by ℵ* A B C etc. After ἀπέθανεν some MSS read καὶ ἀνέστη, some have ἀνέζησεν instead of ἔζησεν, and there are several combinations of these possibilities. The problem seems to have arisen in that after "died" the scribes looked for a verb that plainly indicated resurrection. We should take ἔζησεν as ingressive, "sprang to life"; it indicates resurrection, but not in the way some scribes expected.

31. ἵνα with the subjunctive.

32. κυριεύσῃ. The verb is used of the lordship that sin will not have (6:14).

dead") is probably due to the order in which Christ's dying and living are mentioned in the earlier part of the verse. And since Christ is Lord over all, dead and alive alike, then clearly eating or not eating, keeping a day or not, come under his direction.

10. Twice in this verse Paul uses an emphatic *you* (cf. GNB, "You, then . . .—why. . . ? And you . . .—why. . . ?"), first of the weak who is inclined to condemn the strong for doing what the weak considers sinful, then of the strong who is tempted to despise the weak (cf. v. 3). The meat eater and the vegetarian, the day-keeper and the non-day-keeper, all alike are subject to the one Lord who will in due course sit in judgment on them all. Any judgments that they may pass are irrelevant, and in the light of the assize they all face they should not presume to anticipate the divine judgment. Both times Paul refers to *your brother* (a term he has not used since 12:1 and which he employs five times in this chapter), an important concept in this discussion. "If the Lord has ordained among us a society of brothers, equality must be observed. Anyone, therefore, who assumes the part of a judge is behaving insolently" (Calvin). It is not a mere acquaintance but a brother in Christ who is being judged or despised.[33] A reason is introduced by *For*,[34] but it is not clear whether the warning against judging others is because those who judge will themselves face judgment in due course (cf. Matt. 7:1; Luke 6:37) or whether Paul means that the brother who is the object of this "judgment" will in due course be judged by God (not by his fellows). Either way the thought is that the verdict that matters is God's. The coming judgment will be universal; *all* are caught up in it and will *stand before*[35] *God's judgment seat*.[36] Some MSS read "the judgment seat of Christ", but it is usually agreed that the right reading is *God's*.[37] The New Testament teaching, of course, is that God will judge us all through the agency of Christ. But even though we reject the reading "Christ's" at this point, it is important to notice how easily Paul moves from "Christ" to "God" in this passage.

11. Now comes a characteristic appeal to Scripture. The apostle quotes from Isaiah 45:23 (LXX) with a small change of word order, preceded by " 'As I live,' says the Lord" from Isaiah 49:18. NIV takes these words in the sense *As surely as I live*, which is the meaning of it. The bowing of the knee is an expression of homage and in this passage indicates "worship". With this is linked *every tongue will confess to God*.[38] This may be understood in the sense

33. For the strong term ἐξουθενέω see on v. 3.
34. γάρ.
35. παρίστημι means "to place beside, stand beside", but it is also used in the technical sense of standing before a judge or a judgment seat (cf Acts 27:24).
36. βῆμα is connected with βαίνω and can mean "a step" (Acts 7:5), hence a raised place mounted by steps, a platform, or, as here, the official seat of a judge.
37. θεοῦ is read by MSS like ℵ* A B C* D G, and Χριστοῦ by ℵc C² P Ψ and others. The weight of the MSS is behind θεοῦ, and it would seem that Χριστοῦ has been imported from 2 Cor. 5:10.
38. ἐξομολογέω may be used in the sense "promise" (Luke 22:6), or for confessing sins (Matt. 3:6 etc.), but it is also used of acknowledging (Phil. 2:11) and of praising (Matt.

"confess that I am God" (GNB) or "give praise to God" (RSV, Moffatt, etc.).
Paul is saying that in the end every one of us will do homage to God.

12. Paul rounds off this part of his argument with a short statement of
which Denney says, "Every word in this sentence is emphatic" (so Cranfield). *So then* introduces the logical conclusion.[39] *Each* makes the judgment
universal: each one of us is caught up in it and there is no escaping it. *Of us*
makes it personal: we cannot see this as applying to our neighbor but not
ourselves. And we should notice that Paul is including himself with his readers. *Give an account* is an expression often used for the keeping of financial
records. A reminder of the judgment we all face is a fitting conclusion to this
stage of the discussion. The fact that each will render account for himself
leaves no room for despising and judging others. The verdict on them is for
God, not us.[40]

2. The Way of Peace and Love, 14:13-23

13*Therefore let us stop passing judgment on one another. Instead, make up
your mind not to put any stumbling block or obstacle in your brother's way.* 14*As
one who is in the Lord Jesus, I am fully convinced that no food is unclean in itself.
But if anyone regards something as unclean, then for him it is unclean.* 15*If your
brother is distressed because of what you eat, you are no longer acting in love. Do
not by your eating destroy your brother for whom Christ died.* 16*Do not allow
what you consider good to be spoken of as evil.* 17*For the kingdom of God is not a
matter of eating and drinking, but of righteousness, peace and joy in the Holy
Spirit,* 18*because anyone who serves Christ in this way is pleasing to God and
approved by men.*

19*Let us therefore make every effort to do what leads to peace and to mutual
edification.* 20*Do not destroy the work of God for the sake of food. All food is
clean, but it is wrong for a man to eat anything that causes someone else to
stumble.* 21*It is better not to eat meat or drink wine or to do anything else that
will cause your brother to fall.*

22*So whatever you believe about these things keep between yourself and God.
Blessed is the man who does not condemn himself by what he approves.* 23*But the
man who has doubts is condemned if he eats, because his eating is not from faith;
and everything that does not come from faith is sin.*

11:25). Chrysostom thinks that this means "shall give an account of what he has done",
and Michel sees the meaning as "the eschatological confession of sins which each must
make before the judgment throne of God" (TDNT, V, p. 215). Käsemann rejects this in
favor of "acclamation connected with *proskynesis*" (p. 373).

39. ἄρα οὖν, for which see the note on 5:18. οὖν is absent from some MSS, as is τῷ θεῷ
at the end of the verse, but Wilckens argues that the shorter text may be secondary.
Metzger's committee found reasons for and against τῷ θεῷ and accordingly included the
words in the text but put them in square brackets.

40. Cf. Barrett, "The strong, then, is right; but if he boasts of his superiority he
instantly becomes as wrong as the man he despises. The weak is mistaken, yet accepted;
and he must not put himself in God's place, and judge the strong." Godet makes an
interesting practical point: earlier Paul has argued in effect, "Judge not thy brother, for
God will judge *him*"; now he is saying, "Judge thyself, for God will judge *thee*."

Paul says explicitly that "no food is unclean in itself" (v. 14) and hammers home his argument that no Christian should act as though the presence or absence of scruples about food is the important thing. All believers should have due regard for other believers whose view is different. Much more important than a particular view of food are things like consideration for other people, righteousness, peace, and joy. This part of the argument is a plea that the Roman Christians differentiate the important from the unimportant and that they act with consideration for others. Love, not particular views about food, must be the guide.

13. The first exhortation in this section seems directed at both the weak and the strong, but thereafter the strong are primarily in view. After all, they have greater scope: they can partake of the food in question or abstain; they can treat a day as special or treat all days alike. It is easier for them to change their practice. They should show consideration for their weaker comrades and promote the cause of peace and unity. But when Paul says *let us stop passing judgment on one another,* he is surely concerned about the weak as well as the strong. It is important that Christians do not arrogate to themselves the right to pass judgment on their fellows, a divine prerogative as Paul has just made clear (vv. 11-12). Indeed, his *Therefore*[41] bases this direction on what he has just said about judgment. The present tense together with his "no longer"[42] implies that the Romans have been doing this and urges them to stop.[43] But his *let us*, characteristically including himself, means that this is not a peremptory command given by someone who adopts a superior position. What he is saying is something to which he must give heed as well as they. What he looks for is the very opposite of judgment, as his use of the strong adversative[44] shows. Jesus warned his followers against actions that would hurt others (cf. Matt. 18:7; Mark 9:42; Luke 17:1-2), and his servant had learned this lesson well. For all its popularity among some Christians, judgment of others is an activity from which believers do well to abstain.[45] Far more important than censuring a weaker brother for some overscrupulous action is it to make a firm resolve not to hinder such a weak brother in any way.

The content of the resolve for which the apostle looks is *not to put*[46] *any*

---

41. οὖν.

42. μηκέτι.

43. Barrett holds that the tense also "supports the view that Paul is addressing a real, not a hypothetical, situation".

44. ἀλλά, which NIV renders *Instead*. It is reinforced by μᾶλλον.

45. The verb κρίνω is used in two senses here. The first time it carries the notion of passing an adverse judgment on other believers; the second time it points rather to a decision that will determine one's own line of conduct (NIV, *make up your mind*). The aorist tense points to a firm decision.

46. τὸ μὴ τιθέναι. BDF comment on the nominative and accusative of the substantivized infinitive that "its reference to something previously mentioned or otherwise well known, is more or less evident" (399 [3]). TH remarks that the implied subject of this infinitive is "you", so that it should not be given an impersonal construction as in NEB's "that no obstacle or stumbling-block be placed in a brother's way."

stumbling block or obstacle[47] in that brother's way. It is not enough for a Christian that a certain course is not wrong; he must also consider its effect on other people, specifically on his *brother*, one bound to him by close ties.

14. "I know and am persuaded in the Lord Jesus" (cf. Phil. 2:24) is a very strong affirmation (it is "strikingly emphatic", Cranfield). Paul lets it be known that he has no doubts about this whatever; it must be stated with the utmost plainness. That is quite clear. What is not quite so clear is whether he is referring directly to some teaching of Jesus (as Matt. 15:11; 23:25-26; Mark 7:15), whether he means "on the authority of the Lord Jesus" (LB, NEB mg.), or whether he is saying, "My union with the Lord Jesus makes me certain . . ." (GNB). Since he says "in the Lord Jesus", perhaps some such meaning as that of GNB is in order. He is not so much quoting as speaking out of the richness of his being "in" Christ. His relationship to Christ makes him absolutely certain about some things, of which this is one. "Nothing", he says, "is common of itself".[48] Paul is denying that there is such a thing as ceremonial uncleanness; that is impossible if we take seriously what God has done in Christ (cf. Acts 10:9-15; 1 Tim. 4:4; Tit. 1:15, etc.). All of life is God's, and there is no ceremonial area from which he is excluded. In principle the "strong" are right. Nothing is inherently unclean.

But[49] when someone *regards something as unclean*, the situation is different. If it is a question of food, there is no uncleanness in the thing itself; but if a person regards it as such, then *for him it is unclean*. The person's conscience is such that he cannot partake of the food in question without seeing the action as wrong. Such a person should not eat such a food. He should never do anything that he thinks, however misguidedly, is wrong. This is not because of anything inherent in the thing itself; Paul has already made that plain. No, it is because of his conscience. This does not mean, as Dodd points out, that "Nothing is good or ill, but thinking makes it so", for some things are good and some are evil whatever we may think about them. It is taboos that Paul has in mind.

---

47. The *stumbling block* (πρόσκομμα) is an obstacle in the way; when the foot strikes it the person stumbles. The *obstacle* (σκάνδαλον) refers strictly to the bait stick of a trap; when an animal or bird strikes it this triggers off the mechanism that produces entrapment. Many think that the two words are practically synonyms here, but Leenhardt holds that the former word points to something that is "met with by chance" and the latter to "the result of an intention". It is, however, difficult to think that a strong Christian would intend to trap a weak brother, so some such translation as NIV is in order. The two words occur in 9:33.

48. κοινός means "common", "communal" (as distinct from ἴδιος, "one's own"). It may also be used of "that which comes into contact w. anything and everything, and is therefore *common, ordinary, profane*. . . . Of that which is ceremonially impure" (BAGD). "Of itself", δι' ἑαυτοῦ, is the reading of ℵ B C² etc., while A C* D F G etc. have δι' αὐτοῦ, "through him", i.e., "nothing is impure through Christ" (for he did away with such distinctions). Most agree that the former reading is to be preferred.

49. εἰ μή often means "except", and some so translate it here. But after a negative joined to a noun it may be used in such a way that it refers to the negative alone; then it may be seen as adversative and thus equivalent to ἀλλά (BDF 448 [8]; so Shedd). Lenski renders "only".

15. NIV omits "for",[50] presumably because it makes for a difficult transition. We should probably take it as referring back to verse 13, with verse 14 as something of a parenthesis. The condition is stated realistically;[51] "on account of food" comes next in an emphatic position. On account of something as unimportant as food, Paul is saying, one who is no less than *your brother* is grieved. The strong Christian is not dealing with abstract truths but grieving his own brother in Christ.[52] The verb rendered *is distressed*[53] is a strong term. Paul is saying that the affront to the weak brother's scruples could cause him deep hurt. His sensitive conscience is deeply pained as he observes the strong brother doing what he cannot but feel is wrong. He may also be emboldened to do the thing himself, in which case the hurt is even deeper. Murray points out that more than grief is involved; there is hurt from the violation of religious convictions. His integrity as a believer is at stake. If this happens, the strong brother is not walking[54] (a characteristic Pauline term) in love (a characteristic Pauline idea). For Christians love is the standard and love is the motive.[55]

"Not for your food",[56] Paul goes on, thus stressing the small gain to the strong Christian compared to the terrible loss for the weak one. "Do not destroy that one", he says, and his pronoun is emphatic;[57] "that one for whom Christ died" (cf. 1 Cor. 8:11). It is no less than Christ who did no less than die for that weak brother, and is it too much to ask the strong to abstain from a particular kind of food?[58]

16. Consequently[59] Paul exhorts believers not to let their good be evil spoken of. The big problem here is the meaning of "good". Moffatt renders "Your rights must not get a bad name", and many accept the kindred view

---

50. γάρ.

51. εἰ with the indicative may be understood in the sense "if, as is the case. . . ." Paul is putting it strongly.

52. σου drives it home to the individual. Luther asks, "Why, then, should he be more concerned about his belly and gullet, which are bound to perish, than about his brother who will live for ever?" Brunner warns against "a devout carelessness in doing what one has recognized as right for oneself but which can ruin one's neighbour."

53. λυπεῖται.

54. περιπατεῖς, which NIV renders *you are . . . acting.*

55. Cf. Burton H. Throckmorton, "Paul is consistent in his criterion: one is free *to love;* one is not free *not to love*" (*Adopted in Love* [New York, 1978], p. 104).

56. μὴ τῷ βρώματί σου. Turner takes this as a dative of cause and says, "This dat. is extraordinary" (M, III, p. 242). Moule sees it as instrumental (IBNTG, p. 44).

57. ἐκεῖνον.

58. The bearing of this on the final perseverance of the saints is differently understood. Hodge says, "They are saved only, if they continue steadfast unto the end. If they apostasize, they perish. . . . Saints are preserved, not in despite of apostacy, but from apostacy." Hendriksen understands the passage to mean "you, by means of your unbrotherly conduct, are treating him in a manner which, were it not for God's irresistible grace, would destroy him." Murray points out that "All sin is destructive" and that the sin of the weak "if not repaired, would lead to perdition." The strong must consider this "and not take refuge behind the security of the believer and the final perseverance of the saints." Whichever way we understand it, the strong are being given a serious warning.

59. οὖν, "therefore".

that Paul is speaking of the liberty the strong enjoy in Christ (Calvin, Murray, SH, TH, and others), a view which H. Moule expresses in these terms: do not let your liberty "be railed at, as only a thinly-veiled self-indulgence after all." Others hold that the words are addressed to the Romans as a whole, the weak as well as the strong, and that therefore the meaning cannot be liberty. It must be something like "your salvation" (cf. Lenski), a view which Luther puts this way: "what you are in God and what you have from God." Or it might be the gospel (Hendriksen, Cranfield; cf. Chrysostom), for this will be brought into disrepute if the strong hurt the weak for the sake of so little. Any of these is possible, but perhaps there is most to be said for the third. It is not clear whether the evil speaking is seen as coming from inside or outside the church. If the former it will be the weak criticizing the strong, but it seems more likely that Paul is thinking of the harm that would come to the Christian message if people outside could see that some Christians had so little care and concern for others in the membership.[60]

17. *For* carries on the argument and gives a reason for the preceding. It is because *the kingdom of God* is what it is that those who are in it should behave as Paul has suggested. This is the only use of the expression *the kingdom of God* in Romans. Indeed, Paul does not make a great deal of use of the concept (1 Cor. 4:20; 6:9-10; 15:50; Gal. 5:21; Col. 4:11; 1 Thess. 2:12; 2 Thess. 1:5; cf. 1 Cor. 15:24; Eph. 5:5; Col. 1:13); all told he uses the word "kingdom" only 14 times (Matthew has it 55 times; Mark, 20; Luke, 46; and John, 5). When he does use it, he mostly refers to the kingdom in its future aspect (the present may be only here and in 1 Cor. 4:20). The *kingdom* is distinctive,[61] and Paul brings this out by contrasting *eating and drinking*[62] (which apparently mattered so much to some of the Romans) with *righteousness, peace and joy in the Holy Spirit*. His *but* is the strong adversative,[63] which sets the two in sharp contrast. The three qualities he names are all important concepts with the apostle, and the combination is striking. But there is some dispute as to exactly how they should be understood here. It is possible to see a reference to the righteousness in Christ that is God's gift, to peace with God and to the joy that God gives (as Hodge, Shedd, and Cranfield). Or the three may refer to ethical qualities: "righteousness as fulfilled and peace promoted and preserved by believers . . . joy in the believer's heart" (Murray; cf. SH, Barrett).

---

60. On this whole subject Barclay remarks, "A new age would dawn in the Church if we remembered that our rights are far less important than our obligations".
61. Earthly kingdoms do not give us the pattern for the kingdom of God: "Those kingdoms make their kings, who are nothing without them; here the King makes the kingdom, which is nothing without him" (Lenski).
62. Strictly βρῶσις and πόσις (both here only in Romans) denote the acts of eating and drinking, though both can signify the appropriate concrete, i.e., food and drink, and some see this meaning here. But NIV is probably correct. For a similar view about food cf. 1 Cor. 8:8. There is a rabbinic saying: "In the future world there is no eating nor drinking nor propagation nor business nor jealousy nor hatred nor competition, but the righteous sit with crowns on their heads feasting on the brightness of the divine presence" (Ber. 17a). But Paul is talking about the kingdom now, and the rabbis about the world to come.
63. ἀλλά.

The former is favored by the primacy of God in the kingdom of God; it is not a kingdom brought in by our efforts but by what God has done and is doing. The latter arises naturally enough from the context, which refers to the actions of Roman Christians. It seems likely that Paul is not differentiating sharply between these two views and that he is using the expression in a way that suggests both (cf. Denney). The concluding words *in the Holy Spirit* are probably to be attached to all three concepts and not to be confined to *joy*.[64]

18. Again Paul carries his argument along in logical sequence.[65] *Anyone who serves Christ* points to more than merely nominal service; it indicates wholehearted commitment.[66] It is significant that Paul does not say "he who eats rightly" or "he who is considerate of his brother" or the like, but "he who serves Christ". Everything is related to Christ. There is a problem regarding the Greek rendered *in this way*, which properly means "in this". We expect a plural to cover all that has been listed,[67] and the question arises as to what "this" means. It may be the principle involved, or "in the Holy Spirit" (who has just been mentioned), or "the whole idea of spiritual privilege" (CBSC). Perhaps better is the view that it is the righteousness, peace, and joy that have just been mentioned, the singular being used because they are viewed as a unity. The person who serves like this *is pleasing to God* (this is the kind of service that God demands) and is also *approved by men*. This is in contrast to being "spoken of as evil" (v. 16). The word *approved*[68] means "able to stand the test", "approved by testing" and indicates that the person in question, being pleasing to God, has survived the test and should be approved by his fellows, believers and unbelievers alike.[69]

19. As a result of all this[70] Paul exhorts his readers to pursue[71] (a verb

---

64. Cf. Conzelmann, "The addition ἐν πνεύματι ἁγίῳ characterises righteousness, peace and joy as blessings of eschatological salvation; there is no reason to relate it to joy alone" (TDNT, IX, p. 369 n. 90; he also says, "the eschaton determines the present"). BDF 272, however, affirm the link with χαρά and also find this unusual, for "Prepositional attributives going with anarthrous substantives are usually avoided for the sake of clarity." Turner comments on the rarity (M, III, p. 221), but he also finds a reason for the anarthrous noun here in that it comes at the end of a list of anarthrous nouns (p. 176). Lenski sees the anarthrous noun as a proper name "which needs no article."

65. γάρ, which NIV this time renders *because*.

66. The verb δουλεύω means "serve as a slave". This indicates that the servant in question belongs entirely to Christ.

67. A number of MSS have the plural, but the reading seems secondary and most accept the singular.

68. δόκιμος.

69. Lenski holds that the dative should be understood not as "approved of men" but "approved for men"; those approved are approved by God and thus are valuable for men. This is true, but it does not appear to be what Paul is saying.

70. ἄρα οὖν, for which see the note on 5:10.

71. διώκωμεν is read by C D Ψ etc. while διώκομεν has the support of ℵ A B G^gr etc. Metzger's committee found it "extremely difficult to answer" the question of which reading is to be preferred. The attestation of the indicative is better, but the context favors exhortation. Indeed, so strong is this consideration that W. Foerster speaks of the indicative here as "impossible" (TDNT, II, p. 416). In ancient MSS ω and o are often confused. This, taken with intrinsic probability and the fact that an exhortation seems required, convinces Cranfield that we should accept the subjunctive. This seems the best course.

which indicates more than a slight interest; it means earnest application) *what leads to peace* (more literally "the things of peace"). In the New Testament the most important thing about peace is that Christ has brought about peace with God, but in passages like this one the thought is rather that of peace with one another. Here the word is used in parallel with edification so that it clearly means peace with other people. It is the responsibility of those at peace with God to pursue the kind of conduct that will promote peace with people. *Edification*[72] is a term which properly means the erection of a building, but in the New Testament it is used in the metaphorical sense of building people up. It is mostly a Pauline conception (Paul has it 15 times out of 18 in the New Testament). Paul saw the building up of Christians in the faith as most important (cf. 1 Cor. 14:26, "let all things be done for edification"), and further that it was something in which every believer could have a part. So here he exhorts the Roman believers to build one another up. Their aim should be to help one another rather than to criticize or despise.

20. By putting "not for the sake of food" in the emphatic position Paul again draws attention to the very small gain which some were evidently striving to obtain. Not for such a small matter should anyone *destroy the work of God*. He has just spoken of the importance of "building up", and he uses a verb which envisages the naturally opposite process and which NIV renders *destroy*.[73] *The work of God* is a very unusual expression, found only once elsewhere in the New Testament and then in a different sense (John 6:29, where "the work of God" is that we believe; the plural "the works of God" is more frequent). There is wide divergence as to the way we should understand it here. Thus Boylan holds that it refers to what God does in the individual Christian, while Barrett denies this and sees a reference to the church. Wesley combines the two ideas: "Which He builds in the soul by faith, and in the Church by concord." Michel sees a reference to the cross (as in v. 15b), Cranfield to what God does in the weak brother, and Haldane to what he does in the believer. Without some further explanation we cannot be sure of the apostle's full meaning, but he is certainly including what God has done in the weak brother, for it is that that is to be built up or broken down. There may be a fuller meaning, but we cannot be sure.

"All things are clean", Paul goes on to say (NIV inserts *food*, but while the main thrust of the present argument concerns food, Paul uses a wider term). *Clean* means free from anything that soils or corrupts. The apostle moves to the singular when he refers to what is "bad",[74] evidently as he moves in thought from the general application to all things to the present problem for the individual. The construction is elliptical and the precise

---

72. οἰκοδομή.
73. καταλύω means to "loose down". It may be used of loosing the clothing, harness, etc. when the traveller halts for the night (Luke 9:12), or for a more radical loosing like the demolition of the temple (Mark 14:58; 15:29).
74. κακόν.

meaning is in some doubt. Paul may be referring to the weak or to the strong. The meaning might be "All things are clean but they bring evil to the person who eats with a sense of offending" (cf. Phillips, food "can be harmful to the man . . ."), or the very similar "evil happens to the man. . . ." But the meaning might also be ". . . it is wrong for any one to make others fall by what he eats" (RSV). Cranfield argues that the context favors a reference to the strong, but Murray holds that the meaning is that the weak is in trouble if he eats. Barrett sees a difficulty in that the eater may well be the strong (cf. v. 21) who is thus laying a stumbling block before the weak, or the words may refer to the weak person who has been made to stumble by the example of the strong. He concludes, "It may be, perhaps, that the vagueness and obscurity of Paul's sentence is due to the fact that he is thinking of both possibilities, and expresses himself so as to allow for both." In view of the difficulty in tying the meaning down it may be well to adopt some such view and keep open the possibilities.[75]

21. Paul does not say "It is not good to eat meat",[76] but "It is good not to eat meat"; he is setting forth the course of action that will help the brother. His use of the aorist tense for his infinitives may be significant.[77] There is nothing wrong with the eating and drinking as such. They are to be avoided when they cause offence but not necessarily at other times. Paul is relating his teaching to a given situation. With the eating of meat Paul links the drinking of wine, but he does not specify in what way this might cause offence as he has done to some extent with eating (v. 2; he does not actually say that the weak abstain from the use of wine, though that seems implied; but he may be putting a hypothetical case). It may be that some specific practice associated with wine troubled some of the Romans (e.g., being offered to a pagan deity as a libation). Or Paul may simply have been using this as an expression to indicate that in the matter of diet he was ready to go to any lengths to avoid giving trouble to weaker believers. There is another elliptical construction (nothing in the Greek corresponds to NIV's *or to do anything else*, though this gives the sense of it; cf. BDF 480 [1]).[78] The important thing is to take such action that we do not lead anyone to stumble; that is, we must not encourage them to perform actions they can only do in defiance of their conscience.

22. Paul opens this verse with an emphatic *you*, which makes the ap-

75. διὰ προσκόμματος has caused discussion. διά is used "to denote manner", here "with offence" (BDF 223 [3]; so M, III, p. 267). This may mean that the offence is with the weak who eats with a guilty conscience (Hodge, Murray) or with the strong whose eating brings trouble to others (RSV, GNB, SH).

76. The word for meat is κρέας, "flesh meat", here and in 1 Cor. 8:13 only in the New Testament.

77. "It is good not to eat meat *for once* (in a specific instance) if it might cause offense; it is not a question of continuous abstention" (BDF 338 [1]). Turner comments that τό + infinitive (as in v. 13) is rare in the Ptolemaic papyri and in the New Testament outside Paul (M, III, p. 140).

78. He simply says μηδὲ ἐν ᾧ, where Turner discerns a causal use of ἐν. Käsemann speaks of a "remarkable relative attraction" (p. 378; what is the antecedent?).

plication personal. Throughout this chapter he has varied his address; he used the first person plural in verses 13 and 19, the second plural in 13 and 16, the second singular in 15 (twice), 20, 21, and 22. There is thus something of a preference for the more personal and individual singular. "You," he says, "have the faith that[79] you have to yourself", where he displays prominently the quality of faith. He is not speaking here of saving faith but presuming it. He is thinking rather of the faith that enables anyone who has it to follow without hesitation or scruple a course of action which his weaker brother cannot follow. That faith he should not parade, but exercise it where only he knows about it: "The faith that you have, keep between yourself and God" (RSV).[80]

Paul pronounces a blessing on *the man who does not condemn himself by what he approves*. Some translations have "happy" instead of "blessed" (so KJV). But the term[81] has a religious content that is lacking in "happy"; it is not just an emotion but the very blessing of God.[82]

23. Over against the strong, blessed in the freedom he enjoys under God, Paul sets the weak, plagued with doubts.[83] If this man eats[84] he stands condemned.[85] The reason for this condemnation is that *his eating is not from faith*.[86] It is important that we act in accordance with our fundamental Christian beliefs, for "any action that is not based on faith is a sin" (Moffatt).[87] The apostle is condemning conduct that springs from motives like selfishness or greed or fear. Faith is that by which one receives salvation, but it is also basic to the whole Christian way of life. Faith is a humble reliance on God, on God alone, for salvation and for the living out of the implications of that salvation. What cannot be justified by being in accord with our relation to Christ is sin.[88]

---

79. The majority of the MSS (including some good ones such as D G P) omit the relative ἥν, and Godet, e.g., rejects it accordingly. Its occurrence in ℵ A B C etc. may have been due to a desire to remove a certain abruptness (Metzger), or its omission may have been accidental. Without it the text might be a statement ("You have faith. Keep it to yourself before God") or a question ("Do you have faith? Keep it . . ."). The probability is that it was original.

80. Cf. Barrett, "True faith is an invisible relation between man and God, a confidence in God so complete that the man who has it knows that no religious scrupulosity can add to the security of his relation with God. But the moment 'faith' begins to parade itself as a visible thing which can be demonstrated by such acts as eating flesh and drinking wine, it ceases to be faith and becomes weakness." Cf. also Parry, "the doubter must not claim the freedom he does not feel" (CGT).

81. μακάριος.

82. Denney comments, "It is a rare felicity . . . to have a conscience untroubled by scruples . . . he who has this felicity should ask no more."

83. See the note on διακρίνω in 4:20.

84. The aorist φάγῃ points to a single action rather than the continuing practice.

85. κατακέκριται. BDF 344 note that the perfect in general assertions or imaginary examples is rarely used in the New Testament, as in classical, and that this example is "entirely in conformity with classical usage."

86. The Greek is very concise: ὅτι οὐκ ἐκ πίστεως, where ἐκ seems to denote origin; cf. Phillips, "his action does not spring from his faith". That kind of action necessarily means condemnation.

87. Paul's πᾶν is a comprehensive neuter; it is quite general.

88. The words attributed to Jesus in the addition to Luke 6:4 in Codex Bezae are

Some take this as very general and see it as meaning that all works done prior to justification are sinful. Augustine is usually cited for this view, and it is put forward in modern times by Lenski and others. But we should bear in mind the warning of Chrysostom, "Now all these things have been spoken by Paul of the subject in hand, not of everything." In the context Paul is referring to those actions of a believer that do not spring from a right faith. Whatever be the truth of actions done before one becomes a believer, Paul is not discussing them here. His concern is with the believer who sometimes does things that are not motivated by faith. It is those things that have the nature of sin.[89]

---

often cited. To a man working on the Sabbath Jesus is reputed to have said, "Man, if you know what you are doing, you are blessed; but if you do not know, you are accursed and a transgressor of the law" (cited from Metzger on Luke 6:5).

89. A number of MSS have the doxology at this point, and there is evidence that at one time the epistle ended here. For a discussion of these questions see the Introduction, pp. 21ff.; see also Metzger, pp. 533-36.

Romans 15

3. Christian Unity, 15:1-13

¹We who are strong ought to bear with the failings of the weak and not to please ourselves. ²Each of us should please his neighbor for his good, to build him up. ³For even Christ did not please himself but, as it is written: "The insults of those who insult you have fallen on me."ᵃ ⁴For everything that was written in the past was written to teach us, so that through endurance and the encouragement of the Scriptures we might have hope.

⁵May the God who gives endurance and encouragement give you a spirit of unity among yourselves as you follow Christ Jesus, ⁶so that with one heart and mouth you may glorify the God and Father of our Lord Jesus Christ.

⁷Accept one another, then, just as Christ accepted you, in order to bring praise to God. ⁸For I tell you that Christ has become a servant of the Jewsᵇ on behalf of God's truth, to confirm the promises made to the patriarchs ⁹so that the Gentiles may glorify God for his mercy, as it is written:

> "Therefore I will praise you among the Gentiles;
>   I will sing hymns to your name."ᶜ

¹⁰Again, it says,

> "Rejoice, O Gentiles, with his people."ᵈ

¹¹And again,

> "Praise the Lord, all you Gentiles,
>   and sing praises to him, all you peoples."ᵉ

¹²And again, Isaiah says,

> "The root of Jesse will spring up,
>   one who will arise to rule over the nations;
> the Gentiles will hope in him."ᶠ

¹³May the God of hope fill you with all joy and peace as you trust in him, so that you may overflow with hope by the power of the Holy Spirit.

ᵃ3 Psalm 69:9   ᵇ8 Greek *circumcision*   ᶜ9 2 Samuel 22:50; Psalm 18:49   ᵈ10 Deut. 32:43   ᵉ11 Psalm 117:1   ᶠ12 Isaiah 11:10

There is no break in sense as Paul carries on with his treatment of the strong and the weak, but in this section of his argument he puts somewhat more stress on the importance of unity among Christians. He does not use the word "love", but the conduct and the attitude for which he looks are best understood as the outworking of that love of which he has written so feelingly in the earlier part of the letter. There is something of a change at the end of verse 6, and some scholars see a new division of the letter as beginning there, with the example of Christ before us in the earlier verses and the relation of Jews and Gentiles in those that follow. Such a division is certainly in order, but the whole passage is concerned in one way or another with the unity that ought to be characteristic of believers.

1. Paul continues with his subject.[1] His *we* is emphatic[2] and indicates both that the strong have a significant role and that Paul numbers himself among the strong. It is true that he has the habit of classing himself with those of whom he is speaking (see the note on 3:5), but the language here makes it clear that he regards himself as one of the strong. He is concerned that the strong should take up the right attitude toward the weak. His terminology changes a little and he refers to the "able" and the "unable"[3] rather than to the "strong" and the "weak", but there is no reason to think that he has moved to a consideration of two different groups. Here he is concerned that the strong take seriously their obligation[4] to use their God-given strength in the service of the God who gave it and therefore in that of their weaker fellows (cf. Gal. 6:2). In every age it has been easy for the strong to find reasons why they should take little notice of the weak.[5] Indeed, it is a constant in the infinite variety of human cultures that the strong tend to use their strength as a means of easing their burdens and making the weak bear them as well as their own. Even in the Christian church they all too easily see it as unfair that their conduct should be modified on account of considerations that seem of no importance to them, even though those considerations form insurmountable problems for their weak brothers. They do not realize that their strength is given them in order that it may be used to help others.

But they are to *bear with the failings of the weak*.[6] This means, of course,

---

1. This section is linked to the previous with δέ, which most translations simply ignore, though LB has "Even if".

2. ἡμεῖς. Wilckens comments on this.

3. οἱ δυνατοί and οἱ ἀδύνατοι. The former term is used of the chief men in Acts 25:5 (cf. 1 Cor. 1:26), but here it is rather Christians who are "firm in conviction and faith" (GT; cf. 2 Cor. 12:10; 13:9). ἀδύνατος may be used of what is "impossible" (8:3), but here it means those who are impotent, without power (as in Acts 14:8).

4. He uses the verb ὀφείλομεν, "we owe it". It is a strong word and makes clear that Paul does not think the strong have a choice in the matter. In another letter he asks "What do you have that you did not receive?" (1 Cor. 4:7), and something like that is also true of his view of the strong; they are not the naturally powerful but those to whom God has given ability.

5. Cf. H. Moule, "A dominant school, in any age or region, too easily comes to talk and act as if all decided expression on the other side were an instance of 'intolerance,' while yet it allows itself insufficiently severe and censorious courses of its own" (pp. 393-94).

6. τὰ ἀσθενήματα τῶν ἀδυνάτων βαστάζειν. The verb βαστάζειν is used for carrying

that they should tolerate rather than criticize the weak, that they should endure the irritation caused by the practices of the weak. But it means more. It means that they should "carry" the weak. This is more than that they "ought to help the weak to carry their burdens" (GNB). They are to support and sustain the weak (cf. Moffatt, "We who are strong ought to bear the burdens that the weak make for themselves and us"). There may well be a reference (as, e.g., Michel thinks) to Isaiah 53:4;[7] whether this is so or not, the strong are to take firm action to assist the weak. This is very important in the Christian church, for the church is a very inclusive body, made up of people old and young, rich and poor, intellectually able and handicapped, of every race and class. It is not easy to maintain a sense of "family" in such a group, and the strong bear a heavy responsibility for bringing it about.[8] We should also bear in mind that "strong" and "able" are relative terms; in the Christian church we are all "strong" in some respects and in some situations. What Paul is saying is not something we can easily set aside, regarding it as advice for someone else.

The negative side of carrying the weak is that we are *not to please ourselves*. This does not mean that we are never to do anything that we want to do, but that we are never to do what pleases us regardless of its effects on others. Consideration for weaker Christians takes precedence over what we ourselves would like to do.[9] Elsewhere Paul can cite his own example; he practises what he preaches (1 Cor. 10:33; cf. Rom. 8:8; Phil. 2:4). Selfishness is always a barrier to effective Christian work,[10] and of course it breaks up Christian unity, which is such an important consideration throughout this discussion.[11]

2. As Paul continues his exhortation, he does not use a connecting particle. *Us* could mean "us Christians" or "us strong people", but probably the former, for *each* seems to make it universal in its Christian application and,

---

literal burdens (Mark 14:13); interestingly it is used for carrying the cross physically (John 19:17) and spiritually (Luke 14:27). ἀσθένημα is used only here in the New Testament; it means "weakness", here "of conscientious scruples caused by weakness of faith" (BAGD).

7. Though the verb there in LXX is φέρω. But in Matt. 8:17 it is quoted in a form that employs βαστάζω.

8. Gore thinks that "probably in part . . . we have ceased to think of the real fellowship of the naturally unlike ‑fellowship in all that makes up human life—as a necessary part of the Christian religion. But to St. Paul there was no Christianity without the reality of catholic brotherhood." The "fellowship of the naturally unlike" is a very real part of being Christian.

9. "The originality of Christianity is here brilliantly manifested. The Greek sage aimed at an ideal of autarchy; the voice of conscience was sufficient for him and he despised the opinion of others" (Leenhardt, who further comments, "love gives birth to humility").

10. "Il faut sortir de soi" (Lagrange).

11. MM find the idea of service underlying ἀρέσκω in this and some other New Testament passages; Abbott-Smith sees this meaning in the inscriptions and accepts it here. That service is involved is implied throughout the passage, but "please" seems to be the meaning of the verb.

further, the duty he lays down is something the weak should do as well as the strong. *Us* again puts Paul in the same class; he is not standing aloof. The *neighbor* makes the application very wide (GNB seems in error with "our brothers"; Paul is not limiting the application of this principle to the Christian brotherhood). But he immediately limits it with *for his good*. This principle must be applied with care, for great harm is done when Christians assume that in all circumstances they know what is good for other people. It must be done with humility. But it is necessary, for we may find it very easy to please people by doing or permitting something that is really harmful in the long run.[12] The point is that we must constantly seek to do what is for the good of others rather than what is for our own good. This does not mean that the weak control the church—that they have only to express a scruple and all rush to conform. That would mean that the church would be permanently tied to the level of the weak and that life and growth would cease. Paul is not laying down a rule of conduct but enunciating a principle of tender concern. The strong must respect the weak; they must not hurt them and at all times they must strive for what is for their good. A genuine concern for the weak will mean an attempt to make them strong by leading them out of their irrational scruples so that they, too, will be strong. Moreover, Paul can repudiate quite vigorously actions that can be understood as "pleasing men" (Gal. 1:10; Eph. 6:6). He is not writing about seeking human approval but about subordinating our own profit to the good of others. *His good* will mean something like "his spiritual profit" (some think "his salvation"; cf. 14:16).

The meaning of *good* is further brought out with the addition of *to build him up* or "with a view to edification."[13] Christians must always have in mind the importance of building one another up in the faith, and the attitude of the strong to the weak is to be guided by this consideration. For "edification" see the note on 14:19. It is an important concept.

3. A powerful incentive to this kind of conduct is that Christ is our example.[14] He *did not please himself*, which points to the way he set the interests of others before his own. The verb is a constative aorist, which means that the whole of Jesus' earthly life is in view (cf. BDF 332 [1]: "in his whole earthly life"). The Gospels show that Christ lived to do the will of the Father (cf. "not my will, but yours be done", Luke 22:42), which meant the service of others. The line of argument is like that in Philippians 2:4-5, where Paul speaks of the importance of acting in the interests of others and goes on:

12. There is also the point made so well by Harrisville: "I am not summoned to abandon my own appetite conceived as a criterion for my behavior, in order to embrace as a criterion the appetite of my neighbor."

13. πρὸς οἰκοδομήν. Moule classifies πρός under "transferred senses . . . *tending towards, leading to, concerning, against, in view of*", here "*making for upbuilding*" (IBNTG, p. 53). GT thinks it denotes "an intended end or purpose".

14. καὶ γάρ may mean "for also", but it is more likely that καί here means "even" (as NIV). *Christ* has the article, "the" Christ, and it is possible that we should understand it to be a title accordingly. But Paul does not seem to use the word in this way (see the note on 1:1). We need not doubt that he well knew that the word was a title, nor that on occasion what the title signified was present to his mind, but we cannot press it.

"Your attitude should be the same as that of Christ Jesus". Hodge remarks that Christ's example "is constantly held up, not merely as a model, but a motive."

It is significant for the way Paul's mind works that he does not appeal to any of the incidents in Jesus' life which illustrate his point, but simply quotes Scripture. For him the Bible ends all argument. If there is a relevant passage, then he need do no more than draw attention to it, and that is what he does now.[15] The Psalm was uttered by a godly man of old who found people insulting God and who became the victim of those insults himself.[16] So with Christ. People insulted God, and it was those insults that Christ bore as he suffered for his people. Paul could have drawn attention to what is more significant, that Christ bore the wrath of God in bringing us salvation. But the wrath was not apparent to those who saw what was happening, while the insults were heard by all who were there (cf. Matt. 27:39-44). Paul will have in mind the evil deeds that were done against Jesus, the insults in act as well as in word, and that throughout his life. In the Psalm the godly man has a consuming zeal for the house of God, and this means that he is the butt of those who do not obey God. It was like this in the life and death of Jesus,[17] and Paul sees him as the pattern and motive for Christians. In the light of what Jesus has done, can the strong in Christ's church insist on having their meat and the weak keep up their condemnation of their fellows?[18]

4. Paul explains why he can appeal to Scripture in this way. *Everything that was written in the past* means "all that was written in Scripture"; it is not an endorsement of every piece of literature that comes down from earlier ages. But we should bear in mind that *everything*[19] is comprehensive: Paul is not saying that there are some good things in the Bible, but that all of it was written for[20] our[21] instruction (cf. 4:23-24). "Our" evidently has some empha-

---

15. Notice the ἀλλά with which he introduces his quotation: Christ did not please himself *but*, on the contrary. . . . Paul goes on to quote from Ps. 69:9 (LXX 68:10), exactly as LXX. Other verses of this Psalm are cited also in 11:9-10; John 2:17; 15:25. Clearly the first Christians saw it as an important part of Scripture for understanding what the Christ came to do.

16. ὀνειδίζω means "reproach, revile, heap insults upon" (BAGD); ὀνειδισμός is the corresponding noun.

17. "Man's enmity against God was pure evil, pure absurdity, the totally irrational and inane . . ." (Cranfield, who also points out that the wrath of God was the most terrible part of what Christ had to suffer, but it was not irrational).

18. Murray points out that Paul "adduces the example of Christ in his most transcendent accomplishments in order to commend the most practical duties".

19. ὅσα, "whatever things"; NIV is not an exact translation but gives the sense of it. Notice that προεγράφη is followed up by ἐγράφη, "a classical idiom by which the preposition in a compound is omitted, without weakening the sense, when the verb is repeated" (M, I, p. 115). προεγράφω is used in a different sense in Gal. 3:1.

20. εἰς conveys the thought of purpose, "with a view to".

21. This is Paul's one use of ἡμέτερος in Romans (it is found once each in 2 Timothy and Titus, and eight times in all in the New Testament). His "our" refers to the Christians, which leads to the conclusion, "This statement is a bold generalization expropriating all Scriptures for the infant church" (Denis Farkasfalvy in William R. Farmer and Denis M. Farkasfalvy, *The Formation of the New Testament Canon* [New York, 1983], p. 105).

sis: although it was written in earlier ages it was intended for *our* instruction (cf. 1 Cor. 9:9-10).[22] The reason[23] for their being written was that *we might have hope*. The present tense of the verb points to continuous possession, and the article before *hope* seems to show that it is not the general hope of mankind of which Paul is writing, but the specifically Christian hope, the hope that is given by what Christ has done in winning our salvation, the hope that leaves no doubts and sustains Christ's people in the darkest days (see the note on 4:18).[24]

Paul speaks of two things important in bringing this about: *endurance* and *the encouragement of the Scriptures*. It is not clear whether we should take both *endurance* and *encouragement* as deriving from the Scriptures (as GNB, "through the patience and encouragement which the Scriptures give us") or whether we should see Paul as specifically linking only *encouragement* with the Scriptures (as Moffatt, "by remaining stedfast and drawing encouragement from the scriptures").[25] Of course the Christian's *endurance* and *encouragement* both come from God, and it may well be said that Scripture has a part in producing both. The question here is whether Paul is linking them both with the Bible or only one; his construction seems to show that only *encouragement* is here said to derive from the Bible. The apostle often speaks of *endurance*[26] and of *encouragement*.[27] Both are important. We need steadfastness in our Christian life and we need the encouragement the Bible can give; our life is a very poor thing without either.

5. Now comes a characteristic Pauline interjection of a short prayer; Paul often interrupts his argument in this way to pray. He speaks of "the God of steadfastness" (or "endurance"), which probably means that God is the

---

22. διδασκαλία may be used in the active sense, "instruction", or in the passive, "that which is taught"; here it is the active (BAGD). The word occurs 15 times in the Pastorals, and 19 times in the Pauline corpus out of 21 times in the New Testament.

23. ἵνα.

24. Cf. William Watty, "May I therefore suggest that this is our unique contribution to the world of to-day? It is to offer the Biblical message of hope from the God of hope to a world of shattered hopes" (ET, LXXXVII [1975-76], p. 50).

25. Paul has διά before τῆς ὑπομονῆς and another διά before τῆς παρακλήσεως. It is this repetition of the preposition that seems to show that the two are separated. If he were saying that both qualities are derived from Scripture we would expect only one διά. Käsemann says that the first διά "denotes an accompanying circumstance, the second is causal . . . . Scripture gives comfort and leads to patience" (p. 383). NEB has "that through the encouragement they give us we may maintain our hope with fortitude", but there seems no reason for linking "hope" with "fortitude".

26. ὑπομονή is found in Paul in exactly half its New Testament occurrences (16 out of 32; six in Romans); see the note on 2:7. It is often taken to mean "patience", but this is too negative a virtue for this word. It is rather "fortitude" or *endurance*. Griffith Thomas quotes A. Beet on the importance of this word in the present context: "Our Christian character is seldom so severely tried as when we are put to inconvenience by the spiritual childishness of members of the Church."

27. παράκλησις is found in Paul 20 times out of 29 in the New Testament, three being in Romans. See the note on the corresponding verb in 12:1. It is often understood of comfort (as KJV), and it can refer to exhortation, but *encouragement* seems right in this place.

source of steadfastness in his people (which accounts for NIV's insertion of *gives*) rather than that he himself is characterized by this quality (though that, of course, is true). Parry points out that the use of the genitive after "God" (i.e., "the God of —") is "confined to S. Paul (exc. Heb. xiii.20; 1 Pet. v.10) and to prayers". Paul has expressions like "the God of love and peace" (2 Cor. 13:11), "the God of peace" (Phil. 4:9; 1 Thess. 5:23), and "the God of hope" (v. 13). With this is linked *encouragement* (cf. 2 Cor. 1:3, where God is the God "of all encouragement"). The implication of all this is that God is the giver of steadfastness and encouragement to believers. Paul is not exhorting believers to pull themselves together and manifest these qualities, but rejoicing in God who gives them. In the Christian understanding of things they are always the gift of God, not the result of human achievement.

Paul proceeds to pray that God will *give*[28] what NIV calls *a spirit of unity*. More literally it is "to mind the same thing", but NIV gives the sense of it, for it is not so much identity of opinion of which he is writing here (the strong and the weak do not agree on a number of things but they can still be prayed for in this way) as harmony among themselves.[29]

As you follow Christ Jesus is another paraphrase, for the Greek means something like "according to Christ Jesus".[30] Paul is not saying that Christian unity is a general community product. He is not looking for unanimity in itself, for people sometimes agree in error. He is praying for the unity that accords with Christ, and that is a unity that God alone can give. Hence it is the object of this prayer.

6. There is a purpose in this unity.[31] Paul prays that *with one heart*[32] *and mouth*[33] his correspondents may glorify God. There were certainly tensions in the Roman church, and the presupposition that the strong and the weak were

---

28. δῴη is the optative, which Burton finds 35 times in the New Testament, mostly in prayer as here (MT, 176).

29. Cf. G. Bertram, "The fundamental demand of Pauline exhortation is a uniform direction, a common mind, and unity of thought and will" (TDNT, IX, p. 233). The same expression is found in 2 Cor. 13:11; Phil. 2:2; 4:2 (some MSS of Phil. 3:16), but the addition ἐν ἀλλήλοις is found only here. Notice the change to the second person plural. Paul has been linking himself with his correspondents in the first person plural, but from here on he addresses them as "you".

30. κατὰ Χριστὸν 'Ιησοῦν, where κατά "can also stand simply w. the acc. of the pers. according to whose will, pleasure, or manner someth. occurs" (BAGD II.5.a.α). W. Michaelis says that the expression "means according to the will rather than the example" (TDNT, IV, p. 669 n. 18)

31. As the use of ἵνα shows.

32. ὁμοθυμαδόν, a term used ten times in Acts and elsewhere in the New Testament only in this passage. H. W. Heidland notes that it derives from ὁμό-θυμος, "with the same emotion", "with the same mind". As used in secular Greek it is often used of political unity, and this not as based on "a similarity of inclination or disposition but upon an event which comes on a group from without" (such as the hostility of one who might attack). Christian unity "is not the expression of a religious disposition of man; it is the response to God's action for the world and the community in Christ" (TDNT, V, p. 186).

33. ἐν ἑνὶ στόματι, where ἐν may be instrumental or locative "since words are certainly formed here" (M, III, p. 252).

h.ving some difficulty in getting along with each other underlies this whole section of the letter. But when the church gives itself over to glorifying God there is a deep and satisfying unity. That is what Paul looks for.[34] *Glorify*, of course, means "ascribe glory to" or "praise"; this is the creature taking up the appropriate position over against the Creator.

God is here called *the God and Father of our Lord Jesus Christ* or, as KJV has it, "God, even the Father of our Lord Jesus Christ", an expression that recurs elsewhere (2 Cor. 1:3; 11:31; Eph. 1:3; 1 Pet. 1:3).[35] The question is whether God can properly be called "the God of our Lord Jesus Christ". Some think that this is improper. They prefer to understand Paul as speaking of our God, who is also the Father of our Lord (cf. O'Neill). But in his genuine humanity there is a sense in which God is rightly understood as the God of Jesus, and indeed on the cross Jesus addressed the Father with the words "My God, my God . . ." (Matt. 27:46; Mark 15:34). So also the risen Lord spoke to Mary Magdalene of "my God and your God" (John 20:17). We also come across the expression "the God of our Lord Jesus Christ" (Eph. 1:17). So there is no reason why we should not follow the natural sense of the Greek and understand Paul to be referring here to God as the God as well as the Father of Jesus Christ. This brings out the genuine humanity of Jesus and reminds Christians that it is Jesus who has brought us the perfect revelation of God. We know him as the Father of Jesus Christ, and unless we know him in this way we do not know God as he really is.

7. *Accept one another* is surely addressed to the whole community. Paul is not now dividing his readers into the strong and the weak. Käsemann points out that in this section "the tensions and debates vanish completely from view" and that Paul is proceeding to show that his doctrine of justification is seen in God's having mercy on the Gentiles (p. 384). The verb rendered *accept*[36] means wholehearted acceptance. David H. C. Read has a sermon in which he emphasizes this point and refuses even such a word as "welcome" as a translation. He reminds us that "Acceptance is never easy", but also that "we have been accepted".[37] That is Paul's point. *Just as*[38] *Christ accepted* us, we

---

34. Boylan points to an ambiguity in that the words might mean "be of the same mind in order to praise with one accord" or "be of one mind when according to Christ Jesus it unites to praise God." Whichever way we take it, Paul is emphasizing that believers are to be united, and to be united in praising God.

35. τὸν θεὸν καὶ πατέρα τοῦ κυρίου ἡμῶν Ἰησοῦ Χριστοῦ. The question is whether καί is to be taken as "and" or "even". Grammatically either is possible, which means that our decision has to be taken on the general sense of the passage.

36. προσλαμβάνω has the notion of warm welcome about it (cf. its use in 14:1, 3; Philem. 17).

37. ET, LXXIV (1962-63), pp. 375-77.

38. καθὼς καί is seen by Turner as "adverbial or epexegetical καί (*that is, even*)" (M, III, p. 335). Cranfield argues that it is causal, giving the reason for accepting one another, rather than comparative, following the example of Christ.

are to accept other believers. When Christ has accepted someone, are we to say that we will not take him as a Christian brother? Our attitude to others must flow from the transformation wrought in us by Christ. There is a textual difficulty as to whether we should read "you" or "us" after "received".[39] Most accept "you" as the harder reading, but not much depends on our decision. But perhaps we should say that earlier Paul has been speaking as one of the strong, whereas here he stands off, so to speak, and addresses the whole community. His point is that all are to accept those who differ from them. This follows well on Paul's prayer, for "Nothing glorifies God as much as the unity of His children, which alone is in harmony with His essential will of love" (Leenhardt). And it leads well into what follows, for Paul sees the purpose of Christ's accepting of them as "the glory of God". God's glory was promoted when Christ received us sinners, and it is further advanced when we who are by nature sinners and wrapped up in our own concerns instead receive our brothers and sisters in Christ with warmth and love.[40]

8. *For I tell you*[41] introduces a reason for the foregoing, namely that *Christ has become a servant of the Jews on behalf of God's truth*. The verb *has become* should apparently be taken as in the perfect tense,[42] indicating a permanent state: Christ continues in his capacity as "a servant of circumcision".[43] His function as the Jewish Messiah is permanent. "Servant" is the word used for a deacon in the church and more widely for lowly service in general. The word order puts some emphasis on "servant"; in his coming to bring salvation Christ did not appear in might or in glory, as might have been expected, but he came as a servant (cf. Mark 10:45; Luke 22:27; Gal. 4:4-5). "Circumcision" here means that he served the Jews (cf. Matt. 15:24), but we should not overlook the fact that circumcision was the sign of the covenant. This way of putting it brings out the fact that Christ was the minister of the covenant of which circumcision was the seal (so Murray), that covenant with Abraham which Paul earlier argued was of such relevance to the Gentiles (ch. 4). Paul is reasoning that Jews and Gentiles comprise the totality of the Christian church. Christ took the lowly place (became a "servant") to bring salvation not to the one or the other but to both. Both are precious. Believers are warned that no member of

---

39. ὑμᾶς is read by ℵ A C Dᵇˑᶜ G etc., and ἡμᾶς by B D* P 048 etc.

40. There is another uncertainty here, namely whether we should take "to the glory of God" as qualifying "accept one another" (as Cranfield, Hodge, etc.) or "Christ received you" (Murray, Lenski, and others). Certainly both are true, and it is not impossible that Paul takes the words as applying to both (cf. Hendriksen, Barrett).

41. λέγω γάρ. The point could have been made without using this verb, so clearly Paul means it to have some emphasis. Cranfield objects to NEB's "I mean" as being "too weak"; he prefers "I declare".

42. γεγενῆσθαι is read by ℵ A C² D¹ etc., while the aorist γενέσθαι has the respectable support of B C* D* G and others. But it seems much more likely that scribes would alter the perfect to the aorist than the reverse, so the perfect is generally accepted.

43. διάκονον περιτομῆς.

the church may safely be despised.[44] *On behalf of God's truth*[45] is not the easiest of expressions, and a variety of translations have been suggested: "in the interest of God's truth", "in order to prove God's honesty", "to show God's truthfulness", "in vindication of God's truth", and others. The problem is the preposition; BAGD say that here it means "in order to show that God's promises are true" (1b). Clearly Paul is saying that the work of Christ in some way advanced God's truth, but his form of words allows of too many possibilities for us to pin him down to one precise meaning.

To confirm[46] *the promises made to the patriarchs*[47] sums up what Jesus did with respect to the Jews. Paul has had a good deal to say in the earlier chapters of this letter on the way God worked out his purposes in and through the patriarchs, and he has made it clear both that the promises God made are of permanent validity and that they find their fulfilment in Christ. This he reiterates at this point.

9. The Greek at this point is difficult.[48] But however we resolve the grammatical problems, Paul is bringing out the truth that God's mercy has brought the Gentiles salvation and that this leads them to praise him. Some scholars emphasize the oneness in God's action to the two groups. They see the fulfilment of the promises to the patriarchs and the mercy shown to the Gentiles as not two acts, but one: "the confirmation of the promises comes by the call of the Gentiles" (CGT). It is also to be borne in mind that Israel's salvation, just as much as that of the Gentiles, depends on the mercy of God. Others suggest that we have here a pair of contrasts: the patriarchs are set over against the Gentiles and faithfulness to the promises corresponds to mercy. It would seem that there is more to be said for the former view, for Paul has often argued that the coming of the gospel to the Gentiles is not in

---

44. Cf. Smart, "just as Christ by humbling himself to be the servant of his Jewish people made possible the fulfillment of the promise of the Old Testament—that Gentiles and Jews would one day be united in the service of the one true God—so now an imitation of his humility by Christians could dissolve the lesser barriers between the strong and the weak in the church at Rome." Barrett suggests that the Jews "especially when described as the 'circumcision', may be regarded as the most awkward and irritating of scrupulous persons. He thus provides an example for all strong Christians (cf. *v.* 3)."

45. ὑπὲρ ἀληθείας θεοῦ.

46. For εἰς τό with the infinitive see the note on 1:20; the construction generally denotes purpose, and this gives good sense here (though result is not impossible, as CGT). βεβαιόω means "make firm, establish" and thus here "prove the promises reliable, fulfill (them)" (BAGD).

47. The genitive τῶν πατέρων means the promises belonging to and thus made to (not made by) the patriarchs.

48. There seem to be two possibilities. One is to take δοξάσαι as dependent on γεγενῆσθαι and coordinate with βεβαιῶσαι: "Christ became a minister of circumcision to confirm the promises and so that the Gentiles might glorify. . . ." The other is to see δοξάσαι as dependent on λέγω and coordinate with γεγενῆσθαι: "I say that Christ became a minister of circumcision . . . and that the Gentiles might glorify. . . ." Both are awkward, for in each case there is a change of subject. Either is possible, but perhaps the decisive consideration is that "the statement about Christ controls the sentence". This leads Barrett to favor the first solution.

contradiction of the Old Testament but in fulfilment of it. Mercy for the Gentiles is involved in the Old Testament.[49]

Paul now launches into a series of quotations from the Old Testament which are surely meant to support what he has said in verses 8-9 (and not simply in v. 9). He quotes from the law, the prophets, and twice from the Psalms, so that he calls all the recognized divisions of Scripture to witness to the point he is making, that the Gentiles have their place in God's salvation. There is something of a progression. The first quotation has the note of confession, as the Psalmist praises God among the Gentiles. The second calls on the Gentiles to rejoice with Israel. In the third the Gentiles praise God independently of Israel. And in the fourth we find that the cause of it all is the "root" of Jesse, the only one on whom sinners can hope.

The first quotation is from Psalm 18:49, almost exactly as LXX. The Psalmist says he will "confess" to God,[50] which means that he will praise him. It would be natural for a Hebrew singer to praise his God, but this one wants to do it among the nations. The Psalm is a song of victory which looks for the praises of God to be sung throughout the world. Evidently the mention of the Gentiles is what attracts Paul. The Psalm goes on to say, *I will sing hymns to your name*.[51] Delling regards the Psalm as relevant to Paul's aim: "The praise of Gentile Christians for God's mercy to them in Christ is provided here with scriptural support" (TDNT, VIII, p. 499).

10. Calvin holds that Paul is here quoting from Psalm 67:5, but most interpreters agree that the passage he has in mind is Deuteronomy 32:43 (cited from LXX).[52] The passage stresses the note of joy as Moses calls on the nations to join in happy praise of God on account of his greatness and his defeat of all his enemies. But for Paul the significant thing is not the cause of the rejoicing but the call to Gentiles to rejoice along with Israel. God has brought the blessings of salvation to both, and it is well accordingly that they rejoice together.[53]

11. Now comes a quotation from Psalm 117:1 (again from LXX). This

---

49. The Gentiles praise God ὑπὲρ ἐλέους, where ὑπέρ is used "to denote the moving cause or the reason" (BAGD 1d).

50. ἐξομολογήσομαί σοι. The verb is used of confessing, e.g., confessing sins (Acts 19:18), from which there arose the idea of acknowledging (Phil. 2:11). This in turn led to the idea of praising, and the word is used in LXX of praising God, especially in the worship of the temple.

51. ψάλλω referred originally to plucking the strings of a musical instrument; later it appears to have been used of singing with accompaniment and then simply of singing. There is nothing in the Greek to correspond to NIV's *hymns*; the translators have assumed (not unreasonably) that it is hymns that would be sung to God. See the notes in BAGD *sub* ψάλλω and the article by G. Delling, TDNT, VIII, pp. 489-503.

52. He introduces it with λέγει, which may mean "it (Scripture) says" or "he (God) says" or "he (Moses) says". But since Paul sees God as the author of Scripture and the inspirer of Moses, the difference is not material.

53. εὐφραίνω is a general word for rejoicing; it may be used, e.g., for festive meals (Luke 12:19; 15:24). But it may also be used of holy joy, as in rejoicing at God's final victory (Rev. 12:12).

time there is no reference to Israel and the words are simply a call to the Gentiles to praise God. The two lines are parallel and express much the same thought. We should not look for great differences in meaning between the two verbs for *praise*, nor between *Gentiles* and *peoples*.[54]

12. Now Paul moves to the prophets with a quotation which he tells us is from Isaiah (11:10; again from LXX). This speaks of *the* (not "a", as KJV) *root of Jesse*, a way of referring to Jesus as the descendant of the great king David (and hence of David's father). We would normally use *root* for the origin ("the root of Jesse" would be that from which Jesse derived his being), but manifestly the word is not used in this way either in Isaiah or here in Romans. Rather, it points to one who springs from Jesse, one for whom Jesse is the origin. We may perhaps discern the reason for this way of speaking when we reflect that in Palestine drought would threaten the life of a plant, so that its root system would be its best guarantee of survival. The root came then to be used not only of the root itself but also of that which springs from the root.[55] So from a household that looked far from royal there would emerge God's Messiah, and the point of this particular prophecy and of Paul's quotation of it is that that Messiah would be one on whom the Gentiles could set their hope. For Gentiles as for Jews it was the descendant of Jesse who would be the Savior.

That the root of Jesse *will arise*[56] *to rule over the nations* means that he will be a mighty king. But he will not be a tyrant; *the Gentiles*[57] *will hope in him.* Throughout this section of the epistle the note of hope is strong, and it is fitting that Paul should choose this to characterize the blessed state of the Gentiles in question.

13. As in verses 5-6 Paul interjects a little prayer as he comes to the end of his argument. In this case it is all the more fitting in that we have now come to the end of the massive argument of the epistle as a whole (the rest of the letter is taken up with personal matters of one sort or another). We should not think of Paul as primarily a controversialist; he was a deeply pious man and it is characteristic that he finishes not with some equivalent of Q.E.D. nor a shout of triumph over the antagonists he has confronted but with prayer.

There is a connective (KJV, "Now")[58] which NIV does not translate but which marks a transition to something new, something distinguished in some way from the preceding. It is a mark of the importance attaching to hope

54. The words for *praise* are αἰνέω and ἐπαινέω. The other two words are ἔθνη and λαοί.

55. C. Maurer comments on Isa. 11:10, "From the pitiable remnant of the house of Jesse there will come forth, as from the remaining stump of a tree, a new shoot which will establish the coming kingdom of peace and righteousness" (TDNT, VI, p. 986; he also speaks of "the idea that the root as *pars pro toto* includes the shoot"). In both Isa. 11:10 and here he takes the genitive as one of derivation (p. 989 n. 24).

56. ἀνίστημι is used transitively in the sense "raise up" (as in Acts 9:41); the intransitive tenses (as here) have the meaning "arise".

57. ἔθνη lacks the article, but this word "is especially liable to be anarthrous" (M, III, p. 181). NIV translates the term once as "nations" and once as "Gentiles", but there is no difference in meaning.

58. δέ.

in the New Testament[59] that Paul characterizes God as *the God of hope* (cf. v. 5). This means both that he is the origin of hope and the object of hope ("who inspires hope and imparts it to his children", Harrison). Becoming a Christian means leaving a whole way of life and in faith starting a new one. Not having been along that way before, the beginner cannot know to what it will lead; he can only go ahead in hope and in the power of the Holy Spirit. Paul prays that God will *fill*[60] his correspondents *with all joy and peace*. Joy is one of Paul's great concepts, the term occurring in his writings 21 times whereas no other New Testament writing has it more than John's nine times. It is linked with faith (Phil. 1:25) and is part of "the fruit of the Spirit" (Gal. 5:22-23).[61] For *peace* see the note on 1:7; it is linked with joy in 14:17 and in the list of the fruit of the Spirit as well as here. The two go together. Peace here is the inward state of peace that God gives his people rather than the peace with God that is its prerequisite. Paul adds, *as you trust in him;*[62] faith is basic to the Christian way. The specifically Christian joy and peace are impossible apart from trust in Christ.

Paul goes on to the purpose[63] of his prayer, namely *that you may overflow with hope.* He looks for a full measure of hope in his readers, not a tentative step in that direction. This is the third mention of hope since the end of verse 12, and it is all the more significant in that we have just heard of "the God of hope". There is a strong emphasis on hope, an emphasis we should not miss in an age so lacking in hope. Perhaps Leenhardt draws our attention to the basic reason that hope is in short supply in our modern world when he says, "No one can really hope unless by faith he turns away from the past, that is, from himself, to offer himself to God who is the Creator and Dispenser of the world to come." Whether this is the basic reason or not, there is no denying that hope is fundamental to the Christian life and that it is always to be understood in connection with faith. It is also to be understood in connection with *the power of the Holy Spirit* (for *power* see the note on 1:16). The believer's experience of hope is always connected with the Holy Spirit and never a personal achievement of his own (cf. 14:17).

59. And which we all too often miss. Thus Hunter speaks of hope as "the modern Cinderella in Paul's triad of Christian graces".

60. πληρῶσαι is another optative (see the note on v. 5), which is very appropriate in prayer. Paul looks for no niggardly supply but for God to fill his correspondents with these Christian virtues.

61. Conzelmann points out that in Paul "χαρά is never a profane mood. In Paul it is bound up with his work as an apostle. . . . Joy is the actualisation of freedom, which takes concrete form in fellowship" (TDNT, IX, p. 369).

62. ἐν τῷ πιστεύειν. For the construction see the note on 3:4. It is not common in the New Testament outside Luke; it occurs four times in Paul (M, III, p. 145, where the meaning here is seen as causal, "because you believe"). The words are viewed by Michel as a gloss (they are lacking in a small group of MSS headed by D F G), but Black dissents strongly: "so far from these words being a gloss . . . they recall the central theme of the Epistle. Faith is the way into the kingdom of joy and peace."

63. See the note on 1:20 for the construction εἰς τό with the infinitive. Cf. Turner, in Paul this "expresses hardly anything but purpose" (M, III, p. 143).

VII. CONCLUSION, 15:14–16:27

Paul's great treatment of justification has ended. He has shown something of its necessity, of what Christ has done to bring it about, of the necessity of trust in him, of what it means in terms of Jew and Gentile, of the importance of living day by day as those who have been justified by faith. Now the apostle turns to matters like his reason for writing the letter, his travel plans, and sending greetings to people he knows. At the beginning of this concluding section there are some resemblances to what he wrote in 1:8-15; clearly his mind went over these things again.

A. THE MINISTER OF THE GENTILES, 15:14-22

14I myself am convinced, my brothers, that you yourselves are full of good-ness, complete in knowledge and competent to instruct one another. 15I have written you quite boldly on some points, as if to remind you of them again, because of the grace God gave me 16to be a minister of Christ Jesus to the Gentiles with the priestly duty of proclaiming the gospel of God, so that the Gentiles might become an offering acceptable to God, sanctified by the Holy Spirit.

17Therefore I glory in Christ Jesus in my service to God. 18I will not venture to speak of anything except what Christ has accomplished through me in leading the Gentiles to obey God by what I have said and done— 19by the power of signs and miracles, through the power of the Spirit. So from Jerusalem all the way around to Illyricum, I have fully proclaimed the gospel of Christ. 20It has always been my ambition to preach the gospel where Christ was not known, so that I would not be building on someone else's foundation. 21Rather, as it is written:

> *"Those who were not told about him will see,*
>   *and those who have not heard will understand."a*

22This is why I have often been hindered in coming to you.

a21 Isaiah 52:15

14. *I . . . am convinced* translates a perfect tense which points to a con-tinuing state of confidence in the Roman Christians.[64] Paul is giving his considered opinion. His warmth toward his correspondents comes out in his address *my brothers* (which seems to mean more than the general address "brothers"), and he follows this with *I myself,* which is strongly emphatic.[65] Chrysostom understands the significance of this approach in this way: " 'I

---

64. πέπεισμαι. The verb means "convince, persuade", and this perfect passive shows that Paul is completely convinced. There are no lingering doubts.
65. After saying "Now I am persuaded, my brothers," he adds καὶ αὐτὸς ἐγώ. It is possible to see adversative force in δέ (which NIV omits) as if to say, "I have admonished you strongly, *but* —". More probably it is transitional; it is hard to see a contrast with the immediately preceding.

508

myself,' that is, I that rebuke, that accuse you", and this is probably the point of it. Since Paul has written some very weighty things, it might well be that the Romans on reading them would feel that Paul thought them deficient in their understanding of the Christian way. But at the beginning of his letter he had said that their faith was well known (1:8), and his words here show that he is in full agreement with that assessment. There are to be no doubts about his warm approval of the Roman church. Actually the letter itself is evidence of the same thing—it is not a letter for people who do not take their faith seriously or are not prepared to think deeply about it. And Romans differs markedly from the Corinthian correspondence in that there are no rebukes for the recipients, no indication of a deficient understanding or practice of the Christian way.

So Paul goes on to speak of the Romans as *full of goodness, complete in knowledge and competent to instruct one another*. This is a courteous introduction to this section, and in view of the opinion held in some circles that Paul was a rather abrasive person it is worth noticing that this is typical.[66] When he says that they are *full of goodness* he is not speaking of an occasional virtuous action; *full* means plentiful supply. The Romans were outstandingly good.[67] It is not easy to distinguish between *full* and *complete*.[68] But *knowledge* takes us on to the intellectual understanding of the Christian faith. Paul is not referring to knowledge in general, but that genuine comprehension of Christian teaching which is allied with a deep concern to do what is good. That is the way the problem of the weak and the strong will be solved (and many other problems as well; it is perhaps significant that when he writes to the Corinthians Paul compliments his readers on their knowledge, but does not mention goodness, 1 Cor. 1:5). The Romans also have the ability[69] *to instruct one another*, where *instruct* means more than "teach"; it has rather the idea of "admonish" with the thought of correcting what is amiss.[70] Here it points to "the reciprocal brotherly ministry of the members exercising pastoral oversight with a sense of congregational obligation" (Behm, p. 1022).

15. The Roman congregation, then, is in good shape. But if they are so

66. Thus Knox can write, "the 'thanksgiving' in every Pauline letter is a model of courtesy and charm".

67. ἀγαθωσύνη is not a classical word but one found only in LXX, the Pauline writings, and later ecclesiastical writers (so Leenhardt). It points to "moral excellence as well as goodness. . . . Its possession constitutes the content of the life of the Christian" (W. Grundmann, TDNT, I, p. 18; he goes on to speak of its use as "controlled by . . . the Christian's radically new possibility of life"). Cf. the description of Barnabas (Acts 11:24).

68. μεστοί and πεπληρωμένοι. The perfect participle gives the thought of a completed action (MT, 154), but the adjective means much the same. We should probably see a stylistic variant.

69. δυνάμενοι.

70. νουθετεῖν "describes an effect on the will and disposition, and it presupposes an opposition which has to be overcome. It seeks to correct the mind, to put right what is wrong, to improve the spiritual attitude" (J. Behm, TDNT, IV, p. 1019). In the New Testament the verb is found only in the Pauline writings and in a speech of Paul in Acts 20:31.

good, why write? Paul proceeds to the answer. He recognizes that what he has written[71] is audacious,[72] adding *on some points,* an expression that may be taken in more ways than one. Paul may mean that on some points he has written boldly (as against others which are less controversial); this takes *on some points* with *I have written.* But we may instead take it with *boldly* to give the meaning "somewhat too boldly" (Hodge) or with *remind,* where the meaning would be "partly by way of reminding you" (CGT).[73] Paul's verb for *remind* is unusual.[74] There is the tactful assumption that the Romans are knowledge-able in the faith and that Paul has not been putting novel teachings before them. He does not specify what it is of which he has been reminding them, but it will surely be the great truths of the gospel and of the way the Christian life should be lived. Barrett sees this as "more than tact; the believer who has accepted the Gospel knows the essence of the truth, but he may—and gener-ally does—need many reminders." It is probable that Paul's treatment of the great things in this epistle brought before the Romans many things they had not realized before (as has happened to Christians in every century since!). But the essence of it all in the gospel of our Lord Jesus Christ is something that has always been basic in Christian experience, that of the Romans as of all other believers. Paul was enlarging their horizons but he was also reminding them of things they already knew. This he says he does *because of the grace God gave me.* He is fond of the idea of grace (see the note on 1:5) and he has already spoken of God's special gift of grace to him, the grace of apostleship (cf. 1:5; 12:3). The aorist points to a gift at a definite time, and that time will be that of his call to be an apostle.

16. Paul proceeds to the purpose[75] of that grace, namely that he should be *a minister of Christ Jesus to the Gentiles.* The word for *minister*[76] is one that is

---

71. ἔγραψα means "earlier in this letter"; Turner points out that in the New Testa-ment we get ἔπεμψα as an epistolary aorist, but that ἔγραψα is probably not used in the same way; as here, it means earlier in the letter (M, III, pp. 72-73; so also BDF 334).

72. τολμηρός means "bold, daring, audacious" (BAGD). The comparative here may mean "very boldly" or "the more boldly" (Turner takes it as the "Comparative for Positive"; M, III, p. 30). δέ may be adversative (Shedd), introducing a contrast with the preceding and thus something of an apology, or it may introduce an explanation and mean "and now" (Harrisville).

73. The Greek is ἀπὸ μέρους, "in part"; NIV's *on some points* is a trifle too definite (Murray regards this view as "scarcely warranted", preferring "boldly in some measure"). While some such understanding is often held, the other ways of taking the Greek are both possible.

74. ἐπαναμιμνήσκω is found only here in the New Testament. SH comment on it, "The ἐπί seems to soften the expression 'suggesting to your memory.'" Chrysostom thought the word "means putting you in mind in a quiet way", while Gifford sees it "used with a delicate courtesy".

75. That seems to be the significance of εἰς τό with the infinitive (see the note on 1:20). Lenski takes it as result, but there seems no valid reason for denying purpose, the usual meaning of this construction.

76. λειτουργός originally meant someone who does public service at his own ex-pense, but in Christian literature it came to be used of the service of God (cf. the related word in 13:6).

elsewhere used of the service Christ renders (Heb. 8:2), but also of that performed by Epaphroditus (Phil. 2:25). Paul took very seriously his call to minister to *the Gentiles* (cf. 11:13; Gal. 2:9). He never renounced his Jewish heritage; rather, he gloried in it, but never in such a way that he forgot that his calling was to be God's minister to the Gentiles (cf. Acts 22:21). He goes on to refer to this service in priestly terms,[77] a most unusual way of referring to Christian service (here only in the New Testament; Paul uses a different piece of sacrificial imagery about himself in Phil. 2:17). But it is interesting and significant that Paul does not use the expression in connection with any liturgical practice but explicitly with *the gospel of God*. It is a striking way of affirming that the proclamation of the gospel is a solemn and sacred act.[78] The genitive *of God* means that the gospel originates with God,[79] another way of bringing out its sacredness.

The purpose[80] of this is that *the Gentiles might become an offering*. Paul uses the word for *offering*[81] again only in Ephesians 5:2; it is not a common word with him. It is used in LXX for the sacrifice offered on the altar. The expression here is "the offering of the Gentiles", where the genitive is appositional and signifies "the offering which is the Gentiles". The imagery is unusual for Paul (or for that matter for any of the other New Testament writers). It is his way of saying that he preaches the gospel to the Gentiles so that they come to offer themselves to God (cf. 12:1); instead of some slain animal ascending to God in the flames of a physical altar there is the spiritual ascent to him as Gentile people offer themselves, their souls and bodies, as a reasonable sacrifice to God (a kind of fulfilment of Isa. 66:20).[82] It points to the thoroughgoing commitment which Paul demanded of his Gentile converts.

This offering is said to be *acceptable*[83] to God. The Old Testament knew of sacrifices that God would not accept (e.g., Isa. 1:11ff.), and Paul is distancing the offering of the Gentiles from such offerings. With this he links *sanctified by the Holy Spirit*. Paul's Jewish opponents would have regarded all Gentiles as

77. ἱερουργέω means "to act as a priest"; MM see that service in this passage as "sacrifice". GT defines the term as "to perform sacred rites" and says it is "used esp. of persons sacrificing . . . trans. *to minister in the manner of a priest, minister in priestly service*".

78. Calvin speaks of "consecrating the gospel", but this does not seem to be the thought. It is not that Paul "consecrates" the gospel, sets it apart to be holy, but rather that it is already holy, holy in itself, so that his proclaiming of it is a sacred act.

79. Turner takes it as "subjective gen. of origin or cause" (M, III, p. 211).

80. ἵνα with the subjunctive.

81. προσφορά.

82. Cf. Leenhardt, "the priesthood is assumed by the apostle not because he sacrifices at a new altar to offer a new sacrifice, but because he proclaims the gospel and becomes the instrument by which the Holy Spirit associates believers with the sacrifice of the cross." Most see Isa. 66:20 as referring to Gentiles who escort Jews from the Dispersion back to Judea, but Edward J. Young, e.g., sees "your brothers" as Gentile converts and explains the passage as meaning "None of the elect, whether from the Jews according to the flesh or from among the Gentiles, will be left behind" (*The Book of Isaiah*, III [Grand Rapids, 1981], p. 534).

83. εὐπρόσδεκτος, from εὖ + πρός + δέκτος, "well received" and thus "acceptable".

"unclean", so his use of the term *sanctified* is very significant. Most agree with NIV in seeing this as meaning *by the Holy Spirit*, but Lenski rejects this in favor of "in union with the Holy Spirit". It may be that we should think of the union with the Spirit as showing the sanctification, but there is no great difference.[84] The point is that the Gentiles are accepted by God and are holy in the fullest sense. We ought to notice here the way the three Persons of the Trinity are introduced. This is not yet the full doctrine of the Trinity, but it was from such expressions as these that the church in due time came to formulate this doctrine.

17. *Therefore*[85] introduces the consequence. Because of what God has done in him towards the Gentiles Paul has reason for exultation (or boasting).[86] NIV has *I glory*, but Paul uses the noun, not the verb, and links it with "have" ("I have boasting"). This construction puts some emphasis on "the durative action" (CGT).[87] *Glory* (or boasting, or exultation) is *in Christ Jesus*; all that Paul has done he has done in the strength of Christ, which means that Paul is not boasting in his own achievement but in what God has done through him. And what has been done has been done *in my service to God*, which is NIV's rendering of an unusual Greek expression.[88] Paul is claiming, then, that he has matter for exultation in what he has done in Christ in the things that refer to God.

18. He adds an explanation,[89] saying that he will not dare[90] to speak of certain things. Because the Greek is awkward, commentators differ as to the best way of understanding it. It may be that he is saying here that he "has no intention of presuming to refer to anything other than what Christ has wrought through him" (Cranfield). Or the awkwardness may be due to the combination of two thoughts: "(i) I would not dare to speak of this if it were not Christ's work (rather than mine); (ii) I would not dare to speak of this if it were not Christ's work through me (rather than anyone else)" (Barrett; cf. CGT). Whichever way we take it, the main thrust is clear enough: Paul will

---

84. Paul says ἐν πνεύματι ἁγίῳ, the point at issue being the meaning of ἐν.

85. οὖν.

86. καύχησις can have either meaning. Paul uses it of his own activity, but this is not quite boasting as we use the term, for he boasts always in what God has done, not in his human achievement. Bultmann speaks of the apostle as developing "more radically the OT paradox that man can truly boast only when he looks away from himself to God's acts" (TDNT, III, p. 650). See further the note on 2:17.

87. There is a difficult textual question here. τήν is read before καύχησιν by B C D E F G, but it is not found in ℵ A L. If we read it, the article will be a demonstrative, pointing back to v. 16 and yielding the meaning "I have this boast"; if we do not read it, the sense is "I have a boast in Christ". We should probably take the article as original, for the reading without it looks like "a simplification which can hardly be original" (Käsemann, p. 393).

88. τὰ πρὸς τὸν θεόν (cf. Heb. 2:17; 5:1). BDF 160 take this as an adverbial accusative, though the same expression is accusative of respect in Heb. 2:17; so also M, III, p. 221. It means "with reference to what concerns God" (BAGD *sub* πρός III.5b).

89. γάρ.

90. NIV has *venture*, but the verb is cognate with "boldly" in v. 15 (τολμήσω and τολμηρότερον). We should not miss the point that there were some things Paul dared to communicate and some he did not.

glory only in what Christ has done through him. He is sure that Christ has done[91] great things through him,[92] and he is glad that he can draw attention to those things. But he is not trying to attract adulation. It is what Christ has done that is his theme.

What Christ has done has been to bring about "the obedience of the Gentiles",[93] that is, obedience to the command implied in the gospel (in 1:5 Paul had spoken of "the obedience of faith"). This obedience meant that they had left their former way of life and committed themselves to the service of Christ. "By word and deed" will refer to what Paul said and did (as NIV), not to any activity of the Gentiles.[94] Christ accomplished his purpose through the apostle's words and his deeds.

19. This is further elaborated. Christ acted in *the power[95] of signs and miracles*,[96] a rare combination in Paul (it is frequent in Acts). He uses it of himself on one other occasion (2 Cor. 12:12), of the "counterfeit miracles, signs and wonders" of the man of lawlessness (2 Thess. 2:9), and that is all. Here he says that his ministry among the Gentiles was accompanied by miraculous events. He regards them as "the signs of an apostle" (2 Cor. 12:12), and this is well attested in Acts (cf. Acts 13:6-12; 14:3, 8-10; 19:11, etc.). With this Paul joins *through[97] the power of the Spirit*. This may be another way of referring to the miracles; it is the fact that the Spirit is at work to make them "signs" that gives them their significance. But the Spirit's power is not confined to the miracles, and Paul may well be referring to the spiritual efficacy of his whole evangelistic activity.[98]

So[99] introduces the result, but there is some uncertainty as to Paul's precise meaning in the following words. Paul claims to have preached the

91. *Accomplished* translates κατειργάσατο (see the note on 1:27). This verb takes the accusative of the thing done, so ὧν is evidently attracted into the case of its omitted antecedent.

92. δι᾽ ἐμοῦ directs attention to Paul's work rather than that of others, but also makes it clear that it was not done "by" him but "through" him.

93. εἰς ὑπακοὴν ἐθνῶν. εἰς introduces purpose, and ἐθνῶν is a subjective genitive. What was done was done with a view to producing obedience from Gentiles (cf. 1:5, where see note).

94. Brown takes it of the Gentiles: true conversion is " 'in word,' that is, manifested in profession, 'in deed,' that is, proved by conduct corresponding to the profession" (p. 569). This is true, but it is not what Paul is saying.

95. A few MSS read αὐτοῦ (P46 D* G), "in his power", and Barrett regards this respectfully. It is, of course, Christ's power, but we should probably not accept this reading. The note of power is stressed here with the repetition of ἐν δυνάμει. Paul is sure that the divine power was at work in his ministry.

96. σημείων καὶ τεράτων. NIV's *miracles* for the second term is misleading, for both terms mean miracles. σημεῖον points to the miracle as significant or meaningful, while τέρας concentrates on the wonder. The miracles are often called "signs", but the term "wonder" is never in the New Testament used of them by itself; it is always in combination with "sign".

97. ἐν may be taken to mean "in" the Spirit's power (cf. v. 16).

98. Cf. Leenhardt, "it is Christ who is the hidden Author of the 'signs and wonders' and it is Christ who gives the Holy Spirit by whose power testimony is given to the Lord."

99. ὥστε.

gospel *from Jerusalem all the way around*[100] *to Illyricum.* Paul's great work started when he was sent out from Antioch (Acts 13:1-3), so the reference to Jerusalem is puzzling. As far as we know, he did not do any considerable work in the Jerusalem area. He may possibly be referring to his early preaching in that city (Acts 9:28-29), but that was not concerned with Gentiles and it is the Gentiles of whom he is speaking here. He had a vision in the temple associated with his call to preach to the Gentiles (Acts 22:19-21), and in Jerusalem he was given the right hand of fellowship for his work among Gentiles (Gal. 2:9). But Jerusalem was regarded as the starting point of all Christian preaching (cf. Luke 24:47), and it may be this that is in mind. Illyricum is modern Yugoslavia and Albania. As far as is known, Paul had not preached there. But since he seems to have done little in Jerusalem either, perhaps the best solution is to see these as excluded: he had preached from the boundary of Jerusalem to the boundary of Illyricum. He is stating the limits of his preaching so far, not claiming to have preached in both.

In the area he has defined Paul claims to have *fully proclaimed the gospel of Christ.*[101] Since Paul had done no more than preach in a number of the larger cities, this can scarcely mean that he felt that the whole of the area named had been evangelized. He is saying that he has done what he, the apostle of the Gentiles, was required to do. He had preached in strategic centers throughout the area named and established churches. No doubt there was much still to be done, both by way of preaching to those not yet converted and of building up in the faith those who had come to believe. But that was not Paul's responsibility as a pioneer evangelist.[102]

20. NIV omits the first two words of this verse,[103] which qualify and explain what Paul has just said. He is not claiming that he has "fully pro-

---

100. μέχρι (μέχρις is never used in the New Testament before a consonant, though μέχρι sometimes precedes a vowel) signifies "as far as" and may be used of time or place or measure or degree. Moule says that in the New Testament it is not found in a purely adverbial sense, but always as a preposition meaning "up to, as far as" (IBNTG, p. 85). κύκλῳ strictly means "in a circle", "round about", but does Paul mean "from Jerusalem and a circle round about it" or "from Jerusalem round to Illyricum"? An objection to the former suggestion is the lack of an article with κύκλῳ. In any case, the general probabilities favor the second view. Knox suggests that Paul has in mind the circle of "the nations around the Mediterranean Sea" with the thought that part of the circle (from Jerusalem to Illyricum) has been completed (JBL, LXXXIII [1964], p. 11). But Paul never mentions north Africa, not even Egypt, so this is unlikely. A. S. Geyser argues that the expression is not meant to be taken historically or geographically; it is Paul's way of authenticating his apostolate; like Acts 1:8 it is a way of referring to preaching to the ends of the earth (NTS, VI [1959-60], pp. 156-59). But this ignores the fact that in the context Paul is referring to real places like Rome, Spain, and Jerusalem. It seems a most unlikely solution.

101. His verb is πεπληρωκέναι. BAGD class this use of the verb under "*bring* something. *to completion, finish* someth. already begun". Cf. the similar use of the verb in Col. 1:25. R. Jewett remarks that this is "the kind of thing an ambassador would claim in completing the visits on the route to the ultimate goal" (*Interpretation*, 36 [1982], p. 17).

102. Griffith Thomas comments that the method "might almost warrant the assertion of the principle, 'Take care of the cities and the villages will take care of themselves.'"

103. οὕτως δέ. οὕτως here seems to refer to what follows (cf. BAGD 2), while δέ is adversative, "But in this manner. . . ."

claimed" the gospel in an absolute sense but in the sense that accorded with his ambition to preach it where Christ was not named. The reference to ambition is interesting.[104] The verb is used by Paul on two other occasions and by no one else in the New Testament. He says that he "makes it his ambition to have no ambition" (1 Thess. 4:11; alternatively "seeks restlessly to be still") and that it is his ambition to be pleasing to the Lord (2 Cor. 5:9). Clearly he is not ambitious in the sense in which the world normally uses the term. Whether we understand the verb in the sense of ambition or of eager striving, Paul is saying that his constant aim was the lowly one of being a pioneer evangelist. He wanted to preach the gospel only where Christ was not "named".[105] This means more than "utter the name"; it refers rather to accepting what the name stands for, acknowledging Christ ("named as Saviour", Olshausen).

The purpose[106] of this was to avoid *building on someone else's foundation*.[107] We should be clear on what this means. It is Paul's own personal calling that is in view: he is not saying that this is what all Christians should do. He is well aware of differentiation of function in the service of God. There will be those who plant and those who water, and they are both working together and working together with God (1 Cor. 3:6-9). There are those who lay the foundation and those who build (1 Cor. 3:10ff.). He is simply saying that his own calling is to plant the seed or to lay the foundation. This necessarily involves others working later, but it differentiates Paul from them, at least in the way of regular labor. He does not mean that on occasion he will not do anything to build up people whom others have won for Christ. This whole letter is proof of the contrary; Paul did not found the church at Rome, but he had no hesitation in trying to help the Roman Christians (1:11, 13). He is saying that his essential calling is to found new churches, and this means going into areas where others have not been. He is to preach the gospel to those who have not heard; to go to those who had already heard would be to renounce the calling God had given him.

21. Characteristically Paul finds a passage of Scripture that expresses this (Isa. 52:15, LXX).[108] We should interpret *Those who were not told*[109] *will see*

---

104. The verb is φιλοτιμέομαι, meaning strictly "to love honor" and thus "be ambitious", but also used in the sense "to strive eagerly" (see LSJ).

105. ὠνομάσθη.

106. ἵνα.

107. ἀλλότριος means "belonging to another"; as such it is opposed to ἴδιος, "one's own".

108. This is the last of 64 quotations from Scripture in Romans in the list given in the UBS Greek New Testament. We cannot take this list as the last word on the subject, for the boundary between a free quotation and the expression of one's thoughts in scriptural language is not easy to pin down; others would perhaps give somewhat different lists. But no one will question the fact that Romans is exceedingly rich in quotations from Scripture. In this list it has more quotations than any other New Testament book (next is the much longer Matthew, which has 61).

109. ἀναγγέλλω means "announce", "make known". It has no special connection with the gospel (though cf. 1 Pet. 1:12), but it certainly is applicable to evangelization.

in some such sense as "understand", as the next line makes clear with its use of precisely that verb.[110] It is not clear why we have an aorist of the proclamation in the first line and a perfect of the hearing in the second. There can scarcely be a difference.

22. *This is why*[111] refers not to the immediately preceding, but to what was said in verse 20 or earlier (Cranfield refers it to v. 19, and Lagrange to everything from v. 17 on). It was on account of his determination to obey God's call to him that Paul had been unable to go to Rome earlier. Though he had wanted to make the journey, evidently there had always been the demand that he preach in some new area and he could not deny the compulsion to follow God's leading in such a matter. So Paul says he had *often*[112] *been hindered*[113] *from coming to you* (cf. 1:13). Parry sees a reference to Paul's "delicacy; he will not seem either to have neglected the Church in Rome; or to force himself upon them."[114]

B. PAUL'S PLANS, 15:23-33

> [23]*But now that there is no more place for me to work in these regions, and since I have been longing for many years to see you,* [24]*I plan to do so when I go to Spain. I hope to visit you while passing through and to have you assist me on my journey there, after I have enjoyed your company for a while.* [25]*Now, however, I am on my way to Jerusalem in the service of the saints there.* [26]*For Macedonia and Achaia were pleased to make a contribution for the poor among the saints in Jerusalem.* [27]*They were pleased to do it, and indeed they owe it to them. For if the Gentiles have shared in the Jews' spiritual blessings, they owe it to the Jews to share with them their material blessings.* [28]*So after I have completed this task and have made sure that they have received this fruit, I will go to Spain and visit you on the way.* [29]*I know that when I come to you, I will come in the full measure of the blessing of Christ.*

110. συνήσουσιν, a verb which means "bring together" and so "understand".
111. διό.
112. τὰ πόλλα. Käsemann comments, "Common in Greek but singular in the NT, τὰ πόλλα means 'frequently' and almost 'regularly'" (p. 397). Moule wonders whether the meaning is *"those many times* (of which you are all aware), or *the majority of occasions, more often than not"* (IBNTG, p. 108). He gives no answer and perhaps none can be given. Cf. πολλάκις (1:13).
113. ἐνεκοπτόμην. The verb means "to cut into" and thus "to impede by cutting off the road"; it is used for hindering in any way. Burton remarks, "When an Imperfect refers to an action not separated from the time of speaking by a recognized interval, it is best translated into English by the Perfect" (MT, 28). Wuest sees the tense as implying a succession of hindrances.
114. τοῦ ἐλθεῖν is the genitive following verbs meaning "to hinder" (cf. Hodge). BDF 400 (4) comment on the absence of μή after this verb, "so that the dependence on the verb is clear".

30I urge you, brothers, by our Lord Jesus Christ and by the love of the Spirit, to join me in my struggle by praying to God for me. 31Pray that I may be rescued from the unbelievers in Judea and that my service in Jerusalem may be acceptable to the saints there, 32so that by God's will I may come to you with joy and together with you be refreshed. 33The God of peace be with you all. Amen.

Paul enlarges on his desire to go to Spain, which would mean passing through Rome. That will give him the opportunity of visiting the church in that city on the way and perhaps making it his base. But before he can do that he is taken up with his collection of money from the Gentile churches to assist the poor Christians in Jerusalem. It is clear that he saw this as very important. In the end trouble at Jerusalem led to his arrest, so that when he got to Rome it was as a prisoner making his appeal to Caesar, something very different from what he envisaged.

23. But now begins a sentence which is broken off and never completed (NIV inserts some words at the beginning of v. 24 to smooth the construction). This opening draws attention to changed circumstances. Paul no longer sees a place[115] to work in the *regions*[116] where he then was. This does not mean that he could not find a place where he could preach a sermon or two or where he could help build up the faithful. He means that there is no scope for his specific ministry of planting churches where the gospel had never previously been preached. Some have drawn this into an argument that Paul expected that he would cover all the nations of the world and that the parousia would then come. This, however, is not implied in anything he says, and it comes up against the fact that the apostle must have been conscious that there were many nations, such as the Parthians and the German tribes, where he had not been and had no prospect of going. He was not doing something to bring about the parousia but discharging his obligation to plant churches in virgin territory. With this he links his longing over many years to see the Roman Christians.[117]

24. *I plan to do so* is NIV's insertion to smooth out a difficulty; there is nothing corresponding to any of this in the Greek. Paul simply goes on,

---

115. τόπος means "place" in the sense of locality, but it came to be used to mean "opportunity", as here.

116. κλίμα means a "district" or "region", but precisely what kind of region is unclear. W. M. Ramsay examined the term and concluded that it signifies "a comparatively small geographical division" (*A Historical Commentary on St. Paul's Epistle to the Galatians* [Minneapolis reprint, 1978], pp. 279-80).

117. ἐπιποθία means a strong desire; it occurs here only in the New Testament (and as a variant reading at 2 Cor. 7:11). It is cited only here in LSJ, and SH say it occurs nowhere else. It is certainly a rare word. τοῦ ἐλθεῖν is epexegetic (M, III, p. 141). ἀπό is used of separation in time as well as in space (cf. Luke 8:43; Acts 15:7).

when[118] *I go to Spain.*[119] He expresses the hope that in passing through[120] he will be able to *visit* the Roman Christians.[121] He also hopes that the Romans will *assist* him on his journey. Paul does not explain what this means, but his verb is one which can be used for sending one forward on a journey with a variety of pieces of assistance.[122] Some think that Paul was looking for prayers and good wishes only, and this may indeed be the case. But it seems somewhat more likely that he hoped to have Rome as his base for his work in the western regions. Until now Antioch had functioned as his base, but this was too far from places like Spain. It would be a very great help to Paul if the Christians at Rome could see their way clear to acting as his home church, so to speak, while he went forward into unknown territory (in the spiritual sense) in the regions to the west.

After I have enjoyed your company for a while is a tactful and paradoxical expression[123] that combines two thoughts: (1) to be in Rome among the Christians will be a great pleasure to Paul, and (2) he does not plan to stay long. Paul makes it clear that his visit would not be a boring interlude which he would have to endure—he would enjoy it. He could never have his fill of the company of the Christians. But he did not intend to impose on the Romans—he was on his way.

25. There is some emphasis on *Now, however.*[124] Those are the plans, but now—there is something else to be done. He pictures himself as already on the way to Jerusalem (the present tense is used for the future to give greater

---

118. ὡς ἄν, "w. the subjunctive of the time of an event in the future, *when, as soon as*" (BAGD IV.c); "on my imminent journey to Spain" (BDF 455 [2]). Moulton remarks, "'when I am on my way' (durative) transfers into the subjunctive the familiar use of present for future" (M, I, p. 167).

119. Paul's word is Σπανία, though the more common Greek is Ἰσπανία (the Greeks also called it "Iberia"). The Latin form was *Hispania*. It denoted the whole of the peninsula south of the Pyrenees. Did Paul ever get to Spain? That depends on whether he was released from his Roman prison and able to implement his plan for evangelism in that land. Toward the end of the first century Clement of Rome speaks of Paul as having reached "the limits of the west" (τὸ τέρμα τῆς δύσεως; v. 7), which to a Roman would probably have meant Spain. There is also a reference in the Muratorian Canon to "the departure of Paul from the City on his journey to Spain" (cited from J. Stevenson, ed., *A New Eusebius* [London, 1963], p. 145; "the City" means Rome). These are interesting references, but they fall short of proof.

120. διαπορεύομαι has the meaning "pass through"; here it is used absolutely.

121. This is an unusual use of the verb θεάομαι, which is normally employed in the sense "see".

122. His verb is προπέμπω, which BAGD define as "*help on one's journey* with food, money, by arranging for companions, means of travel, etc."

123. Paul combines ἀπὸ μέρους, "in part", with ἐμπλήσθω, "be filled"; the verb means "to fill full" (Moule sees the preposition as denoting intensification [IBNTG, p. 88]); "to be filled in part" indicates his conviction that he would never reach satiety no matter how long he enjoyed the company of the Romans. Cf. Chrysostom, "That is, no length of time can fill me or create in me a satiety of your company."

124. νυνὶ δέ, which is probably not a resumption of the νυνὶ δέ of v. 23 but a new beginning.

certainty). Paul speaks of going there *in the service*[125] *of the saints there*.[126] The expression is quite general and could refer to service of any kind, but no doubt Paul is speaking of the collection he had caused to be taken up among the Gentile churches for the poor Christians in the holy city. His other references to it show that he attached the greatest significance to it (Gal. 2:10; 1 Cor. 16:1-4; 2 Cor. 8–9). Curiously Luke has but one casual reference to it in his account of what went on when Paul got to Jerusalem (Acts 24:17), but Paul saw it as very important, though he never tells us precisely why. Evidently the Jerusalem Christians (or some of them) were very poor, and their need would be a significant factor. Dodd reminds us that the Jerusalem church had been poor from the beginning when the few wealthy believers sold their possessions to give to the poor. This he considers a "partial and voluntary communism." He proceeds, "But they carried it out in the economically disastrous way of realizing capital and distributing it as income (Acts ii.44-45, iv.34–v.5). So far as we can gather, no practical steps were taken to replace the capital thus dissipated; and when hard times came, the community had no reserves of any kind." This may be part of the story, but we must bear in mind that Jerusalem was not a wealthy place so that the Jews in the Dispersion were in the habit of sending money to relieve the needs of their compatriots in Jerusalem. The Christians, of course, would be excluded from this largesse, so that in a city characterized by poverty they would tend to be poorer than the poor. This would only be made worse by the persecutions they experienced (e.g., Acts 8:1). All in all, the Christians in Jerusalem were a very needy group. Paul, in association with Barnabas, had been involved in an earlier aid project in a time of famine (Acts 11:27-30; 12:25).

But there was more to it than that. Paul evidently saw the offering as symbolizing the unity of believers. It was a token of fellowship between Christians in the heartland of the Jewish way and Gentile believers. Some early Christians held that all converts ought to be circumcised and to live according to the Jewish law; Paul had a continuing controversy with people who held such opinions. His collection would show that those who rejected this hard-line conservatism were nevertheless bound to Jewish believers in ties of Christian love.

Bruce detects eschatological significance in the offering. He draws attention to prophecy in which the Gentiles escort Jews from the Dispersion to Jerusalem as an "offering . . . to Yahweh" (Isa. 66:20; cf. Zeph. 3:10). But Paul had in mind "something more magnificent and surprising", for "the offering which he will present to the Lord consists not merely of Jews from the Gentile

---

125. The participle διαχονῶν. Cranfield regards this as expressing purpose rather than being durative as Michel holds.

126. Paul says simply τοῖς ἁγίοις (NIV has inserted *there*). Some hold that "the saints" means Christians in Jerusalem or Jewish Christians, but this is not borne out by use (cf. 16:2; 1 Cor. 6:1, etc.). It refers to believers generally, wherever they may be, though in this case, of course, it is those in Jerusalem who are in mind.

lands but of Gentiles themselves."[127] Jerusalem was the place where this offering should be made. The Gentiles could not be taken *en masse* to that city, but the collection could be taken there as a symbol of the offering of the people who gave it.

There may well have been other considerations. But the New Testament tells us enough to let us see that for Paul the taking of this money to Jerusalem was not a routine piece of financial administration. It had deep significance, and it was important that it be done rightly. It was worth postponing his longed-for visit to Rome until he had done all that was necessary for the proper presentation of the money.

26. *Macedonia and Achaia* of course means the Christians in those provinces; the usage is not common, but the meaning is plain enough. Paul's collection was apparently from his Gentile churches generally, and it certainly included others than those from these two areas (cf. 1 Cor. 16:1-2). It is not clear why he singles them out for mention here. Be that as it may, he says that they *were pleased* to help, which points to more than stolid acquiescence.[128] These Christians were happy to help. They made *a contribution*, where Paul's choice of word[129] points to something more than money. The term is the ordinary one for "fellowship" (and is used, e.g., of "the fellowship of the Holy Spirit", 2 Cor. 13:14) and will indicate here that the money was not a soulless gift, but the outward expression of the deep love that binds Christian believers in one body, the church[130] (it is used similarly in 2 Cor. 8:4; 9:13). The gift was for "the poor of the saints[131] who were in Jerusalem", where the form of expression indicates that not all the Jerusalem saints were poor. But there were enough of them to make the gift worthwhile.

27. Paul repeats that the Gentile Christians *were pleased to do it*,[132] putting emphasis on the goodwill that found expression in the gift. He himself had brought some pressure to bear, as we gather from the Corinthian correspondence, but that does not mean that the gift was not made with a willing mind. After all, there was no compulsion apart from moral obligation: the

---

127. See his New Zealand Tyndale Lecture for 1966, published in *Tyndale Bulletin* 19 (1968), pp. 3-25. The quotations are from pp. 23 and 24.

128. εὐδοκέω is sometimes used in the sense "decide" (as JB), but here it surely conveys more than that. The verb means "be well pleased" (BAGD). Cf. the cognate noun in 10:1.

129. κοινωνία, "communion", "fellowship". BAGD give meanings like these and go on to "3. abstr. for concr. *sign of fellowship, proof of brotherly unity,* even *gift, contribution. . . .*" The word "even" is significant.

130. "Paul had had differences with the Jerusalem church. He had not been willing to alter his gospel in the light of these differences, but neither would he consent to a divided church. There could be differences of opinion, but there could be only one church" (Burton H. Throckmorton, Jr., *Adopted in Love* [New York, 1978], p. 109).

131. The genitive τῶν ἁγίων is partitive (cf. IBNTG, p. 43).

132. H. E. Dana and J. R. Mantey maintain that the translation "for" for γάρ "has been greatly overworked." They hold that in this passage "it is properly translated as emphatic" in RV (RV has "Yea"). On this view the conjunction is giving emphasis to the thought (DM, p. 243). Cf. BDF 452 (2).

Christians could not be made to contribute.[133] The fact that they did shows their pleasure at being able to help needy brothers and sisters. Paul goes on to say[134] that there was in fact an element of debt; the Gentile believers were the "debtors"[135] of believing Jews. Paul introduces his explanation of this with a conditional clause, *For if the Gentiles have shared. . .* , where the implication is that the condition has been fulfilled.[136] What they *shared*[137] is put in general terms, *spiritual blessings,* but there is no doubting that Paul means the gospel above everything else. That was the supreme privilege; nothing in all this world is to be compared to the gift of God in the gospel, and the gospel came first to the Jews. When the Gentiles received it, it was because Jewish missionaries proclaimed it to them and invited them to share in its blessings. It is reasonable, then, that the Gentiles should serve[138] the Jews with their *material blessings.*[139]

28. Taking the collection to Jerusalem was the immediate task, but Paul looks for its consummation[140] and sequel. He speaks of "having sealed to them this fruit", which NIV understands in the sense *made sure that they have received* it. This may be the way to take it, but the meaning of "sealing" in this context remains doubtful. It is known that produce such as wheat and barley was put in sacks and sealed; this was the last thing done and indicated that everything was in order. It may be that that is the way we should understand it: Paul's seal meant that the money was there in full amount. A somewhat similar view is that which starts from the seal as a mark of personal authentication; Paul's seal was his guarantee that all had been done well. It has been held that Paul's very presence certified the gift and set the seal on his apos-

---

133. "Charity is an obligation but it is not a tax" (Murray).

134. NIV renders καί with *and indeed* (as do RSV, NEB); GNB has "but, as a matter of fact". These are all ways of bringing out the truth that "The force of 'and' in this context is emphatic" (TH).

135. ὀφειλέται, a term used of those who owe money but also of those bound by some obligation or duty.

136. εἰ with the aorist indicative.

137. The verb is κοινωνέω, cognate with κοινωνία rendered "contribution" in the previous verse. Paul is bringing out the fitness of the contribution the Gentiles were asked to make. The verb may be used either of the giver or the recipient.

138. NIV reads *to share,* the translation just used for κοινωνέω, but the verb here is λειτουργέω, a verb whose original use was for "the direct discharge of specific services to the body politic. Citizens with an income above a fixed level had by law to accept these at their own expense, or else they could do so voluntarily, whether for motives of patriotism or vainglory or both" (TDNT, IV, p. 216). The word was used of the service of God in LXX, a usage that the New Testament writers took over. Here the form the service of God takes is the service of his people. Paul has used the cognate noun in 13:6; 15:16.

139. ἐν τοῖς σαρκικοῖς. Adjectives in -ικός signify "-like"; this one means "belonging to σάρξ, of the nature of σάρξ" (BDF 113 [2]; cf. M, III, p. 378). It can signify "carnal" and is sometimes used in a derogatory fashion in Christian writings. But here the meaning is "things pertaining to this life" or the like. It is not pejorative.

140. His verb is ἐπιτελέω, meaning "bring to an end", "complete". It can be used of completing almost anything, but BAGD note that it is used "Esp. of the performance of rituals and ceremonies" (2). SH also notice this use and hold that, combined with the use of λειτουργέω, it suggests that Paul sees in the collection "a solemn religious offering".

tleship. Knox holds that when the money has been given and received in the right spirit "Paul will have ended his divinely appointed work in Asia Minor and Greece; the 'fruit' of his mission will have been 'sealed.'" There are other views, and at this distance in time we cannot be sure of the precise significance of the sealing. But it is clear that in some way it pointed to official assurance that all was well.

Once the money is delivered, Paul says, *I will go to Spain and visit you on the way.* More accurately he says, "I will go off to Spain through you." His verb is the usual verb for going away, and we have already had occasion to notice his plan to make Spain his next place of mission. But "go away through you" is not what we would have expected, though, of course, it is quite intelligible.[141]

29. Paul closes this part of his letter on a note of quiet certainty (*I know*); his certainty is one of faith, but none the less certain for that. He looks to the time when he will come to the Romans,[142] and he expresses his confidence that that will be *in the full measure of the blessing of Christ.*[143] He was engaged in the service of a Christ who was faithful, one on whom Paul could place the utmost reliance. So whatever happened, he was sure of the blessing of the Lord. It is pointed out that these words are a mark of authenticity, for no one who knew how Paul in fact arrived at Rome would have put it quite that way. We may well feel that in the providence of God the divine blessing rested on the apostle even in his time as a prisoner in Rome, but it is certainly unlikely that anyone else writing after the event would have chosen to put it in these words. It is not quite clear whether Paul thought that the blessing in question would rest on him or whether he meant that the work he would do would be a blessing to the Roman Christians. Probably neither is out of mind and there is truth in both.[144]

30. It is not uncommon for Paul to request prayer from his correspondents (2 Cor. 1:11; Eph. 6:19; Col. 4:3; 1 Thess. 5:25; 2 Thess. 3:1), so this passage is quite in character. On this occasion something of what the collection for the saints meant to the apostle comes through in a very impassioned exhortation to pray. *I urge you* (or perhaps "I implore you", NEB) is normal enough in a pressing request, but *by our Lord Jesus Christ* is not.[145] Cranfield may well be right when he says that the expression (together with its immedi-

---

141. Moule classes this use of διά under the heading "extension through" and sees the meaning as "via" (IBNTG, p. 55).

142. Moule points out that the participle might mean "when I come" or "if I come" (IBNTG, p. 134), but the sense of the passage makes "when" much more likely than "if".

143. πλήρωμα signifies "fulness", "full measure". G. Delling takes it here as "almost adjectival: with the 'full' blessing." He goes on, "The noun, however, underlines the overflowing wealth (Vg *abundantia*) of the blessing with which Christ accompanies His apostle" (TDNT, VI, p. 302).

144. D. M. Baillie chooses this text for a sermon on "The importance of a complete Christianity" (ET, LXVII [1955-56], pp. 121-22).

145. BDF class this use of διά as "Idiomatically with urgent questions = 'by'" (223 [4]). It is the use we have in 12:1.

ate sequel) "indicates the authority invoked and the ground of appeal in Paul's urgent entreaty." A second *by* leads to the thought of *the love of the Spirit,* an expression which might mean the love the Spirit enkindles in believers, the love the Spirit has for them, or even love the believers have for the Spirit. Not many hold to this third view (cf. Barrett, "the genitive cannot be objective"), but either of the other two is possible. Murray holds to the second view, but the New Testament more often refers to the love the Spirit brings about in Christians (cf. Gal. 5:22), and that seems to be the most likely understanding of the words here.

Paul is not looking for a formal and tepid prayer but for a wholehearted involvement, which he describes in terms of conflict: *to join me in my struggle.*[146] There is a very real struggle going on between the forces of good and evil, and a most significant part of that struggle is prayer. Thus E. Stauffer can say, "the form of the battle is prayer. In prayer there is achieved unity between the will of God and that of man, between human struggling and action and effective divine operation. In prayer, too, there is fulfilled the fellowship of conflict and destiny between man and man. In prayer one man becomes the representative of the other, so that there is here opened up the possibility of one standing in the breach for all and all for one" (TDNT, I, p. 139). It is this kind of powerful praying for which the apostle looks.

He specifies that he wants prayer *to God* and *for me;* neither is strictly necessary, but they help fill in the picture. We should not leave this verse without noticing once again the mention of the three Persons of the Trinity. This natural placing of the three together would lead in time to the enunciation of the doctrine of the Trinity.

31. Paul moves to the content of the prayer for which he looks,[147] namely that he *may be rescued from*[148] *the unbelievers in Judea.*[149] Paul was evidently well aware of the fact that there were fanatical Jews in Judea who would oppose him vigorously (cf. Acts 20:22-23; 21:11), and in due course events proved his fears well founded. In obedience to God he would go up to Jerusalem despite the danger, but he did not plan to thrust himself into peril and he prayed to be delivered from it.

---

146. συναγωνίσασθαι is a strong term meaning "fight along with"; it points to serious involvement. Cf. Minear, "He appealed with great urgency for supporting prayers from the Roman brothers. To those who discount the significance of intercessory prayers this may seem a negligible motive; but not to the apostle. He believed that such prayers could be of great effect" (p. 4).

147. ἵνα might be used in the sense of purpose, "in order that I may be delivered", but more probably it signifies the content of the desired prayer. NIV inserts *Pray,* but this is not in the Greek; the sentence carries on from the previous verse with "that".

148. ῥυσθῶ is perhaps better rendered "delivered from", "preserved from"; Paul is asking that he not fall into the hands of his opponents, not that he may be rescued after they have taken him. The verb may be followed by ἐκ (7:24) or ἀπό (as here).

149. For the verb ἀπειθέω see the note on 2:8. The participle may be taken to mean the "disobedient" here (as Goodspeed), but this is one of the passages where BAGD think the meaning "be an unbeliever" "seems most probable"; the disobedience of the people in question consisted in their refusal to believe.

523

With this he joins the prayer that his *service in Jerusalem*[150] *may be*[151] *acceptable to the saints there.* From our standpoint it is difficult to see why there should be a problem: the saints in Jerusalem were in need, the Gentile Christians had taken up a collection specifically to meet that need, so why should not the money be welcomed with enthusiasm and gratitude? But we must bear in mind that the Jerusalem church appears to have been very conservative. That was where the view was most strongly held that Gentile believers must be circumcised and taught to observe the law of Moses. Paul was regarded by some members of the Jerusalem church as a dangerous innovator, a man who was disobeying God by taking lightly the obligation to obey the law that God had given through his servant Moses. The money Paul brought might be seen by some who held views like this as a bribe wherewith the apostle hoped to buy a condonation of his breaches of the law. The Jerusalemites would think that by accepting the money they would be endorsing what Paul had done among the Gentiles; in other words, they would be countenancing his work.[152] Perhaps also they did not want to be helped by people like Gentiles. Such reluctance would be somewhat curious because the Jerusalem people had asked Paul to help the poor (Gal. 2:10), and that was exactly what he was doing. When in due course Paul reached Jerusalem he was welcomed by "the brothers", specifically by James and his fellow elders (Acts 21:17-25), but these leaders showed concern about the reaction of the rank and file. The church at Jerusalem as a whole does not appear to have been very helpful and, for example, no assistance of any sort is recorded after the apostle's arrest.

32. It seems that Paul is here recording what he hoped would be the answer to the prayers of the Romans. *So that* indicates purpose.[153] Paul looks forward to coming to the Romans with joy *by God's will.* Leenhardt understands this to mean that "he does not propose to proceed on his way to Rome unless he can do so with the joy of having found a kind welcome at Jerusalem." But this seems to be reading too much into the expression. It is unlikely that Paul would leave himself so dependent on men when he felt that God was calling him on. It is more probable that his determination to proceed to Spain was firm and that this included a stop in Rome. He calls for prayer that his service in Jerusalem might be acceptable so that his coming to Rome would be a happy one *(with joy* immediately follows *so that).* He looks for refreshment

---

150. *Service* is διακονία (see the note on 11:13); while the term is a general one, Paul clearly is referring to the collection taken up to serve the need of the saints. εἰς Ἰερουσαλήμ means "to the saints in Jerusalem", not to the inhabitants generally.

151. γένηται, "become", has the force of "prove to be".

152. Achtemeier comments that acceptance of the money "would be an acknowledgment that just as they have rightfully received a share of the material blessing of the gentiles so the gentiles rightfully received a share of the spiritual blessings of Israel. . . . More than that, the acceptance of such an offering would be a clear acknowledgment that Paul's apostolic mandate is valid".

153. ἵνα could be taken as introducing a further part of the prayer, but, as Denney puts it, this ἵνα "seems to be subordinate to, not co-ordinate with the preceding one."

with the Roman Christians;[154] he anticipated no difficulties or dangers when he came among them.

33. Now comes a little benediction such as is not uncommon in Paul's letters (cf. vv. 5-6, 13; 9:5, etc.). He describes God as *The God of peace* (16:20; 2 Cor. 13:11; Phil. 4:9; 1 Thess. 5:23). True peace is associated with God so fully that Paul can characterize God by it. Paul expresses the wish that the God of peace be with *all* the Roman Christians. It is characteristic of Paul to make his wish all-embracing. *Amen* is probably added on general principles. There is no need for it where there is no congregational response. But it was evidently conventional at the end of a prayer, and this wish falls into that category.[155]

---

154. συναναπαύομαι is found here only in the New Testament. It usually has a meaning like "lie down together with" and is often used of married couples (BAGD). But here it clearly means rest in general.

155. Manson holds that this was the original end to the letter. It would certainly form a suitable ending, though we should notice that none of Paul's accepted letters ends in this way. It is better to take the verse as a prayer wish inserted into the letter as Paul moved on.

Romans 16

For a discussion of the question whether chapter 16 was an original part of this epistle or whether it was a separate letter which has somehow become attached to Romans see the Introduction, pp. 24ff. As I have tried to show there, there are good reasons for seeing this chapter as an integral part of the letter from the beginning. And it is a significant part of the letter. The multiplicity of greetings to people of whom we know nothing apart from their being listed here roots the letter in a specific context. It was a letter to real people and, as far as we can see, to ordinary people; it was not written to professional theologians (though through the centuries scholars have found the epistle a happy hunting ground). As we consider the weighty matters Paul deals with, we are apt to overlook the fact that it was addressed to people like Ampliatus and Tryphena and Rufus. Clearly Paul expected this kind of person to be helped by what he wrote, a fact which modern experts sometimes overlook.[1] And it is fitting that this letter, which has given us so much solid doctrinal teaching, should end with this emphasis on persons, on love, and on a reminder that humble servants of God perform all sorts of active ministry.

C. Commendation of Phoebe, 16:1-2

> [1] I commend to you our sister Phoebe, a servant[a] of the church in Cenchrea. [2] I ask you to receive her in the Lord in a way worthy of the saints and to give her any help she may need from you, for she has been a great help to many people, including me.

[a] 1 Or deaconess

People did a good deal of travelling in the first-century Roman empire and, since they often went to places where people they knew had friends, used letters of commendation. There are references to them in the New Testament (cf. Acts 18:27; 2 Cor. 3:1; 8:18-24; 3 John 9-10). Such letters did not, as far as our information from the ancient world goes, contain greetings (one greetings expression is known in such a letter but no more), but letters of a

---

1. Barth comments that the letter "would be altogether incomplete if it did not itself make clear that it was addressed to particular men possessed of human names and bearing a human countenance."

completely different sort sometimes contained commendations. The commendation of Phoebe at the end of a letter dealing with other things is quite in character. It seems likely that she was the person entrusted with the task of taking the letter to the Roman church, for a commendation of someone not with the letter normally refers to a future arrival (cf. 1 Cor. 16:10; Col. 4:10). The Christians were noted for their hospitality, and letters of recommendation were necessary as a way of guarding against fraud.[2]

1. The opening does not read like the beginning of a letter, but as something that follows on from a preceding passage.[3] *I commend* makes use of the verb normally employed in such recommendations.[4] *Phoebe* is the pagan name[5] of a woman otherwise unknown. When the early Christians became believers, they did not bother to change names associated with heathen deities (any more than we do with the names of the days of the week; for that matter we still use the names of pagan deities such as Diana). Phoebe is called *our sister*, a normal description of a female believer; believers were "family".

She was also *a servant of the church*[6] *in Cenchrea*. Several translations call her "a deaconess" (as RSV; cf. NEB, "who holds office"). It is not easy to defend that translation, for the word "deaconess"[7] is not found until much later. But Paul's word,[8] besides meaning "servant", is the word for "deacon" (it is the word used, e.g., in Phil. 1:1), and it may well be that Paul is describing Phoebe as a deacon of the church at Cenchrea. Some commentators hold that there would not have been female officebearers as early as Paul's time

2. We see the kind of thing that had to be guarded against in Lucian's story (somewhat later than this) of a certain Peregrinus, a swindler and a cheat, who discovered the Christians, and found out that "if any charlatan and trickster, able to profit by occasion, comes among them, he quickly acquires wealth by imposing upon simple folk" (Lucian, *Peregrinus* 13; cited from Loeb edition, V, p. 15). Letters of commendation were some sort of guard against this sort of thing.

3. The conjunction δέ (which NIV omits) may introduce a contrast ("but") or mark a transition ("and"), but we do not expect it at the opening of a letter. This does not of course prove that chapter 16 always followed chapter 15, but it is a point against chapter 16 ever having existed by itself. A few MSS omit δέ (principally D* F G), but it should be read. Cf. Käsemann, "The δέ, which is certainly original (Michel), undoubtedly implies continuation (Ridderbos) and is thus the introduction to a new section" (p. 410).

4. συνίστημι, which MM say "is very common in the papyri, and is used with a great variety of meanings." The first they select is "From its original meaning 'set together,' 'combine,' συνίστημι passes into the sense of 'bring together as friends,' 'introduce,' 'recommend'". GNB here translates "recommend", and Moffatt "introduce". BDF 93 note this as one of the few "certain examples of the -μι conjugation" in the active and regard it as "a polite social formula".

5. It is the feminine form of φοῖβος, a name given to the god Apollo, "the Bright One" (LSJ). Such names were often given to slaves, who of course retained them if they were set free. Phoebe may have been a freedwoman.

6. Interestingly, this is Paul's first use of ἐκκλησία in Romans; he uses it five times in this chapter.

7. διακόνισσα. This is implied by Pliny's reference to *ministrae* whom he had tortured (Epp. x.96.8). Deaconesses are mentioned in *The Apostolic Constitutions*, where they are admitted to communion ahead of the virgins and the widows.

8. διάκονος. οὖσαν indicates her current position.

and thus argue for the meaning "servant" here. But the social conditions of the time were such that there must have been the need for feminine church workers to assist in such matters as the baptism of women or anything that meant contact with women's quarters in homes. The form of expression here makes it more likely that an official is meant than the more general term "servant", though in view of the wide use of the term for the general concept of service this is far from being proved. Phoebe is certainly called a deacon; the question is whether this is an official position or general service.[9] She came from *Cenchrea*, which was the port of Corinth towards the east on the Saronic Gulf (Corinth was on the isthmus between the Gulf of Corinth, with Lechaeum as its port, and the Saronic Gulf). Paul is mentioned as having been there (Acts 18:18).

2. *I ask you* is NIV's insertion; Paul simply says "in order that", introducing the purpose[10] of his commendation, namely that the Romans *receive her in the Lord*.[11] The expression "in the Lord" recurs in verses 8, 11, 12 *(bis)*, 13, and 22, while "in Christ" is found in 3, 7, 9, and 10. Some have seen a difference in meaning, but this seems unwarranted; the variation is surely stylistic. But it should be noticed that the life in Christ is emphasized throughout this chapter. To receive someone "in the Lord" means more than simply to receive that person into one's house; there is the reminder that what Christians do they do in Christ. They are to give Phoebe a welcome *worthy of the saints*, which may mean the kind of welcome that is appropriate for saints to give or the welcome that is fitting for saints to receive.

To give her any help she may need is more exactly "to stand by her in whatever matter she has need of you".[12] We know nothing of Phoebe's circumstances and needs, but clearly they were such that Paul anticipated that she would need assistance in the capital and further that he expected the

---

9. Barrett holds that the distinction between "the 'part-time helper' and the minister set apart to the service of the Church was not as sharply drawn as it is today, and it may therefore be that the question whether Phoebe was a 'deaconess' or a valued church worker is wrongly put." There may be something in this, but even in the first century there appears to have been a distinction between those who held official positions and those who did not. Gore cites Origen, "Here we learn that female ministers are recognized in the Church." Wilckens similarly sees here "one of the earliest witnesses to the formation of the diaconate", and A. Oepke thinks that this description of Phoebe "indicates the point where the original charisma is becoming an office" (TDNT, I, p. 787; in a footnote he adds, "Esp. if καί . . . is genuine", as it surely is). Cranfield regards it as "virtually certain that Phoebe is being described as 'a' (or possibly 'the') deacon of the church in question", and that this passage is to be classed with Phil. 1:1; 1 Tim. 3:8, 12.

10. ἵνα is telic. Moule discusses it under imperatival ἵνα and includes it with those which "can plausibly be explained by an antecedent verb, stated or implied, of saying, wishing, etc., and therefore permit the ἵνα to be more or less consciously *final*" (IBNTG, p. 145).

11. The verb is προσδέχομαι, which carries the notion of welcome. BAGD see "welcome someone in the Lord" as meaning welcome "as a Christian brother or sister".

12. The verb παρίστημι in its intransitive uses means "stand beside" and so "stand by to help".

Romans to be able to help. "Matter" is a very general term[13] and does not allow us to see very closely what the lady's needs were. But she had come on quite a journey, and we may guess that there was something important behind it.[14]

We cannot say more, but Paul goes on to make it clear that Phoebe was someone special.[15] She had helped many people, himself included, though in precisely what way he does not say. The word he uses[16] is the feminine of a word which SH note was "used like the Latin *patronus* for the legal representative of the foreigner. In Jewish communities it meant the legal representative or wealthy patron." But we cannot reason from that that Phoebe was the legal protector of the Christians at Cenchrea, for a woman could not hold that position. The word must be used figuratively in this place. But it is a word that points to an important person. We should reflect also that it was most unlikely that a woman would travel alone and that Paul says nothing about travelling companions. If she had had any, Paul would surely have commended them to the Romans also. The inference is that Phoebe travelled with a retinue of servants, and this, too, points to a woman of means. There were not many wealthy people in the church of the day, but it seems that Phoebe was one of them.

D. GREETINGS, 16:3-16

>3*Greet Priscilla[a] and Aquila, my fellow workers in Christ Jesus.* 4*They risked their lives for me. Not only I but all the churches of the Gentiles are grateful to them.*
>
>5*Greet also the church that meets at their house.*
>
>*Greet my dear friend Epenetus, who was the first convert to Christ in the province of Asia.*
>
>6*Greet Mary, who worked very hard for you.*
>
>7*Greet Andronicus and Junias, my relatives who have been in prison with me. They are outstanding among the apostles, and they were in Christ before I was.*

13. πρᾶγμα means "that which is done, *deed, thing* . . ." (BAGD). It may be used in the sense "undertaking", and sometimes even of a specific undertaking like a lawsuit (1 Cor. 6:1). Moule comments on the grammatical problem of ἐν ᾧ . . . πράγματι that the omission of the antecedent "is common enough" and that "where necessary, the relevant noun is then placed *after* the relative pronoun" (IBNTG, p. 130).

14. Marcus Loane mentions the possibility that the reason for the journey was "no more than a change of residence." He goes on, "The terms of his introduction seem to imply that a graver cause was at stake, perhaps a law-suit with regard to her property" (*God's Mere Mercy* [Blackwood, South Australia, 1986], p. 118).

15. Howard notes this as one of the passages where a change of accent means a change of meaning (αὐτή might be read as αὕτη; M, II, p. 60). But the evidence for αὕτη is not weighty enough to carry conviction. Cranfield agrees that we must accept αὐτή "in its emphatic sense" with the meaning "she herself" (cf. BDF 277 [3]).

16. προστάτις.

8Greet Ampliatus, whom I love in the Lord.
9Greet Urbanus, our fellow worker in Christ, and my dear friend Stachys.
10Greet Apelles, tested and approved in Christ.
Greet those who belong to the household of Aristobulus.
11Greet Herodion, my relative.
Greet those in the household of Narcissus who are in the Lord.
12Greet Tryphena and Tryphosa, those women who work hard in the Lord.
Greet my dear friend Persis, another woman who has worked very hard in the Lord.
13Greet Rufus, chosen in the Lord, and his mother, who has been a mother to me, too.
14Greet Asyncritus, Phlegon, Hermes, Patrobas, Hermas and the brothers with them.
15Greet Philologus, Julia, Nereus and his sister, and Olympas and all the saints with them.
16Greet one another with a holy kiss.
All the churches of Christ send greetings.

a3 Greek *Prisca*, a variant of *Priscilla*

Apart from Prisca and Aquila we know nothing of any of the people in this list. There are 24 names and two people who are not named. Of the 26 nine are women,[17] and if we add Phoebe there is a very impressive number when we reflect on the character of the male-dominated society of the day. Some of the names are Jewish (Herodion, Apelles), some are Latin (Ampliatus, Urbanus), though most are Greek. It is perilous to argue from this to the nationality of each of the individuals named, for in the first century people not uncommonly bore more than one name as they moved in the cosmopolitan society of the empire. But the effect of the whole list is to emphasize the universality of the church. It is not a society of people from one nation or class or social grouping.

3. Paul begins his greetings with one for Prisca and Aquila. NIV mg. is perhaps a trifle misleading when it says that Prisca is "a variant of Priscilla", for it is Prisca that is the base word of which Priscilla is a diminutive. Luke favors the name Priscilla, whereas Paul seems always to use Prisca.[18] Prisca is mentioned before her husband on four occasions out of six (Acts 18:18, 26; Rom. 16:2; 2 Tim. 4:19; Aquila is first in Acts 18:2; 1 Cor. 16:19), from which some have deduced that she came from a higher social stratum, and others that she was more able than her husband. Aquila (the name is the Latin for "eagle") was a tentmaker from Pontus who had evidently settled in Rome, but had been compelled to leave when the Emperor Claudius expelled the

17. Prisca, Mary, Junia, Tryphena, Tryphosa, Persis, the mother of Rufus, Julia, the sister of Nereus.

18. In some passages there are MSS that read Priscilla, but in every case it seems that Prisca is correct. Bengel comments on Paul's usage, "in the Church the name, *Prisca*, is more dignified." For some reason NIV always conforms Paul to Luke's usage.

Jews (Acts 18:2). It was their common trade that brought him and Paul together and began a friendship that lasted. They went with Paul to Ephesus (Acts 18:18), and remained there when he went on. They were evidently a fine Christian couple, for they were able to instruct the redoubtable Apollos in the faith (Acts 18:26). They had a church in their house in more places than one (v. 5; 1 Cor. 16:19). It is sometimes objected to what the New Testament tells us about them that they seem to be travelling too widely, but we should remember what Parry calls "the migratory habits of Jews engaged in business" (CGT) and the fact that they were active in spreading the gospel. In this latter task they may have been on the move as much as Paul was. Paul refers to them here as his *fellow workers*,[19] a term always used in the New Testament of people who worked together in the fellowship of the gospel. This is made clear here by the addition *in Christ Jesus*.

4. NIV begins a new sentence, but the Greek simply carries on with "who".[20] These people *risked their lives* for Paul,[21] and he expresses his thanks to them for what they did (the only place in the New Testament where the verb "to thank" has a human object). He adds that *all the churches of the Gentiles* share his feelings. Evidently what they did was widely known, but unfortunately we do not share that knowledge. Paul lets us know that there was an occasion when he was in great danger in Ephesus (1 Cor. 15:32; cf. Acts 19:23, 30-31). There may possibly be a connection, but we have no way of knowing whether there was and, if so, what it was. The expression indicates that Prisca and her husband were widely known among the Gentiles.

5. The greeting is extended to cover *the church that meets at their house*[22] (for other such house churches cf. 1 Cor. 16:19; Col. 4:15; Philem. 2; cf. also Acts 12:12). There were no church buildings in the first century (not until the third century on our present information), so it was natural for Christians to meet in private homes. Some have thought the expression means something like "family worship"; they see a reference to a godly family and remind us of conversions of households (e.g., Acts 16:15; 1 Cor. 1:16). A household would include all the members of the family, perhaps other relatives, slaves, and employees. But under first-century conditions there seems no reason to limit a house church to those linked with the householder in some way. It seems that other Christians would join a house church (where else could they worship?). Nothing is known of how and where the whole church in a city like

---

19. συνεργός.

20. οἵτινες, the relative of quality. It often does not differ significantly from οἵ, but here, where Paul is pointing to the outstanding qualities of his friends, it may have its original force. BDF hold that in vv. 3ff. ὅς and ὅστις vary "according to whether a simple assertion is made (ὅς) or a characteristic (ὅστις) given" (293 [4]).

21. τὸν ἑαυτῶν τράχηλον ὑπέθηκαν. The singular here may favor the view that the usage is metaphorical (Gifford). ὑποτίθημι means "put under", pointing to the metaphor of putting the neck on the block under the threatening axe.

22. τὴν κατ᾽ οἶκον αὐτῶν ἐκκλησίαν. BAGD see this use of κατά as that which "serves to isolate or separate by" as in 14:22 or Paul's living in a private dwelling (Acts 28:16).

Rome would meet (Paul speaks of "the whole church" as meeting in Corinth, 1 Cor. 14:23, so it did meet). Nor do we know the relationship of a house church to the church as a whole. It was not a schismatic assembly, for greetings are sent in a letter to the church as a whole.[23]

Paul also greets *Epenetus* (SH cite the name from inscriptions in Asia Minor and in Rome). Paul calls him "my beloved"[24] ("beloved" again in vv. 8, 9, and 12), so evidently he was very dear to the apostle. He is called *the first convert to Christ in the province of Asia*.[25] Paul's word means "firstfruit" rather than "first convert", and we should see in this the thought that "firstfruit" implies later fruit; it carries with it the thought of a greater harvest.

6. Greetings are sent to *Mary*.[26] While her name could possibly be Latin, it is generally agreed that she was probably Jewish. Mary is the name of a number of women in the New Testament, but there is no reason to identify this Mary with any of the others. Whatever her nationality, she was distinguished by the fact that she *worked very hard for you*. There is no indication of the direction her many labors took, but Paul is clearly referring to Christian service of some kind. The past tense shows that he has in mind some past endeavor. It is interesting that Paul both knows of and is appreciative of service rendered to the Roman Christians.

7. Next come *Andronicus* (the name means "man of victory") and *Junias*. NIV thus makes the second name that of a man, but this seems unlikely.[27] The patristic commentators seem to have taken the word as feminine ("Junia") and understood the pair to be man and wife.[28] Paul calls them his "kinsfolk", which may possibly be meant in the sense of *relatives* (as NIV), but more probably means "fellow Jews" (as in 9:3). The term recurs in verses 11 and 21, and it seems unlikely that there were so many members of Paul's family in Rome or with him when he wrote (especially since these two were Christians before Paul). He goes on to say that they were "fellow prisoners" of his,[29] which may mean that they were in jail together or that they had shared the same fate (not necessarily at the same time). We have no record of this, but Paul tells us that he was in prison often (2 Cor. 11:23; Clement of Rome says

---

23. See further Robert Banks, *Paul's Idea of Community* (Sydney, 1979).

24. τὸν ἀγαπητόν μου.

25. ἀπαρχὴ τῆς ᾿Ασίας εἰς Χριστόν. Some MSS have ᾿Αχαίας instead of ᾿Ασίας, but there is no doubt that ᾿Ασίας is the correct reading.

26. The MSS vary between Μαρίαν and Μαριάμ; the former could be Latin (the feminine of Marius) or Jewish, whereas the latter is clearly the equivalent of Miriam and is Jewish.

27. ᾿Ιουνιᾶν could be a contraction of the masculine Junianus, but no other example of this contraction is known. It is more likely that it is the accusative of the feminine ᾿Ιουνία. Ray R. Schulz, in an article entitled "Romans 16:7: Junia or Junias", argues strongly for the feminine form (ET, 98 [1986-87], pp. 108-10).

28. Thus BDF 125 (2), "the ancients understood a married couple like Aquila and Priscilla".

29. συναιχμάλωτος (again in Col. 4:10; Philem. 23) strictly means a fellow prisoner of war. Paul may be indicating that they were engaged together in a grim warfare against evil.

that Paul was in prison seven times, 1 Clem. 5:6), so there were ample possibilities for this. It is possible that the expression is to be taken figuratively, but there seems no good reason for this. It is likely that we should understand this couple to have suffered the same fate as Paul had undergone at the hand of the authorities.

Andronicus and Junia are also *outstanding among the apostles*,[30] which might mean that the apostles held them in high esteem or that they were apostles, and notable apostles at that. The former understanding seems less likely; it "scarcely does justice to the construction in the Greek" (Harrison).[31] It is fairly clear from the New Testament that there was a wider circle of apostles than the Twelve, and it would seem that this couple belonged to that wider circle. Some find an argument from this that we should understand the second name as masculine, holding that a woman could not be an apostle, but we should bear in mind Chrysostom's comment: "Oh! how great is the devotion of this woman, that she should be even counted worthy of the appellation of apostle!"[32] This couple[33] were very early on the Christian scene, for Paul says that they were[34] Christians before he was and his conversion must have taken place within a year or two of the crucifixion.[35] That puts them among the earliest of all believers and makes it probable that they originally were Jews from Palestine.

8. *Ampliatus* is another of those beloved by Paul; once again we discern the warmth of affection with which the apostle regarded his fellow workers. The name is a common one according to Lightfoot,[36] often connected with the

30. ἐπίσημοι ἐν τοῖς ἀποστόλοις. σῆμα denotes a mark or sign, so these are "marked" or "notable" people. I have discussed the meaning of apostle in *Ministers of God* (London, 1964), pp. 39-61.

31. SH say it was apparently taken "by all patristic commentators" in the sense distinguished as apostles. They further think that the presence of these apostles in Rome suggests "perhaps one of the methods by which the city had been evangelized."

32. Cranfield comments on Paul's view of women: "That Paul should not only include a woman (on the view taken above) among the apostles but actually describe her, together with Andronicus, as outstanding among them, is highly significant evidence (along with the importance he accords in this chapter to Phoebe, Prisca, Mary, Tryphaena, Tryphosa, Persis, the mother of Rufus, Julia and the sister of Nereus) of the falsity of the widespread and stubbornly persistent notion that Paul had a low view of women and something to which the Church as a whole has not yet paid sufficient attention."

33. The relative this time is οἵ; earlier in the verse it was οἵτινες, but there seems no difference in meaning.

34. The verb γέγοναν is listed by Moulton as tolerating "the company of adjuncts that fasten attention on the initial point" (M, I, p. 144). The perfect also indicates the continuing state.

35. George Ogg dates the crucifixion as A.D. 33 and Paul's conversion as A.D. 34 or 35 (*The Chronology of the Life of Paul* [London, 1968], p. 200). Martin Hengel likewise dates his conversion as A.D. 32-34 (*Between Jesus and Paul* [Philadelphia, 1983], p. 11), and N. A. Dahl puts it "only a couple of years after Christ's death" (*Studies in Paul* [Minneapolis, 1977], p. 2).

36. J. B. Lightfoot has an important excursus on "Caesar's Household" in his *Saint Paul's Epistle to the Philippians* (London, 1908), pp. 171ff. in which he comments on several names in this list. Those on Amplias come on p. 174.

Emperor's household. A number of commentators draw attention to a tomb dating from the late first century or early second century in the catacomb of Domitilla, the earliest Christian catacomb. It bears the inscription AMPLI-AT[I]. Parry comments, "The single personal name suggests a slave: the honour of an elaborately painted tomb suggests that he was very prominent in the earliest Roman Church: the connexion with Domitilla seems to show that it is the name of a slave or freedman through whom Christianity had penetrated into a second great Roman household" (CGT). We cannot be certain that this is the tomb of the man Paul greets, but it is an intriguing possibility.

9. *Urbanus* is a common slave name which Lightfoot finds common also in the imperial household. Like Prisca and Aquila he was a *fellow worker* of Paul's, though we have no information as to where they had worked together. *Our* may mean Paul and the Romans, or Paul and Timothy (cf. v. 21), or all who work for Christ. The name *Stachys*, which means "ear (of grain)", is "comparatively rare" according to Lightfoot, though he does find one person of this name holding an important office in the imperial household (p. 174). "My beloved" may mark this man out as a personal friend of Paul's.

10. *Apelles* is a name found among the imperial household (Lightfoot), but also borne by Jews (its likeness to Abel may have made it a natural name for Jews looking for a suitable additional name; cf. Saul who was also Paul). Bruce says that it "was sufficiently common among the Jews of Rome for Horace to use it as a typical Jewish name". This man was *tested and approved*.[37] We have no way of knowing what test he had undergone, but he was a man of tested excellence and Paul approves of him accordingly.

The apostle goes on to refer to *the household of Aristobulus*. This is the name of a grandson of Herod the Great who ended his days in Rome, apparently as a private citizen. He was on friendly terms with the Emperor Claudius, and it is not unlikely that on his death his slaves passed to the Emperor. If they did, they would collectively retain the name "those of Aristobulus".[38] There would be many Jews in such a household, and this may have opened up the way for the gospel. However it happened, it is of interest that there were Christians in such a household in Rome.

11. The name *Herodion* is obviously connected with Herod and is thus a link with the household of Aristobulus; Herodion may even have been a member of that household. The name would tell us that he was a Jew even had Paul not added that he was "my kinsman", which probably means "fellow Jew" as in verse 7.

Narcissus was the name of a wealthy and powerful freedman who had been prominent under Claudius but put to death early in Nero's reign. His

---

37. τὸν δόκιμον. In 1:28 we read of "a reprobate mind", ἀδόκιμον νοῦν; here we have the very opposite. Cf. Jas. 1:12.

38. οἱ ἐκ τῶν Ἀριστοβούλου. Turner says of this genitive of proper names: "The possession of slaves by a family may be indicated by this construction" (M, III, p. 169; so also BDF 162 [5]). See Lightfoot's note, pp. 174-75.

slaves would have passed to the Emperor and have been designated by the name Narcissus. Lightfoot mentions an inscription referring to a member of this household (p. 175). Narcissus was not of the character that we associate with Christian profession, so it is interesting that even from that household there came those who were "in the Lord".

12. Because the names *Tryphena* and *Tryphosa* are similar sounding it has been conjectured that they were sisters, and even that they were twin sisters. Either proposition may be true, but, of course, we have no way of knowing for certain. Both names come from a root meaning "live delicately, luxuriously". Paul is perhaps using some gentle irony when he commends two ladies called "Delicate" and "Dainty" for the fact that they *work hard*.

His present tense points to a continuing labor, while he uses the past tense of *Persis*. It may be that she was old or that some factor like sickness had interfered with her productive capacity. Be that as it may, Paul is appreciative of her very hard work.[39] He calls her "beloved" (as in vv. 5, 8, and 9); evidently she was very dear to him. The name, incidentally, means "Persian".

13. *Rufus* ("red") was a common Latin name and indeed one of the most common slave names (SH). We read in Mark's Gospel of a man called Simon who was the father of Alexander and Rufus (Mark 15:21). Now it is usually agreed that that Gospel was written with Rome very much in mind, and evidently the point of mentioning Simon was that he was the father of two people well known in the Roman church. It is not improbable that this is the man Paul greets, though again we must be cautious, for there is no way of verifying this. This Rufus was *chosen in the Lord*.[40] All Christians are, of course, "chosen in the Lord", and it is accordingly unlikely that that is the sense of the expression in this place. It would not differentiate Rufus from any other Christian, but it seems that Paul is singling him out, not placing him in the same category as all others. We should see him as a "choice" believer (cf. French *élite*).

Paul also sends a greeting to Rufus's *mother, who has been a mother to me, too*. NIV gives us what appears to be the sense of it, but Paul says "his mother and mine".[41] It is possible that he and Rufus were siblings, but there seems no reason for making the assumption. Rather, it would seem that on some occasion of which we have no knowledge Rufus's mother had been very kind to Paul. It seems that people were more ready to claim an extended family in that day than we are (cf. Mark 10:30), so that Paul's usage is not exceptional.[42]

---

39. The verb κοπιάω is used to mean "labor to the point of weariness"; thus hard work is ascribed to all three of these women. In the case of Persis Paul inserts πολλά, but he gives us no indication of the distinction he makes between hard work and very hard work.

40. τὸν ἐκλεκτὸν ἐν κυρίῳ.

41. On ἐμοῦ here BDF 284 (2) note that "Emphatic ἐμοῦ does not appear in the NT except in combination with another gen."

42. J. I. H. McDonald quotes a third-century letter in which Aurelius Dius writes "to Aurelius Horion, my very dear father". He sends his greetings to a number of people including several brothers and sisters, but also "to my mother Tamiea. . . . I greet my father Melanus and my mother Timpesouris and her son . . ." (NTS, XVI [1969-70], p. 370). He thus greets two fathers and two mothers.

14. Now comes a group of five names, otherwise unknown, but commonly names of slaves and freedmen. It is possible that they form a group, such as a house church (there are *brothers* linked with them). They may have been slaves of one man or freedmen. *Asyncritus* (apparently a rare name) means "incomparable", and *Phlegon* "burning".[43] This latter is cited from Xenophon as the name of a dog (Lagrange); it was also used for slaves and freedmen. *Hermes* was the name of the Greek god who was called Mercurius by the Romans; it was a common name for slaves. *Patrobas*, a shortened form of Patrobius (BDF 125 [1]), was not a common name. It was the name of a wealthy freedman of Nero who was later put to death by Galba. His reputation is such that he is unlikely to have been a Christian, but one of his dependents may have borne the name. *Hermas* is the contraction of a number of names and thus was comparatively common.

15. Next to be greeted is *Philologus*. The name means "fond of words", which may be the equivalent of "Chatterbox" or may refer to a secretarial occupation. Lightfoot cites it from the inscriptions of the imperial household. *Julia* was probably the commonest of all Roman female slave names (SH); she may have been the wife (or sister) of Philologus. *Nereus* is a name "possibly marking one of Nero's freedmen" (M, II, p. 350; Howard adds that the name is "as old as Homer"). The name of *his sister* is not given, but Paul greets her, too. The final name in this section of the letter is *Olympas;* it is clearly a Greek name (and a contraction of some longer name). With this group there is associated a group of *saints;* Paul sends a greeting to *all* of them.[44] Possibly we have here members of another house church.

16. Paul urges them all to use a *holy kiss* as a greeting (mentioned again in 1 Cor. 16:20; 2 Cor. 13:12; 1 Thess. 5:26; "a kiss of love", 1 Pet. 5:14). The kiss was, of course, a regular greeting in the society in which the early Christians moved (cf. Mark 14:45), and we should understand it in this way and not as a liturgical action like the "kiss of peace" which was taken into the service of Holy Communion.[45] This probably came about because the time when Christians came together and thus exchanged a greeting tended to be that of worship. It is usually held that men kissed men and women women, but Tertullian refers to a wife being kissed by "any one of the brethren" (*To His Wife* ii.4). Clement of Alexandria speaks of people who "make the churches resound" with kissing; he points out that "the shameless use of a kiss . . . occasions foul suspicions and evil reports" (*Instructor* iii.12). This led to its restriction and general abandonment. H. Windisch thinks that "It is to be

---

43. Ἀσύγκριτον is from alpha-privative and συγκρίνω, "compare", while φλέγω means "to burn". Whether such names had any particular significance is not known.

44. Moule sees in τοὺς σὺν αὐτοῖς πάντας ἁγίους "a striking exception" to the rule that when πᾶς means "all" it is "not enclosed within the article-noun unit", for here the expression "surely = πάντας τοὺς ἁγίους τοὺς σὺν αὐτοῖς" (IBNTG, p. 93 n. 3).

45. This is attested by Justin, I Apol. 65: "Having ended the prayers, we salute one another with a kiss", and by other ancient writers; in the Apostolic Constitutions it is given its place in the liturgy after the prayers: "And let the clergy salute the bishop, and the laymen the laymen, and the women the women" (R. H. Cresswell, ed., *The Liturgy of "The Apostolic Constitutions"* [London, 1900], p. 51).

assumed that the holy kiss was customary in the churches", so that Paul means "that on the reading of the letter it should take place at the request of the absent apostle" (TDNT, I, p. 501; see also Gamble, pp. 75-76).

Paul further sends greetings from *All the churches of Christ*, an expression not found elsewhere in the New Testament. Paul does not explain which churches are involved, but it is probable that the expression reflects the fact that the delegates from the churches were gathering to take the collection to Jerusalem (Acts 20:3-5). In any case Paul would have let the leaders of the churches know of his plans and the provincials would have been glad to send their greetings to the church in the capital and perhaps give some backing to Paul. It reflects the fact that at this time most of the churches were in the East, so that a greeting from that area could be taken as a greeting from "all" the churches.

E. A Doctrinal Warning, 16:17-20

> [17]*I urge you, brothers, to watch out for those who cause divisions and put obstacles in your way that are contrary to the teaching you have learned. Keep away from them.* [18]*For such people are not serving our Lord Christ, but their own appetites. By smooth talk and flattery they deceive the minds of naive people.* [19]*Everyone has heard about your obedience, so I am full of joy over you; but I want you to be wise about what is good, and innocent about what is evil.*
> [20]*The God of peace will soon crush Satan under your feet.*
> *The grace of our Lord Jesus be with you.*

This rather strong warning about false teaching is held by a number of scholars to be an interpolation into the letter or perhaps a Pauline fragment from another writing. They regard the tone as distinctly sharper than anything elsewhere in this letter and find nothing in the context to justify it (why should Paul insert such a sharp warning between two sets of greetings?). But the differences should not be exaggerated. Murray points out that the tone is not so very different from that in other places (e.g., 2:1-5; 3:8; 9:19-20, etc.). And as for its placing, Paul has just spoken about the kiss of peace; a warning against divisions that would spoil harmony follows naturally on that reminder of unity. He has also referred to "all the churches of Christ", and when he thinks of the churches he had founded, could he forget the people who had caused trouble and fomented division with their false teachings? In the light of those troubles it would be natural for him to warn the Romans to be on their guard against false teachers they might well face. Again, Romans is a long letter and it must have taken quite a while to compose it. It is possible that news was brought to Paul just before he finished it that made him think a warning was in order. Some have suggested that it was at this point that Paul took the pen in order to authenticate the letter and his concern overflowed in this warning. Any or all of these considerations may be relevant, and they lead us to see that the objections are not insuperable.[46]

Exactly what was the danger against which the warning is given? A variety of answers is given. Thus some think that the troublemakers were Judaizers, while others see them as libertines or proto-gnostics. It is possible that they were not a homogeneous group and that more than one kind of false teaching is in mind. The words are too general for us to be certain, and in any case it is the fomenting of faction on which Paul concentrates his attention. Some (e.g., Dodd) think that the false teaching was already in Rome, but it is usually held that, whatever the teaching was, it had not yet made its appearance there; Paul is speaking of a possibility and warning against it.

17. *I urge you* is the language of appeal, not of command;[47] Paul is inviting his readers to heed what he says, but he is not giving a peremptory order. He wants his readers to *watch out for* troublemakers, where his verb[48] is quite a strong one. Chrysostom explains it in these terms: "that is, to be exceedingly particular about, and to get acquainted with, and to search out thoroughly." They should not adopt a casual attitude to false teachers. Paul can use the same verb for a right attitude to good teachers (Phil. 3:17); the word denotes close attention, not opposing or following as such. There is an article with *divisions* (and another with *obstacles*); it is "the well-known divisions" and not some hypothetical danger of which Paul warns. Evidently the troubles were widely known.[49] Paul puts a strong stress on unity and regards the dissensions as *contrary to the teaching you have learned*. The *teaching* clearly refers to common Christian teaching; it cannot refer to anything like "Paulinism", for Paul had never been to Rome. It is the common stock of Christian instruction, and Paul plainly aligns himself with it. He puts emphasis on *you*; from what he has heard of the Roman church he knows that its members have been well grounded in the faith (cf. 1:8; 6:17). They have had good teaching and have *learned* it well. He reminds them of its importance. Any new teachers whose instruction did not conform to that good teaching must not be followed. *Keep away from them*, the apostle says. They are teaching error; it is important to have nothing to do with them.[50]

18. *For* introduces the reason for the foregoing. *Such people* makes it clear that the warning is against more than one form of false teaching. It is not "these" people, as though a definite group, but anyone of this kind. The false

---

46. Barth speaks of this section as "A last urgent appeal, which is, however, no foreign element in the Epistle." See further my discussion in the Introduction, pp. 27-28.

47. παρακαλῶ as in 12:1 (where see note); 15:30.

48. σκοπεῖν.

49. διχοστασία means "a standing aside" and thus apart from others (it is one of "the works of the flesh" in Gal. 5:20). σκάνδαλον is the bait stick of a trap, and then trouble generally (see the note on 9:33).

50. ἐκκλίνω may be used of turning away from good (3:12) or from evil (1 Pet. 3:11). The MSS are divided here, some reading the aorist (which would point to a decisive turning), others the present (which indicates the continuing attitude). Most scholars favor the present, but not a great deal turns on the decision.

teachers *are not serving*[51] *our Lord Christ, but their own appetites*. This last word translates a term that more exactly means "belly" (cf. Phil. 3:19). It is unlikely that this means that they were gluttons (would it be necessary to give a warning against such obvious sin?). Paul may mean that they were preoccupied with food laws, or that they exercised an indiscriminate self-indulgence, or a greed arising out of general egotism.[52] NIV takes "belly" to stand for the *appetites* in general.[53]

Despite such base conduct they manage to deceive people by their plausible way of putting things. *Smooth talk* renders a word found here only in the New Testament and which BAGD explain as "smooth, plausible speech".[54] *Flattery* is a word always elsewhere in the New Testament used in a good sense,[55] but here NIV gives us the sense of it. Paul is describing people whose conduct is base, but whose words are excellent. Such people may easily *deceive*.[56] The *naive* are the guileless, the innocent, perhaps we could say here the simple. They are people who are innocent, indeed, but not because of a reasoned understanding of what is good and what is evil. They are too simple to know and thus they readily fall prey to the plausible deceiver. Paul looks for Christians to avoid both gullibility and cynicism.

19. "For"[57] (which NIV omits) is difficult, for what follows is not obviously a reason for what went before. Perhaps Paul is expressing his confidence in the Romans ("For 'I have no fear about you'"), or the connection may be "This warning is serious for you are widely known and they will be sure to make an attack on you" (cf. Godet). *Obedience* is an important concept in Romans (see the note on 1:5), and Paul assures his readers that their obedience is widely known. It has reached[58] to all. "Therefore",[59] he says, "I rejoice over you", where there is some emphasis on "you". Clearly Paul knew of no great blemish in the Roman church. He adds his wish that they be

---

51. δουλεύω means "be a slave to" (this is more than διακονέω); the people in question were slaves, but not slaves to Christ. This leads some to the view that they were libertines.

52. Denney detects an allusion to "a self-seeking spirit, rather than an allusion to any particular cast of doctrine."

53. Cf. Michel, who regards it as equivalent to "flesh". Goodspeed renders "base passions". Parry comments, "He does not say ἑαυτοῖς because they are not even serving their own true interests."

54. χρηστολογία. BAGD cite a Latin saying (found in several commentaries) that the word refers to one who "speaks well and does ill". It is "the language of a good man hypocritically used by a bad man" (Shedd).

55. εὐλογία (which gives us our word "eulogy"). In the New Testament it generally means "praise" or "blessing".

56. ἐξαπατέω is a strengthened form of ἀπατέω; it is used in 7:11 of sin's deceit of Paul and in 2 Cor. 11:3 of the serpent's deceit of Eve.

57. γάρ.

58. ἀφικνέομαι means "arrive at, reach". When Paul says that their obedience has reached "to all", he means that the report of their obedience has been very widespread (cf. 1:8).

59. οὖν.

wise about what is good,[60] *and innocent*[61] *about what is evil.* There may be a reminiscence of some words of Jesus (Matt. 10:16); Paul has similar teaching elsewhere (1 Cor. 14:20). Hodge quotes from Grotius a neat summing up of what Paul is looking for: "too good to deceive, too wise to be deceived."

20. Now comes a little devotional section with a prophecy and a prayer for grace. Paul speaks of God as *The God of peace* (as in 15:33), a significant title over against the "divisions" of verse 17. This God of peace, however, is pictured in a warlike activity, that of crushing Satan. We should bear in mind that our English idea of peace, like the Greek from which it is borrowed, is a negative idea, the absence of war. But we must not read our idea of peace back into the Bible. The New Testament writers tended to take their idea of peace from the Old Testament, and for the Hebrews peace *(shalom)* was a positive idea, the idea of wholeness, of well-roundedness. It was the prosperity of the whole life, a positive and not a negative idea.

Now one feature of this wholeness was spiritual prosperity, the over-coming of evil, and thus Paul can speak of God in terms of peace when he says that God is at war with the evil one. Part of the true concept of peace is that of defeating evil, and that is what the God of peace does. Paul is not praying that God will defeat evil but prophesying that he will in fact do this; this is a prophecy, not a prayer. Notice that it is God who does the crushing, but that Satan ends up under the feet of believers (cf. Chrysostom, " 'under your feet,' so that they may obtain the victory themselves, and become noble by the trophy"). The metaphor is a vivid one and looks for the complete triumph of the Christian (for the connection between "under the feet" and triumph, cf. Heb. 2:8). There may be an allusion to Genesis 3:15 (if so, it is to the Hebrew, for LXX is different). NIV says this will happen *soon,*[62] which is taken by some to refer to a speedy eschatological happening (e.g., Käsemann, p. 418) and seen as an activity in the present world by others (e.g., Haldane, Wilckens). Nothing in the context indicates that Paul is looking to the parousia, and it is better to see the promise of a victory over Satan in the here and now.

The grace of our Lord Jesus be with you (with some slight variations) is the way Paul normally ends his letters. He may expand this somewhat (as in 2 Corinthians) or abbreviate it a little (as in Colossians), but there is always the

---

60. A number of MSS read μέν after σοφούς; BDF comment on such readings, "the inclusion of μέν throws the emphasis on the second member (indicated by δέ); therefore, where the emphasis is on the first part and the second is only an appendage, μέν is not to be read" (447 [5]). Clearly the emphasis here is on the second member, so the tendency of scribes would be to insert the word. It should be rejected.

61. ἀκέραιος means "unmixed" (alpha-privative + κεράννυμι) and thus "pure", metaphorically "simple", "guileless"; Trench sees the "fundamental notion" in the word as "the absence of foreign admixture" (*Synonyms*, p. 206).

62. ἐν τάχει. This may well mean *soon*, but Lenski argues that it signifies "swiftly", not "shortly"; Godet also denies that the word and its derivatives denote imminence (which is rather εὐθύς), and holds that what is in mind is not so much the nearness of the event as "the celerity with which it is accomplished."

prayer for *grace* (for this term see the note on 1:5). There are problems about the ending of this epistle, but it certainly seems as though this was seen as the end. It may well be that Paul took the pen and wrote these words himself. We know that he wrote something at the end of every letter; it was the way he authenticated it (2 Thess. 3:17). Sometimes he draws attention to this and sometimes he does not, but there is no reason to doubt that he always did it.[63] It is quite possible that Paul wrote these words, then passed the pen back to Tertius for a postscript. Something unusual has happened at the end of this letter, and this is a very possible understanding of it.

F. GREETINGS FROM PEOPLE WITH PAUL, 16:21-24

> [21]*Timothy, my fellow worker, sends his greetings to you, as do Lucius, Jason and Sosipater, my relatives.*
> [22]*I, Tertius, who wrote down this letter, greet you in the Lord.*
> [23]*Gaius, whose hospitality I and the whole church here enjoy, sends you his greetings.*
> *Erastus, who is the city's director of public works, and our brother Quartus send you their greetings.*[a]

[a]23 Some manuscripts *their greetings.* [24]*May the grace of our Lord Jesus Christ be with all of you. Amen.*

21. Earlier Paul had greeted certain friends in Rome by name. Now he passes on to the Romans greetings from friends of theirs who happen to be with him at the time of writing. First is Timothy, whom he describes simply as *my fellow worker*.[64] This man, the son of a Jewish mother (and therefore accepted as a Jew) and a Greek father, Paul circumcised and took with him on his missionary travels (Acts 16:1-3). He evidently became a trusted and highly valued helper, for he is mentioned as being with Paul a number of times in Acts and his name crops up in every one of Paul's letters except Galatians, Ephesians, and Titus. And, of course, he was the recipient of two of them himself. Paul's many references to him show that he was very dear to him. A number of times Timothy was joined with Paul in the authorship of letters. On this occasion we do not hear of him until now, possibly because he had not been with Paul when the apostle began the letter, possibly because the nature of the letter was such that it had to be seen to come from Paul alone. At any rate he is interested in Rome, and he sends his greetings.

---

63. Deissmann draws attention to a letter dated A.D. 50 in which the body of the letter is in one hand and the conclusion in another (LAE, pp. 170ff.). Nothing in the wording shows that two people were occupied in the writing; had the letter not survived we would not know. It is fair to conclude from such evidence that this was a recognized way of authenticating letters written to dictation.

64. ὁ συνεργός μου. BDF 268 [1] see the article here as having the force "my *well-known* co-laborer".

Greetings come also from *Lucius*, who may (or may not) be the man mentioned in Acts 13:1. The name resembles "Luke",[65] but it is not identical with it and there is no real reason for equating them. This *Lucius* we must leave as otherwise unknown to us, but the name is Roman, which may hint at a reason for his greeting the Roman church. But it is not a very convincing reason, for the next two names are Greek. *Jason* was the name of Paul's host at Thessalonica (Acts 17:5-9), but the name is not uncommon and we do not know whether this was the same man or not. There is a Sopater in Acts 20:4 and given that this is a recognized shortening of *Sosipater*, and remembering that Paul commonly uses people's correct names, while Luke tends to use the abbreviated forms, it is not impossible that this is the same man. But it looks as though Luke's Sopater is one of the Gentiles taking the Gentile collection to Jerusalem, while Paul's man is expressly said here to be one of his *relatives*, and thus a Jew. So we should probably not identify them. The term rendered *relatives* is the one Paul has used before in 9:3; 16:7, 11 and which seems to mean "fellow countrymen". We cannot insist that the people mentioned were in fact members of Paul's family.

22. It was Paul's habit to use an amanuensis when writing his letters, though he did write a little himself towards the end. This is the one occasion on which we hear of the scribe, for Paul lets him convey his own greetings to the Roman church. The fact that his name is Latin may mean that he had some kinship with this church, but for whatever reason he sends his own greetings. It is a little human touch. That the apostle allows this to be done in connection with such a weighty letter as this sheds light on the relationship between the apostle and his helpers. Tertius calls attention to himself with the emphatic *I* and tells the reader that he wrote the letter. There is a teasing little problem with *in the Lord*, which is usually taken with *greet* but which in the Greek follows immediately on "wrote the letter".[66] It is also true that in this chapter "in Christ" or "in the Lord" occurs repeatedly in verses which convey greetings (vv. 3, 7, 8, 9, 10, 11, 12 [twice], and 13), and not once is it connected with the greeting. It may well be that Tertius meant that he wrote the letter "in the Lord", which, of course, immediately raises the question of what it means to "write in the Lord". If this is the way to take it, we should see the writing of the letter, not as a mechanical project, but as something Tertius undertook as a piece of service to his Lord.[67]

23. *Gaius* was a not uncommon name; we find it in Acts 19:29; 20:4;

65. This man is Λούκιος; the other Λουκᾶς, which Paul uses of "the beloved physician" each time he mentions him (Col. 4:14; 2 Tim. 4:11; Philem. 24). Deissmann argues for the possibility that the two are the same man (LAE, pp. 437-38), but not many have been persuaded.

66. ὁ γράψας τὴν ἐπιστολὴν ἐν κυρίῳ. The article τήν, of course, means "this".

67. Gordon J. Bahr connects "write" with "in the Lord", but takes the Lord here as Paul, not as Christ. He then sees the meaning as "I, Tertius, who write the letter in the service of (my) master [Paul], greet you" (CBQ, XXVIII [1966], p. 465). But in a chapter where "in Christ" and "in the Lord" occur so often it is very unlikely that on this one occasion the Lord should be Paul.

3 John 1. But there seems no reason for equating the man who sends his greetings to Rome with any of these. Rather, he is likely to be the Corinthian Gaius whom Paul baptized (1 Cor. 1:14). He may be the man named Titius Justus in Acts 18:7, for that man received Paul in Corinth; this accords with his description here as "host".[68] Further, the name Titius is a *gens* name which is likely to have been preceded by a praenomen (his name could well have been Gaius Titius Justus; so Cranfield). Paul speaks of Gaius as host to *the whole church* as well as to himself. This may mean that the church met in his house or that he habitually provided hospitality either for local church people or for travelling Christians like Paul.[69] Clearly he was better off than most of the early Christians.

Erastus (meaning "beloved") is unlikely to have been Paul's travelling companion (Acts 19:22; cf. also 2 Tim. 4:20), for his position in Corinth would have made that difficult. He was clearly an important person, though possibly not *the city's director of public works*, as NIV makes him. The word used of his office seems rather to indicate something like "treasurer".[70] But the aedile (or director of public works) held office for a year only, and he normally had held other offices previously. There seems no reason why we should not think that our Erastus was the city treasurer at the time Paul wrote and that he later was honored with the office of aedile.[71]

Joined with Erastus in sending greetings is *Quartus*, described as "the brother". Nothing more is known of this man. *Brother* presumably means "Christian brother", though it is possible to think he is someone's sibling (for all the males in the chapter could be described in the same way). Bruce wonders whether he could be brother of Tertius, for that name means "third" and this one "fourth", but Cranfield finds this "an exercise of free fancy". We simply do not know.

24. NIV mg. includes words which some MSS have as verse 24 and

---

68. ξένος. The word means "strange, foreign", and this appears to be the only New Testament passage where it does not have this meaning. But there can be no doubt that here it means giving help to strangers, i.e., being host. The word is discussed in TDNT, V, pp. 1-36.

69. Lagrange favors travelling Christians, as does Parry, who dismisses the idea that the church met in Gaius's home on the grounds that "It is not probable that they had only one such place." This may well be the case, though we should bear in mind that we have no actual information on where the first-century church met for worship.

70. οἰκονόμος, "the city treasurer" (BAGD). An inscription has been found in Corinth which reads "Erastus in return for his aedileship laid (the pavement) at his own expense" (J. Murphy-O'Connor, *St. Paul's Corinth* [Wilmington, 1983], p. 37). The pavement in question is first-century, and this may be our Erastus. The office of aedile was such that its holder might well be deemed "Director of Public Works", but he was not treasurer. Of course it is quite possible that the one man held both offices at different times. Haldane comments, "It shows that Christians may hold offices even under heathen governments, and that to serve Christ we are not to be abstracted from worldly business."

71. Gerd Theissen discusses the problem and favors the view that the Christian Erastus was first treasurer and later aedile in Corinth. He points out that the name "is not otherwise attested for Corinth, by inscriptions or literature" (*The Social Setting of Pauline Christianity* [Philadelphia, 1982], p. 83).

which are substantially a repetition of part of verse 20 (the differences are that this verse has a fuller description of Christ and it includes the word "all"). In modern critical editions this section is universally rejected. For its content it is sufficient to refer to the notes on verse 20.[72]

G. DOXOLOGY, 16:25-27

> [25]*Now to him who is able to establish you by my gospel and the proclamation of Jesus Christ, according to the revelation of the mystery hidden for long ages past,* [26]*but now revealed and made known through the prophetic writings by the command of the eternal God, so that all nations might believe and obey him—* [27]*to the only wise God be glory forever through Jesus Christ! Amen.*

The doxology is found in some MSS at the end of chapter 14, by one at the end of chapter 15, by some at this point, by quite a few both here and at the end of chapter 14 (for details see the Introduction, n. 82), while some omit it altogether. Some hold that Paul wrote it, and others point out that Paul normally closes a letter with a benediction rather than a doxology. Accordingly it has been conjectured that it was composed as a suitable ending when the 14-chapter edition was formed and considered too valuable to be lost when scribes encountered the 16-chapter edition. Another view is that it was added to Romans in a New Testament which had this epistle as the last; it would then have served as a fitting close to the Pauline writings in general. Some are impressed by the liturgical tone of the passage and seek its origin in worship. There may be something in this, but we should keep in mind the point made by Brevard S. Childs: "The doxology is not a liturgical response of the letter's recipients to Paul's words, but a liturgical response of Paul to the subject of his book."[73] There are other ideas, but there seems little point in canvassing them. The point for us is that we have the doxology at this point in the 16-chapter edition and it is fittingly studied here. It is beyond doubt that these verses express Pauline ideas, and those who hold that it was not written by Paul agree that it contains Pauline language, even quotations from Paul. It is better to take it as simply the close of Romans as we know it and see what we can learn from that.[74]

---

72. Gamble argues that this verse is authentic. He is able to cite letters which have parallels to the doubling of the final benediction, and he shows that this verse tends to be absent when the doxology is found at the end of this chapter, but not when it is found elsewhere (pp. 88, 129-32). It thus formed the end of the letter but was readily deleted when the doxology was added. T. Zahn also argues strongly for the genuineness of this verse (*Introduction to the New Testament*, I [Edinburgh, 1909], pp. 408-10).

73. *The New Testament as Canon: An Introduction* (London, 1984), p. 254. O'Neill speaks of it as "a splendid liturgical doxology".

74. Parry thinks that the doxology "sums up, tersely but completely, the main conception of the Epistle, and reproduces its most significant language." Similarly Shedd thinks that it "is strikingly Pauline in its elements."

25. *To him who is able* reminds us of the power of God, and this in that he can *establish* believers.[75] Once again Paul refers to *my gospel* (cf. 2:16; 2 Tim. 2:8). This means that it is the gospel he preaches, a gospel he has not only heard about but has made his own. It is not to be understood as meaning that Paul had a gospel different from that of the church in general. He can insist that he preaches what the others preach (1 Cor. 15:11). The gospel of which he speaks is the gospel other people had preached and the Roman believers had come to accept. It may be that Paul put a little more emphasis on its application to the Gentiles and perhaps on the freeness of divine grace, but it was essentially the same gospel.

With it he links *the proclamation of Jesus Christ*,[76] which stands for much the same thing but from a different point of view. It seems probable that we should take *according to the revelation* with *the proclamation* rather than with *to establish you* (so Denney, SH, Cranfield). The gospel is revealed truth, not human wisdom. Paul goes on to speak of *the mystery* (see the note on 11:25), which points to the gospel as something that people could never have worked out for themselves. The truth that the Son of God would come from heaven to live and die for us and that we enter into salvation only by faith in him is not obvious and could be known by us only when and as God revealed it. This mystery was "kept silent through times eternal". Paul's choice of verb is intriguing,[77] and the use of the perfect tense means that the silence is permanent. We should understand that the silence of God is not some deprivation, the absence of noise or speech, but something positive, what P. Dewailly calls God's "plenitude and concentration".[78] The silence of God stands for God's hiddenness, the truth that his innermost being is not open to the scrutiny of mortals. He may choose to make himself known, but that does not mean that everything about him has been revealed. There still remains that about God which is beyond our perception and our understanding. The silence endured "through times eternal",[79] which appears to be a reference to the eternity of

75. στηρίξαι, "set up, fix (firmly), establish" (BAGD); cf. its use in 1:11.

76. κήρυγμα means the content of the Christian message generally. Ἰησοῦ Χριστοῦ is an objective genitive, "the preaching about Jesus Christ". Moule sees the possibility of a subjective genitive, "preaching which He Himself delivers". This would be understood either of the teaching of Jesus or of Jesus as preaching through the apostles (CBSC). But an objective genitive has much more support.

77. σιγάω. This is the one transitive use of the verb in the New Testament.

78. NTS, XIV (1967-68), p. 115. He has argued that God's silence is no more only the absence of speech "than health is only the absence of sickness, or peace the absence of war" (p. 112). Harrisville similarly comments: "The silence thus does not signify privation, absence, but plenitude, something into which a word may enter, but without putting an end to the silence . . . . God remains hidden, even for those to whom he makes himself known."

79. BDF 201 note that the temporal dative is contrary to classical usage and that "Its position is secure . . . only with transitive verbs along with scattered examples with the passive, while the accusative is retained with intransitives" (cf. M, III, p. 243).

God rather than to the time from creation to the coming of Christ (as some think).

26. *But now* there is a difference:[80] the mystery has been revealed. The change to the aorist tense is significant; it points to a definite event, the coming of Christ. Leenhardt points out that the *now* "should be heard in its full resonance; it expresses the eschatological character of the present moment, a drama in which the action of God is embodied in man's history in order that he may be directed towards his true end." The gospel has been made known, and been made known to the Gentiles (cf. 1:5). *The prophetic[81] writings* most naturally refer to the writings of the Old Testament prophets, though some think of the prophets of the New Testament period and Godet of the writings of the apostles. But it seems that Paul is saying that the real meaning of the Old Testament has become apparent only through the coming of Christ, which, of course, is a constant theme of the New Testament writers.[82] And this took place by divine *command*,[83] the command of *the eternal God*, where the adjective at least hints at changelessness. The mystery has been revealed but lately, but that does not mean a change of mind in the regions celestial. An eternal God works out an eternal purpose. This purpose is "with a view to the obedience of faith"[84] and "unto all the Gentiles".[85] The verse ends with "having been made known", which NIV correctly links with "revealed".[86]

27. Most translations agree with NIV, *to the only wise God*, but it is a question whether we should understand it as GNB, "To the only God, who alone is all-wise".[87] However we translate, there is no doubt that Paul thinks of God as the only God and also as the only God who is wise. To this God is ascribed glory forever through Jesus Christ. There is no cessation of his glory:

---

80. δέ is adversative, marking the contrast between the time of revelation and all that preceded it.

81. The adjective προφητικός is found again in the New Testament only in 2 Pet. 1:19.

82. Cf. SH, "The unity of the Old and New Testaments, the fact that Christ had come in accordance with the Scriptures (Rom. i.1, 2), that the new method of salvation although apart from law, was witnessed to by the Law and the Prophets (. . . Rom. iii.21), the constant allusion esp. in chaps. ix-xi to the Old Testament Scriptures; all these are summed up in the phrase διὰ γραφῶν προφητικῶν."

83. ἐπιταγή occurs seven times in Paul and nowhere else in the New Testament (here only in Romans).

84. εἰς ὑπακοὴν πίστεως, as in 1:5 (where see note). εἰς denotes purpose.

85. εἰς πάντα τὰ ἔθνη may mean "among all the Gentiles", but more probably εἰς means "as far as" the Gentiles; i.e., it reaches throughout the world.

86. τε is probably meant to connect the two participles.

87. μόνῳ σοφῷ θεῷ, where the question is whether Paul means "the only God" and "the wise God" or "the only wise" God. BDF 243 speak of the adjective μόνος and the adverb μόνον as "occasionally confused", and to take this as one of those occasions gives us justification for the sense of NIV.

it is forever. And the Christian knows that glory is to be ascribed to God on the basis of what Christ has done. It is that that enables us to see what a glorious God this God is. *Amen* rounds off the doxology with a firm affirmation.[88]

88. NIV gets rid of a difficulty by giving no equivalent of ᾧ. But the MS evidence for it (with the meaning "through Jesus Christ, to whom be glory", NEB mg.) is very strong and cannot be dismissed on purely textual grounds. This reading ascribes glory to Christ and leaves the sentence unfinished, but most commentators agree that in this doxology glory is being ascribed to the Father and further that it is unlikely that the book should close with an unfinished sentence. We could, however, take ᾧ as "resumptive" (so Robertson, p. 437) with a meaning like "To the only wise God, through Jesus Christ, to him, I say, be glory for ever" (Hodge). But to most commentators the difficulties seem too great. The ᾧ is regarded as an error which may have been introduced because in doxologies it so often comes in at just this point, or perhaps Tertius slipped it in from force of habit. BDF, with the support of B, think it should be deleted "not only because of anacoluthon, but especially in order to connect διὰ 'I. Χρ." (467).

General Index

Abba, 315-317, 327
Abimelech, 126
Abraham, 5, 9, 19, 37-38, 42, 139-140, 145, 159, 170, 174, 193-216, 335, 348-349, 352-355, 360, 373, 393, 398-399, 411, 423, 503
Abyss, 383-384
Acceptance, 478, 502-503
Achaia, 520
Achilleus, 26
Adam, 19, 87, 177, 190, 199, 227-242, 251, 254, 261, 278, 283, 288, 321, 348
Adoption, 314-315, 324, 348, 424
Adultery, 136, 138, 272
Advantage, of Jews and Gentiles, 151-152, 163-165, 480
Affection, 98-99, 270, 378
Affliction, 220, 447
Ahab, 291, 401
Akiba, 123, 166
Alexander, 536
Alexandria, 13
Altar, 399-400, 433, 511
Ambition, 515
Ambrosiaster, 3, 125
Ammon, 353
Amos, 37-38
Ampliatus, 26, 527, 534-535
Analogy, 270
Andronicus, 533-534
Angel, 320, 341, 460
Anger, 119, 305
Anguish, 346
Antinomianism, 18, 27-28, 116, 247, 272
Antioch, 6, 12, 17, 514, 518
Apelles, 535
Apocalyptic, 101, 135, 156, 177, 234, 238, 339, 410
Apollonius Dyscolus, 182
Apollos, 532
Apostle, 38-39, 48-49, 437, 510, 513, 534
Apostolic authority, 11-12
Apostolic foundation, 11-12
Approve, approval, 93-94, 132, 436, 489, 492, 498, 535
Aquila, 14, 25-26, 531-533, 535

Aristobulus, 25, 535
Aristotle, 64, 125, 200, 458
Armor, 453, 472
Ashtoreth, 401
Asia, 26-27, 533; Asia Minor, 522
Assurance, 319, 338, 343, 401
Astrology, 341-342
Asyncritus, 537
Athens, 22, 79
Augustine, 1, 125, 221, 230, 271, 280, 284, 379, 474, 493
Augustus, 40
Authority, 11-13, 386, 390, 432, 437, 459-467, 523
Autobiography, 276-277, 284

Baal, 401
Balaam, 421
Baptism, 2, 9, 246-248, 252, 273, 385, 473, 529
Barnabas, 519
Base of operations, Rome as, 280, 282, 284
"Belly," 540
Benediction, 525
Ben-Hadad, 401
Benjamin, 398-399
Bernard of Clairvaux, 306-307
Blasphemy, 138
Bless, 449
Blessing, 199-200, 492, 522
Blind, 133
Blood, 146, 181-182, 215, 224, 338, 433
Boasting, 85, 98, 131, 185-186, 195-196, 219-220, 414-415, 512
Boldness, 510
Body, 89, 247, 257-258, 309, 312, 324, 433-434, 438-439, 474, 520; of Christ, 273; of death, 296-297, 312; of sin, 251-252, 433
Branches, 411-417
Breves, 21-22
Brother, 62, 270, 272, 311, 333, 347, 377, 419, 433, 443-445, 461, 483, 486-487, 489, 491, 503, 508, 521, 524, 544
Burial, 247-249, 273

549

Index of Authors

AUTHOR INDEX

Index of Scripture References

NEW TESTAMENT

INDEX OF SCRIPTURE REFERENCES

INDEX OF APOCRYPHAL WRITINGS